3

920 SIM

Mrs Simpson

Film

Kate: The Life of Katharine Hepburn
Marlene: The Life of Marlene Dietrich
The Films of Orson Welles
Orson Welles: The Rise and Fall of an American Genius
Charles Laughton
Marlon Brando
Hollywood in the Forties (with Joel Greenberg)
The Celluliod Muse (with Joel Greenberg)

Literature

The Adventures of Conan Doyle

Poetry

A Distant Star
Spring and Death
The Earthbound
Noonday Country
The Voyage to Brindisi

Anthology

Australian Writing Today

Politics

Trading with the Enemy
American Swastika
Rose Kennedy
Howard Hughes: The Secret Life
Murdering Mr. Lincoln

CHARLES HIGHAM

MRS SIMPSON

Secret Lives of the Duchess of Windsor

SIDGWICK & JACKSON

First published as *Wallis: Secret Lives of the Duchess of Windsor* in 1988
by Sidgwick & Jackson Ltd

This revised, expanded and updated edition published 2004
by Sidgwick & Jackson
an imprint of Pan Macmillan Ltd
Pan Macmillan, 20 New Wharf Road, London NI 9RR
Basingstoke and Oxford
Associated companies throughout the world
www.panmacmillan.com

ISBN 0 283 07382 9

1 3 5 7 9 8 6 4 2

A CIP catalogue record for this book is available from
the British Library.

Typeset by SetSystems Ltd, Saffron Walden, Essex
Printed and bound in Great Britain by
Mackays of Chatham plc, Chatham, Kent

For Richard V. Palafox and Dorris Halsey
Special acknowledgement to Dr Gerald Turbow

Contents

Contents

Prologue

It has been called the auction of the century. Long before the sale, which took place on 2 April 1987, the jewels had flashed and glittered in glass-covered cases in Manhattan, Monaco and Palm Beach; the press had been filled with announcements and descriptions. A. Alfred Taubman, Michigan millionaire and owner of Sotheby Parke-Bernet, was putting on the biggest jewellery show on earth. He chose an appropriately lustrous setting: the Hôtel Beau Rivage, overlooking Lake Geneva, which not only housed Sotheby's headquarters but offered, next door, at the Hôtel Richemond, a handsome accommodation for the influx of the rich who would bid for the romantic gems. Taubman erected a red-and-white-striped marquee in the lakeside gardens of the Beau Rivage: a grandiose circus tent for what was, in fact, a circus. On previous evenings Taubman had thrown a series of parties to allow the potential buyers and their representatives to view the jewels at leisure; shrewdly, he had selected the hour of 9 p.m. for the auction itself: an hour when darkness had fallen, and the soft lights, cunningly arranged inside the marquee, would flatter the women's faces. Only a few complained about the fact that they had had to eat dinner at an uncivilized early hour.

The men were in black tie, the women in designer gowns. Among those present was the Countess of Romanones, the 'spy in red', an old friend of the Duchess of Windsor's who had been a secret agent in Portugal and Spain during the Second World War. Also attending was Grace, Lady Dudley, formerly a Radziwill and thus related to the Kennedys by marriage; another of the duchess's best friends, she had risen from Yugoslavian origins to become a prominent figure in international society. There were scions of the former royal families of Europe, whom the Duke of Windsor had befriended and whose treatment he had deplored, among them the Princess of Naples and Prince Dimitri of Yugoslavia. There were the Infanta of Spain, Baron Hans Heinrich Thyssen, Princess Firyal of Jordan, singer Shirley Bassey and divorce lawyer Marvin Mitchelson. Elizabeth Taylor was on the telephone from her Beverly Hills poolside. Many stars had people standing in for them, annoying the paparazzi who had rushed to the spot and, after an hour of photographing fading royalty or aristocracy, must have felt like rushing lemming-like into Lake Geneva.

The auction was late in starting; the rich have never been noted for their punctuality, and there was competition among several of them as to who would enter the marquee last. Finally, as the clock moved towards 10 p.m. Nicholas Rayner of Sotheby's, the perfect choice with his elegant good looks, wearing a 1930s-style black tie, well-tailored dinner jacket and red breast-pocket handkerchief, walked up to the podium with a gold gavel in his hand. He glanced up at an illuminated screen that showed, in flashing scarlet against black, the amount asked to open the bidding for the first item, a sapphire, gold and ruby clip shaped like a curtain tassel. A pretty girl appeared, carrying a black velvet mount upon which rested the precious clip. It went for 70,000 Swiss francs, at least ten times its actual worth. It is safe to say that nobody present was interested in the real value of anything offered, nor did anyone think of the items as investments. The participants were there to satisfy a fantasy, to share a dream.

The atmosphere soon began to resemble a cross between Ascot, a Manila cockfight and a Madison Square Garden heavyweight championship. Many auctions are notable for their silence, like that of a crypt or a gay bar. A scratch of the head, a subtle wave of a gold pencil, even the raising of a well-watched eyebrow would normally indicate bids that might run well over a million. But this time people behaved as though they were at an auction in a bad movie. They shouted, they screamed, they fought, they gesticulated, they waved catalogues or fists or fingers at the podium with all the hysteria of the witnesses of a shipwreck or a major fire. The staff, chosen for their clean-cut public school faces and slim figures, gestured from the telephones to indicate that millionaires in other countries were demanding that they get in the last bids. After thirty-one lots had sold, $3 million had been put down. A lorgnette framed in diamonds sold for $117,000; it wasn't worth a penny over $5,000. The modest cufflinks, coat buttons and studs of the Duke of Windsor went for $400,000, at least forty times their actual value. When everybody finally trailed out two-by-two at the witching hour, the auction had already raised close to ten times what it should have. The next night, when Nicholas Rayner banged his gavel for the last time, the total sales were almost $51 million.

Those who dipped into their purses and pockets wanted not only to possess the belongings of royalty – though ironically the Duchess of Windsor had never been allowed to use the title 'Her Royal Highness' – but also to partake, albeit vicariously, of an age in which society was society, the rich were (in the collective fantasy, at least) almost uniformly glamorous, and, while the rest of the world was on the breadline, the party never seemed to end. They wanted mementos of the love story of the century shining on their necks and wrists.

Thus, in death, Wallis Windsor was even more famous than she had been in life. She had been the most talked-about woman of her age, yet so much about her remained a puzzle. As I began my research, the character of this remarkable woman emerged more clearly, not least through the numerous US State Department documents and passport files and Public Record Office documents, particularly those from the papers of the late Lord Avon (formerly Anthony Eden). None of these appeared to have been examined before. More and more clearly I saw her determination, her steely will, her fight to overcome her own deficiencies; her love of intrigue, and her energetic dabbling in espionage; her pride in herself as an adventuress and a dominant woman who more than held her own in a world of men; her taste, her authentic glamour despite her lack of conventional beauty, and her love of the rich and splendid things of life. My greatest challenge was to determine the secret that allowed this woman, born illegitimate and handi-capped by lack of both inherited money and strongly desirable physical attributes, to achieve great wealth, incomparable fame, magnificent houses and the lifelong love of a king that brought her very close to the British throne. I hope that this book will supply the answer to the mystery.

I have been fascinated by the Windsors from the age of five when, as the excessively precocious child of Sir Charles Higham, advertising tycoon and member of parliament (who would die when I was seven and who had married, like Henry VIII, six times), I was brought from the nursery by my German nanny to the opulent red drawing room of The Mount, our family home, to attend what I was informed was to be a momentous occasion. The men were in black tie, wreathed in clouds of smoke from expensive cigars; the women wore backless evening gowns, their shoulders vanishing in explosions of ruffles.

The combination of perfume and tobacco smoke made me dizzy; the decor of red plush furniture and Chinese carpets swarming with dragons and exotic birds made me feel even worse. I sat on the edge of a Victorian chair, having been told that I must fix my attention on a speckled walnut cabinet that stood under a Gothic landscape painting. The cabinet was the family shrine: a radio-gramophone.

Father turned on the switch, and everyone at last stopped talking. We heard a voice announce the king. I understood nothing of what he said, in an American-cockney voice adopted partly from his lady love and partly from a succession of nannies. (Some fifty years later, I discovered that the only language he spoke with a perfect modulation was German.)

When the speech was over – the abdication speech which would become one of the half-dozen most famous broadcasts in history – there was a murmur of conversation. I am told that my godfather, the bestselling novelist Gilbert Frankau, broke into tears, that the staff was sobbing in the background, and that more than one visiting European aristocrat had mist on his monocle. I had no idea what 'abdication' meant. I was probably thinking about my pet goldfish, whether my father would continue to keep me a kidnap victim (I had been snatched from Mother in a Rolls-Royce Silver Ghost, hidden and almost smothered under a heavy sable rug), or whether I would be able to finish, under the bedcovers, unravelling with a penknife a stubborn tennis ball (later I would discover that it had a sticky, toffee-like, mysterious something at its centre).

*

For years I had been thinking of writing about the Windsors. Every book is a new adventure; my three visits to England in ten months in 1987 to research the first edition of the book were as much an exile's journey of rediscovery as they were voyages of investigation. The England I had fled long ago had disappeared, to be replaced by a kinder, warmer and more appealing country. Along with its empire, Britain had lost its stiffness and its stern, heartless formality. I was rewarded by examples of kindness that made me feel as much at home as if I had never left. I enjoyed lunch with the Duchess of Marlborough and dinner with the legendary Margaret, Duchess of Argyll, as well as country visits to Sir Dudley Forwood, former equerry and secretary to King Edward VIII, and his fascinating wife, and to Adrian Liddell Hart, son of the London *Times* correspondent Basil Liddell Hart. I had pleasant days at the home of Hugo Vickers, who showed me evidence of the Windsors' charm in a recording made of them in London and who gave me much valuable advice. I shall not forget visiting Alfred de Marigny (falsely accused and acquitted of the murder of Sir Harry Oakes) and his enchanting wife Mary at their home in secret-filled, luxurious River Oaks, Houston, Texas.

Among others who helped, I must single out James P. Maloney, who in Washington, DC, spent countless hours exploring obscure documents, struggling against the restrictions of the Freedom of Information Act and poring over shipping lists of the Dollar Lines, the Royal Canadian Pacific Lines and the Cunard Lines, over naval intelligence files, passport files, immigration records from Seattle and New York and thousands more abstruse documentary sources that no other biographer or historian had examined. Simultaneously, I spent sometimes frustrating but more often exciting months at the University of California Research Library and the Von Kleinsmid Library of the University of Southern California, as well as the Glendale and Pasadena public libraries, reading through scores of old magazines and examining such items as the 1924 guest lists of the Astor House Hotel, Shanghai, issues of the *South*

China Morning Post and *Hong Kong Telegraph* and reports of the Prince of Wales's Ball at San Diego's Hotel del Coronado sixty-five years ago.

As I continued the work, I was surprised to find that Wallis had covered her tracks with great expertise, even giving the name of the hotel in which she stayed in Shanghai as the Palace and not the Astor House, and concealing the name of her travelling companion for reasons that will become clear to the reader.

The conclusions reached in the book are, of course, mine and should not be taken to reflect the views of those who aided me.

In San Diego I had a series of enjoyable meetings with Mrs Dale St Dennis, charming granddaughter of Wallis's cousin and friend Corinne Montague Mustin Murray, who gave me first access to letters in which the duchess gave a vivid account of her life. Her father, Vice Admiral Lloyd Mustin, had found them. The Maryland Historical Society and Radcliffe College came up with more letters, the latter supplying the correspondence of Mary Kirk Raffray, Wallis's school friend, who later married Wallis's second husband, Ernest Simpson. The late Sir John Colville, former secretary to Sir Winston Churchill, was a mine of information. So too was the late John Costello; Nigel West proved to be informative on the intelligence background. The late Charles Bedaux, Jr, loyally did his best to soften my judgements upon his late father, who had committed suicide in 1944 following charges of treason and who had been the duke and duchess's host at the Château de Candé when they were married in 1937. Robert Barnes of Baltimore was very good on the genealogical background. The late John Ball helped me with the Sir Harry Oakes murder case, and I was further assisted by Dr Joseph Choi, a forensic expert. Richard A. Best did some early research. Herbert Bigelow, Boris Celovsky, the late Comte René de Chambrun, Mrs Evelyn Cherfak, Jim Christy, the late Richard Coe, Rabbi Abraham Cooper, the Earl of Crawford, the late Kenneth de Courcy, Alain Deniel, Todd Andrew Dorsett, the late Tony Duquette, Leslie Field, Martin Gilbert, Barbara Goldsmith, Count Dino Grandi, Henry Gris, Betty Hanley, Lord Hardinge, Kirk Hollingsworth, John Hope, Lord Ironside, Anna Irwin, Michael Kriz, Samuel Marx, Mrs Milton E. Miles, Philippe Mora, Roy Moseley, Lady Mosley, Luke Nemeth, the Duchess of Normanby, Donatella

Ortona, Chapman Pincher, Peter Quennell, Clark G. Reynolds, Kenneth Rose, Jill Spalding, Roberta Stitch, Mrs Beatrice Tremain, John Vincent and the late Frederick Winterbotham all gave of their help. I am also most grateful to Gillian Paul for her expert advice in England. Finally, the excellent physical training methods of Richard M. Finegan, fine typing of Victoria Shellin, and the very skilled editing and warm encouragement of Thomas W. Miller were indispensable.

For assistance in obtaining the information for the new edition (2004) I am especially grateful to my Washington researcher Jill Cairns-Gallimore, who worked long and gallantly to find obscure records not seen outside of the National Archives in decades; to John Taylor, wise and illustrious head of the Modern Military branch of the same archive, colleague, supporter and friend; Dorris Halsey, incomparable literary agent, sage advisor; Bob O'Hara, diligent London researcher, and Jessica Gerger in the same city; Eleanor Davies Tydings Ditzen, in her late nineties a fountain of information; Scott Libson and Tanya Chebotareff; Michael Neal in Paris, notable bookstore manager, good historian; Chi-Chi Barthelemy, French friend and contact; Andrea Lynn, indispensable source of the vanished diaries of Constance Coolidge; Martin Allen, excellent and incorruptible author; Aline, Countess of Romanones; Professor Jonathan Petropoulos; Dr Herbert Reginbogen; Joel Greenberg; Jean Paule and Michael Sutherland of Occidental College, Los Angeles; Margaret Shannon; Madgid Madgidi; Dr Mildred de Riggi; Carolyn Ugolini; Heidi Sugden; Jane Singer; Nigel West; Fulton Oursler, Jr, and Harry Cooper of Sharkhunters. And it was a pleasure to work again with my original American editor Thomas Ward Miller and with new British editors, Jacqui Butler and Emma Marriott in London, as well as with the fine theatre director Michael Clark Haney, and with Udana Powers, master of word processing.

In the year 2003, after an interval of sixteen years, I was approached by American and British publishers to write an enlarged edition – hence the present, considerably enhanced, book. The publication of the collected papers of Joseph P. Kennedy, former ambassador to London, and father of the later president, in 2002, with unprecedented details of royal reactions to the Windsors, rendered such a publication mandatory; and my chance discovery of Andrew Lynn's excellent *Shadow Lovers*, about the love affairs of H. G. Wells, led me to the unpublished diary of Constance Coolidge, which in turn revealed the existence of an astonishing story of attempted blackmail and extortion, set in Paris in the troubled March of 1938, that took me months to unravel.

In addition, at the suggestion of a friend, I contacted the remarkable Eleanor Davies Ditzen, daughter of US ambassador to Russia Joseph E. Davies, who told me of the Duchess of Windsor's prolonged and unknown affair with William Christian Bullitt, Davies's replacement as emissary to Moscow and the famous ambassador to France from 1936 to 1940, who new documents show was a Nazi collaborator. In the course of researching this unknown romance, I found in Washington, through Jill Cairns-Gallimore, the massive FBI files on Elsa Schiaparelli, the great Italian dress designer, whose salon the duchess and the ambassador used for their liaison.

Other leads brought me to the previously unavailable files of Kenneth de Courcy, Duc de Grantmesnil, at the Hoover Institution of Peace and War at Stanford University, California, which confirmed the existence of the much argued-over China dossier in which King George V and Prime Minister Stanley Baldwin explored the duchess's activities as prostitute and drug dealer in China in 1924; and I was led by complicated threads to the little-known archives of Russian émigrés at the Bakhmeteff Archive at Columbia University, New York City, courtesy of Tanya Chebotarev, where one remarkable letter from the Queen of England attacking the Windsors had survived generations of weeders in England, and where the highly explosive letters of the Duke of Kent to Prince Paul of Yugoslavia have been preserved. The British historian Martin Allen, a leading authority on the subject, gave me his views on the alleged assassination of the Duke of Kent supplied to his father by Squadron Leader Frederick Winterbotham of the British Secret Intelligence Service.

In June 2003, I stumbled on a forgotten memoir housed in the labyrinthine stacks of the Doheny Library of the University of California. Princess Viktoria Luise, Duchess of Brunswick, daughter of Kaiser Wilhelm II of Germany, illuminated for me as nobody else could have done that Hitler's and King George V's approved choice of wife for the future King Edward VIII was Viktoria's daughter, Princess Friederike of Prussia. Had that wedding taken place, and Wallis Simpson been royal mistress, the course of history might have been changed. How could England declare war on Germany when the granddaughter of its former ruler, and the choice of Hitler and King George V, was on the English throne? That the British royal family had forgiven their cousin the Kaiser by 1935 is clear from the sheer number of German members who appeared at the silver jubilee of King George V that summer and the following January at his funeral, not to mention the flood of royal congratulations sent to his Dutch place of exile on the occasion of his eightieth birthday in 1939.

In October 2003, in the course of a final factfinding mission to Europe, I visited the apartment building at 36 Boulevard Emile Augier at which the blackmail plot by 'Madame Maroni' took place. Bleak and forlorn, it stood in a neighbourhood that had known far better days. Across the street, a tall black-painted iron railing stood, protecting not other buildings but a scene that could have come from a Jean Cocteau film: a scene from a nightmare.

Long before, some fifty years ago, a railway station named La Muette (the woman who cannot speak) had existed nearby, and now the deep siding through which the steam trains ran, replaced by the ubiquitous Métro, had become a jungle of uncontrolled weeds, enormous red and yellow flowers, some of them twenty feet high, huge bushes displayed black prickles and flaking lichen-covered trees. When I walked into the building, a lady concierge who was almost too classic – hair in a bun, clothes gipsyish, manner suspicious – asked me my business. Soon afterwards, an elderly male resident appeared and questioned me even more closely. I replied accurately – but made no mention of blackmail. As I left, very fast, the sky, already dark, turned a deep, ominous black. No setting for a blackmail plot could have been more perfect.

From my new research and travels, I believe I obtained a deeper understanding than hitherto of a powerful motive that drove both the Duke and Duchess of Windsor: to preserve and enhance the royal connections through Hitler that would result in the destruction of the Soviet Union, itself the destroyer of Tsar Nicholas and his wife Alexandra, blood kindred of Windsor himself.

It was after this a complicated journey to learning of the Nazi connections, of which I was not aware in 1988, of the Duke of Windsor with his brother the Duke of Kent, and their cousin Queen Victoria's great-grandson Prince Philipp of Hesse, the basis of the aforementioned blackmail plot of 1938. Philipp was the favourite and emissary of Hitler; his wedding to Princess Mafalda, daughter of King Victor Emmanuel III of Italy, with Mussolini presiding over the civil ceremony, provided the support of the Hitler–Mussolini alliance of which the Windsors and the Kents were so much a part. This royal tapestry of pro-Fascist loyalties provided much of my new text, and seemed to make a 2004 edition eminently desirable.

1

A BALTIMORE CHILDHOOD

The world into which Bessie Wallis Warfield was born out of wedlock, on 19 June 1895,[1] was without aeroplanes, radio, television, movies, automobiles, income tax, chain stores, supermarkets, cafeterias, ice cream sundaes, crossword puzzles or bathing trunks. Almost everyone attended church on Sunday. Mail deliveries were made by horse and buggy, and blacksmiths still hammered out horseshoes; America had fewer than 75 million inhabitants, and much of the nation breathed the atmosphere of the frontier.

The United States was recovering painfully from a disastrous depression. The once buoyant and brash New World had long been stifled under a shroud of gloom. The chief causes of the panic of 1893, in which millions liquidated their stockholdings and banks collapsed by the dozen, were over-expansion, excessive confidence and the unbridled investments of the tycoons known as the robber barons. President Grover Cleveland was unable to find a salve, much less a solution; the Treasury had to fight to stop the constant drain on gold.

Yet the shabby-genteel backwater of Baltimore in which Wallis's family lived showed few obvious signs of distress. The Warfields were at 34 East Preston Street, a narrow, four-storey terraced house fashioned of grey Maryland brick. The kitchen was in the basement; the parlour, hidden from prying eyes by hand-made Irish lace curtains and rich, dark red satin drapes, was on the ground floor; at the back there was a dining room flanked by African mahogany sideboards; the library was on the first floor; the family rooms were on the second floor; and the servants' quarters at the top of the house.

The matriarch of the clan was Anna Emory, the widow Warfield. She was in her sixties and her hair was snow white, piled high and fixed at the back by a black lacquered comb.

Her sole companion, other than her overworked and harshly disciplined cook, maids and butler, was her bachelor son Solomon. Three other boys had moved away: two of them, Emory and Henry, to get married, and one, Teackle, to live in a small apartment.

Solomon Warfield's households, which included his handsome farms Manor Glen, where he shot game, Mount Eyrie and Mount Prospect, and the 109-acre Parker-Watters Place, with its aviary of a hundred rare birds, still had slave quarters where blacks were maintained in substandard conditions. Solomon was to all appearances a pillar of rectitude, with his close-cropped, carefully parted black hair, his square-cut, neatly moustached face, imposing physique and erect bearing, his hand-made suits and chamois gloves; he was cold, haughty and disdainful in the Warfield tradition. Yet it was whispered that this smart Baltimore gentleman was a lecher in private, and there were few women, married or not, on whom his cool eye lit who escaped his advances. His list of actress and opera singer mistresses in New York, where he retained a hideaway apartment on Fifth Avenue, was an open scandal.

Anna Warfield's youngest son (she also had two married daughters living in Baltimore) was Teackle Wallis. Teackle was an anomaly in the clan. Not a black sheep – the Warfields could have stood that, and sent him off to Canada or California – but something unforgivably unAmerican: he was a physical weakling who had no athletic ability and even had to leave college because of his ill health. The normally robust strain of Warfield genetics had faltered when a failing Henry Mactier, at the age of sixty-two, had fathered this ill-fated child.

At eighteen, Teackle suffered from consumption. Instead of sending the boy to an expensive sanatorium, his brother Sol insisted he should learn the banking business from the ground up. Teackle was forced to toil as a clerk, with green eyeshade and leather sleeve protectors, at the Continental Trust, while his brothers were already insurance executives working for Henry Mactier Warfield II.

In those days, tubercular patients were forbidden to cohabit with women. The benign family physician, Dr Leonard E. Neale, must surely have given advice in the matter of celibacy to the young man. But at twenty-five Teackle made the mistake of falling in love; some time in the early 1890s he met the pretty, golden-haired, lively and adorable twenty-four-year-old Alice Montague, whose ancestry, like the Warfields', went back to the Normans at the time of William the Conqueror. She always claimed that both families were descended from knights in the army that invaded England. Alice was the daughter of William and Mary Anne Montague, an insurance man and his wife, of 711 St Paul Street.

When even a kiss from a tuberculosis sufferer was considered dangerous, possibly even a cause of death, Alice needed all her young courage to enter into a romantic liaison with her lover. He seems to have given no thought to the consequences to her, but in fact she did not contract the disease. Somehow, in cheap hotels or parks at night, they escaped the watchful eyes of their families and consummated their relationship. Horror of horrors, Alice became pregnant. Dr Neale reached that conclusion two months after the conception.

In an Episcopalian family, birth out of wedlock was a disaster. It meant potential disgrace, social ruin and possible expulsion. Neither the Warfields nor the Montagues would risk exposure to such scandal. The baby must not be born in Baltimore, nor would the official Warfield family history, then being written and published finally in 1905, include the names of father, mother or child. Nor would Dr Neale or cousin Mactier, also a physician, preside over the birth.

In the early months of 1895, the young couple left for Blue Ridge Summit, a popular resort that stood high in the mountains that straddled the Pennsylvania–Maryland border. The excuse for this ignominious exile was that the resort was said to be good for consumptives. Warfield money ensured there would be no mention of Alice's pregnancy or the child's birth in the Blue Ridge or Baltimore papers. Alice would remain indoors for the entire length of the stay.

Blue Ridge Summit had grown considerably as a health resort and spa since the railroad had gone through in 1884. When the steam train chugged into the Summit station that spring day in 1895, Teackle and Alice were met by a coach drawn by four white horses, which conveyed them by standard arrangement to their new home, a cabin of the Monterey Inn known as Square Cottage. It was about as architecturally pleasing as a dog's kennel. The town offered Saturday-night dances lit by Chinese lanterns, trail horse-back rides, and Sunday parades with high hats and parasols, but the couple experienced none of these pleasures.

On 19 June 1895,[2] Alice was seized by the first contractions. Dr Lewis Miles Allen, a postgraduate student of Dr Neale, arrived by train from Baltimore to ensure a safe delivery and no scandal. On seeing the baby, Dr Allen said, 'It's all right. Let her cry. It'll do her good.' He did not say, and he spent much of his life saying he had not said, 'She's fit for a king.'

Not only was the birth the only Warfield or Montague advent that was never featured anywhere in print, but the baby, named Bessie Wallis[3] Warfield, was the first Warfield not to be baptized. The family's Episcopalian advisers decided not to permit baptism; birth out of wedlock was sufficient reason, Baltimore church authorities confirm, for this grave verdict. When Wallis came to be confirmed at Christ Church, Baltimore, on 17 April 1910, the baptismal record was falsified in order to secure her confirmation, and as a result of her unbaptized state two of her three marriages, including the one in 1937 to the Duke of Windsor, were religiously invalid. In the eyes of the Church she would suffer eternal damnation as an unbaptized person.

A marriage was finally arranged for Teackle and Alice seventeen months after Wallis's birth. It could not in any circumstances take place in a church. This in itself was a disgrace – no Warfield or Montague marrying for the first time had ever been denied a church wedding – nor could there be a dowry, a trousseau, a municipal office wedding or a ceremony in either the Montague or Warfield family homes. The solution was to have the ceremony performed in the rectory living room of the Episcopalian minister, the Reverend Ernest Smith, who suspended his finer feelings in order to perform his disagreeable task. The wedding took place on 19 November 1896. Alice wore a sable-trimmed green silk afternoon dress, with hat and gloves to match, and she carried a small posy of violets;

the groom wore a plain grey suit. No member of their families was present; there was no best man or matron of honour, and nobody to give the bride away. There was neither wedding party nor honeymoon.

The unhappy couple moved first to Teackle's lodgings at 28 Hopkins Place and thence to the Brixton Residential Hotel, a faded family hostelry on Park Avenue with rooms rented out at $1.50 a week. There the enfeebled boy, often prostrated, debilitated and flushed, in the grip of fevers, no doubt brought anxious glances from the other boarders. How Alice must have felt is beyond comprehension. Nursing a child, with a husband whose days were numbered and whose coughing could cause her own and her child's death, she faced every day with fear and anxiety that not even her stubbornly cheerful and optimistic nature could quell.

The Warfield ranks closed; the decision was made that parents and child should travel, presumably incognito, to Teackle's mother at 34 East Preston Street, which they did as soon as Alice was sufficiently recovered from post-natal complications to take the train. Teackle lasted only six months; he died in November 1897. Just before he passed away, he asked to see Wallis's baby picture – he was not permitted to touch or kiss the child.

Corseted and starched, brooding over her substantial landholdings, Anna Emory Warfield remained a despot. By the time Wallis was five, the child was up with the family at dawn for prayers. Breakfast was announced at eight each morning by the banging of a brass Indian gong. Immediately afterwards, Mrs Warfield summoned her staff of six bonneted and aproned maids and instructed them in the business of the household. Mrs Warfield carried with her a chatelaine of keys; when a maid wished to take linen from a closet or fetch the season's preserves, she had to apply formally for the use of the key. Each night at precisely the same hour Uncle Solomon would return and would inspect the rooms for dust, disorder or other evidence of incompetence. Sometimes Uncle Henry and his wife Aunt Rebecca would visit from next door to look at the child with her large, eager, violet eyes.

Wallis was an outgoing, mischievous and buoyant child. Alice adored her; she had her photographed week by week as she grew, so that by 1900 more than three hundred pictures of the little girl filled her grandmother's room. She called them the 'Wallis Collection', after the London gallery. Wallis was a Warfield: a born snob. According to Cleveland Amory, she named her first dolls after Mrs Astor and Mrs Vanderbilt, the reigning queens of New York society. Her first reading was about fashion, the theatre and the fashionable world, and of English kings and queens. She behaved royally from the first: instead of saying 'Mama' she said 'Me Me'.

The atmosphere at 34 East Preston Street was tense and unpleasant for Alice Montague Warfield. Uncle Sol never ceased to make her aware that she was living on charity, but at the same time he was casting lecherous glances over her voluptuous young body. In 1901 Alice left, taking Wallis with her, and moved back into the Brixton Residential Hotel.

Uncle Sol's meagre allowance did not cover the hotel bills, so Alice had to work. She could not type or book-keep; her only skill was as a dressmaker. She joined the Women's Exchange, a charitable organization, altering children's clothes for a small weekly fee. At least she could make Wallis's dresses on the Exchange's sewing machine during her lunch hours.

In 1902, Alice's sister Bessie came to the rescue. Warm, sweet, plump Bessie had been widowed the previous year when her husband, an auctioneer named David B. Merryman, had died suddenly from pneumonia at the age of forty-three. Lonely in her big brick house at 9 West Chase Street, she adored Alice and Wallis and made a cosy home for them.

That same year, Wallis became a pupil at Miss Ada O'Donnell's kindergarten at 2812 Elliott Street. It was there that the child's character began to emerge. She was determined to be first in everything. She was seven years old when Miss O'Donnell asked the class, 'Who tried to blow up the Houses of Parliament in London?' A boy seated at a desk behind Wallis jumped up and yelled, 'Guy Fawkes!' – just as she was about to give the same correct answer. Furious, she smacked him hard over the head with her wooden pencil box.

Ninety-four-year-old Mrs Edward D. Whitman, formerly Susan Waters White, daughter of a distillery owner, remembers Wallis well at Miss O'Donnell's:

She was as busy as a cartload of monkeys. Oh! She was bright, brighter than all of us. She made up her mind to go to the head of the class and she *did.* She was poor, mind you. The Warfields had nothing. Servants? Anyone could afford those. But she had no pocket money, not a penny. She loved the country. She would stay with us at our estates, Robinswood and Knowleboth are still standing – and she would have a great time with us – we were *eleven* children. She *loved* to play Jacks. At night, she'd get excited over the fireflies. She loved a story we would tell: how an English Lord came to stay and said, 'Oh look at all the lights, where do they come from?' And grandfather would say, 'Don't you have any more mint juleps!'

In 1906, Alice was back at East Preston Street, leaving Wallis in the care of Bessie. Two years later she moved again, with Wallis, into the Preston Apartments and began letting back rooms – an unthinkable disgrace in Baltimore society, especially since she let them to good-looking young male students, including, for a time, her Montague cousins. She was lax in collecting rents, so much so that she had difficulty in paying her own; over-generously she served her tenants expensive meals such as Terrapin à la Maryland or Lobster Cardinal free of charge.

She taught Wallis to cook; the bright, prattling little girl was able to manage a Lady Baltimore cake or a pecan pie at the age of ten – and heaven help anyone who stood in her way or failed to smack their lips over her efforts. One of the boarders, young Charles E. Bove, a medical student, recalled years later that Wallis was always busy in the kitchen, fussing over the stove and the dishes. She had her black hair drawn back in fancy braids. Because of that and her sharp, high-cheekboned features, he dubbed her 'the Squaw' and 'Minnehaha'. She believed her mother's story that she was indirectly descended on the Warfield side from the Indian princess Pocahontas.

At ten, Wallis went to the fashionable Arundell School for Girls at 714 St Paul Street, just a few houses away from her maternal grandparents. When pupils laughed at her because her mother took in boarders, she would hit them with her heavy walking shoes.

The head teacher at Arundell was a Miss Carroll. Wallis often defied her authority, earning herself a reputation as both impertinent and haughty. She also used bad language, to the stupefaction of her teachers. Though spanked at school and at home, Wallis remained proud, stubborn and unregenerate. She worked maddeningly hard at everything from basketball to needlework to cookery to history lessons. Though she was not pretty, and was prone to theatrical headaches and fainting spells when attention strayed from her, she was popular because of her enthusiasm, vitality and charm. With her angular, efficient body, her boyish shoulders, her 'Indian' hair and face and her jutting chin, she was, according to one fellow pupil, different from the other girls: 'special'. Always immaculately groomed, she knew that any slackening of deportment would earn her a smacking with a hairbrush or a plunge in an icy bath. Her pencils were sharpened to fine points. She was never seen with chewing gum or half-eaten apples. Her blouses and pleated skirts were immaculately ironed.

Even daunting Uncle Sol could not rattle her. Knowing how she hated mathematics, he subjected her to a mathematical quiz each Sunday night at East Preston Street. One Sunday she suddenly drew herself to her full height and said, 'The square on the hypotenuse of a right triangle is equal to the sum of the squares on the other two sides.' Uncle Sol dropped the carving knife on the beef dish with a clatter.

NOTES

1 Not 1896, as given in all sources.
2 The date is documented in the census report on the Warfield household taken in 1900. No birth certificate exists.
3 Not Bessiewallis, as given in most sources.

2

A STUBBORN YOUNG LADY

As she grew older, Wallis developed a new characteristic. She would plunge recklessly into some daring adventure, only to panic when she had gone in too deep. A fellow pupil at Arundell recalled, 'One night she prodded us to spy on a Masonic ceremony. A police guard caught us and threatened us with arrest. Wallis panicked and we fled. She told us she was going to drown herself in a creek! We all teased her about that speech for years.' Another pupil said, 'She seemed a fly-up-the-creek little girl. I mean she screamed a lot at parties . . . she had smartness and style without real beauty or hard, good common sense.'

Wallis was fiercely angry in 1907 when, after eleven years of widowhood, her mother took a lover. John Freeman Rasin was the ne'er-do-well, thirty-seven-year-old eldest son of the leader of the Baltimore Democratic party. He had not married before and was the worst possible prospect as a husband: a big, moon-faced, portly alcoholic who liked to lie in bed all day reading comic strips and drinking beer. His excessive love of the bottle had given him kidney and liver ailments. But he had been kind and generous to Alice and Wallis, and he offered Alice, who still carried the stigma of her first marriage, the chance of a proper home and a father for her child.

During the courtship, which Wallis treated with sulks and fainting fits as she saw her exclusive domain invaded, Alice moved to a better address, 212 Biddle Street. There, in defiance of all conventions, she spent the nights with Rasin in the guest bedroom, just a thin wall away from her eleven-year-old daughter. When Alice announced that Rasin was going to be her husband Wallis flew into a tantrum, screaming hysterically. It was quite obvious to her that the world had come to an end. She announced she would boycott the wedding – until Aunt Bessie Merryman talked her into going. Aunt Bessie could talk Wallis into anything.

The ceremony took place at 3 p.m. on 20 June 1908, at 212 Biddle Street; once again, there could be no question of a church wedding. On this occasion the Warfields and the Montagues did attend. But Wallis could not bring herself to see her mother married. When nobody noticed her display of sulks, she left the parlour during the ceremony and began tearing the wedding cake to pieces. She was determined to steal the traditional ring, thimble and newly minted dime that were contained within it, but was surprised at her task just as she located these elusive treasures. The whole wedding party burst into laughter at the sight of her.

She behaved better at the wedding of her favourite cousin, the gorgeous, blue-eyed, blonde Corinne De Forest Montague, in 1907 – a glamorous affair because Corinne was marrying the ruggedly handsome thirty-three-year-old Henry Croskey Mustin, a pioneer navy pilot. There was a full white-uniformed guard of honour. Wallis vowed that when she was married she would have a similar husband, and an even grander wedding.

At twelve, Wallis was a rebel and a tomboy, almost too bright to be bearable. With her sharp voice, her constant barrage of questions, her air of confidence and boldness, and her theatrical attacks of sickness, she was considered a handful. She dutifully endured the religious practices of the eiscopalian Warfields and Montagues, who made sure she was confirmed even though she had, of course, never been baptized. She struggled through the endless round of prayers at morning, noon and night and the irritating advice of ministers led by the Reverend Francis Xavier Brady, who had no more idea of the feverish, romantic daydreams that went on in a young girl's head than would the man in the moon. At a time when young girls were supposed to think of nothing but sewing, cooking, preparing menus, dressing and playing basketball, Wallis was already pursuing boys (who were used to doing the pursuing themselves) and planning a future as a doctor, scientist or explorer.

She adored many things passionately: riding around the back roads in her donkey cart, dressing in smart new shirtwaisters, and wearing lace-up boots. Above all, she loved the taste, the smell, the feel of wealth. She was addicted to her richer, prettier cousins: Lelia Barnett, whose home was the big Wakefield Manor in Virginia, with its four-pillared Ionic portico, and Corinne, now settled in a nice house in Washington and soon to go to Florida. Wallis liked fine Irish linen, lace doilies, solid silver napkin rings, Waterford crystal, Crown Derby plates, orchids, tapestries, chandeliers, jewels – diamonds, emeralds, rubies – and money.

In 1911, Wallis went to the exclusive and snobbish Burrland, at Middleburg, Virginia, a family country property turned into a summer camp. While there, enjoying the antebellum mansion and its thousand acres of grounds, she fell in love for the first time. The object of her 'pash' – as a crush was then called – was the teenage Lloyd Tabb, the slim, dark, athletic, good-looking heir to a fortune. The other girls at Arundell and Burrland were jealous of her prize catch. They asked each other how she, the least pretty of them all, had managed to hook the handsomest boy they knew.

Her secret was that she researched her prey. She, who had no interest in football, found out every school score Tabb had made. She knew in how many minutes he had swum to victory at competitions, what kind of ice cream he liked and that he enjoyed skating in winter. His friends secretly helped her in her conspiracy of seduction.

She knew how to praise, how to build up the adolescent male's ego. Although it was thought immodest, she boldly felt biceps. She also knew how to charm the Tabb family by gurgling over their glorious pillared antebellum house, Glenora. She spent long, golden summer afternoons there, when she and Lloyd read Kipling's empire poems to each other, or shared the pages, one reading a few paragraphs, then passing the task to the other, of the popular *Monsieur Beaucaire*, Wallis's favourite novel by Booth Tarkington, about a commoner at the court of Louis XV of France. Significantly, she liked stories about kings and queens and how the lowly could attract their attention; Mark Twain's *The Prince and the Pauper* was another favourite of hers, and she was a-flutter over the daring Indian love lyrics of 'Laurence Hope'. Lloyd would never forget Wallis joining his family in close harmony sessions on the Glenora wooden veranda. Years later he said:

> Curiously enough, Wallis rarely joined in the singing, though she manifestly enjoyed the efforts of the others. She was one of the best at thinking up new numbers for us to render. Having made a few suggestions, she would lean back on her slender arms, head crooked appreciatively, and by her earnest attention make us feel we were really rather a gifted group of singers.

Tabb gallantly didn't mention that Wallis was tone-deaf. Her skill was the ability to seem to enjoy musical accomplishment in others – she had the charm of considerateness.

Lloyd had a bright red Lagonda sports car in which Wallis loved to go out. The first night he took her for a spin in it, she said, as he kissed her on her Biddle Street doorstep, 'Ah, the leader of the younger set honours me with his presence!' and she threw back her head and laughed. Lloyd never forgot those words – or Wallis.

In 1912, Wallis went to Oldfields School. She had decided it was superior to its rival, Arundell, though to leave one for the other instead of going ahead to graduation was considered shocking. She even had the boldness to go to Burrland that summer from her new school, brazenly confronting the class and basketball teams she had summarily abandoned. In her memoirs she wrote that she graduated from one school to go to the other, but the truth is that the two establishments took students from the ages of seven to eighteen.

Oldfields was the most expensive girls' school in Maryland, and Uncle Sol had to dig deep into his pockets to send her there. But she reckoned he could afford it as president of the Seaboard Air Line Railway and, by now, six other railroads. The school was housed in an eighteenth-century white clapboard farm building on two hundred acres on the banks of the Gunpowder River. It had been founded in 1867 by the Reverend Duncan McCulloch and his wife Anna, whose family owned the farm. Anna, known as Miss Nan, was the principal when Wallis was enrolled.

Wallis's best friends at Oldfields and Burrland summer school were the heiress Renée du Pont of the du Pont Chemical family and the ravishingly pretty Mary Kirk of Kirk Silverware money. Together the three girls, known as the 'Three Musketeers', decided to make the best of the strict, drab, heavily religious atmosphere of the school under its noble, black-clad head teacher and proprietress. Days were spent in learning whole chapters of the Bible, reciting prayers, studying sewing or having cookery lessons. But there were lighter moments: visits by Renée's father, Senator du Pont, who distributed $20 gold pieces to the girls; trips to Burrland in a jolting hay wagon that left everyone cheerfully bruised; playing in tableaux in the gym; putting on a vaudeville show at Middleburg with Wallis's heiress friend Lucie Lee Kinsolving as a moustached Don Juan singing 'Dear, Delightful Women' while Wallis and Mary fainted with delight; picnics at midnight when Wallis and Mary crept out of bed with Aunt Bessie's smuggled-in hamper of olives, beer(!), cakes, sweets and peanut butter and enjoyed the feast in a field; putting on blue stockings to go to a Sunday horse show; having tintype likenesses done; going to a costume party with Mary Kirk as the famous cartoon character Buster Brown and Wallis as Buster's beloved Mary Jane; going to Washington to see the great actor Sir Johnston Forbes Robertson in *Hamlet*, the girls shrieking with excitement on the railway platform as the teachers argued over the tickets, and then spending a glorious night at a hotel with Wallis and Mary yelling downstairs and waking up the whole school to demand ginger ale and sandwiches well after midnight.

There were 'rags' and dances and going-away shower parties and graduation parties, and, of course, dashing Lloyd Tabb in his red Lagonda and Wallis's second-best beau, rangy young Tom Shyrock, who went riding with her. Tom said later: 'Wallis took the highest jumps without batting an eyelash. There was something regal about the way she sat on a horse. I was rightly proud of my riding, but I had to take my hat off to Wallis.'

Like millions of young girls at that time, Wallis had a crush on the legendary Prince of Wales, the golden-haired, seventeen-year-old heir to the British throne. She had dozens of pictures of him in her room, cut out articles about him, and followed his movements incessantly. Lloyd and Tom took this schoolgirl silliness in their stride.

In 1914, Wallis left Oldfields. Alice, who had lost her husband, and was visibly much aged, took an apartment at 16 Earl Court, Baltimore, in Warfield-haunted Preston Street. At eighteen Wallis now had to make her society debut, which would – custom required it – be followed as soon as possible by marriage to a rich and attractive young man from an old Baltimore family. First, she insisted, she would go to the Princeton Ball with her cousin Lelia of Wakefield Manor, as the date of Lelia's frail but good-looking brother Basil Gordon. Basil, who was dating another girl, said the idea was out of the question. Wallis ranted and raved until Basil arranged for his best friend to break a date and take her. Wallis changed from tantrums to ecstasy. She and Alice fussed for hours over what she would wear. Wallis favoured blue organdie; Alice preferred pink. Wallis won by discovering that she would be the only girl at the dance wearing blue.

Now came a greater challenge: the major event of the year for any young woman in Baltimore.

3

RUNNING UP THE LADDER

The Bachelors Cotillon was the summit: entrance to the ball ensured a girl's place in society. Only forty-nine young women out of five hundred could be invited to this occasion, which tradition-ally took place at the Lyric Theatre on the first Thursday in December. World events had seemed dreamlike and distant to Wallis: the 1906 San Francisco earthquake, the 1907 financial panic, the advent of Halley's comet, the sailing of the Great White Fleet, the race to the North Pole, the Baltimore Democratic Con-vention, even the sinking of the *Titanic* in 1912 and the outbreak of world war in 1914 seemed unreal. But the Cotillon – that was real. Wallis, unable to sleep, alternately hysterical with excitement and afraid and depressed, could think only one thought: would she be among the forty-nine chosen?

At last, the great morning arrived, and she tore open the envelope. It contained the precious invitation card! Now all she had to do, war or no war, was somehow obtain a wardrobe, a family member as escort, and a corsage.

Wallis had to sweet-talk old Uncle Sol into backing her to the limit, and she sallied forth in the family Pierce-Arrow to the crucial appointment at his offices at 'Solomon's Temple', the rebuilt Continental Trust Building. She sat like a princess, gazing out from the sumptuous limousine as the chauffeur in grey livery drove her to her destination. Money! Was there anything like it?

Uncle Sol received her in ostentatious style and listened to her pleas. He knew as well as she did there was no way a Warfield girl would not make a splash at the Cotillon, and gave her the incredible sum of $20 – enough to buy at least thirty dresses. Wallis made her way to Maggie O'Connor, Baltimore modiste, and invested her entire, newly acquired fortune in one dress and one alone.

It was an exact copy of a white satin Worth gown made in Paris for the famous society dancer Irene Castle. Wallis stood for hours while it was fitted to her angular form. She spent more hours learning the one-step and the just-introduced tango. She greatly improved her waltzes. Her mother waltzed with her at home; various beaux led by Lloyd Tabb whirled her across country club dance floors until she fancied she was as proficient as Irene Castle herself.

Of course she must, she simply must, have the best possible escort on the big night. It was traditional to have an uncle or an older cousin dance with the debutantes. But Wallis would have none of that. She would have her handsomest, most dashing and youngest relative: her rugged, twenty-seven-year-old cousin Henry Warfield, who was already half in love with her anyway. That settled, there were weeks of teas and lunches and dances and meetings and hour-long phone calls, with Alice going mad because she couldn't use the telephone.

Finally, 7 December came around. Wallis, after prolonged fussing and spinning around in front of mirrors, was at last satisfied that she looked like a dream. At the appointed hour cousin Henry, looking like a million dollars in white tie and tails, roared up to 212 Biddle Street in Uncle Sol's Pierce-Arrow.

She was danced off her feet for hours. Each time a new partner joined her, she gave him her absolute and undivided attention, never talking about herself. As a result, the young men came back to her again and again, though she was probably among the least pretty debs in the place, but she was bright and bewitching and she knew it.

In the wake of that glorious night, Wallis now considered herself a woman. Alice acted as her chaperone on date after date. Wallis was man-mad; she risked tongue-wagging by having a bewildering succession of romances. Asked to sum her up in one word, a contemporary says, 'Fast'. She especially liked uniformed men – and in 1915, with war in Europe, and after the *Lusitania* went down from a German torpedo, more and more boys in the social set were at the Annapolis naval academy or West Point military academy.

After Grandma Anna's death, Wallis found that she had been left $4,000 in the will. She was guiltily excited, and in no mood to stay in mourning for months on end. Worse, Carter Osburn, whom she had almost made up her mind to marry, was posted to Mexico with General Pershing's army to fight Pancho Villa. Wallis made a theatrical farewell with tears and fluttering handkerchief as his train pulled out of the depot.

She filled the months of family mourning for Anna by writing love letters to Osburn, which he read by the light of hurricane lamps in lonely Mexican encampments after days of scouting or skirmishes. But it irritated her that she couldn't date or go to dances. Even learning contract bridge was no consolation.

At last she found an opportunity to get out of town. On 20 January 1914, her cousin Corinne's husband, Lieutenant Commander Henry C. Mustin, had sailed into Pensacola, Florida, as master of the battleship USS *Mississippi*. He had been appointed to help establish a naval aeronautic centre for flight and ground training for defence operations as America lumbered towards war. Corinne had often written to Wallis about life at the newly formed base: the first in American history, just a few years after the Wright brothers made their pioneer flight at Kitty Hawk. In November 1915 Corinne reported excitedly that Mustin had been the first man to be catapulted from a ship – in the AB-2 flying boat, off the rolling deck of the USS *North Carolina*.

Wallis, with her mania for servicemen and her addiction to the army–navy football game, was excited by Corinne's news and still more so when Corinne asked her to come to Pensacola and stay with her. Wallis begged her depressing family to let her go. A family meeting was held, with Aunt Bessie and Alice pleading her cause to stern, black-clad Uncles Sol, Henry and Emory and cousin Mactier. The women won. Pensacola it would be. And Uncle Sol owned part of the railroad that would take her south-west to the Florida panhandle; that would ensure her a free first-class ticket.

Corinne met her at the Gregory Street station and drove her to the white-painted wooden house, part of a long row of similar bungalows, overlooking the huge, landlocked, palm-fringed bay and the aeronautical station with its hangars, slipways, derricks and machine shops.

Wallis was in her element. Pensacola, the major Gulf town of the north-east Florida panhandle, with a hundred miles of un-spoiled, snowy-white beaches to east and west, was predominantly Spanish in flavour.

Wallis very much liked Henry Mustin. Older than Corinne, he was at this time forty-two, wrinkled and dark from spending so long on an open fuselage in the tropical sun. His infectious grin and strong voice were pleasing, and he looked impressive in his flying helmet and goggles. He was having problems with the Navy Depart-ment that caused an angry exchange of letters between him and Washington. His chief quarrel was with Captain Mark L. Bristol, director of naval aeronautics. Mustin wanted more autonomy and better operational management from the Capitol. It was an uphill fight every day.

Wallis stayed with the Mustins and their three children, occupy-ing a big, sunny guest room and helping Corinne with the cooking and housework. On Saturday nights she went with the Mustins to the San Carlos Hotel, where there were dances to a palm court orchestra in the big, Spanish-style dining room. Once again she attracted many beaux through her expert one-stepping and tango-ing, and focusing on their interests to the exclusion of her own.

Early in May, after weeks of sunbathing, swimming in clear, clean water, picnicking, movie-going and dancing, Wallis was asked by Corinne to stay in for lunch to meet three young airmen. They were coming to the house as a special favour. Wallis, on the porch, saw the officers in starched white uniforms stride up. She was excited; they were all good-looking, but one of the three was riveting and irresistible.

Mustin introduced him to Wallis as Earl Winfield Spencer. She wrote later, 'He was laughing, but there was a suggestion of inner force and vitality that struck me instantly.' At lunch, when most of the discussion about aeronautical matters went right over her head, Wallis couldn't take her eyes off him. As she looked at his shoulders and their gold braid he made it clear, by the merest indication in his eyes, that he knew what she felt about him; she hung on every word he was saying, and he noted that, too. She wanted to know all about flying.

His close-cropped black hair stood *en brosse* above a high forehead; his piercing, bold, arrogant eyes, sharp nose and firm, jutting jaw were very attractive; his expression was proud, challenging and fierce. His body was tanned, lithe and muscular, and his posture erect and assured. His demeanour did not suggest gentleness, courtesy or ingratiating charm. He appealed to Wallis, going to her head like champagne. She was always drawn to tigers.

After lunch he sauntered up to her the instant they were alone and asked her to dinner the next night. He brushed aside her demurs and told her he would be calling on her; then he left. The casual, almost contemptuous arrogance of the young man left her breathless. She was in a daze; she felt no warning signals.

Spencer had been born in a small town in Kansas on 20 September 1888. His father was a Chicago stockbroker, whose American antecedents, like Wallis's, went back to the early 1600s. Big, brawling Earl Senior was formerly on the Ithaca, New York, baseball team and had been a big-game hunter in his day, bagging buffalo, wolves, deer and antelope, whose heads bristled from the walls of the family home at 109 Wade Street, Highland Park, Illinois.

Winfield was his eldest child. The others were Gladys, Ethel, Egbert, Dumaresq and Frederick. Win was the bad seed in the family, though Wallis did not know it then. After enlisting at the Annapolis naval academy in 1905, he earned a long list of demerits in his conduct record for, among other things, dirty shoes and uniform, room dirty and badly swept, bathing trunks falling down at a swimming match, lateness at meals and drill and choir practice, skylarking in corridors, rowdyism and moving furniture without authorization. Yet he was popular, especially in naval academy vaudeville shows, in which he excelled in drag. He was a good footballer, and he was cheerleader and head of the Christmas parade; 'a merry devil, a singer nicknamed Caruse,' said the naval academy magazine. He was also a secret bisexual whose predilection, if discovered, would have resulted in his expulsion.

His face stares out at us from the group photograph of the class of 1910: moody, dark and petulant among all the open, fresh faces, his jug ears standing out almost at right angles from the head and slightly undercutting the primitive, threatening, somewhat simian handsomeness of the whole.

Fond though she was of Corinne, with her innocent, china-doll eyes and flow of bright tittle-tattle, Wallis was glad to escape with Win, unchaperoned whenever possible, for blameless romantic trysts at night. Henry Mustin was brooding and silent, obsessed with his battles with Washington, and there was a sense of strain in the household. Wallis always found it difficult to relate to children, and Corinne's offspring, including the high-spirited eldest boy, Lloyd, who was at the toy train stage, baffled and irritated her, lovable though they were.

Through Win, Wallis met many of the men at the base, and she was captivated by their bravery; she flirted with many but it is unlikely she allowed intercourse. John Towers, base commandant; George D. Murray, whom years later she would know again; Chevy Chevalier; Jim Rockwell; and Dick Saufley – they and their girlfriends and Wallis and Win went picnicking and dancing together in a life of buoyancy and frivolity. It was good to be alive, and young and carefree.

But then, out of a clear, blue Pensacola sky came horror. On 24 May 1916, Wallis joined a crowd at the beach to see Lieutenant Jim Rockwell, one of the youngest of Win's set, take off in a practice flight. His training plane soared into the sun, to a height of 150 feet. Suddenly there was a choking sound. The plane plunged in a nosedive into the sea. Wallis and the other spectators watched in agony as the body of the twenty-six-year-old man was dragged from the waves.

Fifteen days later, Dick Saufley, also twenty-six, took off on a flight of several hours around the bay. Wallis and hundreds of Pensacolans went out by the boatload to Santa Rosa Island to watch him. After almost nine hours in the air, three struts loosened and the plane crashed, killing Saufley instantly. For almost thirty years after that, Wallis refused to fly.

That night, Mustin was dark and thunderous, complaining of the lack of safety features in authorized plane designs, talking of inquests and official inquiries, holding emergency conferences and making telephone calls.

Wallis tried to find escape on Sundays. She and Win played golf, looked for shells on the beach and went to see movies at the big, fancy stucco Isis movie house – she loved Buster Keaton and Harold Lloyd comedies – where she ate popcorn and cuddled with Win in the darkness. Still considered flighty, she dated other men, including Chevy Chevalier, with giddy, wild abandon. Wallis was a 'sport'.

Soon she realized Win was in love with her; he exploded into jealous rages when she dated Chevy. She was in love with Win, too, and she told Corinne unabashedly she longed for him. Corinne knew the inevitable would happen.

Given the restrictions of the time, and the disaster of her mother's indiscretion with Teackle Warfield, there could be no question of her going 'all the way' with Win, no matter how urgent his pleadings. Finally he proposed, as she had hoped he would, on the country club porch late one night after the last picture show. She told him she must think about it and discuss it with her mother and Uncle Sol. He told her – he did not ask her – not to keep him waiting too long.

In June, she went home. Win saw her off with a lingering kiss that made her blush and flee into the train. Back at the Baltimore apartment, Alice was full of predictable warnings. But Wallis was set on her path and nothing would stand in her way. She had a persuasive argument: Win's family was rich and socially prominent; Win could ensure her a future.

In August, Win took Wallis by train to Illinois to meet his family: large, imposing, big-game-hunting Earl Senior, his mousy British wife, Agnes, and their other five children. They approved of Wallis at once; the Warfields were not unknown in Chicago. Win bought Wallis a diamond engagement ring, and the announcement of their intentions appeared in the Baltimore papers on 25 September 1916. The wedding date was set for 8 November. How would Wallis sleep until then?

4

A STYLISH MARRIAGE

Wallis was determined that her wedding would be the most glamorous in Baltimore's recent history – a far cry from her mother's pathetic and shameful marriage. Uncle Sol – who was richer than ever, having bought no fewer than nine more railroads and about to start the Florida and Northwestern that would go 238 miles across the state to West Palm Beach – provided both dowry and trousseau. Corinne arrived from Pensacola, breathless as ever with excitement, to help Wallis pick out her clothes.

They went to the expensive Lucile's of Paris in downtown Baltimore where Wallis chose a gown of white velvet that would open at the waist to show a daring filmy petticoat of Brussels lace worn by her grandmother Anna Warfield at her wedding. Wallis would have a coronet of orange blossom and a lace-fringed tulle veil, a bodice of embroidered seed pearls, and long, bell-shaped tulle sleeves. Win gave her a diamond pin for her corsage of orchids and lilies of the valley and she would carry a bouquet of the same flowers.

Lelia Barnett and several Montagues and school friends gave parties for her. On the eve of the wedding Wallis and her entourage and members of the family went to see the Dolly Sisters in the big, saucy hit *His Bridal Night* at the Lyric.

Wallis had decided that the wedding should take place romantically after dark at the Christ Episcopal church. The beautiful building was lit, according to Wallis's instructions, by beeswax candles; she would have nothing as cheap as tallow. The lighted tapers and lilies, the bower of white chrysanthemums and roses created an appealing atmosphere as Wallis entered, to the strains of the organ, on the arm of Uncle Sol. She was followed by the matron of honour, Ellen Yuille, a friend from Oldfields, and by six bridesmaids, Mary Kirk, Lelia Barnett, Renée du Pont, Ethel Spencer (Win's sister) and two others, all in pink and blue. Win was accompanied by a navy guard of honour, including Chevalier, in full dress uniform; his youngest brother, Dumaresq Spencer, the family favourite and its handsomest member, was best man.

The Reverend Edmund Niver made Wallis and Win man and wife. The couple ran down the steps to a shower of rice and were then driven to the Hotel Stafford for the reception. Wallis gave gold rings to each of the bridesmaids; they later used them as teething rings for their children. As the couple took off for their honeymoon, Wallis threw her bouquet at Mary Kirk and the guests showered the bride and groom with white rose petals.

The newly-weds travelled via the Shoreham Hotel in Washington and the Shenandoah Valley Inn to the newly built and lavish Greenbriar Hotel at White Sulphur Springs in the mountains of West Virginia, where Wallis had spent many a childhood holiday and which she had visited just the year before.[1] It was a spectacular train journey uphill to the expensive and exclusive hostelry.

They were shown into room 528 on the top floor, which commanded an unobstructed view of oaks, maples and fir-clad mountain slopes wreathed in mist. It was already time for dinner and they changed at once. She wrote later that Win, impatient on discovering that Virginia was a dry state, dragged a bottle of gin from his suitcase. But he knew it was dry; he had been in West Virginia before.

His alcoholism was an established fact. There is no doubt that he drank heavily on the honeymoon, both at the Greenbriar and in New York, where they saw Wallis's favourite army–navy football game and the Ziegfeld Follies, and in Atlantic City, where the widowed Alice had a little 'weekender' cottage. They took a train back to Pensacola in December, and once again Corinne met the express and drove them to the San Carlos Hotel. They stayed there a few days and then moved to the Widow Covington's house at Baylen and Gonzalez until the repairs of a recent hurricane's damage were partly finished at 6 'Admiralty Row' – a wooden bungalow just a few houses down from the Mustins' home, and of almost identical design, with a view of the ocean and a small veranda.

Always correct, neat, disciplined and proud, Wallis found that Win's behaviour was starting to grate on her. He stored water in gin bottles to upset Henry Mustin, who kept a dry base, when he made his Saturday morning inspections. Win caused excitement at the San Carlos Saturday-night dances by performing impromptu in a straw boater, carrying a cane, as an amateur song-and-dance man, fronting the orchestra in imitation of George M. Cohan. On off-duty days he liked to dress up in loud checked knickerbockers, lurid sweaters and brogues. He constantly swilled beer. He would use the excuse of toasting the flag before a flight; then he would have another drink to boost his courage, and a third afterwards 'to settle down'. Martinis served before lunch and dinner were concealed in open Campbell's soup tins and served in cups and bowls.

Wallis hated the drinking and feared that Win would crash. When two ensigns collided in mid-air in a daredevil drunken stunt, she panicked. Every time Win went up on a practice flight, she felt worse. Corinne was her chief consolation, but on 31 January 1917, much to her despair, Henry was transferred to Washington to be executive officer of the USS *North Dakota*, and Corinne went with him. Wallis found herself very much alone in the long, empty, sun-drenched, humid days.

She was consoled by the friendship of Gustav and Katherine Eitzen, a genial timber merchant and his wife who had a big house on the bay, by their daughter Carlin and by another friend, later Mrs Fidelia Rainey, who said: 'Wallis loved the movies. Every single afternoon we would stop and buy bags of hot peanuts from the vendor and then go to the Isis Theatre to watch the picture – often the same one for a week. It kept her mind off Spencer flying.'

One afternoon, Wallis returned home to learn that Win had crashed his plane but had been fished, almost unharmed, out of the bay. She was learning the pain and stress of a difficult marriage. Wallis already hated flying, and for the rest of her life she was to loathe the idea of war.

On 6 April 1917, America entered the First World War. Win

applied at once for active service in France. It was a shock to Wallis that he would want to leave her, but he had a fierce desire to get involved in the fighting. His brother, beloved Dumaresq, was already in the Lafayette Escadrille, and Egbert and Frederick were on their way to join the American Army Expeditionary Force for service in the trenches.

Win was refused permission to go overseas, probably because of his record as an alcoholic: the navy wanted its image in Europe untarnished. Win was furious and took his rages out on Wallis; he grumbled when, on 8 May, he was directed to leave Pensacola and travel to Boston to train recruits at the newly formed naval militia station at Squantum. He was promoted to lieutenant junior grade, and his salary was increased.

After a brief visit to Oldfields School for the fiftieth anniversary celebrations on 2 and 3 May, Wallis and Win took a flat at the Mulberry Apartments near the Boston Common. Wallis drove Win to the base every morning and picked him up at night; because of drunken-driving incidents, he was forbidden to have a licence. She filled the time in between by going to museums and attending criminal trials.

The Squantum experience was short-lived. By October someone in the Navy Department had realized that the late autumn and winter climate of Boston would make it unsafe to train pilots there, so the recruit operation was shifted overnight to Hampton Roads, Virginia. Wallis was pleased; she would be close again to her cousins Lelia and Corinne and to her mother. But instead of the expected posting, the navy ordered Win to San Diego in faraway California, to be in charge of training cadets at North Island.

The Naval Air Station there had come about as a result of a joint Army and Navy Board report. On 20 July the new training school had been named Rockwell Field, in honour of Second Lieutenant Louis C. Rockwell of the 10th Infantry, who had been killed in a training flight in Maryland in 1912. Because the Air Service was now growing very rapidly, officers and enlisted men were transferred there at too great a speed, and the lack of discipline and organization was a serious problem. Two companies of the 21st Infantry, followed by the 19th company of the Coast Artillery Corps, formed the backbone of Rockwell Field's personnel.

Potash fields of kelp were commandeered, and hangars, construction works buildings, bungalows and offices thrown up. On 20 August, the War Department took complete control. On 8 September, the navy moved in, occupying two old buildings and the Curtis seaplane hangar. By this time there were 413 officers, 144 cadet officer trainees and 1,576 civilian enlistees at North Island.

This new appointment of Win's was almost certainly a relief as well as an irritation to Wallis; Win would not be sent to a probable death on the war front. She began packing for the long journey west.

The trip, which started on 3 November, involved a change of trains in Chicago – from the Baltimore and Ohio to the Santa Fe *Chief* – and an overnight stay at the Blackstone Hotel.

At long last, the Spencers arrived in Los Angeles, and then on 8 November took the train to San Diego, a pleasant, sleepy town of a hundred thousand inhabitants, with a beautiful winter climate on the edge of the blue-grey Pacific. The palm trees reminded Wallis of Florida, but the colours were more subdued and delicate. Wallis and Win moved into the rambling Hotel del Coronado, a hotch-potch of Victorian gingerbread with rich African mahogany fixtures and a driver-equipped Otis cage lift of ancient vintage. The semicircular dining room was handsome, and the rooms, including the Spencers', looked over rolling lawns and dwarf palms to the sea.

While Win spent his days at offices downtown, Wallis looked for an apartment. Eventually she found 104 The Palomar, 536 Maple Street, with a fine view of an imitation Spanish fountain patio[2] and Balboa Park, which still showed many signs of the big 1915 Exposition which had been held there. No. 104 was one of only two apartments with a view and one of the very few with a separate bedroom.

In those first few months, Win was busy setting up the training school at the newly commissioned naval air station on North Island. He trained not only pilots but also mechanics. Soon he added marine and military personnel and raw recruits out of Los Angeles. For a while he stopped drinking, but news of the death of his brother Dumaresq in an aerial dogfight in France on 16 January 1918 drove him into depression and gave him guilty feelings of inadequacy because he had not seen active service with his sibling. He began to drink again.

Win and Wallis moved often – an indication that they were restless and unhappy. They went back to the Hotel del Coronado, the second floor of which was commandeered as officers' quarters by the navy, and then to Pine Cottage, later renamed Redwood Cottage, at 1115 Flora Avenue. With its tiny, twelve-foot-long living room, sun porch and minuscule bedrooms, and its quaint, gabled exterior, it was like a witch's house in a Grimm fairy tale.

They went on to the slightly larger 1029 Encino Row and then to 1143 Alameda Street, their home for over three years.

Wallis celebrated her twenty-second birthday on 19 June 1917. She cannot have felt much happiness in the event. Win was subject to rages, sulks and deep brooding silences; were his bisexual impulses plaguing him? And Wallis did not want to have children, though Win, like any navy man, wanted sons. Not only did all the Montague women she so envied, whom she had emulated by 'marrying navy', have families, but so did several of Win's siblings. His disappointment was gnawing and lasting. Wallis's flirtatiousness with any man in uniform, too, vexed him greatly; at a mere twenty-eight he was already growing coarse and plump, his face that of a man fifteen years older, his once-proud chin buried in fat. Drink cost him his looks and his figure.

San Diego was a backwater; Wallis was tired of making her clothes on a Singer sewing machine. She was lost; there seemed to be no escape. She fell out of love.

In June 1918, Wallis travelled to New York to be a bridesmaid at the wedding of her school friend Mary Kirk to the French commercial and military delegate Captain Jacques Achille Raffray. The trip cheered her up; when she returned, she began to make friends in San Diego, including Katherine Bigelow, whose husband had been killed in action in France; Rhoda Fullam, daughter of a naval officer who was later promoted to rear admiral; Mrs Claus Spreckels, rich in land and sugar interests; young Marianna Sands; and Grace Flood Robert.

On 11 November that year, the San Diego *Union* was delivered, along with the milk bottle, to the doorstep of Wallis's house. She picked it up and read the news that the war had ended in Europe. Hundreds of San Diegans ran from their homes in their night-clothes, screaming and yelling.

After that great day, Win was more grim and depressed than ever. His drinking grounded him now; there was no war on, so his job at North Island seemed pointless; he was insulting to Wallis when they went out to parties and made snide remarks about her cooking when they were at home. A clumsy dancer, he was furious when men came over to their table at navy parties to whisk flirtatious Wallis across the floor to the popular new numbers by Irving Berlin and Jerome Kern. He charged Wallis with adultery; to be sure that she didn't visit or entertain other men, he often locked her in the house.

On 8 December 1919, Mustin took command of the Air Detach-ment, Pacific Fleet. He had moved to Coronado ahead of Corinne, who followed in mid-January 1920. Wallis rejoiced in Corinne's presence there.

On 7 April 1920, a big event took place. The Prince of Wales was in San Diego with his cousin Louis Mountbatten on his way to Australia aboard the battle cruiser *Renown*. He arrived early in the morning and received the Mayor, L. J. Wilde, and the Governor of California, William E. Stephens, along with the press, on the boat deck. Addressed by Wilde as 'Your Royal Highness', he told him to 'cut out that stuff' in an odd, half-American, half-cockney accent he had developed because he hated the plummy diction of the British upper classes.

Slim, short, golden-haired, charming and informal, the young prince conquered San Diego at once. He came ashore with Mount-batten at 2.30 p.m., shook hands with the war veterans, and addressed some twenty-five thousand people at the Stadium, while close to seventy thousand thronged the pavements to watch him in the motorcade.

Wallis must have been galled by the fact that she was not invited to the elaborate luncheon held on board the battleship *New Mexico* in honour of the prince, followed by receptions aboard the *Aroostook* and HMS *Renown*. The guests were taken out to the vessels by minesweeper. The Towerses, the Mustins and their friends the Charlie Masons and the Pete Mitschers were included. Why were the Spencers not? It is inconceivable that Wallis would have missed out on such an opportunity. It is probable that Win's drinking and misbehaviour, and clashes with the authorities, had resulted in this example of cruel social punishment.

Wallis was in attendance with Win that night at the Hotel del Coronado for the Mayoral Ball. But in another major blow to her pride, she was not included on the banquet guest list. She and the Mustins were among the thousand guests who thronged the ballroom, which was hung with Californian wild flowers and the British and American flags. The band of the USS *New Mexico* played current hits; a local adagio dance team performed exhibition waltzes and the 'Whirlwind One-Step' and the men in full dress uniforms and women in expensive gowns soon joined them on the floor, forming, according to the San Diego *Union*'s somewhat overwrought society correspondent, 'a scene of kaleidoscopic gaiety'.

Wallis only saw the prince far off, in Royal Navy tropical whites, shaking hundreds of hands. He left early – to go, according to some eyewitnesses, to Tijuana to sample the local pleasures. That was typical of him; he hated receptions and banquets and wanted only to enjoy life.

Although it must have been exciting for Wallis to catch a glimpse of her girlhood idol, the episode was swallowed up in the darkness of her marriage. In May Alice came out to visit Wallis and found her in tears; Win was staying out all night and frequently broke the furniture when he came home. One afternoon Alice arrived at their house to find Win shaking Wallis; they had been arguing because Wallis did not feel like joining him in a game of golf. He announced that he was going back to Florida, saying that he was in love with a girl there. Wallis begged him to stay; but by November he had obtained his transfer and left.

Wallis suffered for four months without a word from Win. Then, in the spring of 1921, he was appointed to the Navy Department in Washington under Rear Admiral William A. Moffett. Win asked her to come and join him; and she agreed. Henry Mustin had finally made it into the department, and she wanted to see Corinne again. Alice was now working at the Chevy Chase Country Club as a social hostess and was dating a legal clerk, Charles Gordon Allen.

Wallis moved with Win into the Brighton Apartment Hotel on

California Avenue. She soon regretted the decision. Win's scream-ing fits were unendurable and woke up the hotel at night; he locked her in the bathroom and left her there for hours; he fell down drunk; he had affairs with other women and, perhaps, with men. Finally, it became obvious to Wallis that she had to obtain a divorce.

There had never been such a scandal in either the Montague or the Warfield families. Alice and Aunt Bessie were shocked, and tried to talk her out of her decision. The Episcopalian Church would countenance no such thing. But Wallis's mind was made up. Just because nobody divorced in her family was no reason for her to be bound for the rest of her life to a man she hated.

She went to see Uncle Sol, now the biggest railroad baron in the south, in his offices at the Continental Trust. He was furious, horrified; he screamed, 'I will not let you bring this disgrace upon us!' Then he softened a little and asked her to try again.

She did, but it was hopeless. She would prepare a dinner as carefully and expertly as she could, and Win would not turn up for it.

On 19 June 1922, Win told Wallis he was moving out to the Army and Navy Club. Wallis called Alice; her mother came to the hotel; Wallis tearfully showed her cupboards empty of Win's cloth-ing. Alice stayed overnight. The next day Wallis called the club. The reply was, 'Commander Spencer will not care to talk to you.' Alice waited an hour; then she called him herself. She urged him to come and have a family conference. Win said, 'It's useless to talk about my returning. I have made up my mind to live my own life as I see fit.'

Anguished, deeply disappointed and depressed, Wallis moved in with her mother, at 2301 Connecticut Avenue. Win moved to Rauscher's Hotel. That autumn Alice asked Win to come to her apartment for a chat. There, he told her flatly that he was in love with another woman. 'I'm far happier away from Wallis,' he said. Then he left, declining Alice's invitation to stay for dinner.

He began to drink more heavily than ever. In February 1923 his extramarital affair collapsed. Win quarrelled constantly with the navy and, like Henry Mustin before him, was grounded: he was transferred to warship service as master of the *Pampanga,* of the South China Patrol of the Asiatic Fleet.

The *Pampanga* was a 1,400-ton, leaky, thirty-six-year-old former Spanish gunboat of dubious seaworthiness that patrolled the then war-torn Canton delta. She was the only vessel small enough to slip through the narrow, marshy estuaries where fire and mass bloodshed occurred. The vessel had great holes in the hull, caused by Chinese guns during frequent offshore battles; there were no showers, just a bucket of water on a string, and no proper toilet, just a primitive head; there was no proper ventilation, so in the summer heat the men had to sleep half naked on mattresses on deck. The ship and her fellow vessels of the South China Patrol were delegated by the navy secretly to ship Standard Oil petroleum into the mainland and publicly to protect American businesses and missions in a nation torn apart by rival warlords and by Russian-inspired revolutionaries. Each captain also had an intelligence mission and a charter to rescue endangered missionaries or Standard Oil personnel. Every day priests were being butchered by various rival and murderous factions, and war with America or Britain was threatened.

Grounded from flying, in charge of the lousiest ship in the navy, Win began drinking more heavily than ever.

Wallis made the best of the separation. The fact that her husband was on active service and that China was too dangerous a place for a young woman made her position more acceptable than that of a would-be divorcée; she met many old friends again and through two of them from San Diego, Marianna Sands and Ethel Noyes, she entered diplomatic society. Although she would deny it at a crucial stage later on, she spoke fairly good German, having studied it at Oldfields; and she had a smattering of French.

At a reception at the Italian embassy Wallis set her cap for, and won, the attractive Italian ambassador himself. The forty-five-year-old Prince Gelasio Caetani had at least two popes and two cardinals among his ancestors. The son of Prince Teamo and the American Ada Bootle Wilbraham, he had graduated in civil engineering from the University of Rome in 1901; he became a geologist and authority on mining and in 1910 based an engineering firm, Burch, Caetani and Hearsley, in San Francisco.

In the First World War, he had served in the Italian army and won several decorations. A convinced nationalist, he was a passionate supporter of Fascism and participated in the march on Rome in 1922. He was appointed to Washington in 1922; Mussolini saw in him the ideal person who could succeed in winning the interest and sympathy of the American ruling classes: he had a vast network of connections in eastern cultural and moneyed circles. Caetani worked hard on the extinction of the Italian war debt and the establishment of strong relations with the Italo-American military and navy. With Mussolini's money he built a new embassy, an ornate imitation of a Renaissance palace.

There is no question that it was Caetani who first and most deeply got Wallis interested in his Italian dictator master and in the Italian system of government; exercising such influence was his main purpose in becoming involved with her, apart from the strong sexual bond between them. He knew she moved at every level of Washington society and that she could purvey Fascist ideas, albeit in a somewhat superficial manner, wherever she went. That fact was confirmed by a reliable source in Rome who was a close friend and associate of Caetani's. But the affair did not last; Wallis soon settled for friendship.

She had a more serious relationship with Felipe Espil, the thirty-five-year-old first secretary at the Argentine embassy. Espil was rich and smooth, a classic Latin lover who danced the best tango in town. His black hair was plastered to his head with brilliantine. His eyes glowed like Rudolf Valentino's. He had an oval, pale olive face with full, sensual lips, a short neck and a slim but muscular body. He wore a monocle. He was the biggest catch in Washington.

Wallis wasted no time. Husband or no husband, she had to have him. She got herself invited to a dinner party at which he would be present. Espil was everything she had been told he would be. But she was afraid that, with the competition from so many gorgeous single young women, she wouldn't have a chance. With her square-cut face and flat, masculine figure, what hope did she have? But she was determined to try; nothing and no one, not even the most shapely Washington belle, would stand in her way. The ugly duckling set out to get Felipe Espil into bed with all the determination of Wellington planning the battle of Waterloo.

She summoned up her courage and asked her hostess and Espil, but not his date, to an eggnog party at her mother's apartment. He came, alone as requested – Wallis left nothing to chance – and she set out to fascinate him with her wit and charm. He was captivated and, to gasps all round, asked her to lunch at the Hamilton Hotel. She accepted, only to find herself in the midst of the Soixante Gourmets, a group whose functions she had previously attended with other young diplomats, most of whom were there. But nobody minded; it was catch as catch can in the young Washington society of those days.

With her usual gift for flattery, for making a man feel he was a cross between Socrates and Apollo, she won Espil away from the society beauties who pursued him. And although he cried poor, Espil had in fact risen through powerful family connections in the government of President Hipolito Irigoyen, a radical suppressor of the workers and German sympathizer who had kept his country out of the First World War despite large British interests in Buenos Aires and German attacks on Argentinian shipping. Irigoyen ruled over a country crippled by a corrupt administration and haunted by mass poverty. Espil was an appeasement diplomat who wanted to avoid all future wars. Wallis listened and learned.

Their affair became the scandal of Washington. Mrs Lawrence Townsend, the reigning queen of society, refused to invite Wallis to the annual Townsend Ball, considered the social event of the year. When Wallis complained, Espil said to her, 'I can't ask Mrs Townsend to invite my mistress!' Wallis was furious. But she managed to push her way into other events to which Espil was invited, and she even dared to go to the Argentinian Ball as his guest.

Then Wallis met her nemesis.

NOTES

1 In her memoirs Wallis said she told Win she scarcely remembered the place. But her name in the 1915 register belies the statement.
2 The apartment did not have a patio of its own, as described in her memoirs.

5

CHINA

Felipe Espil, who had not been faithful to Wallis, met and fell in love with the society beauty Courtney Letta Stilwell, of the famous political and military family. When she found out, Wallis was furious. In an excess of jealousy she attacked Espil, clawing his cheeks until they bled. He dropped her at once; and she decided to give up Washington, where her defeat had made her a laughing stock.

There is a substantial documentary file on her at the time, preserved at the State Department, which shows that she stayed with Captain Luke McNamee, the chief of Naval Intelligence, and his wife, the painter Dorothy McNamee, at their Georgetown house. It was a typical preliminary move to test confidentiality and to be briefed in secrecy. Harry W. Smith, chief clerk at the naval intelligence headquarters, interviewed her carefully on 9 July 1923. That month she sailed to France and England aboard the *President Garfield*, accompanied by her cousin Corinne. In Paris she made contact with William E. Eberle and Gerald Green, both intelligence liaisons for the US Navy at the embassy; she proceeded to London and Rome.

It was a custom at that time to engage trusted navy wives, briefed at headquarters, as unofficial couriers, to carry classified documents to Europe and the Far East. Couriers were necessary because all telegraph messages transmitted to the US Navy in China were intercepted and read, and the cyphers were broken; all radio messages were transmitted from a central tower in Manila and again could be read. Thus the only way to transmit information was by trusted immediate members of the families of naval personnel. Upon her return from Europe, Wallis was seconded to link up with Win Spencer in China. Captain Henry R. Hough, who had taken over from Captain McNamee when the latter was put in charge of intelligence at the Panama Canal, personally signed the papers that authorized the trip. In the meantime Spencer had been appointed a naval intelligence officer of the South China Fleet, combining his job of gunboat captain of the *Pampanga* with that more important office. His headquarters at Shameen Legation Island, Canton, were crucially situated since Sun Yat-sen and the Communists were constantly attacking missionaries and annexing American properties in the region. Win was to join Wallis in Hong Kong on 8 September; she would link up there with Mary Sadler, wife of the intelligence officer Rear Admiral Frank H. Sadler of the USS *Sacramento*. The two women would proceed with classified messages to Shanghai, where American interests were endangered by Russian-controlled warlords.

Wallis was given another intelligence clearance and put aboard the troop carrier *Chaumont*, a former double-ended Hog Island ferry, carrying 1,200 enlisted men to Pearl Harbor, Guam and Cavite. Under the command of Captain F. L. Oliver, the vessel was moored at Pier 10, Brooklyn Navy Yard, on 17 July 1924, when Wallis, according to the log, came aboard at 4.30 p.m. She was berthed with Ruth Thompson, fiancée of Lieutenant R. E. Forsyth, who was going to join her husband at Cavite, and two other women. A cousin of Win's from Chicago, Lieutenant Douglas E. Spencer, was aboard, seconded to Cavite with his wife and five-year-old son. The ship was crammed with marines and infantry doughboys.

The *Chaumont* steamed out of Brooklyn at midnight, stopping for a few hours at anchor offshore because of boiler trouble; the vessel made landfall at Hampton Roads, Virginia, later that day. Two days later the ship entered the Panama Canal in suffocating heat and berthed at Cristobal and Balboa; the crew, crammed into stifling quarters with as many as ten to a cabin, began to grow unruly and clashed in fistfights with the marines aboard. A gang of below-decks ensigns tossed a film intended for the officers' mess into the canal. A doughboy attacked and beat a quartermaster and was court-martialled and confined to the brig. The daylight canal transit was delayed; the British battleships *Hood, Repulse* and *Adelaide* were steaming into the locks, and the *Chaumont* had to anchor in Gatun Lake. Wallis, hating the trip, exhausted and feverish, had a miserable, brief sojourn in Panama City. Two days out into the Pacific, on the 28th, a man was killed and flung into the sea. More court martials followed as the drunken and disorderly crew came close to outright mutiny.

The voyage into Pearl Harbor, Hawaii, was tricky, involving the navigation of a dangerous coral reef in a violent, gusty squall. Wallis stayed one week in Honolulu; the vessel sailed on 13 August. At Guam Governor Henry B. Price received her and the other wives with the *Chaumont*'s officers at an official reception; three days later Price was piped aboard the vessel to make the rest of the journey to Cavite.

After a stifling, monotonous voyage of several weeks, the *Chaumont* at last made landfall off San Miguel Light and Manila Bay on 30 August. Wallis had to be billeted at naval headquarters because she was one of the few wives continuing to Hong Kong. There had been riots along the wharves following student demonstrations the week before. She was put aboard the *Empress of Canada*, the famous 'jinx ship' of the Canadian Pacific Line, on 4 September.

Wallis's arrival in Hong Kong on 8 September was one of the great experiences of her life. Black fishing junks with square, slatted sails spined like bats' wings, and huge yellow eyes painted on the prows, came out to greet the *Empress*, followed by single-oared sampans filled with tiny brown boys who dived into the oily green water to fish up coins tossed by the passengers from the decks. Ahead, Wallis saw the looming mountain called The Peak, dotted with wooden shacks and fronted by the ostentatious office buildings of British banks and mercantile companies. There were the sounds of dogs barking, sirens blaring, children screaming, men crying their wares. And the peculiar musky scent of Hong Kong, composed of sandalwood, cinnamon, jute, urine and tar.

The *Empress of Canada* docked at 4.30 p.m. According to navy tradition, Win was in the *Pampanga* gig alongside when the vessel berthed at the Royal Naval Anchorage. Win was under orders from Admiral Thomas Washington, fleet commander, to have all possible repairs done because his vessel would be required at Canton and Shanghai.

The week Wallis arrived in Hong Kong, civil war, which had been threatened for several months, exploded in full force across China. The country was without an effective government. The dominant presence was Sun Yat-sen, leader of the Kuomintang or People's party, a Canton administration composed of the quarrel-some sons of the merchant and landowner class who were opposed to the rival military government in Peking. Sun Yat-sen and his splinter government had come under the influence of the Soviet Union through the Russian agent who called himself Michael Borodin, and by January 1924, at the first Party Congress, power was delegated to a Central Executive Committee that reflected the similar government in Moscow.

Within the Kuomintang there were violent conflicts, and the right-wing elements, led by the rebel generals, began that summer to clash head-on with the Canton forces. Simultaneously, there was growing resentment over the presence on Chinese soil of large numbers of British, French and American residents. In the previous century, China's rulers had granted permanent leases at nominal sums to foreign powers in the notorious unequal treaties that had established in most of the major cities well-protected, militarized and armed settlements that were not subject to Chinese law. China was a country divided in every possible direction, haunted by famine and plague and brutal warfare, sold out to European enterprise while the people suffered in appalling physical conditions.

Hong Kong, though nominally independent from mainland China, reflected the tensions of the giant nation across the straits. There were constant outbreaks of violence in the Crown Colony. When Wallis arrived, typhoid was raging and there was a record heatwave. With fire and gunshot surrounding her, Wallis moved into the Repulse Bay Hotel and then, reconciled with Win, into a navy-owned Kowloon apartment that came equipped with cook and maid. Win was busy during that visit of a few weeks. He had to have the *Pampanga* coaled, provisioned, repaired and ready for emergency sailing orders – at least a sixteen-hour-a-day job.

On 16 October, the sailing orders arrived. It must have been painful for Wallis, after managing to patch up her shattered marriage, to realize that Win was travelling into conditions of extreme danger. He had been seconded back to Canton, and that tormented city was now plunged into terror and bloodshed. The so-called Red Army, a disorganized rabble of labourers, dock workers and mercenaries, had swept through the city, the insurgents pillaging and raping as they ran with torches through the labyrinth of streets lined with wooden houses. They massacred the Merchant Volunteer Corps, a hastily thrown together vigilante army known as the Chinese Fascists. Five days of street fighting had left a thousand dead in the streets, many of them women and children burned to death in incendiary fires lit by arsonists, or struck down mercilessly by machine-gun bullets. When Win sailed into Canton harbour, the sky was black with choking, acrid smoke.

In a shambles of violence, famine and disease, the *Pampanga* docked at the militarily protected Shameen Legation Island, her three-pounder and one-pounder guns ready to shell the shore. Three British gunboats followed the ship into the docks, and stubborn Wallis was on board one of them, probably the *Bee*. She was not going to be left behind. She joined Win at the naval quarters in the British–American settlement, the only billet available to navy wives at the time; the island was closed to foreign civilians. Both water and food were in very short supply. After Wallis became ill from a kidney disorder brought on by the toxic water, she was evacuated to Hong Kong on 28 October.

With missionaries and evacuee doctors and nurses aboard, the *Pampanga* returned to Hong Kong on 3 November for provisioning. Then it sailed to Kongmoon on the 30th to protect American interests and to ship Standard Oil to the region.

Something curious took place that month. According to a dossier prepared on Prime Minister Stanley Baldwin's orders by MI6 for King George V and Queen Mary in 1935 (when it became crucial to prevent Wallis becoming Queen of England), Wallis was introduced by Win to the 'singing houses' of the Crown Colony. They were run by an American woman, Gracie Hale, who, with her peroxided hair, false eyelashes, heavily rouged cheeks and plump but attractive figure, was still going in the 1930s, when she gave an interview to the Dutch author Hendrik de Leeuw for his book *Cities of Sin* describing her earlier career when Wallis was in Hong Kong. The singing houses were luxurious brothels; the inmates, recruited from the China seaboard, were trained from their early teens in the arts of love. The client was entertained with stringed instruments, delicately erotic songs and dances of rare beauty.

There were two kinds of singing (or 'singsong', as they were sometimes known) houses. The best known were the 'purple mansions'. The only one of these establishments which admitted foreign women was in Repulse Bay. As the client entered, a smiling male slave in a blue cotton robe would appear, bowing deeply. He ushered the arrival into an immense square room with green and white draperies covering the walls.

Beyond the entrance hall was a long corridor which led to another hall filled with sumptuously upholstered chairs and settees. The doors and walls were decorated with latticework and scrolls in Chinese. There were cabinets of expensive mahogany, containing shelves of valuable china ornaments. The girls were customarily dressed in blue or red silk. The upper floor consisted of a series of tiny but elegantly furnished rooms where the prostitutes awaited their customers. Some houses had individual names, such as 'Fields of Glittering Flowers' or 'Club of the Ducks of the Mandarins'.

Other houses of prostitution were known as *Hoa Thing*, or 'flower boats', and were moored or floated in the harbour. The boats were sixty to eighty feet long and fifteen feet wide; inside they were lavishly carpeted and furnished, and crystal lamps dangled from the ceilings. It was customary for an individual to hire the entire boat for the evening and to begin with a multi-course dinner at 9 p.m. When dinner was over, the guest would take his companion of the night across a small wooden platform to one of a series of boats attached by ropes to the mother vessel.

According to those who have seen the Chinese dossier, Wallis was taught 'perverse practices' in these houses of prostitution. The practices can only mean lesbian displays and the art of Fang Chung. This skill, practised for centuries, involves relaxation of the male partner through a prolonged and carefully modulated hot oil massage of the nipples, stomach, thighs and, after a deliberately, almost cruelly, protracted delay, the genitals. The exponent of Fang Chung was taught where the nerve centres of the body were, so that the brushing movement of the fingers had the effect of arousing even the most moribund of men. Fang Chung was especially helpful in cases of premature ejaculation. By the application of a specific touch, between the urethra and the anus, climax could be delayed. Masseuses delayed intromission as long as possible to remove the fear of failure in intercourse that afflicted men suffering from dysfunction.

According to a close friend of Wallis's, she had no sooner had an opportunity to apply this technique than Win left her in order to share an apartment with a handsome young painter. By mid-November Wallis was on her way to Shanghai aboard the *Empress of Russia* with the charming, forty-two-year-old Mrs Mary Sadler, wife of the now Admiral F. H. Sadler, commanding officer of the USS *Saratoga* and head of naval intelligence (as arranged long ago in Washington).

Long before the *Empress of Russia* docked on the 22nd, streams of brownish yellow mud could be seen darkening the water of the East China Sea, announcing the fact that Shanghai was built on marshy river flats. The vessel steamed slowly up the Whangpoo River, past frail wooden villages, weeping willow trees and rolling green paddy fields under a khaki sky. The river was so crowded with small craft that the ship could barely edge between them. At last Wallis saw the looming brick chimneys of the Shanghai Power Company belching smoke. There was a stink of sulphur and coal. She disembarked by tender, across water filled with old newspapers, dead birds and dung. Ahead of her lay the Bund, the famous waterfront esplanade with its jerry-built bank and office buildings and its jumble of electric signs. She walked up the steps from the jetty as the luggage was brought by the deckhands and piled up on the wharf. A line of rickshaws stretched as far as the eye could see; the drivers, their ribs exposed against dry yellow skin, shrieked for custom. There was a cluster of wheelbarrows, pushcarts and bicycles; coolies trotted about with enormous bamboo poles slung over their narrow shoulders.

Wallis and Mrs Sadler undertook the short trip to the fashionable Astor House Hotel; with civil war raging, soldiers and police stopped them every few yards to examine their passports. When at last they reached the hotel, they found a shabby grandeur. It was made up of four brick houses linked by stone passageways. The lobby was huge and red-carpeted, lit by ancient cut-glass chandeliers. There was a circular leather couch in the centre surrounding an enormous brass bowl containing ferns. There were red ceramic lions, red plush and gilt seats, and bronze bowls of paper lilies. Fans revolved slowly in the ceiling, disturbing flies. The rooms were like cabins, with bunks as well as beds; the corridors were painted with portholes and *trompe l'oeil* seascapes – an idea Wallis would one day use at her house in Paris. The manager was Captain Harry Morton of the Royal Navy (retired), who ran the hotel like a ship, with trumpet fanfares to announce meals. Wallis and Mary Sadler stayed at the Astor House for ten days.

Shanghai was an amazing spectacle in the grip of war. Each day there were skirmishes and killings. Although the international settlement was protected by US and British marines so that the old, privileged life could continue, there were bursts of gunfire less than a block from the Astor House. Flames engulfed the shanties and tenements, and screams and shouts could be heard from the native quarters as the police suppressed the maraudings of the locally notorious Green Gang. There were opium dens and brothels and sinister dark alleys, but there were also black-tie parties at the grand mansions of the very rich, including the sumptuous home of the Jewish merchant prince Sir Victor Sassoon, which was staffed by some seventy-five servants. There were lavish department stores, including the Sun Sun, the Sincere and the Wing On, that offered all the treasures of the Orient. Wallis bought ivory elephants with their trunks up for luck, carved ivory boxes and a Chinese screen.

She eagerly entered into the exciting social life of the city. Behind the walls and the bristling lines of infantry, the British and American tradesmen and the colonial officers defiantly enjoyed a life of luxury and ease at the Eiwo racecourse and the clubs and hotel *thés dansants* while opposing forces fought for possession of the sprawling native quarters of the metropolis.

A report on Wallis's activities at the time, issued just one day before Pearl Harbor, has turned up in the FBI files, declassified on appeal to the Associate Attorney General, after seven years of waiting, on 30 April 1987. Although the informant was confused about Commander Spencer's rank and location, the report is intriguing in other respects; the long time during which it had to be considered and reconsidered for possible release by one committee after another indicates that it was not regarded as the work of a mere gossip or aggrieved crank.

FBI, December 6, 1941:
Confidential. Memorandum for D. M. Ladd by P. J. Wacks of the Bureau (Washington).

On September 26, 1941, at 2.30 p.m., [blank] contacted the writer in the latter's office concerning the Duchess of Windsor. [Blank] advised that the first husband was a midshipman [sic] of the United States Navy whom the Duchess met in San Diego, California; that the midshipman was subsequently ordered to Singapore [sic]; that the Duchess followed him to that city where she frequented various night clubs and contacted various naval officers of both the United States and British navies; that the British authorities received information that the Duchess was attempting to obtain information concerning Naval secrets from the British officers she met; that as a result of her activities her husband . . . was transferred from that post of duty.

Was this mere idle gossip? The informant was a person who must have known something. But what? If Wallis was spying for some enemy power it can only have been Russia, which was America and Britain's opponent in China. The late John Costello, author of *The Pacific War*, an able historian, told me that Foreign Office rumours, recently confirmed by a reliable source in London, stated that Wallis was used by the Soviets during her sojourn. It is all a fascinating subject of conjecture, impossible to authenticate at this stage.

The American-born biographer, historian and editor Leslie Field, who had recently been working at Buckingham Palace in consultation with Her Majesty the Queen on a book about the royal jewels, told me in 1987 that the China dossier contained still further damaging information about Wallis. Mrs Field stated on tape that Wallis was involved in extensive drug peddling at the time and that these activities were not determined until years later when, on royal instructions, the Hong Kong authorities managed to obtain the facts from various individuals in China who were aware of them. Also, Mrs Field reveals, Wallis was backed by wealthy men as a high roller at the gambling tables. In view of the fact that at the time gambling in China was totally corrupt, and very often the 'right' people were allowed to win at the tables, it is not surprising that she succeeded in winning substantial sums at baccarat, roulette and blackjack. Mrs Field says that Wallis was notoriously a kept woman, and that even during her marriage to Win she was bedded by rich men, including a Chinese general.

Wallis and Mary Sadler went to Peking on 4 December 1924; American women were not permitted at the time to travel to the capital, except on official business. The obese warlord General Feng Yu-hsiang, who rejoiced in wearing Napoleonic braided uniforms and carrying a telescope, had seized power in the city and had driven the 'Boy Emperor' of China into hiding at the Japanese Legation when the British Legation refused him entry. The rival warlord, Marshal Cheng Tso-lin, had marched out of Peking, taking with him twenty-five thousand troops. The confused and volatile situation was about to erupt into severe violence. Sun Yat-sen had just returned from Japan, mustering support for a coup d'état which was to wrest power from Feng and would be aided by Marshal Cheng.

The railway tracks had been so badly damaged by the warring forces that the famous Blue Express could no longer make its way from Shanghai to Peking. Wallis and Mary had to take the SS *Shuntien,* a 1,200-ton vessel of the B&S Company, under the command of Captain Einar Christiansen, to Tientsin via Weiheiwei and Chifoo; at Tientsin they would change to a train for the rest of the journey. The voyage, beset by typhoons, was an agony of rolling decks, crashing dishes and furniture, and stifling heat.

As an indication of the importance of their mission as couriers, Wallis and Mary were met on 10 December at the Tientsin dock by Clarence E. Gauss, orientalist and consul general, who later became the widely admired Second World War ambassador to Free China. Gauss told them that the US Army had commandeered the train to Peking, but that Cheng's forces were posted along the tracks.

Mary Sadler fell ill with stomach trouble and returned to Shanghai. Wallis reached the Tientsin Central National railway station on the morning of the 11th. The ramshackle station was an infernal spectacle of typhoid and famine victims, rabble soldiery, hysterically crying children and exhausted women fighting for seats. Wallis had been given a special military authorization and still carried a special intelligence-authorized naval passport. At 12.10 p.m., when she boarded the eight-coach Inter-Allied train reserved for official or military personnel,[1] she was subjected to a close examination, and at Pei Tsang station, the first whistle stop, Cheng's troops came aboard, marching up and down the corridors.

It was a ghastly journey. The engine was old and rusty; the cold was intense in this northern region and the windows, shattered by gun shots, let in icy winds; there was no food or water; the toilets were mere holes in the floor. The soldiery under First Lieutenant E. M. Brannon was out of control and drunken; there were constant engine breakdowns followed by screeches of brakes and mysterious, fierce cries as the train lingered for hours in featureless low hills and by grave mounds and paddy fields, awaiting refuelling and repairs. A journey that should have taken only ninety minutes took thirty-eight hours.

Long before the train chugged into Peking, Wallis could see the lines of Marshal Cheng Tso-lin's machine guns along the tracks. When she finally arrived she was met, in the clanging darkness of the station – which was in the grip of a power failure – by Commander Louis M. Little of the Marines. She must have been carrying very important documents; it was a rule that a commanding officer was never to leave a major military post in civil war without some hugely pressing reason, such as contacting a courier.

As Little's grey armoured navy car drove through the plaza and the Hatamen Gate to the protected Legation Quarter, the first thing Wallis would have seen was a line of heads stuck on thirty-foot-high bamboo poles: signals by General Feng, who was now camped in the western hills awaiting possible battle with Marshal Cheng and Sun Yat-sen, that he would brook no rebelliousness in the city.

Peking was in the grip of terror. When Wallis checked in to the Grand Hotel, a riot of chinoiserie, the papers were reporting that Feng's enemies were being dragged into the parks and decapitated by sword without benefit of trial. Day by day, a tense and anxious

British and American population awaited word of Sun Yat-sen's imminent arrival and a full-scale outburst of Communist activity against all foreigners. Suspense hung over the ancient city with its walled cities within the city, its vast gateways and yellow and blue roofs, its cruelly cold, dusty winds from the plain, its dominating colour of recently dried blood.

The Grand Hôtel de Pékin was an oasis for Wallis and the other bedraggled arrivals from Tientsin. The lobby had a curio shop, a French bookshop and an ornamental fountain. The grand marble staircase rose to the glass doors of the Imperial Ballroom. Soon she would discover the dining room with its minstrels' gallery and British dance orchestra.

Her room looked over the Legation Quarter, which was guarded by a line of blue-clad American Marines. Beyond the quarter she could see the old Tartar wall, with its L-shaped watchtowers and ornamental gates, and the shiny blue tiles of the Temple of Heaven. On the hour rang the iron bells of the ancient Tower of Kublai Khan, and at four every afternoon, according to time-honoured tradition, a thousand pigeons were released from wicker baskets into the ice-blue winter sky; the tiny bamboo flutes tucked under the birds' wings created an eerie, plaintive sound.

While in Peking, Wallis became romantically entangled with Alberto da Zara, the suavely handsome, blond, thirty-five-year-old naval attaché at the Italian Embassy. Da Zara was descended from a long line of cavalry officers, from whom he had inherited his valiant and gallant manners as well as a deep knowledge and love of horses. She first met him at the embassy compound during an at-home which took place every Friday evening.

Well educated and with a grasp of several languages, every summer in his youth he was sent abroad, where he built up a number of international contacts. In 1907 he had fulfilled an adolescent dream and enrolled at the Annapolis naval academy, where he met and became acquainted with Earl Winfield Spencer.

In May 1922, he was assigned command of a ship, the *Carlotto*, berthed at Hankow, China; he sailed on to Shanghai in November of that year. His memoirs[2] contain vivid descriptions of military missions along the Yangtze River and of the social life of China at the time.

He took up his post of naval attaché in Peking a few months before Wallis arrived, in the spring of 1924. In his book he observed: 'The prospect of commanding a barracks and to carry out the role of naval, military and aviation attaché in a country without a navy or aviation, and with an army of feudal militia did not appeal.' Horses were his passion, so Wallis joined him enthusiastically at the racecourse. She had no real interest in horses; as usual, she knew what she was doing. He wrote in his memoirs: 'The winter of 1924–1925 was a great season for Italian participants in the Peking Horse Shows . . . without distinction of age or sex, of profession or social status, everyone cheered for someone: a horse or rider, an athlete or team, a club or city; ministers and consuls, customs officers, bank directors, industrialists, great dames and young beauties.' He added gallantly: 'Among these, one of the most frequently present fans was Mrs Wallis Spencer. In those days she wore a classical hairdo which fit the beauty of her forehead and her eyes, with her hair, as the Americans say, off the face, stroked, as I would say, to which she has kept faithful until the present day. Already then she expressed a fondness for the colour which would become famous as Wallis blue. It matched her eyes.'

Wallis became deeply fascinated by da Zara. He was a poet, an addict of d'Annunzio, to whose works he introduced her. Authoritative as a commander, he was discreet and generous. Wallis loved his proud, independent, untamed spirit. His aide in China, Lieutenant Giuseppe Pighini (now a retired admiral) remembers da Zara's affair with Wallis vividly:

Mrs Simpson and da Zara had a very close relationship which from love developed into lasting friendship. Da Zara used to say about her that although she was not beautiful she was extremely attractive and had very refined and cultivated tastes. Her conversation was brilliant and she had the capacity of bringing up the right subject of conversation with anyone she came in contact with and entertaining them on that subject. This quality of conversation and her great knowledge and love of horses were things which she had in common with da Zara.

Soon the affair cooled, but Wallis remained friendly with da Zara. Pighini remembers that for years da Zara carried an autographed photograph of Wallis wherever he went; it was signed, 'To You, Wally'. In 1938, when da Zara's ship the *Montecaccoli* was docked in Melbourne, a reporter found the picture by snooping in the cabin and published a story about it in the Melbourne *Age* the next day. Da Zara was furious.

Alberto da Zara undoubtedly cemented Wallis's love of Italy and her conviction of the value of Fascism as the only possible block to Communism that would, in turn, soon cement her to the Prince of Wales.

Wallis discovered the Imperial Yellow City, the Forbidden Violet City, and the fairy-tale beauty of the sea palaces built on icy lakes spanned by marble bridges and dotted with frosted lotus leaves. She had letters of introduction to French intelligence and German officials combatting Soviet influences in the region, and to the elegant aesthete and architect Georges Sebastian, a Romanian who had been raised in London and Paris. A beau from Paris days, Gerry Green, was intelligence liaison at the US Consulate and took her dancing in the Grand Hôtel de Pékin dining room. One night Wallis saw a familiar face among the other dancing couples at the Grand Hôtel: Katherine Bigelow, now Katherine Rogers, the young widow who had befriended Wallis in Coronado, southern California, just six years before. Katherine's husband, Herman Rogers, was a US intelligence officer attached to the embassy (his family confirms this fact). Rogers was a classic example of the man who had everything; his only flaw was that he was a very unconvincing novelist. He was the son of the millionaire railroad tycoon Archibald Rogers, whose estate, Crumwold Hall, was two houses away from Franklin D. Roosevelt's at Hyde Park, New York. Tall, handsome and athletic, Rogers had been educated at Groton and Yale. He had retired at the age of thirty-five and after his marriage to Katherine, whom he had met originally in France during the first World War, had decided to devote the rest of his life to travel, leisure, trying to write the 'great American novel', and the acquisition of culture.

In the normal tradition of intelligence contacts, the Rogerses billeted Wallis with them at their house, 4 Shih Chia Huting, in the Legation Quarter. They did everything possible to make her feel at home; she had her own rickshaw driver and her own maid. At weekends, Herman and Katherine drove her to their rented Buddhist temple in the foothills of the mountains that doubled as a lookout post on General Feng's army. Wallis joined them for riding and poker, contract bridge and the inevitable mahjongg. However, the circumstances of her stay were not as idyllic as she later claimed.

According to a friend of Wallis's, she entered into a bizarre *ménage à trois* with Herman and Katherine. This created great tension and differences, followed by quarrels; the mutual jealousies and conflicts of feeling deeply upset her.

And at the same time there was the war. Gunshots, explosions, fires and the screams of men and women were all fully audible from the Legation Quarter. Sun Yat-sen arrived on New Year's Eve, mortally stricken with cancer of the liver; his grievous condition cancelled out his plans for a coup d'état, and he made an uneasy truce with General Feng while lying in agony in a local hospital. There was fear that when he passed away China would disintegrate into even more meaningless violence, and only the rising military figure of Chiang Kai-shek would offer hope for a sustained government. When Sun Yat-sen died on 11 March, Peking was plunged into mourning. Black banners fluttered from the battlements and delegations arrived from all parts of the civilized world to pay their last respects.

The cold of Peking was almost unbearable. The only heat in the Rogerses' house was supplied by copper braziers whose feebly glowing coals did little to relieve the chill and filled the rooms with unpleasant, acrid fumes. Wallis's favourite rickshaw driver was crushed by a car, and by April there were outbursts of violence reminiscent of those in Shanghai. But the worst problem Wallis had to deal with lay in her own self. The stress of her situation with Herman was by now unendurable. Even the attentions of Alberto da Zara did not satisfy her. There was no alternative but for her to leave as soon as possible.

When Wallis returned to Hong Kong by train on 21 March, Win had just left the *Pampanga* and was about to command the *Whipple* at harbour in Shanghai and then en route to the United States. They tried to patch up their relationship once more and took a busman's honeymoon aboard the *President Grant* to Shanghai on the 23rd. That she was under special orders, from Rear Admiral C. V. McVay of the South China Fleet, is clear from the fact that navy wives, along with all other civilians, were forbidden entry to Shanghai at that time. Much of the city had been occupied after a violent conflict in which Marshal Chi Hsieh-yuan defeated the army of Marshal Chang and drove twelve thousand of his followers out of the city and into the International Settlement. As the Shanghai Volunteer Corps clashed with the Chi militia the gutters ran once more with blood, and the journey from the wharf to the quarters where Wallis and Win were billeted was exceedingly dangerous.

On 23 May, an incident occurred in that city that placed Wallis and every American there in jeopardy. Three months earlier Chinese mill workers under Japanese management had gone on strike; the ensuing conflict between labour and management resulted in violence. Now the workers had come out again; a ferocious battle was fought with sticks and guns in which one worker was killed and seven injured. The British-controlled Shanghai Municipal Council failed to discipline the Japanese but instead arrested the strikers. Following a memorial service for the murdered worker, there was a mass demonstration by three thousand students. A British commanding officer ordered members of the Sikh Indian militia to fire into the crowd; eleven Chinese students were killed and thirty-five others were injured. The result was an unprecedented outburst of 'anti-foreignism' across the nation, and a general strike. In Hankow, on 10 and 11 June, British and Japanese troops killed fifteen and wounded a hundred Chinese. On the 23rd, the British killed or injured hundreds more on Shameen Island and the *Pampanga* was shelled from the shore. By now Win had sailed to the United States as commander of the *Whipple*, while Wallis was stranded in Shanghai, unable to sail for weeks and subject, as a courier, to being kidnapped and murdered by militant Communists at any time.

While in Shanghai, Wallis met and became involved romantically with another handsome Fascist, the moody, proud, twenty-one-year-old Count Galeazzo Ciano, a keen supporter of Mussolini. His father, Admiral Ciano, had taken part in Mussolini's famous march on Rome and was among the figures involved in the murder of the anti-Fascist politician Matteotti. Later, Galeazzo Ciano would be the

Italian Foreign Minister. Fascinated by China, the count was on a reconnaissance trip to Peking. At the time he was a student in Rome; by 1927 he would be vice-consul.

According to Mrs Milton E. Miles, whose husband was an officer on the *Pampanga* and later became an admiral, 'Wallis went up the coast to Qunhuangdao, the beautiful summer resort where the Great Wall of China meets the sea. Ciano came down from Peking to spend a lot of time with her there. It was the gossip among us navy wives in Hong Kong; it was an open scandal.' Wallis became pregnant by Ciano. Since she was still married to Win, giving birth to a child out of wedlock would have destroyed her chances of getting an equitable divorce and could have been so great a disgrace that it might have caused him to be cashiered from the navy. According to Mrs Miles, Wallis attempted an abortion that destroyed her chances of ever having a child and caused her severe gynaecological problems that dogged her for the rest of her life. Mrs Miles remembers that, when she arrived in Hong Kong to join her husband, he told her that Wallis had been in the gynaecological ward of the Women's Hospital.

Wallis returned to Shanghai on the *Empress of Canada* to recover. The strike was continuing, although American ships were allowed in and out of the harbour. In a severe rainstorm on 29 August Wallis sailed, in very poor health, in a first-class cabin aboard the Dollar Lines *President McKinley* via Kobe, Yokohama and Honolulu to Seattle. When she arrived on 8 September she went immediately into hospital.

Win had meanwhile left his command of the *Whipple* and was about to assume command of the USS *Wright* at Hampton Roads, leading a torpedo-boat squadron. Wallis remained in touch with him; concerned about her health, though apparently not knowing the cause of her illness, he met her in Chicago and they made an attempt at a reconciliation. They returned to Washington by train together in mid-September; soon he was transferred to the *Wright*. They remained good friends.

Win, like Wallis, had established strong connections with the Mussolini administration in Italy. That autumn he entertained the Italian soldier and airman Italo Balbo, the early Fascist leader and associate of Ciano's who at the time was building up Mussolini's air force. Balbo had been in charge of the Blackshirt militia, and with Ciano's father he had been a leader of the march on Rome. His friendship with Win continued until his death in 1940, when he was shot down in error by an Italian artillery post at Tobruk. In 1936 Win was awarded the high decoration of Cavaliere of the Order of the Crown of Italy for his assistance to Mussolini in matters concerning the Italian air force.

Wallis stayed with her mother in Washington for three weeks, recuperating slowly. From time to time she travelled to Wakefield Manor, Front Royal, which was scarcely changed from the days of her childhood. Her cousin Lelia was living there with her husband, General George Barnett, who had just retired after eleven years in San Francisco as commandant of the US Marines in the Pacific. The Barnetts took Wallis under their wing; they put her in touch with their able attorney, Aubrey 'Kingfish' Weaver, of Weaver and Armstrong, Front Royal.

Weaver told Wallis that at Warrenton, across the Blue Ridge Mountains in Fauquier County, Virginia, divorces could easily be obtained on the basis of the husband's desertion. It would be a simple matter to have Win write a letter backdated to June 1924, stating that he would not live with her again. The letter would be headed 'USS *Pampanga*'.

She would have to establish residence in Warrenton for at least a year, and she must not leave the town for longer than a few weeks. Wallis listened carefully, but she had a fit of nostalgia and made yet another effort to patch up the marriage. She wrote to Win on the USS *Wright*; he met her at Aubrey Weaver's office at Front Royal. He told Wallis he wanted to be free.

In a spirit of resignation, Wallis travelled to Warrenton on 3 October 1925. The town was close to Middleburg, where she had been at Burrland, and it was in the heart of fox-hunting country. Horse shows were the major social events of the community. Conversation hinged upon the studbook and the saddle.

Wallis stayed with the socially prominent horse owner Mrs Sterling Larrabee at her historic home, Oakwood. Corinne Mustin, who had just married Captain George Murray following the death at sea of Henry C. Mustin, had arranged the introduction. After some weeks Wallis moved to the fifty-year-old Warren Green Hotel, a red-brick imitation colonial building with a double-deck veranda and a glassed-in sun porch. Although the hotel had seen better days it was still, with its plush seats, potted ferns and lobby decorated with flowered wallpaper, possessed of a musty Victorian charm. Wallis moved into room 212 on the second floor, overlooking the square and the Fauquier National Bank. The furniture was uninspiring, with brass bed, dressing table, water jug and bowl, and cracked leather chair; she got permission from the manager to refurbish it for a long stay. When she had put out her boxes and elephants and her Chinese screen she felt a little better.

Wallis was close enough to the scenes of her early life to find friends whom she had known at the beginning. Phoebe Randolph, who had been at Arundell as her classmate, was now Mrs Henry Poole, of local note, and Florence Campbell, who had been a friend of hers and Mary Kirk's at Oldfields, was now Mrs Edward Russell and a leader of society. Both entertained her at their homes. Wallis also caught up with her handsome early beau, Lloyd Tabb, and with Lewis Allen, the doctor who had delivered her and who now exhibited prize mares and geldings at the Warrenton horse shows.

At Christmas 1926, Wallis answered an invitation from her old friend Mary Raffray and her husband Jacques to stay with them in New York at their house in Washington Square. Her decision to travel there resulted in a meeting that was to change her life and propel her on her most dangerous adventure so far.

NOTES

1 See *US Military Intelligence Reports, 1924–5*, University Publications of America, Frederick, Maryland.
2 *Admiral's Skin*, Mondadori, 1949.

6

ERNEST

Late on the afternoon of Christmas Day, Jacques, Mary and their friends and relatives were gathered round the tree when the doorbell rang and Jacques went to answer it. Two men walked in; one of them made so little impression on Wallis that within days she had forgotten his name or what he did for a living. But the other man had the same strong effect on her as Winfield Spencer had some ten years earlier.

Jacques introduced him as Ernest Aldrich Simpson; he had a fake British accent and a slightly haughty manner. His brown hair was lightly flecked with gold. He had mild, sympathetic, dark blue eyes, pink cheeks and a square jaw. Like Win, he had a dark moustache. Well built, he walked with a cocky, confident military swagger. He was twenty-nine years old.

As the evening went on, and presents were unwrapped and dinner served, Wallis became intrigued. Simpson had a polished, suave manner, an air of good breeding and intellect, and a well-balanced disposition that lacked the underlying sense of danger that had unwisely drawn her to Win. The chief problem was that he was married, to the former Dorothea Parsons Dechert, daughter and granddaughter of well-known Massachusetts Supreme Court judges, and the couple had a young daughter, Audrey.

Ernest Simpson was a partner in Simpson, Spence and Young, a company that bought and sold ships. The firm had extensive dealings on both sides of the Atlantic, with offices in London and agents in Hamburg, where it worked in close alliance with the

Hamburg–America Line, and in Italy, where it made deals with Mussolini's government. Simpson had left Harvard without graduating, to follow the impulse of an intense love of England; both his parents came from the British Isles. He joined the cadet battalion of the Coldstream Guards. Then, at the end of the First World War, he was compelled, due to his father's negligent management, to surrender his commission and take up the reins of the company. But he remained ultra-British in New York: he walked the avenues in bowler hat, Guards tie and plain, dark suit, carrying a tightly rolled umbrella as if he were in Mayfair.

This impeccably dapper and correct young American gentleman had a secret, so carefully kept that not even his own daughter knew it. He was Jewish. His father had changed the family name from Solomons because he feared, not without reason, that the business world would close its doors to a new and struggling Jewish company. Because both he and his father were fair of complexion and the masquerade could be sustained, Ernest neglected to tell his first wife and he joined several clubs that never admitted Jewish members. He was especially careful to conceal the truth in Germany, where anti-Semitism was even more pervasive than it was in the ruling and commercial classes of Manhattan and London.

Wallis had no inkling of Ernest's racial background. Throughout her life her attitude towards Jews was ambiguous and changeable; she would eventually be close to members of the two richest (and inter-related) Jewish families, the Sassoons and the Rothschilds, yet she could, according to the author Stephen Birmingham, scream out about 'kikes'. In this she was typical of her time; Cecil Beaton was equally known for using this term; in 1938 he scandalized the world by using it in a notorious cartoon.

Wallis should have returned to Warrenton to sustain the residency requirements called for by the divorce, but instead she boldly embarked on a liaison with Ernest, despite the fact that Dorothea Simpson was present at his East 68th Street house. Wallis and he had much in common. Both enjoyed good books (he was better read than she); both liked to collect figurines and knick-knacks; both knew a great deal about silver and china. Ernest was an expert in many fields, including painting, poetry and music. He was representative of a now endangered species: the businessman of culture. He took Wallis to museums, galleries, bookshops and libraries; she learned all he had to teach her.

He had other advantages. He appeared to be financially secure. He had perfect manners and knew how to order wines and food. It was true he smoked – she hated smoking – but he liked only the finest pipe tobacco, Havana cigars and Sobranie or Turkish cigarettes. He had a couple of expensive touring cars. He was respectful, even subservient, and Wallis had never been able to release the dominating side of her personality in the way she wanted.

Their relationship began to develop through games of bridge and poker and a trip to the army–navy game. But Wallis felt it was a dead end. Ernest refused to consider a divorce. There was the existence of his child. Wallis broke with him for a time. First, she moved from the Raffrays' house to a tiny room at the British-style New Weston Hotel. Then she tried to sell an article to *Vogue*; it was rejected. She enrolled at a secretarial college but soon left. She was beginning to feel sorry for herself.

She was partly consoled by meeting an old friend from San Diego days, the ugly but charming Benjamin Thaw, who was in charge of the Latin American Division of the State Department and was married to Consuelo Morgan, elder sister of the famous twins Gloria Vanderbilt and Thelma Furness. Consuelo, Gloria and Thelma were gorgeous, the spoiled and wilful children of the diplomat Harry Hays Morgan. When Consuelo was seventeen, Mama Morgan had arranged for her to marry the wealthy French aristocrat Count Jean Marie Emmanuel de Maupas du Juglart in Brussels, where H. H. Morgan was consul general. Two years later the couple was divorced; Consuelo was charged with adultery.

By the mid-1920s, Gloria and Thelma were the buzz of society; they had inherited a smouldering, dark, Latin glamour from their Chilean grandmother. Refusing to wear the short skirts of their era, they paraded through society parties *à deux*, with their hair severely dressed, long strands of pearls, industrial-sized diamonds and dramatically pale complexions. Thelma married James 'Junior' Vale Converse, grandson of a founder of Bell Telephones; the marriage didn't last. Gloria married Reginald Vanderbilt, a horse-fancying society lush and the number one catch in New York. He had inherited $30 million in 1901. When his uncle Alfred went down on the *Lusitania*, he got half a million more.

In 1923, Consuelo married Benjamin Thaw; the Thaws were one of the reigning families of Pittsburgh. Soon afterward Gloria's child, known as Little Gloria, was born. In 1925 Reggie Vanderbilt died of drink; Thelma then married Lord (Marmaduke) Furness, owner of the Furness-Withy shipping line that ran cruise vessels from New York to Bermuda. Benny Thaw arranged for Wallis to stay in Pittsburgh with his cousin, the immensely rich, eighty-five-year-old Mary Copley Thaw; at the same time he was talking about Wallis with some other friends, the Morgan Schillers, who were looking for attractive women to work for them, improbably selling construction elevators.

Staying with Mary Thaw had its pleasant aspects but it also had its problems. Mary's mansion, Oaklawn, was an immense Gothic pile filled with antiques, gloomy landscape paintings and a collection of Corots. There were seventy rooms, a dozen live-in servants and a Parisian chef. Mary was deeply troubled. She was suing her grandson for $600,000 which she claimed he had extorted from her. She was being blackmailed for some alleged shady business dealings. Above all, she was tortured by the manic presence on the scene of her dissolute son Harry K. Thaw, who in 1906 had shot and killed New York's most prominent architect, Stanford White, on the Madison Square Garden roof in a dispute over the famous showgirl Evelyn Nesbit Thaw.

While Wallis was at Oaklawn, Thaw, who had been saved from the electric chair by Mary's money and influence, and had spent years in a mental hospital, kept arriving without warning in hysterical, terrifying rages. He would take off to New York, where his ex-wife, Evelyn Nesbit, had a nightclub; storming into the club, he would knock all the bottles and tables to the floor and stamp on the broken glass.

Wallis was unable to get the job with Morgan Schiller because of her poor grasp of mathematics, necessary in dealing with specifications, and she returned via New York to Warrenton. Depressed during that spring of 1927, she was consoled when Aunt Bessie, who was now acting as paid companion to Mary B. Adams, owner of the Washington *Evening Star*, offered her a free trip to Europe. Just before sailing, on 16 June, Wallis made her official divorce application through her Front Royal lawyers.

The European trip was meaningless and bland. In Paris, in late October, Wallis heard that her Uncle Sol had died of heart failure in Baltimore. He had been very annoyed by her divorce proposal, and he had been severely depressed by the $3 million worth of damage to his railroads caused by the Florida hurricane in July that year. The constant struggle with rival railway interests and his exhausting lobbying in the Florida cities had worn him out. At first Wallis, who owed so much to him, was sorry that she had not been able to attend the funeral; but she was greatly displeased by the will when it was read a few days later. Uncle Sol had left her only the interest from $15,000 worth of shares in his railway companies and in the related Alleghany Company and the Texas Company. Having expected a slice of his $5 million she furiously began a lawsuit against the trustees of the estate, in the form of a caveat. Using her proxy, Josephine Warfield, granddaughter of her Uncle Henry, she charged that Solomon Warfield was mentally incompetent and emotionally disturbed at the time he made the will and that his signature was forged.

In December 1927, Judge George Latham Fletcher granted her divorce in Warrenton; among the depositions by her mother and others was the letter Win was supposed to have sent from China, complete with American postage stamps, a detail that the judge chose to overlook. There is no question that this was a collusive divorce, since Wallis's statement that she had not seen Win in four years was contradicted by the evidence and she had omitted any mention of China from her deposition, thereby perjuring herself. She was lucky that in later years British officials, including a Lord Chamberlain and a King's Proctor, somehow failed to note those significant postage stamps.

Now that Wallis was free, she turned her mind back to Ernest Simpson and returned to New York to resume her affair with him. Dorothea learned of this while she was ailing at the American Hospital in Paris, and filed divorce proceedings there. Prematurely grey-haired and frail, years later this Massachusetts gentlewoman allowed herself to say to the author Cleveland Amory, 'Wallis was very smart. She stole my husband while I was ill.' Later in 1928 Ernest decided he would take up the managing directorship of his company in London; his father was becoming increasingly negligent and was also involved in a somewhat questionable liaison with a woman in Paris.

Wallis needed time; she was fond of Ernest, but she wasn't in love with him. The Rogerses came to the rescue; they had moved from Peking back to their ancient haunted villa, Lou Viei, in Cannes, in the exotic hillside suburb known as Californie, and, past conflicts and emotional complications forgotten, invited her to stay with them. The villa had been partly remodelled by Barry Dierks, a talented American architect.

Wallis arrived in perfect winter weather; Californie was a riot of hibiscus, frangipani and coral trees, and at night the scent of flowering jasmine filled the air. The villa was festooned with creepers and had a striking view of the Mediterranean. Herman and Katherine took Wallis out, with various eligible bachelors, dancing at the Palm Beach Club or sailing on chartered yachts under the stars. The Riviera was dreamlike in its charm and tropical loveliness, and Wallis again bathed in the luxury of great wealth.

She discussed with Herman and Katherine whether she should marry Ernest, and they urged her to follow her instincts. It didn't take long for her to make up her mind. Ernest offered freedom from want and a safe haven. Word that his divorce had been granted meant that he was free. She had no money; he was up and coming in British financial circles. She cabled her acceptance of his long-standing proposal and left for London in late June 1928.

Her timing, as always, was perfect. Just as she had arrived in China in the midst of civil war, so she reached London in time for the height of the social season, which officially began on 1 July. It was a dazzling month. The Prince of Wales, who continued to fascinate Wallis and whom she had not seen since that crowded night seven and a half years earlier in San Diego, had just launched a series of parties at York House, his grace and favour home at St James's Palace. He was busy shattering the pomp and circumstance of court life by featuring at these fancy shindigs a dance orchestra, a vaudeville show and cabaret dancers, and by inviting oceans of the *jeunesse doré* of London.

At the dinner tables of Mayfair, which Wallis now frequented, the conversation hinged on royalty, 'in' people, sex, tennis and horses. Few would dream of discussing slums, mass unemployment or the rising cost of living. In 1928 Mussolini was the idol of London society. Among his keenest supporters was Winston Churchill, who made a statement in Rome, quoted in *The Times* on 21 January 1927: 'If I had been an Italian, I am sure I would have been wholeheartedly with you from start to finish in your triumphant struggle against the bestial appetites and passions of Leninism.' George Bernard Shaw was among many who agreed; referring to Mussolini's most famous political murder, he said, in a letter to Friedrich Adler on October 1927, 'The murder of Matteotti is no more an argument against Fascism than the murder of St Thomas à Becket is an argument against Feudalism.' Almost everyone of influence in London society agreed. In hindsight, infatuation with Mussolini can only seem both dangerous and misguided. Fascism was a corrupt and repressive system, both fraudulent and incompetent. Mussolini was an empty-headed, posturing, preposterous bully with no visible charm; his entire foreign policy executed by Ciano in later years was a denial of the principles of the League of Nations. From beginning to end, the British (and French) policy towards Italy was one of conciliation and concession instead of stern rebuke and reminder. In the event, one can hardly be surprised that thinking people lost faith in those gurus who felt that the Italian system was a valid answer to the evils of Communism. In view of Wallis's romantic involvements with Prince Caetani, Count Ciano and Alberto da Zara, it is easy to see how she was inveigled into a belief in that corrupt and invalid political system, and how she shared her conviction of its merits with the Prince of Wales.

Born while his great-grandmother Queen Victoria was still on the throne, the prince was obsessed with the Empire; he knew that one day he would be the ruler of one-third of the world and of millions of people for whom the monarch was almost a divinity. His father, King George V, was a remote and regal figure who seldom condescended to visit him and his brothers, Albert, Henry, George and the retarded John, and his sister Mary, in the nursery; according to the custom of the age the king left the children to the infrequent attentions of a succession of nannies, of whom very few were not sadistically cruel.

King George treated the three oldest boys very much like cadets on a battleship quarterdeck. As the Prince of Wales later wrote, they were always 'on parade'. If their sailor suits or tartan suits were even a fraction in disarray, the king reprimanded them with savage anger; if they put their hands in their pockets, those pockets were sewn up. They had to wear the strangling, stiff Eton collars that cut into their necks like saws. They wore long stockings and buckled shoes; even when they swam, they had to be covered from head to foot. The body, in those times, was an object of shame; except in the bath, it had to be concealed utterly. Sex was only for procreation; women were not supposed to enjoy its pleasures at all.

As a result of the repressions of his boyhood, at an early stage the good-looking Prince Edward became a rebel. In time he would revolutionize fashion and release the human male from the constrictions of centuries. He would do away with stiff collars, waistcoats, morning coats and gaiters; he would encourage open-necked shirts, shorts, and even walking around in public stripped down to trousers.

He was an appealing little boy, golden-haired, slender – the world's Prince Charming. As he grew up, only his youngest surviving brother, George, who was tall and dark whereas he was very short – no more than five feet five – was his equal in looks. Both brothers had a feminine streak: at Oxford, where he was a poor student, the Prince of Wales was linked by gossip with his tutor, Henry Peter Hansell; they were familiarly known as Hansel and Gretel. Queen Mary taught the boys to crochet from an early age; much was made of this by the critics, though in fact it was a British custom of that period to instruct male members of a family in what today would seem to be a predominantly feminine skill.

The Prince of Wales was fond of Austria and Germany; he much regretted the divisions in the royal family that preceded World War I. So did his mother, the German but London-born Princess of Teck. George V's cousin and the prince's godfather, Tsar Nicholas II, had been murdered by the Bolsheviks at Ekaterinburg; he never forgot that, and he was committed from the beginning to wiping out Communism. Another cousin of his father's, Kaiser Wilhelm II, fascinated him; he became very friendly with the Kaiser's family, spoke German, and spent much of his youth in Germany. The prince's favourite cousin was the Eton-educated Charles, Duke of Saxe-Coburg-Gotha, who would one day play a sinister role in his life.

In the 1920s, the prince undertook his famous Empire tours. No royal figure before or after covered so much territory or shook so many thousands of hands. His small, slim figure with its golden crown of hair became the world's symbol of the promise of youth.

He was the most sought-after eligible bachelor of his age, surpassing even Valentino in the immensity of his popularity among young women of all nations. In January 1923 it was announced in the press that he would marry Lady Elizabeth Bowes-Lyon, whose face, under a chaplet of spring flowers, stared prettily out of an ornamental oval. A week later her engagement to his brother Albert was announced; later of course she became Queen Mother. The following year Queen Marie of Romania tried to match the prince with her daughter, Princess Ileana. In 1926 Lady Alexandra Curzon, who would soon marry his equerry Edward 'Fruity' Metcalfe, was named as being engaged to him. That same year George, Duke of Kent was linked to the Infanta Beatriz of Spain, and in 1928 to Princess Ingrid of Sweden.

Max Beerbohm, artist and aesthete, created a now quite forgotten sensation in June 1923; with powers equal to those of Nostradamus, he predicted the abdication of fourteen years later. He exhibited at the Leicester Galleries in London a cartoon of the Prince of Wales in 1972 already abdicated from the throne, a wretched old man married to the gaudy socialite daughter of a landlady. There was a storm of criticism over the cartoon, but Beerbohm refused to withdraw it from the exhibition and later sold it to the actor-manager Sir Gerald du Maurier.

The prince's every movement made headlines; during Wallis's stay in Hong Kong, Shanghai and Peking the papers were full of him almost every day. His chronic tendency to fall off horses, his love of driving steam trains, and his fondness for the Charleston and the Black Bottom and for New Orleans classical jazz were widely featured.

By the time Wallis came to London, the prince was in his early thirties. He was wilful, spoilt, charming, and furious when crossed. He was decades ahead of his time in his obsession with fitness, a trim waist and a well-toned, carefully trained physique. He spent hours fussing over his waistline and did thirty minutes of callisthenics every morning; while everyone around him ate themselves into potbellies with heavy meat dishes, sauces and puddings, he nibbled lettuce leaves and fruit and ate only one full meal a day. He loved sport and visiting nightclubs; a typical day in his life would begin with breakfast, consisting of an apple, followed by a brisk game of tennis, lunch (more fruit), an afternoon of golf or polo, then dinner of steamed fish or chicken; it would end with an evening spent at his favourite nightclubs, surrounded by the golden youth of the era and with a pretty, eligible débutante on his arm.

The prince had recently been in Paris, where he had been involved in a steamy affair with the notorious Marguérite Laurent, the Princess Fahmy Bey, an exotic beauty who, on the third floor of the Savoy Hotel, on the night of 9 July 1923, at the height of a gothic thunderstorm, had shot and killed her husband, a voluptuous Egyptian, in a fit of jealousy brought on by his apparent interest in another woman. A porter wheeling a luggage trolley heard the shots and found Prince Fahmy in silk pyjamas, bleeding from the mouth. The princess flung the smoking revolver at the dying man's feet and surrendered to the hotel detective. Ably defended by the lawyer Sir Edward Marshall Hall, she was acquitted on the grounds that she had been provoked; after inheriting several millions, she moved to the Ritz in Paris, where the Prince of Wales flew his biplane to visit her for many a romantic weekend.

At the same time he was still involved, after many years, with Mrs Freda Dudley Ward, who in 1918, despite the fact that she was married to a Liberal whip in the House of Commons and had two children, had allowed herself to enter into a prolonged liaison with the prince. She was introduced to him, oddly enough, by Ernest Simpson's sister, Maud Kerr-Smiley. More gossip again averred that the prince was bisexual and that he had enjoyed a romantic liaison on an Empire tour with his celebrated cousin, Louis Mountbatten, while Edwina Mountbatten had found consolation with an odd assortment of partners including the famous black nightclub pianist Leslie 'Hutch' Hutchinson.

On 10 June 1930, in a letter to Dora Carrington, the homosexual author Lytton Strachey would write:

> I went yesterday to see the Duveen room [Tate Gallery]. . . .
> There was a black-haired tart marching round in india-rubber
> boots, and longing to be picked up. We both lingered in the
> strangest manner in front of various masterpieces – wandering
> from room to room. Then on looking around I saw a more
> attractive tart – fair-haired this time – bright yellow and thick
> hair – a pink face – and plenty of vitality. So I transferred my
> attentions, and began to move in his direction when on looking
> more closely I observed that it was the Prince of Wales – no
> doubt at all. . . . I fled – perhaps foolishly – perhaps it might
> have been the beginning of a really entertaining affair.

This, of course, indicates no more than the feverish imaginings of a brilliant flibbertigibbet. Was there anything in all this? The truth probably is that the sexually ambivalent prince at that time had not had an actual homosexual experience; that he was considerably lacking in virility despite his romantic image in the eyes of millions of women; and that even by the late 1920s he was what the French call a *demi-vierge*. Uncertain and insecure, he was an unsatisfactory lover, and his homosexual leanings, deeply repressed, were revealed in what became an almost hysterical aversion to anyone homosexual. Nevertheless, gay figures of society continued to weave daydreams around his golden head and slim, perfectly proportioned figure. He was the very stuff of salon gossip when Wallis Spencer began to make her way in London society.

Ernest Simpson might not be exciting, but he had entry to at least the middle levels of that society when Wallis, who was tired of wandering, weary of struggle, married him, after a very brief engagement, not out of love but out of apathy. The marriage took place at Chelsea register office on 21 July 1928. Her mother, who was suffering from a cancerous condition of the eye, could not make the journey from Washington, and she had already made it clear that she did not approve of Ernest, possibly because she had found out his secret that he was Jewish or because his company was beginning to be shaky financially. Not a soul arrived from the United States, not even Corinne or Lelia or Mary Raffray or

Consuelo, whose husband Benny had applied for a transfer to Paris. The witnesses were Ernest's father and Maud's son Peter, who apparently disliked Wallis as much as she disliked him. The setting was drab and dirty, and the wedding reception was held not at the elegant Grosvenor House, where most such occasions took place, but at the humdrum Grosvenor Hotel, a somewhat seedy pile situated in the hurly-burly of Victoria Station.

It was an unpromising start to the marriage. But at least the couple left for the Continent in style aboard a handsome new Lagonda tourer complete with uniformed chauffeur. Throughout the honeymoon trip, which began in Paris and then went all over France and Spain, Ernest continued to teach Wallis much about art and architecture. He walked her off her feet, combing through galleries and museums and palaces.

Back in London, the Simpsons found a house at 12 Upper Berkeley Street, Mayfair. This was a pleasant address, not far from the delights of Hyde Park and Green Park. It was rented to them furnished for twelve months by Margot, Lady Chesham, and with the lease came a cook, maid, butler and chauffeur. Such was the accepted mode of upper middle-class life in those long-lost days.

Maud Kerr-Smiley made Wallis feel more or less at home in London, whose climate she hated. Maud gave a series of parties for her and Wallis responded in kind. Wallis voraciously read the many London newspapers, following especially every movement of the Prince of Wales. Although she pretended to herself and others that the British obsession with royal doings was absurd and misguided, the fact is she had a hunger which drove her back again and again to read the Court Circular, the officially authorized daily account in *The Times* of what the royal family was up to every day of the week. Her health was poor; she suffered from colds; her marriage was uninspiring and she was sad much of the time.

During the autumn of 1928, the prince was continuously in the news. He was planning a visit to Egypt and to the rest of Africa, a trip that would include a safari in Kenya and a liaison with the aviatrix Beryl Markham; he enjoyed her favours on alternate nights with his brother Henry, Duke of Gloucester – a scandal that was carefully suppressed by the royal spin doctors; he appeared in public without a waistcoat, which set a new trend; he was seen helping a small boy dig worms at the seaside; and he joined the war veterans at Ypres in France for a memorial service at that scene of bloody conflict. These seemingly trivial matters summed up his interests: his love of Empire and his need to preserve the security of the Suez Canal, the channel whereby the trade routes to India were maintained; his informality and love of children and the poor; and his obsession with the horrors of the First World War, which he regarded as futile and stupid and the result of unnecessary conflicts between his grandfather, King Edward VII, and his father's cousin, Kaiser Wilhelm of Germany. That war had cost England the flower of its youth, and the Prince of Wales, who had been on the front in France, was determined, with all his heart and soul, that such a holocaust of bullet and bomb and gassing should never happen again.

All this Wallis could determine by reading his speeches, particularly the impassioned address at Ypres. She still hated war; it had caused her great anguish at Pensacola, and she had never forgotten the death of her husband's brother Dumaresq Spencer in action in France. And then in Canton, China, she had seen first-hand the terror and danger of bloody battles between Communists and Chinese Fascists. She could not fail to sympathize with the Prince of Wales's neutralism from the beginning.

There was another matter which she soon heard about and which did not find its way into even the most garish newspapers. While still entangled with Freda Dudley Ward and the Princess Fahmy, the prince found a new light of love: Thelma, Lady Furness, the twin sister of Gloria Vanderbilt and the younger sister of Wallis's friend Consuelo Thaw. Thelma had sultry, dark good looks inherited from a partly Latin ancestry. Her American accent did the rest – the Prince was always infatuated by Americans. He met her at a cattle show; he had known Consuelo and her husband Benny he said, when Benny was a diplomat in Buenos Aires. Thelma moved boldly into Fort Belvedere, the prince's house on the edge of Windsor Great Park, and redecorated a guest bedroom as her own – in shocking pink, with the Prince of Wales's emblematic three white feathers at the top of each of the four wooden posts of her bed. The prince was greatly amused by this example of vulgarity. They entered into childish games: they bought teddy bears at

Harrods and exchanged them as peace offerings after quarrels; they did embroidery together, an art taught them both by their mothers; and they called each other Poppa and Momma – Momma for the prince. Their sexual relationship appears to have been infantile and unsatisfactory: Thelma later complained to friends that the prince had a very small endowment and was a very poor sexual performer. Spitefully she called him, as did so many others, 'The Little Man'.

Wallis learned that in December 1928 the prince had to return abruptly from his trip to Dar es Salaam, Tanganyika, because his father was grievously ill; Mussolini, to whom he would always be grateful, supplied transportation. Wallis, by accident or design, caught a glimpse of him one murky afternoon as he left York House, St James's Palace, in the polished black royal Daimler to go to Buckingham Palace to attend his sick parent. She claims she was on her way to pick up her husband in the City when she beheld this sight; in fact Ernest was always brought home by chauffeur, and the palace was not on the direct route from Upper Berkeley Street. It is probable, therefore, that like so many fans she was simply waiting to catch a glimpse of the prince.

Life moved on slowly for Wallis; Ernest was a lecher who made advances to women at parties. She accepted this. They kept accounts together, and they enjoyed dinner parties and bridge games and backgammon. The only shadow on her life was the illness of her unhappy mother, who, Aunt Bessie wrote, had aged badly and in her fifties was already an old woman. In early 1929 Wallis and Ernest sailed to America on the *Mauretania* to visit Alice, whose appearance shocked them. They returned for a chauffeur-driven tour of England, but the pain and sorrow remained.

The lease ran out on the Upper Berkeley Street house after a year, and Lady Chesham, who was now reconciled with her husband, a captain in the Royal Hussars, from whom she had been separated, wanted the house back. Wallis and Ernest moved into a temporary flat in Hartford Street, and were house-hunting when news came from Washington that Alice was dying.

Wallis travelled alone on the *Olympic*. With her usual timing, she arrived in the midst of the Wall Street crash. The news was received aboard ship, and it was impossible to sell her shares in time. She lost almost all her $15,000 from the Warfield estate; her caveat under the name of Josephine Warfield was not heard until the following year, when it failed.[1]

It took only a day or two to learn that most of Ernest's American holdings had also been wiped out. It was a grievous week, and Alice's death on 2 November was the ultimate blow. Alice left nothing; she was intestate. Charles Gordon Allen, her present unhappy husband, was also penniless, his meagre savings wiped out by the crash. Wallis sailed back to England under a heavy cloud.

Fortunately Simpson, Spence and Young did not depend on America; the company continued to buy and sell ships at a profit in Germany, Italy and the Scandinavian countries. The Simpsons managed to scrape together enough money to buy some furniture, and Wallis and Ernest found a fine flat at 5 Bryanston Court, in George Street; it was spacious and comfortable, and it came with a complete staff of servants, who were housed elsewhere on the premises. The flat had a small entrance halla large drawing room, a dining room that could seat fourteen, three bedrooms – a master bedroom, a second bedroom, and a guest room – two bathrooms and a large kitchen. Wallis decorated the rooms tastefully, with the exception of the guest room, which she fixed up with a huge round white bed and pink sheets and pillows. Guests entering the drawing room saw to the left an overstuffed brocade armchair and behind it a mahogany table with a Chinese vase brought from Peking; ahead a Chippendale cabinet filled with small Chinese ornaments; also straight ahead a Regency mirror over a conventional fireplace; and to the right a Queen Anne chair with a striped silk seat and a large, silk-covered sofa. Bookshelves built into the wall displayed Ernest's collection of Dickens and A. A. Milne, author of *Winnie the Pooh*, his favourite book, whose central figure he resembled in more ways than one.

Throughout much of the autumn and winter of 1929, the Prince of Wales's activities consisted of performing stunts in planes, remodelling his houses with Thelma and planning another trip to Africa, which took place in January 1930. Wallis followed his movements daily: his long voyage to Cape Town through gale-swept seas; his feverish cold; his elephant hunt near Nairobi; and in March a recurrence of malaria. What she did not know was that

Thelma Furness, who had taken off with her husband on a separate safari, joined the prince in late February in Kenya. On a lion hunt organized by the Governor Thelma slipped away from Lord Furness after a day of hunting lions and joined the prince's own safari of forty. At night their romance allegedly grew in intensity; twenty-eight years later she wrote in a book co-authored with her twin sister, Gloria:

> This was our Eden and we were alone in it. His arms about me were the only reality; his words of love my only bridge to life. Borne along on the mounting tide of his ardor, I found myself swept from the accustomed mooring of caution. Each night I felt more completely possessed by our love, carried ever more swiftly into uncharted seas of feeling, content to let the Prince chart the course, heedless of where the voyage would end.

This account scarcely fits with her complaints later on that he was sexually inadequate as a partner; she was probably indulging in fantasy. The onset of the prince's malaria was brief; Thelma was on her way back to England when he recovered. He filmed elephants in their native haunts in Uganda, narrowly escaped a charging beast, filmed rhinos in the Congo, and flew to Aswan and Cairo to see the ancient Egyptian monuments. The plane used on his Cairo trip crashed the day after he left it, killing the occupants. He was back in England in April.

In October 1930, Benny and Consuelo Thaw moved from Paris to London, where he became First Secretary at the US Embassy. At the same time, and to Wallis's delight, Corinne Mustin Murray also turned up in the city; her husband, George Murray, was assistant naval attaché. Wallis felt much more at home in London now. She became part of an American colony that tended to meet at least twice a week and exchange news of home.

Through Benny and Consuelo, Wallis met Thelma Furness. Bearing a son, Tony, to Lord Furness made no difference to Thelma's continuing royal liaison, and Furness, who was immensely rich from his Bermuda honeymoon ships despite the crash, was enjoying a continuous honeymoon with beautiful young women in the south of France. As if surrounding the prince on all sides, not only did Thelma spend her weekends at Fort Belvedere but Gloria

Vanderbilt, with her daughter, Little Gloria, set up house at the imposing Three Gables, which was directly opposite Fort Belvedere and could be watched from the royal windows.

Even Mama Morgan, Laura Kilpatrick, the sisters' colourful mother, moved into Three Gables to make the siege complete. Meanwhile, inspired by Thelma's American enterprise, the prince redid Fort Belvedere from top to bottom, installing central heating – a great luxury in England then – a Turkish bath, a gymnasium and a swimming pool. The prince would arrive romantically with Thelma at this Gothic hideaway by plane, his new King's Flight pilot, Flight Lieutenant Edward Fielden, expertly touching down on Smiths Lawn at Windsor Great Park.

Wallis became a friend of Thelma's; possibly she felt that through the connection she would obtain a foothold at court. At all events the two women met for lunch, usually at the Ritz, and enjoyed the gossip of the hour; when, in mid-January 1931, Consuelo and Benny Thaw invited Wallis to Burrough Court, the Furnesses' house at Melton Mowbray in Leicestershire, centre of the fashionable fox-hunting country, she accepted at once. The Thaws made an exciting promise: the Prince of Wales and his brother Prince George, who every year attended the Quorn Hunt from their nearby house, Craven Lodge, were expected to be in the house party. Lord Furness was on safari in Africa at the time.

At the last minute, Benny's mother fell ill in Paris and Consuelo flew over to take care of her. Wallis, Ernest and Benny decided to go up to Melton Mowbray by train. It was well into January and the weather was too foggy for safe driving.

Wallis was nervous about meeting the Prince of Wales and spent a day at the hairdresser's. By Saturday she could face herself more or less calmly – the Bryanston Court flat was full of mirrors. But she was still terrified: that she wouldn't make the right impression; that she would be out of place, as she had been in Warrenton, in an environment in which horses and hunting were the main topics of conversation; and that she wouldn't be well enough to dazzle – she was coming down with a miserable winter cold.

At last she was ready. With the long-suffering Ernest she drove to St Pancras station, where they met Benny Thaw for the trip. Wallis felt increasingly unwell on the journey. As the train chugged through fog and drifting snow, she was coughing and sneezing uncontrollably; she was sure she had a fever. She suddenly realized she had no idea how the prince should be addressed. Benny told her the correct form was 'Sir'. It dawned on her that she didn't know how to curtsey; Benny must teach her at once. In the swaying, rattling, sooty train Benny Thaw, career diplomat and First Secretary at the US embassy in London, managed a very clumsy curtsey. Wallis felt too awful even to laugh. But she copied Benny, and by the end of the trip she had mastered the art to perfection.

The train steamed into Melton Mowbray in a dense yellow fog. Thelma had sent a car. The chauffeur struggled with painful slowness through the damp and icy murk. At last he stopped in front of a large, gabled house with an imitation Tudor look. 'Stockbroker Tudor' as Osbert Lancaster would later dub this architectural style. Averill Converse, Thelma's stepdaughter by a previous marriage, was at the door instead of the butler to greet the arrivals. Averill told her guests that Thelma had gone over to Craven Lodge to return with the two princes. Wallis could only sneeze and cough miserably as she and Ernest went to their rooms to freshen up.

Averill entertained her guests to a prolonged afternoon tea. The hours ticked away on the grandfather clock; Wallis began to wonder if the princes would ever turn up; if they were marooned somewhere in the fog. Finally, after two hours, at 7 p.m., she heard the sound of a car drawing up on the gravel drive, followed by a babble of voices. The butler opened the front door.

NOTE

1 But she was offered, and accepted, an alternative settlement.

7

THE PRINCE

Dark, vital, gorgeous, Thelma strolled in with the princes. It was the first time Wallis had seen the Prince of Wales at really close quarters: the faraway figure moving through the crowds at the Hotel del Coronado and the barely glimpsed, sad-faced presence in the royal car leaving St James's Palace, the personage of the newsreels and the newspapers and the magazines – was actually saying 'Good evening' to her and shaking her hand. She curtseyed. She looked hard at him, with a burning curiosity.

Wallis liked him at once. He was even smaller than he seemed from photographs. He looked very fit but was narrow, delicate and slender in build. His hair was a shining gold; his eyes a tired, haunted blue with premature pouches under them, the result, Wallis would later discover, of heavy drinking and insomnia. Almost childlike at a distance, his face was puckered and deeply lined because of too much exposure to the tropical sun on his travels to the limits of the Empire. He had even, white teeth, frequently displayed in an infectious, quizzical smile that few could resist. The prince was dressed in a loudly checked tweed suit. He was informal, relaxed and laughing. His face in laughter was open, innocent and joyous; in repose it was intensely sad, possessed of a secret pain. Part of that pain was caused by the recurring sexual problems which Thelma Furness would later and quite ruthlessly discuss in international circles.

It was already night. Dinner would be served at nine. To make her royal guests welcome, Thelma prepared a second tea, forcing

Wallis, who dieted grimly, to tackle yet another round of scones, cake and England's favourite beverage. The conversation was desultory. At last Wallis and Ernest went to their rooms to dress for dinner while Thelma went to the nursery to tuck her baby son, Tony, and his cousin, Little Gloria Vanderbilt, into bed; Gloria Senior was abroad in France. The conversation at dinner offered little inspiration to Wallis: it centred on hunting, which she continued to dislike, hounds and the studbook. She felt as bored and alienated as she had been at Warrenton. She was still suffering from her cold, and she was a long way down the dining table from the prince.

Feeling only slightly better after sleeping late the next morning, Wallis, still sniffling into her handkerchief, walked downstairs to find the Prince of Wales chatting with his devoted aide, Brigadier General Gerald F. 'G' Trotter, a grizzled charmer who had lost his right arm in the Boer War and whose uniform sleeve was pinned to the front of his tunic. At the luncheon table Wallis found that there were no place cards; boldly, she sat next to the prince. For something to say, he observed, 'You must miss central heating, Mrs Simpson.' To which, with startling effrontery, she replied with a falsehood: 'To the contrary, Sir, I like the cold houses of Great Britain.' Then she added, 'I am sorry, Sir, but you have disappointed me.' The prince looked understandably startled by this impudence. 'In what way, Mrs Simpson?' he asked. While, no doubt, the expressions of Ernest, Thelma, 'G' Trotter and the other guests were pictures of shock and dismay, there was no stopping Wallis now. She said, 'Every American woman who comes to England is asked that same question. I had hoped for something more original from the Prince of Wales!'

Wallis had grasped shrewdly from the first moment she looked into the prince's weak, sensitive, pale blue eyes that he wanted to be dominated by strong people; he liked to be confronted head-on. Her cool, expert calculation paid off. The prince was unable to shake off her sharp remark; she had caught his interest, and she knew it.

Dinner that night was an elaborate occasion. Dozens of the local gentry and their ladies gathered in the dining room for hours of horsey conversation. The next day Wallis, Ernest and Benny

returned to London. Perhaps because the meeting with the prince
had awakened thoughts in Wallis that she would rather suppress,
her behaviour over the next few days was nervous and drastic. She
fired her chauffeur because of some slighting remark he had made
to Ernest; she got rid of a maid and gave notice to the cook. She
was consumed with a new ambition: she must meet the prince
again. An ideal occasion would be her official presentation at court.
When an American acquaintance, Mrs Reginald Anderson, suggested she should be presented, she accepted immediately, even
though Mrs Anderson as a personality left her somewhat cold. Her
cousin Lelia Barnett had come to London in the autumn of 1929
for such a presentation, and Wallis had helped to dress her. Thelma
Furness had been presented; so had Consuelo and Gloria. Wallis
would not be left behind.

The conditions of presentation had a moral stringency typical of
the reign of King George V, whose high standards of conduct
contrasted oddly with the decadent self-indulgence and promiscuity
of fashionable London in the 1930s. For years, no divorced woman
was received at court. By 1931 a divorcee could be presented, but
she had to prove that the fault of adultery, cruelty or desertion lay
with the husband. Any suspicion of collusion would be frowned
upon, which narrowed the field considerably.

In order to crawl through this needle-eye of official acceptance,
which meant a good deal more to her than she pretended, Wallis
anxiously wrote to Mrs Sterling Larrabee, her former hostess at
Warrenton, to obtain the necessary divorce documents from the
Warrenton court house files. Why she didn't write to her lawyer,
Aubrey Weaver, at Front Royal is a mystery, although she often had
a poor memory for names. No sooner had she written to Mrs
Larrabee than panic seized her, and she sent a letter to Aunt Bessie
expressing her interest in the prince, with a cable insisting that
nothing be said about the meeting at Melton Mowbray. She was
afraid of a leak to the press. Then, unpredictably, after issuing this
stern request, she couldn't resist bragging about her encounter.
She wrote to Mary Kirk Raffray in New York about it and then
impulsively gave Bessie permission to talk to Lelia Barnett, and she
told Benny Thaw who told Corinne . . . It was clear that she was in
a spin of nervous excitement mixed with tension and scarcely knew

what she was doing. And yet she claimed in her memoirs that royalty meant nothing to her.

Mrs Larrabee proved to be a friend and sent the divorce decree to London. But since she was no expert at obtaining documents, she failed to obtain the all-important depositions of Alice and Wallis herself; Wallis most anxiously sent her back to the court house to obtain the depositions and send them on.

Meanwhile, the Prince of Wales and his brother George had left England, travelling via Paris to Spain and then across the Atlantic to the Caribbean and South America. The journey, taking many weeks, had the double benefit of aiding British trade problems south of Panama and spiriting the star-crossed bisexual George away from a dire situation with a boy in Paris. In the prince's absence Wallis wasted no time in capitalizing on her royal encounter. As word got around that she had met the prince, she received invitation after invitation, dragging with her the exhausted and irritable Ernest, who hated late nights after a hard day's work at the office.

Her social ambition was ferocious, obsessive. Among the Simpsons' hosts that spring of 1931 were Lord and Lady Sackville, who invited them to stay at their fabled estate, Knole. At the same time, Wallis began cultivating Thelma much more intensively, clearly realizing how that friendship would bring her very close to the throne. And she also got to know Gloria Vanderbilt, who was spending more time in England, and the colourful Nadeja, known as Nada, Lady Milford Haven. A glamorous White Russian, Nada Milford Haven shared with Thelma and Gloria membership of a high-powered group of society lesbians who were the cause of constant hothouse gossip in the Mayfair salons.

On 15 May, Thelma threw a grand welcome-home party for the two returned princes at her house in Grosvenor Square. The guests were excited as Thelma walked in, resplendent in a silver gown, with the Prince of Wales. As the prince approached Wallis, he whispered to Thelma, 'Haven't I seen that lady before?' Thelma reminded him that he had met Wallis at her house. He shook hands with Wallis as she rose from her curtsey and he told her how much he had enjoyed their previous encounter. She smiled; he continued to pass down the line.

A few days later, the Lord Chamberlain, who had accidentally overlooked the telltale American postage stamps on Win's faked letter from Canton, approved Wallis's presentation at court. Wallis was overjoyed. She could think of nothing else but the big event coming up in June. However, she had a distraction: Her friend Mary Kirk Raffray, who was separating from Jacques, announced that she would be arriving on the *Mauretania* in a few days. Wallis was far too busy to welcome this visit; the dark side of her nature was in evidence as she fretted about the arrival of her oldest and dearest friend.

Mary had a rough crossing, but she overcame seasickness to carry on elaborate flirtations with several handsome young bachelors aboard. She arrived at the railway station in London with no fewer than five beaux escorting her, then dropped the lot as she sped off with Wallis through the crowd. Wallis had an invitation to lunch at Consuelo and Benny Thaw's, and there was no way she was going to miss it. Suitcases and all, she whisked the exhausted Mary off to Consuelo's house to meet Thelma and Nada. On the way, she confided that the Thaws' was used by the prince and Thelma as a love nest.

Mary scarcely had time to powder her nose as she was whirled by high-strung Wallis from tea party to dinner party; they didn't get home to Bryanston Court until well into the early hours. Mary fell exhausted on to the ghastly circular guest room bed with its pink sheets, pink plush covers and wide satin eiderdown. Wallis spent the next few days in a constant spin with Mary. The occasional dinners at Bryanston Court had an offbeat flavour – Ernest stiffly dressed up in white tie and tails and the two girls in lounging pyjamas and robes. Felipe Espil, Wallis's old flame of Washington days, was now first secretary at the Argentinian embassy and frequently entertained the Simpsons and Mary. On Derby Day, 3 June 1931, the sleek US diplomat William Galbraith and his brusque, abrupt wife Katherine took the excited Wallis and her gang to Epsom Downs to see the race from the top of a rented London doubledecker bus, lunching off champagne, caviar and cold chicken from picnic hampers.

At last the presentation day arrived: Wednesday, 10 June. In a state of hysteria, Wallis borrowed Thelma's fan made up of three ostrich feathers, the traditional symbols of the Prince of Wales required of every presentee. A white dress was also essential. She was too tall to fit into Thelma's, so she wore Consuelo's instead. Thelma lent her the train. She bought an aquamarine and crystal necklace cross and a corsage brooch. The wealthy American Lester Grant lent her and Ernest his touring car.

The Andersons and the Simpsons left Bryanston Court early to beat the tremendous traffic jam in the Mall. Crowds had already formed and peered into the luxurious interior of the car, trying to see the occupants. It was the first time Wallis had seen Buckingham Palace. She was enthralled. The chauffeur drove through the iron gates, parking the vehicle in the courtyard. Wallis and her party went to a special entrance, passing through a vestibule where liveried flunkeys took the ladies' wraps. From there, the guests walked slowly up the red-carpeted grand staircase that was lined on either side by Yeomen of the Guard in their Elizabethan costumes and made their way down a chandeliered corridor to the red-and-gold ballroom. Wallis was fascinated by the throne dais. The king and queen were seated side by side in front of the gold-embroidered canopy of crimson velvet, beneath which they had sat at the Delhi Coronation Durbar of 1911. Under the canopy's top were embroidered in gold the royal lion and unicorn, and on either side white-fluted pillars supported a display of noble classical figures.

The king was in full-dress uniform; the queen in a beaded gown of white satin with a choker necklace of pearls and diamonds. The Prince of Wales stood behind the throne. The indispensable 'G' Trotter led Wallis's party to seats near the front. Soon, the room was completely full. At a signal from the conductor of the palace orchestra, the presenters and presentees formed a line passing the thrones, the ladies curtseying one by one to the royal couple. Later everyone repaired to the state apartments, and the prince joined his parents in talking briefly with the guests. Wallis heard him say to his great-uncle, the Duke of Connaught, 'Something should be done about the lights. They make all the women look ghastly.'

After the presentation, Thelma invited Wallis, Ernest and the Andersons to join her and the prince for a nightcap at her house. Wallis boldly challenged the prince on his remark about the lights. He expressed surprise that his voice had carried so far; he had underestimated the intensity with which she, feigning indifference, was hanging on his every word. Once again, with great cleverness, she had piqued his royal interest.

As the Simpsons left Thelma's house at 3 a.m., their chauffeur was waiting to take them home. But the prince offered to drop them off in his own car. Wallis dismissed her driver. At Bryanston Court she invited the prince to come up for another drink. He declined with a smile; he was on his way to Fort Belvedere. But he indicated that he would certainly take her up on the offer another time.

Soon after this memorable evening, Consuelo Thaw offered the delighted Wallis the chance of a trip to the south of France. The idea was that this would be a party for women only; Benny and Ernest would be left in Paris, and Gloria Vanderbilt would join the women at the Hotel Miramar in Cannes. Wallis accepted, apparently unaffected by the fact that the entire adventure had sapphic potentialities. Mary Raffray accompanied Wallis part of the way. In Paris, while Wallis and Mary and Ernest Simpson were crossing the street, a cab, swinging round the corner too fast, struck Mary head-on and threw her to the ground. Wallis, horrified, hurried to her side. Rushed to Gloria Vanderbilt's apartment by ambulance Mary, crying hysterically, was then transferred to the American Hospital at Neuilly. Cables flew to and fro; Mary's rich Aunt Minnie, who lived in Paris, offered to take care of her. At last Wallis felt that Mary was sufficiently recovered and she proceeded to Cannes. Mary returned to New York, her health permanently impaired.

Wallis was embarrassed to find an uncomfortable situation in the south of France. She discovered that she had to share a room with Consuelo. What that led to was uncertain, but one morning Gloria Vanderbilt's maid, Maria Caillot, strolled into Gloria's room for no particular reason and found Gloria and Nada in negligees enjoying a passionate French kiss. Wallis found that men were totally discouraged by this steamy ménage, and she had to go out hunting for eligible males. When Ernest, who may have had an inkling of what she was getting herself into, summoned her back to London to go to Lord and Lady Sackville's house party, she packed up her things and fled.[1]

Back in London, a depressed Wallis found that Ernest's business was falling apart. Her extravagances had drained whatever was left over from Uncle Sol's trustee settlement, and now she had reduced her unhappy husband to such a state of penury that he had to dismiss the chauffeur and sell the car. Keeping up with the rich tore away at her nerves and made the weekly accounting a torment. Once again, her insistence on late night parties wore Ernest, who had to be up at eight to go to his office by Tube, to a frazzle. He began to look haggard and pale, and dark circles formed under his eyes.

In the autumn of 1931, Wallis was feeling terrible. She was ill from inflamed tonsils and had to have them removed. Consuelo came to see her every day; her solicitude seemed to go beyond that called for by normal friendship – her interest in Wallis had not waned. Wallis dreaded her visits. It was a grim, foggy November; for weeks Wallis lay in bed, exhausted by the operation, unhappy and unsettled by her penurious condition. Word from the Prince of Wales was a long time coming, but at last her impatience was rewarded. In late January 1932 the winter gloom was lightened by the longed-for invitation to go to Fort Belvedere. The Simpsons drove down in a borrowed car through snow-covered countryside to Sunningdale in Berkshire, arriving in the early evening. The road cut through forest trees until, at a moment of dramatic unexpectedness, it opened out into a gravel driveway and then to the brightly lit turrets and battlements of the fairy-tale castle. Lamplight was glowing in the tall windows, and at the sound of the car engine a liveried footman appeared, to open the door and take the luggage. With typical informality the prince, dressed in a kilt, was at the door in person to greet his guests.

He led the rejuvenated and happy Wallis with Ernest through an octagonal ante-room with a black-and-white marble floor to the elaborate drawing room surrounded by Canalettos. Rich golden yellow satin curtains were drawn against the night; the atmosphere was cosy, snug and very American under Thelma's influence. There were chintz-covered armchairs and Chippendale tables and a grand piano. Even though a fire was roaring away cheerfully in the grate, the central heating was on full blast. Thelma was there, along with 'G' Trotter and the Thaws. The prince insisted on taking the Simpsons to their room. When they returned after dressing for dinner they were astonished to see the prince, watched tenderly by Thelma, embroidering with infinite care a backgammon table cover. He said, looking up bashfully, 'This is my secret vice. The only one, in any case, I am at pains to conceal.'

Dinner took place in the handsome, panelled dining room decorated with pictures of horses by Stubbs. Wallis was very amused to see that the prince kept his cigarette case in his sporran. After the meal the guests joined their host in games of cards and in trying to piece together a giant jigsaw puzzle. Then they danced cheek to cheek to the latest foxtrots and rumbas. At last came the moment Wallis was waiting for; the heir to the throne asked her to dance. 'I found him a good dancer, deft, light on his feet, with a true sense of rhythm,' she wrote years later.

In March 1932, Wallis's old friend from Peking, Georges Sebastian, issued an invitation to the Simpsons to visit him in his elegant house at Hammamet in Tunisia. When Wallis glumly wrote to tell her host that she was without funds, he sent her the tickets. It was a pleasant trip, and Georges an excellent host. Not long afterwards Aunt Bessie arrived, and she treated the Simpsons to a trip around Europe. But despite these adventures Wallis was still under severe stress; her marriage wasn't working, and the financial problems and a frustrated longing to see more of the Prince of Wales left her again in a poor state of health, suffering from ulcers. As a result, the trip with Aunt Bessie was cut short.

Wallis was also distracted with what became an open scandal that summer: Consuelo Thaw's affair with a charming foreign woman. In view of Benny's position at the US embassy, this was not only a torment to that correct and decent man but it also exposed the embarrassed Wallis to untoward gossip because of Consuelo's consuming interest in her. She began to edge away from Consuelo. And she had a further problem still: in those summer weeks the Prince of Wales found a new female distraction: the celebrated aviatrix Amelia Earhart, who had just made international headlines by being the first woman to cross the Atlantic in a solo flight. Apparently disregarding Thelma, the prince ostentatiously took Amelia dancing; she was married, and once again he was showing an unhealthy fascination with married women. He took Amelia to the Derby, causing a flurry of excited comment in the American press; the British newspapers primly avoided any mention of this new romance. The *New York Times* noted that he danced with Amelia at the Derby Ball – again and again and again.

He treated Thelma badly that year; he was looking for new fields to conquer. He travelled to Mussolini's Italy without her, giving crowds the Fascist salute as he arrived in Venice, where he danced repeatedly with a young Hungarian beauty and then joined her for a swim at the Lido the following morning. He inspected the Italian and British fleets at Corfu; then he proceeded to Monte Carlo, where on 25 August he was seen repeatedly dancing cheek-to-cheek with an American girl, Mrs Barbara Warrick, while young French maids pelted them with flowers from the casino balcony. He continued to Sweden, accompanied now by Prince George, where he publicly flirted with the beautiful Princess Ingrid and where there was much baseless talk of an engagement. After a quick trip through Ireland, where there were threats that he might be blown up by the IRA, he returned to England and flew north to look at the dreadful labour conditions that vexed and disturbed him.

During the prince's long absence abroad, Wallis was increasingly unhappy, frustrated and distracted at Bryanston Court. She still fought with her staff, firing and rehiring servants; she continued to be sickly and fretful, and her ulcers caused her much pain and discomfort. However, she was consoled by the fact that the prince wasted little time after he returned before inviting her and Ernest to Fort Belvedere. In January 1933 Wallis made another visit to the Fort, but it is clear from her letters that by then she was irritated by Thelma's continuing hold over the prince; she wrote an edgy note to her Aunt Bessie, clearly distracted by the sight of Edward and Thelma embroidering in unison. She didn't realize that the prince very much had his eye on her.

In March 1933, she knew. It was not customary for royal persons to send messages to passengers on ships unless those passengers had already been promoted to the role of court favourite. When Wallis sailed that March aboard the *Mauritania* to visit Aunt Bessie in Washington, a Marconigram was received for her aboard ship, wishing her bon voyage and a safe return. News of the wire rapidly spread around the ship, ensuring for her the maximum of attention from officers and crew. She regarded the entire trip as an opportunity to escape from her stultifying marriage. She enjoyed the attention of many men, and she spent much of her time in Washington carrying on a series of giddy romantic liaisons; she added a new series of beaux on the return voyage. It is clear that it was hard for her to return to a monogamous situation, even though dear, dull, devoted Ernest met her when the ship docked at Cherbourg.

After her return, Wallis's relationship with the Prince of Wales underwent a change. Evidence for this can be found in an episode involving Henry Flood Robert, the son of Grace Flood Robert, Wallis's old friend from Coronado days, who arrived in London to take part in the International Monetary Conference. Wallis, Ernest and Grace, who was staying with them, met Henry off the train. Wallis prepared an excellent American meal for him, including fried chicken. It was an exciting occasion; Wallis was delighted to recall the good old days in southern California. Oddly, Thelma Furness was present on her own, as out of place as Ernest was in a tide of reminiscence that neither could share. Mr Flood Robert will never forget what took place at four o'clock that afternoon:

> Suddenly the door opened and the maid came in. She announced that the royal car was at the door. And that Madam was expected to come at once to Fort Belvedere as the Prince of Wales was waiting for her! Wallis immediately, and right in front of Ernest and Thelma, picked up her coat and handbag without a word and walked out, leaving us all so stunned we couldn't speak. I looked at Ernest and saw a tear in his eye. I couldn't look at Thelma. My heart went out to Ernest, but I admit I said to Mother as we went to our hotel, 'More power to Wallis!'

A certain inscription on a bracelet given by Edward to Wallis three years later, but now in the possession of the Countess of Romanones, indicates that it was not long after that incident that the relationship between Wallis and the prince became a sexual one. The countess will not reveal the exact words of the inscription, which marks a significant anniversary, but says only that it contains a highly intimate reference to 'a bathtub'. According to the late Sir Dudley Forwood, later equerry to the Duke of Windsor, the relationship between Wallis and the Prince was bizarre. He said, in 1987:

The techniques Wallis discovered in China did not entirely overcome the Prince's extreme lack of virility. It is doubtful whether he and Wallis ever actually had sexual intercourse in the normal sense of the word. However, she did manage to give him relief. He had always been a repressed foot fetishist, and she discovered this and indulged the perversity completely. They also, at his request, became involved in elaborate erotic games. These included nanny–child scenes: he wore diapers; she was the master. She was dominant, he happily submissive. Thus, through satisfying his needs, needs which he probably did not even express to Mrs Dudley Ward and Thelma Furness, she earned his everlasting gratitude and knew that he would be dependent on her for a lifetime.

Others disagree with this view, among them Alberto da Zara's lieutenant, Giuseppe Pighini, who said in 1987: 'I was told by close friends of Wallis that indeed she in fact did introduce the Prince to techniques which made it possible for him to have satisfaction during intercourse. He was so emotional that before he would climax too quickly and thus could not consummate sex.'

That same year, Adolf Hitler rose to power in Germany. From the beginning he was determined to secure an alliance with Great Britain, whose foreign policy was leaning towards his chief rival among European dictators, Mussolini. He embarked upon a policy of interesting the British royal family in re-cementing their fractured alliances with their cousins in Germany. With great shrewdness, and in order to secure the support of the army, which maintained its traditional allegiances to the old Prussian Junker class, he did not confiscate the massive properties of Kaiser Wilhelm II, cousin of King George V. Although the Kaiser remained in exile at Doorn in the Netherlands, his sons and daughters-in-law were comfortably maintained under the Führer's protection in Berlin. Of these, Hitler's favourite was the Crown Princess Cecilie, the tall, buxom, Wagnerian daughter-in-law of the former monarch. It was at her home, Cecilienhof, a looming Gothic folly filled with potted plants and pictures of dead Hohenzollerns, that the young Prince of Wales had spent happy days in his childhood. Her son, Prince Louis Ferdinand, was twenty-five years old in 1933 and an employee of Henry

Ford in Dearborn, Michigan; Ford was a keen admirer of Hitler, and Hitler had Ford's picture on his desk in the early, struggling days of the Nazi party at the Munich Brownhouse. Tall, handsome and dark-skinned, with silky black hair, Prince Louis Ferdinand was considered by the Führer an ideal emissary to London. He had a romantic background calculated to appeal to the Prince of Wales: he had just had a romance with the French film star Lili Damita, who was soon to marry another of Hitler's idols, Errol Flynn.

His host, the entertainingly scurrilous Sir Robert Bruce Lockhart, kept a careful diary of Louis Ferdinand's meetings with the Prince of Wales in London that season; the German visitor also met Wallis, who liked him. On 11 July 1933, the two young men met at York House, St James's Palace. They talked partly in German and partly in Spanish. Bruce Lockhart reported in his diary on 12 July, 'The Prince of Wales was quite pro-Hitler and said it was no business of ours to interfere in Germany's internal affairs either re Jews or re anything else, and added the dictators are very popular these days, and that we might want one in England before long.' Bruce Lockhart did not report on Prince Louis Ferdinand's response to this statement. It should be noted that at the time, due to King George V's uncertain health, the Prince of Wales was taking his place at some official functions and was expected to succeed him before too long. Perhaps he himself was the dictator he had in mind. Soon afterwards Louis met Prince George, noting shrewdly, as Bruce Lockhart recorded, 'He is artistic and effeminate and uses a strong perfume. This appeals to me.'

The kaiser appreciated his grandson's visit to the British capital. He wrote to Bruce Lockhart on 22 July:

> My special thanks to you for your kind efforts in getting the Prince into touch with members of the Royal Family . . . It would be particularly agreeable if, through this visit, the German–English relationship is furthered . . . The remark of the Prince of Wales, that we have a right to deal with our affairs as we deem it right, shows sound judgement. Prince Louis Ferdinand would no doubt have agreed with him on this point.

Although Prince Louis Ferdinand was secretly anti-Nazi and later joined the German resistance, his presence in London as a presumed symbol of Hitler's support of royal alliances ironically influenced the Prince of Wales and, through him, Wallis. If anything were needed to convince the Prince of Wales that the Führer's intentions were to restore the old family alliances, those doubts were removed. From then on, he and Wallis seldom wavered in their naive belief in Hitler's intentions and desires for a lasting peace. On Armistice Day, 11 November, the Prince of Wales confided in Count Albert Mensdorff, the former Austrian ambassador, telling the count of his fondness for Nazism. Mensdorff wrote:

> It is remarkable how he expressed his sympathies for the Nazis of Germany. 'Of course it is the only thing to do, we will have to come to it, as we are in great danger from the Communists here, too . . . I hope and believe we shall never fight a war again, but if so we must be on the winning side, and that will be the German, not the French . . .' It is . . . interesting and significant that he shows so much sympathy for Germany and the Nazis.

By a juxtaposition of significant quotations, it can be seen that the prince's politics, then and later, were coincidental with those of Sir Oswald Mosley, head of the British Union of Fascists. In his memoirs, while advocating, among other things, that Goering should have come to England to secure widespread support for Nazi Germany, Sir Oswald wrote emphatically:

> I was prepared to do anything to prevent a war by maintaining good relations between English and Germans, provided it was compatible with my duty to my own country. [We should have let] the Germans go to a possible clash with Russia, which, if it happened, would have smashed world Communism [in the 1930s], pointed Germany in the opposite direction to us, and kept its vital energies busy for at least a generation while we had time to take any precautions which might prove necessary.

In an article in the *New York Daily News* of 13 December 1966, the then Duke of Windsor wrote:

> My Hanoverian and Coburg forebears were German. There was much in the German character that I admired. At their best as, alas, at their worst, they are a virile, hard-working, efficient

nation. I acknowledge now that along with too many other well-meaning people, I let my admiration for the good side of the German character dim what was being done to it by the bad. I thought that the rest of us would be fence-sitters while the Nazis and the Reds slogged it out ... the immediate task ... was to prevent another conflict between Germany and the West that would bring down our civilization.

Wallis agreed with these attitudes of Mosley and the prince from the beginning.

In December, Thelma Furness made what for her would be a fatal decision. She returned to the United States to join her twin, Gloria, who was much vexed by conflicts with the Vanderbilt family, for an escapist trip to Hollywood to visit their old friend, Constance Bennett, who was starring in a film entitled *The Affairs of Cellini*. Thelma had enjoyed an abortive if steamy career as a movie actress in the silent period and had once had an affair with Constance Bennett's father. Wallis took Thelma to a farewell lunch at the Ritz. Referring to the Prince of Wales with a rather questionable degree of concern under the circumstances, Wallis said, 'Oh, Thelma, the Little Man is going to be so lonely.' To which, improbably and perhaps innocently, Thelma replied, 'Well, dear, look after him while I'm away. See that he doesn't get into any mischief.' Thelma wasn't being naive and absurdly trusting; she was blinded by her colossal ego and infatuated by what she believed was her unlimited power to hold the prince from any distance. She didn't realize, apparently, that he had been getting up to some mischief with Wallis already.

Thelma sailed to New York in a dream state, in a first-class suite brimming with hothouse flowers from Fort Belvedere. The prince was petulant and irritated that she should have chosen to leave him, even for a few weeks, thus disobeying his royal command. The day after she sailed, he called the Simpsons and invited them to a dinner party at the Dorchester Hotel in honour of a local representative of the National Broadcasting Company (NBC), his old friend Fred Bate. The prince carried on all through the meal about the working-class people of the Midlands, their unemployment problems, their courage and their misery. Wallis seized her opportunity. Although she lived in a world in which the matter of men on the dole and the breadline meant little or nothing to her, she pretended to be touched by the prince's stories of hardship. She hung on his every word. When he went on to discuss his role in the future of the British Empire, she provided expert flattery. He wrote in his memoirs that by the time dinner was over, he was convinced that she was a woman with a social conscience.

Still fretting over Thelma's absence, apparently not satisfied by whatever brief encounters he could manage with Wallis alone, the prince became a man obsessed. He called the Simpsons at all hours of the day and night, sometimes as late as 4 a.m., just to talk; always an insomniac, tortured by his own private complexes and by the frustrations of his royal impulses, hating to be left alone even for a moment, he would turn up at Bryanston Court without warning. Wallis would then have to wake up her staff, housed in another part of the building, to satisfy his whims. He drove poor Ernest, whose days were spent trying to deal with the matters of a crumbling business, to a state now bordering on nervous breakdown.

Wallis decided to make the best of this uncomfortable situation. By now the Prince of Wales was utterly dependent on her; she held the upper hand. She knew how to make him laugh, and no matter what hour of the night he turned up she would regale him with witty, risqué stories and observations. Sometimes he would accompany her and Ernest to such popular London night spots as the Embassy Club. There, in the overcrowded cellar room favoured by high society, with everyone in evening dress clustered at packed tables around the tiny dance floor, the genial host Luigi in attendance, and Ambrose's glittering band playing the latest quicksteps and foxtrots, the prince and Wallis would engage each other in high-pitched, raucous conversation while Ernest sat exhausted and befuddled, in cigarette smoke thick as fog.

By December 1933, Ernest was greatly distressed. His frustration and stress emerged in a breakout of boils that had to be painfully lanced. While he was ailing, Wallis was preparing American 'popovers' – rather like small Yorkshire puddings – for the prince in her kitchen. Just before Christmas Wallis dragged herself from her sickbed, where she had been lying with a cold, because of an irresistible invitation: Consuelo had arranged another party for her and the prince.

In mid-March 1934 Thelma Furness was at a soiree given at the Pierre Hotel in New York by her friend, the socialite Mrs Frank Vance Storres. At dinner the hostess shrewdly placed Thelma next to the twenty-three-year-old Prince Aly Khan, heir to the immense fortune of his father, the pro-Hitler Indian potentate known as the Aga Khan. Aly was the ultimate lady-killer of the day. Lithe, muscular, dusky-skinned, and handsome, he was a bronze Apollo whose life was polo ponies, fast cars and beautiful women. His reputation as a lover was second to none in society. Only Porfirio Rubirosa, the Dominican playboy, could match his boudoir reputation in later years. His father had sent him to Cairo at the age of eighteen to be trained by the madams of the great bordellos in the art of Imsak, the art of withholding climax and the Egyptian equivalent of Fang Chung. A night with Aly Khan was like winning the Irish sweepstakes. Later, a journalist commented that, like Santa Claus or Father Christmas, Aly Khan 'came only once a year'.

He was instantly attracted to Thelma. He liked dark, smouldering, vaguely Latin women, and she was looking her best that night. Right at the table in front of her escort, he suggested they go off together the moment they were past the coffee stage. She told him she had to pack that night because she was sailing in two days for England. He gave her a burning glance, peering into the depths of her soul, and said, 'Put your trip off for a week.' She was no fool; she said she would be sailing on schedule. He wasn't to be stopped. He asked her what she was doing the following night. She suggested he call her late the next morning.

She was wakened at her town house by a messenger bringing in an enormous bouquet of red roses with a note in a distinctive hand that read, 'Call you at 11.30 a.m. for our dinner tonight. Prince Aly Khan.' He did call, and she couldn't resist it: she had dinner with him. The next day, she sailed. When she got to her veranda-deck suite on the *Bremen*, it was filled with roses from one end to the other and Aly had scribbled on a card for each bouquet.

The next morning, when she woke up, the *Bremen* was at sea. The telephone rang. It was Aly, presumably calling from New York.

He suggested lunch. She laughed at this absurd idea. How about in Palm Beach? To her astonishment, he replied, 'I'm on board.' And he was. After that, how could she resist him?

On the crossing, she had ample opportunity to learn the difference between an ardent but sexually insecure and childish Prince of Wales and a copper-skinned bedroom bombshell with an anatomical chart of the female body stored carefully in his pretty head. Thelma arrived in London looking ten years younger.

*

The prince had spies everywhere, and evidently some of them were on board the *Bremen* because Thelma was in trouble from the moment she landed in England. In her reckless vanity, glowing from her lover's attentions, she had apparently forgotten that royalty does not brook disobedience or infidelity. The Prince of Wales turned up at her house in London and insisted she explain herself. How could she betray him with an Indian?

It is clear that all the prince's colonial racist snobbery was aroused, along with his wounded pride. The fact that he was already conducting an affair with Wallis didn't seem to strike him as in the least contradictory. Aly wisely moved on to Paris. Then Thelma, in her blindness, foolishly called Wallis and asked, on the verge of tears, for some womanly advice.

It was Wallis's moment of power, and she seized it with relish. As Thelma swept in to 5 Bryanston Court, dramatically pale and tense as only she could be, Wallis told her maid to leave them alone and on no account to disturb them, no matter what the emergency. Thelma poured out her story: Aly Khan, the Prince of Wales's displeasure, her distress at his verbal punishment of her. Wallis, with expert, finely judged calculation, said, 'But Thelma, the Little Man loves you so very much. The Little Man was lost without you.'

At that moment, the maid walked in. Wallis glared at her furiously. 'I thought I told you I was not to be disturbed,' she said, with a jagged edge to her voice. The maid replied, 'I know, madam, but it's ... His Royal Highness, the Prince of Wales!' Thelma looked as though the Tower of London had fallen on her head. Wallis went to the telephone without a word.

Thelma strained her ears to listen. All she could hear was Wallis saying, in a tight, tense voice, 'David, Thelma is here.' David was the name by which all his close friends called him. Then Wallis returned. Thelma could see from her face that nothing further would be said about the call. Chilled and depressed, and realizing that her reign was coming rapidly to an end, Thelma left soon afterwards.

The next weekend, the prince invited the Simpsons to Fort Belvedere. It was an agonizing two days for Thelma. The prince was cold to her and scarcely listened to a word she said. By contrast, and right in front of Ernest, he was deeply and affectionately attentive to Wallis, who treated him rather the way that a nanny would treat a spoilt child. The worst happened at dinner that night. The prince picked up a lettuce leaf with his fingers to nibble it. Wallis slapped his hand and told him brusquely to use a knife and fork in the future. He smiled sheepishly and blushed like a schoolboy. Thelma looked at Wallis, who answered her gaze with an icy, triumphant stare. Wallis was revelling in her victory; that cold, haughty glance told Thelma she was finished. Lady Furness understandably took to her bed. The prince poked his nose through the door later that night. She whispered from her pillow, 'Darling, is it Wallis?'

'Don't be silly,' he snapped. But he didn't return that night.

Meanwhile Wallis, no doubt to the dismay of the Fort Belvedere staff, whose kitchen prerogatives were absolute, had actually invaded that sacred domain. When the prince, looking for her, at last located her there, she presented him with a plate of eggs she had scrambled herself. He sat down at the kitchen table in front of the cook and maids and ate the eggs on the spot. Thelma left at dawn.

After that, Wallis unhesitatingly left Ernest behind on many dates with her royal paramour. The writer Somerset Maugham's wife Syrie, the interior decorator who had helped Wallis re-do Bryanston Court, gave a party to which the Prince and Wallis were invited. Very late in the evening, they repaired to the library together. Suddenly they were startled by the sound of voices raised in the corridor outside. 'Where's David?' a voice shrilly demanded. It was Thelma, insisting on seeing the prince, and using his nickname.

'I'll find him for you,' Wallis heard Syrie Maugham reply.

But at that moment Thelma flung open the library door and saw the heir to the throne and his American mistress locked in an embrace. Furious, she stormed out, to find consolation with Aly Khan in the south of France.

Early in 1934, Wallis's star rose rapidly. She was pleased to be the rage of London society as the prince's reigning lady, and not a soul believed the carefully arranged fiction that their relationship was platonic (although it now appears that they were still merely involved in sexual game playing and had not fully consummated their relationship). Suddenly, all of Wallis's financial worries disappeared; backed now by substantial sums from the royal purse, she and Ernest could afford everything they wanted – though she shrewdly cried poor in letters to Aunt Bessie. Humble, quiet Ernest was apparently quite prepared to continue with this arrangement. He seemed almost to be honoured by the imperial bounty that descended upon his wife. There is not even evidence that he found consolation with a mistress of his own.

Somewhere between a sheep and a saint, this foolish, fond American royalist simply got on with his daily business. It was typical of that era and place that a husband would accept the fact that he and his wife were going separate ways. Society seemed to regard marriage as a mere convenience, a conventional front covering any manner of untoward behaviour. Yet Simpson's reaction seems abnormal: he was in love with Wallis, and the reaction of most men would have been an excess of jealousy and hatred followed by a demand that the marriage should be ended. The situation seemed to suggest that his relationship with Wallis was essentially sado-masochistic, just as her relationship with the prince would in many ways be.

One of Wallis's new-found friends and supporters among London hostesses was the celebrated Lady Colefax. Tiny, dark and squat, Sibyl was a brilliant patroness of the arts, at whose dinner parties the young John Gielgud, Cecil B. De Mille, and Osbert and Edith Sitwell could easily be met. Bernard Shaw, Arnold Bennett, Somerset Maugham and Max Beerbohm were frequently at her exquisite Georgian house in Chelsea, with its eighteenth-century furniture and green-and-yellow silk hangings. Wallis always looked forward to walking through Sibyl's tiny walled garden with its blaze of flowers to the French-windowed living room with its air of skilfully acquired culture: the beginnings of taste.

No less prominent a hostess was Lady Cunard, yet another American *arriviste* who had managed to climb to the top from humble San Francisco origins. Emerald had married Sir Bache Cunard, heir to the Cunard steamship line, and had conveniently shunted her ageing husband off to his country estate while she queened it in London. Tiny and birdlike, with dyed canary-yellow hair, enormous spots of rouge on each cheek, and Cupid's-bow painted lips, she talked in a twittering voice and never sat still, darting all over the room as she provoked her guests with audacious and risqué remarks. Her lover was the conductor Sir Thomas Beecham, and she was the chief patroness of Covent Garden, with its resident ballet and opera companies. Her passions were Hitler, Shakespeare and Balzac, not necessarily in that order. She hated her daughter Nancy, who was left-wing and had an erotic interest in blacks.

Emerald's parties at her house at 7 Grosvenor Square were the focus of growing Nazi influence in London. Her drawing room, glowing with Marie Laurencin paintings, was alive, night after night, with excited conversation about the merits and demerits of Mussolini, of the British prime minister, Ramsay MacDonald, and of the new Führer.

It was Emerald who, wittingly or unwittingly, began to embroil Wallis in Nazi connections that would dog her for many years. One of Emerald's leading protégés, and her personal court favourite, was the ebullient White Russian Gabriel Wolkoff, brother of the late Tsar Nicholas II's admiral of the fleet. Gabriel, or Gaby, as he was known, was the chief set designer at Covent Garden, specializing in particular in the Wagner operas which Hitler loved and which Sir Thomas Beecham also favoured.

Admiral Wolkoff owned a humble London tea shop. He was the centre of a group of rabidly anti-Semitic, intensely pro-Hitler White Russian refugees and others who were determined to crush the Soviet Union by rallying to the cause anyone and everyone in Britain who might share their point of view. Admiral Wolkoff's daughter, Anna, was a plain but determined young woman who worked as a dressmaker for Princess Marina of Greece. It was at Marina's suggestion that Wallis also engaged Anna. And it was at about that time or soon afterwards that Anna became a Nazi agent; by 1940, she would be sending crucial secret intelligence to Italy for use in Berlin.

The association was sufficient to interest the Secret Intelligence Service. Nor did the SIS fail to note that among the very first individuals to whom the prince introduced Wallis were the ambassadors of Italy and Germany. Count Dino Grandi, the Italian emissary, has stated through his diplomatic associate Egidio Ortona:

> I was the first ambassador who asked the Prince and Mrs Simpson together at my embassy at 4 Grosvenor Square, the purpose being the breaking of the ice which surrounded her. In fact, the dinner was not a smashing success, as a cool attitude prevailed among the guests toward the American lady. My wife, Countess Grandi, even teased me about the whole thing, saying, 'You're always up to strange things!' The morning after the dinner, as early as 8:00, we received an enormous bouquet of roses from the Prince with a note of thanks to us.

Soon, the coolness of the Grandi circle disappeared. Grandi confirms that he was invited on several occasions to Fort Belvedere for happy, informal gatherings at which Wallis was present, and that both Wallis and the prince were deep admirers of his thuggish boss, the Italian dictator.

Simultaneously, the prince was determined that Wallis would be part of the German fascist circle at the highest levels in London. The Princess Ann-Mari von Bismarck, widow of Prince Otto von Bismarck, the German chargé d'affaires, has written to this author as follows:

> I remember how our association began. It was at Ascot. We separated from the crowd in the Royal enclosure. Ambassador Leopold von Hoesch told me he was in a troublesome dilemma. The Prince had asked him if he would arrange a dinner party at the German Embassy for him. Naturally, the Ambassador complied. The Foreign Office in Berlin was content. Then, the Prince asked point-blank if Mrs Simpson could be added to the list of guests! This was certainly a problem; it was also a royal

order. Ambassador von Hoesch told me how worried he was that the German government might find it an unforgivable faux pas to include Mrs Simpson. Not to speak of the British Foreign Office and the Royal Family of England!

I remember discussing this matter for an hour and a half with the Ambassador, impervious of the people around us. I tried to relax him and suggested he report to Berlin that the Prince had asked him to invite Mrs Simpson. He did not want to be disloyal to the Prince. We discussed all possibilities. Finally, I said, 'As the dinner is for the Prince, it is important to enjoy it, and if Mrs Simpson is not asked he will be bored, or, perhaps, not even come at all.'

The dinner took place. I do not know whether or not approval was given in Berlin and at Buckingham Palace, but I would assume that the Palace was not approached. I was sitting next to the Prince because since von Hoesch was unmarried I was acting as his hostess. We were at large round tables, and my husband was sitting at the table behind me with Mrs Simpson. The result was that, while the Prince was talking to me, he kept turning around to look lovingly at Mrs Simpson and to make sure that she was enjoying herself. The evening was a great success. I loved and admired both the Prince and Wallis. She was extremely witty, and I could see how she amused him.

Von Hoesch, the polished and genial German ambassador to the Court of St James, was the homosexual bachelor heir to a substantial manufacturing fortune. This career diplomat of the old school was typical in criticizing the upstart Hitler in private but at the same time working consistently and deviously to carry out his master's undesirable wishes. His kitchen was among the finest in London; his parties were splendidly organized; his budget from the Foreign Ministry in Berlin was arguably the most lavish accorded to any diplomatic representative. Hitler was determined to secure the devoted interest and admiration of the British aristocracy, and he gave specific instructions that no expense was to be spared in entertaining the cream of British society.

Certainly, the Führer was concerned that von Hoesch should cement the good feelings of the Prince of Wales. According to his diplomatic associate Paul Schwarz, von Hoesch was aware that more than any other music the prince loved the melancholy, thrilling strains of the gypsy czardas. As a result he hired, at great expense and on many occasions, the gypsy band of the Hungaria Restaurant to play for Wallis and Edward at small, exclusive soirees at his home. He invited the couple to join him at a reception for Hitler's special adviser on foreign affairs and ambassador without portfolio, the well-tailored but fatuous Joachim von Ribbentrop. Ribbentrop was fascinated by Wallis. To mark the first anniversary of their meeting, Schwarz recorded, Ribbentrop sent seventeen red roses with notes of open admiration every morning, all year round, to Wallis at Bryanston Court. She did not return them. It was widely believed in London that she entertained him frequently at her home, with her Jewish husband present. There was even talk of an affair that lasted seventeen nights. Ribbentrop represented his master in expressing great fascination for the new royal mistress. Before too long Hitler would be obtaining films of Wallis and running them with ecstatic pleasure at his hunting lodge at Obersalzburg.

This one-sided romance interested the Secret Intelligence Service. Yet another association proved to be provocative to the anti-Hitler faction in the British Secret Intelligence Services.

According to Sir Dudley Forwood, that relationship was the Prince of Wales's love affair with his equerry, Edward 'Fruity' Metcalfe, one of the few servants of the Crown who was denied a knighthood in later years, perhaps because of his sexual and political affiliations. (It is possible the affair was platonic.) Metcalfe was tall, lean, lantern-jawed and horsey; he had a sportive, rather grating, jocular personality that went with the loud Harris tweeds and an addiction to military uniforms.

Born in Ireland, son of the head of the Irish Prisons Board in Dublin, he was described by the future Edward VIII in infatuated terms in the memoir *A King's Story*, as 'gay, handsome, sympathetic and understanding'. From the beginning, King George V hated him, perhaps because he suspected a romantic involvement with the heir to the throne at a time when men of those inclinations shot themselves; perhaps because he disliked Metcalfe's tendency to encourage the Prince of Wales's addictions to night clubs, louche dives and heavy drinking.

Despite an early marriage to the fascist Lady Alexandra Curzon, known as 'Ba-Ba Blackshirt', sister-in-law of Sir Oswald Mosley, a marriage that produced children, Forwood insisted that Metcalfe was an active homosexual and that he had a physical affair with the Prince of Wales then and later. Forwood told me:

> Of course I wasn't in the bedroom but there was every sign of intense love between him and my master. My master worshipped the ground Fruity walked on – no royal person ever felt that way about a mere servant. He was in agony whenever Fruity wasn't with him. His absences drove my master nearly mad.

On September 22 1922, the prince wrote Metcalfe in anguish during one of his trips, 'I miss you terribly when you are away.' On September 1 1925 he dashed off an equally pained note begging Metcalfe not to leave England for a post in India to which King George had furiously sent him. Their activities as brother athletes at steeplechasing, running, swimming, golf and tennis, as well as mutual photograph-taking while stripped half-naked in locker rooms, had all the earmarks of a 'Greek' relationship and again and again the king insisted they break it off. When he refused to pay Metcalfe's salary, the prince first restored then doubled it.

By 1934, the relationship was dangerous politically. Like his wife, Metcalfe was a Nazi sympathizer, an admirer of Hitler and a friend of such Fascists as William Joyce, who in the Second World War would broadcast for Hitler as 'Lord Haw-Haw', and would die for that crime on the gallows. If anything were needed to draw the Prince of Wales more deeply into the Nazi camp it was this superficial, silly, frivolous and viciously anti-Semitic companion.

Although Wallis shared Metcalfe's political views, she hated him intensely. Forwood stated that she was jealous of Metcalfe, which, he said, can only have emerged from the conviction Forwood shared with her, that the two men were sexually involved.

At the same time, Metcalfe's membership in the pro-Hitler January Club, and its outright support of the Prince of Wales, was a minor danger to British security compared with another matter that surfaced at the time. Hitler and Ribbentrop embarked upon a plan, not opposed by King George V and Queen Mary, to unite England and Nazi Germany in a permanent alliance by engineering a match for the Prince of Wales that would give Hitler a free hand in Europe and preclude any future war with England. This could bring about a permanent Anglo-German alliance of the kind advocated by the January Club (and by the majority of the British Establishment) that would cause the wished-for destruction of the Soviet Union.

The bride upon whom Hitler enthusiastically settled, and who was eminently acceptable at Buckingham Palace, was the beautiful Friederike, Princess of Hanover, granddaughter of Kaiser Wilhelm II and daughter of the Duke and Duchess of Brunswick, close friends and cousins of King George and queen Mary. Since all were directly descended from the prolific queen bee Victoria, Friederike was considered the perfect wife for the future English monarch. In 1911, her mother had similarly been proposed as the wife of the selfsame Prince of Wales.

In January 1934, Friederike was a pupil at North Foreland Lodge, an exclusive girls' school near Broadstairs in Kent. She was invited to London so that the king and queen could give her a looking-over at Buckingham Palace; they approved her unhesitatingly. Once back in Germany, the Brunswicks were advised by Ribbentrop that Hitler shared King George V's approval of the match and insisted that it take place as soon as possible.

According to the Duchess of Brunswick in the cleaned-up British and American version of her memoirs, *The Kaiser's Daughter*, she and her husband were appalled by the idea, defied the Führer and cancelled his plans. Nothing could be further from the truth; in the German original she wrote that her daughter wanted it. Princess Friederike was on the British royal family's list of approved brides (until late 1937, when she became engaged to Prince Paul of Greece), as a potential Queen of England, and not a single Buckingham Palace or Foreign Office press statement ever contradicted it.

Had the marriage taken place, with Wallis as back-street mistress, a situation very common in British royal history, it is doubtful whether the Second World War would have occurred. How could England declare war on Germany with Hitler and King George V's own choice, and the granddaughter of the former ruler of Germany, installed upon the English throne? In the circumstances, it is ironical that King Edward VIII, in his determination to make Wallis queen, upset the very alliance that he had wanted so desperately all his life. In the circumstances, King George's hatred of Wallis for upsetting this marital applecart can well be understood.

Among the strongest supporters of this romantic royal alliance were the wealthy and influential members of the royal House of Hesse, cousins of the Prince of Wales and of Princess Friederike, and very close to the Prince of Wales's youngest brother, Prince George, later Duke of Kent. They were great-grandsons of Queen Victoria and the sons of the Duchess of Brunswick's sister Margarethe, the youngest daughter of the kaiser. They would play a crucial role in the Prince of Wales's and Wallis's Nazi–royal alliances aimed against Communism and seeking an Anglo-German *rapprochement* then and in the future.

The two oldest boys, Philipp and Wolfgang, were twins, born on 6 November 1896. Long before Hitler came to power, they were firmly in the Nazi camp. Both were admirers and friends of Hitler and Herman Goering. Hitler, with his streak of repressed homosexual hero worship, was captivated by Philipp, whose fair-haired, muscular good looks and pure Aryan royal blood had him in a state of unreasoning adoration.

From his early manhood, Philipp developed a love of Italy, and, as an architect of sorts, designed many buildings in that country. Like the Prince of Wales and Prince George of England he was bisexual, and had an unmasculine addiction to interior decoration. During the rise of Hitler he was often in Rome, where he was engaged to Princess Mafalda, daughter of King Victor Emmanuel III, to raise money from Mussolini, who presided over the civil ceremony of their spectacular marriage in Italy in September 1925.

Throughout the 1930s and until 1942, Prince Philipp was the chief personal and political link between Hitler and Mussolini. Profoundly anti-Semitic, bent upon Hitler's cause, he became, on the Führer's orders, both governor and storm-trooper führer of the Hesse province; later, he would secure Mussolini's agreement to Hitler's annexation of Austria. He cleared the way also to Mussolini's reluctant acquiescence in the German conquest of Czechoslovakia. Prince Philipp never tired of seeking to secure, through the cooperation of the Prince of Wales and his brother Prince George, a permanent alliance with England ('The Jews,' he said, 'must be fought in all countries.') His other chief alliance was with Prince George's brother-in-law, the weak, duplicitous and vacillating Prince Regent Paul of Yugoslavia, who was sent to Africa under arrest in 1942 by Winston Churchill for betraying his country to Germany.

And there was yet another threat of scandal at the time. Sandra Rambeau was an international American adventuress and Nazi agent, and the amour of the Prince of Wales, Prince George, and of Hitler's favorite, the bisexual General Franz Ritter von Epp.

Born in Springfield, Missouri, on 26 January 1909, the daughter of a naval commodore, she became a spectacular beauty, with dark, wavy hair, smouldering grey-green eyes and a perfect figure. Abandoning high school without graduating, working successively as telephone operator, waitress and dancer in the touring Monte Carlo Follies all over Europe, she met von Epp in Berlin while appearing with the show, and quickly lured him from a male lover who was part of the homosexual Ernst Roehm group that Hitler purged.

Von Epp was a member of the same political sect to which the Hesses subscribed; he became head of the Nazi Colonial Office, which sought the restoration of German colonies removed after the Second World War as part of a permanent peace arrangement with England. He was also head of AMT VIII of the German Secret Intelligence Service under Admiral Wilhelm Canaris, who, as double agent for England and Germany, was in pursuit of that unholy alliance.

Sandra Rambeau met the Prince of Wales and Prince George in Paris and in 1934 they both were romantically involved with her. As late as 4 April 1938, George referred to her indirectly in a conversation in London with US ambassador Joseph P. Kennedy, when he said that his brother King George VI complained that he (like their sibling Edward) was 'involved with' an American woman. According to the substantial FBI files on Rambeau in Washington, Prince George gave her a number of the crown jewels, including an inherited signet ring with his royal initials on it.

Travelling restlessly from London to Paris and Berlin, Rambeau found still a fourth romance, with the glamorous Major General Bishnu Shumshere Jung Badahur Rana, self-styled Prince of Nepal and black sheep son of that country's prime minister. High on the British Foreign Office list of political undesirables, later ejected from England, Bishnu wound up finally in the Bahamas, in 1942, as an associate of the Duke and Duchess of Windsor when they, Nazified exiles also, were governor and first lady there.

On 10 June 1939, when touring Canada, King George VI told Canadian premier Mackenzie King, as recorded in King's diary:

> My own family relations in Germany have been used to spy and get particulars from other members of my family.

Nobody could have put it more succinctly – or accurately.

Fruity Metcalfe attended, at the end of May 1934, a Fascist Blackshirt dinner at the Savoy Hotel; dressed to the teeth, he was photographed by the society magazine the *Tatler*. The guest list included Count and Countess Paul Munster, also close to the Prince and Wallis, and at whose castle they would eventually spend their honeymoon. The Fascist leader Sir Oswald Mosley and his wife Lady Cynthia (sister of Alexandra Metcalfe) were present; and last, but by no means least, William Joyce, who would one day become a traitor to England as 'Lord Haw Haw', the best known of British Nazi broadcasters from Germany in the Second World War.

At that time, the pro-Hitler January Club, to which all the aforementioned individuals belonged, was under investigation by both MI5 and the Jewish Defence League. The British Union of Fascists, of which the January Club was both seedbed and participant, was financed directly by Mussolini; the funds were channelled and laundered via Minculprop, the Ministry of Culture and Propaganda of the Italian government, headed by Wallis's former lover Count Ciano, who by now was Mussolini's son-in-law and Foreign Minister.

On 27 May, the same night as a January Club dinner, the prince and Wallis were at Sibyl Colefax's in the company of the Hungarian-born film tycoon Sir Alexander Korda; the actress Merle Oberon; Lord Dalkeith (later the Duke of Buccleuch); and another of Wallis's new friends, the interior decorator Elsie Mendl, and her husband, Sir Charles. Two of those present, Korda and Elsie Mendl's husband, were working for the Secret Intelligence Service and noted the fact that at the party the Prince of Wales expressed his keenest admiration for Nazi Germany. Neither Sir Robert Bruce Lockhart nor the vivid diarist Henry 'Chips' Channon, an American snob obsessed with the rich and titled, failed to note Wallis's choice of friends or her royal consort's frequent verbal indulgences in pro-Hitlerism.

One of Wallis's strongest friendships at that time was with Elsie Mendl. Wallis adored this stylish, witty, irresistibly charming blue-haired doyenne of interior decoration. Lady Mendl influenced Wallis considerably in her upward climb. When Wallis first came to London, probably because of insecurity, she was a somewhat strident, harsh, high-pitched presence on the scene, as the shrewdly perceptive Cecil Beaton noted in his diary. Lady Mendl taught her to tone down her personality to suit British requirements. She encouraged her to speak in a softer, more southern drawl instead of in harsh accents and to dress very simply, to accentuate the angular lines of her figure rather than striving to work against her physical deficiencies. Wallis's severe, classical clothes became her trademark and emblem.

Whereas dresses in the mid-1930s tended to be fussy and exaggerated, Wallis made sure hers were subdued and reserved, in pastel colours or in plain blacks and whites. Even her hats were restrained. Lady Mendl replaced Syrie Maugham's white-on-white designs at Bryanston Court with her own subtle and varied colour schemes. She taught Wallis how to entertain and how to present her meals, explicitly forbidding soup; her motto was 'Never build a meal on a lake.' Soon Bryanston Court, aided by the royal purse, lost its slightly Early Pullman look and became a riot of spectacular effects, indicative of Lady Mendl's capacity to go to the very edge of overdecoration and then stop short. And of course the friendship provided an opportunity for Sir Charles to keep an eye on Wallis's activities and associations.

Pressing on with fierce ambition, Wallis further asserted her power in the summer of 1934. Having disposed of Thelma Furness, she now proceeded ruthlessly to make sure that nothing more was heard from Mrs Freda Dudley Ward. The prince had not officially disconnected his relationship with Mrs Dudley Ward. Freda's daughter Penelope, later the wife of the film director Carol Reed, and rumoured falsely to be the child of the Prince of Wales, fell ill.

Freda hoped for some word from York House or Fort Belvedere, some expression of concern or even interest. There was none. At last Penelope rallied, and Freda called York House to inform her ex-lover that the danger was past. The switchboard operator informed her that orders had been received not to put her through. She never spoke to the Prince of Wales again.

Wallis concentrated grimly on the servants. Members of the royal staff enjoyed certain privileges that had remained unchanged from generation to generation. They tended to set the rules of the various households, instruct the lower-level staff, and delegate duties right down the line to the lowliest echelons of the kitchen and the cellars. Of these Osborne, the butler in the Fort Belvedere household, was pre-eminent. He had been the prince's batman in the First World War, and from there he had gone on to assume his present position, which was considered unassailable, absolute and final. To his horror, he, who took orders only from royalty, was informed by the Prince of Wales that henceforth he would receive his instructions from Mrs Simpson, an American commoner! This was insupportable. However, unless he wanted to be dismissed Osborne had no alternative but to accept this galling humiliation. Wallis instructed him to undertake all the flower arrangements at the Fort himself, instead of delegating this unmasculine task to the maids. This was a complete break with tradition. She drew up the menus for each day of the week, even though she was present at the Fort only on weekends. This task had always been the prerogative of the housekeeper and Osborne, working in collaboration. Not content with the decor that had been decreed by the Prince of Wales and Prince George, Wallis and Lady Mendl invaded room after room, pulling up carpets, taking down curtains and storing furniture. Then they redid the Fort from top to bottom, oddly enough retaining only one room as it had been before: Thelma's pink folly of a bedroom, with its absurd bed decorated with the Prince of Wales's feathers on each post.

Wallis clashed furiously with Finch, the butler at York House. This formidable personage had played a leading role in the Prince of Wales's childhood. He had been the prince's valet from the earliest days, and saw himself as a combination of nanny and surrogate father, repeatedly persuading the prince to cut down on his drinking, late nights, wild parties and loose women. This impeccable, upright north countryman, the very epitome of gritty rectitude, now found himself being bossed by a foreign woman with little regard for his finer feelings. She not only took over everything at York House, even down to ordering over a hundred gifts for Christmas, but also insisted that Finch learn to mix, serve and put ice in drinks in the American manner; the very presence of ice in a glass was anathema to the old retainer. When Finch refused to obey instructions he was dismissed. His successor, Crisp, also failed to last. Osborne hung on, but only by a thread.

The staffs of the two households favoured by the prince grew to hate Wallis for her busybody interference. They dreaded the return of their master and mistress at three or four in the morning from the Embassy Club, the Kit Kat or other night spots; laughing loudly, they would call up maids and butler and cook to get out of bed and prepare a snack or otherwise attend to their imperious needs. King George V and Queen Mary were punctilious in their relationship with their staff. They attended meals at the same time every day, and the matter of instruction to the various levels of household staff was always adhered to. Wallis and the Prince of Wales rode roughshod over such arrangements. Wallis was always punctual, and irritated by the prince's lax attitude towards appointments and mealtimes, but she seemed to have no understanding or consideration when it came to the employees.

That summer of 1934, the prince decided to flout convention to the limit and invite Wallis on a trip to Spain and France that was sure to attract attention from the press. Not the British press; royal persons in those days could always rely upon the utmost discretion from Fleet Street. But the American reporters in particular could not fail to note his expedition with an American married woman; he seemed to care little about this, or about the fact that Ernest Simpson would not be included in the royal party. The inclusion of Aunt Bessie Merryman was a sop to critics. She would supposedly be a chaperone, but few were deceived.

The prince rented a house, the Castel Meretmont, outside Biarritz, the fashionable resort in south-western France. Piloted by Flight Lieutenant Edward Fielden, the prince arrived at Le Bourget in Paris at 5.30 p.m. on 1 August 1934; he was accompanied by his equerry, the Hon. John Aird. Wallis, as always afraid of flying, proceeded in a good humour with Aunt Bessie, 'G' Trotter, and the rest of the party by boat train across the English Channel. The prince joined them for the train ride to Biarritz. The Castel Meretmont proved to be spacious and comfortable, and after the first day reporters politely withdrew to the edge of the grounds, content to watch the movements of the royal party through field glasses.

On 5 August, Wallis and the prince were enjoying a drink at a swimming pool bar on the Biarritz seafront when a boy of ten began screaming from the deep end that he was drowning. The prince flung off his jacket, dived in and rescued the boy, to general applause and the mother's tearful thanks. The news spread rapidly, and the press swarmed in as the prince and Wallis left the bar. The prince was furious, shouting that the story was 'lies, all lies', and pushing his way to the royal car. It was clear that he was embarrassed because of Wallis's presence; he was terrified they would be photographed together. They were.

When the story appeared all over the world the next morning, the French government elected to give the prince the Lifesaving Medal. He refused it. He and Wallis went into seclusion for a week at the Castel Meretmont. Then, on the 15th, they went out in wind-driven rain to dine with the celebrated Marquis and Marquise de Portago at the opulent Villa Pelican. At the party the prince told Wallis and the others that he was weary of Biarritz and was going to fly to Cannes to join Prince George, who was now engaged to Princess Marina of Greece. George and Marina had been in Vienna, visiting the leaders of the Austrian government. On cabled instructions Edward Fielden flew the royal aircraft from London, in stages, to pick up the royal party. However, it is probable that Wallis's hatred of flying influenced what the prince decided to do next.

He now proposed to make his way to Cannes by sea. It says much for his dedication to Wallis that he would rather miss his own brother and future sister-in-law – by sailing instead of flying – than make her uncomfortable by taking the short air trip across Spain to France. He decided to obtain a vessel in Biarritz and charter it for a voyage around Gibraltar. He planned to arrive at Cannes in time to fly to Marseille, where he would say farewell to his brother

Prince Henry, later Duke of Gloucester, who was on his way, aboard HMS *Sussex*, to Australia and New Zealand. The only ship available was the ancient, battered 700-ton ocean-going steamer *Rosaura*, which after thirty years of service as an English Channel steamer, struggling gamely through the choppy seas between Newhaven and Dieppe, had been bought by Lord Moyne, an explorer and ethnographer, as a scientific exploration vessel to be used mainly in the south seas. The steamer was temporarily laid up in Biarritz harbour for refuelling, provisioning and repairs.

The prince asked Lord Moyne if he might charter the *Rosaura*. Moyne felt unable to decline the royal request. However, he issued a warning that the weather conditions for the voyage were extremely unfavourable. The Bay of Biscay was notorious for its violent storms, one of which was blowing up at that precise moment. The Prince of Wales refused to listen to Lord Moyne's sage advice, and the captain, under Moyne's personal command, set sail on 26 August. The moment the vessel butted out into the sound it was greeted by a tremendous burst of lightning and thunder. For four days and nights Wallis was virtually confined to the cabin in conditions as harrowing as those she had experienced aboard the Chinese tramp steamer *Shuntien*. Not the least of her anxieties was caused by Lord Moyne's pet monkey, which made a nuisance of itself, continuously screeching and darting about. The *Rosaura*, decks awash, put in at Corunna on 1 September. The prince and his party made their way ashore, and took a car to Santiago de Compostela to see the sights. They visited the tomb of the Peninsular War hero Sir John Moore, one of the Prince of Wales's childhood idols, and lit candles for him in the church. The next day they travelled on to Vigo and thence, accompanied by the local Portuguese and British consuls, proceeded to the border of Portugal. They were greeted by the Portuguese diplomat Pistango Vasconcelles, an old friend of Wallis's from Washington days.

The rain continued for most of the trip, but the royal party proceeded regardless to Tuy and Oporto to see the famous vineyards. The group lingered on in the region until, on the afternoon of 3 September, a large crowd of local women in traditional costume greeted them at Viana del Castello and presented the startled prince and Wallis with a two-foot-tall doll in embroidered skirt and blouse.

The voyage around Gibraltar was rough. On the 7th, the prince and his party sailed on to Majorca, where they motored to the Hotel Formentor on the north side of the island. They swam from the beach, returning at dusk to see the *Rosaura*, lit from stem to stern, anchored in a bend of the bay. The next day they visited the cathedral and cloister of San Francisco; they spent the weekend exploring caves, picking up seashells and climbing rocks.

At last the vessel, shipping water, was comfortably moored at Cannes. Somewhere between Oporto and France the relationship between Wallis and the prince had intensified still further, but only on his side. He was by now so deeply in love that he would have been perfectly happy to let the voyage go on forever; ambitious Wallis coolly accepted his madness. Having cabled his brother Prince Henry to await his arrival at Marseille, and having instructed Edward Fielden to fly in from Paris to await his pleasure, the prince impetuously decided to stay where he was, with the woman he loved. He sent Fielden back to London and his brother sailed to Australia without seeing him.

Despite having announced to the press via John Aird that he would not be leaving the *Rosaura* in harbour, but would be continuing the voyage immediately, the prince advised Lord Moyne that he would be lingering on in Cannes for several days. Then, dogged by newspapermen and photographers at every step of the way, he walked ashore with Wallis at midnight on the 11th. They were driven by the local British vice-consul, John Taylor, and his wife to the local Palm Beach Club, where they danced one rumba after another until 4 a.m. The next night they accepted an invitation from Herman and Katherine Rogers for a midnight supper and a swim by moonlight off the chartered yacht of a wealthy couple from St Louis.

On the third day, the prince and Wallis boldly moved into the Hotel Miramar together. At 1 a.m. the prince summoned the night manager to his suite and told him to wake up the staff of the local branch of Cartier and instruct them to go to the shop. He slipped out of the hotel through a back door and made his way to the shop, where he bought not only an emerald and diamond charm for Wallis's bracelet but also many other items that he held in reserve for presentation to her later on. Then he returned to the hotel and got Wallis and the entire party out of their beds, announcing to Lord Moyne that he wished to proceed immediately to sea.

As the vessel moved out into the moonlit ocean, the prince embraced Wallis and pressed the Cartier charm into the palm of her hand. She was flattered but not moved. The *Rosaura* continued to Nice and Genoa, in calm seas, arriving on 17 September. The prince had wired ahead for reservations, and the royal party took a fleet of cars to Lake Como, situated at the foot of the Alps. The group stayed at the Hôtel Villa D'Este. The weather was glorious; the white sun burned on the mountains and the lake water was a dazzling blue. Each morning the prince and Wallis went out in a rowing boat on the still water; on the first afternoon they took a speedboat all the way up to Bellagio. Next afternoon they played golf in Monteforno; the day after that they took a long drive on spectacular mountain roads. On 21 September the party motored to Lake Maggiore and took a launch trip from Stresa to the Borromeo Islands. There, the prince finally threw away restraint and allowed himself to be photographed by the press as he walked around naked except for a pair of shorts.

On the 23rd, the party boarded the Orient Express at Domodossola; Mussolini had provided a luxurious private car for them. The prince had cabled Edward Fielden to pick him up in Paris; he was anxious to get home in time to see the RMS *Queen Mary*, the newest of the Cunard ships, go down the slipways for the first time on Clydeside. Leaving the others in Paris at the Hôtel Meurice, he flew to Windsor Castle, landing at Smiths Lawn, on the way to the royal residence at Balmoral. John Aird went with him; Wallis and the others followed on the USS *Manhattan* from Cherbourg. But it seemed that the prince could not tear himself away from Wallis even then. Before he left for the *Queen Mary*'s launching, he turned up at Southampton with gifts and loving words for Wallis and her aunt.

NOTE

1 In a bizarre echo of this curious episode, years later Wallis had a
picture of two naked women making love, which she displayed in the
bedroom of her successive homes in Paris.

8

MOVING TOWARDS THE THRONE

In the autumn of 1934, Prince George, the Prince of Wales's youngest surviving brother, and Princess Marina of Greece were at the centre of the world's attention. They were to be married on 29 November. The royal family was greatly relieved. For years untoward rumours had circulated about George, and some of them appeared to have a basis in truth. It was stated that he had had an affair with a black actress. And according to the late Laura, the Duchess of Marlborough, one of her husbands, Michael Canfield, who died young, was Prince George's illegitimate son and had been handed over to Cass Canfield, head of the American publishers Harper & Brothers, later Harper and Row, who raised him.

To this heady scenario were added some even more colourful ingredients. In his diary the incorrigible Sir Robert Bruce Lockhart mentioned that tales were being told around London of an affair between the prince and a young boy in Paris and that blackmail was involved. According to several sources, Prince George gave the boy magnificent, personally inscribed Tiffany and Cartier cigarette boxes and lighters. The Prince of Wales had to make a disagreeable journey to France to pay money to retrieve these damaging items, but the boy sold him copies, retaining the originals. There was also talk of an involvement with Noël Coward and with a smouldering youth of Latin American origin. Everyone was greatly relieved when Prince George fell in love with the exquisitely beautiful Princess Marina. But he still slept with Sandra Rambeau.

On October 24, leaving Wallis at the Hôtel Meurice in Paris, the

Prince of Wales and Prince George flew together, taking turns at the controls of the royal biplane, to attend the funeral of King Alexander of Yugoslavia, who had been assassinated on the 9th of that month by a Macedonian terrorist in Marseille; the killer, who was opposed to Alexander's Nazi connections, ironically also murdered the anti-Nazi French Foreign Minister, Léon Barthou. It was on this sombre funerary occasion, with all Belgrade in mourning, that a major step was taken in the British–German royal connection that involved both Hitler and Mussolini.

Since the young King Peter succeeding to the throne was under age, his royal cousin Prince Paul was made regent; Paul's wife, Olga, was the pro-Nazi sister of the Duchess of Kent; Paul had arranged the Kent marriage. According to *Current Biography* for the year of 1941, a widely quoted comment at the time was, 'The Duchess of Kent brought Balkan fashions to London – while Princess Olga brought Hitler's emissaries to the White Palace [in Belgrade].' In fact, though he has been protected by most historians, Paul was himself nervously in support of Hitler, if only for self-protective purposes, and Kent and the Prince of Wales found in him a kindred spirit along with another guest at the funeral, Prince Philipp of Hesse, führer of the storm troopers. Another guest was Field Marshal Hermann Goering, who reported to Hitler on the meetings with the prince, Kent and Philipp with considerable enthusiasm and a request that Paul should visit Berlin at the earliest possible opportunity. Hitler made the offer, and Paul accepted at once.

On 27 November, two days before the wedding, a celebration ball was held at Buckingham Palace. King George and Queen Mary insisted that the Lord Chamberlain remove Wallis's name from the guest list. This was very upsetting to Wallis, and Edward was furious when he found out; as a result, he arrived with Wallis and swept through the vestibule with her, determined that she would meet his parents. 'He smuggled her into the Palace,' King George later said to Count Mensdorff.

Wallis was anxious to upstage the beautiful Marina, who was dressed unpretentiously in white satin; the queen was in silver brocade. Most of the ladies were dressed in subdued colours in keeping with the dignity of the occasion. Wallis appeared in a creation of violet-coloured lamé with a green sash. While many, including the monarch and his consort, stared at her in cold dismay, Prince Paul, regent of Yugoslavia, made a point of telling her she was the best-dressed woman in the room. Her jewels, presents from her lover, glittered at neck and wrist. She also wore a tiara of diamonds, hired from Cartier's.

Prince Christopher of Greece wrote in his memoirs:

> The Prince of Wales laid a hand on my arm in his impulsive way.
> 'Christo, come with me. I want you to meet Mrs Simpson.'
> 'Who is she?'
> 'An American. She's wonderful.'

With sheer effrontery, the prince introduced Wallis to his parents. She curtseyed while they stared at her. She had no warmer a reception from the Duke of York, next in line to the throne, or his wife, the former Lady Elizabeth Bowes-Lyon. The Duchess of York took an instant dislike to Wallis. She was offended by what she felt to be Wallis's blatant and vulgar behaviour and the garish colours of her dress. Wallis was equally unimpressed. She was irritated by the Duchess of York's sweet, slightly high-pitched voice, pink Scottish face and plump figure. Of course, the Duchess later became the beloved Queen Mother.

Christmas brought new problems for Wallis. She had the audacity to select the 250 Christmas gifts for the Prince of Wales's staff herself. Many of the employees were annoyed by this. There was further unfavourable gossip about the prince's present to Wallis – a diamond pin with two square-cut emeralds. He also gave her a cairn terrier puppy that was named Mr Loo, but was as often called Slipper. The prince compounded his various faux pas in the eyes of his households by inviting Wallis's personal staff from Bryanston Court to join his own servants around the Christmas tree at York House. It needs no feat of the imagination to envisage the tension on that occasion.

Wearied by the prince's almost constant attentions and still obsessive visits and phone calls, much as she wanted to be the prince's lady, Wallis was almost relieved when he spent the season with his family at Sandringham. Then, in January 1935, she made one of her most serious mistakes. She began imitating the Duchess of York with a harsh, mocking style that recalled her schoolgirl burlesques at Oldfields. One afternoon Elizabeth walked into the drawing room at Fort Belvedere and stood frozen. Wallis was performing an aggressive parody of her voice and gestures. Elizabeth stormed out. Wallis was not forgiven.

That same month, the Prince of Wales and Prince George, now the Duke of Kent, had an interesting visitor from Berlin. Kent had just returned from Munich, where he cemented relations with his wife Princess Marina's brother-in-law, Karl Theodore, Count von Toerring-Jettenbach, husband of her pro-Nazi sister Elizabeth, who conveyed through a special agent to Berlin that Kent was reconciled to Germany's extensive rearming. He invited to London the Baron Wilhelm de Ropp, a peripatetic double agent and emissary of the Nazi theorist Alfred Rosenberg, who, during a visit to London in 1933, had placed a swastika wreath on the Cenotaph. De Ropp's purpose in coming to London was to meet the royal brothers in order to give them a complete picture of the qualities of Hess, Rosenberg and the other leaders. Sir Robert Bruce Lockhart would write in his diary later that the Duke of Kent was 'strong in the German camp'.

The Prince of Wales decided to embark upon another trip to Europe with Wallis and a group of friends. The journey was to be a combined vacation and adventure in politics. That year, the situation on the Continent was exceedingly delicate. The Foreign Office had embarked upon a policy, emanating from the prime minister Ramsay MacDonald, which seemed to appease both Hitler and Mussolini in their territorial ambitions in order to secure for the future the British balance of power in western Europe and the defeat of communism. The Foreign Office wanted at all costs to keep Mussolini and Hitler apart and to discourage them from a full-scale alliance which could imperil British hegemony. Among the British government's urgent concerns was to preserve British power in the Mediterranean and to prevent the blockade or seizure of the Suez Canal, which provided the all-important trade route to the British colonies in East Africa, and to India, the chief jewel in the crown of the Empire.

Britain was playing a dangerous game of conciliation with

Mussolini, whose activities were increasingly felt to be inimical to British interests and a threat to the British fleet. At the time, Mussolini was taking a position adverse to Hitler because he feared Hitler would upstage him in the European theatre. It was felt by both dictators that the possession of Austria, itself a weak, poverty-stricken and politically flaccid nation, would swing the balance of power definitively in the direction of the country which achieved it. Britain was tending to encourage Italian influence in Vienna because Hitler must at all costs be kept within a certain circumference of power. The game was played in Whitehall for high stakes, and the Prince of Wales, both by assignment and by personal design, became part of that game.

Always an Empire man, aware of the importance of India in the Commonwealth, in his own mind the prince was doing his best to execute British foreign policy in making the trip when he did. However, it was not customary or desirable for royal personages to meddle in politics in this manner, no matter how well-intentioned the purpose might be. The prince's intention was to encourage the Austrians and their neighbours the Hungarians to maintain as firmly as possible their Italian connection and provide a block against Hitler's advances south. The venture was approved by a friend of his, Sir Oswald Mosley, whose British Union of Fascists was still being financed by Mussolini and Count Ciano via the Italian propaganda minister. Wallis was a convenient 'cover' for this mission to Vienna and Budapest. In view of the fact that, by his own admission in his memoirs, the Prince of Wales turned to her for advice in everything, and that we have it on his own cognizance that she was fully informed politically and read all London newspapers from cover to cover, it is impossible to believe she was not aware of the purpose of the journey. But no proof of her knowledge exists.

The trip began as a holiday. The royal party travelled from Paris on the Simplon Express to the skiing resort of Kitzbühel in Austria. The prince and his companions were supposed to travel through the Augsburg pass, but an avalanche swept down ahead of them, blocking the track. Instead they were transferred to another train which, sent by the Austrian government to the town of Wörgl, took them a hundred miles off course. They had to wait several hours in freezing conditions for the train to arrive.

On 5 February, they reached Kitzbühel, where a crowd of newspaper correspondents and photographers was waiting. The prince responded in fluent German to the speeches by the mayor and prefect of police. They checked into the Grand Hotel. The swirling snowflakes and leaden skies created a picture of Gothic gloom. Fifteen people had been killed in avalanches, and a resort hotel and eight homes had been swept away.

While at Kitzbühel, Wallis and the prince made the acquaintance of a person whom Wallis liked; he was to play an important role in their lives. He was the young, witty and handsome Dudley Forwood, whose neatly trimmed moustache, sturdy figure and smart suits instilled confidence in everyone who met him. He was the junior attaché to Sir Walford Selby, British envoy and minister in Vienna. It was customary to send an attaché or first secretary to attend on visiting members of the royal family when they arrived within the borders of a foreign nation. At the Grand Hotel, Forwood joined the royal entourage, which included Bruce Ogilvy, the son of Lord Airlie, who disapproved of Wallis; the Colin Buists; and the equerry, Commander Lambe.

After an abortive skiing lesson, Wallis stayed in the hotel playing bridge, backgammon and poker with the others in the royal party, while the prince went out in severe wind and sleet to ski from morning to night.

On 9 February, the sun broke through and the sky was a sudden icy blue. That night a radiant Wallis appeared with the prince at a Tyrolean costume ball, sharing him with several pretty girls in traditional folk dances. The party lingered on for a week, leaving Kitzbühel on the midnight express for Vienna on 16 February.

It was a charged time. Austria had emerged from the First World War a broken and dispirited nation. Starvation, financial ruin and spiritual despair were followed by a conviction that the only hope for the future lay in an alliance with Germany. Some Social Democrats and Christian Socialists, though ostensibly to the left of centre, were entirely for friendly relations with the Nazis. When Hitler came to power he made it clear that, as a native of Austria, he expected Austria to be absorbed into the Third Reich. When it was evident that Germany would not accept the country as an equal, Austria turned to Mussolini. All policy was carried out in the closest consultation and collaboration with the Italian dictator. Parliamentary government was abolished; socialism was crushed by the fascists. Just days before the prince and Wallis arrived in Vienna, socialists and communists had demonstrated and distributed leaflets in the Vienna suburbs, and ten had been arrested. There was rioting, marking the anniversary of the defeated Social Democratic revolution of the year before. More arrests followed; the day after the royal party's arrival police and socialists clashed violently at Floridsdorf, and forty-five more were arrested during radical meetings.

There were mixed demonstrations outside the Bristol hotel where the royal party was staying; some workers felt that the Prince of Wales was on their side; others felt he was pro-fascist. Leaving a nervous Wallis behind, he took off on the 17th for his first visit to the Chancellery to meet President Miklas, Chancellor von Schuschnigg and Vice-Chancellor von Stahremberg. George Messersmith, American minister to Austria, who had spies at their meetings, reported on the political content to the State Department later that month. The purpose was to establish the solidarity of the so-called Balkan Entente, that group of southern European nations which joined in uneasy alliance with Italy in opposing Hitler's influence. However, as Messersmith pointed out in his report, the Prince of Wales was anxious that the Labour party in England might not approve of his contact with the Austrian fascist government, and for this reason he insisted that the high-level meetings be downplayed or ignored in the press. The prince, Messersmith's report continued, also made a special visit to the immense and elaborate workers' apartments, built by the former socialist regime.

He and Wallis proceeded by train to Budapest. The Hungarian capital, then at the height of its sophistication and gaiety, was ablaze with light to greet them. There, the pro-Mussolini government was even more repressive than in Austria. Conducting an uncomfortable love–hate relationship with its neighbour nation, Hungary was also firmly allied with the Balkan Entente at the time.

The prince had meetings with Admiral Horthy, the regent, and the ferocious General Julius von Gombös, whose repressive regime (he would soon dissolve the existing government) had already offended many informed commentators. Once again the prince discussed the Hapsburg restoration and the necessary anti-Hitler alliances with Italy. At the same time he and Wallis enjoyed the baroque pleasures of the Danube Palace Hotel, the casino and shops filled with antique Hungarian jewellery. The future King of England startled the clients at the St Gellert Thermal Bathing Palace by appearing before them stark naked.

The visit was a success from every point of view. Both Austria and Hungary were now more firmly bound into the Italian orbit because of the prince's influence, thereby restricting Hitler's power. When the prince and his party returned on 28 February to Paris, a huge crowd greeted them at the Gare de l'Est. Police seized cameras and smashed bulbs, but several photographs appeared. When Wallis and the prince got off the boat train in London, they fled through the crowd to York House to change hastily for dinner at Lady Cunard's. It had been an exciting, exhausting trip.

And there was a new excitement ahead: a matter of the gravest concern to the throne.

As a latter-day Victorian puritan, in marked contrast to King Edward VII, George V, whose own sexual record was far from blameless, had much to deal with in his immediate family. Though even he might have balked at condemning his sons for indulging in 'normal' sexual activity on the sly, he was most emphatically opposed to their choice of certain partners. He had had to face the fact that his sons the Prince of Wales and the Duke of Gloucester had shared the bed of the aviatrix Beryl Markham, who was notorious for her affairs; he had had to put up with the Prince of Wales's and the Duke of Kent's romance with Sandra Rambeau; Kent's fling with the Paris ephebe David Edge, and sundry others; and with Kent's and the Prince of Wales's dalliances with Noël Coward. The fact that Kent had married Princess Marina of Greece had come as something of a relief, especially since two of her sisters were married to men who might help preserve a lasting peace with Germany. But worst of all was the Prince of Wales's liaison with

Wallis, a married woman of bad reputation, an obvious gold digger and an exponent of what were called, in those prelapsarian days, perverse sexual practices.

The king, with his Silver Jubilee looming, married to an even more correct and upright Queen Mary, embarked on a project which was, to say the least, against his character. This was to obtain, not to put it delicately, the dirt on Wallis Warfield Simpson.

Although once, in a fit of pique, he said that he hoped Edward would never marry, he clearly continued to hope for his son's union with Princess Friederike, a match that might prevent another world war in his lifetime. The horror of the trenches, the mud, the rats, the shells, the bloodshed, the conflict between German cousins, the loss of a world of grace and cultivation, the destruction of the flower of England's manhood – these haunted the minds of everyone of George V's generation, and he would, it is fair to say, have given almost anything to prevent it happening again.

And so, in early 1935, the king contacted Lord Trenchard, an old and devoted friend and commissioner of the London Metropolitan Police. Trenchard, the immensely distinguished creator of the Royal Air Force, was, like his royal master, a dogged puritan. In the course of revising the bureaucratic structure of Scotland Yard, he had improved the quality of the force, instituted a police training school, and cut the dead wood from the rank and file. What he emphatically did not have his officers do was pursue errant ladies of leisure in and out of bedroom sexual-combat zones, obtain information on co-respondents that could lead to a divorce or undertake any other squalid duties more suitable for a private detective agency. What the king asked Trenchard to do was investigate Wallis Simpson as if she were a common prostitute.

Trenchard cannot have relished the task. In fact, from the beginning, despite his energetic reforms, it is certain he had not enjoyed his job of dealing with crime; the air force was his love.

His daily work at the Yard was already onerous and unpleasant without this sordid extra burden; but he was a gallant old soldier and he would never fail to satisfy his king. He had in fact resigned two years earlier, wanting to enjoy a life of well-earned retirement, but the monarch had insisted he remain, first to take care of security at the marriage of the Duke and Duchess of Kent, both of whom were potential targets of pro-communist terrorists, and later for the preparations for the jubilee.

Scotland Yard's Special Branch was used to protect, rather than to expose, members of the royal family. It began its investigation into Wallis the late spring of 1935; the hard-working Superintendent Albert Canning was in charge. Canning discovered from various friends of hers that Wallis was sleeping with a man whom they would not for some reason name. It didn't take long for Canning to discover that her lover was a Ford Motor Car Company sales executive named Guy Marcus Trundle.

Handsome, dashing, thirty-five years old at the time, Trundle was little more than a gigolo, since Wallis had given him the Prince of Wales's money for his sexual services. Reflecting their American boss Henry Ford's notorious anti-Semitism and love of Hitler, Ford employees had to be non-Jewish, politically to the extreme right and approving of the corporation's building of trucks and armoured cars for the German army, a process that did not cease with the Second World War. Hitler worshipped Ford, gave him honourable mention in *Mein Kampf*, and had a picture of him at all times on his desk. Thus, Trundle must have been a true-blue Aryan fascist at heart, and a man to whom Wallis could relate.

Married at the time, described by many of Canning's informants as a 'bounder' or cad, Trundle seems to have been disliked by everyone to whom Canning spoke. The question is: where could she and Trundle have conducted their affair?

Hotels, with their gossipy staffs, would not be the answer, since the Prince of Wales might hear of that. Wallis's social friends could not be trusted to supply houses or apartments. Since Trundle was married, they could not meet at his home, which was a royal property near the birthplace of the Duchess of York in Bruton Street; certainly Wallis could not bring him to 5 Bryanston Court. The most likely rendezvous, as is indicated by her subsequent liaison with William Bullitt, US ambassador to France, was a dressmaker's: the one place where the Prince of Wales would not follow her.

Her regular dressmaker, the Nazi agent Anna Wolkoff, had a small establishment in Mayfair; but another friend, Elsa Schiaparelli, the celebrated Italian fashion designer, whose clothes Wallis began wearing in the mid-1930s, had just opened a salon at 36 Upper Grosvenor Street, very close to one of Wallis's former residences. In 1990, Jean Negulesco, the Hollywood film director, told me that the building, now a block of flats, in which he had owned an apartment from 1950 on, was famous among his circle as the place where Mrs Simpson met her lover, and where Schiaparelli (whom he knew in Paris in the late 1930s) protected them both.

Schiaparelli would be an ideal cover because she was also a Nazi sympathizer. The FBI and State Department files on her at the National Archives in Washington show that she operated continuously on behalf of Hitler and, most importantly, in view of the Wallis connection, shared Wallis's French Nazi lawyer, Armand Grégoire; he was working for Wallis as early as 1934.

One curious aspect of Canning's report is that Wallis was said, while carrying on this affair of her own, to be jealous of a certain 'Austrian or Hungarian' woman in the Prince of Wales's life. The woman was not named; it was not customary to name royalty in Scotland Yard investigations. The likelihood is that the woman concerned was Princess Friederike of Hanover, who was in Vienna and London at the time. 'Austro-Hungarian' would be an understandable police description of a daughter of the Duke of Brunswick, if Canning, as is likely, had little grasp of European genealogical niceties.

In the middle of the police investigation into Wallis, Lord Trenchard resigned finally and unequivocally on 5 June 1935, perhaps (his grandson doubts it) because he disliked this continuing sordid royal assignment, though he did linger on until December to assist his successor, Sir Philip Game. Game, after an unfortunate term as Governor General of Australia, was considerably demoted by his appointment as commissioner. He now had to assist the king by conducting, in cooperation with the Secret Intelligence Service, an investigation into Wallis's life in America with which the monarch could trump her ace when the time came.

With startling hypocrisy and effrontery, Wallis managed to keep up a pretence to the Prince of Wales. On 15 June, in the midst of her affair with Trundle, she sat for a portrait by Cecil Beaton and gave it with a loving inscription to the prince. It appeared in *Vogue* magazine for 10 July. On 27 July, she gave him another portrait of herself by Man Ray, inscribed, rather oddly, 'SO BIG'. Since the prince was scarcely known for his endowment, was this a ghastly, private joke, designed to keep him guessing, and a sly and surreptitious reference to the more virile Guy Trundle?

One of George V's few abiding interests, outside field sports, was China; he had a knowledge of that country so formidable that Lord Killearn, British ambassador to Egypt, visiting him at Buckingham Palace at the time, was astonished by it and recorded it in his diary. In addition, Stanley Baldwin, who became prime minister in June, had a deep interest in China, which he had visited in the 1920s. Armed with prior knowledge, both king and premier were well equipped to instruct the Secret Intelligence Service's China agent, Emmanuel Cohen, to proceed to unearth Wallis's career in that country.

Scotland Yard and the SIS supplied all of the facts that were necessary in Hong Kong, Shanghai and Peking, while other agents in Baltimore, San Diego, Pensacola and New York City obtained details of gambling, sexual promiscuity and drug dealing. Baldwin delivered the resulting dossiers to the king; because of Queen Mary's sensibilities, it was left to her beloved friend and gentleman-in-waiting, the distinguished and morally impeccable Honourable John Coke, son of the Earl of Leicester, to show her the dossiers himself. He recorded later that her shock and dismay were indescribable.

In January 1951, when the much vexed question of Wallis being allowed the title of Her Royal Highness came up, Winston Churchill summoned Coke to his holiday home in Marrakesh, where he was working on a popular history, to ask him point blank why it was still being denied. Coke reminded him that in 1936, in the last month of King George V's life, Coke himself had heard Queen Mary say that in view of what he had shown her in the dossier, Wallis must never be queen. She, the Duchess of York, and the Duchess of Kent, agreed on this matter at the time.

From that day to this, historians and biographers have denied the file's existence, one exception being Kenneth de Courcy, Duc de Grantmesnil, a friend of John Coke and the Prince of Wales, who knew from Queen Mary and from Coke that it did exist, but believed that it was a forgery. This is absurd; neither King George nor Baldwin nor John Coke would have forged it; they were not criminals by nature.

It is important to note that the royal family so deeply trusted Coke that he never left their employ. If he had been a party to a forgery arranged by Baldwin, he would have been removed and perhaps given a remote Commonwealth post, the usual treatment for erring royal servants. He remained equerry to Queen Mary to the end of her life and gentleman-equerry to King George VI (who would never have had a forger in his service) until he died. Nor did Winston Churchill reject him when he came to Marrakesh in 1951; Churchill retained great respect for Coke.

The sceptics remain vocal; in his 1991 authorized biography of King Edward VIII, Philip Ziegler incorrectly asserted that everyone seemed to have known someone who saw the dossier but nobody saw it themselves, thus injuring Coke's memory.

During the spring of 1935, Wallis went everywhere at night triumphant, blazing with emeralds. Henry 'Chips' Channon noted that at a lunch party on 4 April Wallis 'already had the air of a personage who walks into a room as though she almost expected to be curtseyed to. She has complete power over the Prince of Wales.' On 31 May, the Prince and Wallis were guests of Lady Cunard in her box at the Royal Opera House, Covent Garden. When the first interval came, Wallis said sharply to the Prince of Wales, 'Hurry off now, David. You'll be late for the London County Council Ball. And take that cigar out of your breast pocket. It doesn't look very pretty!'

That spring, London society was in a twitter over the forthcoming Silver Jubilee of King George. Enormous sums were being spent to make the grimy city look reasonably festive; the buildings were bedecked with flags and flowers, and bonfires were lit the length and breadth of England. The king made it clear to his erring son that Wallis would not be welcome at the Jubilee Ball; as a divorced person, she would also be forbidden access to the royal enclosure at Ascot and would be denied any other privileges over which the royal family had any control.

The king confronted the prince directly in the matter of Wallis. The prince gave his father his word of honour that he had never had sexual intercourse with her. This, of course, may have been literally true if he and Wallis were still merely indulging in fetishistic sexual games that did not involve the total consummation of their relationship. The prince insisted that Wallis was 'a fine person' and had made him 'supremely happy', unlike Thelma Furness, who was, he disloyally said, 'a beast'. He insisted once more that Wallis was not his mistress and begged that she be allowed to enter the royal enclosure and make an appearance at the Jubilee Ball. The king replied that, in view of the fact that the relationship with Wallis was (as he incorrectly believed it) strictly platonic, he would arrange for the Simpsons to be invited. Lord Wigram, the monarch's private secretary, wrote in his diary: 'The Prince's staff were horrified at the audacity of the statements of [HRH] the Prince of Wales. Apart from actually seeing HRH and Mrs S[impson] in bed together, they had positive proof that HRH actually lived with her.'

The ball took place on 14 May. According to tradition, the prince should have opened the evening by dancing with his mother. Instead he created a stir by walking straight up to Wallis and whirling her around the floor for the second number. To make matters worse, he even danced with her straight past his parents, who gave her a look of steely distaste. She was mortified.

After the ball, Wallis, the prince and a party of friends went dancing at the Embassy Club until 4 a.m. The novelist Mrs Marie Belloc Lowndes noted that Wallis kept both the prince's and Ernest Simpson's cigars in her jewelled handbag and handed them out like sweets to naughty schoolboys. When Mrs Lowndes told her husband on her return home, he said, 'I've heard of the price of shame, but never that it took the form of a cigar.'

Wallis was determined that she would see the Jubilee procession to St Paul's Cathedral. York House did not have a satisfactory view. On the morning of the procession, the Prince of Wales telephoned his father's assistant secretary, Helen Hardinge, the wife of Major the Hon. Sir Alexander Hardinge. The Hardinges lived in a grace-and-favour house near York House that had an excellent position from which to see the procession. He told Helen Hardinge, 'Two of my scullery maids badly need to see the parade. Could you make room at one of your windows?' Mrs Hardinge obliged. When she and her husband left for St Paul's, the two 'scullery maids' arrived. They were Wallis and Lady Cunard. Mrs Hardinge was furious.

Throughout that month, members of foreign royalty, including a number of relatives of the monarch, were pouring into London for the Silver Jubilee celebrations. Hitler correctly saw the jubilee as an ideal opportunity to cement the pro-Germanism of so many figures in British royal and aristocratic circles. Aware that the government was still leaning in the direction of Italy, seeking to restrict him in the interest of the British balance of power, he strove to correct the situation by selecting a royal flush from the faded deck of cards that the deposed German royal family of Hohenzollern had become. It would have been a mistake to send the ailing kaiser to London, because the British public would have risen in its wrath against the former enemy. Instead, Hitler shrewdly sent the kaiser's daughter-in-law, Crown Princess Cecilie, her daughter Victoria, and her son Ernst August, along with the prince's favourite, Charles, Duke of Saxe-Coburg-Gotha, who was in the SS. These figures, entirely embroiled in Hitler's cause, if only to protect their assets, could be relied upon, the Führer felt, to make the necessary impression at Buckingham Palace. Wallis inevitably encountered them at the time. Among her new friends were the Prince and Princess von Bismarck, and among the other crucial connections to the royal German cousins were their devoted hosts, Sir Harold and Lady Zia Wernher. Lady Zia was the White Russian sister of Nada Milford Haven. Sir Harold was head of Electrolux in Britain, and thus an associate of the Swedish multi-millionaire Electrolux tycoon Axel Wenner-Gren, royalist and friend of Field Marshal Goering, who would later play a crucial part in the lives of Wallis and the prince. At the end of May Leo von Hoesch gave an elaborate party at the embassy in Carlton House Terrace for Wallis, the Prince of Wales, the Bismarcks, Princess Cecilie and the Wernhers.

At the dinner, Wallis was intrigued to hear Princess Cecilie urge the prince to make public his desire for closer alliances with Nazi Germany. She suggested that an ideal occasion might be his scheduled address at the Queen's Hall to the veterans of the First World War who were members of the British Legion. The Legion was already in close touch with its German counterparts, and it was anxious to repair the damage done in the First World War by stretching the hand of friendship across Europe. The prince agreed that this idea was excellent. It apparently never occurred to him that, by entering into such a commitment, he would expose the double game he was playing with the European powers and greatly annoy his friends in Vienna and Budapest as well as the French government, which was already hand in glove with Mussolini.

On 19 June 1935, to resounding cheers, the prince, without Wallis, walked up to the podium at the Queen's Hall and delivered a speech to the Legion that included words that made explicit his desire to have the conflicts of the Great War forgotten. He was given a standing ovation; most of his audience was still haunted by the horror of the trenches. Even as he spoke, German veterans, carrying swastika flags and the blessings of the Führer, were on their way to Brighton where, a few days later, they marched through the streets and appeared at a dinner, hosted by Prince Otto von Bismarck, at which a message was read to them in German from the Prince of Wales. At a ceremony at the town hall, Reich League leader Klaus Korres said, 'The Prince of Wales is the man of the moment, not only in his own country, but throughout Germany. Heil Hitler!'

The prince's Queen's Hall speech caused a storm of controversy. King George was furious, particularly since it was so important to continue with the appeasement policy vis-à-vis Mussolini in order to protect the Mediterranean and the Suez Canal. More importantly, it was essential that members of the royal family did not express themselves publicly on political issues. The prince's speech only served to illustrate his naive and confused political position. Wayward and defiant, he was being meddlesome and irritating in every possible way. Goering and General Count von der Goetz, head of the Reich League of German Officers, sent approving telegrams. A week later, at a vast assembly of two hundred thousand people at Nuremberg, Goering said, after savagely denouncing the Jews, 'Germans were profoundly cheered by the declaration of the British heir apparent. He can be sure the German front soldier and the German people grasp most eagerly the hand offered them.'

Questions were asked in the House of Commons by Aneurin Bevan, Labour member of parliament for Ebbw Vale, who assailed the new Conservative Foreign Secretary, Sir Samuel Hoare, on the matter. Hoare made it clear that the prince had acted on his own, without either sanction or indirect authorization of any sort. Yet, in a sense, Hoare's somewhat righteous response was flawed by hypocrisy, since only six days before the prince's speech the Anglo-German Naval Agreement had been concluded, allowing Hitler, in contravention of the Versailles Treaty, to rebuild the German fleet to thirty-five per cent of British strength.

At the same time, Britain's relationship with Italy, so warmly encouraged by the prince, became threatened by the foreign policy of Anthony Eden. Count Grandi recalls that, after a meeting with Eden in Rome, Mussolini beckoned him and in a hard and resolute tone said, 'The English and the French have declared their absolute disinterest in the fate of Austria . . . Soon the Nazi flag will wave over the Brenner frontier. This is painful but inevitable. Machiavelli wrote, "If you can't kill your enemy, embrace him." Some bad day we will be obliged to embrace the Germans. It will not be a pleasant embrace.' Grandi continues:

> Mussolini realized that Eden, while taking a belligerent attitude to us, also showed a certain blindness regarding our problems in Africa. Mussolini said to me, 'From this moment on, there will be a shift in our foreign policy. Since we are unable to save Europe, we will move into Africa.'
>
> English opposition to our actions in Africa vis-à-vis Abyssinia was indecisive. The English neither said no nor yes to our plans for the conquest of Ethiopia. In June 1935 British interests were centred on internal politics because of the imminent general election. But as the year went on, the feeling against Italy intensified.

The Prince of Wales brought whatever influence he had to bear in high circles to counteract the increasing opposition to Italian colonialism. In this, given her friendship with Grandi, Wallis was in complete concurrence. And yet there was still the contradiction in both cases that Wallis and the prince were flirting with the Germans in London. Wallis achieved yet another friendship that provoked the anti-German elements in Whitehall: on 29 June, she was a guest of Lord and Lady Londonderry at a time when Londonderry was writing letters of admiration to Hitler (whom he had visited) and was quite unabashedly in support of the Nazi regime. On 15 July, with the Prince of Wales's blessing, members of the British Legion were in Berlin, where they were received with gracious consideration by the Führer.

During this period of enormous publicity and conflicting currents in the world of politics, the Prince of Wales was under great stress. He depended more and more on Wallis for her support, but she still retained an ambiguous attitude towards him. On the one hand, she enjoyed flouting convention, basking in public attention and increasing her personal power. On the other, as a chilling letter written at this time to Aunt Bessie makes clear, she was certainly not in love. She was in fact increasingly distressed by the prince's infantile dependence on her – despite the fact that she had engineered the situation – and his still insistent phone calls and visits. Easily bored, brittle and restless, she impossibly wanted everything: a stolid and loyal husband and a fully enslaved prince; respectability as well as notoriety; the comforts of privacy – and social prominence. The royal need to be satisfied in every possible way had proved catching.

In a conversation with US ambassador to London Joseph P. Kennedy on 13 June 1938, as recorded in Kennedy's diary, Sir Edward Peacock, in charge of the royal finances as Receiver General of the Duchy of Cornwall, stated that at this time the Prince of Wales began sending out royal moneys from the country, most particularly to America where, despite the Depression, good investments were more readily available than in England. Like Hitler and Goering, the prince invested substantial sums in railroad common and preferred stocks in north-eastern America.

In July, plans were afoot for another political journey to Europe undertaken in the guise of a holiday. Using the pseudonym of Lord Chester, which fooled nobody, the prince took off with Wallis and friends to France, arriving on 7 August at Cannes by the Blue Train. Their friends vice-consul John Taylor and his wife met them. Apparently indifferent to the prince's support for Hitler's anti-Semitic regime, Sir Philip Sassoon had remained an intimate friend, and he arranged for them to stay at the house of his sister, Lady Cholmondeley; her Villa le Roc was next door to Maxine

Elliott's famous Château de l'Horizon. The handsome white house was situated by the sea, with an indoor pool, like that on an ocean liner, ingeniously contained within the rocks on which the house was built. There was also a private yacht slip.

The royal party swam, aqua-planed, played golf and took a local cruise down the coast aboard the yacht *Sister Anne*, owned by the Singer sewing machine heiress, the Hon. Mrs Reginald 'Daisy' Fellowes. However, there was an undercurrent of danger and tension in those golden, sunlit days. There were fears that communist assassins might shoot and kill the prince. He and Wallis were under guard day and night, unable to leave the villa without both French and British special agents and a detective from Scotland Yard, David Storrier. The guard intensified when, on 1 September, a very scared Wallis and the prince set off on the *Cutty Sark*, the million-pound yacht of the pro-Nazi Duke of Westminster, one of the richest landowners in England, with vast property holdings in London. The voyage was an act of folly, since the vessel moored at terrorist-haunted Corsica. As it happened, the communists did not act, and on 9 September, after weeks of sun and sea and parties with, among others, Herman and Katherine Rogers, the controversial couple took off for Budapest.

They stopped briefly en route at Geneva, spending the morning at watch factories and the afternoon at a meeting with the private secretary of Sir Samuel Hoare, who filled them in on Hoare's activities at the League of Nations. Italian forces were poised to invade Abyssinia, the enormous and impoverished cotton-growing kingdom of Emperor Haile Selassie, in East Africa. Hoare was prepared to allow Mussolini a free hand in that region for a variety of reasons, among them the guaranteed protection of substantial British economic interests including railways and farms, and an unwritten guarantee that the Italian dictator would not blockade the Suez Canal and launch an attack on the British Mediterranean Fleet and Gibraltar.

On 11 September, Wallis and the prince arrived in Budapest. The headlines there were full of Hitler's speech the day before to the Nuremberg Rally, condemning Jewish Marxism and the centrist Moderate party and promising harsher methods against both in the future. Once more, the prince had meetings with Regent Horthy, and he joined President Gombös for luncheon. He was continuing with his clumsy double game of sustaining the Italian connection to make sure that, in keeping with British foreign policy, there would be no interference with Mussolini's colonial expansions. The couple proceeded to Vienna, where the prince again combined visits to the Spanish Riding School, tea parties and nightclubbing with high-level discussions at the Chancellery.

There was a quick trip to Munich to appease the Germans and then a hair-raising car ride over the Trans-Alpine Highway to France. While in Paris, the couple firmed up two associations. The first of these was with Albert Frédéric Armand Grégoire, who was described in a confidential Sûreté report of 9 April 1934 as 'one of the most dangerous of Nazi spies'. Continuing as Wallis's lawyer, he represented Simpson, Spence and Young's business with the north German Lloyd shipping line and the Hamburg–American Line in France. He was also the lawyer of Elsa Schiaparelli, Ribbentrop and Otto Abetz, later the German ambassador to Paris, as well as Sir Oswald Mosley's chief contact in that city.

Robust and swarthy, with a duelling scar across his left cheek, Grégoire had been born in Metz, Lorraine, in 1894. He had been awarded the Iron Cross, first class, by Kaiser Wilhelm II, and had become a close friend of the crown prince and of Crown Princess Cecilie. He was a founder and director of Marcel Bucard's fanatical Franciste movement, one of the leading fascist cells in France. Under the pseudonym of Greg le Franc he contributed pro-Hitler articles to *Le Franciste*, the inflammatory official journal of the movement. In the issue of January 1934 (vol. I, no. 2), he had written:

> Naturally, we hope with all our heart for an alliance with Nazi Germany. We fully realize that this alliance constitutes the only possible means of avoiding the universal corruption of the world. We estimate that this alliance is possible, easier in fact to realize than an alliance with the British, our hereditary former enemies, with whom we have far less in common than we have with the Germans.

Wallis's use of the notorious Grégoire as a contact and lawyer (in 1937 she would have him represent her in a major libel suit) was a disaster, and the watch on her by the Secret Intelligence Service intensified. While in Paris, Wallis and the prince also became friends of Pierre Laval, premier of France. Devious, unreliable, famous for his greasy look and his washable white tie that was never washed, Laval was married to a charming and elegant wife. He followed a policy of trying to please the Balkan nations, the Germans and the Italians while secretly pitching one against the other. His dream was to give the Germans a free hand to smash the Soviet Union while keeping Hitler and Mussolini apart to preserve the French balance of power. He despised the British, despite their agreement with him on this issue.

*

While in Paris, Wallis was at last propelled into the highest levels of European power. Hitherto, the Prince of Wales had excluded her from meetings with heads of state, leaving her to go shopping while he indulged in duplicitous games of European politics. Now he made a move which was not only scandalous in the eyes of Bucking-ham Palace but also significant in illustrating the confidence he placed in Wallis and his need for her to become his royal consort. He arranged for her to attend a luncheon for Laval given by the British ambassador, Sir George Clerk, at the embassy on 1 October.

The timing of the luncheon was significant. For weeks, Anthony Eden, as Britain's representative at the League of Nations, had been conferring with Laval on the delicate matter of the secret French alliance with Mussolini, which Eden opposed. That January, in Rome, Laval had entered into an agreement with the Italian dictator that would subsequently give him a free hand in Ethiopia. Now, the Prince of Wales chose to confirm that he would stand behind Laval in the outright support of Mussolini's colonial ambitions, a fact to which Laval would testify in August 1945 when he stood trial on charges of treason against France.[1]

It was a unique occasion: the heir to the throne being accom-panied by his mistress to a political encounter sanctioned by a British ambassador. Laval's son-in-law, the distinguished Paris law-yer Comte René de Chambrun, a direct descendant of Lafayette, in 1987 revealed to this author the secrets of the meeting.[2] During the conference the prince promised to secure the approval of his father, the king, and of his government for Laval's policy vis-à-vis Mussolini. In return, the Comte de Chambrun states, Mussolini would be made to promise that he would not enter into an alliance with the Führer that would endanger Britain and France. At the same time, Laval's assurance was required and given that he would allow Britain to use French ports if at any stage in the future there should be a direct conflict with Italy in the Mediterranean.

The Comte de Chambrun regarded this meeting as an indication of the boldness and intelligence of both his father-in-law and the Prince of Wales. But he had overlooked a significant detail. One day before the embassy conference, Hitler had given assurances to Laval, widely published in the international press, though ignored by subsequent historians, that he would not take action against France no matter what arrangements Laval made with Italy. Those assurances had been made through Sir Samuel Hoare. It was clear from this announcement that Hitler was already planning to enter into an alliance with Mussolini in order to secure a permanent foothold in the Mediterranean and joint control of Austria and the Balkans.

During the next few days, Wallis, the Prince of Wales and Laval, in the company of Madame Laval and Laval's daughter Josée, exchanged many visits. The Lavals came to dinner at the Hôtel Meurice, and Wallis and the prince went to the Lavals' house. Once again, including Wallis in such a high-level series of meetings was extraordinary; she was being treated as princess, fellow politician and diplomat. At one meeting, at which Wallis was not present, Laval suggested that the prince should try to make an arrangement with Germany which would bring Mussolini and the Führer together. Laval said that he was sure Mussolini would accept an honourable agreement and suggested to the prince that he should talk to the king. The prince replied, 'My father doesn't meddle in politics, but I will certainly talk to him.'

It was now clear to the prince that it was not necessary to play a double game between the German and Italian dictators – that they could be brought together to a common purpose. That this purpose was the breaking of the Franco–Soviet pact, the prevention of the spread of Bolshevism and the crushing of the Soviet Union was made clear to the author by the Comte de Chambrun.

Meanwhile, the Duke of Kent was busy on the same political agenda. Shortly after the craven Prince Paul of Yugoslavia appointed a fascist prime minister who doubled as Foreign Minister in the sinister persona of Milan Stoyadinovich, and made an infamous deal with Hitler's government for bauxite, coal and grain, Paul met Laval to approve the Italian invasion of Ethiopia. Also at the meeting were Prince Philipp of Hesse, whose father-in-law King Victor Emmanuel would soon illegally be made emperor of that country, and Kent, who was staying in Munich at the home of Count Toerring, his Hitlerian brother-in-law. It takes no feat of the imagination to see what alliances these devious intriguers discussed.

The day after the meeting at the British embassy, the plans of the Prince of Wales and Pierre Laval came to fruition. The British granted Mussolini passage for 150,000 troops through the Suez Canal. He invaded Ethiopia, wreaking devastation and destruction. His troops used mustard gas, forbidden by international law because of its horrifying effects, which included blindness, madness and death.

Simpson, Spence and Young had a vested interest in pursuing the issue of the invasion of Ethiopia. The Italian commander, Treves, was a close associate of a partner of Ernest Simpson's. The firm was trying to obtain a loan on the London Stock Exchange to finance the development of a cotton-growing industry in that country. Treves and the firm persistently besieged the Treasury for permission to exploit the appropriate territory. In this, documents show, they were directly backed by the Italian government through the trade attaché to the embassy in London. The argument for obtaining the loan was that if the cotton industry of Ethiopia were financed by a country other than Britain, this would create a serious competitor to the Egyptian cotton industry, which was under British control. The application was not favourably received as the Treasury saw it as a combined move by Ciano and Wallis's husband. It is hardly surprising, in view of this latest manoeuvre, that the Secret Intelligence Service's efforts were now concentrated even more on Wallis. On 7 September, Wallis was to add a revealing touch to this matter when she wrote to Aunt Bessie, 'If war between Italy and Abyssinia takes place, perhaps shipping will take a leap and I'll be able to come over [to America].'

Back in London, according to Laval's statement under oath at his trial, the prince took the matter of Mussolini and Hitler to King George V. The monarch then allegedly agreed that nothing must be done to stop the Italian dictator in his path of conquest. However Anthony Eden, possibly out of guilt for having smoothed the path to the destruction of a hapless nation, began to press for sanctions against Italy at the League of Nations. In this, he was violently opposed by the Prince of Wales. Six months later the prince would be telling Ambassador Dino Grandi that he wanted the Italians to know he was on their side and that he regarded the British government's attempt to support the League's sanctions policy as 'grotesque and criminal'. He never ceased to maintain, in later years, that Mussolini should never have been interfered with. Count Grandi recalled in 1986:

> Several meetings and discussions took place between myself and leading figures of British government upon the sanctions issue. Sir Robert Vansittart shared with Eden the view that the application of sanctions was not merely designed to give us an indication of the British attitude, but also was indirectly an indication to Nazi Germany to desist from its territorial ambitions. However, the only effect it had, unfortunately for all concerned, was to push us directly into Germany's arms.
>
> I tried to warn Eden of this, without success. I had several very difficult meetings with him. Following the meetings, I felt it necessary to confer with the Prince of Wales. I always went through Mrs Simpson. I would telephone her at home, and ask her if she could make the necessary arrangements. She did so, and the meetings took place around ten o'clock at night. The prince was always very receptive to what I had to say and lent a very attentive ear. This was true also later, when he became king.

During the autumn of 1935, the old king was ill, worn out by the stress of maintaining a gruelling series of official appointments that taxed his waning strength beyond endurance. The matter of Wallis was among the greatest of his burdens. On 31 October, he and Queen Mary spoke with great sadness and fierceness about the prince to the former Austrian ambassador to London, their old friend Count Mensdorff. They told Mensdorff about the prince bringing Wallis into Buckingham Palace against their will. 'That woman in my own house!' King George exclaimed. The monarch continued, 'My son's former mistress, Lady Furness, was also frightful. The first, Mrs Dudley Ward, was a much better class and a lady of good society. [My son] has not a single friend who is a gentleman [and] does not see any decent society.'

Count Mensdorff said, 'The prince has so many attractive qualities, charm and giftedness.'

To which the king replied, 'Yes, certainly. That is the pity. If he was a fool we would not mind. I hardly ever see him and don't know what he is doing.'

The Prince of Wales made still more questionable associations. Jewish Defence League documents show that he was in touch with Dr Frank Buchman, an American clergyman who headed the so-called Oxford Group, or Moral Re-armament Movement, which had millions of followers all over the world. Dr Buchman, a close friend of Himmler's with whom he had stayed in Germany, was soon to become notorious for his statement: 'I thank heaven for a man like Adolf Hitler.' Among Dr Buchman's British admirers were Sir Samuel Hoare, Prime Minister Baldwin, the Earl of Clarendon, the Marquess of Salisbury and the Earl of Cork and Orrery.

In the meantime, the British Union of Fascists expressed its continuing admiration of the Prince of Wales. Although Sir Oswald Mosley was careful not to be too overt in his relationships with Wallis and the prince, he was at his most drastically active in this period. Even during the jubilee celebrations, his Blackshirt brigades had given the fascist salute to King George. Hundreds of meetings were held every week in various parts of Britain. Jews and Communists were beaten up by Mosley's gangs. And Jews were among the leaders of the movement, including the well-known boxing champion Kid Lewis, Mosley's Gauleiter. In addition, the Nazi party established its own headquarters in London and was equally interested in the Prince of Wales. Rudolf Hess, deputy to the Führer, was in charge along with Ernst Wilhelm Bohle, British-born chief of the AO,[3] the organization of Germans living abroad.

As 1935 drew to its close, the king weakened still further. He was greatly distressed by the death of his beloved sister, Princess Victoria. Hitler sent a message of sympathy.

In December, the Prince of Wales, with Wallis, flew to Paris to confer once more with Pierre Laval on the matter of Ethiopia and the continuing appeasement of Mussolini. This visit was understandably kept secret, and has only now been revealed by Comte René de Chambrun. Sir Samuel Hoare joined in the discussions at Rambouillet. Laval proposed that the war should be brought to an end with the following arrangement. Ethiopia would be granted three thousand square miles of largely useless territory in Italian Somaliland. Mussolini would be granted a huge slice of the African nation's richest cotton lands. This obnoxious arrangement was supposed to be kept hidden until the matter could be presented to the League of Nations. However the accomplished 'Pertinax' (André Géraud), foreign correspondent of the *Echo de Paris* and contributor to the *Daily Telegraph,* somehow succeeded in obtaining the text of the Hoare–Laval agreement and published it in both newspapers. It was instantly denounced in the House of Commons, though none of the members knew of the Prince of Wales's role in the matter. Hoare was violently abused and gave a speech of futile explanation before the Commons. The prince rashly took the step of supporting Hoare publicly by appearing in the Distinguished Strangers' Gallery to hear the speech. He allegedly applauded it, thus attracting untoward attention amid a chorus of boos.

According to the late Count Grandi in 1986:

> Hoare made a fool of himself over the Hoare–Laval issue. English public opinion was not prepared by a cautious and shrewd government policy, so the pact idea fell startlingly upon the British people, like a dash of cold water against burning steel. It was a terrible mishap. Had the proposals been accepted, Italy would have been satisfied and Mussolini would never have joined Hitler. Nor would he have extended his empire.
>
> Mussolini later tried to let it be believed that he had refused the Hoare–Laval proposal, but that is not true. He called a Grand Council meeting on December 10, and the acceptance of the Hoare–Laval proposal was on the agenda. I will never forget calling from London with news of what was going on in

the House of Commons. Mussolini interrupted the Grand Council meeting to talk to me, and expressed great astonishment and disillusionment.

In his frequent meetings with Grandi at the time, the Prince of Wales was unquestionably in total accord on the matter. To the end of his days he would tell anyone who would listen (and the editor and author Frank Giles went on record on this matter in his memoirs) that the biggest mistake ever made by England was in the matter of Mussolini and Ethiopia.

Wallis also remained in agreement. Nor could she forget that the Foreign Minister of Italy, Count Ciano, was the father of her dead child. She was happy despite her pro-Fascism, and she spent Christmas with the Jewish Sir Philip Sassoon at Trent Park. Meanwhile, the prince was at Sandringham with his parents. In the wake of the China dossier and the research in Baltimore, the atmosphere was even more charged than usual. The prince made a touching effort to assuage his father by ordering the royal caterer, Frederick Corbitt, to obtain a dozen avocados as a Christmas present to the King. Corbitt had the formidable task of finding the elusive fruit in the midst of a savage English winter. According to Corbitt's memoirs (some historians have questioned the veracity of the story), when the avocados arrived the prince had them served with vinaigrette to the king, who ungratefully snapped, 'What in heaven's name is this?' His father's lack of appreciation for the gesture radically upset the prince, who telephoned and wrote to Wallis that he was utterly depressed and distraught with the situation in his family.

The Prince of Wales stood in for his father at several official functions. He was not at all eager when asked what would happen after he assumed the throne. Frequently he said to friends, 'My brother Bertie would make a much better king than I would.' He even addressed the Duchess of York in private as 'Queen Elizabeth'. He talked of moving to his ranch in the Canadian Rockies for the rest of his days.

January was a typically harsh month in England; the country was swept by snow and sleet and driving winds. The old monarch developed bronchitis, a condition aggravated by his unfortunate habit of smoking heavily. On 16 January, the prince, who had been shooting in Windsor Great Park, walked into the drawing room at Fort Belvedere and handed Wallis a note. It was in Queen Mary's handwriting and read: 'I think you ought to know that Papa is not very well.' The queen went on to suggest that the prince should come to Sandringham for the weekend, but should be careful not to reveal his concern to his ailing father.

The prince took Wallis's hands in his. They knew the king was dying. Soon the Prince would be King of England. Would Wallis then divorce Ernest Simpson and become queen?

When the prince arrived at Sandringham, he found his father, painfully thin and frail, seated in an old Tibetan robe, shivering before a big log fire. The king was scarcely able to recognize his son. A team of physicians led by the royal doctor, Lord Dawson of Penn, had determined that, in addition to the bronchial catarrh from which the monarch was suffering, there were signs of cardiac weakness that were sufficient to cause alarm. Lord Wigram, the principal private secretary, had been informed that the king would not live much longer. He discussed with the Prince of Wales and the Duke of York the arrangements that would take place for the succession. The following day, the two princes drove to London to confer with the prime minister, Stanley Baldwin. The queen was especially concerned about the upkeep of Sandringham. A joint stock company was discussed, to which the Prince of Wales and the Duke of York would contribute funds. However, the Prince of Wales expected to inherit a life interest in Sandringham and Balmoral when he became monarch. The maintenance of both residences would be drawn from Crown funds. The queen was upset; she also dreaded the thought that her son might give the jewellery of the late Princess Victoria, whose death had greatly upset King George, to Mrs Simpson. She made sure that the will divided the jewellery between the Princess Royal and the Duchesses of York, Gloucester and Kent.

On 17 January, with the king in a limbo state between life and death, as Baldwin revealed in a conversation with Joseph P. Kennedy, the US ambassador's son on 13 June 1938, the Prince of Wales, instead of staying by his father's bedside with all the available members of the family who were not travelling abroad, went to

Downing Street to tell Baldwin he had hoped to get out of being king but had never had the courage to discuss it with his father – then, with Baldwin in a state of shock, he upset the prime minister even further by taking off with Wallis, to a nightclub.

On 19 January, the king began to sink into his final sleep. He murmured to Lord Wigram, 'How is the Empire?'

'All is well, sir, with the Empire,' Wigram replied.

At noon, the king managed to sign a document permitting the appointment of a council of state. While Wallis waited by the telephone at Bryanston Court, the Prince of Wales flew back to Sandringham with the Duke of York, and after dinner he and his brothers York and Kent drew up plans for the funeral. At 10 p.m., the king was already in a coma. If he lived past midnight, it was realized, his death announcement would miss the morning edition of *The Times*; in view of this unfortunate possibility, and his grievous suffering, it was decided to terminate his life immediately. At eleven o'clock, Lord Dawson – improperly, according to the law, which forbade euthanasia – injected three-quarters of a grain of morphia and one grain of cocaine into the king's distended jugular vein when the nurse in attendance refused to undertake the task. Within fifteen minutes the royal life was extinct, and before the BBC broadcast of the news at ten minutes after twelve, *The Times* was advised. The Prince of Wales called Wallis, who was with Lady Mendl's assistant and protégé, Johnny McMullen, at Bryanston Court.

Through the night and much of the next day, the prince called the anxious but irritable Wallis countless times, telling her of each successive stage of the preparations for the next few days. There was some discussion of a possible cremation, which, according to some authorities, would have set a precedent, but this was not followed through. Everyone remembered the ghastly episode of the burial of the Duke of Teck, when the body, afflicted by a septic condition, burst open with a loud report during the funeral procession. Because of this disagreeable memory, it was decided to embalm the king.

The Prince of Wales left with the Duke of York by plane for London to discuss matters with the Accession Council, and to be officially declared king. Meanwhile, the royal coffin rested at Sandringham church. On 22 January, the official public proclamations took place in London. At the new monarch's specific request, Wallis, fascinated, watched the ceremony from a tall window at York House.

As the guns thundered, Wallis felt a firm hand gripping hers. The king stood next to her. He had again broken all tradition by coming to watch his accession with her.

They were seen driving off together in the royal car; he dropped Wallis off at Bryanston Court before continuing to Buckingham Palace. At 2.30 he was on his way to Sandringham. Upon his arrival there he joined his mother and the rest of the family to hear the reading of the will by the royal solicitor, Sir Halsey Bircham. To the new king's horror, he was not included. Clause after clause was read out, and every few minutes he would interject an anguished, 'Where do I come in?' Sir Halsey was obliged to say that he did not. Lord Wigram stated that he had not been left an inheritance because it was presumed that he had built up a substantial sum from the Duchy of Cornwall. The king was beside himself with rage. He exclaimed, 'My brothers and sister have all this money and I have nothing!' At that time he had amassed from the Duchy of Cornwall an estimated £1 million worth of investments and property. Moreover, he had of course inherited the life interest in Sandringham and Balmoral.

As it happened, the new monarch was very well off indeed. The Duchy of Cornwall earned him at least £364,000 a year. He would receive £425,000 from the Duchy of Lancaster and £2,355,000 from the Civil List. Sandringham and Balmoral were worth at least £5 million. He also had the use of Buckingham Palace, worth £15 million, and containing £10 million worth of gold plate alone. The palace boasted a collection of old masters worth £5 million. The king had investments that included a ranch at Calgary, Alberta, with several hundred head of shorthorn cattle, and very substantial stocks in Jewish companies, obtained for him by the Rothschilds.

Wigram was exceedingly disaffected with the new king because of his behaviour over the will. He made it clear that he would resign from his post in six months and emphatically would not act as private secretary to the new monarch. His sentiments were shared by a very high proportion of employees on the royal staff, who were appalled by the fact that the king seemed more concerned with his own financial welfare than anything else. Two days later the king stormed into the offices of the Duchy of Cornwall demanding immediate reassurance that no portion of the income, drawn in part from the rentals of the impoverished people of London, would be denied him. He was coldly informed that it would not.

In the meantime, the body of George V had been brought to London to be carried in a simple procession through the streets to Westminster Hall. Something ominous occurred on that sombre journey: because of the jolting of the gun carriage that carried the dead monarch, the jewelled Maltese cross surmounting the Imperial Crown, which had been fixed to the coffin over the royal standard, came loose and fell into the gutter.

A much more elaborate procession, attended by a vast throng of mourning citizens, took place a few days later.

The body at last reached Westminster Hall. For days and nights, close to a million people trooped past the coffin. Officers of the Household Brigade stood at the four corners of the platform and funerary candles glowed in the subdued light. In the early hours of one morning, when the crowd had gone, the king, perhaps feeling a twinge of conscience because of his behaviour, hit upon the touching gesture of summoning his brothers to stand with him in vigil in between the officers. On another morning, he and Wallis came in through a back door and stood in silent contemplation. According to Ribbentrop's biographer, Paul Schwarz, a German agent managed to film them and send the film to Hitler, who giggled uncontrollably as he watched it. He was already in possession of moving pictures of the royal yacht cruises the previous summer and, like Eva Braun, was mesmerized by Wallis's hair, carefully made-up face and exquisite clothes. He told Frau Ribbentrop he deeply admired Wallis.

In the midst of these sad rituals, with London black-draped in the spirit of mourning, the new monarch somehow managed to fit in meetings with representatives of Nazi Germany. Even before his father was dead he had met Leopold von Hoesch and told him that he intended visiting Hitler's Olympic Games that summer.[4] He also squeezed in an audience for several groups of German servicemen and, while his father was scarcely cold in his coffin, had a fireside encounter at York House with Charles, Duke of Saxe-Coburg-Gotha. He told his Eton-educated cousin, a member of the SS, that he wanted to meet Hitler, that he had the highest admiration for Rudolf Hess, and that Ribbentrop had done a very good job with the Anglo-German Naval Agreement. He said that von Hoesch, though a 'good representative of the German Reich', was a 'bad one for Hitler's Third Reich', and that he as king would require 'a representative National Socialist from Germany as ambassador, who, through his personal rank in society, would belong naturally to the gentry, and who could be regarded as a representative of official policy and the confidante of Hitler'. This statement suggested an urgent need for von Hoesch to be replaced by the prince's and Wallis's intimate friend the Prince von Bismarck, formerly of the Reichstag, who was to take over as chargé d'affaires in March.

One of the king's first acts as monarch was to order, in person, from Lendrum and Hartman in Mayfair, an exact copy of the royal Buick which had been manufactured in Canada. The second Buick, with identical licence plates and with the royal insignia on the bonnet, was for Wallis's exclusive use. This was widely considered an outrage in court circles. Wallis acquired a whole series of enemies that January. Chief among her existing enemies were the severely correct Major the Hon. Alexander Hardinge and Mrs Hardinge. Helen Hardinge, a woman of old-fashioned moral character, a member of the distinguished Cecil family, detested Wallis. Several of the royal ladies-in-waiting refused to shake hands with Wallis. When Wallis came up to one of them with her hand outstretched, the woman dropped her handbag and bent to pick it up to avoid the contact.

On 28 January, Hitler gave an elaborate memorial service for George V in Berlin, improbably finding himself in church for the occasion. He gave Princess Cecilie the place of honour next to him, and Himmler, Goebbels, Goering and the rest of the cabinet were in attendance.

That same night, the king gave the customary ceremonial dinner that followed a royal funeral; this was held at Buckingham Palace. Among the guests were the Regent of Yugoslavia, Prince Paul; the

Italian Prince of Piedmont; and the Austrian Vice-Chancellor, Ernst von Stahremberg. Hitler had sent Baron Constantin von Neurath, former ambassador to the Court of St James and a close friend of Queen Mary's, to represent him along with Charles of Saxe-Coburg-Gotha. At the dinner, served in the Gold Dining Room, the king shook everyone's hand rather perfunctorily. But when the turn of von Neurath, Saxe-Coburg-Gotha and von Hoesch came, he held up the whole receiving line for twenty minutes, totally breaking protocol, while he talked with them animatedly in German. Every-one noticed this; everyone was meant to. Clearly, the king felt confident that Mussolini and Hitler were now moving so closely together that this gesture would not offend the Prince of Piedmont. He calculated correctly.

He had refused to permit the Russian envoy, Maxim Litvinoff, to sit at the dining table where his cousin Grand Duke Dimitri of Russia was placed. Instead, he received Litvinoff and all the other non-royal figures at a separate reception later in the evening. He pointedly ignored Litvinoff, summoning him to a separate meeting at Buckingham Palace, where he asked him, 'Why did you kill my cousin Tsar Nicholas?'

Litvinoff cunningly replied, '*I* didn't. I was among the con-servatives.'

The king proceeded to irritate almost everyone in his house-hold. He had already annoyed many retainers by changing the clocks, which had been set half an hour fast from the time of his grandparents to save daylight hours for shooting, back to their normal time. He instructed Frederick Corbitt that lunch would no longer be served at one, as it had been for over a century, but would be eaten whenever the mood took him, usually at half past two. This put severe pressure on the kitchens. He made it clear that the staffs at all the royal houses must be ready to answer the ring of a bell at any hour of the day or night. He consulted Wallis on the royal budget. She advised him to make a clean sweep of the staff, cutting out dead wood and giving anyone inessential a ten per cent wage cut. To the lasting disgust of Wigram and the Hardinges, he dismissed many old and ailing retainers. Together, he and Wallis decided that court clothing should be modified and that morning coats should be eliminated. They appeared at York House without warning in the kitchens, maids' quarters, wine and food cellars and basement, conducting cursory inspections and making radical changes. Years later, the king told Commander Grattidge that he had been amused to find in the bowels of Buckingham Palace a group of tiny men responsible for stoking the boilers like primitive cave-dwellers who never came up for air.

Always a dieter, he cut the food purchases of each of the royal households by two-thirds; he was served salads, fruit and small portions of meat. His and Wallis's only indulgence was a delicious Scandinavian dessert called *Rødgrød,* made of crushed raspberries, redcurrants and rice. He was a little hesitant in bringing Wallis to Buckingham Palace, but one evening he gave her a tour. They decided that the entire antiquated edifice should be remodelled in a modern manner and that, outrage of outrages, it should be redecorated from top to bottom by Lady Mendl. As it turned out, this idea was never executed. By the time Lady Mendl had finished her drawings, the king was off the throne.

His rebellious informality was so extreme, and his submission to Wallis so absolute, that he did the unthinkable. When she left his royal residences, often after spending most or all of the night, on her snapped instructions he would dash past his staff all the way out of the front door and often in rain and darkness, to frantically hail cab after cab until one would draw to a halt. The driver, recognizing the monarch, would respond to the shrieked words, 'Stop! I'm the king!' with a stare of astonishment that was even more wide-eyed when that elevated being actually opened the door for his notorious mistress and assisted her inside. It is fairly safe to say that no English ruler has acted in this manner before or since.

Rear Admiral Sir Lionel Halsey of his household was let go; the king also disposed of Sir Louis Greig, another loyal courtier, and tried to take his house in Richmond Park from him – but George V had long since made sure that Greig was given a 99-year lease and the property was no longer subject to royal confiscation. Brigadier General G. F. Trotter was another victim; the list grew longer every day.

And the king's meannesses were appalling. Even Wallis, who disliked and was jealous of Dudley Forwood, objected when the monarch made him pick up papers from the carpet on his hands and knees, papers the king had deliberately spilled there. When Forwood announced that members of the staff were drinking imported Evian water, Edward sent an announcement to the kitchen saying that Evian was only to be drunk at the royal table and anyone caught quaffing it would be dismissed on the spot without references. They were.

The King of England, according to custom, would receive official dignitaries one at a time. This practice greatly aggravated the new monarch, who instead required groups of officials to appear before him simultaneously, much to the annoyance of many of them. He disposed of the private car supplied by the railways and travelled in ordinary carriages. He did away with a stenographer and typed his own correspondence with two fingers until the sheer number of letters to be answered made him give up. He ran up colossal telephone bills at the palace. When Wallis was irritated by the telephone service, he told her to call the Postmaster General to have the problems fixed. They were – at least for the time being.

The world was excited and impressed with the new monarch. In the United States enthralled millions watched the newsreels of his accession. One of his keenest admirers was my father, Sir Charles Higham, who, in an interview at the Waldorf-Astoria Hotel in New York, accompanied by me, his baby son, said:

> King Edward is a young people's king. And England is coming to be a young people's country, as the gap in the ranks of her youth, caused by the war, is being filled with intelligent young- sters. Edward will be their idol. He can ride, dance, fly, mix with the commoners, deal with diplomats. What can't he do? He is fully equipped for his job, if a king ever was.

The German press enthusiastically agreed. Above all, the Italians gloried in the new monarch.

*

Wallis was under a considerable strain during those first weeks of her lover's reign. Yet she seemed to enjoy the new game of being the king's mistress, writing to Aunt Bessie that she was 'laughing a lot inside'. Although her apologists have denied it, she had designs on the throne already, since on 1 February she wrote to her aunt for the Warfield and Montague family trees, determined that they would stand up against these '1066 families here'. Only a week later she seemed to realize the folly of any thought of becoming queen, writing to Bessie that it would be a good idea if the king were to marry someone of appropriate background. She also made clear that she would *never* relinquish her power.

There was still nothing in her letters of the time to indicate the slightest degree of love or even affection for the new monarch, only a cold conflict in herself over whether or not she should seek further heights. By contrast the king, despite his crowded schedule, seemed to hate every minute he was apart from Wallis; he sent her a stream of letters, inscribed on black-edged mourning stationery printed on behalf of his father, expressing an infantile, obsessive adoration, sprinkled with a private code in baby talk.[5] Some time in the late winter he backed his written admiration with a bold financial gesture. He settled £300,000 on Wallis, almost exactly one-third of his entire life savings. According to *Time* magazine, he later panicked at the size of the gift and reduced it to £100,000. Wallis informed her Aunt Bessie Merryman that the financial arrangements, which Wallis had no doubt requested, had been taken care of. Soon the king would be spending thousands of pounds on jewels for her.

In February, Ernest Simpson wished to obtain membership at the masonic lodge in which both the king and the Duke of Kent, who was grand master, had supreme influence, and over which Sir Morris Jenks presided. Jenks turned Simpson down. The King demanded to know why. Jenks told him that it was against masonic law to accept a cuckolded husband as a member. Once again, the king insisted that his relationship with Wallis was platonic. This, of course, was a mere technicality. As a result, Ernest was admitted. He was also given the unfulfilled promise of a baronetcy.

Some time that month Ernest went to York House to visit the king; he was accompanied by a witness, Bernard Rickatson-Hatt of Reuter's. According to Rickatson-Hatt, during the course of the evening Ernest, who was by now in love with Mary Raffray, boldly told the monarch that Wallis would have to choose between them and asked the king what he meant to do about it. Did he intend to marry her? The king replied, 'Do you think I would be crowned without Wallis at my side?' Ernest agreed to end the marriage provided the king promised to be faithful to Wallis and look after her.

If this conversation (the veracity of which has been questioned by certain historians) had ever been leaked, it would have finished Wallis's chances of divorce the following year; a collusive arrangement would have been exposed by the King's Proctor, who had to rule on the matter, and the most famous marriage of the century would never have taken place.

NOTES

1 At his trial at Nuremberg, Ribbentrop tried unsuccessfully to summon the Duke of Windsor as a witness.
2 Only part of which appears in the minutes published in Sir George Clerk's decoded report to London in the British foreign policy documents.
3 *Auslandsorganisation*.
4 He was dissuaded from attending by the Foreign Office.
5 His favourite word was 'einum', which, according to a reliable source, was a cross between 'eenie' and 'meenie' in the toe-counting nursery rhyme.

9

ALMOST GLORY

In March 1936, the Earl of Harewood, husband of the Princess Royal, the king's sister, delivered a speech to the British Legion which was a far cry from the king's speech the previous summer. He attacked Hitler's reoccupation of the demilitarized Rhineland, in defiance of the terms of the Versailles treaty. Among other things, he was seeking to influence the Legion away from its Nazi associations. According to the present Lord Harewood, the king wrote a stinging rebuke to his brother-in-law denouncing him for the speech and saying, 'How can I make my contributions to foreign policy if my own relatives make irresponsible statements?'

That same month, Wallis took off for Paris to order her spring wardrobe from Mainbocher. Wallis saw a good deal of Mrs Beatrice Cartwright, heiress to the Standard Oil fortune; Standard Oil had substantial holdings in Germany and continued to collaborate with the Third Reich throughout the Second World War.[1]

While Wallis was in Paris, the situation in Europe was darkening. The nineteen infantry and three artillery battalions of Hitler's army now stood on the edge of France, yet the French public seemed apathetic, still carrying memories of the misery and exhaustion of the First World War, and anxious to avoid even a show of hostility to the threatening forces of the Führer. In London the sentiment of the financial leaders was, as British Foreign Office documents made clear, overwhelmingly pro-German and anti-French. That Wallis shared their views is clear from a statement made in a letter to her Aunt Bessie, in which she expressed the hope that the

Germans would ill-treat the French couturiers and others who were causing her problems. Her attitude to the French was ambiguous: on the one hand, she loved French food, the Hôtel Meurice, Mainbocher's fashion salon and the glamorous world of French society; but on the other hand she regarded the country as hopelessly corrupt, weak and ineffectual, a natural victim of the stronger forces of Germany.

As for the King of England, in a report marked 'Strictly Confidential' the London correspondent of the *Berliner Tageblatt* wrote, through the German embassy, to his foreign editor on 18 March: '[The monarch] has caused a number of important people in the Government to come and see him, and has said to them: "This is a nice way to start my reign!"' He was referring directly to Hitler's reoccupation of the Rhineland. Ironically in the context, Wallis expressed concern to her aunt that, in view of the deteriorating international situation, Ernest Simpson, who was continuing to do business with Nazi-controlled shipping companies in Hamburg, might be interned.

Mary Raffray arrived in London. She had seen a good deal of Ernest in New York the previous autumn, when they had become involved in a secret love affair. She was keeping a careful record of Wallis's association with Ribbentrop, which she insisted to her family was also a love affair. She 'hated' Wallis for it, she wrote to her sister Anne in St Louis. In a curious reversal of the double standard, Wallis apparently objected to Mary's affair with Ernest; but at the same time she and the king clearly saw the liaison as a perfect way of disposing of Wallis's marriage and clearing the way to remarriage. As early as mid-March the monarch began to plan the divorce, consulting a number of trusted advisers on the best way to proceed. He was, of course, greatly discouraged by those in his circle, and he frequently lost his temper over their objections to Wallis as the future queen. One of those whom he dismissed that spring was the honourable and devoted 'G' Trotter, who also felt the executioner's axe because he was thought to be in touch with Thelma Furness. According to several sources, Trotter fell on very hard times and was even reduced to becoming an assistant in a department store. The king never lifted a finger to help him.

On 9 April, Maundy Thursday, a sacred occasion each year at

Westminster Abbey, when the reigning monarch gave alms to the poor, Edward deliberately infuriated the Archbishop of Canterbury by having Wallis attend in a back-row section usually reserved for visiting foreign royalty.

As her power grew, Wallis began to behave with even greater boldness. An extraordinary situation developed among herself, the king, Ernest and Mary. They were involved in what rapidly became a flagrant *ménage à quatre*. Ernest and Mary stayed with Wallis and the king at Fort Belvedere and at Lord Dudley's house, Himley Hall, and the king would spend evenings at Bryanston Court while Ernest and Mary shared the guest bedroom. On 23 April Mary wrote to her sister Anne:

> I meet the king often, dined at York House . . . and spent a weekend at the Fort . . . Saturday night he took us all to Windsor Castle; at the Earl of Dudley's we met Lady Oxford [Margot Asquith], Lady Cunard, Ribbentrop, and Lady Diana Cooper . . . Wallis is in the thick of things, received and toadied to by everyone on account of her influence with the King. (This you must absolutely not repeat.)

Ribbentrop was in London frequently that spring; while he still had the seventeen red roses delivered every day to Wallis at Bryanston Court, he was arguably the most popular party guest in London. Emerald Cunard, Laura Corrigan and Lord and Lady Londonderry – Wallis's set – entertained him constantly; he became popularly known as the 'Londonderry herr'. Ribbentrop was also very close to 'Chips' Channon and his wife, who paid court to him. Channon, though a gifted writer, had little power of perception when it came to dealing with leading Nazis; he was intoxicated by the idea of having a member of the German government at his dinner parties. In his diary entry for 10 June 1936, Channon wrote that Ribbentrop resembled 'a jolly commercial traveller'. Mrs Ronald Greville, a friend of Queen Mary's and later of King George VI's and Queen Elizabeth's, was another of his favourite pro-Nazi hostesses. Everywhere he went, he was lavishly praised for his and the Führer's defeat of unemployment and Bolshevism; some even dared to praise him for the official German policy on the Jews.

It was widely believed (among the alleged witnesses was Mary

Raffray) that Wallis was by now having an affair with Ribbentrop and that he was paying her directly from German funds in Berlin to influence – as if that were necessary – the king. Certainly, as Mary testified in a long, detailed account given to her sister Anne at the time, and subsequently written by Anne as a report to the biographer of Edward VIII, Frances Donaldson,[2] Ribbentrop was constantly in the apartment at Bryanston Court; and it is hard to believe that in this case the thick smoke of gossip had no fire as its source. No such relationship could have made its way into the official files in case their contents should leak back to Ribbentrop's wealthy wife, the champagne heiress Annelise Henkell, and cause her to undermine his position by creating a public scandal. Frau von Ribbentrop had young children; she had a jealous, possessive nature; and she must not be allowed to ruin Ribbentrop. As for Wallis, we know from her letters that she was not in love with the Prince of Wales; she was enjoying her power, but at the same time was fearful that he might want to marry her. No absolute proof exists of the relationship with Ribbentrop, but the people of Wallis's set were certain of it.

On 27 March, Edward gave Wallis her finest gift of jewellery: a Van Cleef and Arpels ruby and diamond bracelet; inscribed on the clasp were the words 'Hold Tight' and the date, a sly reference perhaps to the Casanova Clip, her method of enhancing weak erections by a tight grip of the fist at the base of the penis on entry, followed by internal muscular contractions, which Wallis had, according to the late Sir Dudley Forwood, brought to a fine art. On 2 April Wallis threw an elaborate party at Bryanston Court for the author and diplomat Harold Nicolson. In a blaze of white orchids and arum lilies she received her guests, who included the king, the American wit and broadcaster Alexander Woollcott ('She has the King like *that*,' he noted in his diary), and, audaciously, the arch-rivals Lady Cunard and Lady Colefax, both of whom wanted to monopolize the king. They were furious; Wallis evidently enjoyed the black joke of bringing them together under her roof. It was typical of her mischievousness and sheer nerve that she brought off this soirée.

That month, she and the king invited the Duke of Connaught, a royal great-uncle, and his friend Lady Leslie to Fort Belvedere for afternoon tea. According to a memoir by Lady Leslie's daughter Anita, the party strolled in the grounds; when the group returned to the house, Wallis's shoes were muddy from the damp soil. Without warning, she commanded the king, 'Take off my dirty little shoes and bring me another pair!' To the stupefaction of the two guests, the monarch knelt down and smilingly complied.

On another occasion, the king arrived with Wallis at a party at Lady Cunard's. He had been drinking Vichy water all through dinner, but decided to add a few drops of brandy at the coffee stage. Unable to find a bottle opener, he turned to Wallis. She instructed Ernest to take his own opener from his keychain and do the job for her lover.

Frequently, the king irritated his guests and Wallis by playing bagpipes after dinner at parties at the Fort. One evening, in front of a fashionable crowd, Wallis made so severe a face at him during his performance that he stopped dead, blushing like a schoolboy. It was by now clear to everyone that he no longer had a will of his own. He would even yield to Wallis's entreaties to accompany her to the Royal Opera House at Covent Garden. The audience rippled when he arrived with Wallis and friends and took his place in Lady Cunard's box. He loathed opera and slipped out time and time again during the performance to chain-smoke cigarettes and fret while Wallis, who remained tone-deaf, gave the impression that she was enjoying the performance. Actually, her enjoyment was chiefly in noting that the audience was barely looking at the stage; most eyes were fixed firmly upon her.

The king had several meetings with the committee of the Civil List that spring, discussing what provisions would be made for the 'future queen'. He ran into resistance on the matter but persisted in pressing the subject, much to everyone's irritation. Major the Hon. Alexander Hardinge and Mrs Hardinge were determined to block the marriage at all costs. They tried to contact the king's legal adviser, Walter Monckton, to enlist him in their cause, but he was in India. They continued to manoeuvre behind the scenes.

The king added Sir Robert Johnson, deputy master of the Royal Mint, to his long list of enemies. Sir Robert was in charge of the British coin designs. It was understood that in each successive reign the monarch would be photographed from the side opposite to that of his predecessor. It was a tradition that went back centuries. George V had been photographed from the left. But when the king discovered that the design for his own coins was based upon a rare photograph of his right side, he flew into a temper and, convinced that his right profile was hideous, demanded that a change be made immediately. He won.

He provoked still further criticism when, on 20 April, he sent a telegram to Hitler on his birthday, wishing the Führer well for his future 'happiness and welfare'. Five days earlier, Ambassador von Hoesch had died of a heart attack. He was replaced immediately by the king's and Wallis's intimate friend, the mild and bespectacled Prince Otto von Bismarck, who was acting chargé d'affaires until Ribbentrop took over that autumn. It was known that Bismarck was a frequent guest at Fort Belvedere, which suggested a very serious possible breach in security.

The reason for this fear in Whitehall was clear. Day after day, from the beginning of the reign, red dispatch boxes had been sent down from London to the Fort. They contained from British embassies all over the world secret documents relating to the international situation. These were for the eyes of cabinet ministers and the monarch, and were not made available to anyone else. It became a scandal that the king, bored by paperwork and troubled by eyestrain, would leave crucial documents scattered about, some of them marked by the stains of tea and coffee cups. It was suspected that certain crucial information in these documents was making its way back to Berlin. Wallis was thought to be the leak. In a biography of Prime Minister Stanley Baldwin by Keith Middlemas and John Barnes the following passage appears:

> About Mrs Simpson, greater suspicions existed. She was believed to have close contact with German monarchist circles . . . she was under close scrutiny by [Sir Robert] Vansittart [permanent undersecretary of the Foreign Office], and both she and the King would not have been pleased to realize that the Security Services were keeping a watching brief on her and some of her friends. The red boxes sent down to Fort Belvedere were carefully screened in the Foreign Office to ensure that nothing highly secret should go astray. Behind the public facade, behind

the King's popularity, the Government had awakened to a danger that had nothing to do with any question of marriage.

In the files of the FBI in Washington, a report, entitled 'International Espionage behind Edward's Abdication', contains this statement: 'Certain would-be State Secrets were passed on to Edward, and when it was found that Ribbentrop actually received the same information, immediately Baldwin was forced to accept that the leakage had been located.' The same report categorically states that Wallis was responsible for this breach of security.

In his biography *This Man Ribbentrop*, Paul Schwarz, a member of Ribbentrop's Foreign Office staff, reported that secrets from the dispatch boxes were being widely circulated in Berlin and that materials germane to British national security and sent by a British ambassador to Germany, Sir Eric Phipps, were making their way back to the German capital. Again, Schwarz seemed to imply, Wallis was responsible.

Sir Robert Vansittart, the controversial *éminence grise* of British intelligence, took charge. Tall, broad-shouldered, ruggedly athletic, exuding decency and warm common sense, Vansittart succeeded the very able Sir Ronald Lindsay as permanent undersecretary at the Foreign Office in 1930. He was arguably the most daring, free-thinking, brilliant and piercingly perceptive political figure of his time apart from his close friend and neighbour Winston Churchill. As John Connell wrote in his book on British diplomacy, *The Office*:

> He was [capable of] swiftness of analysis ... linked indissolubly to an equivalent swiftness in his desire for action. He was impatient if the action which he believed to be obviously necessary did not immediately and resolutely follow upon the assessment of a situation which he had made or the advice which he had offered. This caused more timorous and less decisive men to regard him as imprudent and injudicious.

Poet, gambler and bon vivant, Vansittart was a close friend and partner of Alexander Korda's; in the late 1930s, as his associate and boss in London Films, he hired Korda for the Secret Intelligence Service along with other German-speaking Hungarian employees of that company. Vansittart had been in the foreign service in Paris, Teheran, Cairo and Stockholm, and he had the clearest head in London where the German menace was concerned. He was the unofficial head of MI6, which was nominally run by Admiral Sir Hugh Sinclair until 1939. Connell wrote: 'He was a leopard whose fate it was to be harnessed with a team of domesticated but sly and vindictive tabby-cats.' He was Wallis's implacable enemy from the day that he was convinced she was a Nazi collaborator.

How did Vansittart reach the conclusion that Wallis was responsible for leaking crucial documentary information to the German government? According to the late historian John Costello, the Russian secret agent Anatoly Baykalov was the source of this intelligence. The statement is confirmed in Richard Deacon's impeccably researched *The British Connection*. He wrote:

> Baykalov had [a] trump card up his sleeve, one which he played very skilfully during the later years of the Baldwin government and which paved the way towards the abdication ... Baykalov reported to MI5 that Mrs Simpson was a secret agent of the Germans. He noted that she was very frequently at the German embassy ... The information was passed to Baldwin by his Secret Service Liaison Minister, J. C. C. Davidson.

Posing as a White Russian, Baykalov was part of the same set that included Wallis's dressmaker Anna Wolkoff, which would explain his knowledge of the matter. He appears to have acted as a double agent for the British. He took the information about the leak to the Russians and also in February 1936 to J. C. C. Davidson, who was now Chancellor of the Duchy of Lancaster. Davidson in turn took the information to Vansittart, who then conveyed it to Stanley Baldwin.

Vansittart had two reliable plants in the German embassy who could inform him when any material arrived for transmission to Germany in the diplomatic bags. Wolfgang zu Putlitz was one of these spies; later, when posted at The Hague, he would reveal the Duke of Windsor's leakage of important information on a British War Council meeting. Putlitz worked in association with another British spy, the German press attaché Iona von Ustinov, father of the actor and playwright Peter Ustinov. Nigel West wrote in his book *MI6* (the history of the Secret Intelligence Service): 'For . . . years, zu Putlitz kept Ustinov . . . in touch with everything that took place within the German Embassy in London.'

Wallis would have had to use the Italian embassy as a conduit for the information. What could have been her motive? Sir Eric Phipps, British ambassador in Berlin, had greatly excited the king's displeasure because of his missives and telegrams which indicated an intense dislike and mistrust of the Hitler regime. She would not have risked acting without royal authorization; it seems likely that the king himself wished this information to flow back to Germany in order to fortify opposition to Phipps and to undermine Phipps's secret policies.

On 4 May, Wallis sent a long, emotional letter to Aunt Bessie, complaining of the awful strain she had been under with the king and Ernest tearing her apart for a year and a half; how painfully difficult it was to placate and amuse two men at the same time and to fit into their separate lives; how she was constantly tired, nervous and irritable. Even though, she went on, she, Ernest and the king discussed their curious relationship on a reasonably friendly basis, and even though Ernest appeared to regard his position as a cuckold with complacency, she herself could no longer endure much more mental and physical stress. She knew she had outgrown Ernest; if she were to give up the king she would regret it, and should the king become romantically involved with another woman she would cease to have the power and possessions she now enjoyed. The letter is a harshly astonishing revelation of her ambition.

On 27 May, the king invited Prime Minister Baldwin and his wife to York House to meet his 'future wife'. Among the guests were Charles and Anne Lindbergh. Lindbergh had just returned from Germany, where he had been given a grand tour at the specific request of his friend Marshal Goering. Some time after the dinner Lucy Baldwin told her husband, 'Mrs Simpson has stolen the Fairy Prince.'

Walter Monckton, the king's legal adviser, returned to London from India. The Hardinges brought their influence to bear on him, but he was adamantly loyal to the king, almost certainly rejected charges of espionage against Wallis, and would only do what the king wanted. He knew that no power on earth could shake the monarch's obsessive love of Wallis. On one occasion that spring Monckton was with the monarch looking over a depressed property of the Duchy of Cornwall in London when he noticed the king staring with intense yearning out of one of the windows. He asked, 'What are you looking at, sir?' The king replied that Wallis was in that general direction. Even a brief absence from her that day was tormenting to him.

Another incident was widely discussed in London. In an effort to patch up the conflict between Wallis and his brother and sister-in-law, the Duke and Duchess of York, the king decided to take her to visit them at the Royal Lodge at Windsor. Wallis talked to them and at first they began to melt a little. She made a fuss over their children, the Princesses Elizabeth and Margaret Rose. But then Wallis destroyed all possibility of a reconciliation. The nursery governess, Marion Crawford, recalled in her memoirs that right in front of her host and hostess and their daughters, Wallis walked to the window and announced that the view would be greatly improved if certain trees were cut down or replanted and part of a hill bulldozed. The recommendation was not appreciated.

During the summer of 1936, severe censorship was applied to any mention of Wallis in England. The newspaper magnates, loyal to the king, introduced a self-imposed edict that precluded either photographs or articles which would disclose the relationship between her and the monarch. Foreign periodicals and journals were sent by their distributors to a special office where passages referring to the king and Wallis were scissored out. When the British news weekly *Cavalcade* daringly brought out an issue covering in five columns the life of Mrs Simpson, the issue sold very well but was finally dragged off the stands and confiscated. Nevertheless, black market copies of European magazines found their way into many homes in society and were read with much surreptitious giggling over the breakfast tables.

On 30 June, Superintendent Albert Canning of Scotland Yard, still pursuing Wallis on orders from Lord Trenchard and Sir Philip Game, advised Game that the Communist party of England was very much concerned with the king's relationship with Wallis and that, at a meeting led by the political firebrand Harry Pollitt at the City of Leeds Peace Conference, Pollitt had shouted, to general cheers and laughter, 'If gas masks are to be given out [in a future war] we should demand the same gas masks for our wives as will be given to Mrs Simpson.' This was at a time when the press lords of England, led by Lord Rothermere of the *Daily Mail* and Lord Beaverbrook of the *Daily Express* followed the policy, dictated by both king and prime minister, of behaving as if the notorious American woman did not exist.

One of the king's most characteristic acts that summer was to call a meeting of his Privy Council in late June to discuss the situation in which Mussolini had brutally subjugated and pillaged Ethiopia. In ten minutes, he suspended sanctions instituted by his father against Italian trade from 15 July, thus greatly benefitting Ernest Simpson. He ordered Sir Samuel Hoare, First Lord of the Admiralty, to withdraw war vessels from Italian waters, and he stood back while Mussolini forced Turkey, Greece and Prince Regent Paul's Yugoslavia to withdraw their sanctions.

By midsummer, all confidential documents were being withheld from the king and were not even passed from the Foreign Office as far as Major Hardinge. The Foreign Secretary, Anthony Eden, was responsible for this restriction, along with Sir Robert Vansittart. Eden had no time for the king, and the feeling was mutual.

Eden, still gravely concerned over the appeasement of Mussolini, and distraught that no punishment of the Italian dictator would be permitted by the government of which he was a member, had two alternatives at this stage. Either he could accept the majority decision of the cabinet or, if he felt sufficiently strongly about it, he could resign. Unquestionably he should have resigned, but, as was revealed later in his career, he tended to be morally irresolute in a crisis. It was not until 1938 that he finally resigned over the official appeasement policy. The cabinet was instrumental in arranging the abrogation of Mediterranean naval pacts with Greece, Turkey and Yugoslavia that were supposed to have ensured collective security against Mussolini. At the same time, Mussolini and Hitler had drawn together in what would turn out to be a fatally dangerous alliance. And just to be sure that Italy had unlimited power in the

Mediterranean, where it was secretly involved in a submarine war with the Soviet Union,[3] the King planned another political 'holiday' in Europe.

Shortly before he left with Wallis, the deposed Sir Louis Greig discovered that the couple was staying at Blenheim Palace, ancestral home of the Dukes of Marlborough, with Ernest Simpson confined to a separate room. There, Greig determined, the three hatched up details for the arrangements for Wallis's upcoming divorce, for which Simpson would receive a large sum of money. Mary Raffray, who would use the pseudonym of 'Buttercup', would oblige, for a financial consideration, as his sexual partner for the night and witnesses would be secured to testify to this. Evidently, the king still did not know that Wallis continued to sleep with Guy Trundle.

While the travel preparations were under way, an extraordinary incident took place. On 16 July, the king attended a military review in Hyde Park, inspecting on horseback a fine array of guardsmen in their scarlet uniforms. He reminded them of their heroic traditions, which went back 250 years to the period in which their leader and patron was the Duke of Marlborough. He spoke of the horrors of war, encouraging his troops in their hopes that they would never suffer from fire and gunshot as their predecessors had. 'With all my heart I hope, and indeed I pray, that never again will our age and generation be called upon to face such stern and terrible days. Humanity cries out for peace and assurance of peace,' he said. It was a ceremony that took place only once every fifteen years.

In bright sunshine the battalions marched past the king. The monarch rode behind the bandsmen at the head of the Brigades of Guards for the journey round Hyde Park Corner to Buckingham Palace. As the parade moved under the Wellington Arch, a man in the second row of spectators raised a gun and pointed it directly at the king. A policeman's horse backed into the man's line of fire, and he impetuously tossed the unused revolver under the hooves of the king's horse. 'Damn fool!' the king exclaimed as someone screamed, 'Get the killer, don't let him go!' Three policemen apprehended the would-be assassin and hustled him off. Grim but calm, the king continued to ride to the palace.

It turned out that the assailant was one Jerome Bannigan, an

Irishman living in Glasgow, who used the pseudonym George Andrew McMahon. A disgruntled alcoholic of unstable temperament, Bannigan had already been sentenced to twelve months in prison for the libelling of two police officers whom he accused of blackmail. The conviction had been quashed by the Court of Criminal Appeal. He was allegedly distressed because a magazine he edited, entitled *The Human Gazette*, had been emasculated in an act of censorship by the authorities. He claimed in a rambling story that he had been directed to kill the king by a political group that was Nazi in origin. This absurdity was treated with contempt, and after a brief trial he was sentenced to serve twelve months in jail.[4]

On 21 July, a storm drenched the guests at the first garden party at Buckingham Palace in six months. The king cancelled the receiving line until the following day. Four days after that he sailed for France on the Admiralty yacht *Enchantress* to dedicate the Canadian war memorial at Vimy Ridge. In a solemn ceremony he unveiled the expensive white stone monument before fifty thousand veterans, and, in a speech worked on extensively by his friend Winston Churchill, he spoke eloquently of the glorious dead and once more appealed for lasting peace.

He planned to spend some time on the Riviera at the Château de l'Horizon, home of the former Broadway star Maxine Elliott, before undertaking a Mediterranean cruise. However, the Popular Front's left-wing Léon Blum had become premier of France after an interregnum that followed the collapse of the Laval government the previous January. It was feared that certain Communist elements attaching themselves to the Blum administration might attempt to kill the king, and he was advised by the Foreign Office to bypass the Riviera. Instead, he chartered the 1,391-ton *Nahlin*, the luxury yacht of the eccentric millionairess Lady Yule, who had a house full of stuffed animals and an animal graveyard in her garden. Under the command of Captain Doyle, the yacht would travel through much of the eastern Mediterranean, where the Italians and the Russians were engaged in their secret war; at 4,700 tons the royal yacht *Victoria and Albert* would have been too large to make her way up the narrow inlets of Dalmatia.

It was a dangerous time to travel. The Spanish Civil War had broken out. The situation in the Balkans was potentially volatile.

Yet nothing would stop the king in his determined effort to embark upon yet another misadventure in politics in the guise of a holiday trip. He was still determined to appease Italy, despite the fact that that nation's imperial policy was still flagrantly opposed to British interests in the Mediterranean. Once again, in keeping with foreign policy, his clumsy, amateurish but on the whole well-meaning concern was to secure the permanency of the trade route to India through the Suez Canal; shortly before his departure he entertained Farouk, the teenage heir to the Egyptian throne, in order to receive reassurances vis-à-vis Suez. He was also pleased to approve Baldwin's crucial appointment of his old friend Sir Samuel Hoare as First Lord of the Admiralty. This was no idle choice. He needed Hoare to help him secure Italy's permanent cooperation and freedom to continue its anti-Soviet submarine war and to reinforce Gibraltar, Malta and Cyprus. Moreover, the king considered the heavy armament installations in Yugoslavia of the British company Vickers. In Greece he could contact King George and General John Metaxas, newly arisen dictator and Mussolini admirer. He would also meet Kemal Ataturk, dictator of Turkey, to ensure that the Turkish army and navy would be allied to Britain for the indefinite future.[5] There were fears that the Turks might be building or even floating submarines to assist their allies the Russians against Italy.

As usual, the king flew to Calais, while Wallis and the rest of the party came by Channel steamer. On this occasion the king used one of his hereditary titles, the Duke of Lancaster. The royal party took the Orient Express, again in a private car supplied by Mussolini, via Salzburg in Austria, arriving at the Yugoslav frontier at Jessenice late in the afternoon. The travellers were met by the regent, Prince Paul, and by John Balfour, British chargé d'affaires in Belgrade. The king stepped out to chat with the regent and Balfour. Sitting in the private car, Wallis was surprised to find it was being shunted around a siding to join the royal train. There was grave concern that Edward and Wallis would be murdered either by communists or by Croat terrorists. When Edward and Wallis broke their journey briefly to drive out into the country in the royal car to have tea with Paul and the Princess Olga, who did not approve of Wallis, the chauffeur, on instructions, drove at a frantic pace, scattering chickens and goats in every direction. The authorities were afraid that if the royal party was in a slow car, the Croats might strike.

The purpose of the meeting was not merely social. The timing had been carefully thought out and the meeting had been pre-planned, despite statements in both Wallis's and the king's memoirs that it was the result of Paul's insistence on interrupting their journey south. Two months earlier Dr Hjalmar Schacht, Hitler's leading economist and financial wizard, had been in conference with Prince Paul on the matter of massive armaments contracts; at the same time Mussolini had been in close touch with the prince to achieve similar political and economic relations. As a result, when King Edward and Wallis arrived in Yugoslavia half that country's exports and imports were the result of German and Italian deals. It is clear that again the King of England wanted to be reassured that the fascist alliances established in Bucharest would not affect the British balance of power in Europe, especially in the Mediterranean basin. Prince Paul had no difficulty in giving that reassurance.

Wallis and the king then proceeded to the Dalmatian coast, joining the *Nahlin* at Sibenik. The weather was perfect, and the yacht, extensively refitted on royal instructions and freshly painted white from stem to stern, made a magnificent sight in the harbour against a background of vivid blue sea and sky. Twenty thousand people in traditional costume greeted the royal party as the group made its way by car to the docks. Stories about Wallis had been appearing regularly in the local press; everyone knew she was the king's mistress. Cries of 'Long live the king!' rang through the warm and humid air as the white vessel slipped from her moorings and moved out into the glittering sea.

During the next three days, politics was set aside as the royal party, with two destroyers as escorts, enjoyed small Adriatic ports and experienced the visual pleasures of the mountainous, magical coast. Wallis would never forget one particular evening when the *Nahlin* was moored at a pier directly under the shadow of a looming mountain peak. Several thousand peasants came to greet the yacht, carrying torches in a long procession that wound down the cliffside paths, while the sound of singing filled the night. At Dubrovnik another great crowd surrounded Wallis and the king as they went shopping, crying, 'Long live love!' Despite the heat and humidity, the closeness of the cabins and the lack of wind to aid the yacht's passage, Wallis was enjoying her role as surrogate queen, and the king was overjoyed to be giving her a taste of what it meant to be a royal person.

Among the guests on the cruise were the minister of war, Duff Cooper, and his wife Lady Diana; they had joined the yachting party en route. Neither was particularly enamoured of Wallis, nor was she of them. They found it sinisterly prophetic that Wallis was already wearing, on a gold necklet on her wrist, exact copies of the two crosses worn by the king. Diana noted in her memoirs that the couple occupied the main suite (actually, a converted library from which all the books had been removed) at the bow of the vessel, while the numerous guests were crammed into the stern.

The monarch insisted on behaving like an ordinary tourist. As the *Nahlin* nosed through the Corinth Canal he stood stripped down to shorts on deck, provoking hundreds of camera shots, as well as severe and puritanical criticism in London. King George of Greece came aboard for two hours to meet Wallis; related to the British royal family, he had known Edward on and off for many years. Then the couple went ashore with George to meet his British mistress, Mrs Jones. The situation in Greece was very tense. Only two weeks before, General John Metaxas had seized power in Athens, appointing himself premier and minister of army, navy, air and foreign affairs. He had cut off all telephone and telegraph communications, censored the press and sent police to break up trade unions. In a few days he would dissolve parliament. Both he and King George had cemented relations with Italy and Germany; again, it was important for King Edward to receive assurances that British interests would not be affected by the new regime. He did.

The royal party continued to Athens, where the king and Wallis walked their feet off exploring the Acropolis and the Parthenon. While Wallis shopped, the king and Duff Cooper visited General Metaxas for two hours and had afternoon tea with him. According to a survey of the tour made by the American magazine *Living Age*, during the course of the meeting they arranged a substantial British loan to Greece through Hambro's Bank, which in effect helped to put Britain more firmly in the Hitler–Mussolini camp.

Back on board, Lady Diana Cooper witnessed a bizarre scene. The king suddenly sank to his knees to drag the hem of Wallis's evening gown from under the foot of a chair. Instead of expressing her gratitude, Wallis stared at the monarch and snapped, 'Well, that's the *maust* extraordinary performance I've ever seen!' And then, to the astonishment of all concerned, she launched a sharp attack on the king, criticizing the way he had handled the Greek monarch and his mistress. Diana wrote in a letter, 'Wallis is wearing very, very badly. Her commonness and Becky Sharpishness irritate.' It was not the first time Wallis had been compared to the heroine of *Vanity Fair*. Diana noted in her diaries that Wallis kept picking on the king quite coldly, with boredom and irritation. Later, the engineer of the yacht wrote an unpublished book about the cruise which indicated how bad-tempered and restless both the king and Wallis were and how they constantly badgered and bullied the crew.

'The good ship *Swastika*,' as Malcolm Muggeridge later dubbed the *Nahlin*, now proceeded on her journey to Turkey, hitting a bridge on the way. Wallis watched, laughing, as the king was spilt into the water when his small rowing dinghy capsized in a heavy swell. Picnicking, rock-climbing, collecting shells and swimming in the warm and still sunlit sea, the royal party proceeded to Turkey, where the group received an especially tumultuous welcome. The Turkish destroyers *Adapepe* and *Kojapepe* met the royal yacht off Imbros at 8 a.m. on 3 September. General Altay of the Turkish army came aboard by launch with a message of welcome from the Turkish dictator, Kemal Ataturk. Turkish destroyers joined the two British destroyer convoy ships accompanying the royal cruise up to the landing stage at Seddul Bahr. Wallis and the king spent two hours walking through the British and Australian graveyard at Gallipoli. This caused much annoyance in Australia and New Zealand because many in those countries blamed the British, and in particular Winston Churchill, for the inefficiency that had caused the Anzac troops to be sacrificed in the battle against the Turks in that region during the First World War.

At noon, the *Nahlin* anchored off the Dalma Bagtche Palace. The king and Wallis were greeted by Kemal Ataturk, along with the premier, the Foreign Minister and the Turkish ambassador to the Court of St James. The royal party climbed into open cars and drove at headlong speed past cheering crowds to the British embassy for a meeting with the ambassador, Sir Percy Loraine. Again, what seemed to be merely a courtesy visit was crucial in terms of securing British interests in the region. After several months of negotiations, the League of Nations had at last agreed to permit the Turks to overcome post-Great War agreements and to refortify the Bosphorus. In view of Turkey's recently cemented political and economic alliances with the Soviet Union, and her proximity to Egypt and the Suez Canal, the situation was felt to be potentially dangerous to British interests. During his meeting with the Turkish dictator, the king succeeded in acquiring the contracts for the Dardanelles refortifications for Britain right under the nose of Hitler's Dr Schacht, as well as outfoxing Skoda, a Czech company.

That night, Ataturk put on a Venetian regatta for the royal party, with the Turkish fleet lit from stem to stern, and a display of fireworks that illuminated the dome of Santa Sophia in a blaze of multicoloured lights. It was an unforgettable night to cap an unforgettable visit.

The king and Wallis proceeded to Bulgaria, whose King Boris was yet another Hitler associate and admirer. The visit was absurdly mooted as an incognito affair but overnight turned predictably into a gala event. On this occasion, the couple's behaviour was appalling. Not only did they boldly sleep together in the private car of the imperial train, supplied by Boris to take them from the border to the capital city of Sofia, with himself as royal engine driver, they also refused to get out of bed on arrival in the early morning, even when they were informed that hundreds of schoolchildren were outside the railway station with flowers of greeting and a brass band.

Many in the crowd tried to peer into their bedroom but fortunately a lesson in bizarre biology was avoided because the blinds were pulled firmly down. The king contemptuously ordered a British–African servant in his retinue to appear and wave and speak to the crowd. In a country noted for its racism, this was a deliberate insult, but the insult backfired; the children had never seen a 'Negro' before, and jumped up and down in excitement at the sight. As King Boris's chief of protocol, Stoyan Petrov-Tchomakov, reported in December 1965 in the *Monthly Bulgarian Review* published in Buenos Aires, 'They [the kids] were quick to seize the unique opportunity [to see] a live specimen of the African race.'

The king astonished his hosts by snapping pretty local girls with his Leica camera; in a sly reference to the nanny–baby relationship he had with Wallis, he responded, during a visit to the Imperial Palace, to a grumble from the king's four-year-old daughter that she had to go back to the nursery with the slyly significant words, 'And so, my dear, do I.' He didn't improve matters when he dubbed the queen's lady-in-waiting Helen Petrov-Tchomakov 'Petrol', the royal secretary Georghi Hanschief 'Handkerchief' and the king's close friend and aide-de-camp Alexei Bugharov 'Bugger off'. The Secret Intelligence Service used all three names as codes for these officials in the Second World War.

Wallis and the king were met at Vienna by a royal car especially transported from London. As always, they checked into their favourite Hotel Bristol. The American hostess and columnist Elsa Maxwell was in the lobby when they walked in, followed by an immense number of suitcases and trunks. Miss Maxwell noticed Wallis's fixed, purposeful stare and hard, determined manner.

On the morning of 9 September, Wallis and the king visited the Vienna Fair, lingering at the British-Indian Pavilion. They went on to visit President Miklas and Chancellor von Schuschnigg. The political situation in Austria was exceedingly volatile. In June Hitler and Schuschnigg had signed alliance agreements with guaranteed mutual political association, and Italy had concurred with the arrangement. This caused widespread discontent among the Jews and socialists in the country, and on 10 September, the second day of Wallis's and the king's visit, there was a riot in which parts of Vienna were set on fire by militant rebels. Previously the king could always use the excuse that he was in league with Schuschnigg in order to avoid an alliance between the Austrians, the Italians and Hitler. But now he was lending his personal support to a government that was totally committed to Hitler. At the same time he seemed to find nothing untoward in the fact that he and Wallis visited one of the most prominent figures in the Jewish financial community, Baron Eugene Rothschild, and his American wife, Kitty, at their country house, Schloss Enzesfeld. To increase the irony, that night he and Wallis attended a full-scale performance of Wagner's masterpiece, *Götterdämmerung*, which was Hitler's favourite opera; they were accompanied by the composer's daughter, the pro-Hitler Winifred Wagner. The king also hunted chamois, visited Heinrich Neumann (the Jewish doctor who had refused to attend Hitler) for the king's ear trouble, which had been exacerbated by sea bathing, and appeared at a public Turkish bath with an embarrassed David Storrier of Scotland Yard and six leading Vienna detectives; all eight men disported themselves in the nude, with guns, before the astonished patrons.

Wallis and the king returned to the opera house to see Wagner's *Flying Dutchman*; on this occasion the king spent most of the performance outside the royal box smoking impatiently. He was more comfortable dining at the famous restaurant the Three Hussars, revisiting the beloved Rotter Bar and enjoying the waltzes at the Bristol.

After a week-long stay, the couple took a train to Zurich, from where the king flew to London and Wallis and the rest of the party continued on the express. George Weller, the *New York Times* correspondent in Athens, wrote on 6 September, 'In Edward's visits [in the Mediterranean] four nations envisaged a new strong British policy. They asked themselves whether a synthesis of Edward's sincerity and Hitler's zeal might not be a better protection than the League of Nations. They might not be greatly averse to being dominated by the British and Germans.' Weller had put his finger correctly on the main purpose of the voyage of the *Nahlin*.

Back in London, Wallis and Ernest finally parted company. Ernest moved to his club, and Wallis took a room at Claridge's Hotel. She had a meeting with her solicitor, Theodore Goddard, who had already begun divorce proceedings. Goddard informed her that he had decided not to have the case heard in London because the calendar was so filled that it might be a year before the divorce could be granted. Instead, he had settled on Ipswich in Suffolk. Wallis would be represented by the celebrated barrister Norman Birkett, KC.

The king invited Wallis and Herman and Katherine Rogers, who had been with them on one leg of the *Nahlin* cruise, to stay with him at Balmoral. Among the other guests were the Duke and

Duchess of Kent, Lord and Lady Mountbatten, the Duke and Duchess of Marlborough and the Duke and Duchess of Sutherland. Cancelling a scheduled opening of the infirmary at Aberdeen Hospital, the king disappeared from the castle to drive to Aberdeen station to pick up Wallis and the Rogerses. The train was late; despite his disguise of enormous motoring goggles, everyone recognized the monarch except a policeman who reprimanded him for leaving his car in the 'No Parking' zone. Wallis had never been to Balmoral before.

Wallis seemed to rejoice in the fact that she occupied rooms that had originally been used by Queen Victoria, Queen Alexandra and Queen Mary. The incongruity evidently amused her as she issued forth in shorts each morning with the king and began shopping in the local village of Crathie.

She returned in a good mood to London while the king held his first Privy Council outside London at Balmoral. At the same time plans were well advanced for his coronation, which was to take place on 12 May 1937. Hotels were completely booked along the six-mile parade route. Department stores planned hundreds of thousands of pounds' worth of decorations. Lloyd's of London was busy with the contingency of a postponement, guaranteeing various firms against risk. It was announced that Westminster Abbey would be closed to the public from 4 January to allow the Office of Works to prepare the ancient edifice for the ceremonies. The abbey organ had already been taken apart for repairs.

At the beginning of October, Wallis sent congratulations to Sir Oswald Mosley and his new wife Diana, sister of the Hitler-fancier Unity Mitford, on the occasion of their wedding in Dr Goebbels's house in Berlin, with Hitler in attendance. After a brief stay at Claridges Wallis moved into a Regency house, 16 Cumberland Terrace, which was Crown property; it was sub-leased from the tenant, who was going on a world cruise. Enormous and sumptuously furnished, the Nash-designed house had a huge upstairs drawing room overlooking Regent's Park that Wallis filled from end to end with her favourite flowers. She began to refurbish rooms with the help of Lady Mendl. Simultaneously, Neville Chamberlain had arranged to lease his home in Eaton Square to Ribbentrop.

As Wallis moved into Cumberland Terrace on 7 October, under the closest surveillance by the Secret Intelligence Service, she looked up at the roof, where stood figures representing Love, Justice, Wisdom and Victory. Associated Press announced that, up to that date, the king had given £200,000 worth of jewels to Wallis and that £10,000 worth of silver fox furs had been imported by a British company from Julius Greene of New York as his gift to the royal mistress. On the 11th, the king officially took up residence for the first time at Buckingham Palace.

The king called in the proprietors of the London newspapers and succeeded in obtaining a promise that Wallis's imminent divorce hearing at Ipswich would be treated with the utmost discretion in the press. However, the American press was unrestricted, and by the second week of October, every hotel in the Suffolk town was crammed with reporters from the major American cities. As a result, representatives of European newspapers had to find rooms in nearby villages.

During her brief stay at Cumberland Terrace before moving to Suffolk, Wallis was under royal protection. On 20 October, she went to her hairdresser, Antoine, in Dover Street. Inspector Storrier had placed her brand-new Buick, the exact copy of the monarch's that had been ordered in January, behind Cumberland Terrace; but this feeble attempt to hide her departure from the house failed, and crowds were waiting when she emerged. She was followed by car and bicycle to the salon, and when she ran, looking flushed and uncomfortable, into the car to make the journey to her bank, the inspector had to clear the pavement for her. That night, Wallis moved to a cottage at Felixstowe, near Ipswich, an uninspiring place overlooking a pebble-strewn beach and a slate-grey sea. The king disappeared from a shooting party at Sandringham to make her welcome, leaving his brother-in-law, the Earl of Harewood, and Sir Samuel Hoare to continue without him. Wallis's companions were her old friends George and Kitty Hunter, whom she had known from her earliest days in London and whose Mayfair flat she and the king had used for romantic evenings. Wallis was under the constant guard of David Storrier. The king visited her one more time during that difficult week of waiting.[6]

On the 23rd, the king went to London to have dinner with his mother at Marlborough House. He found her quietly distraught at the prospect of his marriage to Wallis should the divorce from Ernest Simpson go through. It proved impossible to sway her in the matter. The hearing in Ipswich was set for Saturday the 24th. Wallis had a sleepless night on the Friday. She paced the floor of her room at Felixstowe, tortured by many thoughts. She was not happy about losing Ernest; nor was she happy at the prospect of being forced to become queen. She would have been content to have retained the role of royal mistress, like Mrs Fitzherbert in the reign of King George IV or Mrs Keppel in the reign of King Edward VII. In her reckless pursuit of power, position and money, in her cool, dominating exercise of power, she had got out of her depth. Where was this madness that she had engineered going to lead her?

To prolong Wallis's agony, her case was postponed until Tuesday 27 October. The judge had too full a calendar of minor malfeasances, including poaching rabbits, to deal with her all-important matter, and, suffering from a bad cough and cold and the worst of tempers, Mr Justice Hawke was in no mood to take her case out of the natural sequence. While Wallis went through the torments of the damned at Felixstowe, the Ipswich bars overflowed with heavy-drinking reporters who were becoming increasingly irritable and frustrated. At last, the time arrived: 2.15 on 27 October 1936. Mr Justice Hawke was ushered in by two military trumpeters playing a fanfare on their silver instruments. Ironically, the musicians were from the band of the Coldstream Guards, in which Ernest Simpson had served in the First World War. A uniformed marshal in black and scarlet announced the judge, bewigged, coughing and blowing his nose into an outsize handkerchief. Wallis, looking extremely pale and exhausted in a small navy blue felt hat and double-breasted coat and skirt of matching blue, made her way from the Buick through the crowd to the witness stand. She was accompanied by Norman Birkett, in his famous shabby wig and enormous horn-rimmed glasses, and his second, the chubby, red-faced Walter Frampton. Ernest was not present, nor was he represented by counsel; his solicitor, North Lewis, was, however, present.

Hawke, looking grim, his mouth a hard, resistant line in his red and heavily jowled face, spoke in a muffled voice for the next few minutes through his linen handkerchief and a blizzard of coughs and sneezes. This was scarcely helpful to Wallis's already frazzled nerves. She stood with her right blue kid glove already removed to take the oath. Her American accent struck an incongruous note in the drab British court room. Although her hands were kept firmly from trembling by her will, she betrayed her tension in a characteristic gesture, flicking her tongue around her mouth.

Under oath, questioned by her counsel, she told of her happy marriage with Ernest until the autumn of 1934, when he began to go away for weekends. She described an episode that took place on Christmas Day 1934, in which she found a note on her dressing table in a woman's handwriting. She didn't say what was in it, and it was handed to the judge. It was an almost certainly manufactured two-page letter from Mary Raffray thanking Ernest for a gift of roses. Wallis said it had caused her 'considerable distress'.

She went on to say that at Easter of the present year she had found a letter on identical blue stationery intended for her husband. She improbably asserted that Mary Raffray had written both this love note to Ernest and a simple letter to Wallis from the south of France, and had 'accidentally' put them into the wrong envelopes.

Two waiters who had worked at the Hôtel de Paris in Bray stated that on 22 and 23 July 1936 they had served breakfast in bed to Ernest and a woman. She was Mary Raffray. Norman Birkett stood and asked the judge for a decree nisi. Hawke, visibly in a bad temper, had interrupted Wallis's testimony several times for no particular reason except his obvious distaste for her. He did not respond immediately to Birkett's request. Wallis cast the barrister an anxious glance.

'I assume what your Lordship has in mind—' said Birkett.

'What is it I have in mind?' the judge snapped.

'That this is ordinary hotel evidence,' Birkett said. 'But the lady's name has been divulged in the petition to My Lord, and notice was served on her.'

The judge then said, 'I suppose I must come to the conclusion that there was adultery in this case. Very well, decree nisi.' It would be six months more before there was a decree absolute.

Wallis, surrounded by police who had been sent on royal

instructions from Scotland Yard to shield her from the photographers, walked nervously and quickly down the stairs and into her car. The ordeal had taken less than nineteen minutes. She hadn't even had to face an audience in the public gallery. The king had had it cleared. He had not instructed the newspaper owners in vain. There was scarcely a mention of the granting of the divorce decree in the British press. The king, who was at Buckingham Palace that night, called Wallis to congratulate her.[7]

The king presented a pleased Wallis with an engagement ring. She had heard of the fabled Mogul emerald, one of the finest stones of its kind, whose provenance went back to the ancient rulers of India. She had to have it, and the king had contacted the great jeweller Jacques Cartier in Paris to obtain it for her. Cartier had undertaken a worldwide search, which led him and his spies to Baghdad. There, a syndicate was prepared to sell the stone for a substantial price. It was brought to London by courier after being exquisitely set by the Cartier specialists. According to one version of the story then in circulation, the king declared that the price was too high and that he would pay only half of it; whereupon Cartier withdrew the emerald, cut it in half, and presented the smaller stone to the monarch.

Wallis returned to Cumberland Terrace, which had been prepared for her by her cook and housemaid. The removal firm Carter Patterson had brought over much of her furniture from Bryanston Court, including many of her things from China; in addition, the king had sent over many royal possessions including sumptuous furnishings, mirrors, bed linen, china and silver. That night Wallis dined with the king at her home. He told her of a very unsettling incident that had taken place. A few days before the divorce, Prime Minister Baldwin had turned up at Fort Belvedere in his tiny black car and, after much meaningless talk, had got down to business and asked the monarch to persuade Wallis to abandon the proceedings. Wallis was appalled. Not only did she not intend to marry the king, but she was, for all her boldness, not prepared for a full-scale confrontation and conflict with the prime minister of England.

Little did she foresee the storm that lay immediately ahead.

NOTES

1 Mrs Cartwright would soon meet and marry the Nazi collaborator Frederick G. McEvoy, the closest friend of the film star Errol Flynn. Mrs Cartwright was known to the US State Department for her Nazi sympathies.

2 The contents of the report have been supplied by Kirk Hollingsworth, nephew of Mary Raffray. The actual document has apparently disappeared.

3 The Italian submarines were disguised as Spanish.

4 It is possible that Bannigan was backed by the IRA, which was at that time under communist control.

5 Stories that he was reluctant to visit Turkey and was forced to do so by Sir Percy Loraine, British ambassador to Ankara, cannot be substantiated by documentation.

6 Simultaneously, an anonymous representative of Prime Minister Stanley Baldwin engaged the services of a Washington, DC, lawyer, Raymond Neudecker, to investigate the records of Wallis's divorce from Win Spencer in 1927. Evidently the prime minister, who was already opposed to any thought of the king's marrying Wallis, was determined to find some evidence of iregularities in the 1927 hearings. However Aubrey Weaver, her lawyer of the time at Front Royal, succeeded in having Judge Peck Alexander of Warrenton seal the files on the case. It is possible that Wallis prearranged this. The files remained inaccessible until the present author obtained them in 1986.

7 In a bizarre coincidence, on exactly the same day Win Spencer was divorced by his second wife, Miriam, in San Diego, California. She charged him with cruelty, desertion, drunkenness and breaking up the furniture in their home.

10

ABDICATION

Even now, Wallis continued to sleep with Guy Trundle. It was one thing to cuckold a prince; it was quite another to cuckold a king.

On 13 June 1938, Sir Edward Peacock told US ambassador Joseph P. Kennedy that Wallis was sleeping with a 'young man' throughout the reign and that this 'embittered the Cabinet more than ever'. Kennedy recorded this in his diary that night.

Wallis was in the Distinguished Strangers' Gallery to see the king open his first parliament. The traditional speech from the throne reviewed events and legislation during the past session. He referred to the forthcoming coronation, the Imperial Conference, the treaty of alliance with Egypt, the International Conference at Montreux, the tragic events in Spain, the grave concern caused by hostilities between Japan and China, the bilateral naval agreements between England and Germany, and the strengthening of the defence forces. He also mentioned the continued growth of trade, employment problems, the Physical Training and Recreation Act, progress in slum clearance, improved conditions of work in factories, defence loans and the subsidies to shipping. He announced that he would proceed immediately to India after the coronation ceremonies and would repeat the lavish Delhi Durbar in which his parents had been proclaimed Emperor and Empress of India in 1911. This was clearly a symbolic revelation of his continuing concern with Empire; it tacitly reaffirmed the views of enlightened commentators that his main concern in appeasing Mussolini and Hitler was to keep open the traditional trade routes to the east. Count Grandi recalled in 1986:

> At a ceremony connected with the opening of parliament, I stood talking to the king and to the Archbishop of Canterbury. As I walked in, I heard people applauding me. The archbishop said to me, 'You do realize, sir, the applause is for your person and not for the country you represent.'
>
> To which I replied, 'But I am not a person, I am my country and its flag.'
>
> To which the king then responded, 'Well said! Well said!'

This publicly stated expression of support for Mussolini was discreetly left unmentioned by the ever loyal British press. Grandi continues, 'The Prince of Wales reassured me, "There will never be a war between Italy and England."'

An ominous rainstorm had swept away all plans for the procession of the monarch from Buckingham Palace to parliament and back again. The king celebrated the occasion by sending a four-foot-high basket of flowers to Wallis, composed of her beloved white chrysanthemums, pink and red roses and sprays of autumn leaves. It arrived in the van of a company granted the royal warrant and therefore displaying the lion and unicorn, and was followed an hour later by an identical van with a supply of liquor and non-alcoholic drinks. By this stage the king was probably beyond caring whether anybody noticed or photographed these vehicles or not.

He was almost certainly equally indifferent to the fact that people might notice that the house Wallis occupied was being furnished bit by bit with silver, pictures, mirrors and even china from Buckingham Palace and Fort Belvedere. It is questionable whether the king had the right to make presents of these family heirlooms to Wallis or anyone else. Later, many of these items would be removed to his and Wallis's homes in France. Simultaneously, records show that he had paid jewellers over £100,000 of his savings from the Duchy of Cornwall to supply Wallis with her beloved gems. There were those who felt that this extravagance was in direct contradiction of his apparent concern for the sufferings of the British working class in the depths of the Depression.

On 6 November, Wallis caused a ripple in the audience at

Covent Garden when, in emeralds, black satin and green-and-gold brocade, she sat with the Channons, Lady Diana Cooper and Sir Victor Warrender, former vice chamberlain and Comptroller of King George V's household, in Emerald Cunard's box. She seemed unabashed by the attention. That week was saddened by the departure to Berlin of Prince Otto and Princess Ann-Mari von Bismarck; the farewell parties went on and on. Hitler, probably influenced by the fact that Bismarck was still under constant surveillance by the Secret Intelligence Service and Sir Robert Vansittart, had decided to replace the prince with Ribbentrop.

Aunt Bessie arrived in November to give Wallis moral support. On the 12th, the king went to Portland harbour to inspect the Home Fleet from the decks of the flagship *Nelson*. Floods plunged the royal train into two feet of water, and the driver at the wheel of the royal Buick could barely plough through the drenched, badly drained streets of the dock town. Rain poured down all afternoon as the king boarded the aircraft carrier *Courageous* and made the inspections, soaked to the skin, refusing both raincoat and umbrella. On the night of the 13th, he returned to Fort Belvedere in a good mood. He embraced Aunt Bessie and Wallis, only to be called away by a couriered message from Buckingham Palace; he did not disclose its contents to Wallis until the following afternoon. The note was from Alexander Hardinge, who issued a dire warning. He said that there was only a matter of days before the press would break its promise of silence on the subject of Wallis. He went on to state that Baldwin and the cabinet were meeting that day to discuss the situation, and that they might resign. It would be difficult for the king to form another government; the only remaining alternative would be a dissolution of parliament and a general election, resulting in considerable damage to the Crown. It would be best, to avoid this circumstance, if Wallis were asked to go abroad.

The Hardinges had been plotting this manoeuvre from the very beginning. The king responded with anger. When Wallis said she would be happy to leave the country, he told her she would do no such thing and said that nothing would stop him from marrying her. She begged him to change his mind. He would not. He said to her that if the government would not approve the marriage, he would be ready to leave the throne. She began to cry. She told him it was madness to think along those lines. He was adamant. He would immediately consult Sir Samuel Hoare and Duff Cooper, and he would summon the prime minister. Wallis agreed to stay. It was a decision she lived to regret.

On 16 November, the king left for a tour of the south Wales coalfields, one of the grimmest areas of the British Isles, where severe unemployment and poverty had existed for many years. Welcomed wherever he went, possessed of a burning concern to improve the local conditions, he greatly upset his cabinet by making the public statement, 'Something should be done.' Not only were kings discouraged from doing such things as dabbling in international politics and marrying twice-divorced women, they were not supposed to express to their ministers their opinions on social reform.

Nor were they supposed to take their mistresses on the royal train. In her 1971 memoir *Three-Cornered Heart* the wealthy American socialite Anne Fremantle recorded a conversation she had had with the Lord Lieutenant of Monmouthshire in which he had expressed his shock that Wallis was in bed with the king in the sleeping car. Later, she and her husband discussed the matter with the Archbishop of Canterbury, who told them that the act of illicit sexual intercourse on the royal train would preclude forever the possibility he would preside over the couple's marriage at Westminster Abbey or anywhere else. Beside this, the king's habit of knocking on the doors of out-of-work miners' cottages with the words 'I am the king; may I come in?' seemed only mildly shocking.

On the third day of the tour, Wallis left the train and hastened back to London by car. She had been asked to a lunch meeting with the right-wing Esmond Harmsworth, son of the newspaper tycoon Lord Rothermere, who would soon be her neighbour in the south of France, at Claridges.

He suggested to Wallis that she should abandon any idea of being queen; she reassured him that no such thought had ever been on her mind. He recommended to her the idea of a morganatic marriage, which would keep her in England without being constantly exposed to scandalous comment. Her presence in the UK would, of course, be an advantage from the Nazi point of view. There had been precedents for this in British history. Should such

Wallis in 1915, aged nineteen.
She had more beaux than any other girl in Baltimore.

Above: Wallis with her bridesmaids and maid of honour for her marriage to Win Spencer in November 1916.

Left: Lieutenant Earl Winfield Spencer, Wallis's first husband. Their divorce was granted in 1927.

Opposite: Wallis Simpson dressed for her presentation at court in June 1931, holding the obligatory Prince of Wales feathers.

Top: Ernest Simpson,
Wallis's second husband
from July 1928 to
May 1937.

Far left: Freda Dudley Ward:
she was told in 1934 that
her telephone calls to the
prince would no longer
be put through.

Left: Thelma Furness,
Edward's lover from 1928,
who introduced Wallis
to the prince.

Opposite:
The Prince of Wales and
Mrs Simpson in 1935.

Top: With Mrs Herman Rogers during their Adriatic cruise, 1936.
Above: At the Villa Lou Viei in December 1936,
with Lord Brownlow (left) and Mr and Mrs Herman Rogers.

Top: Cecil Beaton arriving in Tours for the wedding of Wallis and the Duke of Windsor. *Above*: Major Edward 'Fruity' Metcalfe and Lady Alexandra arrive in Tours for the wedding, June 1937.

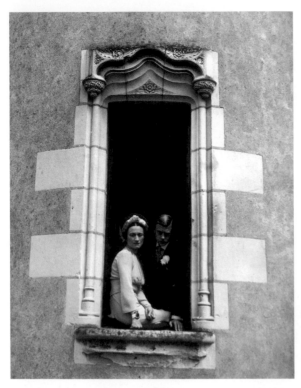

Left: The wedding day,
3 June 1937.
Photograph by
Cecil Beaton.

Below: Wedding picture
with 'Fruity' Metcalfe,
the best man, and
Herman Rogers.

an arrangement be made, Wallis would be entitled to be a duchess or to receive another title. However, she would not be permitted to be included in the Civil List in terms of her personal income; should she have heirs, they would not be entitled to any part of the royal inheritance. Nor could the children of the marriage inherit the throne.

Wallis was surprised and intrigued by the suggestion. She left the matter open at the end of lunch, giving no opinion but at the same time by no means rejecting the idea. That was as good as saying that she accepted it.

When the monarch returned from the Welsh mines for a party at the Channons', Wallis asked him whether he would accept the Harmsworth plan. He responded adversely, but in a subsequent discussion with Harmsworth he began to show some interest. However, when he summoned Baldwin to Buckingham Palace to discuss the matter, the prime minister made it clear that the obstacles to such an arrangement would be formidable, perhaps insurmountable. A morganatic marriage would have to go through very difficult channels. The cabinet would have to approve it; special legislation would have to be passed in the form of a parliamentary bill. And Baldwin, who presumably thought it impolitic to mention the fact, no doubt bore in mind the potential danger in such an idea emanating from a highly questionable political source. This danger was known in the inner circles in Whitehall, but judiciously never mentioned in print.

According to the diaries of Chips Channon, another incident occurred that week. The king called for the Dukes of Kent and Gloucester and told them that he was going to marry Wallis. The Duke of Kent was supposed to have exclaimed, 'What will she call herself?'

'What do you think, the Queen of England of course,' the king allegedly replied. And he added, 'Yes, and Empress of India, the whole bag of tricks.' His brothers were flabbergasted.

During the crisis, one of the few supportive figures upon whom the king and Wallis could rely was Walter Monckton, who continued as Attorney General to the Duchy of Cornwall, which associated him directly with an important source of the monarch's income. In view of the fact that the king was obsessed with money and terrified that he might lose substantial funds were he to abdicate, Monckton's support of him was crucial. Bespectacled, somewhat scholarly in appearance, Monckton had the look of a don who spent a lifetime in smoke-filled common rooms, but when his vivid, humorous and heartfelt smile illuminated his ascetic face he became another creature entirely. He was, above all, steadfast and loyal, a rare example of a humanist lawyer; a royalist to his fingertips, he was deeply concerned with the king's welfare and clearly refused to believe Vansittart's and Hardinge's suspicions of Wallis as a Nazi contact.

Day after day in the last week of November, the king summoned Monckton to Buckingham Palace, a procedure that involved an almost cloak-and-dagger series of movements. The king was determined that Monckton should not say anything that could be overheard by Hardinge, who was, he felt, spying constantly for Vansittart and whose offices adjoined Edward's Belgian Suite on the ground floor. Under instruction, Monckton had to park his car at the back of the palace and then take the Privy Purse entrance and ascend by lift to the top floor. From there, he had to walk across the vast building to the front and then take another lift which descended directly into the Belgian Suite. This subterfuge was useless, since members of the palace staff reported on Monckton's every movement to Hardinge, who one evening pointedly invited him to his office for a drink.

In his supposedly secret meetings with Monckton, the king made clear that nothing would shake him in his complete emotional, physical and mental involvement with Wallis. Monckton saw at once that any argument with his old friend was totally pointless. 'If they want someone exactly like my father, they can have the Duke of York,' the king said, hinting that he was fully prepared to abdicate in his brother's favour.

Monckton could not help but respect the king's extraordinary devotion, which went beyond his love of Empire and his desire to be in a position of power. Furthermore, Monckton had the greatest respect for Wallis. He knew that she had caused the king to stop his heavy drinking and had cut down his smoking. He also knew, as Winston Churchill did, that whereas the king had been miserable, neurotic and tortured before he met Wallis, he was now released from the bondage of his sexual and emotional problems and was a fulfilled and confident man. In the face of such a transformation, how could the monarch's gratitude be in any way limited by considerations of duty, honour and state?

Monckton issued sage advice. He suggested to the king that he should not take any drastic action until the decree absolute of the divorce in April 1937. The coronation would soon follow, when a decision could be made more prudently and from a position of greater power. However, the king replied that this was out of the question. He could not go through a major religious ceremony as head of Church and state and the Commonwealth while he had in mind that the oaths of office could soon be rendered invalid by a decision to proceed with his wedding in defiance of world opinion and the cabinet. As Lord Birkenhead wrote in his life of Monckton, '[The king] hated and was repelled by the thought of being crowned under false pretences.' Monckton was impressed that the king was not prepared to be dishonest, however much he might be disrupting protocol and even the royal course of duty.

On this basis, Monckton felt confident in seeking to achieve a compromise between 10 Downing Street and the Palace. His was no easy task. Nor was he helped by the fact that Queen Mary was tortured by the situation and appalled by the thought that her eldest son might abdicate, leaving the throne to her second son, Albert, who, shy, physically frail and completely lacking in public charisma, would be extremely uncomfortable in high office. She was not without humour in the circumstances. At one of her meetings with Baldwin, on 15 November, she said, 'This is a pretty kettle of fish!' The Duke and Duchess of York were extremely uneasy during the crisis. The duchess, still deeply dissatisfied with the very presence of Wallis on the scene, would have preferred to have her dislodged completely, but clearly that was an impossibility. She did not relish the idea of her frail husband experiencing the pressures and strains of being king. The Dukes of Kent and Gloucester were also tortured by the thought of a possible abdication.

Winston Churchill decided that Wallis had to go. ('That bitch!' he called her later.) In what he believed to be the best interests of the king and in an attempt to save the throne, he connived at a plot to drive Wallis out of England. In this he was, according to his later secretary, Sir John Colville, aided and abetted by Lord Beaverbrook, owner of the *Daily Express*. Beaverbrook, who had been en route to a proposed holiday in Arizona, returned abruptly at the royal request but then proceeded to double-cross his monarch in the most abject manner. Sir John Colville confirmed that Beaverbrook pretended to offer the king his support, which amounted to little more than the discretion of his newspaper in dealing with the crisis, while a member of his staff cooked up a bomb plot, supposedly emanating from Amsterdam, in which a paid Australian assassin would murder Wallis. The same man arranged for threatening letters to be sent to her saying that vitriol would be thrown in her face, a substance which would scar and blind her for life.

At the same time, Kenneth de Courcy, a friend of the king and Wallis, stepped in. He was honorary secretary of the Imperial Policy Group, a royalist entity founded in 1934 by Sir Reginald Mitchell-Bank that included among its members such figures as Lord Mansfield, Lord Bertie of Thame, Alan Lennox Boyd, the Earl of Glasgow, Sir Charles Petrie and Lord Phillimore. In those years the IPG had sought at every level of government to convince the governments of France, Italy, Austria and Spain that, despite official pronouncements, Britain's actual if secret foreign policy was to keep out of all European conflicts in order to give a free hand to Hitler and Mussolini against the Soviet Union. Needless to say, this rash disclosure ensured a more binding relationship between de Courcy and the king and Wallis, while greatly irritating both Vansittart and Hardinge. De Courcy was close to George and Kitty Hunter, those friends of Wallis when she had first come to London. The Hunters got wind (probably from information supplied by Sir Robert Vansittart) of the proposed assassination plot against Wallis. De Courcy remembered in 1987 that he brought word of the plot to Aunt Bessie at Cumberland Terrace. The frightened Bessie burst into tears. 'She called the king, who was at Fort Belvedere; he told her not to worry. But Wallis was utterly terrified when she received the news.'

One night, Wallis screamed, having been awakened suddenly by the sound of breaking glass. Somebody employed by Beaverbrook had tossed a brick through the windows of the house next door.

From then on, she spent most of her time in a state of terror between Claridges and Fort Belvedere, and Scotland Yard was instructed by the king to double her protection.

By 29 November, Wallis was on the verge of a nervous breakdown. Even Aunt Bessie's presence could not soothe her jangled nerves. When friends, headed by Sibyl Colefax, came to see her, she was on the edge of tears. At last she realized that in her reckless ambition she might well have damaged her health. The king burst into hysterical rages, condemning her enemies and protesting his undying love of her. The London sunset was a portentous blazing red. Wallis began to think seriously about leaving England. But she was too ill at Fort Belvedere to consider doing anything for the time being. She mentioned possibly returning to the United States; the king said he would follow her on the next ship. On the 30th she wrote to her friend Foxy Gwynne that her heart had been acting up and she wasn't having any callers. She would remove herself and only return when 'that damned crown has been firmly placed'.

On 1 December, the Right Reverend A. W. F. Blunt, Bishop of Bradford, made a speech at the annual diocesan conference. He invoked the grace of God to inspire the king to do his duty faithfully. He expressed the hope that the king was aware of his need of God's grace; then he added, 'Some of us wish he gave more positive signs of such awareness.' He criticized the statement by the Bishop of Birmingham that the coronation should be attended by a wide range of clergymen. He suggested that in the present situation the religious significance of the coronation ceremony would literally be endangered. The floodgates were opened to adverse comment in newspapers throughout the nation. Despite the king's supposed control of the press, a number of editorials sternly reminded him of the sacred trust of his high duty. It was clear that he had not succeeded in persuading the newspaper owners to follow his line of thought; they were too mindful of their readers' Christian sentiments and concern with moral values.

Baldwin even went to the extent of failing to send the king the minutes of the cabinet meetings at which the crisis was discussed. When the king opened the red dispatch box, all he could find was an obscure document about arms to Spain. However, he had a spy in the cabinet, who informed him that Baldwin had totally written off the morganatic marriage proposal at the last cabinet meeting without even attempting to present it to parliament. The prime minister had forced through the decision that either the government must accept Wallis as queen or the king must abdicate. It was following this meeting that a full-scale constitutional crisis broke.

On the evening of 3 December, the Duke and Duchess of York arrived at Fort Belvedere for a most urgent discussion on what would happen if the king were to abdicate within twenty-four hours. That same night Baldwin met the king, who drove to Buckingham Palace for a stormy encounter in which the monarch made clear that he would not budge an inch. The next day, the High Commissioners for Canada, Australia and South Africa put enormous pressure on the king. Headed by the Australian high commissioner, who represented the strict Roman Catholic prime minister, Joe Lyons, they made it clear that the dominions would never accept Wallis as queen or even as morganatic wife. She herself longed to withdraw; she hated the rejection. Even Canadian High Commissioner Vincent Massey, whose brother, the actor Raymond Massey, was an old poker-playing friend of Wallis's and the king's, was obliged to convey the grimmest warnings to the Palace. In each of the Commonwealth countries the newspapers were blunt in their outright assault upon the issue. This was grievously distressing to Wallis and to the king, who had been perfectly happy to have Baldwin throw open the issue to the Empire. It was clear that, hour by hour, his position was becoming increasingly untenable, and by 3 December all the costly and elaborate preparations for the coronation came to a standstill.

The Duke of York was overcome by the horror of what was to come. He detested the idea of being king as much as his older brother had, and began talking loosely about abdicating in advance and (passing over his dull brother, the Duke of Gloucester) throwing open to plebiscite the idea of the egregious Duke of Kent as successor – still the wild card in the royal pack. Kent, endlessly flying to Munich to maintain his Nazi connections through his brother-in-law Count Toerring, was mooted for years for all kinds of thrones – Romania, Greece, Hungary, Poland – the list was long.

Like it or not, and afraid of the effect on his health and even his reason, York had to face a ghastly future of ritual and responsibility. Returning from a trip to Scotland by train on 3 December, he saw at the railway station newspaper placards glaringly announcing the dreaded words, 'THE KING'S MARRIAGE'. He drove straight to his mother Queen Mary in a state of nerves and she did her best to remind him sternly of his necessary future. He left her in near-suicidal despair. At another meeting six days later, he broke down, knelt before her and sobbed in her lap like a child.

There was a flurry on the postage stamp market as thousands of people rushed to buy complete sets of the commemorative issue in the event that the stamps should be rendered obsolete within the week and thus increase considerably in value. Simultaneously, the king's friends in Berlin supported him once again. On Hitler's express instructions Dr Goebbels issued a communiqué forbidding any German newspaper or radio station even to mention the constitutional crisis. Hitler was deeply disturbed by the situation: he was counting upon the king to maintain a special relationship with Germany in the future. Similarly Mussolini was most disappointed, and Count Grandi in London conveyed that disappointment to the monarch. When these positions of the newly formed Axis powers appeared in the American press, it was of no help to the king's cause in Whitehall.

Day and night throughout the crisis, meetings were held by the Imperial Policy Group. Kenneth de Courcy recalled the extreme tension among the members of the group as they tried to find some way through the mesh of problems involved. A preliminary meeting of interested and influential peers and members of Parliament was held in the London house of de Courcy's mother, and subsequent meetings were held at de Courcy's office in Old Queen Street. The group sent representations to the Bishop of London, to Lord Salisbury and to Walter Monckton in an effort to ameliorate the situation. The purpose was clear: the group wanted to force the king to call upon the government to resign or, at the very least, to pressure it into a position from which it would have to resign. The king would then send for Winston Churchill – who himself may have been unaware of these plans – to form a new government; the IPG was convinced there were enough individuals in both the House of Commons and the House of Lords to achieve its purpose.

De Courcy told me he believed that Churchill would have swept into power with an overwhelming majority. He would immediately have achieved massive public support and would have put Britain on a much firmer footing vis-à-vis Germany and Mussolini.

However, the IPG was doomed to failure. Monckton proved obstructionist. A major problem was that Thomas Dugdale, MP, informed de Courcy and another member, Lord Mansfield, that there was a flaw in Wallis's divorce case which might make the decree absolute impossible; he also informed his visitors that the Secret Intelligence Service had a case against Wallis which, if they could see the file, would entirely change their attitude: a direct reference to the China dossier, Grégoire and Wallis's Italian and German links. Should the SIS suspect that Wallis was a Nazi contact, they must prepare to deliver this fatal trump card at the right moment; the group's entire case for the royal marriage and the accession of Winston Churchill to the premiership would collapse.

Faced with this revelation, de Courcy and the Imperial Policy Group understandably felt weakened in their resolve. Furthermore, Monckton failed to convey their purpose to the king. Either he felt that they were too maverick and unreliable or he was by now sensing that the monarch was quite ready – or would even prefer – to depart from his sacred office; or he may have got wind of the plot against Wallis and feared that if Churchill did assume the premiership she would have no chance of becoming either queen or morganatic wife.

Wallis and the king's meetings at the time were gloomy and foreboding. *The Times*, under the editorship of Geoffrey Dawson, was bitterly assailing her. One evening, as the couple walked around the flagstone path at Fort Belvedere and a damp English fog crawled up from Virginia Water, the king explained to her that there was no middle way: it was either abdication or permanent separation. Wallis was beyond exhaustion, beyond being able to endure any more. She began to make arrangements to leave the country, and in London her staff was under instruction to pack up her belongings.

Wallis now wished she had left when the first inklings of disaster reached her. On Saturday, 3 December, she made arrangements to move to Herman and Katherine Rogers's villa at Cannes; by long-distance telephone they had agreed, as so often before, to provide her with safety and refuge. The king told her that he would supply her with a companion and bodyguard for the journey – the slight, subdued (and very rich) Peregrine ('Perry'), Fourth Baron Brownlow. He was a dear, reliable, trusted friend. The royal chauffeur, George Ladbroke, would drive them to Newhaven, where they would embark for Dieppe. Inspector Storrier of Scotland Yard was on leave, so Inspector Evans would be her official protector. Wondering whether she would be killed en route, Wallis hastily increased her jewellery insurance and drew up a will in her bedroom at Fort Belvedere, leaving most of her possessions to Aunt Bessie, her two devoted maids and a few personal friends. Her solicitor, George Allen, assisted her with the document, which was drawn up on blue Fort Belvedere stationery. In the late afternoon the king, along with Winston Churchill, Walter Monckton and others, was at the Fort finishing work on the abdication broadcast. Wallis left so hurriedly that there was barely time to say goodbye to the king (who gave her a ladybird bracelet charm with the message 'Fly Away Home'), Aunt Bessie and her personal staff. To her great distress, she had to leave behind her dog, Slipper. In anguish, white with tension, she kissed the king and held him close. He told her she must wait for him no matter how long it would be. He would never give her up.

Her car moved out into the fog. Passage had been booked for her and Brownlow under the names of 'Mr and Mrs Harris'. In the wake of Wallis's departure for the Channel ferry, the king drove to Buckingham Palace to meet Baldwin. He told him about the broadcast and placed the text in his hands. Meanwhile, Wallis refused to slow down her departure, despite the increasing fog. Wrapped in sable against the cold, she sat grimly staring into the night. The ferry left at 10 p.m. She knew there would be no sleep that night. During the journey she urged Lord Brownlow to find a way to make the king forget the marriage completely, end the crisis and retain his throne. She had in mind returning at some stage after the coronation to take up the position of royal mistress.

The fog continued during the Channel crossing and into France. Wallis and Brownlow checked into the Hôtel de la Poste in Blois at 11 a.m. on 4 December. She took a room for a few hours and lay down on the bed. According to Lord Brownlow, Wallis felt a pang of loneliness and asked him to lie in the second bed in her room to keep her company. She cried, he recalled, with 'primeval' pain. He took her hand gently but the tears would not stop.

On the 5th, to avoid the reporters who had got wind of her movements and pursued her from the coast, Wallis was forced to abandon a plan to go to Paris to see Lady Mendl because it was clear that she would be intercepted by newspaper men. She was still terrified of assassination. Ladbroke took a circuitous route south, to make sure that there was no danger. They travelled through Evreux in Normandy. At the old coaching inn in that town, the Hôtellerie du Grand-Cerf, she asked Brownlow to put through a telephone call to Fort Belvedere. She had made an arrangement with the king to use code names in case she was overheard. After a long wait, Brownlow succeeded in getting through. Wallis could barely hear the king's voice through a blizzard of static. She said, 'On no account is Mr James to step down.' In other words, the king must not abdicate. She went on, 'You must get advice. You must bring in your old friends. See Duff Cooper; talk to Lord Derby; talk to the Aga Khan [all these names in code]. Do nothing rash. I will go to South America or some-where.' It was so difficult for the king to hear her that she was forced to scream the words. When she left the hotel, she was horrified to find she had left her notes for the conversation in the telephone booth. Brownlow warned her that if she returned to retrieve them she would be recognized. It was a miracle that she had not already been identified. So, in a mood of great distress, she decided to leave the notes behind. A considerate manager locked them up in his office safe, apparently not even yielding to the temptation to read them. The following year they were retrieved for her by Harold Nicolson.

Back in England, the increasingly discredited Sir Oswald Mosley scarcely helped the king's cause by stating that he was entirely on his side and that the abdication issue should be submitted to the people for a referendum. This announcement only lent strength to Baldwin and to Sir Robert Vansittart and Alexander Hardinge.

On 5 December, Winston Churchill sent a memorandum to the king from his home, 11 Morpeth Mansions, advising him not to leave the country under any circumstances and that no final decision should be made until after Christmas, probably February or March. That same day the Archbishop of Canterbury urged 'silence and caution' in the matter of the crisis until the king's decision was made public.

By now, according to a diary kept by Mrs Thomas Dugdale, wife of Baldwin's parliamentary undersecretary, the king 'was in a very nervous condition, threatening to do some violence to himself'. Geoffrey Dawson's *Times* was thundering more loudly than ever. The prime minister, accompanied by Dugdale, had driven down that day through the fog to Fort Belvedere to confer with the king yet again.

That same day Baldwin held a special cabinet meeting at 10 Downing Street. Crowds stood in the driving rain as the ministers got out of their cars. Sir Samuel Hoare came first; he was followed by Chancellor of the Exchequer Neville Chamberlain, Sir Kingsley Wood, Duff Cooper and Anthony Eden, among others. As they left the building hecklers greeted them, shouting, 'Edward's right. Baldwin's wrong!'

Hundreds more swarmed outside the gates of Buckingham Palace, yelling: 'We want Edward!' A group appeared at the Piccadilly house of the Duke and Duchess of York, chanting in unison, 'We want Eddie and we want his Missus!' A band of women marched from Marble Arch to the palace with huge banners upon which, in red and blue letters, was the slogan: 'After South Wales you cannot let him down. Come to the Palace and cheer him. Let the King know we are with him.' Later in the afternoon the crowd outside the palace began singing, 'For he's a jolly good fellow!' Two hundred stood at the corner of Whitehall and Downing Street after sunset, screaming, 'We want our king!' They were rapidly broken up by the police. Meanwhile, Lord Rothermere's papers had on their front pages the enormous headline in black letters, 'God Save the King!' The world was breathless; the American ironist H. L. Mencken called it 'the greatest news story since the Resurrection'.

Also on 5 December, Winston Churchill wrote to Neville Chamberlain, chancellor of the exchequer, describing his meeting with the king at dinner at Buckingham Palace the night before. He said that the monarch began the meal in a lighthearted mood but soon succumbed to depression and had two prolonged mental blackouts during which he completely lost the thread of the conversation and was visibly on the edge of a breakdown.

Years later, Sir Edward Peacock told Ambassador Kennedy of a meeting the next day between Prime Minister Baldwin and the King at Fort Belvedere. Baldwin described the meeting to the essayist and biographer Harold Nicolson as tearful and sentimental, with both men dissolving, like Alice in Wonderland, into a puddle of tears. In Peacock's version, Baldwin pointed out that Wallis wasn't 'the type to be queen', whereupon the monarch snapped back at him, 'So I can have her as mistress but not as wife. That's fine hypocrisy!' Baldwin had had enough. He shouted, in a direct reference to the China dossier, 'If a king wants to sleep with a whore that's his private business. But the Empire is concerned if he now makes her queen.'

The king's reaction to this exchange was to set up even more investments for Wallis in America. He told Peacock he didn't want her to 'wind up like Lady Hamilton', the mistress of Lord Horatio Nelson, who had died in poverty. When he tried to give Wallis a freehold in certain royal properties, including the New Gallery Cinema in Regent Street, the Criterion Restaurant, His Majesty's Theatre and the Regent Palace and Strand Palace Hotels, Peacock made clear that these were not to be bartered or given away, and that there was no possibility of her acquisiton of them being approved by the Commons or the Lords. Furious, the king gave up.

The other members of the royal family remained in seclusion, not leaving their separate houses. The king consistently deferred meeting with his anxious brother the Duke of York, who realized that huge responsibilities lay just a step away. Sleepless, wretched, the king had no energy to see anyone except his prime minister.

Meanwhile, Wallis continued her journey south through France. The weather was appalling, a driving wind blowing a mixture of snow and sleet against the windscreen of the Buick. The party breakfasted at the Hôtel de Paris in the town of Moulins. As the group continued, through increasingly hazardous driving conditions, the car became filled with the strong smell of Scotch whisky. Lord Brownlow, who had thrust a small glass hip-flask into his overcoat pocket, had accidentally shattered the bottle and the whisky had drenched him. When he opened the window to release the smell, the snow blew in and he had to close it again.

Wallis and her companions continued to the grim old city of Lyons where the press caught up with the car, alerted by a pedestrian of whom Brownlow had rashly asked the way. They were chased relentlessly through the city, the pursuing vehicles emitting a deafening sound of klaxons, but they managed to flee successfully to Vienne. It was 1.30 p.m. A single reporter, Jean Bouvard of *Paris-Soir*, managed to secure an interview with Wallis as she arrived at the Restaurant de la Pyramide. She replied in schoolroom French, scarcely improved since her days at Oldfields, 'You French people are very sympathetic but very bothersome. I have not been able to get any sleep for two days. In the hotel where I stayed last night there were twenty-four newspaper men. I want rest, lots of rest. . . . I can't make any statement. The king is the only judge. I have nothing to say except that I want to be left quiet.'

Wallis entered the restaurant through a back door with the aid of her old friend Madame Point, proprietor of the Pyramide. Madame Point had arranged a private room on the first floor for lunch. Wallis was able to call the Rogerses and tell them that they could expect her within hours. Madame Point was a good business-woman. She summoned the reporters and told them she was considering changing the name of her restaurant to Mrs Simpson's.

Wallis achieved her escape from the press in a manner that would have done justice to the Count of Monte Cristo. Above the kitchen sink was a window which was just large enough for her to squeeze through. In order to do so, she had to climb on to the kitchen table while Lord Brownlow and Madame Point supported it. Inspector Evans and Monsieur Point stood in the alleyway to catch Wallis as she jumped down. They all dashed to the waiting Buick and took off again through driving sleet.

Meanwhile, Wallis's maid Mary Burke had arrived by train at Cannes with Wallis's sixteen trunks and thirty-six suitcases. Wallis stopped again at the town of Brignoles to buy medicine and to telephone the Rogerses once again to confirm that she was indeed on the way. Lord Brownlow tried to rouse the occupants of the local post office, but at first there was no response. Then windows burst open and the occupants screamed with fury at him as he asked desperately where a telephone could be found. The group finally located one and Brownlow, beating at the instrument in helpless rage and screaming down the mouthpiece, at last managed to get through to the Villa Lou Viei.

At 2 a.m. on the 6th, while the king was sleepless and agonized at Fort Belvedere, the Buick at long last arrived at the wrought-iron gates of the Rogerses' villa at Cannes. Hundreds of spectators were waiting, and the car could barely edge its way through the crowd as the police strove to control the hysteria of the people, who had stood for many hours in the rain in expectation of Wallis's arrival. Wallis was on her knees on the car floor, a heavy rug completely concealing her.

When Wallis and Lord Brownlow walked into the hall, the Rogerses greeted them with immense relief. They had been fearful of some incident or fatal collision on the way, and their own stress was almost the equal of Wallis's. Though pale, exhausted and fragile-looking in her brown hat and three-quarter-length sable coat, Wallis was relieved to note that Mary Burke was safely installed at the house and that the trunks and suitcases had been placed in her suite. There were ladders and pots of paint everywhere because up to that very night painters and electricians had been doing up six bedrooms and bathrooms. Wallis walked with her host and hostess into the gloomy living room, where an enormous log fire was roaring in the grate in an attempt to dispel the damp. She collapsed into a chair.

In London, the mass demonstrations continued. The younger people of England were very much on the king's and Wallis's side. Supporters of the Labour party now found themselves in a curious alliance with the fascists. In Berlin the blanket of silence continued. Germans anxious to learn news of the latest developments in the crisis had to obtain their newspapers from Austria. Walter Monckton tried a last-ditch stand, recommending that legislation should be passed through parliament allowing the decree nisi of the divorce to be declared absolute immediately, without the necessary six-month waiting period. This idea was rejected out of hand.

When the king drafted a proposed broadcast calling the nation to rally behind him in his love for Wallis, Baldwin refused to permit it. The prime minister again wrote off the question of a morganatic marriage, and he would not agree to change the traditional status of the king's consort to permit Wallis to assume certain privileges. He advised the Commonwealth nations of his position, and they and Dawson's *Times* went along with him in his determination to prevent Wallis from becoming the king's bride. Beaverbrook and Rothermere continued to urge a delay until the matter could be weighed in a more detached spirit, preferably after the coronation. Winston Churchill suggested to the king that he should ask for a brief respite and retreat to Windsor Castle, firmly closing the gate to the prime minister. Then Churchill would send Baldwin a letter urging him not to hurry the king to a decision and stating that time was imperative. Even while Churchill began manoeuvring in this direction, the king, walking up and down alone in his bedroom, knew he could not possibly consider fighting Baldwin. Any delay would only cause more agony to him and to Wallis. He couldn't fight the Commonwealth. He might even be risking civil war. He could no longer rule over a united nation. It would be torn by controversy, anger and bitterness for the rest of his reign. Moreover, not only would Wallis be in danger if he forced the marriage, but her unpopularity among the political parties and the more righteous figures of the Church of England would make her position untenable.

On 6 December, Wallis wrote to the king expressing her anxious conviction that he should not abdicate. She was afraid that if he did, she would be put 'in the wrong light to the entire world because they will say that I could have prevented it'. In the course of a long and confused letter, Wallis went on to suggest that the entire matter should somehow be postponed until the autumn of 1937. She suggested that the king should urge Baldwin to accept the postponement. She repeated that she was 'terrified of what the world will say', and she incoherently repeated her idea of the postponement again and again. Even her spelling went to pieces as she talked of the king making 'an eight-month sacrifice' for his people by holding off from the decision. Part of the reason for her desire for the delay was to escape the situation herself; she wrote to

Sibyl Colefax at a later date, clearly indicating her continuing need to flee to parts unknown. Her panic was so overpowering that she was sleepless, exhausted, devastated by terror.

After a sleepless night himself, the king at last decided, on the 7th, that he would abdicate. Once he had made the choice he was flooded with relief and happiness. Whereas only two days before he had been on the verge of suicide, he knew now in his heart of hearts that he had made the correct decision. The two things that mattered most to him in the world were the British Empire and Wallis. By choosing Wallis, he would save the Commonwealth. He summoned Monckton and said, 'I want you to go to London immediately and warn the prime minister that when he comes to the Fort this afternoon I shall notify him formally that I have decided to abdicate.'

Monckton reminded him of what this step would mean. He told the king that within days he would be no more than a private citizen and, since he intended to go into exile, he would be pursued relentlessly by reporters. Furthermore, he must not see Wallis until her divorce became absolute, or he would risk the possibility that his enemies would bring pressure upon the King's Proctor, who was in charge of decisions relating to whether a divorce decree could be passed through as absolute without any obstacles.

That day, Winston Churchill appeared in the House of Commons protesting the king's cause, only to be greeted with screams of 'Sit down!' and 'Shame!' Although Baldwin had lost some of his notes, several of them in the toilet, and dropped others on the floor, banging his head on a table as he rose from picking them up, he recovered himself and gave what was probably the most accomplished speech of his career. He correctly stated the moral and political issues involved, achieving a dignity that even his many enemies were forced to admit was peerless. He was the hero of the hour in the eyes of all except the most fervent Labourites and the single communist member, Willie Gallacher.

Wallis was consumed with guilt and terror. When she got wind of the king's intention to abdicate she wrote an impassioned letter, insisting that he reconsider her offer to back out of the situation completely. Her enemies, led by the Duke and Duchess of York, Baldwin, Vansittart and the Hardinges, were convinced she was devising this appeal as a way of securing permanently the monarch's devotion. They refused to believe her sincerity when they learned of the gesture. She sent the letter by airmail, and on the 7th called the king at Fort Belvedere to read him a statement she was issuing to the press; she had been assisted in writing it by Lord Brownlow and Herman Rogers. In the statement Wallis offered 'to withdraw forthwith from a situation which has been rendered both unhappy and untenable'. Lord Brownlow read the statement to a large number of international newspaper reporters at a press conference at the Hôtel Majestic in Cannes. While the statement was being delivered, Associated Press noted: 'In her haven of refuge of the Villa Lou Viei, a dim light glowed in Mrs Simpson's bedroom. Faintly silhouetted against it, a slender figure paced back and forth as the American divorcee awaited the next move – Edward's acceptance, or his refusal to surrender her love even at the cost of his throne.' The author of this piece did not realize that the king had already made his decision and that nothing Wallis or anyone else said would shake his inexorable resolve.

In the meantime, Sir Horace Wilson, special adviser to the king and diplomatic liaison between various conflicting political groups including the Labour party, the British Union of Fascists, the Anglo-German fellowship, the Link and even the communists, prepared a sixty-four-page report for the chancellor of the exchequer, Neville Chamberlain, on the Duke and Duchess of Windsor and the circumstances of the abdication. His concluding statement was damning. It read:

> The Prime Minister not being available, I think I should refer to the point I made as to Mrs Simpson's 'plans' for the future. It is clear to me that it is her intention not only to come back here but (aided by what she expects to be a generous provision from public funds) to set up a 'Court' of her own and – there can be little doubt – do her best to make things uncomfortable for the new occupant of the Throne. It must not be assumed that she has abandoned hope of becoming Queen of England. It is known that she has limitless ambition, including a desire to interfere in politics: she has been in touch with the Nazi movement and has definite ideas as to dictatorship.

The essentials for her plans are (a) that she secure her divorce and (b) that she is provided with a sufficient income.

As regards (a), about which she is very anxious, it is unnecessary for me to say anything. As regards (b) we have some means, at least, of saving the country from grave future trouble.

By the 8th, the king still had not abdicated. Nor had any public statement been made that he would do so. However, the king's decision had already filtered out through the grapevine. Mosley's Blackshirts demonstrated at Buckingham Palace. At the same time Wallis's solicitor, Theodore Goddard, decided to fly to Cannes in a last-ditch effort to persuade Wallis to give up the king completely. Baldwin and one of his allies in the crisis, Sir Horace Wilson, were behind Goddard's mission. The king was furious when he learned of it, and he forbade Goddard to go, but Goddard was under the prime minister's orders. Despite a heart condition Goddard got into a plane normally used for official business, with a shaky engine that threatened to give out at any minute, and undertook a harrowing flight through thunderstorms. He was accompanied by Dr William Kirkwood, his personal physician, who was also a gynaecologist.

At the same time, the king at last agreed to see his brother the Duke of York, who had arrived at Fort Belvedere without being invited. It was necessary to discuss with that shy and awkward man the responsibilities that would be his within a few days. Both men were desperately weary. Their state of mind was not improved by the equally impromptu arrival of Baldwin, who walked in with Dugdale and Monckton at 5.30 p.m. To the king's horror, Baldwin arrived with a suitcase. The monarch was annoyed to think that the hated prime minister would have the nerve to want to spend the night at the Fort. The king had already decided that any further discussion was useless. After a meaningless dinner Baldwin left, pale and depressed, to take his final leave of the king whose moral integrity he had so strenuously tried to preserve.

The king looked fresh and happy that evening. Now that he had made up his mind, he enjoyed his first sound sleep for longer than he could remember. Yet the newspapers continued to say that he had not made up his mind.

At Cannes on the night of the 8th, Wallis received Theodore Goddard. Lord Brownlow was furious that he had been sent. Brownlow had made it clear that the gynaecologist Dr Kirkwood would not be welcome in the house. The presence of such a person could only give rise to rumours that Wallis was pregnant. Goddard then said to Wallis that she should immediately withdraw the divorce action against Ernest Simpson. If she did that, the crisis would be over. As it turned out, she required little persuasion. In her state of nervous exhaustion, she would have been happy to disappear to New Zealand or Argentina and never be seen again. She replied that she would do anything to keep the king on the throne. Goddard expressed his pleasure at her response. Wallis turned for advice to Lord Brownlow, who said, 'If the king does abdicate, his object will be marriage; for you to scrap your divorce will produce a hopeless climax and an all-round tragedy.' However, Wallis was prepared to do what Goddard asked. She tried to telephone the Fort. The king could not be reached. He returned her call at noon. Wallis said to him, 'I have agreed to withdraw my divorce petition.' The king responded both independently and through the solicitor George Allen that the matter had already progressed beyond the point of rescue. The abdication documents were drawn up. The king said to her, 'You can go wherever you want. To China, Labrador or the South Seas. But wherever you go, I will follow you.' It was now clear to Wallis that nothing would shake the royal resolve.

Wallis wondered what she should do next. She thought she might go back to Peking. For the time being she could go to Italy, by special train, to stay with Lord and Lady Berkeley, old friends of hers with a villa in Rome and police protection. Did she think of her old lover, Count Ciano? Still determined to save the situation and bring about some form of marriage, Lord Rothermere asked Esmond Harmsworth, who was then on the Riviera, to intercede with Wallis, but Harmsworth could provide no adequate reason why she should change her mind. Goddard returned defeated to London.

On the morning of 10 December, the king held a meeting with his brother the Duke of York, Monckton and other advisers on the matter of his financial future. He was entitled to a life interest in

Sandringham and Balmoral. The suggestion had been made that he should return these properties to the Crown upon his abdication. However, he did not prove to be cooperative. Instead, he would compel his brother to pay him £25,000 a year in return for releasing the two houses. He would be required to pay part of the pensions of those retainers at Sandringham and Balmoral whom he had discharged or who were retiring of their own free will or at the appropriate age. Through intermediaries, Baldwin conveyed an even sterner proviso. In return for these financial considerations, the king must never return to England unless he were granted special permission by the government. The implication was that if he refused to obey the request, he might be very restricted in terms of income under the provisions of the Civil List.

The king was displeased. The news that he would not henceforth receive the income from the Duchy of Cornwall was a matter of great distress to him. He had apparently forgotten that an abdicated monarch was not entitled to that emolument. It was stated that he very nearly withdrew the abdication at that moment. But instead he signed the Instrument of Abdication: 'I, Edward VIII, of Great Britain, Ireland, and the British Dominions beyond the Seas, King, Emperor of India, do hereby declare My irrevocable determination to renounce the Throne for Myself and for My descendants, and My desire that effect should be given to this Instrument of Abdication immediately.' As the king inscribed his signature on the document in front of his brothers, the Dukes of York, Gloucester and Kent, he felt marvellous – 'like a swimmer surfacing from a great depth', as he wrote in his memoirs.

That same night, thirty fascists, four of whom were in Blackshirt uniforms, were seen in Regent Street. They broke up and proceeded in twos and threes to Buckingham Palace. By 9 p.m. five hundred pro-Nazis had joined them. Some two hundred youths and girls stood chanting, 'We want Edward!' and 'One two three four five, we want Baldwin, dead or alive!' At intervals they gave the fascist salute, cheered and sang patriotic songs and the national anthem. Just before ten several youths, headed by one in fascist uniform, led eight hundred demonstrators to 10 Downing Street. Other fascist demonstrators picketed the House of Commons with placards reading: 'Sack Baldwin. Stand by the king!' At the same time they gave the fascist salute. Towards midnight the Blackshirts were screaming, 'Long live the king! Long live Bessie Warfield!' The next day, according to Scotland Yard reports, three thousand attended a meeting in Stepney at which Sir Oswald Mosley demanded that the abdication issue should be put to the people. Windows were smashed in Bancroft Road. There was a struggle between fascists and anti-fascists in the street.

According to Sir Edward Peacock, in statements at meetings with US ambassador Kennedy, and according also to Sir Dudley Forwood and the late Laura, Duchess of Marlborough, the king began to panic when Peacock pointed out to him the loss of money that would follow after the act of abdication. He might, he feared, lose much of his inheritance, of which Peacock was custodian, since he had no male heir, and any sums due to him under the provisions would have to be accorded him by his brother, who hated Wallis most bitterly.

The Labour party was particularly anxious for the king to reverse the abdication, and the king told Peacock he might consider that, and yield to the idea of morganatic marriage after all. The leading socialist John Strachey approached Claude Cockburn, the well-known Irish left-wing editor of the *Week*, an aggressively free-thinking journal, with an intriguing if mysterious suggestion. He and Lord Louis Mountbatten, a royal cousin, would provide Cockburn with sensational facts, authorized, Strachey said, by the king, that would terminate the abdication and give Cockburn the scoop of a lifetime. The story would be delivered to him on a certain midnight – by a royal motorcyclist sent straight from Fort Belvedere.

Cockburn and his staff waited breathlessly for the king's specific instructions at the appointed hour. But no cyclist arrived and, greatly annoyed, the editor had to put his paper to bed without a lead story. The question is: what was the mysterious (and absent) journalistic scoop?

Cockburn in his memoirs, *A Discord of Trumpets*, wrote that he had no idea; his son, the political journalist Alexander Cockburn, remains equally baffled, and the Cockburn papers are inaccessible in storage in Ireland. The most likely solution is that the king knew nothing about the matter; that Mountbatten and Strachey decided to release the story of Wallis's affair with Guy Trundle to Cockburn, sending it by a man disguised as a royal messenger, thus forcing the king to give up any idea of marrying her, and thus keeping him firmly on the throne as the 'people's monarch'. Popular with the working classes, he would, they thought, serve the cause of Labour better than that of the Conservatives. But at the last minute the conspirators panicked and backed off from the plan.

The king lunched with Winston Churchill, whose existence in the political wilderness was doomed to be extended because of his loyalty to the monarch. Churchill helped the king make some last-minute alterations to the abdication speech, upon which Walter Monckton had already worked extensively. As Churchill, on the verge of tears, left the house he quoted two lines of poetry: 'He nothing common did or mean/Upon that memorable scene . . .' The lines were by the poet Andrew Marvell and referred to the beheading of King Charles I. After lunch, the king had a further meeting with the Duke of York, who was seeking once more to overcome his nervousness and his fear that his stammer would handicap him badly when he had to broadcast or make public speeches. The Duke of York suggested that his brother should now assume the title of Duke of Windsor. The king was delighted with the suggestion and accepted it immediately.

In the late afternoon, Monckton arrived from London, having taken the text of the broadcast to Baldwin for his verbal approval. Baldwin asked for a total rewrite and the insertion of a sentence saying that he had given the king 'every consideration' during the crisis. The king was irritated by the audacity of this request by his arch-enemy, but felt that in the interests of propriety he should make the inclusion. Before leaving for Windsor Castle to make his ten o'clock broadcast, the king called Wallis to tell her that he would be going to Switzerland and staying at a hotel near Zurich.

Wallis told him she was shocked that the British government would not have provided him with a safe haven where he could enjoy privacy. If he were in a hotel, he would face the same nightmare she was enduring, a state of being totally under siege. He would never have a minute's peace from press or public. Instead, at Lady Mendl's suggestion, Lord Brownlow could arrange for him to stay with his old friends the Baron and Baroness Eugene Rothschild at their castle, Schloss Enzesfeld, near Vienna. Wallis said she would call him immediately to make the necessary arrangements. She did; they agreed at once. The American-born Kitty Rothschild was especially overjoyed by the idea.

Accompanied by the adored dog, Slipper, the king said goodbye to his staff at Fort Belvedere. The suitcases were carried to the royal Buick. As it swung down the driveway with Ladbroke at the wheel, the king looked back at his beloved Fort, realizing he might never see it again. In a few days, the furniture would be stored; most of it was to remain in storage for almost a decade. The wrench was painful. The Fort had been his home for so long; he had poured so much of his thought and skill into remodelling it, creating an oasis, a haven from the cruel world. The car drove on to Royal Lodge, Windsor, where his mother, Queen Mary, his brothers and his sister, the Princess Royal, were waiting for him. The conversation at dinner was awkward; the Duke of Kent, always highly emotional, broke down and sobbed uncontrollably at the table; the Duke of York was on the verge of tears. As the meal concluded, Monckton arrived to accompany the king to Windsor Castle. Meanwhile, Herman Rogers had managed to reach Monckton and inform him that the Rothschilds would be delighted to have the king as a house guest.

Ironically, the monarch's old enemy Lord Wigram was now deputy constable and lieutenant governor of Windsor Castle; impassively he greeted the king and Monckton as they entered the great hallway. In the Augusta Tower, the director of the BBC, Sir John Reith, surrounded by a technical team, was waiting with what was described by one eyewitness as 'a basilisk stare'. The tower room had been set up as a temporary studio. Then, at 10 p.m., the king spoke, warmly, confidently, released from his torment. He made it clear that the decision to abdicate was his and his alone; that the woman he loved had tried to the last minute to persuade him to take a different course; that his brother the Duke of York would take his place on the throne 'without interruption or injury to the life and progress of the Empire. And [Winston Churchill's addition] he has one matchless blessing, enjoyed by so many of you and not bestowed on me – a happy home with his wife and children.' The king went on to mention, no doubt with a sinking feeling, how the ministers of the Crown, 'and in particular Mr

Baldwin', had always treated him with full consideration. He concluded:

> I now quit altogether public affairs, and I lay down my burden. It may be some time before I return to my native land, but I shall always follow the fortunes of the British race and Empire with profound interest, and if at any time in the future I can be found of service to His Majesty in a private station I shall not fail. And now we all have a new king. I wish him, and you, his people, happiness and prosperity with all my heart. God bless you all. God save the king.

With the Rogerses, Wallis listened to the broadcast in the drawing room of the Villa Lou Viei. By her own account she was quietly grief-stricken, but Katherine Rogers told her friend Fern Bedaux that in fact Wallis flew into a tantrum, shouting with rage and smashing things. She hated the idea of abdication. She had wanted to be the king's mistress and to keep her husband; she had wanted to be powerful without the burdens of power and the agony of guilt. Raised like so many Americans to believe that the fulfilment of any ambition was possible and that the world was her oyster, she had learned, she wrote, 'the dregs of my cup of failure and defeat'. She had discovered that a prime minister and a cabinet and a Secret Intelligence Service bent upon her destruction left her no chance, no hope of survival. Moreover, for the rest of her life she would be accused of destroying her monarch and of bringing down his rule. It was in that knowledge that she went to her room alone for a night of very great pain.

11

EXILE

The Duke of Windsor, as he would now be known, though the title was not gazetted until May, had a last meeting with his mother and his three brothers; Queen Mary was, as always, superbly controlled, but the Duke of Kent was still visibly distraught and said at one stage, 'This is quite mad.' He was extremely upset at the thought of not seeing his brother again for an incalculable length of time. As the new Duke of Windsor left the house, he remembered his manners and bowed to the new king.

The duke had two last-minute visitors. The first was Winston Churchill, who bade him a warm farewell. The second was Count Grandi, who expressed the sympathy of the government in Italy. Neither of these visits was recorded in the press of any country; Count Grandi revealed them to the present author in 1987.

The drive, with Ladbroke at the wheel of the Buick, to Portsmouth to take the night ferry to Boulogne was dragged out because of the increasingly foul weather. The duke occupied himself by talking with Monckton, whom he had asked to travel with him to the dock, about the arrangements in Europe. He also read a letter from his sister-in-law Elizabeth, Duchess of York, who had been ill in bed but, for all her hatred of Wallis, was full of good wishes. And he told Monckton how deeply he loved his mother; there was no indication in his voice of bitterness because of her attitude to the woman he loved.

The fog, drizzle and sudden bursts of rain delayed the vehicle's arrival at Portsmouth dock. Ladbroke drove past Nelson's flagship, the *Victory*, which had become a tourist attraction, and realized he was lost. As he searched for the right entrance, the Unicorn Gate, the duke pointed out various ships to Monckton, giving particulars of their histories. They drove on, looking for HMS *Fury*, which at the last minute had been substituted for *Enchantress*; according to some versions, the latter vessel was rejected because of the unfortunate associations of the name.

The duke boarded *Fury* accompanied by Major Ulick Alexander, keeper of the Privy Purse, who had been delegated to take charge of his financial affairs, and by his new equerry, Sir Piers Legh. He was welcomed aboard by the fleet commodore, Admiral Sir William Fisher, and two other admirals. In his cabin, the duke said farewell to his assistant private secretary, Sir Godfrey Thomas. The duke took Monckton's hands in his; never had he known a more devoted friend.

The ship sailed at 2 a.m. The Channel crossing was choppy; the duke remained secluded in his cabin. He was met at Boulogne by the Orient Express, which had been specially diverted to make the connection. The train's comptroller, Roger Tibot, greeted him as he boarded; the duke had asked that a private car should not be provided on this occasion, but rather a simple first-class compartment; fortunately this ruse, plus the diversion of the train, threw the reporters off the scent. The duke told Tibot he did not want to take any meals in the restaurant car and insisted that Tibot have the sleeping-car attendant serve him in the compartment. The duke took his light and unpretentious breakfast, lunch and dinner on trays which were set upon suitcases that filled the space between the facing seats. This was distressing to Tibot, who was used to the former king entering the dining car, after the other passengers had left it, to enjoy an exquisitely prepared repast.

Meanwhile, Wallis was far from comfortable at the Villa Lou Viei, which she had liked much better in 1928. The house was over six hundred years old. The guest bedrooms were on split levels, with an ancient stone wall that ran up between the floors. The thick outer walls retained the clinging dampness of the Mediterranean winter. The living room, which seemed dark even in spring and summer, was cavernous, dank and cheerless despite its chintz-covered chairs and bowls of green plants on the French provincial tables. There was even, Wallis learned for the first time, a ghost: Herman swore he had seen the original builder of the house flitting in a shadowy form through the corridors and rooms. The residence, which once had seemed a glowing refuge, now looked more and more like an expensive dungeon.

The Rogerses did everything possible to cheer Wallis up. But all she could see as she stared glumly out of the windows were five *gendarmes* and three British policemen walking up and down, and beyond Herman's well-tended vegetable garden the misty, rain-swept slopes that led down the hill to Cannes. Even the cuisine was depressing; the old couple who acted as butler and cook busied themselves to little effect in the badly kept-up kitchen. Wallis began to wish she were somewhere else. In the meantime her cook, chambermaid and chauffeur had taken the ferry to Dieppe with a dozen suitcases and trunks and left at once by car for Cannes. They arrived two days later. She got in touch with Georges Sebastian at Hammamet in Tunisia, but finally decided not to make the move. She was very annoyed the next day when a shoal of letters arrived, many of them threatening and some of them actually stating that the assassination plan had not been abandoned. As a result, the Cannes chief of police was called in for consultation. He stationed himself outside her rooms in person, concerned that if anything happened to her it would bring disgrace upon his community. On 12 December, Wallis wrote to the duke that she had heard there was 'an organization of women' who had sworn to kill her. She urged him to arrange for full protection at all times; she was under armed guard.

The duke proceeded to Vienna on the Orient Express on 13 December. He was met there by the British minister to Austria, the genial Sir Walford Selby, and by a party of journalists who behaved with uncharacteristic reserve. Among these was Douglas Reed, later the author of the book *Insanity Fair*, who observed that in spite of everything the forty-year-old duke still looked amazingly boyish, innocent and untouched by time and stress.

Another who was present was the attaché Dudley Forwood, who had first met Wallis and the Prince of Wales at Kitzbühel. At the duke's request, Forwood would soon become his equerry and private secretary; in the meantime Sir Walford Selby put him in charge of the royal arrangements. The duke wanted to proceed to

the Rothschilds' Schloss Enzesfeld immediately. But it wasn't possible, because protocol required him to present his respects to
President Miklas. With Forwood the duke proceeded to pay those
respects; a further requirement was that afterwards the president
must appear at the British Legation to present his own respects.
This tiresome ritual went on and on. Sir Dudley recalled:

> When I informed the duke of the latter requirement, he said,
> 'Oh! Miklas had better be asked to lunch!' But there was a
> problem. Lady Selby was a good but extremely stingy hostess.
> No matter who it was, if there were guests for lunch they only
> got one lamb chop each. I was very concerned that something
> better would be done for this important occasion. But the chef
> was under orders to supply a maximum of four lamb chops. So
> there could be no change. Learning of this, the duke informed
> me that I did not need to have lunch!

The Rothschilds sent their chauffeur to pick up the duke and his
party and drive them to Enzesfeld. Dudley Forwood was among the
entourage. The duke had been at the schloss briefly the year
before, suffering from a bad cold. Forwood remembered:

> I returned to Vienna almost immediately, but then I had to
> return because there were so many problems at the schloss.
> First, none of the duke's personal entourage spoke German,
> though of course he did. That made it difficult for them to
> communicate with the staff. The equerry, the Hon. John Aird,
> left, recalled to Buckingham Palace by the king. The other
> equerry, Sir Piers Legh, stayed on, but he wasn't at all in tune
> with the duke. He was an older man, very nervous and tense,
> horrified by the abdication, not at all sympathetic to Mrs Simp-
> son, and upset by the fact that he couldn't speak German. So,
> in this very difficult situation, I was asked to return and become
> equerry. I accepted at once.

Forwood soon learned the ritual of serving a royal master, a term
which he still uses in reference to the duke. In the morning the
valet would wake the duke, whereupon Forwood would enter the
bedroom and announce the order of the day's business. He must
bow as he did so; on the occasions when he failed to do so, the

duke quietly reprimanded him. A very important matter was that of the royal clothing. Sir Dudley wrote that when the duke played golf, he would change into golfing clothes; he would not wear that outfit at lunch, but had to change into a suit and tie; if he wished to garden in the afternoon, he would again have to change. And then of course in the evening there would be the obligatory black tie or, for special occasions, white tie and tails.

But from the beginning, despite the onerous challenges involved, Forwood was utterly devoted to the duke. He would, in 1987, hear not a word against his 'master'. One of his most vivid memories of Enzesfeld is that the duke called Wallis several times a day. The Duke seemed reluctant to restrain himself, pouring out his agony to her, while the telephone bills in those expensive times averaged the equivalent of between £60 and £80 a week; as he talked to her, he could see in his room dozens of photographs of her that he had brought from Fort Belvedere. Although pleased to accommodate him, his host and hostess had mixed feelings about him, and he about them. Kitty Rothschild was still a very attractive woman, but the Duke did not find her particularly intelligent; he had always joked that she had become Protestant with her first husband, Roman Catholic with her second and Jewish with her third.[1]

Wallis continued to suffer from the torments of the damned. She wrote to the duke, 'So much scandal has been whispered about me even that I am a spy that I am shunned by people so until I have the protection of your name I must remain hidden.' She expressed her desire for more and more obscurity, a pathetically futile wish in the circumstances. she also wrote of her hopes that the love she shared with the duke would win out against all obstacles.

In England, Emerald Cunard and Sir Philip Sassoon disowned the exiled couple outright. Following hypocritical statements of sympathy and sorrow from Stanley Baldwin in the House of Commons, the Archbishop of Canterbury delivered a moralistic and protracted BBC broadcast on 13 December, remarking, inter alia, of the former monarch:

Even more strange and sad is it that he should have sought his happiness in a manner inconsistent with Christian principles of marriage and within a social circle whose standards and ways of life are alien to all the best instincts of his people. Let those who belong in this circle know that today they stand rebuked by the judgement of the nation which had loved King Edward.

His comments made the archbishop singularly unpopular, and not only among the duke's still-loyal friends. His broadcast had the disagreeable flavour of a righteous churchman kicking an unfortunate man when he was down. Two days later the Labour member of parliament Ellen Wilkinson, both in the Commons and in an article in the newspaper the *Sunday Referee*, went a step further. She said:

> There had been growing uneasiness about political tendencies around [Mrs Simpson], or perhaps it would be fairer to say, in groups that had been using her influence over King Edward for their own purposes. . . . Eager to be behind Mrs Simpson was a set that makes little secret of its enthusiasm for the political and social doctrines of a power not particularly friendly toward Britain. Prime Minister Baldwin recently described what he called a dangerous mentality in politics as being 'the enjoyment of power without responsibility'.

As a sop to the public (and perhaps to avoid a libel suit), Miss Wilkinson added that she wasn't implying that either the duke or Wallis knew what was being done to them politically. This scarcely soothed the troubled brows of the two victims of the speech and the article.

At the same time, yet another blow fell. Francis Stephenson, an obscure and ancient legal clerk, intervened in what seemed to be a fairly straightforward legal procedure towards the granting of the decree absolute of the divorce. He claimed to be able to show cause as to why the divorce should be stopped. What information he had, if any, was never made clear, and he subsequently was silenced. However, the likelihood is that he had got wind of the royal collusion. Wallis was in a state of shock when she learned of the intervention. She wrote to the duke, 'I didn't think the world could put more on two people whose only sin is to love.' She added that she looked a hundred years old and weighed only 110 pounds, and that England had made her '[a] wreck . . . The world is against me and me alone.' She wondered if she could survive the ordeal.

Wallis must have worried that the truth would come out about her earlier collusion in the matter of Spencer and that somebody might produce evidence that she was born out of wedlock and not baptized, which would preclude her religious marriage to the duke, even if it might reveal her marriage to Ernest to be invalid. She went out on long and meaningless drives around the curving roads of the three corniches, the hairpin bends and sudden glimpses of the sea temporarily distracting her from her anguish. It was some relief to hear that Aunt Bessie was going to join her for Christmas.

In that time of loneliness and sorrow, it is clear that Wallis at last began to feel a little fondness for the duke. Her letters to him at the time expressed some show of devotion and loyalty, though they still did not have the impassioned affection of his own. At that time Newhold Noyes, who was married to Wallis's cousin Lelia of Wakefield Manor, Virginia, was publishing a series of articles in the United States (and would soon do so in France) based upon what Wallis and the duke had thought were private conversations at Fort Belvedere and Cumberland Terrace in November. The articles were largely empty-headed puffery about the couple's likes and dislikes (Wallis hated cats; she loved open fires and high winds). However, Wallis felt very strongly that the pieces represented an invasion of privacy, over-reacting to them to the extent that she took out a libel suit against Noyes.

She made a serious mistake. Instead of engaging a respectable French attorney, she yet again turned to the Nazi activist Armand Grégoire. Grégoire was still notorious; still listed with the Deuxième Bureau and the Sûreté as one of the leading Nazi agents in France. Espionage files on him currently deposited at the Archives Diplomatiques in Paris and the National Archives in Washington reveal that despite his position as a prominent lawyer, with offices in the Place Vendôme and a socially prominent wife, Crystal, who was an American by birth, he was under ceaseless watch by the authorities. France was still under the socialist government of Léon Blum, and by a peculiar irony the head of Blum's cabinet, Monsieur Blumel, was the brother of Maître Suzanne Blumel, later Blum, who would follow Grégoire many years later as Wallis's lawyer.

The situation was clearly monitored by Herman Rogers, whose position as an American agent was still continuing; Wallis's decision to engage Grégoire enhanced suspicions of her Nazi connections among representatives of MI6 in Paris. In short, she was in worse trouble than ever.

The phone calls and letters continued. And so did the endless threats, causing the Rogerses to change their telephone number again and again. An unpleasant footnote to an already disagreeable month occurred when a news announcement revealed that Wallis's old home at 212 North Biddle Street, Baltimore, had been bought by a lawyer, Harry J. Green, who planned to turn it into a museum.

In Austria, the duke travelled frequently to Vienna both to receive ear treatments from Professor Neumann and to renew his earlier acquaintance with Chancellor Schuschnigg and President Miklas. Now that he was no longer on the throne, he was careful to restrict his discussions with these men to social niceties. He also renewed his friendship with the clever, sophisticated American minister to Austria, George Messersmith, who from his first day in Vienna had kept up, through a network of intelligence contacts and the consistent interception of cables and telephone calls from other embassies, what amounted to a detailed watching brief on the duke. On the evening of 15 December, the duke rose from his sickbed, to which he was confined with severely aching ears and a bad headache, to join Fritz Mandl for dinner. Mandl, the husband and discoverer of the film star Hedy Lamarr, was a Jewish armaments maker who was already supplying Hitler despite his ethnic origin. The duke also met Eugene Rothschild's brother Louis, whom he would later assist to escape from Europe. Lord Brownlow had in the meantime arrived from Cannes with a bundle of notes and reminders from Wallis, only some of which later made their way into the pages of the collected correspondence edited by Michael Bloch.

Two problems, other than the continually tormenting matter of their separation, were paramount in the minds of Wallis and the duke. The first was the question of where they would live once they were married. There was some discussion of their going to the French estate of the Duke of Westminster, who had on a previous occasion given them the use of his yacht. But accepting this idea would have been unwise: the Duke of Westminster still had very strong and notorious Nazi connections. Prince Roman Fancuszko suggested they might like to move to his castle in Poland; and there was talk of their buying Count Bela Zichy's 4,000-acre estate in Hungary. None of these plans seemed practicable, but another thought was taken seriously by the couple. The Rogerses put up the idea that they might want to move, at least for a time, to the Château de Candé at Tours, not far from Paris; the chateau was the home of the naturalized American industrial-systems tycoon Charles Bedaux and his American wife, Fern.

The second problem was the matter of the royal income from the Civil List, which was intended to keep the duke in comfort for the rest of his days. Despite the new king's verbal approval, the matter would take several weeks or months to go through the necessary committee. And there was no guarantee that, at the end of that time, the arrangement would be approved. For the moment, though he still kept it a secret, the duke had the very substantial sum of money he had saved from the Duchy of Cornwall. But even that bounty would not be sufficient, given the standard of living to which he was accustomed, to provide for him indefinitely. At some stage in this period Wallis agreed to give up the £300,000 he had settled on her, exchanging it for £10,000 a year for life. However, the duke was still fretful, obsessed as always with money. In London the devoted Winston Churchill never ceased, either then or during the next few months, to press repeatedly for the cash. As a member of the Civil List committee, Churchill did his utmost to override the objections of the others. He still thought of himself, and always would, as the duke's surrogate father or kindly uncle.

The reporters still clung relentlessly to the grounds of both Schloss Enzesfeld and the Villa Lou Viei. Wallis forced herself to make an awkward appearance one afternoon, giving a brief press conference in which she said little of interest. She was treading water, consumed with boredom and loneliness, unable to sleep; she relished prominence, publicity and admiration and could not bear to think that she was hated as few other women had been hated in history. It was scarcely a relief to her to learn that a wax statue of her in a symbolically scarlet evening gown now stood in a chamber of Madame Tussaud's Wax Museum in London. Visitors noted that her startlingly realistic violet-coloured glass eyes looked balefully across at the Archbishop of Canterbury.

Minor troubles increased. The duke called Wallis frantically to tell her that her beloved Slipper had been mauled by Baron Rothschild's dogs and a vet had had to be summoned to take care of the animal. As Christmas approached, he was not in a mood to enjoy the season. The piles of letters heaping up on his desk surpassed even Wallis's. When he advertised for a secretary, eight hundred women lined up for the job. He finally chose one, addressing her through sneezes and a worsening headache while sipping red wine spiced with cloves, sugar and cinnamon.

When Wallis went shopping, press and public made her trip impossible. Her white hat and ermine coat were spotted as she took a walk along the Cannes seafront, and she had to flee back into the car. Matters did not improve in England: His Master's Voice, which had the royal warrant for reproducing speeches, was forbidden by Sir John Reith of the BBC to issue a recording of the abdication speech. Bootleg copies sold furiously in the United States and on the Continent.

On 19 December, Aunt Bessie arrived at last at Lou Viei; Wallis embraced her in tears. It was a heartfelt, eagerly longed-for reunion. The duke busied himself with preparations for Christmas. He sent Wallis a mink cape; she in turn sent him a possum coat. Recovered from his cold, he reverted to his usual custom of morning exercises and played golf and ninepins, and he even tried yodelling at a small dinner party in the newly constructed bar and dining room. And he was overjoyed when the unhappy Slipper, who had been lying in his tiny kennel, suddenly recovered from his wounds and woke the household to reveal that he had triumphantly cornered and killed a large grey mouse. But his mood rapidly changed. He was again depressed by his loneliness when, on 22 December, he wrote to Wallis expressing his agony at the thought of four months of separation to come. The ten days he had spent at the schloss had almost driven him mad with their slowness and monotony. He wrote that he only lived for their telephone conversations in the evening, that without Alexander Graham Bell's invention life would be unbearable. He complained of the cruel and inhuman newspapers; he talked of the cruelty of life itself. The same day the duke wrote to Aunt Bessie, talking of the last two weeks as 'a nightmare'.

On Christmas Eve, Wallis decided to ignore the press, and made her way with the Rogerses through a large and eager crowd to the Palm Beach casino in Cannes. It was officially announced that she had stayed at home. There was no Christmas tree but she worked hard on the decorations of holly and mimosa. As an unpleasant Christmas gift to the couple, Buckingham Palace issued an announcement that sixty employees at Sandringham, who had been dismissed by the duke, had now been restored to their former positions. The duke appeared in church in Vienna on Christmas Day, joining George Messersmith at the service. Sir Walford Selby read the first lesson, and the duke read, in his excellent voice, still with its touches of American and cockney pronunciation, the first twenty verses of the second chapter of the gospel according to St Luke. He and Wallis exchanged telephone calls. On the following afternoon the duke was mobbed by hundreds of children as he gave Christmas gifts to the children of Enzesfeld. He seemed cheerful, glowing and in good form as he walked out into the driving snow.

Over Christmas, the duke bombarded the king at Sandringham by telephone, according to Sir Dudley Forwood, giving him fraternal advice on how to behave as monarch. This was not particularly well received. But the royal family, whatever its feelings about his advice and about Wallis, did not hesitate to convey to the duke their love and tender thoughts. However, the cost of the duke's calls, which dragged on for hours, greatly concerned the Rothschilds. Kitty Rothschild told George Messersmith, 'Edward has no sense of money. You know, we are not among the rich Rothschilds, and these telephone calls appal me.' One Christmas message added fuel to the fire of the duke's enemies: the one from his friend Lloyd George, the former prime minister of England, who was on holiday in the Caribbean. Lloyd George had visited Hitler and admired the Führer to distraction; so intense was the Nazi support surrounding him in England that the secret service was watching him and his friends day and night.

On Christmas night, Wallis, at the invitation of her old friend Sibyl Colefax, who had remained loyal through the crisis, went with the Rogerses to dinner at the Villa Mauresque, where Somerset Maugham, then at the height of his fame as both novelist and playwright, received them with his celebrated crocodile smile. The evening was rendered somewhat embarrassing by the drunken interruptions of his 'secretary', his alcoholic lover Gerald Haxton. Asked at the inquest following a rubber of bridge why she hadn't used a king of hearts, Wallis replied, 'My kings don't take tricks. They only abdicate.' Wallis did not particularly warm to her host, nor he to her. But he had something in common with her and with Herman Rogers: all three had been involved in intelligence work, Maugham in the First World War.

On 1 January 1937, Aunt Bessie wrote to Wallis's cousin Corinne Murray, who was now back at Pensacola, Florida, telling her of the life at Lou Viei: 'The events of the past month are too big for my feeble mind to tackle,' she said. She went on to say that Wallis was looking very well, but 'too thin, of course', and that she should put on six pounds. She wished the newspapers would stop hounding Wallis; there were so many letters to answer that Bessie herself had to write several, like this one, in her place. But she did note that the tourists had stopped peeping through the gates; only the very curious were still hovering about.

Also on New Year's Day, the duke wrote to Wallis once again expressing his anguish and sense of strain at the separation. That night, on the telephone to her he sobbed like a child, and after he had finally hung up Wallis, clearly touched, dashed off a note to him saying, 'I couldn't bear hearing you cry.'

As January wore on, Wallis's worry that the divorce would not be granted did not cease. The duke was so anxious and irritable that he didn't even go to nightclubs in Vienna, nor did he visit the Rotter Bar. On 21 January, 'Fruity' Metcalfe telephoned from the Grand Hotel at Kitzbühel to suggest that he might come to Schloss Enzesfeld and stay for a while. The duke unwisely agreed. Wallis was consumed with jealousy.

The duke went skiing with Fruity at Semmering; Metcalfe noted in letters to his wife Lady Alexandra in London that the duke was as eager and happy as a schoolboy. He was as insomniac as ever, seldom getting to bed before 4 a.m., and he ran Fruity, whose letters of the time have a breathless quality, off his feet.

All through January, Wallis was writing to the duke, continuing to complain about her position as an outcast and an object of international scandal. She never ceased to grumble about the ill treatment she felt the duke was getting from the king. The boredom and notoriety were eating into her more and more deeply. In her desperation she had turned to an astrologer in Switzerland, but the written horoscope only depressed her with its prophecy of many more obstacles.

On 27 January, Wallis wrote to the duke, saying that she was very distressed that Baldwin would not let the Dukes of Kent and Gloucester pay a visit to the schloss. She charged Baldwin with not only ruining the family affairs but also continuing to humiliate the duke.

Eugene Rothschild went to Paris in the third week of January, transferring most of his funds to the Paris banks, but Kitty did not finally move out until 2 February, when the duke didn't even have the grace to get out of bed to bid her farewell and to thank her for her kindness to him.

On 3 February, Wallis wrote to the duke expressing her distress at the behaviour of King George VI, accusing him of being a mere puppet for government forces which had removed her beloved from the throne, using her as a 'convenient tool'. She expressed her annoyance that her forthcoming marriage to the duke would not be mentioned in the Court Circular; this was a disappointment because she loathed the idea of being undignified and of joining 'the countless titles that roam around Europe meaning nothing'. She wanted the duke to write to the king giving reasons why he should not be treated as an outcast, and to give her a proper title. She disclosed her disgust with the royal family as a whole for denying her any degree of dignity.

It was not until 3 February that the duke made a public appearance at a social occasion, attending, along with Messersmith, the Selbys and Mrs Miklas, a concert given by the young Australian soprano Joan Hammond. The choice of programme was, to say the least, unfortunate. One lied by Hugo Wolf was entitled 'In Retirement', and contained the words, 'Leave me alone, O world, Let my heart remain alone with its pain and its bliss.' Richard Strauss's 'Dedication' began, 'You know, dear soul, that far from you I suffer.

Love makes my heart sick.' In the worst taste of all was the song 'The Little Foreigner' by Cyril Scott. In it, the titular figure declared that she had come from a country far away to London 'to set the Thames on fire'. And the final blow to an already uncomfortable duke came in the song 'The Green Hills of Somerset', in which the refrain was, 'No more we walk by your green hills, no more.'

Two days later, the Princess Royal, the duke's beloved sister, and her husband, the Earl of Harewood, left London for Enzesfeld. According to the *New York Times*, the reason for the visit was to discuss the duke's financial future. Baldwin was still adamant that the duke would receive nothing from the Civil List. The princess and her husband were to bring word of this disagreeable decision and try to soothe the duke's fevered brow. When they arrived, the duke lunched with them at the Hotel Bristol and took them on a tour of several museums. Dismayed by their news that his money had been frozen, he reminded the Princess Royal that he still had possession of Balmoral and Sandringham and would not release them until he was paid. He said bitterly, referring to the ancient palace of the Austrian emperors, 'If the worst comes to worst, I'll always be able to pick up a living showing people around Schönbrunn.' He gave his sister and brother-in-law a free tour of the mouldering edifice, pointing out the pony cart belonging to Crown Prince Rudolf, who had shot his mistress and himself in a famous double suicide. He also showed his relatives the workers' apartments over which he had already embarrassed his fascist friends in Vienna two years earlier.

In February, a series of anguished letters from Wallis to the duke indicate her extreme nervousness about the outcome of the investigation by the King's Proctor into the matter of the divorce from Ernest. One of her letters, dated the 7th, was especially confused and jumbled, filled with a sense of panic. She wanted the duke to intervene with the king on the matter, obviously an impossibility. She blamed everything that had happened upon the queen, whom she persisted in calling the Duchess of York. ('I blame it all on the wife – who hates us both.') It is quite clear from this and other letters that Wallis knew that the granting of the decree was by no means a certainty; it might be revealed that she had in fact had a form of sexual relationship with the duke. Had she (as Michael Bloch, who edited the collected letters, avers) had only the most chaste relationship with the duke, her letters would have assumed an entirely different character, based upon a certainty that no one would expose her in an act of adultery.

On 12 February, Wallis, feeling a little better, made her 1937 social début on the Riviera at an elaborate party given by Henry Clews, Jr, a wealthy New York socialite. The affair, at the Palm Beach casino, was enlivened by a commotion when some tourists who had crashed the event tried to snoop through the curtains drawn round the table at which Wallis and the Rogerses were seated with their host and hostess. In a splendid black lace gown and pearl necklace, a present from the duke, Wallis danced twice with the Greek casino owner, Nicolas Zographos.

The next day, the Princess Royal and the Earl of Harewood left Vienna by train. The princess was in tears; the duke shouted angrily at film cameramen who tried to photograph the group on the railway platform, and police seized and smashed the cameras. It was widely believed that at the last minute the Harewoods had tried to persuade the duke to break up his relationship with Wallis. Predictably, any such suggestion was abruptly rejected. But they did prevail upon him to postpone his wedding until after the coronation. And they were compelled to inform him, after talking with London, that there was still no arrangement for his financial prospects and provisions. He told Messersmith he had been treated 'shabbily'. That the duke had ideas of returning to England and assuming the throne once more is indicated by a phrase in a letter dated 18 February to Wallis: 'WE will be back in our full glory in less time than WE think.'

In London, Joachim von Ribbentrop turned up at Buckingham Palace to present his credentials as ambassador to the king and to convey Hitler's good wishes. He told King George about German workers' apartments and social reforms; the conversation was friendly and cordial. At the end of the meeting, Ribbentrop gave the monarch the Nazi salute. It is clear that Hitler's purpose was to obtain the support of the royal family in England regardless of which particular member of it should happen to be on the throne.

On the 24th, the Duke of Kent arrived in Vienna from Munich. The two brothers visited various museums and Schönbrunn Palace, and the Duke of Kent stayed for several days and nights. Lord Brownlow arrived from London on the 26th; he had been badly treated in London because he had backed the wrong royal horse. He was told not only that he would not be lord in waiting to the new king, as he had expected, but also that he was persona non grata at court; men left the bar of his club when he arrived. His name was to be banned from the Court Circular. When he asked the Lord Chamberlain, Lord Cromer, whether he was to be turned away like a dishonest servant without notice, he was told that that expectation was correct. The fact that he had accompanied Wallis was clearly the death-blow to his career, and even to his social life.

At the same time, rumours increased in London and the south of France that Wallis had somehow made off with the emeralds bequeathed to the duke by his grandmother, Queen Alexandra. The suggestion was either that she had wormed them out of the king or that he had retrieved them through the jewellers Garrards in London as a present for her. There was no truth in either assumption; the emeralds were figments of the collective imagination. The truth was that whatever jewels had been left by Queen Alexandra had been divided up among the female members of the family and had never been available to the duke at any time. But the story, which persisted until very recently when it was finally quashed by Leslie Field, increased the hysteria that seemed to accompany Wallis's every move.

The Duke of Kent had arrived in Vienna with bad news. He was obliged to say that there was no prospect of Windsor receiving any money through the Civil List. This news, on top of his sister's a few days before, threw the duke into a state of anger and deep depression. He and Wallis argued over it for hours on the telephone, shouting at each other night after night.

On 2 March, Wallis attended her first fashion show in over a year as Captain Edward Molyneux showed his spring collection at Cannes. She bought thirteen dresses and suits, including a crêpe satin evening gown of greyish blue, with a jacket fastened by three mirror buttons; the most expensive item she purchased was a silver fox coat made of ten skins used lengthwise in straight bands. She wore it to another party at Somerset Maugham's villa that weekend.

The fear of assassination intensified in March. Wallis received another threatening letter, and she had once again been advised by Kenneth de Courcy of the existence of an organization that was determined to eliminate her and that would be well paid for the killing.

There was talk that Wallis and the duke would move to the United States, and the duke even began some preliminary negotiations to buy Cloisters, an immense castellated residence owned by Mr and Mrs Sumner A. Parker outside Baltimore. Nothing came of it. Finally, on the 9th, Wallis left with the Rogerses for Charles Bedaux's Château de Candé; she was accompanied by her maid, Mary Burke, and by twenty-seven pieces of luggage. She stored the rest of her possessions brought from England at the Villa Lou Viei. Charles Bedaux was in the United States at the time, staying at his apartment on Fifth Avenue; Fern Bedaux had broken off a trip to London and worked with tremendous concentration for over a week to prepare for her celebrated guest. An army of servants, augmented by villagers, had dusted and scrubbed and repainted the ancient edifice virtually round the clock. The Buick, which had been garaged for most of the previous weeks while Wallis used the Rogerses' car, swept up the hill to the chateau's immense, arabesque doorway with its iron handles. When the hand-pulled doorbell was rung, the door creaked open to disclose a vast hallway lined by twenty-two members of the staff, all of them uniformed. At their head was Hale, the English butler, dressed impeccably in a hand-tailored suit from Savile Row. The liveried flunkeys wore royal blue and gold coats, black trousers and gold-buckled shoes. The maids were in floor-length, black silk dresses with frilly caps and aprons, and the housekeeper was equipped with a large châtelaine of keys. Chandeliers were glowing from the ceiling on this gloomy, wet Wednesday afternoon. Ten thousand francs' worth of bought flowers sprang from crystal vases. Wallis was accommodated in Fern's own bedroom, which was decorated in ivory silk and satin and overlooked the sombre woods and countryside.

Exhausted by the journey, Wallis spent her first day resting in her room. When she took a step out of doors at dusk, the rain was so heavy that she quickly returned. She called the duke several times during her first twenty-four hours there.

She gave a press conference in the library, carefully avoiding any mention of her marriage plans. Asked, rather oddly in the circumstances, for her views on the Spanish Civil War, in which fascist and communist forces were locked in a deadly conflict, she was clever enough to say, 'I'm sorry for both sides. It will be the ruin of beautiful Spain.' Several reporters noted that she was wearing an enormous sapphire engagement ring on the third finger of her left hand; apparently, she had tired of the Mogul emerald engagement ring that the duke had given her on the night of the granting of her decree at Ipswich and wanted a jewel that was closer to the colour of her eyes.

During the next few days, Wallis accustomed herself to the atmosphere of the Château de Candé. She studied everything Fern Bedaux did with the utmost care; she told Fern that the chateau was the best-run house she had ever stayed in. Fern, a tall, elegant, exquisitely groomed product of Grand Rapids, Michigan, came from old money and ran her household with superb expertise. She was also a stern taskmistress: if one of the maids or manservants was heard talking or giggling outside the kitchen, the offender was immediately sent below stairs. Hale was a fussy but skilful butler. Briskly, with much slapping together of his hands, he ordered about the two footmen, the ladies' maids, the upstairs maid, the downstairs maid and the scullery maid; the only part of the house where he was not in command was the kitchen. That was the domain of Legros, who had formerly been chef to the Duke of Alba, a chief financier of Franco; Legros was considered virtually matchless, and his three-star cuisine would have done justice to any fine restaurant in Paris. After the mediocrity of the cooking performed by the Rogerses' couple, Wallis was at last able to eat some decent food.

Bedaux and his architects had modernized the castle, covering the furniture with eighteenth-century patterned linens that had been found in rolls in the attic when he bought the house from its previous owners, run-down French aristocrats. He had also installed new plumbing and heating, with vast furnaces in the basement. Wallis's bathroom had heated platinum-plated towel rails and an enormous tub equipped with massive gold taps. There was even a gilded fountain to keep newly bought fish fresh; fish were always bought live for the Château de Candé.

Dinner parties at the chateau were small but formal and done with great style. Two cloths were put on for evening meals. The first layer was a cloth of gold; the second was fine Brussels lace. The effect was beautiful; the gold shone through under the glistening light of the candelabra. Meals were served by Hale and the flunkeys in livery. The monogrammed china and silver were of the finest quality. An individual menu was written out in copperplate for each guest and placed on a tiny silver rest in front of him or her. If Hale didn't like someone, he would turn the tray offered from the left so that the guest got the worst piece of fowl or fish; and he would never top up the wine of someone he hated unless he was specifically asked to do so. The fowl were brought to the table 'dressed' (with their feathers on) so everyone could see and feel them. Then they were cooked and served.

After dinner, for smaller occasions, Hale would put dance music records on the radiogram. For larger events, Marcel Dupré, the best-known organist of his day, would perform at the enormous Skinner cinema organ in the living room, its bronze pipes carefully hidden under oak panelling and the music of Bach and Handel emerging through a grille. Sometimes Fern Bedaux would take her guests to the small pavilion in the grounds, a tiny lodge rather like a shooting box. There, Wallis and her friends would join in card games or roll up the carpet and dance to the wind-up gramophone. Fern would stand on the sidelines, not joining in. Wallis could not have been more content in this sumptuous environment. Even her fastidious tastes were satisfied at last.

Meanwhile, on 18 March, there was at last some action on the divorce. The King's Proctor, Sir Thomas Barnes, announced that the case would be discussed in court the following day. Sir Boyd Merriman, president of the divorce court, would hear the matter at 10.30 a.m. The Attorney General, Sir Donald Somervell, would appear to report the result of the investigations by the King's Proctor. Surprisingly, neither Ernest nor Wallis was required to be present. Wallis had a sleepless night over this, but in fact she need not have worried. Somervell announced in court that he had found no grounds for an intervention and that there was no basis for any possible belief that the divorce was collusive. The judge asked if Francis Stephenson, the clerk who had entered a complaint charging that there had been irregularities in the original procedures, was there. Stephenson responded that he was indeed. Small, round-shouldered, with a drooping grey moustache, he admitted he had taken legal action on 9 December. He confirmed, however, that he no longer had any reason for complaint and asked that his original charges be permanently stricken from the record. Asked by news-papermen as he left the building why he had taken the action in the first place, he snapped, 'You can go on wondering! Go away! I have other fish to fry!' It seemed obvious that he had been put up to the task of disrupting the divorce, but had withdrawn because of his feelings as a loyal subject. The irony, of course, was that the divorce in fact *was* collusive; the wonder is that nobody was able to prove it.

There would still be some time before the decree absolute would be granted. Nevertheless, Wallis was greatly relieved to hear that there would be no major obstacles from now on. The duke was equally pleased with the news, but he was as restless and fretful as ever; having virtually forced Kitty out of her own home, he was burdened by the problems of running Schloss Enzesfeld and began making plans to move. By March, the duke's letters to Wallis had become almost literally hysterical. 'God's curses be on the heads of those English bitches who dare to insult you!' he wrote. Sir Walford Selby and Dudley Forwood found him a new residence: a small hotel called Appesbach House near St Wolfgang in the Salzkam-mergut lake district of Austria. It had a private bathing beach, a landing stage, a tennis court and a good view of water and moun-tains. In the previous few weeks the duke had acquired no fewer than seventeen members of staff, including several maids and a valet, two-thirds of whom he was now compelled to dismiss. He was suffering from bad toothache and had flown in Dr Sumner Moore from Wimpole Street to take care of the problem. His ear con-tinued to bother him despite the numerous ministrations of Dr Neumann. His mood was scarcely helped by the fact that Winston Churchill was still running into every possible obstacle in London on the question of the money. On 22 March, the duke wrote to Wallis saying that one day he would 'get back at all those swine [in England]' and make them realize 'how disgustingly and unsport-ingly they have behaved'.

On the 31st, Wallis wrote to the duke, once again attacking his 'wretched brother', and suggesting that if the treatment continued the duke should announce to the world the ill-treatment he had received. She advised the duke to make the king 'ashamed of himself – if possible'.

On 28 March, the duke was given a farewell in the form of a torchlight procession in the village of Enzesfeld. Schoolchildren, followed by members of the local fire service and police, walked through the streets and up to the castle with torches held high, chanting in unison and providing a concert of local traditional music. The next morning the duke drove to St Wolfgang. He was accompanied by Sir Godfrey Thomas and Dudley Forwood. On arrival at Appesbach House, the duke walked out on to his bedroom balcony, staring moodily at the mountains in their veil of early spring mist. He was accompanied by his new cairn terrier, Schnuki; Slipper had already been sent to Wallis by train. He spent the next few days climbing in the mountains with Forwood and visiting local monasteries and the summer residence of the late Emperor Franz Josef. His love of the Teutonic scenery and fascination with the relics of the Hapsburgs were characteristic. He was still moving behind the scenes for the restoration of the Archduke Otto to the Austrian throne.

On 8 April, Slipper, who had a tendency to run around looking for rats and mice, had strayed on to the golf course near the Château de Candé and was bitten fatally by a viper. 'Now the principal guest of the wedding is no more,' Wallis wrote in agony to the duke. He responded in kind, saying, 'My heart is quite breaking this morning my beloved sweetheart from sadness.' They were both devastated by the loss; Wallis couldn't bear the thought of burying the animal, so Herman Rogers took care of it. Lady Mendl and her favourite Johnny McMullen came down to the chateau to console Wallis.[2] Wallis had other troubles too: Fern went off to Paris and London for the visit she had interrupted to receive Wallis, and Wallis was not entirely comfortable living with only the staff for company. Moreover, she was perplexed by the question of her birth records. For over a month, she had been plaguing Aunt Bessie to get her a certificate of some kind, as required by French law, but of course this was not forthcoming. At last, the enterprising

Aunt Bessie found a solution. She would contact the young doctor, Lewis M. Allen, who had been rushed to Blue Ridge Summit to take care of the birth. He signed an affidavit stating the date and time of Wallis's arrival.

On 25 April, 212 East Biddle Street, Baltimore, was opened as a museum. Wallis's bedroom was prominently displayed; 150 people peered into it in groups of six after making their way up the narrow staircase. As it happened, none of the original furniture remained; only the kitchen, with its coal-burning stove, was more or less the same. Wallis's handwritten recipe for apple popovers was propped up on a shelf above it.

Wallis was furious when she learned that the museum offered a lifelike wax figure of herself, dressed in the wedding gown from her marriage with Ernest Simpson that Simpson had stolen and her friend Mary Raffray had sold to the owners through the agency of her friend Gloria Vanderbilt; and, that, to add insult to injury, she was shown kneeling before King George and Queen Mary, her worst enemies. When a reporter asked the museum's co-owner if this was a shrine to the Duchess of Windsor, he snapped back with, 'Only God and His saints are for shrines. Mrs Simpson is neither!' When Thelma Furness told Wallis this (and admitted she got a percentage of the sale of the stolen wedding gown'), Wallis snapped, 'Who does that man think he is? The Archbishop of Canterbury?'

The duke was perturbed by the publication by William Heinemann of a book entitled *Coronation Commentary*, written by Geoffrey Dennis. The duke claimed that the book libelled him, even though today it seems entirely harmless. He actually sued, through the offices of George Allen, successfully seeking to enjoin the publishers from releasing the book. At the same time, Wallis dropped her suit against Newbold Noyes, her cousin by marriage, in the matter of his articles in the American and French newspapers. Armand Grégoire remained her lawyer.

On 14 April, Wallis wrote the most revealing of all her letters to the duke. She stated, referring to the king, 'Well who cares let him be pushed off the throne.' No doubt she expressed sentiments of this sort at dinner tables on the Riviera, ensuring the permanent disfavour in which she would be held by many at the palace. Read in conjunction with the duke's threats in an earlier letter to return to England and resume the throne ('WE will be back in our glory sooner than WE think'), and his plans, which would soon be announced to a London journalist, to form a republic in England with himself as president and Wallis as first lady, it is clear that her statement, seditious from a naturalized British citizen, is not to be taken lightly.

At the end of April, Lord Wigram advised Winston Churchill that the king personally guaranteed he would take care of the duke's income in the future. Lloyd George was given a similar assurance. As a result, neither Churchill nor Lloyd George brought the matter up before the Civil List committee. The duke was greatly relieved to hear the news. But there were still problems to face. British law required that the weddings of British citizens abroad must take place at a local consulate, not at a private residence. Furthermore, it would be virtually impossible to find an Anglican clergyman to perform the ceremony. By this stage, too, the investigations made by Baldwin's detectives must have established that Wallis had been born illegitimate and had no certificate of baptism; in addition, under British law the marriage could not take place until six months had elapsed from the original divorce decree. Nevertheless, Wallis pressed forward with her plans. Since she couldn't face the reporters, she asked for various Paris designers to send her their latest creations for consideration for her trousseau. Squadrons of couturiers' assistants arrived to show her an extraordinary variety of morning, afternoon and evening clothes. Among those who submitted originals to her were Schiaparelli, Mainbocher and Chanel. She finally decided to give Mainbocher the authorization to dress her for the wedding itself; his rivals supplied the trousseau.

Mainbocher named the colour of her wedding dress 'Wallis blue'. She had a total of sixty-six dresses, including several of a bold, not to say vulgar, design with patterns of lobsters and butterflies on white or silver backgrounds. These were in seemingly deliberate contrast to the image she had of being exquisitely tasteful at all times.

Much of the concern that the crucial figures in the Windsor matter felt at this time was expressed in a confidential note, sent from Buckingham Palace, written by Alexander Hardinge to Sir Robert Vansittart. Dated 1 May 1937, it read:

> My dear Van,
>
> As I told you during our talk yesterday, The King was asked by both [ambassadors] Phipps and Selby for instructions as to the attitude which they should adopt in their relations with the Duke of Windsor and Mrs Simpson, after their marriage.
>
> They wanted to know what His Majesty's wishes would be as regards their entertainment, either official or private, or their participation in official ceremonies of any kind.
>
> The King realizes that in the future his representatives may be faced with problems of this sort at very short notice, and it would, in His Majesty's opinion, be desirable that, as far as possible, they should be given instructions in advance.
>
> The King would therefore be obliged if you would kindly submit suggestions for dealing with the different situations which, in your opinion, are most likely to arise.

Vansittart replied on 4 May:

> Very many thanks for your letter of the 1st about the Duke of Windsor.
>
> I entirely agree with the King, if I may respectfully say so, in thinking that HRH should be given as much guidance as is possible in a matter which is entirely without precedent and bristling with every conceivable sort of problem.
>
> Having said this, I need not expatiate upon the difficulty of giving suitable advice or excuse myself for the coarsity of the suggestions which I feel able to make in the circumstances.
>
> Such as these are, they divide themselves into two categories: (1) official, (2) private. As for (1) – e.g., when the Duke and Duchess (to be) are present in a Capital where an official reception is to be given and the question arises whether steps should be taken to see that they are invited to it – I should say that the only course to follow is for HM representatives concerned to ask special instructions in every case, as to which we should of course consult you.
>
> As regards (2), my feeling is that these cases might be left to the discretion of the man in charge at the moment, with the

option, of course, of asking for advice if he needs it . . . What I think we ought to avoid, if we can, is a situation in which the Duke might ask an ambassador or minister to put him and his wife up for a visit. I don't suppose this is likely to arise. Misconceptions might be created if it did, particularly if any interviews or contacts with political personages took place during the stay . . . As a general line, Eden feels that our representatives should treat the Duke of Windsor and his wife rather as they would a member of the Royal Family on a holiday; but that if anything were contemplated which might give to the visit a more serious aspect, our representatives must necessarily refer home . . . In any case, we shall need instructions or confirmation from the King.

Two matters emerge from the somewhat veiled wording used here by Vansittart. First, that there was real fear that the Duke and Wallis would make untoward political connections through their use of the facilities provided by embassies in different capitals; and second, that then, as later, every one of the decisions vis-à-vis the Windsors came directly from the king. It was only possible to reach the latter conclusion in 1987, when these crucially important letters at last became available.

On 2 May, villagers at St Wolfgang turned out en masse for a celebration in honour of the duke. They provided an elaborate pageant of local history, in traditional costumes, the mountainside glittering with a giant swastika that appeared to be on fire. When the duke inquired with false naivety why this Nazi symbol was being used, he was told, no doubt with a touch of cynical local humour, 'It is a demonstration of our sentiments.' On the 3rd, Sir Boyd Merriman, with little ado, made the divorce absolute in London. Within minutes reporters dashed to the telephones to call the duke in Austria. He was overjoyed and immediately had his staff pack up everything; without waiting one more instant than he had to, he drove to Salzburg to join the express for Paris. He boarded at 4.45 p.m., carrying in his arms two wrapped gifts for Wallis, one a bouquet of edelweiss and the other a dirndl. His private car was crammed with the seventeen suitcases that he refused to put in the luggage van; it was almost impossible to move. He was accompanied by his detective bodyguard, Storrier, and a valet; the other members of his staff would follow by separate train. Dr Allen's affidavit of Wallis's birth arrived via the French consul at the local British legation the same afternoon. Also on the same day, the Civil List was published in London, with no mention of the duke.

On 4 May, the duke arrived at Verneuil l'Etang, a small town near Paris; Sir Eric Phipps, now ambassador to France, had arranged for the Orient Express to be stopped there and for his first secretary Hugh Thomas, who much admired the duke, to meet him on the platform. The station was cleared, and the newsreel camera team and reporters who had penetrated the veil of secrecy surrounding the arrival were forbidden to enter the station. The duke left the train with his equerry, Captain Greenacre, the ever present Storrier, and several newspaper reporters who had travelled in the adjoining car. In very good spirits, he chatted briefly with the officers of the Sûreté who were there to ensure his safety and left almost at once for the Château de Candé, escorted by a police car and two *gardes mobiles* on motorcycles.

A crowd was waiting at the gates of the chateau as the duke drove up and rapturously embraced Wallis. Charles Bedaux had arrived a week earlier from New York. Chunky, jug-eared, with the face of a prizefighter who had received several batterings in the ring, Bedaux endeared himself immediately to Wallis and the duke. With charm, charisma and energy he had risen from penury as a tunnel sandhog – an underground labourer – in New York to build a million-dollar business. His highly controversial 'Bedaux B-unit system', aimed at improving efficiency in factories and offices, had greatly helped management in a number of major companies while provoking considerable criticism among the more left-wing elements in the unions for its alleged exhausting effects. Although frequently accused of being pro-Nazi, Bedaux had no more time for Hitler or Mussolini than he did for President Roosevelt or Stanley Baldwin. He was characteristic of the internationalist, pragmatic adventurer-businessmen of the era, crossing all frontiers, ignoring wars as temporary inconveniences, doing business with anyone who would do business with them. His German company had been confiscated, and he was now in the process of trying to win it back. In the course of his efforts, he had become friendly with another skilful internationalist, Hitler's adjutant and First World War commanding officer, the polished and ingenious Fritz Wiedemann.

It was in those first weeks at the Château de Candé that the duke, through Wiedemann, made direct contact with Hitler, asking if it would be convenient to arrange a visit to Germany to study labour conditions there. It was typical of the duke's effrontery and defiance of Buckingham Palace that he would wish to undertake such a mission. It was understood that Ribbentrop was received, as was customary in the case of all ambassadors, by his brother the king and that Anthony Eden, who was still Foreign Secretary, was pursuing a policy of not provoking the Führer; however, for any member of the royal family to embark upon such a visit to Hitler could only cause the utmost distress in Whitehall. The British were still playing for time, hoping to strengthen Britain's position in terms of its military resources while seemingly not disapproving of the Nazi regime. And it was feared that, embittered as he was, the duke might give the game away.

Simultaneously, he rashly selected as his honeymoon venue Schloss Wasserleonburg in southern Austria, owned by Count Paul Munster, husband of Margaret (Peggy) Ward, who was related to the duke's former mistress Mrs Dudley Ward. Munster, a member of the January Club who had dual British and German citizenship, was on Vansittart's watch list. It seemed that the duke was almost deliberately trying to provoke the interest of the Secret Intelligence Service.

The duke asked Sir Eric Phipps to request the French government to grant a special dispensation that would enable the mayor of Monts to perform the civil ceremony at the chateau instead of the town hall in order to minimize publicity and overcrowding. This was approved. At Candé Wallis and the duke, their bedrooms discreetly at opposite ends of the chateau, spent their time playing golf and cards and chatting with their host and hostess. Now that they were reunited, they seemed to all observers to be very happy. Their hosts left them alone for several days, allowing them to enjoy their pleasure in each other in seclusion. They even posed for photographs on the lawn and talked in a relaxed and gracious manner with reporters.

NOTES

1 The political situation in Austria vis-à-vis Nazi Germany was extremely delicate where Jews were concerned. Although nothing approaching Hitler's behaviour towards Jewish people existed in Austria, there was always the threat that the situation might change and the Rothschilds would have to leave.
2 Yet ungratefully, Wallis failed to invite either of them to the wedding.

12

WEDDING OF THE DECADE

The coronation of King George VI and Queen Elizabeth was set for 12 May. It was, of course, out of the question for the Duke of Windsor and his mistress to attend it. On 7 May, the duke and Wallis made their first motor trip out of the chateau. They were chased by newsreel cameramen to the village of Semblançay, where the news teams were perilously perched upon the rooftops, shouting back and refusing to budge when the local police told them to get down. The couple had lunch at an inn and then continued to the village of Vendôme, where they met US consul George Tate at the Grand Hotel. He gave Wallis the sworn statement by the doctor on the circumstances of her birth – described as a 'birth certificate' in the press. As though seriously preparing for a more responsible role as a married man, the duke cut out spirits, replacing them with wine.

Schloss Wasserleonburg was being prepared for the couple's arrival; a new tennis court was laid and the driveway, which was badly potholed, was carefully repaired. Among those who arrived at Candé to offer their congratulations were Lady Brownlow, Mrs Ronald Greville, Mrs Richard Norton and the duke's equerry, Captain W. D. C. Greenacre, just returned from leave in London. The following day Wallis completed arrangements to alter her name back to Wallis Warfield by deed poll. In her application for a marriage licence, she declared herself 'single'.

The duke still retained a futile hope that the Dukes of Kent and Gloucester and his sister Mary would attend the wedding, with the

Duke of Kent as best man. On 11 May, he announced his formal engagement to Wallis at last, strategically timing the press conference at Candé to occur on the eve of his brother's coronation in Westminster Abbey. Wallis displayed the Mogul emerald in her engagement ring; the sapphire had fallen out of favour. Mainbocher arrived with his staff for the third fitting of her wedding gown.

The couple was now informed that the French government, on grounds of courtesy to its British counterpart, would not permit the wedding to be broadcast on the radio. When CBS and NBC applied, they were informed that any attempt to bring microphones to the chateau would be prevented by the police. On the evening of the 12th, Wallis and the duke listened to King George's hesitant postcoronation broadcast; outside, a heavy rainstorm lashed the chateau while the duke knitted a blue sweater for Wallis, plying the needles busily. Neither Wallis nor the duke felt inclined to toast the speech as millions were doing all over the world. A telegram arrived at the chateau close to midnight, announcing that Aunt Bessie had sailed on the US liner *President Roosevelt.* Lelia Barnett made the mistake of giving Aunt Bessie a copy of *Coronation Commentary* as a goodbye present.

In the subsequent days, the question arose of whether Wallis would be given the title 'Her Royal Highness'; for weeks the duke had been pestering the Palace for approval of this. Walter Monckton was doing his best, and so was Winston Churchill, but their efforts were futile. It was determined that the marriage was invalid in the eyes of the Church, which did not recognize divorce. The duke was seeking an announcement of the marriage in the *London Gazette*, which normally contained listings of weddings of which the king approved. There was no response from the Palace on the matter.

Wallis and the duke did not fail to note a most ominous event in London. Count Grandi described it in 1986:

> Something occurred which greatly embittered our national relationship with Great Britain. As we know, the former King had refused to recognize Emperor Haile Selassie on the grounds that he did not wish to provoke Mussolini. But King George VI

invited the former Ambassador of Ethiopia to the Coronation. When Mussolini found this out, he was furious. He impulsively stopped the Prince and Princess of Piedmont, members of the Italian Royal Family, from attending. The British Government interpreted this withdrawal as a deep offence to the Crown of England.

The Prince and Princess of Piedmont were great friends of the Duke of Windsor. It must have been clear to the duke that everything he had feared vis-à-vis the breakdown of relations between Mussolini and the British government was coming true.

On 16 May, Wallis and the duke were guests of their friends the Grafton W. Minots, wealthy Boston and New York socialites, at a nearby chateau. During dinner, as the hostess toasted the happy couple, a bolt of lightning struck the electrical plant next door, ominously plunging everybody in the dining room into gloom. The next night Dudley Forwood set sail for England to escort Aunt Bessie to the chateau.

On the 19th, in Paris, the duke visited the President of France, whom he knew well from the occasion of the funeral of the assassinated Monsieur Doumer and from a luncheon at the President's residence at Rambouillet. At the meeting, he discussed his views on maintaining peace in Europe.

That same day, final word arrived from Buckingham Palace that the king and the prime minister would not permit any member of the royal family to attend the wedding – a depressing end to almost three and a half months of negotiations. For some reason, Wallis decided that she would invite no member of her own family apart from Aunt Bessie. Perhaps she felt that to include her cousins Corinne and Lelia and their families would be offensive to Whitehall, and possibly she was still so disaffected with Lelia's husband Newbold Noyes over his articles that she would not consider inviting him.

The wedding date was set for 3 June. By what one hopes was an unfortunate coincidence, this was the date of King George V's birth. On 16 May, Wallis and the duke signed their marriage contract, guaranteeing that their property would be entirely separate and that no claim would be made on either in the event of a divorce. At first, it was announced by Herman Rogers that there would be no religious ceremony, only a civil marriage performed by Charles Mercier, mayor of the nearby village of Monts. This decision, however, was quickly reversed. There was talk that the Reverend C. H. D. Grimes, rector of the Anglican church of Vienna, would officiate; the duke had read a lesson from the Bible for him the previous December. The Archbishop of Canterbury intervened, however, and Grimes withdrew. The wedding ring of Welsh gold, similar to those worn by several English queens, was brought from Paris. One of the first to see it was the millionaire Cornelius Vanderbilt, Jr, who, in an incongruous touch, declined to stay in the chateau itself, lodging himself instead in a large American trailer outside the main gate. The vulgarity of this action did not escape the attention of the French press.

On 25 May, Mayor Mercier rehearsed Wallis and the duke for the civil ceremony in the music room of the chateau. The couple was still without a minister. When a Liverpool parson offered to preside, the Archbishop of York expressly forbade him. Aunt Bessie arrived, delayed in Paris by a cold, and bustled around the chateau with astonishing energy, causing consternation among the staff. She even dared usurp the supreme power of the omnipotent Hale.

Wallis's friend Constance Coolidge arrived from Baltimore. She wrote to an American acquaintance on the 28th, 'I have never seen anyone as happy as the Duke – like a boy let out of school. He is gay, carefree, laughing, and terribly in love.' At lunch, which he rarely attended ('His Royal Highness is doing you a great honour, Constance, as he never comes to lunch as a rule,' Wallis said), he complained cheerfully about the weather, which had stopped him from playing golf, and said he hadn't enjoyed staying with the Rothschilds because he didn't like Kitty. When Constance asked him if he would want to race horses, he replied, 'I can't. I'm too poor. But the one thing I would like to have if I had a lot of money is a nice yacht.'

After coffee, Hale and two liveried footmen arrived with silver trays completely covered in letters. 'How many are there today?' Wallis asked. 'Only four hundred and fifty,' Hale replied. The letters were filled with poems, music, photographs, insults, threats and requests for everything imaginable, including a discarded pair of shoes. The phone rang forty times in two hours. Representatives of Van Cleef and Arpels arrived from Paris with trays of jewellery, followed by a case of gems, an inscribed gold box from Hitler, an onyx and diamond clock from Herman and Katherine Rogers, and costly gifts from Mussolini, Ciano and Alberto da Zara of China days. Dinner that night, to which Randolph Churchill came, was hot dogs and ginger beer. Constance Coolidge wrote:

> [The duke] wore a Scottish plaid of the Black Watch – black and green kilt, and a sort of white shirt – very smart, and she had ... such jewels: two huge leaves or feathers on the left side of her dress, one in diamonds and the other in rubies, diamond-and-ruby earrings, and diamond-and-ruby bracelets and a ruby ring ... After dinner we went into the living room ... Suddenly [the duke] noticed that Wallis's slipper was undone, and he went down on both knees and tied it up. I caught Randolph Churchill's eye at this moment, and his expression was amusing – to say the least.

When Constance went to bed at 1.30 a.m., quite exhausted from the long evening, Wallis and the duke banged on the door, announced they had come to see if she was all right, sat down on the edge of the bed and started the conversation all over again. The duke announced that the lamp was badly situated for reading, got down on all fours on the floor and crawled about, fixing wires and plugs until the lamp was in a better place. It was typical of his almost childlike naturalness, contrast with his sophistication and guile.

On 29 May, the *London Gazette* printed the following devastating announcement:

> The King has been pleased by letters patent under the great seal of the realm, bearing the date of the 27th of May, 1937, to declare that the Duke of Windsor shall, notwithstanding an instrument of abdication, executed on the 10th day of December, 1936, and His Majesty's Declaration of the Abdication Act of 1936, whereby effect was given to the said instrument, be entitled to hold and enjoy for himself only the title, style or attribute of Royal Highness so however that his wife and descendants, if any, shall not hold said title, style or attribute.

This decision had been passed at a meeting of the cabinet. The prime minister, Baldwin, had refused to take the chair, and in his place the home secretary, Sir John Simon, strongly influenced the setting of this unfortunate precedent. To the end of his life, Sir Dudley Forwood never forgot the moment when the duke was informed of the British government's – and his brother the king's – decision:

> [My master] put down his beautiful head with its golden hair in my lap and sobbed helplessly. His heart was broken, and in a sense it never healed. I never saw such agonizing grief, even from the bereaved, or from those who had been told that they had but a short time to live.

As the Joseph P. Kennedy diaries make clear, the chief influences in the matter were the women of the royal family: the Queen Mary, the queen, the Duchesses of Gloucester and Kent and the Princess Royal, all of whom, to use a term given to Kenneth de Courcy, Duc de Grantmesnil, regarded Wallis as 'a woman of easy virtue', based upon their readings of the China dossier. Queen Victoria is said to have issued an edict laying down the principle that the title 'Royal Highness' was to be enjoyed only by blood relations of the reigning monarch, but in fact this edict had been overridden in at least two famous cases. Her Majesty Queen Elizabeth was a commoner as Lady Elizabeth Bowes-Lyon, but she had been granted the title 'Her Royal Highness' when she became Duchess of York. Lady Alice Montagu Douglas-Scott had also assumed that title when she married the Duke of Gloucester. To this day, no satisfactory documentation has been produced to support a legal basis for the denial of the title to Wallis; in fact, she and the duke spent the rest of their lives ignoring the gazetted notice. The duke insisted – with what to many was an irritating degree of persistence – upon Wallis's being called 'Your Royal Highness' by everyone, and he demanded that she be curtseyed to both in private and on public occasions. In many cases ladies obeyed his command only to please him, fully aware of the fact that their action might bring displeasure at the palace. Wallis was never curtseyed to by members of the queen's household. Members of foreign royal families were forbidden to do so. On her stationery Wallis used the royal insignia, either a coronet surmounted by a lion rampant or two entwined Ws under a royal coronet. She and the duke took the view that as his wife she was entitled to use whatever royal imprints she chose. There were many who disagreed. It was not until 1972 that the College of Arms would officially authorize her use of the royal coronet, and then only after the duke's death.

'The wedding will be very small,' Aunt Bessie wrote to Corinne in Washington, DC, on 31 May. 'Wallis is very well. Thin, but she looks splendidly and she is in fine spirits.' On the 30th Helena Normanton of the *New York Times* boldly asked Wallis about her Nazi connections. Wallis replied, quite contradicting Mary Kirk Raffray, 'I cannot recall ever being in Herr von Ribbentrop's company more than twice, once at a party at Lady Cunard's before he became Ambassador, and once at another big reception. I was never alone in his company, and I never had more than a few words of conversation with him – simply the usual small talk, that is all. I took no interest at all in politics.' Miss Normanton did not have the temerity to question this statement.

More wedding guests began to arrive on 1 June. They included Hugh Lloyd Thomas, first secretary at the British embassy in Paris; Lady (Walford) Selby; Walter Monckton; Fruity and Alexandra Metcalfe; the Eugene Rothschilds; George Allen; and Dudley Forwood. At the last minute a clergyman had been found to officiate: the Reverend R. Anderson Jardine, vicar of St Paul's church in Darlington, County Durham. Although it was claimed that Charles Bedaux had bribed Jardine to defy his Church and conduct the ceremony, Jardine had in fact volunteered by letter. Despite dire threats from his bishop and from the Archbishop of York, he made his way to the chateau and began working on the arrangements immediately. Back in England, Jardine had become infuriated by the press announcement that there would be no religious ceremony; abandoning his breakfast, he had paced agitatedly around the room, gone into his garden and entered an old army tent, where he sank to his knees in prayer. When he rose to his feet, his mind was made up: he would write to Herman Rogers congratulating the duke and stating that he would be prepared to officiate. That Sunday morning, while he was conducting the children's services, he received a telegram from George Allen asking him to call. The following day he met Allen in London; Allen arranged his passport with amazing speed and in the utmost secrecy. The next morning Jardine boarded the boat train. After a brief stay in Paris he was picked up at the local station and driven to the chateau by the duke's chauffeur.

Cecil Beaton was already there, taking photographs of Wallis and the duke. The Rogerses had entertained Beaton with after-dinner films of Peking, the *Nahlin* cruise and Wallis's stay at Balmoral. The chateau was in a turmoil as Constance Spry, the famous florist from London, arrived with her assistant to decorate the residence with flower displays. Wallis watched everything carefully; she was visibly exhausted by the strain of the occasion. But the duke looked fit and suntanned and very happy. The Reverend Jardine drove up and the Rogerses met him at the front steps. Rogers said to him as he shook his hand, 'Thank God you have arrived. Now I shall have something to say to the press.'

A few minutes later, Rogers read to the crowd of reporters in French and English the astonishing announcement that the civil ceremony would be followed by a religious one. This turned the tables on a newspaper hoax that had been proposed, in which the columnist Logan Glendenning would suddenly turn up, wearing a clerical outfit, and perform a fake wedding which would be instantly declared a practical joke. Photographs had even been planned for this vicious leg-pull. The would-be hoaxers were dumbfounded by Rogers's announcement.

Jardine was introduced to the duke and Wallis by George Allen. The duke, dressed in open-neck shirt and shorts, said to Jardine, 'Why wouldn't they give us a religious ceremony? We are both Christians . . . You are the only one who had the guts to do this for me.' Jardine gave a prayer book to Wallis; then everybody began searching for an appropriate 'holy table' in the absence of an altar. In the frantic hunt somebody broke an Italian lamp. Finally, Jardine discovered a hall chest. The problem was that it was faced with plump nude nymphs holding up a fake Renaissance carving. Protesting against the chest's vulgarity, Wallis managed to find a cream-coloured, embroidered silk cloth from one of her linen trunks, and she and Katherine began draping the chest to cover the offending nudes. George Allen came in with two silver candlesticks, but Wallis rejected them as they were to be used for dinner. Jardine asked if there was a cross available. Charles Bedaux replied that he had several, but all of them showed the Christ figure; Jardine refused to have a crucifix. The duke suggested contacting the British embassy or even London for a suitable cross. Another crucifix arrived and was rejected. Finally, Bedaux obtained a plain cross from a local church.

There was a hunt for cushions for the couple to kneel on. Beaton took shots of the duke in Wallis's room, followed by photographs of the couple. The session continued after lunch and well into the afternoon. As the duke and Wallis were standing before a turret window for the wedding shots, a communication from Walter Monckton arrived stating that the duke's last-minute appeal to his brother on the matter of 'Her Royal Highness' had failed.

However, the duke pulled himself together and continued to cooperate with Beaton. When he left that night, Beaton was appalled to discover that a conventional photographer for the London *Evening Standard* had published a photograph ahead of him. Forwood was under great pressure from reporters. In 1987, he remembered one saying to him, 'Do you think the duke has fucked Mrs Simpson yet?' to which Forwood replied, 'I haven't been in the bed.' The reporters laughed. Forwood continued, 'Right up to the last minute the duke hoped that his brothers the Dukes of Kent and Gloucester would come, that somehow the royal family would relent. But they did not. He was deeply, deeply hurt.'

There was a pre-wedding dinner. Everyone at the table was in the best of spirits. Charles Bedaux sat at the head, the duke at the lower end. After separating, the men for brandy and cigars and the women for light conversation, the guests gathered in the library for a recital by Marcel Dupré. Bored as usual by music, the duke left the recital, drew Jardine aside and questioned him, with surprisingly detailed knowledge, on the problems of poverty and unemployment in Durham.

Thursday, 3 June arrived at last. The weather was perfect. 'King's weather', many of the press called it, not quite appropriately. By 7 a.m., a complete ring of police had surrounded the chateau. There were many detectives from the Sûreté. The government had forbidden planes to fly overhead. The entire village of Monts was lined up along the avenue of pines that led to the gates. Jardine went to see the duke at 7.15. He was, Jardine wrote, 'as happy as a schoolboy'. 'I suppose I should have a prayer book,' the duke said, and ran out and fetched one given to him by his mother when he was a child. With tears in his eyes, he showed Jardine the loving message inscribed in it. By contrast, Lady Alexandra Metcalfe later recalled that Wallis looked hard, cold and quietly triumphant now that her hour had arrived.

The civil service took place at 11.42 a.m., and only four news-papermen were permitted to witness the ceremony. The duke's wedding gift to Wallis was a diamond tiara. He wore a black morning coat and striped trousers, with a white carnation in his buttonhole. Wallis looked almost too stiff and formal in Main-bocher's box-shouldered blue outfit. She wore matching jewellery: a diamond and sapphire brooch, bracelet and earrings. The near-sighted Mayor Mercier was extremely nervous, and the duke kept clasping and unclasping his fingers behind his back.

The religious service followed. Above the holy table stood two golden candelabra with sixty-two candles apiece. Two more candles flanked the gilt ormolu mirror at the back of the improvised altar. Marcel Dupré struck up the strains of Handel's 'Wedding March' from *Judas Maccabeus*. During the benediction Dupré played 'O Perfect Love'. Only the duke's excessively loud and high-pitched 'I will' disrupted the composed atmosphere of the ceremony. The Welsh gold wedding ring[1] made Wallis the Duchess of Windsor. There was no incense, no choir, no pomp. Yet no one who witnessed this occasion would ever forget it.

As Herman Rogers walked out to the porch to announce that the wedding was over, and the couple joined their guests in a buffet lunch of lobster, salad, chicken à la king and strawberries, the elderly French housekeeper took a bottle of champagne and ritu-ally broke it against the gate, a local tradition; with characteristic neatness, she then removed the broken glass with a broom. Rogers managed to extract a promise from the reporters that they would not pursue the newly-weds to the railway station.

Back in England, the *Church Times*, the members of St Paul's Anglican church at Darlington and several religious bodies condemned Jardine's action outright. He returned home to a blizzard of criticism and, unswervingly loyal to the duke and duchess, decided in the face of widespread criticism to leave his parsonage and make his way to the United States, where he and his wife opened a modest house of religion which they called the Windsor Cathedral of Los Angeles. They were deported back to England for overstaying their visas in 1942.

Forwood never forgot the events that followed the wedding. The duke and duchess and their large entourage made their way in a convoy of cars to join the Simplon-Orient Express at Laroche-Migennes. They were accompanied by two armed motorcyclists in uniform and a car filled with French *gendarmes*. Another car was filled with English detectives. Dressers, footmen, the household comptroller Monsieur James, the duchess's maids and numerous others followed. Because Forwood had not realized that the police escort would drive at a slow speed according to tradition, he had misjudged the length of time it would take to meet the train. He was already worried about the delay and the fact that the train might be missed when, to his horror, the Duke announced, 'We're going to have a lovely picnic!' Forwood dared not break rank to announce that this might mean missing the express. Following the royal command, every car stopped and a procession led by Wallis and the duke made its way into the fields. The duke told Forwood he wanted the dogs to be let off their leashes so that they could relieve themselves. Forwood said that if that were the case, they might get lost. The duchess agreed with Forwood.

The duke then ordered Forwood to take the dogs on their leashes into a cornfield and, in front of everyone, raise his leg repeatedly so that they would follow suit. By the time he had achieved his purpose, tables had been set up for what presumably would be a royal banquet. But when Monsieur James opened the large picnic hampers, it was discovered that all they contained was peaches. Due to some error in the kitchens of the Château de Candé, the rest of the food had all been sent to the train in advance and only the fruit was passed through in the royal caravan. Everyone had to eat peaches until several people felt ill. It could have been a scene from Saint-Simon's journals of the court of Louis XIV.

By the time this disagreeable feast was over, it became obvious even to the duke that the Orient Express might leave without the party. Everyone piled back into the cars, and the chauffeurs drove at reckless speed to the station. Fortunately, though much to the annoyance of the passengers, the express had been held. Then there was the laborious business of putting 266 pieces of royal luggage aboard; the duke insisted that fifty pieces be placed in his private car, leaving scarcely any room even to move. The car was ablaze from one end to the other with red and yellow roses.

The train's departure was still further delayed because one of the two newly acquired cairn terriers escaped and had to be retrieved. In her hurry, the duchess had left her hat in her car, and another vehicle with numerous suitcases turned up late.

The Orient Express stopped in Venice on the way to Austria. After so many restrictions on their visits to Italy because of the sensitivity of the Foreign Office, under Anthony Eden, the Windsors were delighted to begin their honeymoon there. The Foreign Office had not allowed the duke to visit Italy before since this not only would expose the duke's own Italian connections but also appear to give too overt a message of support for Mussolini to the rest of the world. No doubt this, along with the romantic appeal of the Venetian canals, influenced the royal decision to stop off there. A tremendous crowd greeted them at the station with the fascist salute, to which the duke responded in kind. Forwood recalls that Mussolini had arranged an elaborate escort of gondolas to accompany the royal party to the Lido, where they were accommodated at the Hotel Excelsior. The Windsors had a crowded three and a half hours in the city. It was clear that they were hugely popular in Italy. Gondoliers took them in a brilliantly painted craft down the Grand Canal; they walked through St Mark's Square, where they fed the pigeons; they saw St Mark's Cathedral and the Doge's Palace. They took tea at the Excelsior. They boarded the train in the early evening and, as they waved farewell, a hundred carnations arrived from Mussolini in Rome. As they stood at the window of their private car, the duke once again gave the fascist salute.

The train arrived at Arnoldstein in Austria at 11.45 on the night of the 4th. Dozens of young people dressed in traditional costumes arrived to bid the royal party welcome, but they were rudely turned away by the police. Instead, the Windsors were greeted by six journalists. They stepped off the train in a buoyant mood, accompanied by Dudley Forwood, Chief Inspector Storrier and Inspector Attfield of Scotland Yard. Paul and Peggy Munster were absent, but the countess's Mercedes was there to meet them. The chauffeur drove them up a steep, dangerous road to Schloss Wasserleonburg, which dated back to the fifteenth century. The forty-room Gothic pile stood framed against the southern escarpments of a mountain. As the couple reached the huge grey stone doorway the duke laughed, picked up Wallis and carried her over the threshold to the hall, where thirty servants were waiting. The ancient housekeeper sagely remarked that the fact that the duke had not stumbled meant that the couple would be very happy.

On 8 June, the couple sent a telegram to Hitler, belatedly thanking him for his good wishes and gift on the occasion of their marriage. The following day they thanked Winston and Mrs Churchill for a 'lovely piece of plate' sent as a wedding present. They also expressed their admiration for Randolph Churchill's article about the wedding in the *Daily Express*. They posed happily for photographs; then they sent a note to George Allen asking him about Fort Belvedere. He reported that it would be left unoccupied for the indefinite future. Scene of the alleged leakage of the official documents, tainted by the presence of a woman who was utterly evil in the eyes of both court and Church, it fell into a sad state of disrepair.

On 20 June, the Windsors arrived in Vienna for a stay at the Hotel Bristol. Shortly afterwards Sam Gracie, honorary Brazilian minister in Vienna, and his British wife gave a dinner party for the Windsors at the Brazilian legation. Among the guests were a young secretary of the Italian embassy and George Messersmith. At dinner, Messersmith reported to Washington, Wallis was very bitter about the American press. The duke hung on her every word. It was then that an extraordinary episode took place.

At coffee, Chancellor Schuschnigg's secretary arrived unexpectedly. He called Messersmith aside and gave him a sealed message stating that a train from Germany to Italy had crashed and that naval shells had been found in it, sent by the Berlin Admiralty for use by Mussolini's navy. This was top-secret information, of gravest concern to neutralist Austria and the United States, because it proved that

Germany was directly supplying the Italian war machine. When Messersmith returned to the party from his meeting with the chancellor's secretary, the duke asked Messersmith why Schuschnigg had sent somebody to see him. Foolishly, Messersmith breached the confidence and gave the duke the secret intelligence that had been conveyed to him. Soon afterwards, Messersmith noticed that the duke was talking to the secretary of the Italian embassy, who left immediately. The next day the military attaché at the US legation brought Messersmith an intercepted and decoded telegram that the Italian ambassador, Prezziozi, had sent the night before to the Foreign Office in Rome; it said that the duke had revealed the secret information about the train crash and that 'the cat [was] out of the bag so far as the Naval shells were concerned'. The duke had given away to the Italians the fact that the American government had obtained secret information about Nazi–Italian connections.

On 28 July, the Windsors returned to Venice by train. Once more, the Italians greeted them ecstatically; they could hardly make their way down the Grand Canal as hundreds of gondolas swarmed about them. Hundreds more gathered at the Lido to catch a glimpse of them as they entered the Excelsior. Scores of photographs were taken of them sunbathing and swimming the next day.

By 7 August, the Windsors were back at Wasserleonburg. Plans were advancing further for their trip to Nazi Germany. The diplomat Fritz Wiedemann was behind it. A seeming Anglophile, Wiedemann held firm to the idea of peace with Great Britain for the indefinite future. He represented the group in Germany that supported the idea of restoring the powers of the German royal family. He believed, as much as the Duke of Windsor did, in re-cementing the royal family alliances that had been broken in the First World War. As a political moderate he was not in tune with the extremist elements of the Nazis, but none the less, despite statements to the contrary, he was a devout servant of the Führer. He had several strong connections in London, among them his mistress, the egregious, half-Jewish Nazi agent Princess Stephanie Hohenlohe. Hitler had a surprising sexual interest in her, despite her part-Jewish origin; he was prepared to overlook ethnic prejudice when employing certain loyal servants of the Third Reich.

Later, he would give her the producer Max Reinhardt's castle as a present.

It was Wiedemann, therefore, under direct instructions from the Führer, rather than Charles Bedaux, who was responsible for the Windsors' arrangements for their German trip in the autumn. Dr Robert Ley, Reich union leader, was helping to sort out the details. It was agreed with the duke while he was in Austria that all payments for the trip would be made available from the special funds of the Hitler-controlled Reichsbank. Needless to say, the duke preferred it to be thought that he would be subsidizing the trip himself.

On 19 August, Charles Bedaux, who was in Budapest, called to see Howard K. Travers, chargé d'affaires at the US legation. Bedaux announced that he was acting for the Duke of Windsor and said that the duke wished to study the lot of the lower classes and desired 'to make a complete study of working conditions in various countries'. This seemed harmless enough until Bedaux, somewhat indiscreetly, added the dangerous words, 'with a view to returning to England at a later date as the champion of the working classes'. This was a deadly, dynamite-laden statement. What it implied was that the duke wished to upstage King George VI and re-enter Great Britain, probably to seek political office. With the enthusiastic support of the peoples of Europe and the United States, he hoped to reassemble his vast following in Britain.

The statement that Bedaux made on his behalf had leaked back to London after Howard Travers reported it in a 'strictly confidential' memorandum to the State Department that same day. By that time George Messersmith had returned to Washington as assistant secretary of state in charge of the Balkans, and when he received the document on 10 September there can be no question that he referred it to the appropriate British authorities. The result would seriously affect the Windsors' entire future.

There was another reason for the duke's desire to visit Germany, which was confirmed by Sir Dudley Forwood. He said, 'Why did they go to Germany? I have very strong views on this. It was not to give a public statement of his approval for the Nazis. We went because he wanted his beloved wife to experience a State visit. And the only way such a State visit was possible was to make the arrangements with Hitler.' Sir Dudley did not explain why a visit to Mussolini would not have been equally possible, and perhaps slightly less dangerous. He continued:

> It must be admitted that, whereas the Duke, Duchess and I had no idea that the Germans were or would be committing mass murder of Jews, we were none of us averse to Hitler politically. We all felt that the Nazi regime was a more appropriate government than the Weimar Republic which had been extremely Socialist and under which, we felt, Germany might have turned Socialist. Instead of *National* Socialist, which we felt was the lesser of two evils.

On 2 September, Sir Alexander Hardinge wrote to Sir Robert Vansittart clarifying the Windsors' status.

> His Royal Highness the Duke of Windsor and the Duchess should not be treated by His Majesty's representatives as having any official status in the countries which they visit. For this reason it seems to the King that, except under special instructions, His Majesty's representatives should not have any hand in arranging official interviews for them, or countenance their participation in any official ceremonies.

Hardinge continued by stating that it was the king's wish that the duke and duchess should not be invited to stay as guests in any embassy or legation. Ambassadors or ministers should not meet the couple at a station, and entertainment at the embassy should be strictly private and informal. The Duchess of Windsor must be placed on the right of His Majesty's representative on each occasion. 'Anything of an official nature should be avoided.'

The same day, Vansittart wrote to Sir Geoffrey Knox, British ambassador to Hungary, stating:

> HRH the Duke of Windsor and the Duchess should be treated on the same lines as a member of the Royal Family on a holiday. If anything were contemplated which might give to the visit a more serious aspect, you should refer home at once. It is not considered that you should yourself meet them at the station, but that you should send a senior member of your staff. If they

seem to wish to lunch or dine at the legation, there would be no harm in your inviting them, but you should avoid asking any politically prominent Hungarians to meet them.

The Windsors arrived in Hungary to stay with Bedaux at his Borsodivanka Castle on 9 September. By now, both Washington and the Secret Intelligence Service were again keeping a very sharp eye on them. Messersmith hadn't forgotten the incident in Vienna when the duke had leaked the fact that Messersmith had been informed about the arms shipments from Germany to Italy.

On the 14th, Bedaux was back at the US legation in Budapest, saying that Travers should inform the State Department that the duke would make a public announcement on 3 October. In the statement he would disclose the fact that the duke and duchess would visit Germany at Hitler's invitation for twelve days, beginning on 11 October, and that 'the German government [had] placed two airplanes and eight automobiles at [their] disposal'. The British ambassador in Berlin, Sir Eric Phipps, would be informed on the same day. The Windsors would leave for New York on the German steamer *Bremen* on 11 November, and the duke 'would appreciate being received by the President in order to discuss social welfare'. In his memorandum to assistant secretary of state Wilson, Travers wrote, '[The duke] desires that his forthcoming visit [plans] be kept entirely secret, but will telegraph the British Ambassador in Washington at the same time he informs [the] British Ambassador in Berlin, October 3. The British government is not yet informed of the proposed visits, and he desires to keep them confidential until his October 3 announcement.'

Meantime, despite Bedaux's great air of secrecy, the duke informed Sir Ronald Lindsay, British ambassador in Washington, who was on leave in England, that he would be going to America. Lindsay, in a memorandum of that date to the Foreign Office in London, warned that there might be a subsequent attempt by the duke 'to stage a semi-Fascist comeback in England by playing up to labour in America'.

Sir Robert Vansittart summoned Lindsay to the Foreign Office to show him the secret file on the duchess's espionage activities. What he saw there appalled him. Vansittart told him that instructions had been sent to every British minister and ambassador in the world forbidding them to accommodate the Windsors, give them dinner or present them officially to anyone; at any railway station they were to be met by no one more important than a third secretary. They were to be given only 'a bite of luncheon' – a contemptuous final touch. That was how severe and damaging the contents of Vansittart's files had become.

The degree of Nazi (and more emphatically Italian) collaboration determined by Vansittart was extreme, going far beyond mere sympathy or approval. The Windsors travelled to Bucharest on 13 September. They were in Vienna on the 14th and then continued to Czechoslovakia where they contacted members of the Sports and Shooting Club of Austria, who were visiting there. On 1 November the following year Ribbentrop's *Dienststelle,* or Special Intelligence Service, reported to him that Windsor was president of the club. This cadre of wealthy men was considered by Ribbentrop's intelligence service to be dangerous and illegal, and it was under surveillance by the Gestapo and the Austrian police. The report reads in full:

> On German territory, in the neighbourhood of Salzburg, is situated the Schloss Mittersill, which belongs to the company known as SIMAG, owned by the Princes of Lichtenstein. The aforementioned SIMAG has lent the castle to the Sports and Shooting Club, including its golf course and tennis courts.
>
> The Duke of Windsor is honorary president of the club. From the membership roster, it is clear that a number of noted representatives of the royal families of Europe as well as foreign politicians are members. The club's exclusiveness may be judged by the fact that the membership fees are enormously high.
>
> The club is now looking for German and other supporters. The local police chief and Salzburg civil authorities for state and foreign policy as well as ideological reasons are interested in investigating the activities of the club. According to a report by a Professor Lehotrich of Vienna, a clean-up of the club's activities will be impossible without full German control. As an example, [one royal member] has recently fled Vienna because he was under threat of arrest on charges of homosexuality. In connection with this the [police] report also charges the Duke of Windsor with bisexuality.

That week in mid-September, Wallis and the duke were at Charles Bedaux's Borsodivanka Castle. On the 18th, Cordell Hull, US secretary of state, sent a memorandum to Budapest via Hugh Wilson saying that the president would be happy to receive the duke, but General Watson, the presidential secretary, added in handwriting the note 'subject of course to consultation with the British Embassy at the appropriate time'. He scratched out the words 'who do not want this matter made public'. Hull's memorandum continued, 'It is difficult and even somewhat embarrassing to take a definite position until this government knows the relationship of the British Embassy toward the proposed visit.' By now, all cables in the matter were being sent in confidential code and marked 'No Distribution'. The matter was explosive: in view of the duke's popularity, the US government did not want to seem to be insulting him, but at the same time the security files on the Windsors were so damaging that Washington was nervous of causing offence in Whitehall by arranging for him to be received. Matters were scarcely helped by the fact that the duke wanted to be accompanied on the whole tour by an executive of Eastman Kodak, which was in direct partnership with its equivalent German company for business purposes only. On 14 September, Victor Mallet, British chargé d'affaires in Washington, referred to the Bedaux approach in Budapest in a memorandum to Eden:

> The Duke has now ceased being front-page news over here, but if he were to come out this autumn we shall have all the old ballyhoo revived again. What is more, the tale of his sympathy for the South Wales miners and the consequent wrath of Mr Baldwin, which is still widely believed in the middle west, will be revived by his proposed investigation of the life of the American working man. I can only hope that nothing will come of this suggested trip, but I should be very grateful for any news which you may have about it.

In the FBI files on the Windsors in Washington, a lengthy report shows that an American secret agent named Helga Stultz, planted as an archivist at Hitler's country eyrie of Berchtesgarden, listened to a conversation between Hitler and Robert Ley, Nazi labour leader, discussing the upcoming royal visit to Germany. Ley said he had been in touch with the pro-Nazi former British prime minister David Lloyd George, who had recently visited the Führer for consultations, to discuss what capital could be made from the Windsors' tour.

Hitler told Ley he must convey to the Windsors, and to Lloyd George, that the only hope for the future of the world was if the Duke of Windsor returned to the English throne with Lloyd George as prime minister. He added:

> This cannot happen unless there is a war. Though the British don't want to fight and have no stomach for it, I believe they may blunder into war. If that happens, they will collapse within a year. We will have new rulers to deal with and I am certain (from our talks) that Lloyd George will give us back our colonies without a fuss. He promised he would agree to this.

On 30 September, Oliver Harvey of the Foreign Office in London sent a lengthy memorandum to Vansittart about the Windsors' proposed tour of Germany. The memorandum revealed that the prime minister took the view that it would be impossible to stop the duke from making the visit, but that care should be taken to prevent representatives of the British government taking any action which could be construed as countenancing it. In the same report Harvey revealed that it was known to the king that the German government had arranged the visit and that it was considered at the palace 'most improper that the German Government should take upon itself to arrange such a visit without informing us'. It was felt at the palace that no member of the British embassy staff in Berlin should meet the royal train, 'lest it might appear as giving a British official nature to the tour in Germany'. Vansittart scribbled in the margin, 'I quite agree. This is really a monstrous innovation – for propaganda purposes ... I agree with Sir Alexander Hardinge. We have not been consulted and should therefore stand aloof.'

On 1 October, Vansittart wrote a memorandum to Hardinge confirming that 'nothing can be done to prevent [the visit] but that His Majesty's representatives should not take any action which could be regarded as countenancing it'. He added:

Personally I think these tours, prearranged without a word to us, are a bit too much. And I hope our missions abroad will be instructed to have as little as possible to do with them. If we are to be expected to assist, we are entitled to be consulted, and to have a chance at dissuasion. The direct approach to our missions, without our knowledge, is hardly fair.

In a response of the following day, Hardinge wrote in a postscript, 'I entirely agree with what you say about these tours, and I feel strongly that nothing should be done to make them appear other than what they are, i.e., private stunts for political purposes – they can obviously bring no benefit to the workers themselves.' The same day, Sir George Ogilvie-Forbes, chargé d'affaires in Berlin, cabled from Germany in a mood of anxiety, saying:

> If this visit comes off, I earnestly hope that your instructions will be to accord to the Duke of Windsor courtesies not less than is the authorized practice at Vienna Legation. German Government are certain to make the maximum capital and publicity out of this visit, and it will be extremely embarrassing and painful for me if I am instructed to ignore His Royal Highness's presence, for this will not be understood here . . . While I will of course scrupulously comply with the King's wishes, I trust that [the] above will be taken into consideration.

On 3 October, Ronald Lindsay wrote from his house in Dorset to Vansittart, saying among other things that

> . . . the intended visit of the Duke and Duchess of Windsor to Washington fills me with unmitigated horror . . . Of course the general lines of my conduct will be dictated to me by the Palace and the Prime Minister, and I shall do nothing till I receive from you the necessary indications of what is wished; but it will not have escaped your notice that there is a purely American side to this affair.

He added:

> The visit will be a tremendous sensation – I think it certain that from the first moment [the Windsors] will be in the fullest glare of publicity and will be fairly mobbed wherever they go. The

attitude of the Embassy will be a matter of the greatest public interest.

In my opinion it will be important to allow nothing to transpire indicating that *the visit to America in itself* is in any way disapproved, and I think therefore that I ought certainly to put the Duke and Duchess up at the Embassy while they are in Washington; and I think they should be presented at the White House and that I should at least give them a large Belshazzar [feast].

But I imagine that I should dissociate myself, tacitly, from the undeclared objects of the visit – that is from most of the Duke's activities in America outside Washington.

From the tenor of the memorandum, it is clear that the Duke's extracurricular activities were again thought to be dangerously political.

With the Windsors now in Vienna after a brief trip to Paris, the discomfort of the US government increased. Hugh Wilson, now in charge of the matter at the State Department, wrote a memorandum to Cordell Hull saying that there was clearly 'a distinct political purpose' in the Windsor trip to Germany. The government was still 'not taking sides' in what was, 'after all, a strictly British internal question'.

On 4 October, Vansittart wrote to Hardinge stating it would be preferable for the royal couple not to be entertained at the British embassy. Moreover, the embassy staff should be instructed to refuse any invitations of a ceremonial character issued during the tour.

In a memorandum dated 6 October, Hardinge made clear to Oliver Harvey of the Foreign Office that it was now known for certain that the Berlin government was sponsoring the German tour. Hardinge cabled Sir George Ogilvie-Forbes in Berlin on that day, categorically stating that the king forbade Forbes to attend the Windsors' arrival at the station in Berlin, that no member of the staff should accept any invitations connected with the tour, that Ogilvie-Forbes should have no hand in arranging any official engagements or interviews, that the Windsors were not to be entertained by any member of the embassy, nor should the staff accept invitations from the duke, and that consular officials should not meet the royal party on arrival anywhere. Above all, 'The Embassy must scrupulously avoid in any way giving the appearance that His Majesty the King and His Majesty's government countenance the proposed tour.'

Ogilvie-Forbes replied on the 7th in the following terms:

> The instructions will be carefully carried out. Nevertheless, I feel I should tell you they will leave an unfavourable impression of the attitude of the Embassy and of [His Majesty's government] which the Germans in all probability will view as another snub to a friendly gesture. They will closely watch the measure of recognition the Duke receives from HM missions in other foreign countries.

At last the arrangements for the visit to Germany were concluded. It was announced in the *New York Times* on 9 October that a conversation would take place between Adolf Hitler and 'the English guest', which would be 'an open discussion of those questions interesting the Duke'. These questions would involve 'the new Germany in its varied aspects, its hopes and aspirations and Hitler's hopes for the future'. The Windsors would visit nine cities. The main purpose of their trip would be to study working conditions.

That same day, Sir Ronald Lindsay was summoned by the king to Balmoral for an extraordinary meeting on the matter of the Windsors. The queen was there, and among those also present were two of the duke's worst enemies, Alan Lascelles and the recently knighted Sir Alexander Hardinge. Lindsay pointed out that if the Windsors were not accommodated at the British embassy, it would be regarded by millions of Americans as a snub and an act of disapproval of the duke's interest in the conditions of the workers. The king, Hardinge and Lascelles variously stated that the duke was behaving abominably: it was his duty not to embarrass the king; he was dropping bombshell after bombshell; and what would come next? Lindsay was to write to his wife two days later:

> [In their view] he was trying to stage a comeback, and his friends and advisors were semi-Nazis. He was not straight – he hadn't let the King have an inkling of his plans, and the first news of them was a letter from him to the King's own agent . . .

What if he were to go to a Dominion? Or to cross over from the United States into Canada? There was a lot of talk about a scheme by which I should invite him to stay at the Embassy, and then a swift emissary should speed over and persuade him to decline. This absolutely horrified me and it was, thank God, discarded because [they realized] 'that woman' would never allow him to decline, and because there exists no emissary who would command confidence and at the same time stand the smallest chance of influencing the Duke.

The queen joined in the conversation at the meeting. She expressed grief rather than indignation as she mentioned the duke. 'He's so changed now,' she said, 'and he used to be so kind to us.' She had no good words to say about Wallis. It was clear that the royal family was united in its resolve that the Windsors should receive absolutely no privileges on their American visit. The king and queen would not even allow them to be accompanied by Lindsay when they went to the White House. Lindsay wrote to his wife on 17 October, '[The duke] is being turned into a purely Nazi show, and of course he is known here to have decided Nazi tendencies.' Later, Lindsay managed to arrange through the secret service to have two letters that were written by Bedaux intercepted and smuggled to the embassy. The letters were to private contacts in the United States and indicated that the duke planned to be the leader of an international peace movement, which was considerably more sinister than it sounded.

The Windsors left Paris by train for Berlin, a crowd of three hundred waving them goodbye. When the Nord Express chugged into the Friedrichstrasse station in Berlin, hundreds more were waiting to greet them. The crowd screamed, 'Heil Windsor!' interspersed with 'Heil Edward!' as they stepped down from the platform to be met by Dr Robert Ley, Fritz Wiedemann, the deputy political leader Artur Goerlitzer, and, amid a swarm of uniformed officials and a Gestapo guard, a rather embarrassed third secretary of the British Embassy.

The Windsors checked into the Kaiserhof Hotel. Again, an immense crowd was waiting for them, chanting a specially composed song provided by the Propaganda Ministry. In defiance of the British Foreign Office, Sir George Ogilvie-Forbes, continuing in the absence of Sir Neville Henderson, the British ambassador who had sagely taken leave of absence, arrived at the Kaiserhof to pay his respects. He noted that the Windsors' suite directly overlooked Hitler's Chancellery.

He explained to the duke that the king regarded the visit as purely private and unofficial and laid down the rules vis-à-vis no entertaining and so on. Ogilvie-Forbes cabled Harvey in London, 'I shall . . . be very glad when the visit is over, as the absence of the Embassy from participation is marked and the subject of comment. The Ambassador is fortunate to be away.'

Wallis stayed at the hotel resting while, shortly after noon, the duke visited the Stock machine works at Grünewald. Swastikas flew from the roof as the duke examined the ultra-modern buildings in which three thousand workers enjoyed an elaborate restaurant, an assembly and concert hall, a swimming pool and handsomely planted lawns and flower beds. The duke asked several questions in German and obtained details of factory life from workers whom Dr Ley brought forward one by one. With loud laughs and hearty slaps on the back, Ley encouraged each man to tell the duke about the conditions of work, how disputes were resolved, and how labour and management conferred openly, unhampered by the spirit of class. Several men told the duke of their high wages, physical fitness classes each morning and the nourishing food served in the restaurant.

That afternoon, the duke, along with a thousand workers, attended a concert of Wagner and Liszt given by the Berlin Labour Front Orchestra; it featured the 'Grail Aria' from *Lohengrin*, sung by Hitler's favourite American operatic tenor, F. Eyvind Laholm. At the end of the concert 'Deutschland über Alles' and the 'Horst Wessel' were played, followed by 'God Save the King'. The Duke returned at 4.30 p.m. and went shopping with Wallis.

That night, Robert Ley gave an elaborate party at his thirty-seven-room house in the Grünewald. Among the guests were Dr Josef Goebbels, Ribbentrop, Goerlitzer, Himmler and Hess. Goering could not be there because his brother-in-law had just been killed in the Bavarian Alps. The next day, while Wallis again stayed at the hotel, breaking her solitude only for a brief drive to Potsdam and back, the duke undertook a gruelling inspection tour. An elaborate observation coach, described by Frederick T. Birchall of the *New York Times* as resembling 'a streamlined duck', was used for the journey. It included nine seats, a bar, a small dining area, a wireless telephone and a parlour car. Ley slowed its normal speed of eighty miles per hour to forty along the autobahns so that the duke could get a good view of the countryside.

At the Pomeranian border the coach halted to take aboard the local governor, who joined the party headed by Ley on the journey to Crossensee, headquarters of the training school of the Death's Head Division of the Elite Squad of the SS. The Death's Head band greeted the party, playing the British National Anthem, to which the duke responded with a detailed inspection as the men presented arms and he gave them a full Hitler salute. The sprawling, thatched barracks buildings were dominated by a vast tower with an ancient gateway. Here, the cream of the Hitler Youth studied and trained for four years, undergoing rigorous physical training for five hours a day. The duke's hosts explained to him that the main subjects of teaching were racial biology, German archaeology, history and politics. After lunch, he went on to the Stargard military airport. In Dr Ley's twelve-passenger plane he flew over the Baltic coast to see a four-mile beach and luxury hotel which was being built to accommodate members of the Nazi youth movement. He returned to Berlin at 6 p.m.

That evening, the Aga Khan, having just presided over the League of Nations Assembly, called in at the hotel after dinner. His sympathies were in accord with the Windsors'. Three years later, on 25 July 1940, German Foreign Office documents would reveal that he had planned to join Hitler at Windsor Castle and that he had recommended renewed bombing of England before more bombing took place.

The next day, 14 October, heavy rain prevented the duke from flying to Brunswick; instead, he and Wallis visited the Berlin War Museum and the Pergamon Museum; later, the duke went to a Turkish bath. That afternoon the couple visited the Goerings for tea at the air minister's famous hunting lodge, Karinhall. They saw the plump field marshal's electric train and chatted away happily; Frau Goering never forgot the encounter, writing of it warmly in her memoirs many years later. Forwood remembers:

We had a meal at Karinhall, at which Goering and the Duke and Duchess sat at a high table on a raised dais while the rest of us sat below. Behind Goering's desk there was a large map in marquetry. Except for England, the map was completely covered in colours indicating that it was in the possession of Germany. My master looked at Goering and said, 'Isn't this a little impertinent? A little premature?' Goering replied, 'It is fated. It must be.' I remember the Field Marshal saying, 'My wife is pregnant. If it's a son, a thousand planes will fly overhead. If it's a daughter, only five hundred.' There was one vulgar touch I remember. There were paintings of nude women over his bed.

That evening, the Windsors had a very interesting visitor: Ernst Wilhelm Bohle.[3] Yet another visitor in that crowded twenty-four hours was Dr Goebbels. He had, of course, been host for the Oswald Mosleys when they were married the previous year in his house. Goebbels always regretted the fact that the Duke of Windsor had left the throne. During the Second World War, Goebbels wrote in his diary that he regarded as a tragedy the failure of Germany to make an arrangement with the duke towards permanent alliance. He regarded his meeting with the duke as one of 'the great impressions of my life'. The Duke of Windsor struck him as 'a far-sighted, clever and yet modern man'. He recognized the supreme importance of the social problem in Germany. Goebbels continued, 'He was too clever, too progressive, too appreciative of the problem of the underprivileged, and too pro-German [to have remained on the throne]', and concluded, 'This tragic figure could have saved Europe from her doom. But instead, as Governor of the Bahamas, he had to witness the disintegration of the British Empire and perhaps of Europe and the West altogether.'

On the 15th, the Windsors went to Essen by train to visit a large coalmine (the duke went down 1,500 feet into the bowels of the earth with Dudley Forwood, negotiating a series of awkward steel ladders, with water splashing on his head) and then went on to Krupp's, the leading German armament manufacturers.

A reception was given by the president of the Rhine province that night in honour of the distinguished guests. On the 16th, the Windsors were in Dusseldorf, where they attended a so-called creative folk exhibition. Surrounded by yelling, laughing and frantically gesturing people the duke, flanked by a flying squad of SS men, responded in kind to a chorus of Heils. The duke was impressed and deeply fascinated, but the duchess was bored as the guide, Dr Maiwald, whom the duke had met during the Paris Exposition, explained the exhibits, which covered every aspect of German industry. They saw examples of artificial textiles being made, buna rubber, and displays on the uses of coal, sand, stone and wood. Dr Maiwald said for years afterwards that no other person he had ever entertained knew as much as the duke about the technical details of industry. Yet again the duke gave the Nazi salute as he journeyed through the crowded streets.[4] There was an incident in which an Englishwoman had to be arrested because she was screaming out threats. The Windsors went on to see a miners' hospital, where they talked with injured men; then the duke went alone to see the Krupp colony for workers, unexpectedly dropping in on some old-age pensioners. The Windsors returned to their hotel to go over the details of their American trip. They were still completely ignored by the local British consular representatives.

They visited a concentration camp which appeared to be quite deserted. Forwood says, 'We saw this enormous concrete building which of course I now know contained inmates. The duke asked, "What is that?" Our host replied, "It is where they store the cold meat." In a horrible sense, that was true.'

On 17 October, the Windsors were in Leipzig. Once more, a crowd of several thousand greeted them at the station with the Hitler salute, and this time there were forty swastika banners waved overhead. Ironically, the best hotel in Leipzig was closed because it had a Jewish owner, and they had to take second best in an unsatisfactory hotel. As thousands more stood in the street below their windows, the duke thanked them in German for their kindness, saluted them and then said goodnight. That same evening, he made it clear to Ley that he would not be prepared to meet Herr Julius Streicher, the Nuremberg party chief; the reason can be deduced from an article that had appeared several months earlier in Streicher's newspaper *Der Stürmer*, accusing the duchess of being Jewish.

That same day, Sir George Ogilvie-Forbes in Berlin wrote to Eden, who handed the letter to Hardinge and Sir Ronald Lindsay, discussing a meeting that Ogilvie-Forbes had had on the 15th with Prentiss Gilbert, new counsellor and chargé d'affaires at the US embassy. He reported that Gilbert had discussed with him the matter of the Windsors' visit to the United States, and had mentioned that Bedaux had approached him to get US government approval of the visit and treatment in America of the duchess as royalty. Gilbert told Ogilvie-Forbes that he did not encourage these proposals. Bedaux had made it plain to Gilbert that he would be paying the Windsors' expenses for the American tour; Bedaux also revealed the illuminating fact that following the official visit to the United States the duke would be making similar ones to Italy and Sweden. In Sweden he would be put in touch, by Bedaux, with Axel Wenner-Gren, the multi-millionaire Swedish Nazi supporter and inventor of the vacuum cleaner. The report added:

> [The Swedish millionaire] . . . was interested in world peace through labour reconciliation. Bedaux said it was also intended that HRH should take up this line and even went so far as to express the opinion that HRH might in due course be the 'saviour' of the monarchy! Bedaux also tried behind Gilbert's back to get Miss Frances Perkins, the American Secretary of Labor, to send an invitation direct to HRH, an attempt which has been foiled . . . Much of the above will, I fear, be painful reading, but I feel you ought to know what has been going on here and that it would be as well to keep an eye on Mr Bedaux's activities.

On the 20th, the Windsors' old friend and relative Charles, Duke of Saxe-Coburg-Gotha, gave an elaborate dinner party for them and a hundred guests at the Grand Hotel in Nuremberg. The guests included many of the aristocrats with whom the duke had hob-nobbed during his father's funeral and jubilee. Their host told the Windsors at the dinner that he totally accepted Wallis's right to be 'Her Royal Highness'. His wife and all the other women guests curtseyed to her deeply. Even her place card carried the German equivalent of HRH.

After visiting what the *New York Times* called 'the altars and temples of the National Socialist Cult', the couple continued to Stuttgart, where an awkward incident took place. While returning from a factory visit the duke, who had left Wallis at the hotel, on impulse decided he wanted to see the palace of the kings of Wurttemberg. Dr Ley looked embarrassed, but the duke insisted. When he entered, he was interested to see a huge illuminated map of the world, showing those portions which represented the German colonies 'improperly' seized from the Reich after the First World War. He grimaced with displeasure when he noted that certain of these were now British possessions. He also saw a display of photographs of Nazi storm troops marching through Chicago and New Jersey. He was shown more maps, marked in red to indicate how many Germans lived in certain countries. That night the duke and duchess went to the great municipal auditorium to attend a 'Strength through Joy' festival, where they saw a pageant and play illustrating the glories of German youth; their arrival and departure were marked by frantic shouting, applause and Nazi salutes.

And now at last came the high spot of the trip: the meeting on 22 October with Adolf Hitler, which took place just twenty-five days after Hitler had entered Berlin with Mussolini, joining him in an exchange of toasts at an official banquet. That encounter had sealed the doom of all the early dreams of the Duke of Windsor that, by appeasing the Italian dictator, Mussolini and the Führer would be kept firmly apart. Three days before the ducal visit the Foreign Secretary, Lord Halifax, had visited Hitler, hoping to sustain the British balance of power in western Europe by at least seeming to encourage Hitler's now unbridled ambitions. In the course of the conversation, Halifax had stated that the new prime minister, Neville Chamberlain, wanted to make a permanent settlement with Germany and encourage talks at cabinet level between London and Berlin; Britain would concede to Hitler certain colonies in Africa and would give him a free hand in eastern Europe. Nothing much came of this conversation. As it happened, Hitler had already decided on a policy of obtaining Lebensraum ('living space') by going to war, which he announced to his ministers on 5 November. He would strike west as well as east; but it was part of his policy to pretend to representatives of the British Empire that he wanted only peace with England. From the Führer's point of view, the timing of the duke's visit was extremely appropriate. He knew that the duke, obsessed with Bolshevism as he was, would be very happy to encourage the Führer in his desire to strike at Russia. Hitler was prepared to encourage any folly, even from an abdicated monarch, that would allow him to carry off his supreme bluff in the matter of foreign policy.

Hitler's mistress, Eva Braun, eagerly awaited the arrival of the duke and duchess. Her biographer, Nerin E. Gun, wrote:

> Eva begged Hitler to let her be introduced to the Duchess of Windsor. [She] had subjected her lover to endless eulogies of the ex-monarch who 'had renounced an Empire for love of a woman . . .' . . . According to some, she hinted that Mrs Simpson [*sic*] had something in common with Eva Braun, and that a sincere lover could accept a small sacrifice – not the loss of a crown like Edward, but the risk of a slight blow to his prestige, by marrying the woman that he declared he loved. Hitler pretended not to understand and in order not to aggravate the situation, claimed that the demands of protocol prohibited the meeting.

Hitler looked forward to the meeting. There is no question that in the Führer's grand design for the future Lloyd George, who had visited him the previous year and who was his favourite British politician, would become head of the puppet British government under his control, with the royal family exiled to Canada and the duke restored to the throne with Wallis as queen. Paul Schwarz recalled that he still constantly ran the films of various yacht voyages and of the duke conferring with Wallis at the time of his father's funeral. He never ceased raving to Ribbentrop about Wallis's lack of make-up, 'not bad figure and impeccable grooming and couture'.

At 1.10 p.m., the train arrived at the foot of the mountain at Obersalzburg, where, in the company of Robert Ley and Dr Paul Schmidt, special interpreter for the Foreign Office, they took a trip to Lake Königssee. At 2.30 p.m., the couple was driven up the mountainside in the company of Dudley Forwood; they were fol-lowed to the hunting lodge by three carloads of detectives and SS men. The roads had been completely cleared of tourists; under normal conditions thousands would be seen on the steep incline, making their way up the mountainside to see Hitler's lair. Now only twenty, who had particular influence and had been given special permits, stood waiting at the gates as the procession of cars swept through.

Surrounded by officials, Hitler stood waiting for the Windsors at the bottom of a flight of steps; he was wearing the brown jacket of a Nazi party official, black trousers and patent leather shoes. He conducted the Windsors into the entrance hall, which was dominated by a painting of the nineteenth-century Chancellor Bismarck, grandfather of the Windsors' close friend Prince Otto. As the duke and duchess walked along the passageway behind their famous host, a series of tall, fair-haired, muscular guards, dressed in brass-buttoned uniforms, stood at attention. The Windsors were taken to an ante-room where servants took their coats, then walked down three marble steps into an enormous reception hall. One wall of the room had a bay window which overlooked the Unsterberg mountain. Hitler pointed to the view, a sweeping display of peaks and sloping green meadows where farm workers were toiling with hoes.

As the Führer ordered afternoon tea, the couple had the opportunity to observe the details of the room. The walls were white, relieved by panelling of fumed oak. There was an enormous marble fireplace with great heaps of logs on either side. There were tapestries of figures of the period of Frederick the Great mounted on immense, powerful white horses. The carpet was cherry red, and the marble in the room matched it. The furniture covers were stitched in a series of swastika motifs and Nazi mottoes. There was a grand piano on which stood a bust of Richard Wagner and a large globe of the world. Everywhere there were white and yellow flowers – hydrangeas, zinnias, pansies, roses and carnations. Hitler's special adviser Walter Hewel, his official interpreter Paul Schmidt and his photographer Heinrich Hoffman were present; the last-named took pictures during most of the meeting.

For all except twenty minutes of the two-hour visit, Hitler was with both the Windsors. While tea was being prepared, he showed his guests the entire house and gardens. He pointed out Salzburg from one of the balconies. Albion Ross of the *New York Times* was one of the few reporters permitted to enter the building and receive information as to what was going on. He described the intense interest that the Führer had in both of his guests. Successive biographers and historians have claimed that, aside from some generalized remarks recorded by Paul Schmidt, no word of the conversation between Hitler and his visitors survives. This is incorrect. There was in 1987 a living eye witness. Sir Dudley Forwood, who was present at the encounter, told me:

> The duke was very annoyed because Schmidt had been hired. The duke spoke, as we know, flawless high German. He said to Hitler, in German, 'I do not require this man.' Hitler did not respond correctly, but said to the translator in German that the conversation would be continued as scheduled, and that he expected the duke to speak English. The unfortunate Schmidt had to convey this statement in English to my master. And so it went on. Every few minutes, the duke would say, irritably, to Schmidt, 'That is not what I said to the Führer.' Or he would say, 'That is not what the Führer said to me.'
>
> I vividly recall how the conversation began. My master said to Hitler, 'The Germans and the British races are one. They should *always* be one. They are of Hun origin.' I fear that His Royal Highness had overlooked the Norman Conquest!

On 4 November, William Bullitt, US ambassador to France, would write to President Roosevelt giving an account of the duchess's description of her discussion with Hitler. Hitler told her that the Nazi buildings would one day 'make more magnificent ruins than [those of] the Greeks'. It seems clear that most of the Führer's conversation with the Windsors was deliberately generalized, socially welcoming and inconsequential. However, he drew the duke into another room for a twenty-minute talk that was of much greater moment. The duke himself, in an article published in the New York *Daily News* on 13 December 1966, described what was said:

> My ostensible [*sic*] reason for going to Germany was to see for myself what national Socialism was doing in housing and welfare for the workers, and I tried to keep my conversation with the

Führer to these subjects, not wishing to be drawn into a discussion of politics. Hitler, for his part, talked a lot, but I realized that he was only showing the tip of the German iceberg. In a roundabout way, he encouraged me to infer that Red Russia was the only enemy, and that it was in Britain's interest and in Europe's too, that Germany be encouraged to strike east and smash Communism forever. Hitler was then at the zenith of his power. His eyes were piercing and magnetic. I confess frankly that he took me in. I believed him when he implied that he sought no war with England ... I thought that the rest of us could be fence-sitters while the Nazis and the Reds slogged it out.

It is thus clear that the duke encouraged Hitler in his ambition to strike against Russia. The duke had other suggestions to make. In his table talk on 13 May 1942, according to the record, Hitler said, 'The King [*sic*] offered to meet Germany's colonial needs by allowing Germans to settle northern Australia, thereby creating a powerful shield for British interests against Japan.' That is a very curious statement. It is clear from other documentation that Britain was afraid of a Soviet–Japanese alliance, and in 1939 a group of British businessmen acting as secret agents would be arrested in Tokyo, tried and imprisoned for spying on Japanese officials in regard to this matter. The duke went on to tell Hitler that his brother George VI was 'weak and vacillating and wholly in the grip of his evil and anti-German advisors'. This was, of course, a reference to Sir Alexander Hardinge and Sir Robert Vansittart. The duke also discussed his conversation with Hitler with J. Paul Getty, a close friend of his who also had Nazi connections. In his memoirs, Getty remembered asking the duke, 'Did Hitler listen to you when you spoke with him?' The duke replied, 'Yes, I think so. The way was opened – ever so slightly – for further progress. Had there been any proper follow-through action in London or Paris, millions of lives might have been saved.' He meant that he proposed permanent peace with Germany and (Getty said) mass emigration of Jews from Germany, also advocated by Charles Bedaux and Sir Oswald Mosley, rather than slaughter. Getty added the following revealing paragraph:

Although [the duke] never said as much to me, I had reason to suspect that he was not acting on his own when he went to Germany and spoke to Hitler and other Nazi leaders. It would not surprise me if one day a musty EYES ONLY file is fished out of some top security vault and new light is thrown on the episode.

In part because of his friendships and personal contacts, the duke, and Wallis with him, apparently did not approve of Hitler's genocidal methods or mass imprisonment of Jews, despite the somewhat generalized anti-Semitism, typical of the time, which the Windsors had a tendency to express. The highly charged meeting with the Führer, due to be dismissed as insignificant by enemies of the duke and partisans alike, ended warmly. The *New York Times* noted:

Members of the entourage of the Duke and Duchess of Windsor reported after their visit ... that the Duchess was visibly impressed with the Führer's personality, and he apparently indicated that they had become fast friends by giving her an affectionate farewell. He took both her hands in his saying a long goodbye, after which he stiffened to a rigid Nazi salute that the Duke returned.

After that, Hitler turned to Schmidt and said, 'She would have made a good queen.'

That night, the Windsors dined with Rudolf Hess and his wife in Munich; Frau Hess wrote to friends in Egypt saying how warmly impressed she was, especially with the duchess. She recalled later that she was nervous about meeting Wallis because she felt dowdy; but once they had met she relaxed and enjoyed Wallis's company. The British-born Nazi Ernst Wilhelm Bohle turned up to act as interpreter, cementing his friendship with the Windsors. Hess shared the Windsors' preference for mass Jewish emigration rather than wholesale slaughter. After leaving Munich, Dr Ley returned to Berlin, and two Labour Front officials drove the Windsors to the Austrian border. It is said that, as they arrived, the duchess gave a bag of money to an SS official with the words, 'This is for the Strength through Joy Fund.'

After giving a dinner party to Dr Ley's assistant, Stabsleiter

Simon, and four other officials who had escorted the party around, the couple returned to Paris on the 23rd. That same day Vansittart wrote to Hardinge, referring to the letter from Ogilvie-Forbes sent on the 17th. In a postscript Vansittart said:

> I see . . . in this disturbing letter a reference to visits to Italy and Sweden. You will remember that I prophesied the former, and that was why in my conversations with [Sir Ronald] Lindsay I was very anxious to set no precedents in the United States which would be embarrassing when the inevitable visit to Italy was brought forward.

On 24 October, Bedaux wrote from the Château de Candé, sending Sir Ronald Lindsay, at the Travellers' Club in Pall Mall, the first draft of the Duke of Windsor's schedule of visits. It was to start in Washington on Armistice Day and finish in Los Angeles and San Francisco in mid-December.

Exhausted by their German trip, the Windsors rested for several days at the Hôtel Meurice in Paris, the duke at last mustering enough strength for some indifferent games of golf while Wallis, with a battery of secretaries, continued plans for the American trip.

In a conversation with Ambassador Kennedy on 13 June 1938, Sir Edward Peacock described a telephone call he made from London to the Windsors that week at the Meurice. The matter was pressing; much as he disliked doing it, King George VI, evidently afraid of public criticism – Windsor charged him with stinginess – had been paying the income from the hereditary Duchy of Lancaster (about twenty thousand pounds a year) while at the same time not charging him income tax on that sum; he paid it himself.

Impatient and irritable with this arrangement, the king asked Peacock to call Windsor to ask him to pay the tax; certainly that was a reasonable requirement. The duke picked up the phone; Wallis listened intently on the extension line. Peacock conveyed the royal request; the duke said he wasn't sure if he would oblige. Peacock pointed out that if he refused, the matter could leak to the newspapers (he implied that he would make sure it did) and the Windsors would be plunged into the worst of public scandals. Nervous, the duke asked Peacock to hold the line. He went to Wallis and asked her what she thought. She shouted in anger,

'There will be no concessions!' Peacock could hear her clearly. The duke came back to the phone and told Peacock he could not agree; his brother must pay the tax. Peacock advised the king, who was exasperated; so were the queen, Queen Mary and the Duchesses of Gloucester and Kent. If there were any question of their relenting in the matter of Wallis's royal highness title, this incident ended it.

On 27 October, the duke appeared at the weekly luncheon of the Anglo-American Press Association in Paris, denying that his visit to Germany had had any political significance, which of course was totally false. Asked why he had chosen to sail to New York aboard the German ship *Bremen*, he pointed out that the only reason for the choice was that he had promised not to enter British waters, and the *Bremen* was the only ship that did not enter Portsmouth or Southampton after leaving Cherbourg. On the same day Charles and Fern Bedaux sailed aboard the *Europa* for New York; also on board, by coincidence, was Ernest Simpson, en route to marry Mary Kirk Raffray. His company was selling the SS *Leviathan* for scrap. On the 28th, Winston Churchill wrote to the duke:

> I have followed with great interest your German tour. I am told that when scenes of it were produced in the newsreels in the cinemas here, Your Royal Highness's pictures were always very loudly cheered. I was rather afraid beforehand that your tour in Germany would offend the great numbers of anti-Nazis in this country, many of whom are your friends and admirers; but I must admit that it does not seem to have had that effect, and I am glad it all passed off with so much distinction and success.

The Windsors continued to prepare for America. The State Department in Washington sent out a blizzard of memoranda concerning the visit. Everybody in the government, especially the anti-Nazi secretary of the interior, Harold L. Ickes, was extremely uneasy about the matter. According to Charles Bedaux, Jr, Mrs Roosevelt contacted the labour leaders in Wallis's home town of Baltimore, urging them to boycott the visit on the grounds that the Charles Bedaux system of time-and-motion study in industry was unacceptable and that anyone whom Bedaux sponsored would be unwelcome. On 2 November, Sir Ronald Lindsay met Sumner Welles, undersecretary of state and an opponent of Nazism, in Washington to convey the details of the royal attitude towards the Windsors. He said, inter alia:

> [The king and queen] felt that at this time when the new King [is] in a difficult situation and [is] trying to win the affection and confidence of his countrypeople, without possessing the popular appeal which the Duke of Windsor [possesses], it is singularly unfortunate that the Duke . . . [is] placing himself in a position where he would seem constantly to be courting the limelight . . . [I have found] on the part of all the governing class in England a very vehement feeling of indignation against the course of the Duke of Windsor based in part on the resentment created by his relinquishment of his responsibilities, and in even greater part due to the apparent unfairness of his present attitude with regard to his brother, the King . . . In court circles and in the Foreign Office and on the part of the heads of the political parties, this feeling [borders] upon [a] state of hysteria . . . There has been a widening of this sentiment of indignation because of the fact that the active supporters of the Duke of Windsor within England are those elements known to have inclinations towards Fascist dictatorships, and that the recent tour of Germany by the Duke of Windsor and his ostentatious reception by Hitler and his regime [can] only be construed as a willingness on the part of the Duke of Windsor to lend himself to these tendencies.

Lindsay, expressing his own opinion, said he didn't think the duke was aware of being exploited in this manner, an indication, like the rest of his statement, that he did not fully understand the duke's actual purpose: to be a statesman without portfolio. However, he went on to say that the British government was anxious to avoid taking any action that would make Windsor a martyr; at the same time, he would not be permitted to present the duke to the president, clearly upon royal orders. In response, Welles said that no representative of the US government would accompany the Windsors on the tour; the duke would be received by officials in each city and shown what he wanted to see, and that would be the end of the matter. Welles made it painfully clear that, although the duke would be received informally at the White House, this would not be regarded as a state visit or anything approaching it and no special privileges would be accorded via George T. Summerlin, chief of the protocol division of the State Department, who would act as Washington host. The question of whether the duchess would be called 'Her Royal Highness' arose. The duke had made it clear that he required the title to be used. Sir Ronald Lindsay particularly requested that it should not be. The matter remained unresolved.

The tour would resemble the German excursion in terms of the emphasis on industry and on working and housing conditions.

The Baltimore Federation of Labor unanimously adopted a resolution condemning the Windsors' visit, attacking Charles Bedaux as 'the arch-enemy of organized labour'. At a stormy meeting the Baltimore AFL leader, Joseph P. McCurdy, said, unnecessarily, 'The Duchess, when she lived here, had no interest whatsoever in labour or the labouring classes of her fellow citizens.' Even while he was delivering the speech, the BBC announced that it would not be relaying the NBC broadcast, even though the Canadian Broadcasting Corporation would be participating.

On 4 November, Dr William E. Dodd, Jr, son of the passionately anti-Nazi US ambassador to Germany, said at a meeting of a citizens' committee in Philadelphia, and later in a local broadcast, that the Duke of Windsor might 'try to convince Americans of the achievements of National Socialism in Germany'. More labour organizations attacked the visit, taking their cue from Baltimore, as the Windsors attended an elaborate banquet at the US embassy in Paris; ironically, the anti-Nazi ex-premier, Léon Blum, and his wife were among the guests. The Windsors were disturbed by the fact that Charles Bedaux suddenly crumbled in the face of opposition, offering to withdraw from his role as organizer of the tour. The duke declined this suggestion, but he and Wallis were given pause by a further statement made by Bedaux: 'Out of one hundred chances that [the Windsors] will come, about ninety are gone.' He had just received word that the State Department, in answer to a request by Sir Ronald Lindsay, would not accord the duchess the title 'Her Royal Highness'.

Bedaux's statement, not conveyed to the Windsors in person, reached them most inconveniently and disagreeably by radio. They were very upset indeed. It is clear that if Bedaux had stood firm they would probably still have continued with the trip, and indeed on 5 November, their trunks were still packed. The afternoon of that day Sir Ronald Lindsay telephoned the duke in Paris. Lindsay told him he had noticed with deepest distress the trend of present opinion against the visit. The duke said he was considering dropping Bedaux and touring without him; Lindsay replied that he did not know how dependent the duke was on Bedaux's arrangements with regard to the tour. The duke revealed that William Bullitt in Paris was urging him to go ahead, while Bedaux was urging him to desist. He thought he might perhaps curtail the tour, recasting it on the spot in Washington. Lindsay told him that this would cause dreadful difficulties. Then, ever restless, the duke said perhaps he should just postpone the trip; if he did so, he asked, would he be able to make the tour later? Lindsay replied, 'If you do, you will not be able to do it ever.'

'Are you alarmed?' the duke said.

'Sir,' Lindsay replied, 'I feel the tour will cast a certain discredit on the American view of British monarchy.'

An hour later, the duke telephoned a number which he thought was that of William Bullitt and instead accidentally dialled the private number of Sir Eric Phipps. He began by saying that he was grateful for Bullitt's advice to go to the United States in spite of the campaign against him. Phipps urged the duke to ignore Bullitt's recommendations, and the duke listened.

The following night, the Windsors issued a press communiqué to the effect that they had decided to postpone their trip. In a desperate effort to overcome Nazi charges against them, they unwisely stated that they would be going to the Soviet Union. According to an Associated Press release, authorized by the duke, the purpose of the Russian visit would be 'to balance the German tour' and 'prove to the world that the Duke played no politics'.

Later, Mrs Roosevelt told Lady Lindsay a curious story. The ship that would have carried the Windsors was supposed to dock on 11 November, Armistice Day. The Windsors would have arrived in Washington in time to allow them to go to Arlington and lay a wreath on the Tomb of the Unknown Soldier. Mrs Roosevelt, determined to prevent this, arranged for the train to be delayed deliberately to prevent the wreathlaying.

NOTES

1 A platinum copy was auctioned in 1987 at Sothebys.
2 Born in Bradford, England, Bohle had been raised in South Africa and had renounced his British citizenship just before the Windsors arrived. Intelligent, forceful and domineering, he had joined the Nazi party in 1932. In 1933 he became head of the *Auslandsorganisation,* known familiarly as the AO. It was the organization of Germans abroad. In November that year he was elected to the Reichstag. He was bent upon securing a permanent alliance of all international peoples of German descent against the Soviet Union. Later, he would be secretly instrumental in the flight of Rudolf Hess to Scotland, and he undertook the translations of Hess's letters to the Duke of Hamilton concerning a negotiated peace.
3 The newsreels were tampered with in England to remove his 'Heil-ing' arm.

13

OUTER DARKNESS

It was at this time that Wallis embarked upon the most dangerous emotional and sexual adventure of her life. Abandoning Guy Trundle, she became the lover of the US ambassador to France, William Christian Bullitt.

Bullitt's interest in Wallis was first indicateded on February 22, 1935, when he wrote to Roosevelt saying that, while in London that week, he had received an invitation from 'a very charming Maryland lady' to go to Fort Belvedere but had to decline as he was due in Moscow that week. Little did he know that the charming Marylander whom he would visit several times as her husband's guest at Bryanston Court would ensnare him in a liaison that could have wrecked his diplomatic career.

Philadelphia blueblood, son of a wealthy coal merchant, with George Washington, Pocahantas, and Fletcher Christian of *Mutiny on the Bounty* fame numbered among those he claimed as his ancestors, Bullitt was raised in luxury by his doting parents. He grew up sleek, superficial, and devious – in other words, he had the makings of a perfect diplomat.

Bald from an early age, he was nevertheless attractive, with regular features, lively blue eyes, and a slim figure dressed in tailor-made clothing from Savile Row. His wealth and enormous charm added to his appeal as both social figure and career politician. His passion for Germany began in 1916, when he and his first wife, Ernesta Drinker, were guests in Berlin of the kaiser and his high command. Later, he endeared himself to the up-and-coming Adolf

Hitler when he publicly attacked the Versailles Treaty, which stripped Germany of its power and its colonies at the end of the Second World War, in terms scarcely less incendiary than Hitler's own.

In the early 1930s, his unauthorized efforts to have Germany's war debts waived or reduced by eighty per cent were so dangerous that he came close to being arrested under the terms of the Logan Act, which precluded private American citizens from making arrangements with foreign powers without presidential authorization.

Seeking to obtain inside intelligence on the Soviet Union, which, as a secret anti-communist, Bullitt could well supply, President Roosevelt, with his customary cunning, appointed him ambassador to Moscow, where the Russians sensibly mistrusted him. On 23 December 1923 he had married his second wife, Louise Bryant, widow of the American communist John Reed; the Reeds became the subjects of Warren Beatty's 1981 film *Reds*. Bryant was a lesbian, the lover of the great Broadway star Eva Le Gallienne; in a novel he wrote, based on their relationship, entitled *It's Not Done*, Bullitt portrayed a hero rendered impotent by his wife's frigidity. Rudely, he dedicated it to Bryant.

The truth is that his impotence with his wife was caused by his discovery that he was bisexual; he fell in love, in 1934, with his young and appealing male private secretary, Carmel Offie, a Philadelphian with Nazi connections like himself, whom he first met in Washington and had transferred from a post in Honduras to his embassy in Moscow. In Russia, where sex between males could result in beheading, he daringly conducted his affair with Offie under the protection of the embassy, and installed him in his house, on the excuse that he needed to consult with Offie at all house of the day or night.

He was tortured by his dual nature and for psychosexual treatments he turned to no less than his friend Dr Sigmund Freud in Vienna. Freud shared his detestation of Woodrow Wilson, architect of the Versailles Treaty, and as early as 1925 they jointly produced a sensational book which was not published until 1966, condemning Wilson outright.

Bullitt's connections to the German royal conspirators led by the Hesse family began with the Wilson project and continued for many years as he worked with Freud's cooperation; forming a friendship with Wolfgang, Prince of Hesse, Wolfgang's wife Marie Alexandra, and twin brother Prince Philipp, he spent much time at their Castle Friedrichschof at Krönberg reading the papers of First World War German chancellor, Maximilian von Baden, Alexandra von Hesse's father, to show, through Wilson's correspondence with him, the American president's designing of Germany's complete destruction.

In 1934, Bullitt divorced Louise and left Russia; appointed ambassador to France in 1935, he supported the breaking of a Franco-Soviet pact that liberals believed could have prevented the Second World War. He worked against the anti-Nazi French Popular Front, conspired with the Paris Fifth Column, prompted the French to send 350,000 men to Iraq, Syria and Turkey, thus dangerously undermining the national defence, and gave full support to such flagrantly pro-Nazi figures as the journalist Stéphane Lauzanne, editor of *Le Matin*, a frequent visitor to Hitler, Lauzanne's boss, Maurice Bunau-Varilla, brother of the chief backer of the Panama Canal, and Wallis's lawyer Armand Grégoire, who represented Bullitt as well as Elsa Schiaparelli and Wallis's ex-lover Ribbentrop.

Bullitt had yet another high-level Fascist connection that directly involved the Hesses. At a time when Prince Philipp of Hesse was acting as emissary of Hitler to Mussolini, and Philipp was husband of Princess Mafalda, daughter of King Victor Emmanuel, Bullitt's Aunt Louise married one of the highest-ranking figures of the pro-Mussolini Italian hierarchy, the Duke of Assergio, and set up a fascist salon in Rome that Bullitt often visited.

Exactly when Wallis's affair with Bullitt began is uncertain, but his absence from her wedding, an astonishment in view of his presence as ambassador in Paris at the time, may indicate that at least there were the beginnings of romantic feelings between them even then. The late Charles Bedaux, son of Wallis's friend and host, believed their liaison started in November 1936. The question is, why did Bullitt, who had money, looks, charm and peerless diplomatic status, and could have the pick of Paris females, risk his career by having an affair with the most notorious woman in

Europe? Cuckolding the Duke of Windsor could have made a ruinous news story, followed by an even more sensational divorce.

The answer lies clearly in the fact that he – still involved with Carmel Offie, with whom ironically Wallis often played gin rummy at the American embassy in Paris – needed a woman again, but was threatened, as he had been with his wife Louise Bryant, by the problem of impotence for which Freud was treating him. Wallis, with her Chinese sexual techniques, could arouse and satisfy him, restoring his confidence as a man. After all, had she not done the same for her husband?

The question, as with Guy Trundle, was where Wallis could conduct the affair without the jealous and possessive duke finding out about it. With most society marriages at the time, adultery on the side was considered acceptable, perhaps even desirable. But the Duke of Windsor was neither sophisticated nor amenable. At all costs, the truth must be kept from him.

The answer, again, was Elsa Schiaparelli. Her sumptuous salon at the Place Vendôme had numerous private rooms used for fittings, any one of which could be converted into a bedroom. The American-born designer Mainbocher, with whom Wallis also shopped, was a giddy gossip who could not be trusted to keep his mouth shut. Others who assisted Bullitt in the cover-up were the Nazi emissary Otto Abetz, a friend of Hitler, and his wife, the French patroness of the arts Suzanne de Bruyker. Still another cover was provided by the young attorney Suzanne Blum, a close friend of Bullitt's who would one day be Wallis's lawyer.

Because of Bullitt's fascist connections, Sir Robert Vansittart and Sir Alexander Cadogan of the Foreign Office in London sought – through the Paris SIS agent Wilfred Alfred Dunderdale – a suitable spy who could observe Wallis's relationship at first hand and avoid a royal scandal by making sure the Duke of Windsor didn't find out about it. From his headquarters apartment at 1 Avenue Charles-Floquet, Dunderdale began searching for the appropriate spy. He settled on one of his favourite society operatives, the remarkable Lady Jane Williams-Taylor, whom Wallis knew very well.

The daughter of a Canadian lumber tycoon, Lady Williams-Taylor was the reigning queen of Montreal and Bahamian society, as well as one of the most prominent figures of New York, London, Paris and Palm Beach. Tall and imposing, with a beautifully modulated voice and a strong, single-minded will, she was seventy-two years old when Dunderdale and his team engaged her for her important task.

She was born at Hyacinth, in the province of Quebec, in 1865; her family was quite distinguished; one of her uncles had been tutor to the children of Queen Victoria. She combined a formidably authoritative manner with a contradictory streak of vulgarity; she would at parties point to the crotches of men's trousers and remark on their contents, causing thrills of horror or amusement to pass through the guests; she was noted for the strings of lovers she commanded – handsome one and all, they satisfied her quickly or were discarded as hastily as lame horses from her stable of thoroughbreds.

She settled on a husband, not among the rich, but rather among the poor, whom she could control for life. Frederick Williams-Taylor was handsome, virile, finely proportioned and muscular – just her physical type. A humble clerk at the Bank of Montreal, he rose rapidly through her influence, and his command of finance took him to the very top. An excellent horseman, polished and personable, proficient at tennis, swimming, badminton and bridge, he joined his wife in dazzling society, and nobody was surprised when he was knighted in 1913 for his services to the British Crown.

In 1934, Lady Jane met an admiring Adolf Hitler in Munich, and when she joined Admiral Sinclair's Secret Intelligence Service in London soon afterwards her calling card was that she would pretend to be the Führer's ardent supporter. For years she maintained an oil painting of Hitler at her various homes – Claridges and Hans Court in London; the Ritz in Paris; and Star Acres, her legendary estate in the Bahamas.

Her chief claim to international fame was her granddaughter, Brenda Frazier, one of the most talked-about women of her day. The society debutante and legendary beauty whose photographs and interviews were in almost every woman's magazine in America, Brenda, in league with her husband, John 'Shipwreck' Kelly, worked with Lady Jane in the service of secret intelligence.

On Wilfred Dunderdale's instructions and with the cooperation of Millard E. Tydings, senator from Maryland, and Marjorie Merriweather Post, heiress to the Post Toasties cereals fortune, Lady Williams-Taylor made arrangements to shop at Schiaparelli's, and attend various parties that Wallis and her husband went to, and report on a regular basis the political and sexual connection to Bullitt. At the same time she acted as a decoy, inviting the Duke of Windsor to various afternoon teas and other events so that he would not insist on accompanying Wallis to her fittings at Schiaparelli's. With Constance Coolidge, that close friend of Wallis's, she could ensure that Wallis entered the salon by a secret back door, protected by police, so that the inevitable crowd of celebrity hunters would not mob her.

Throughout the liaison, interrupted frequently by Bullitt's visits to Washington or Berlin, the duplicitous ambassador continued to entertain the duke and duchess to dinners at the townhouse he shared with Carmel Offie at 2 Avenue Iena, and at his country home, Saint-Firmin, at Chantilly on the River Oise, where Offie also lived. He carried off this breathtaking hypocrisy with his usual polished skill. In one letter, he wrote to Roosevelt saying approvingly that the duke was 'still very much in love with his wife'.

Bullitt, up to his eyes in appeasing the Nazis and opposing the Russians, matters in which he found Wallis a continuing ally, in Berlin that month met Goering and his aunt Louise's old friend, Mussolini's ambassador Bernardo Attolico, also a contact of Philipp of Hesse. The result of the meeting was a recommendation to Roosevelt in a letter from Paris on November 23 in which he said, after a lengthy and sly account of the Nazi hatred of the liberal ambassador in Berlin, William E. Dodd, a hatred he shared:

> The only way that I can see that the growth of German strength can be used for constructive instead of destructive purposes is by a general effort to the giving of . . . concessions to Germany as part of a general plan of unification of Europe.

The concessions referred to were the imminent acquisition of Austria and Czechoslovakia. He added, 'The Germans have the most profound desire to improve relations with us and we can influence them.' The next night he found a sympathetic audience in the Windsors when he had them to dinner and Wallis told him of Hitler's remark to her that future civilizations would compare the ruins of the Germany of the time to those of the Greeks – an absurd comparison at best, but received with pleasure by the ambassador.

The failure of Bullitt's plans for the United States tour was a disaster for the Windsors. They had made two mistakes: first, in not undertaking the venture before the German tour, and second, in crumbling so easily under the objections of a small number of trade unions. John L. Lewis, the American labour leader, was, according to Charles Bedaux, Jr, a keen admirer of Bedaux, and certainly there could have been no general strike in the towns which they visited. Their enemies, however, were grateful that the tour was called off.

On 10 November, the Reverend J. L. C. Dart, Anglican vicar at St George's in Paris, announced that he would not welcome the Windsors if they attended the Armistice Day services the following day. He would not fail to provide good seats, but he would certainly not speak to the Windsors. So far as he was concerned, 'Marriage only ends before God when it is ended by death,' and Wallis was still married to her first husband. The Windsors did not appear. Meanwhile, the *New York Times* reported that Buckingham Palace was relieved by the Windsors' decision not to go to the United States, and at the same time the loyalist government in Spain acclaimed it. *Voz*, the loyalist newspaper, said in an editorial: 'The Windsors abandoned their proposed visit to America . . . First it was Mussolini's son, and now the duke and duchess. At this rate no fascist traveller will be able to leave Berlin and Rome.'

Arriving in New York aboard the French ship *Normandie*, Lord Beaverbrook, not content with having driven Wallis out of England a year earlier, said that the duke should 'quit public life'. For some time he and the duchess did. They stayed on for several weeks at the Meurice, in their suite overlooking the long, tree-studded Tuileries gardens and the distant Seine. Chief Inspector Storrier still remained in constant attendance. So did Dudley Forwood.

Several events took place that month. On 9 November, Mary Kirk divorced Jacques Raffray, and nine days later she married Ernest Simpson in a ceremony at her family home in Fairfield, Connecticut. They were to spend their honeymoon in London. He was forty, she was forty-one. Both had tragic futures. Their son,

Henry, was born on 28 September 1939; he was evacuated to the United States, and his mother accompanied him there. She was returning by ship through U-boat infested waters when she had early symptoms of cancer. The ship was diverted because of U-boat action to Lisbon, and she insisted on proceeding to London to work with the Red Cross first-aid stations as a volunteer nurse during the Blitz. Becoming seriously ill, she returned to the United States, but then went back to England to die, at the age of forty-three, on 2 October 1941. Ernest died at sixty-two, of cancer of the throat, on 30 November 1958. It was the same cause of death that took Wallis's third husband.

That same month, the Grand Duchess of Hesse, the duke's cousin, was killed when the plane in which she was travelling to the wedding of Prince Ludwig, her husband's brother, and the daughter of Sir Auckland Geddes, collided with a brickworks chimney in Ostend. The wedding, which the duke and duchess were unable to attend, was held entirely in black, with the bride in a black wedding gown.

In the third week of November, the libel suit filed by the duke against Geoffrey Dennis, author of *Coronation Commentary*, was settled in London. The duke's counsel, Sir William Jowitt, KC, called for dismissal; he stated that the duke had withdrawn the suit in return for unspecified damages and an apology. The chief passage complained of included the statement: 'The lady who is now the plaintiff's wife occupied, before his marriage to her, the position of his mistress.'

On 25 November, the Windsors attended Thanksgiving services at the American church. They sat with William Bullitt, who read President Roosevelt's Thanksgiving Proclamation.

On the 30th, it was mentioned in the press that the Windsors (who had not thought of it) would be going to visit the Argentine. With dry humour, Hardinge wrote to Vansittart, 'There would, of course, be no possible objection to the Duke and Duchess of Windsor paying a prolonged visit to the Argentine.' He clearly hoped they would never come back.

At Christmas, the Rogerses, who had sailed to New York, made arrangements to lend the Windsors Lou Viei on the Riviera. Dudley Forwood and the staff went ahead by car to the villa to prepare everything, while the Windsors followed by train. In the duke's luggage was a complete set of photographs of his visit to Hitler. Two years later the Rogerses' niece by marriage, Mrs Edmund Pendleton Rogers, was visiting France when the duke proudly showed her the same pictures. The duchess seemed quite indifferent.

After dinner on Christmas Eve with several Canadian friends, the duke visited a florist's and bought just under £300 worth of orchids, white violets and lilac for the delighted duchess. However, Christmas Day itself was miserable because the duke had an ulcerated jawbone from neglected teeth and had to undergo orthodontic surgery.

On 28 December, Sir Eric Phipps wrote to Anthony Eden from Paris, referring to a statement made by his predecessor as ambassador, Tyrrell:

> Tyrrell, who has been staying here for a week, told a member of my staff the following astonishing story:
>
> Some time ago, a special correspondent of the *Daily Herald* came over here to interview the Duke of Windsor. Tyrrell was shown the account of this interview, in which it was stated that His Royal Highness said that if the Labour Party wished, and were in a position to offer it, he would be prepared to be president of the English Republic. Tyrrell urged Greenwood to have this left out of any published account of his interview, as he was so shocked and horrified. This Greenwood promised to do, and I understand that, so far, the interview has not seen the light of day. In reply to a question put by a member of my staff as to whether the government knew of the declaration, Tyrrell said, 'I think not the government, but possibly the Prime Minister.' I am not informing anyone of the above except yourself.

The Windsors lingered on in the south of France. On New Year's Eve 1937, they were with their friend the Hon. Mrs Reginald Fellowes when the duke won a substantial sum at baccarat at the Monte Carlo Sporting Club. Three days later, Lloyd George arrived from London for a visit; he reported that it was in the Paris newspapers that the Bishop of Bermuda had ordered the Windsors' portraits taken down from the window of a local shop; when the shopkeeper refused, the bishop tore down and destroyed the photographs himself. Winston Churchill also arrived; the conversation circled around all the problems raised by the royal visit to Germany. On the 7th, the Windsors attended a dinner party given by Maxine Elliott at the Château de l'Horizon. Lloyd George and Churchill were there.

When the Windsors arrived, across a small bridge, they were greeted at the door by Maxine's nephew by marriage, the political journalist Vincent Sheean. Maxine, once a legendary American beauty, still looked attractive with her piled-high white hair and Chanel gown. The duchess, who had been forewarned that Maxine would be in white, succeeded in upstaging her hostess by wearing black. Maxine managed a curtsey, while Vincent Sheean, equally briefed, bowed.

At dinner, the duke sat at the head of the table, and the conversation was brisk. Sheean noted in his memoirs, *Between the Thunder and the Sun*, that the talk revolved around the conditions of the Welsh coalminers and the necessity of improving their plight through legislation. Either unaware – or mischievously aware – of the fact that Sheean was decidedly left-wing and a keen supporter of the loyalists in Spain, the duke praised the social legislation of the Nazis:

> He and the Duchess had been assured by Dr Ley that every mine in Germany had the most ample, and indeed luxurious, arrangements for bathing at the pithead. They had indeed visited these baths on their tour of the Reich some months before. Mr Churchill did not particularly enjoy praise of the Nazi regime, and although he had been remarkably silent throughout the meal (deferring like a schoolboy to the authority of Mr Lloyd George and the Duke) he now spoke up to say that he had proposed compulsory shower-baths at the pithead long ago.

Sheean observed that the seriousness of the interest of everyone present could not be doubted, yet it was 'confounded with an incurable frivolity owing to their astronomical remoteness from the conditions of life of which they spoke'. Clearly, the duke wanted to see the miners 'clean, healthy and contented, as you might wish your horses or dogs to be; to him they were not men and brothers'. Sheean added, with equal shrewdness:

> The Duchess, so slim and elegant, so suggestive of innumerable fashionable shops, dressmakers, manicurists and hairdressers, seemed at the uttermost removed from the pithead of a mine, and I tried to imagine what she must have been like when Dr Ley, all puffed out with . . . the snobbery of a German official, showed her the men's baths in the Ruhr.

The evening became increasingly surrealistic as the hard-bitten journalist watched in a daze of disbelief Churchill, Lloyd George, the duke and duchess, and the few other guests discussing matters of poverty and struggle while surrounded by expensive furniture, glass and silver: 'It was like lunch, I thought, in a traffic policeman's tower; if you turned your back and chewed hard on the ham you were unaware of the street.'

On 9 January, the Windsors returned to the Meurice; three nights later police arrested a man who was trying to penetrate their suite. A Swedish anti-Nazi, he was suspected of attempting an assassination.

On the 18th, the duke interceded with the Spanish government to arrange, through the ambassador, Sir Henry Chilton, for the release from prison of the Franco diplomat Don Javier Bermejillo, whom he and Wallis had known in London when Bermejillo had been on the embassy staff. This fact only came to light because Chilton's wallet was stolen in London and he had to give a list of its contents to the police. They included the duke's written request. This act of assistance to a fascist scarcely improved his image.

On the 26th, after a prolonged search, the Windsors at last found a Paris residence that they both liked; the Château La Maye at Versailles. The property belonged to the American widow of a French politician, Paul Dupuy. Magnificently furnished, it had a tennis court, a golf course and a swimming pool. They took a six-month lease, moved in on 7 February and brought over much of the stored furniture from Fort Belvedere, York House and Wallis's home at Cumberland Terrace. However, they grew tired of the house within two months.

In March, William Bullitt was summoned to Washington by

President Roosevelt, who was far from satisfied with his ambassador's Nazi and Italian connections. He offered Bullitt, with barely disguised humour and contempt, the suggestion that he might run for governor of Pennsylvania. It took all of Bullitt's skills of persuasion to retain his post in Paris.

It was a stormy month in France. The treacherous and slippery premier, Camille Chautemps, presiding over a cabinet feebly composed of right- and left-wing elements, resigned in the face of public fury for his anti-labour policies and the nation was crippled by strikes in industry and transportation. The so-called friend of labour, Léon Blum, was forced to assemble a new government in haste to avoid a national collapse, and for several days the country had no official administration.

Wallis had her rich woman's distractions. Chief among them was the racetrack at Auteuil where she and the duke were guests of the Steeplechase Club president Comte Delaire de Cambacérès, Duke of Parma, and his popular associate, the Marquis du Crozet of Languedoc. There, Wallis often saw her trusted friend Constance Coolidge, the sometimes mistress of H. G. Wells.

Constance was a fascinating if dizzy companion, a Boston blueblood who had been immortalized in a portrait by John Singer Sargent. Beautiful, dark, as promiscuous as Wallis herself, she often entertained the Windsors at her luxurious apartment near the racetrack at 11 Rue Maspero.

Her innumerable love affairs with attractive men were interspersed with brief and ill-fated marriages; first to the American diplomat Ray Atherton, who took her to China just ahead of Wallis's stay there, second to the flamboyant Comte Chapelle du Jumilhac, of the Château du Dreux-Bresée, at Chèze Sur Argos (who later married another American, Ethel Barbey) and third, a step down in the world, to the humdrum California newspaper man Eliot Rogers, whom she shed when he failed to meet her exacting standards in the bedroom.

In March 1938, Constance was the lover of dating the prominent and strikingly attractive political journalist and long-term Berlin correspondent of the pro-Hitler *Le Matin*, Philippe Barrès. His father was the world-famous nationalist and author Maurice Barrès, for whom a street in Paris is named to this day.

Constance herself was profoundly anti-Nazi, recording that month in her diary her horror of Hitler moving through Europe like a fatal disease, a view she kept hidden from the Windsors, perhaps in order to determine what they were up to. Barrès had been a strong supporter of the Nazis; his *Sous La Vague Hitlérienne*, published in 1933, was a somewhat critical but mostly ecstatic account of the Führer's rise to power. But by 1938, when he met and fell in love with Constance, he had already begun to feel disillusionment, seeing a threat to French power and autonomy to which his life, like his father's, was dedicated.

He had left the post of Berlin correspondent when even his mildest critiques of Hitler were relegated to the middle or back pages of *Le Matin*. Now he was preparing to resign as Paris feature writer as he was in conflict with Stéphane Lauzanne, the inflammatory Hitler-supporting editor-in-chief and Maurice Bunau-Varilla, the dictatorial Hitler-loving owner. Like Constance, he put up with the Windsors' fascism, presumably in order to determine how dangerous they were.

One evening at dinner at Constance's apartment at 11 Rue Maspero, the duke annoyed her by saying, all too characteristically, in reference to stories that Czechoslovakia was next on Hitler's list of conquests after Austria, 'It's a ridiculous country. It isn't a nation at all but an invention of [President] Woodrow Wilson's. How could anyone go to war for a place like that?' He was referring to Wilson's 3 September 1918 agreement to grant Czechoslovakia her ill-fated independence from the Austro-Hungarian empire in dissolution; a noble action excoriated by Bullitt in his book written with Sigmund Freud.

On 22 March, Wallis and the duke left by car for the south of France to visit the American millionaire Ogden Codman, to discuss renting his Antibes chateau, Leopolda, named for its former owner, the pro-Nazi King Leopold of the Belgians. Next day, Constance Coolidge had lunch in Paris with the Comte de Cambacérès, who informed her that she should at once attend to a certain important matter concerning the Windsors.

He said he had been contacted by a certain Madame Maroni, who wished to see her quickly. Madame Maroni, he said, lived just a few minutes' walk from Constance's apartment – at 36 Boulevard

Emile Augier, also in the Sixteenth Arrondissement and quite close to the Auteuil racetrack.

Despite the comte's distinction, Constance felt uneasy about this matter. When Madame Maroni called her twice, she told her butler Victor to say she was out. But the woman persisted; her manservant made further calls; and at last Constance gave in. Asked to tea on 23 March, she went that evening instead. Unwisely, she didn't check the social registers (*Tout Paris* and *Bottin Mondain*), which would have shown her that the only Maroni listed in Paris, Fernand Maroni, editor-in-chief of the legendary consevative newspaper *Journal des Débats*, was unmarried and living at 10 Avenue Bugeaud, also quite close to her, in the same Sixteenth Arrondissement near Auteuil.

Once arrived at the apartment building, she wasn't impressed by the ancient and dishevelled concierge in the vestibule; she took the lift to the third-floor flat which, had she consulted the social registers, she would have seen was occupied not by Maroni but by a certain Gustave Badollet of Le Touquet, who was away. The white-coated butler who opened the door left her equally unimpressed and she felt even more uneasy when she met her Italian hostess, who was badly made up with dyed hair and had the atmosphere of an adventuress on the make. The background of vulgar white satin couches and curtains was no more reassuring to the visitor.

The woman talked in hints, suggestions and half-whispers. Essentially, she was saying that she was acting on behalf of a friend who was very highly placed; after a while, she announced that the friend was a duchess. Foolishly, Constance didn't ask for the duchess's name, but listened uneasily while Madame Maroni said the peeress concerned had in her possession letters, documents and photographs of a sensational character that would be of great potential damage to the Windsors and to the royal family of England as a whole. The smell of blackmail lay heavily on the air.

'The papers are not to be believed,' the woman said, as Constance grew more and more uncomfortable. Madame Maroni pressed on; Constance didn't have the sense to ask why, if the friend were a duchess, she couldn't have met the Windsors herself. Maroni said that a 'certain group' was prepared to force her hand to buy the materials and publish them in America unless they were pre-empted; Constance must act at once to protect her royal friends.

Maroni added that all she needed was to see the duke alone. To make him happy she would burn the photographs and documents in his presence – a potential scene of blackmail and high drama that could have come from an overdose of Dostoevsky or of low-grade romantic fiction.

At that moment, the doorbell rang repeatedly; the butler had disappeared and there was no one to answer it; nor did Constance's mysterious hostess bother to excuse herself and go to the door.

Knock after noisy knock followed; at last the door burst open and Constance's butler Victor ran, badly upset, into the drawing room. He was, he said, worried that something untoward had happened to his mistress.

Constance rose from the sofa and told Madame Maroni she would have nothing to do with the matter, thus making it clear that blackmail did not appeal to her. Then she and Victor walked out.

Back at her apartment, badly upset, Constance wrote Wallis a letter to the Hôtel du Cap at Antibes, describing the unsavoury encounter, but thought better of it and didn't mail it. She needed to look further into the matter.

Next day, she had a visit from her friend Dr Edmond Gros, the distinguished physician and director of the American Hospital at Neuilly. She told him the story and he was shocked; he at once contacted his brother-in-law, Stéphane Lauzanne of *Le Matin*. This was a smart decision; if Madame Maroni had incriminating documents connecting the Windsors to a fascist scandal, then she could be silenced by the fascists instead of paid.

Later that morning, Constance's lover, Philippe Barrès, who had just handed in his resignation to Maurice Bunau-Varilla, arrived at her flat and told her that Lauzanne had brought the matter to the *Le Matin* staff's attention but that the story had been quashed immediately – he didn't say by whom. But clearly, the decision was Bunau-Varilla's.

Constance called the Comte de Cambacérès and arranged to have lunch with him and the Marquis du Crozet at the racetrack at Maison-Laffitte. She chided the comte severely for getting her involved in so unsavoury a matter. She made no record of his response.

Still upset, Constance returned to her apartment that afternoon, only to find that a 'police inspector' as she called him was waiting to see her; her diary does not record his name, but it is clear that he was assistant to Superintendent Gilbert Rochès, commissioner of police at the Quai des Orfèvres, the headquarters of the Sûreté, an indication of the importance of the case. Bunau-Varilla and Stéphane Lauzanne had asked him to take charge.

Constance told him the story. The assistant superintendent told her that the only Maroni in Paris was indeed the distinguished editor, Fernand Maroni. Maroni's corruption extended to his being a paid servant of the Lazard Frères banking empire, which connected him directly, and Bunau-Varilla and Stéphane Lauzanne with him, to the internationally conspiratorial Synarchiste movement, which had strong Mussolini connections.

The police officer informed her that the Comte de Cambacérès had unwittingly led her into a trap; the woman was not Madame Maroni, wife of the financial journalist, but an obscure niece; Constance said she was relieved, as she could not believe so important a man would involve his wife in a flagrant blackmail plot.

On a visit next day, the 'inspector' said that the woman had been a maid in the Duke of Windsor's household; that she herself was the mysterious highly placed figure, the so-called 'duchess' who owned the letters and photographs, and that she had a bad reputation in the district.

He added that she had followed the duke from Vienna to Le Touquet, a town two and a half hours by train out of Paris, which he had visited on more than one occasion, and that she had sent him two letters, which he had handed over to the police. It is obvious they were of a similar blackmailing character.

The mention of Le Touquet provides a significant clue. Gustave Badollet, the absent retired industrialist who rented the third-floor apartment in which the Maroni woman spoke to Constance, owned the Villa Savaral in that town, and may well have entertained the Windsors there.

The assistant superintendent went on to say that he had called

Maroni in for questioning at police headquarters at the Quai des Orfèvres; that Maroni had denied any knowledge of the matter and would not allow his divorced wife, the writer Mathilde Maroni, whom he had married in Switzerland, to be asked questions. He had enough power in Paris to prevent that interrogation.

When Constance conveyed this to Philippe Barrès, he wasn't satisfied. Almost his last act as contributor to *Le Matin* was to go with a reporter to 36 Boulevard Emile Augier, to talk to the Maroni woman.

Asking her, as Constance should have done, what exactly she had on the Windsors, she provided the astonishing revelation that the documents and photographs concerned the duke's and the royal family of England's links to Prince Philipp of Hesse.

When Barrès told Constance what he had found out, she would, if she had any political inside knowledge, which she did not, have been in a state of shock. If it were made public that Windsor and Kent had been in intimate contact with Philipp, to the point that they exchanged letters of a dangerous character in favour of Hitler and Mussolini and appeasement of fascism and that they were photographed together, when not one trace of such a direct association was ever made public (or has been since) it could have blown the lid off the British monarchy, especially since Kent was viewed in the world's eyes as an heroically patriotic Englishman. Worse than anything, the woman clearly had evidence that King George VI had personally authorized the Kent–Hesse connection, as would surface in the papers of Neville Chamberlain the following year. This meant that, contrary to popular opinion then and now, the English king was in improbable accord with Windsor and Kent – determined to achieve peace at any cost.

What is certain is that the woman had royal-Nazi connections. As publisher and editor of *Le Matin*, Maurice Bunau-Varilla and Stéphane Lauzanne would be familiar with the Philipp of Hesse association and would want to protect the Windsors to the limit. There could never be any question of 'Madame Maroni's' charges leaking in their newspaper, nor, of course, in the pages of Fernand Maroni's distinguished *Journal des Débats*. And given the political censorship and the libel laws of the time, even such liberal publications as *Paris Soir* or *Paris Match*, of which Philippe Barrès soon became joint editor, would never have published the facts.

Constance, at commissioner of police Gilbert Rochès's request, finally mailed the letter describing everything to Wallis, whose urgent telegram of receipt from Antibes can today be seen in the Coolidge files at the Massachusetts Historical Society. She and the duke must have been in a state of shock, because, despite a national strike, they at once drove on roads crowded with trainless people in cars to a Paris that was virtually paralysed; avoiding both their home at Versailles and the Hôtel Meurice, they checked on 4 April in secrecy to the Hôtel Crillon where they had never before stayed.

The duke immediately contacted Sir Philip Game, commissioner of Scotland Yard, to come to the hotel at once. Game arrived, dropping everything.

Wallis must have been petrified. Game was still in charge of the Guy Trundle affair, of which the duke remained oblivious. The duke also summoned Game's friend and French counterpart Roger Langeron, prefect of the Paris police. After lunch next day with Constance, the duchess called her at home and said she must come with her to the Crillon, to meet the British and French police chiefs.

They asked Constance to tell all she knew; when she was told to describe any woman other than Maroni who was romantically interested in the duke she mentioned an 'Austrian'. She probably meant Princess Friederike of Prussia, now the Princess of Greece. Next day, Gilbert Rochès came to Constance's apartment and took her statement yet again. And that was the last she heard of the matter.

A major problem for the historian examining Constance Coolidge's journal is the identity of Fernand Maroni's mysterious niece.

A slip in Constance's diary entries gives us a clue. When Gilbert Rochès told her who Maroni was, she noted down him saying that, as well as being involved with the *Journal des Débats*, he was also an architect. But he wasn't.

It seems that in his haste to deal with the matter, Rochès had confused Fernand Maroni with his cousin and namesake, the Italian fascist architect Gian Carlo Maroni, who was at the time attending a series of valedictory celebrations in Rome and Florence that followed the death of his friend, the great Italian poet Gabriele d'Annunzio, for whom he had designed Il Vittoriale, the most famous private house in Italy. Gian Carlo Maroni had a direct link to Prince Philipp of Hesse; Philipp was a fellow architect and they both designed for Philipp's wife, Princess Mafalda, and for her father, King Victor Emmanuel III.

Gian Carlo Maroni had several nieces, all of them poor. It is likely that one of them worked as a maid in Philipp's household and stole the photographs and documents from him, at his Castle Friedrichshof; then she stole more from the Windsors, whom she could have joined as a maid in their Austrian–German entourage.

The final question is, what became of the photographs and documents? Normally, the proposed victim of a blackmail plot would prosecute, and the appropriate proof would be filed with the advocates of the court of Paris, pending preliminary hearings and a criminal trial. But in this case, the Windsors predictably didn't press charges; a trial would have exposed far too much.

Instead, the woman was let go, presumably to return to Italy and more work as a housemaid with her uncle Gian Carlo Maroni's assistance. The documents would be held for at least ten years, with copies supplied to the potential plaintiffs, in case they should change their minds and decide to pursue the case before the statute of limitations expired.

The British government perhaps believed incorrectly that the dossier was sent, on orders of the Germans, who occupied Paris in June 1940, to Prince Philipp of Hesse at the time of that occupation; hence the fact that in 1945 the Secret Intelligence Service sent the double agent Anthony Blunt to retrieve them from Philipp's castle. Prince Wolfgang, twin brother of Prince Philipp, would, as we shall see, confirm there were strong links between the Dukes of Kent and Windsor and Philipp that the Blunt intelligence team was looking for. But more of this later.

On 20 April, the Windsors were back on the Riviera; they decided to take a lease on a house which had originally been recommended as the venue for their marriage. This was the Château la Croë at Cap d'Antibes, the home of the British newspaper magnate and Hearst associate Sir Pomeroy Burton. Modernized in

1928, at a then cost of £400,000, the chateau had a twenty-carat gilded bathtub, twelve bedrooms, a swimming pool, two bathing pavilions and a tennis court; it also had a large dining room that seated twenty-four and a magnificent drawing room lined with tapestries and painted panels.

The duke continued to fret over his situation vis-à-vis the royal family. He harassed Sir Walter Monckton and the palace ceaselessly for more money and for the opportunity to return to England with Wallis, where she would be recognized at last as 'Her Royal Highness'. So complete was this obsession, and so absolute the duke's removal from the realities of his own situation, that those who dealt with him could do little more than humour him in what appeared to be a form of madness. Monckton visited the Windsors twice that year, doing his utmost to soothe their fevered brows, returning to the king and queen with not much more than faint reassurances and subdued requests for more consideration for his friends, which were rejected out of hand.

It is easy to see why. The situation in Europe had deteriorated rapidly in Hitler's favour during the past few months. While the Windsors were wrangling over details of their move to La Croë in March, Austria had collapsed completely, failing even to respond when Hitler, having forced the resignation of the Windsors' old friend Chancellor von Schuschnigg, had marched into Vienna. Many opponents of the Nazis who could be identified either committed suicide or were committed to concentration camps. Schuschnigg was arrested without trial. The fact that the duke made no protest at this assault on his favourite European country, and continued to hobnob with certain figures of the Nazi regime in Paris, could only be received badly by the royal couple in London. But Monckton and the ever loyal Winston Churchill seemed to forgive everything. Neville Chamberlain's government was totally impotent in the face of growing Nazi power: appeasement went on.

One unfortunate aspect of Hitler's seizure of Austria was that Baron Louis Rothschild, brother of the Windsors' close friend Eugene, who now commuted between Zurich and Paris, had been arrested by the Gestapo and installed under house arrest with Schuschnigg on the top floor of the Metropole Hotel in Vienna. Louis had been the president of the Creditanstalt Bank when it went bankrupt in 1931, carrying with it substantial amounts of German investors' money. The Nazi government insisted it would not release him until it had received full settlement; storm-troopers had already seized his estates in lower Austria and his house in a fashionable district of Vienna.

His imprisonment greatly concerned the Windsors, who immediately began to take steps to arrange for go-betweens to have an appropriate ransom paid. This would include handing over to Himmler the complete ownership of a Czechoslovakian factory complex, along with sums of money that were being held in Switzerland and France. Since the German government obviously could not deal with any other member of the Rothschild family, it was clear that the Windsors, with their impeccable reputation in Berlin, were ideally placed to undertake the delicate task of freeing the distinguished captive. Others involved in the negotiations were said to have been Fritz Wiedemann and Princess Hohenlohe. In May 1939 Louis Rothschild, his hair completely white, his health adversely affected, would fly to Paris for a reunion with his benefactors.

In the meantime, the Windsors continued to travel restlessly. On 12 July, they sailed with the Herman Rogerses from Cannes to Genoa aboard the chartered yacht *Gulzar*, intending to continue to Rapallo. They terminated the first leg of the journey by meeting Princess Maria, daughter of King Victor Emmanuel, and other members of the Italian royal family. There was a certain black humour in the fact that they chose to make further appearances in a country which was now second only to Hitler's among dictatorships at the same time as King George and Queen Elizabeth were undertaking a state visit to Paris. The gesture seemed almost wilfully tasteless and aggressively affirmative of the Windsors' political position. There were unconfirmed rumours that they had had a meeting with Count Ciano; the Foreign Office was very concerned about the visit, and managed, possibly by threatening to discontinue the Windsors' income, to dissuade the couple from travelling to Vienna or Italian-dominated Tunisia to visit Georges Sebastian. They were also talked out of accepting a Panamanian decoration because of the authoritarian regime in that country.

While the tour continued, the Duke of Kent was acting as an

instrument of British pacification of Hitler and Mussolini. Recently declassified British Foreign Office minutes of 15 July 1938 make clear that his frequent visits to Munich were approved, and that it was desirable he should shortly make a return visit to Germany, where 'a personal gesture of that sort would be appreciated by Herr Hitler'. In return, Field Marshal Goering, whose importance was considered to be equivalent to Kent's, would be invited to London, but the Foreign Office stopped short of a suggestion, source not stated, that German paintings of recent origin should be displayed at the National Gallery in London. It was felt, not without reason, that their artistic quality would scarcely improve British public opinion of the country from which they emanated.

*

Meanwhile, temporarily eclipsing even the Windsors, King George VI and Queen Elizabeth had made a triumphal visit to Paris. They sensibly did not contact the Windsors, who were advised by the Foreign Office to stay firmly in the south of France. As it turned out, the royal tour of the city almost ended in tragedy. A Catalan group, allied with the Spanish falangists, or extreme right-wing fascists, planned to kill the monarch and his wife, pinning the blame on the communist-backed government in Spain.

The plot was hatched in the back room of a popular nightclub, the celebrated Boeuf sur le Toit, and at the Restaurant Le Cour and Café George V, as well as at an apartment rendezvous on the Rue Châteaubriand. A spy, the Marqués Rabalsc, head of the Spanish government's intelligence service stationed at St Jean de Luz, uncovered the plot just in time and despite bureaucratic indifference when he reported it to the British embassy in Paris, managed to get the Sûreté, headed by the overworked Gilbert Rochès, to raid the appropriate clubs and arrest the various conspirators.

Within days, a perfect reason was found for Kent's trip, designed to please the Führer. Queen Marie of Romania died conveniently and Kent and his wife, the duchess, flew at once to attend her funeral in Bucharest, where Goering, Mussolini, Ribbentrop, Prince Philipp of Hesse and Crown Prince Paul of Yugoslavia and their wives were in attendance. After much no doubt useful discussion on the need for peace, Kent left for Munich and his sister-in-law Countess Toerring. And all this just four months after the destruction of Austria. Could pacification of Hitler's policies at the British royal level go any further?

The delights of fascist Italy apparently overcame some of the disgruntlement the Windsors felt over the glory of the British royal reception in the city they had adopted. Besieged by irritable memoranda from the Foreign Office, they impatiently cancelled the remainder of their yacht cruise on 14 August at Genoa, dismissed the captain and crew and boarded the liner *Conte di Savoia*, arriving at Cannes the following day. They returned to La Croë for two weeks, where Wallis did some remodelling of the house. During that period the duke received disturbing news. Schloss Mittersill had burned down, and no doubt the duke was worried that details of his so-called Sports and Shooting Club would be revealed in the press. It was on 1 November that Himmler supplied Ribbentrop with the sensational report on the duke's membership of the club. But nothing ever appeared in print, and it was not until the West German government declassified the files in 1986 that the truth could be determined by this author.

On 22 September, the Windsors left for Paris. The situation in Europe was darkening still further. Czechoslovakia was falling apart, and it would obviously be only a question of time before it was added to Hitler's list of conquests. On 3 August, the British mediator Walter Runciman had arrived in Prague, preparing the groundwork for Hitler's imminent invasion. He was encouraging the leaders of the German-speaking Sudetenland in their determination to assist in the dismemberment of the country. On 12 September, a speech by Hitler at Nuremberg caused an international crisis to erupt, which was followed by the surrender of Britain and France to Hitler's demands. On 2 October, the London *Sunday Dispatch* published a statement from the duke's publicity staff saying, in response to Neville Chamberlain's notorious crumbling before Hitler, 'His Royal Highness has never lost hope [for the solution of the crisis] as he had unqualified confidence in the Prime Minister, although there seemed to be slender hope of success. His Royal Highness was convinced that Mr Chamberlain's personality would prevail and his policy of peace would succeed.'

In this conviction the duke was, it goes without saying, reflecting the majority of conservative political opinion in Great Britain. And that opinion, unhappily, is believed to have been shared by a majority of the public and even of the Labour party.

Once again, that left no one in any doubt about where the duke stood. Nor was anyone surprised when he was seen hobnobbing with Pierre Laval and his wife at parties, or with Otto Abetz, the German diplomat and Hitler fanatic who would soon become ambassador to Paris and play a crucial role in the collapse of the Third Republic.

On 29 September, the duke, without Wallis, held an extraordinary meeting at the Hôtel Meurice, a meeting that was monitored through discs in the walls by the British Secret Intelligence Service. In attendance at the meeting were Hitler's deputy, Rudolf Hess, Hitler's private secretary Martin Bormann, and the Nazi agent and motion picture star Errol Flynn, who had recently been in Spain with the Nazi spy Dr Hermann Erben, going behind the loyalist lines to inform Hitler and Franco, as exposed in such important books as Peter Wyden's history of the Spanish Civil War and George Seldes's *Witness to the Century*. After the meeting Hess wrote to Hitler:

> The duke is proud of his German blood. Says he is more German than he is British. There is no need to lose a single German life in invading Britain. The duke and his wife will deliver the goods.

Records of the meeting remain classified. However, it would be reasonable to deduce that Flynn promised support for the ducal tour of the United States. He had strong connections with Nazi groups in New York (where he was a frequent attendant at German–American Bund underground meetings) and in California, where a Japanese–German network existed, as well as with the Irish pro-Nazi supporters of the IRA, mostly located in the San Francisco Bay area and Marin County. And that Hess and Bormann promised a warm reception from Hitler and from the Nazi leaders as a whole.

Money was a continuing problem for the Windsors. Their £21,000 a year[1], the figure at the time, was barely enough to sustain their extraordinary standard of living. The duchess's addiction to jewellery required constant satisfaction. Her clothes had to be originals by Mainbocher, Schiaparelli, Chanel or Molyneux. The duke auctioned off his entire herd of shorthorn cattle, grazed at his High River, Alberta, ranch, for a total of $10,000. That helped a little, and the investing skills of Eugene Rothschild helped more. Much of the Windsors' money was, ironically, invested in the Jewish-owned Lyons' Corner Houses. The income from these enormously profitable and popular cafes improved substantially as time went on.

On 11 November, the Duke and Duchess of Gloucester, returning from a holiday in east Africa, flew to Paris and joined the Windsors for lunch at the Hôtel Meurice. They went for a drive and stopped at the Eugene Rothschilds' for tea. During the evening they called at a new house which the Windsors had just rented and were redecorating: an imitation Louis XVI residence owned by the Italian Countess Sabini, situated at 24 Boulevard Suchet, facing the wind-stripped autumn trees of the Bois de Boulogne. They would retain this elegant and charming house for many years.

The Gloucesters' visit ended with a farewell at Le Bourget airport. There was no question that the duke used the visit to press for Wallis's recognition and a return to London, but every effort made by the Gloucesters to sway the king and queen in the matter of Wallis's title failed.

On 24 November, Prime Minister Neville Chamberlain and Foreign Secretary Viscount Halifax, who were locked in meetings with French statesmen that would lead to the moral disintegration of the Quai d'Orsay, found time for an evening with the Windsors. The *New York Times* reported that at the meeting the duke and duchess clearly expressed their support of the government's foreign policy.

On 10 December, Prime Minister Baldwin was in Paris to answer yet another futile plea from the Duke of Windsor to have Wallis given the title of Her Royal Highness and to be received by his family in London. In the circumstances, as Sir Dudley Forwood told me, the duke can only be described as virtually insane in the degree of this obsession. That same day, the king wrote Baldwin from Buckingham Palace what was perhaps the fiercest letter of that quiet man's life, stating that he had canvassed people 'of all classes' and that the consensus was clear. The duke must not come to England with Wallis as his companion for even the shortest of visits; that neither his wife nor his mother, Queen Mary, had any desire to meet the Duchess of Windsor; and that any visit made for the purpose of such meetings was out of the question. He closed the letter by stating that the matter was so intimate that he thought this statement would be best conveyed by Baldwin rather than himself; that Windsor might take the refusal in a more friendly manner if it came from the prime minister. This was humorous, to say the least; the king knew that Windsor hated Baldwin even more than he hated him.

On 11 December, at a party in Paris given by Lady Mendl, Lady Diana Cooper and Wallis's friend Mrs Euan Wallace, wife of the parliamentary secretary at the Board of Trade, both curtseyed to the duchess. The Countess of Pembroke objected to this, clearly reflecting the views of Buckingham Palace. She said to the two ladies, 'Nothing would induce me to curtsey to the Duchess, as it is not customary to curtsey to any but royal personages.' Lady Diana later said, 'I only did it to please the Duke.'

On the 17th, the Windsors left for La Croë for the Christmas holidays. Their next-door neighbours for the season were none other than Thelma Furness and Gloria Vanderbilt; it goes without saying that visits were not exchanged. The Windsors' house guests were Lord and Lady Brownlow and children, Aunt Bessie, Sir Charles and Lady Mendl, Johnny McMullen and the Herman Rogerses. Another storm in a teacup blew up when, at an elaborate party given by Somerset Maugham, a couple of the female guests refused to curtsey and were reprimanded to their face by the duke. On the other hand, the opera star Grace Moore did curtsey deeply to the duchess at the Cannes casino following a recital, and this brought a storm of criticism, to which Miss Moore responded with great vigour. Mischievously, the duke sent a cable through the wire services stating, 'Her Royal Highness is displeased at the public criticism of Miss Grace Moore.' This episode, absurd and trivial though it seems, increased the determination against the Windsors at Buckingham Palace.

In January, while Ambassador Joseph P. Kennedy was in Washington, the Windsors invited his wife, Rose, who was visiting Paris, to dinner. She called her husband by transatlantic telephone and asked him if she should accept. He thought it better that she did not, because of the couple's continuing Nazi connections. Accordingly, she declined. Shortly afterwards, Bullitt called her and invited her to his house to meet the couple, saying it was important that Rose attend. She did.

Later, referring to Rose's earlier refusal, Kennedy told an American newspaper reporter, 'I know of no position that I could hold that would involve my wife in any obligation to dine with a tart.' When Kennedy told the queen the story at dinner at Windsor Castle on 14 April, she laughed joyously and said, 'It serves [Mrs Simpson] right.' She added, 'I understand, Mr Kennedy, that the Windsors are talking about my husband and I. Our conscience is clear. They are deplorable!' And Kennedy noted that the decorative motif of the Buckingham Palace ballroom when Windsor was King was a motif of swastikas. The Queen changed it at once.

Early in February, Victor Cazalet, an old friend, visited the Windsors in Paris. They told him that the duke would have gone to see Hitler himself if Chamberlain had not. He noted that the duke still adored Wallis and that she had him under her complete domination. Charming as always, the duke received him in a kilt. He criticized Baldwin to Cazalet because Baldwin had not mentioned Wallis in his famous speech to the House of Commons.

In those early months of 1939, the duke asked Walter Monckton to make inquiries at 10 Downing Street as to how Chamberlain would react to his returning with the duchess for a short visit. On 22 February, a letter from Neville Chamberlain arrived at Boulevard Suchet. The prime minister stated that it was his desire that the visit of the duke and duchess should be successful, and should not provoke heated controversy of any kind. However, he was forced to conclude that controversy would arise if the duke and duchess were to come to England at that time. Of course, this did not mean a permanent postponement, and the prime minister promised to keep a weather eye on the development of public opinion and to give a signal as soon as matters had improved to the point that such a visit would be officially acceptable.

That same day, the French premier, Edouard Daladier, spoke at a Washington's birthday dinner at the American Club in Paris at which the Windsors were present. Introduced by a beaming William C. Bullitt, who stressed that the United States would not 'start a war with any nation', Daladier spoke of permanent peace in Europe despite the fact that Italian troops were mustering on the borders of Libya and French Tunisia. Only sixteen days later, Hitler annihilated the Czech state. And on 8 May, in the wake of that annihilation, the duke, with Wallis at his side, broadcast on NBC from a country inn in Verdun, famous as a battlefield of the First World War; his message was a plea for peace. Although he claimed that his brother the king, who was now on his way to Canada and the United States for a goodwill tour, approved this ill-timed address, nothing could be further from the truth. In fact, the BBC flatly refused to relay it. During the king's tour, Nazi-controlled Sean Russell, head of the IRA in America and an admirer of the Windsors, planned and almost brought off an assassination of the royal couple as they took the train from Windsor, Ontario, to Detroit.

At this stage, King Victor Emmanuel advised his son-in-law, Prince Philipp of Hesse, through the intermediary Axel Munthe, celebrated author of *The Story of San Michele*, who had Nazi leanings, that he wished to abdicate and travel to Washington with a very large sum from the Roman treasury. Munthe contacted Winston Churchill, who at once vetoed the idea. There is no record of President Roosevelt being informed of the plan.

Churchill made a serious mistake. Victor Emmanuel, uneasy with Mussolini at this stage and by no means enamoured of Hitler, would have been an indispensable source for the FBI and the Secret Intelligence Services on Hitler's immediate plans, to which as monarch he had been privy. The proposal was leaked to Berlin, spelling the beginning of Hitler's and Goebbels's inspired suspicion that the royals of Europe in whom they had placed so much trust were preparing to betray them. But it was not until Hitler lost the Battle of Stalingrad, and the royal rats began abandoning the sinking ship, that suspicion hardened into certainty.

That spring, the Dukes of Windsor and Kent came to the edge of a major public scandal. Sandra Rambeau, the beautiful Missourian Nazi agent who had been their lover, while at the same time the lover of General Manfried von Epp and 'Prince' Bishnu of Nepal, was in Hollywood, where her FBI special files kept her from obtaining work. She began talking loosely to her current lover, the actor and British Secret Intelligence Service agent Edward Ashley, about her royal affairs, and he in turn reported them to Frank Angell and Richard Hood of the Los Angeles FBI. They passed on their reports to J. Edgar Hoover, who in turn reported the matter to Sir Stewart Menzies in London. But as before, the British government suppressed all the records and to this day no mention of Sandra Rambeau, despite her full FBI dossier at the National Archives in Washington, survives in England.

On 11 June, with great boldness, the Windsors went to a dinner party at the home of Count Johannes von Welczek, the German ambassador to France, with whom they had been friendly for many years. It was a season of elaborate parties, a summer of golden indulgence on the very edge of war.

By now, the Windsors were fully settled in their home at 24 Boulevard Suchet, a four-storey residence with a small front garden, redecorated with inspired skill by Wallis, with the help of Boudin.

The staff was large and headed by two secretaries; the butler, Hale, who had been wooed away from the Bedauxes; and Dudley Forwood. There were twelve servants' bedrooms, which were always fully occupied.

On 23 June, the Windsors celebrated the duke's forty-fifth birthday at a party in the restaurant on the first platform of the Eiffel Tower. It was also the fiftieth anniversary of the celebrated monument. Among the Windsors' guests was a six-foot-three girl, Jacqueline Vialle, who had been elected Mademoiselle Eiffel Tower in a tallest woman contest. In the middle of dinner Bedrich Benes, military attaché of the Czechoslovak government in exile, who may or may not have been attempting an assassination, was poised 186 feet up the tower outside a window gazing at the Windsors from a perilous metal strut. The party was startled by a horrifying scream. The man had lost his balance, and was clinging to a girder. A minute later he plunged to his death on the pavement below.

In early June, the Duke and Duchess of Kent had received an invitation to attend, in Florence, the most spectacular wedding in years – of Mussolini's admiral, Prince Aimone Roberto, son of the

Duke of Aosta, a crucial figure in fascist–royal politics, and Princess Irene, sister-in-law of Princess Friederike, the former proposed Queen of England, now married to Prince Paul of Greece.

Documents show that the Foreign Office in London urged Kent to undertake the trip in order to confirm the existing and anomalous allegiance between Great Britain and Italy – between Neville Chamberlain and Mussolini, King George VI and King Victor Emmanuel III – when Italy was to all intents and purposes a part of the Axis. If statements made to the *Sunday Times* in 1975 by Prince Wolfgang of Hesse, twin brother of Prince Philipp, are to be believed, the Duke of Windsor had another concern. He wanted Kent to meet Prince Philipp towards the purpose of permanent peace – through an intervention with Hitler.

The Foreign Office's only proviso was that Kent should not show British approval of Mussolini's recent invasion and conquest of the hapless nation of Albania by proposing a toast to King Victor Emmanuel at the wedding banquet as King of Albania and Emperor of Ethiopia, which nation he and Mussolini had, of course, wantonly conquered. Nevertheless, he would join in the toast; so the restriction was meaningless.

On their way to Florence, according to the late Paris socialite Ginette Spanier, the Kents surreptitiously met the Duke of Windsor (they were not talking to the duchess, whom they hated) at the Paris Ritz on 30 June. There, a Croatian terrorist threatened their lives; the anti-Nazi group of Croatian origin was certain that they were on Hitler's business. The Sûreté defused the plot, coming to the Windsors' rescue as they had done the year before in the Maroni affair; Superintendent Gilbert Rochès was in charge of the Place Vendôme, location of the Ritz.

At the last minute, a bizarre invitation had to be brushed off. Mrs George Keppel, the former mistress of King Edward VII, grandfather of Windsor and Kent, offered her summer home in Florence as accommodation during the wedding. The Kents politely declined, stating that they had already been given a suite at the Hotel Excelsior.

No sooner had the Kents arrived in Florence than the British ambassador Sir Percy Loraine warned of another assassination plot. This time a pro-Nazi group was behind it: Croatians were furious that the Duchess of Kent was talking to her sister Olga, Princess Regent of Yugoslavia, to prevent Paul, Olga's husband, from forming an alliance with Mussolini. This plot also was defused; such were the dangers from royal meddlers on both sides of the political spectrum.

After the glowing nuptials were over, the Duke of Kent had his scheduled meeting with Prince Philipp of Hesse, the only one of many encounters referred to by Prince Wolfgang, his brother, in 1975, of which written documentation survives. This meeting was specifically authorized by King George VI.

At the meeting, Kent delivered the king's urgent message, which had not been authorized, indeed had been expressly forbidden, by Neville Chamberlain, and was similarly undertaken without the authorization of the Foreign Office, to convey to Hitler in Berlin. He was to warn the Führer, in King George's words, that 'we mean business', and that Britain would declare war on Germany if Hitler were to invade Poland, a sign of panic on King George's part.

Kent was entirely out of order in saying so. Although Britain had entered into guarantees with Poland, there was still, in Whitehall's eyes, room for negotiation. But hidden inside Kent's warning was a fear much deeper than that of German aims; both he and the king knew that it was only a matter of weeks before Ribbentrop signed a pact with the Soviet Union that would carve up Poland; it was Russia they were as always afraid of, haunted still by the slaughter of their royal cousins, Tsar Nicholas and his family, at Ekaterinburg.

Hence Kent's second statement, which was to urge Philipp to have Hitler dismiss Ribbentrop as a 'perpetual insult to England'. To call for Hitler to dismiss his Foreign Minister was again something that Kent had no right or authorization to do.

Hesse left Florence for Berlin but had to wait until August for an audience with Hitler; this was an early sign that this handsome object of the Führer's adoration had started to lose not only his hair and his looks, but also his influence.

Back in London, the Duke of Kent formed an alliance as dangerous as that with Philipp of Hesse. He had for some time been an intimate friend and mentor of his cousin, the handsome, blond and athletic Prince Friedrich of Prussia, cousin of Princess Friederike, now Queen of Greece, and a favourite grandson of the kaiser.

Beloved of Hitler, the glamorous youth, the toast of pro-Nazi elements in London society, member of the Anglo-German Fellowship and the pro-Nazi The Link, worked as a junior executive at the Schröder bank, a chief backer of Hitler in London, as well as taking classes in history at Corpus Christi College in Cambridge. In a tight-fitting white army uniform, he had been the scene-stealer at the funeral of King George V and the coronation of George VI.

Friedrich was, following the death of his father, and in view of his grandfather's abdication and exile in Holland, the favoured successor to the throne of Germany. The direct heir, his oldest brother Wilhelm, had renounced his rights; his second oldest, Louis Ferdinand, was rejected out of hand by the Reichswehr, the German army faction, chiefly because of his succession of louche love affairs, including a prolonged liaison with Lili Damita, the Hollywood star and wife of Errol Flynn, and because of suspicions of disloyalty to the Führer. Friedrich was, as recently declassified Foreign Office documents show, the choice of the British government for the German monarchy, as part of the royal plans for negotiated peace – a knitting together of the broken strands of royal British and German cousins.

The Duke of Kent urged Friedrich to return to Germany as soon as possible – undoubtedly for the purpose stated, but technically an act of near treason. Even after war broke out on 3 September, Kent was writing to Prince Regent Paul of Yugoslavia through the diplomatic bags, stating his disappointment that Friedrich (Fritzi) had decided to stay. He wrote on 3 December 1939:

> I saw Fritzi who said he couldn't fight for the Nazis, etc. I think he is wrong as he is in the army. He should have gone back and they would have given him work. Now I doubt if he would ever go back again.

Such thoughts were treasonable in wartime.

As the world drifted closer to war, the Windsors returned via Switzerland to La Croë. On 22 August, the announcement that the Nazi government had signed a pact with the Soviet Union appalled the duke; he cannot have been oblivious, however, after some reflection, of the cynicism of this move towards an artificial relationship, engineered by Ribbentrop, which would simply allow Hitler to move as freely as he wished in western Europe and to ship oil and other supplies from Mexico through Siberia.

Whether or not the Windsors knew it, the alliance with Russia was encouraged by Ribbentrop because of his own desire to confront his rival, Rudolf Hess, who agreed with the policy the duke advocated, that of a joint onslaught by Britain, the United States, Germany and Italy on Russia. Stalin seized the opportunity to make the alliance so that he could move into some of the satellite countries such as Bessarabia without being interfered with and could strengthen his army in anticipation of an all-out confrontation. The most serious aspect of this artificial truce between ideological enemies was, from the duke's point of view, that it would no longer be possible for Britain to allow Hitler to move into Poland. Before the pact the British would have been happy to allow the attack if it were to follow that Hitler would then proceed against the Russians.

By the 24th, the Windsors' social set had fled La Croë. Fruity Metcalfe was still there, offering any help that might be required. A squad of Senegalese black troops camped in the grounds along with an anti-aircraft battery. On the 28th, the duke sent a telegram to Hitler, followed by one to King Victor Emmanuel of Italy, urging both to intercede in the interest of securing peace. Even as Hitler marched into Poland, the Führer sent a telegram in response, saying that England was responsible for the situation and that 'if war came' it would be England's fault. However, Victor Emmanuel, presumably with the authorization of Mussolini, cabled that he would do his best to see that Italy remained neutral.

War broke out on 3 September. The Windsors' position was extremely delicate. If they remained in France, they ran the risk that the Germans would kidnap them as accomplices in a plan for the duke to resume the British throne. On the other hand, if they fled to the United States it would reflect appallingly upon them and would suggest that they were cowards. The only alternative was to go to England. They could scarcely do so without at least offering to assist in the war effort, since not offering to help would only add strength to their enemies, led by the Hardinges and Sir Robert Vansittart. From the point of view of the king and queen, there were numerous problems associated with the Windsors' return.

Vansittart and the Secret Intelligence Service would have to keep a close eye on them, as there was always the danger that they might give official secrets to the enemy.

Moreover, there was already afoot in England a disorganized series of movements allegedly bent on overthrowing the throne in the interests of fascism should Britain be invaded and sued for peace. These included the Link, which was headed by Sir Barry Domvile, former chief of naval intelligence; it was made up of a group of right-wing and reactionary politicians and their hangers-on. Two other such groups were the Right Club and the Nordic League, the latter headed by Archibald Maule Ramsay, an anti-Semitic member of parliament for Peebles and Southern in Scotland. These were largely eccentric organizations, with no common leadership and rather scattered resources, but it was well known that if Britain were attacked they would do everything to encourage a general laying down of arms and the setting up of a puppet state. Churchill would be put under house arrest and the royal family exiled to the Bahamas (Churchill, with great dark humour, would instead send the Windsors there). At the beginning of September, Domvile recorded in his diary his excitement at enlisting 'D of W' in the Link. Opinion differed as to whether this was the Duke of Windsor or the Duke of Westminster: it was the latter.

Sir Walter Monckton moved rapidly to assist the Windsors to return to London. After an uncomfortable flight to the south of France, he told the duke and duchess what the situation would be when they returned. No royal accommodation would be offered. Fort Belvedere was in disrepair and uninhabitable; not a soul had touched it from the day the duke left. They must make their own arrangements for a house. The duke would be offered by the king, his brother, one of two meaningless posts, deputy regional commissioner for Wales or liaison officer with the number one British military mission to French General Headquarters under Major General Sir Richard Howard-Vyse.

The Windsors would not fly to London; the duchess remained terrified of planes. In his article in the New York *Daily News* on 14 December 1966, the duke meaningfully wrote, 'The Duchess . . . at Pensacola . . . was witness to many crashes that left her with little confidence in airplanes.' Sir Ronald Campbell was now ambassador to France. He advised the Windsors to drive to the Channel coast, where they would be informed of further arrangements. However, when they reached Vichy and tried to get some more information as to which port they should stay at, Campbell told them to do nothing for the time being. It is clear that arrangements were being made for them to be watched.

They continued to Paris. Finally, they were told to go to Cherbourg, after closing up their house at the Boulevard Suchet for the indefinite future. They reached Cherbourg on the 12th. Ironically Lord Louis Mountbatten, whose politics were the exact opposite of theirs, had been sent by Winston Churchill to pick them up in HMS *Kelly*. Randolph Churchill was also there.

Dodging possible U-boats, the *Kelly* arrived at Portsmouth in blackout conditions; Churchill, as Admiral of the Fleet, had arranged for the Royal Marines band to greet them with the national anthem. Lady Alexandra Metcalfe and Walter Monckton were there to make them welcome; Fruity Metcalfe had been with them throughout the journey. Lady Alexandra had been told by officials at Buckingham Palace that no car would be placed at the couple's disposal. Churchill arranged for them to stay at Admiralty House for the night. Clearly their host and hostess, commander-in-chief Admiral Sir William James and his wife, had been told of the suspicions of espionage surrounding Wallis, who mistook their excessive interest and probing glances to mean simply that she was still considered a notorious abductor of the king.

The Windsors went on to the Metcalfes' house in Sussex, where they posed and smiled for reporters in the garden. At dinner with Ambassador Kennedy on the 11th, the queen told him that the only bad moment on her recent royal tour of the United States was when, in Wallis's home town of Baltimore, a woman stepped up to her with a large bouquet of flowers and for one horrible moment she thought it was Wallis.

She told Kennedy, referring to the Windsors' presence in England, that it was 'terribly embarrassing' to have them in the vicinity; she certainly would not in any circumstances receive 'Mrs Simpson' – as she persisted in calling her. On 14 September, without the duchess, the duke went to see the king. It was a superficially friendly meeting that meant nothing. The duke said he would 'prefer the

Welsh appointment'. The king, already briefed on the problems in Wales, nodded. Queen Mary refused to see the duke, and by royal instruction he was not permitted to visit the Duke of Kent.

The next day, the king visited Winston Churchill, who made it clear he disapproved of the duke's visit to Hitler and his speech at Verdun. He had apparently changed his mind following his previous letter praising that very visit, possibly in view of the changing European situation. However, he was sure the duke would now, as 'one of us', be loyal to the British cause. Where the duke was concerned, Churchill's incurable romanticism again seemed to overrule his famous common sense.

Within twenty-four hours, the Welsh appointment was withdrawn for obvious reasons, on the advice of Vansittart. The very fact that the duke wanted it was sufficient cause for it not to be given. On 14 September, the Earl of Crawford noted in his diary:

> [The Duke of Windsor] was too irresponsible as a chatterbox to be entrusted with confidential information which will all be passed on to Wally at the dinner table. That is where the danger lies – namely that after nearly three years of complete obscurity, the temptation to show that he knows, that he is again at the centres of information will prove irresistible, and that he will blab and babble out State secrets without realizing the danger. I dined with Howe [Francis Curzon, Fifth Earl Howe] at the Club. He is working at the Admiralty, and to his consternation saw the door of the Secret Room open – the basement apartment where the position of our fleet and the enemy is marked out by hour – and lo! out came Churchill and the Duke of Windsor. Howe . . . was horrified.

It was decided that the duke would proceed to France with the rank of major general. Actually, the duke never officially accepted the position, but two advantages can be seen in the decision to make the French appointment. First, it would get the duke out of the British Isles. Second, it would be possible for agents of the Secret Intelligence Service to keep an eye on him while he performed various assignments, including the formulation of reports on French military weaknesses.

The duke went to see the prime minister, Neville Chamberlain, at 10 Downing Street. Chamberlain felt extremely awkward, since he had on his desk much material (and not just hate letters) suggesting it would be unwise to have the duke around in wartime. Chamberlain also undoubtedly knew that the duke was dangerously talkative. The ebullient Leslie Hore-Belisha was minister of war. He was Jewish and certainly cannot have liked the duke's politics. (Hore-Belisha would soon be pushed out of office for allegedly trading improperly in the City and for having criticized the inadequacy of British military strength in France.) When the duke asked if the duchess could go with him to visit the troops in Scotland, a very dangerous request, Hore-Belisha naturally declined. It was inconceivable that, in view of emergency conditions, he would not have been briefed on the security problems involved. It was obvious that the sooner the duke went to France the better. At all events, he must not be permitted to visit British troops there either, because he could so easily give away their secret transit arrangements by talking carelessly in Paris.

Several of the days before the departure of the duke and duchess were spent in London. One afternoon they went to see Fort Belvedere, to find it fallen into disuse, not a sign of life in it anywhere.

In severe weather on 29 September, with Fruity Metcalfe and Captain Purvis of the British army, the Windsors sailed in the destroyer *Express* to Cherbourg. They continued to Paris, deciding not to return to their Boulevard Suchet house, which was still closed and shuttered. Instead, they moved into the Trianon Palace Hôtel in Versailles, partly in order to be close to Lady Mendl. The duke reported for duty on the 30th at the military headquarters under Major General Sir Richard Howard-Vyse. His duties were explained to him with fake seriousness and an air of heavy import: he was to be in charge of an 'investigative mission' surveying the strengths and weaknesses of the French defence forces, including the Maginot Line, and he was to report his considered impressions of French leaders. Although described as an intelligence assignment, this was in fact a survey which had already been undertaken by other officers; Winston Churchill had made a complete tour of the line in mid-August, reporting on its problems, and in January would make another journey of inspection. In meetings with the

British commander-in-chief, Lord Gort, General Gamelin made no secret of the line's deficiencies. As General Lelong, of the French forces, had written to Gamelin on 19 September:

> The assignment of the Duke of Windsor is a matter of pure expediency. They do not quite know what to do with this encumbering personage, especially in England; but they do not wish it to be said that he is sitting on his hands. They have therefore found a way out through Howard-Vyse, who is not too proud of the fact.

Thus a waste of taxpayers' money was undertaken. That Gamelin had no time for it was indicated by the fact that, according to the famous French journalist Pertinax in his book *The Betrayal of France*, Gamelin dismissed General Alexandre Montagne for having told the duke secret information about how the enemy could break through the Maginot Line. It was the only dismissal from the French general's staff at the time. Lord Ironside, son of the late commander-in-chief, said in 1987:

> My father determined that the Duke was a serious security leak. He was giving the Duchess a great deal of information that was classified in the matter of the defences of France and Belgium. She in turn was passing this information on to extremely danger-ous enemy-connected people over dinner tables in Paris. As a result, the information made its way into German hands.

One should add that a most careful examination of the duke's reports from the front, not discovered by his late biographer, Lady Frances Donaldson, but today available from the Public Record Office, indicates that the information he supplied was no more than superficial. In particular, his descriptions of the French gen-erals were no more than might be found in a society gossip column. His account of the defence arrangements, though quite well writ-ten, turned out, Lord Ironside's disclosure makes clear, to be of more help to the Germans than to Whitehall.

Wallis stayed in Paris, helping in a public relations stunt to prepare mess kits including clothing and toilet articles and to knit socks for the French troops. While the Windsors made sure these contributions to the war effort were publicized, it was typical of their impudence and almost humorous perversity that the first person they saw, entertained and visited in Paris was Charles Bedaux. One would have thought even the minimum of common sense would have urged them to avoid any such encounter, in view of the fact that Bedaux, whether guilty of Nazi collaboration or not, was under constant surveillance by British intelligence. The fact that Fruity Metcalfe organized the meeting makes one wonder about his motives.

On 2 October, the queen wrote a very long letter to Prince Paul of Yugoslavia on Buckingham Palace stationery, relating directly to the duke and Wallis's visit to England. Still referring contemptuously to Wallis not as the Duchess of Windsor but as 'Mrs S', she revealed that she had written to Wallis stating that in all honesty and to make things clear she would emphatically not be prepared to receive her; she hoped that the duke would stay in France and not return to England; that there was no place for him in England and that 'the mass of people do not forgive quickly the sort of thing he did to this country and they HATE her!' She added, 'What a curse black sheep are to a family!' The rest of the letter illustrated her horror of the war. The missive was fired less by a burning patriotism than by a need to bring the conflict to a hasty end; for her, the two world wars seemed to run together. She, she wrote, had had the terrifying experience of thinking she saw her brother, dead in the Great War, in a recent dress parade of the Black Watch regiment.

The same day, the Duke of Windsor wrote to Sir Walter Monckton in London, stating that he didn't like the tone of Churchill's broadcast of the day before. That statement gave him away: Churchill had said on the BBC that a defeated Poland would 'rise again like a rock', emerging from the tidal wave of defeat; and he praised the action of British submarines, 'hunting the U-boats with zeal'. Churchill had added that though the war might last for three years, Britain would fight to the end; as proponents of a negotiated peace, these were the last words the Windsors (or Kent) wanted to hear. Five days later, Hitler issued a peace proposal to England which was summarily rejected, on Churchill's specific advice.

On 6 October, the duke had a meeting with the British commander-in-chief, Lord Gort; the Duke of Gloucester was attached to Gort's staff as liaison officer. In a revealing sentence in his diary, the British chief of staff, Major General Pownall, wrote on 7 October, 'There is, for the moment at any rate, an "inhibition" against his going around troops, indeed I believe he was not supposed to come to GHQ, but we can't help saying "yes" when we are told he is coming.' On the 10th, after a tour of inspection, the duke provided a report on the problems of the French defences on the Belgian frontier. The report merely confirmed Churchill's findings in August. When it arrived in London, it was, needless to say, put on a shelf as redundant. On 14 October, Gamelin gave an elaborate luncheon for the duke at the military headquarters at the Château de Vincennes. The duchess was not present; no wives were there. Meanwhile, the duchess decided to reopen her house after all. Astonishingly, she actually entertained Charles and Fern Bedaux at that address, which took a great deal of nerve.

On the 17th, the duke arrived uninvited at Gort's headquarters in Arras; though specifically asked by his brother the king not to do so because of the security situation, he joined his brother Gloucester in inspecting the troops. Unfortunately, according to a United Press release on 8 January the following year, he wore suede shoes with his uniform. He also infuriated Gloucester by returning a salute to which it was his brother's privilege to respond. As a result of this, plus the fact that he had behaved improperly in arriving as he did, the duke was forbidden any further visits to the British front line. On 26 October, he made a further tour of the French troops. But as the war began to look more serious and German attacks were expected, he was increasingly deactivated and sent to places where there was minimal information to be obtained that could be of use to the enemy. He spent most of his time in Paris, where Gray Phillips, an experienced staff officer, had arrived to take up the role of the duke's aide and comptroller. Providing Phillips's services was a gesture by the Palace, but the fact that the duke was in outer darkness was further indicated when neither the war minister, Hore-Belisha, nor King George contacted him when they came to France in November and December. A third inspection tour by the duke of the French forces was equally futile and redundant. Nobody in Whitehall was impressed when the duchess turned up at the front distributing gift parcels to the French troops. The duchess, they knew, had no business being there.

On 11 October, Sir Stewart Menzies of the SIS and his colleagues in Whitehall, in cooperation with the BBC, brought off an ingenious coup, designed to test the Windsors' popularity in Nazi Germany, as well as the response of the German public should England lose the war and the Windsors, as Hitler hoped, be returned to the throne. The SIS team arranged for a fake BBC radio broadcast to be relayed throughout the Nazi empire announcing that there had been a coup d'état in England; that the public had risen up and forced King George's abdication and that Neville Chamberlain and the cabinet had resigned, to be replaced by the supporters of the Duke of Windsor, who would now be returning to Britain to reassume the throne.

The Nazi propaganda minister, Dr Joseph Goebbels, in charge of radio as he was in charge of films and newspapers, dictated the facts to his secretary for his diary in progress. He stated, based on telephone reports received from all over the country, that the German public was swept up into a 'veritable storm of joy'; that people were embracing each other in the streets; and that factories were 'exploding'; even government departments were 'on fire with excitement' at the news.

In her memoirs, Christabel Bielenberg, British wife of a German official, gave an eyewitness account of the matter. She was shopping for vegetables in a Berlin market when she heard a hubbub; people were crying out that England had changed hands and the beloved 'Duke of Vindsor' would at once be restored to the throne; German women shook her hand. Suddenly a police sergeant appeared and announced a broadcast bulletin. A plane with a British peace delegation would be arriving within a few hours at Templehof Airport in Berlin to see Hitler.

Goebbels saw through Menzies's Secret Intelligence Service plot; that it was designed to show the danger of the Duke of Windsor and his threat to the British throne – the degree, in short, of Hitler's and the German people's passion for him. Goebbels himself broadcast that the story was a fabrication; every newspaper in

Germany was ordered to run the headline: FURTHER INSO-
LENCE FROM THE BRITISH MINISTRY OF LIES.

It isn't surprising to note that within hours of the broadcast
King George issued an order restricting Windsor from entering
areas occupied by British troops in France. On 14 October, infuriated by the edict and convinced incorrectly that it had been in
force since before his assignment, the duke fired off an angry letter
to Sir Walter Monckton from Paris, saying that he had heard of the
order 'by accident', and that this was 'a back door intrigue'. He
also addressed a furious note to whoever steamed open the letter.
Given the juxtaposition of dates, it can scarcely be doubted that the
royal order came as a direct result of the SIS broadcast. The duke
wasted no time in disobeying it: a court-martial offence.

When Kim Philby, later to become famous as a Communist spy,
was on special duty for the Secret Intelligence Service in his role as
a journalist, he found the duke at Bruges, suspiciously close to the
German lines, and reported it; seeing him, the frightened duke at
once fled to Paris.

On 4 November, the duke wrote to Hitler, under the name of
EP (Edward Prince), saying that he had information regarding his
trip to the north (to survey the British troops) in disobedience of
his brother's command and that the Nazi Charles Bedaux, on the
way to Germany as his emissary, had the information with him. ('I
am hardly able to stress the importance of the information, which
is why I have gone into so much detail in explaining it to our
friend.') Bedaux handed the letter, and the treasonable intelligence report, to Hitler in Berlin on the 9th. It survives today.

According to the writer Peter Miller, in an article in the *Sunday
Times*, dated 26 January 2003, the Duke of Kent was still involved
in questionable peace negotiations at this time. Although his constant stream of letters to Prince Regent Paul of Yugoslavia emanated
from his home at Coppins, Ivar, Buckinghamshire, Miller states
that he bought a house near Rosyth in Scotland, where he had at
least ten secret meetings with the Polish prime minister in exile,
General Wladyslav Sikorski, who was prepared to offer Kent the
Polish throne in the event of a negotiated peace.

Kent's response to previous offers of thrones had resulted, his papers show, in a consignment of the proposals to the nearest waste-paper basket, and there is no reason to believe that he responded to Sikorski's offer any differently. With Russia as England's ally (disgracefully, since it sliced up Poland with Hitler) no monarch would have been allowed by Stalin to be part of any peace arrangement with his own ally, Germany. As with Italy and Japan, Britain was playing the dangerous game of maintaining full diplomatic arrangements with a member of Hitler's Axis.

Nevertheless, the appeasement group in London led by Sir Robert Vansittart, and Sir Stewart Menzies of the Secret Intelligence Service, took a dim view of the Kent–Sikorski meetings, just as they took a dim view of the Kent–Paul of Yugoslavia letters.

Christmas was depressing, a time for the embattled Windsors to weigh in the balance how much had been lost and how little had been gained. They were under constant surveillance by British agents and undoubtedly they knew it.

On 12 January, while still continuing his affair with Wallis in Paris, William Bullitt was busy cementing his connections with Mussolini. He advised Roosevelt by telegram that he was leaving for Rome to visit his aunt, the Duchess of Assergio. He was also cementing relations between his pro-fascist friend F. Pinckney Tuck and the Italian government. In fact, Tuck became, through Bullitt's Washington intrigues, emissary to Rome and later US ambassador to collaborationist Vichy; Bullitt's other close friend, Gaston Henry-Haye, mayor of Versailles, who, at his request, had provided the Windsors' house there, almost free of rent, would become Vichy ambassador to the United States.

On 26 January, the peace for which Kent and Windsor so profoundly wished was the subject of a letter sent from Prince Paul of Yugoslavia via his aunt, Queen Marie, to King George VI at Buckingham Palace. Paul said that a member of his appeasement delegation in Düsseldorf in Germany had word from a German general that there was to be a coup d'état before winter was over and that Hitler and Goering would be assassinated. Paul thought this might result in an armistice but then he added with typically disgraceful emphasis that of course, after peace was arranged, the Allies should not ask for the restoration of Austria, Czechoslovakia and Poland. Even for the outrageously duplicitous Prince Paul, this was rather extreme.

In mid-January, the duke flew to London for what was described as 'business'. The date of his arrival was altered in the newspapers in order to allow him some extra days of secret meetings. One of these meetings was with Major General John Fuller, who recorded the event in his datebook. Fuller, described as the inventor of modern warfare, was a leading member of fascist-oriented organizations in Britain and had written books and articles praising Hitler. He was under suspicion of being prominent among those individuals in England who supported the idea of a negotiated peace with Germany and would assist the Germans if they were to invade Great Britain. The duke also had a meeting with Lord Ironside at the War Office, where he grumbled about his unhappiness and frustration in his present role. A memorandum was sent on 27 January by Julius, Count von Zech-Burckesroda, German minister to the Netherlands, to the Nazi Foreign Minister in Berlin for Hitler's personal attention:

> Through personal relationships I might have the opportunity to establish certain lines leading to the Duke of Windsor ... He does not ... feel entirely satisfied with this position and seeks a field of activity in which he would not have merely a representative character, and which would permit him a more active role. In order to attain this objective, he was recently in London ... There seems to be something like the beginning of a Fronde [secret organization] forming around W. ... When he was recently in London, I had explained to him through an intermediary why it is completely utopian for England to attempt to effect a change of regime in Germany, and the statements of my intermediary are believed to have made a certain impression on him ... Heil Hitler!

On 19 February, the same diplomat was back in touch with the Foreign Minister. He wrote:

> The Duke of W, about whom I wrote to you in my letter of the 27th of last month, has said that the Allied War Council devoted an exhaustive discussion at its last meeting to the situation that would arise if Germany invaded Belgium. On the military side, it was held that the best plan would be to make the main resistance effort in the line behind the Belgian–French border,

even at the risk that Belgium should be occupied by us. The political authorities are said to have at first opposed this plan: after the humiliation suffered in Poland, it would be impossible to surrender Belgium and the Netherlands also to the Germans. In the end, however, the political authorities became more yielding.

This is a very interesting document. In fact, the Allied War Council did not at its meeting discuss the matter concerned. It was a topic of detailed conversation at a *War Cabinet* meeting in London presided over by Winston Churchill. Some member of the War Cabinet (possibly the ever-trusting Churchill himself) relied upon the Duke of Windsor sufficiently to tell him what was discussed, and in turn the duke treacherously conveyed the information to the duchess, who in turn relayed it to Nazi-associated people in Paris.

For the duke (and more importantly the duchess) to have leaked the secrets of such a meeting to the enemy can only be described as treasonous, assuming that the ambassador to the Netherlands had not invented the story. A career diplomat of the old school, not particularly enamoured of the Hitler regime, Zech would scarcely have had a motive for concocting such a thing. That the Secret Intelligence Service and Sir Robert Vansittart[2] were alerted to this leakage of privileged information can be seen from the fact that Wolfgang zu Putlitz, the British spy who had been at the German embassy when Wallis was suspected of obtaining classified materials at Fort Belvedere, was at Zech-Burckesroda's embassy in The Hague at the time the telegram was sent to Berlin. No doubt this latest disclosure only served to confirm the fears of Wallis's arch-enemy Vansittart. Just three days earlier, there had been another serious leak. In *War Propaganda 1939–1941: Secret Ministry Conferences in the Reich's Ministry for Propaganda*, edited by Willi A. Boelcke, the following entry appears: 'February 16, 1940, Friday: The message of the Duke of Windsor to the King of England [*sic*] about the miserable condition of the English troops at the Front shall be used for the language service.'

The duke had only just returned from inspecting the land and sea defences at Dunkirk on 10 February, and he had noted in his report that the British pilots, among others, were nervous wrecks. Again, Ironside was convinced that the duke and duchess were leaking crucial information to the enemy through contacts in Paris.

The duke's inspection tours continued, and were completed at the end of February. His reports on the French generals continued to be futile. Instead of analysing their technical approach to the war, he restricted himself to meaningless generalities. Commenting on General Condé, he wrote, 'He is shy by nature, and it takes a little time to appreciate his real qualities as a soldier, but an afternoon spent in his company revealed these to be remarkable.' Dealing with General Freydenberg, he said, 'He has a very comfortable appearance and his features are those of a good-looking man. While in no way interfering with his military work, he seems to enjoy his creature comforts.' And so forth in a similar vein. In mid-March the Windsors returned to La Croë. They had offered it as a convalescent home for British army officers, but clearly that idea could not be entertained in Whitehall. It was a fairly commonplace device for enemy agents to milk wounded soldiers for information, and the duchess's membership of the Red Cross was scarcely encouraging to the more sophisticated members of the Secret Intelligence Service. The Red Cross was notorious for unwittingly being a sieve in terms of security, used by Germany in various skilful ways to allow traffic in individuals and information across every border. This is not to say that the duchess used the Red Cross for this purpose – only that she would quickly fall under suspicion of doing so.

On 10 May, the American journalist and playwright Mrs Henry Luce, formely Clare Boothe, was in Paris, and was invited to dinner at the Boulevard Suchet. There was a BBC report that the Germans had bombed London and coastal villages. Mrs Luce said, 'I've driven through many of those villages. I hate to see the British so wantonly attacked.' The duchess replied, 'After what they did to me, I can't say I feel sorry for them – a whole nation against a lone woman!'

On 20 May, her cause was not helped by the fact that her dressmaker, Anna Wolkoff, was arrested in London on Vansittart's advice and charged with having leaked to the Germans the secrets of the British attack on Norway. These secrets had been discussed at the Supreme War Council meeting which Ironside attended and to which the German ambassador to the Netherlands had incorrectly referred. Is it possible that Miss Wolkoff, who certainly had continuing high-level connections, had obtained some of this information from the duchess? She had delivered the crucial intelligence to the Italian Duco del Monte at 6 Cadogan Square.

That month, Chamberlain resigned, and on the 10th Winston Churchill became prime minister of England and formed a coalition government. Pressed by the Labour party leader, Clement Attlee, he instantly acted to destroy the entire group that was planning a negotiated peace with Hitler. A close friend of the Windsors, the Duke of Buccleuch, the brother-in-law of the Duke of Gloucester, was removed from his position as Lord Steward of the royal household. The *New York Times* reported the matter, implying that Buccleuch was part of the appeasement faction in England. The Duke of Westminster was warned not to take part in any serious appeasement efforts. At the same time, Sir Oswald Mosley, Lady Mosley, Archibald Maule Ramsay and several others were imprisoned under the recently introduced regulations. Vernon Kell, head of MI5, was dismissed on 25 May, according to some sources because of the leak of official secrets to Germany, but according to others because of personality conflicts with Churchill. Major General Fuller was warned to be inactive on pain of instant arrest. Sir Samuel Hoare was under grave suspicion of wanting a negotiated peace, and arrangements were made to send him out of the country as ambassador to neutral Spain. Among those who had the greatest misgivings about him was Sir Alexander Cadogan, who had replaced Vansittart as permanent undersecretary at the Foreign Office on 1 January 1938. In a diary entry for 20 May 1940, he wrote, 'The quicker we get [the Hoares] out of the country the better. But I'd sooner send them to a penal settlement. He'll be the Quisling of England when Germany conquers us and I am dead.'

A War Cabinet meeting was held in London on 26 May. During it Lord Halifax, as Foreign Secretary, suggested the idea that there might be a negotiated peace. Entirely echoing the views of the Windsors, he said that the issue now was 'not so much ... a question of imposing a complete defeat upon Germany, but of safeguarding the independence of our own Empire and if possible that of France'. Halifax said that the evening before he had had an interview with the Italian ambassador, Signor Bastianini (who had replaced Grandi) and that Bastianini had suggested a peace conference at which Mussolini would appear in order to obtain peace in Europe. Halifax had responded that he looked upon the suggestion favourably. Churchill dismissed the idea at once. The Lord President of the council said that Italy might send an ultimatum to France threatening that, unless such a conference were held, Italy would join Germany. This was exactly the position taken by the Windsors and by their friend the pro-Hitler Pierre Laval. The matter was discussed at length and was taken up again the following day. Churchill revealed the surprising fact that, whereas he was opposed to a direct approach to Mussolini, he had manoeuvred to have Roosevelt make such an approach, 'ostensibly on his own initiative'. This put a new complexion on the matter. Churchill wanted to avoid any direct negotiation, but was not as adverse to an indirect one as he had appeared the day before. Halifax then revealed that in fact Roosevelt had made the appropriate approach to Rome. The Lord President of the council announced that Sir Percy Loraine, who was now British ambassador to Italy, had sent a telegram advising that Hitler had informed the Italian government he did not want the Italians to enter the war and was sure he could reach a satisfactory arrangement with the French. The secretary of state for air was opposed to any such approach to Italy, and so was the Lord President of the council. The Lord Privy Seal was also opposed. The prime minister talked of the 'futility' of the suggested approach to Mussolini. He added, 'At the moment our prestige in Europe [is] very low. The only way we can get it back is by showing the world that Germany has not beaten us ... Let us therefore avoid being dragged down the slippery slope with France.' After much further discussion the meeting was adjourned. The final outcome was made clear by the prime minister at the end of a meeting on the 28th: 'If we make a bold stand against Germany, that would command their admiration and respect; but a grovelling appeal, if made now, would have the worst possible effect. I do not favour making any approach on the subject at the present time.'

Word of the decision was brought to the Duke of Windsor, who was infuriated. He was still pressing for a negotiated peace via Mussolini, and he was almost certainly in touch with Count Ciano and others in Italy on the matter, in the hope that his friendship with Churchill might prove influential. It did not, of course. Halifax remained unregenerately in support of the peace plan and wrote in his diary that Churchill had talked 'a lot of rot'.

Churchill held another, and secret, meeting at 10 Downing Street on the 28th, at which (minutes were not taken) it was agreed that the Windsors should be brought to Britain immediately, at the very least for interrogation by Cadogan and Vansittart on their peculiar role in Nazi collaboration. However, Churchill's sentimental attachment to the duke overcame his normal sense.

On 23 December 1941, President Roosevelt, in a private conversation at the White House with Fulton Oursler, author and editor of *Liberty* magazine, made the following statement:

> The Duke [of Windsor] was present at the most intimate councils of the commanders in chief of the two armies. He knew everything that was going on. Sometimes he would suddenly decide that there was nothing more for him to do and he would go back to Paris, not just overnight but for three or four days ... I know that there were nine shortwave wireless sets in Paris constantly sending information to the German troops, and no one has ever been able to decide how such accurate information could be sent over those wireless stations.

Quite suddenly, and on the orders of Sir Stewart Menzies, the Windsors were told to leave Paris as they presented security risks, abandoning Fruity Metcalfe, who was on the duke's team, and to make their way to the Villa La Croë at Antibes. This has been described incorrectly as a desertion of duty that could have been a court-martial offence. Removal because of the certainty of treason was worse. Bullitt was left in charge of their Paris house, which he protected when the Germans marched in; actually Ribbentrop, who was at the Ritz, had arranged for that protection already – and so did Winston Churchill.

In a detailed report by Edward A. Tamm, leading FBI executive operative, to J. Edgar Hoover in Washington written on 13 September 1940, he made clear that the Secret Intelligence Service, headed by Menzies in London, was very much in pursuit of the Windsors throughout their trip south:

> The contacts of the Duchess of Windsor with von Ribbentrop from the Villa [la Croë] ... became so serious that it was necessary for the British government to compel them to move. The Duchess was obtaining a variety of information concerning the British and French Government official activities, which she was passing on to the Germans ... immediately upon their checking into a hotel in Biarritz, a British Secret Service man turned on a radio on a German commercial station and heard a news commentator in Berlin state that the Duke and Duchess had moved into [the Palace] hotel where they were occupying suite 104-E. This was in fact the suite occupied by the Windsors and they had been there hardly a matter of minutes when this announcement was heard.

The report went on:

> The British Secret Service [*sic*] ascertained that the Duchess had informed von Ribbentrop of her itinerary, schedule, etc., prior to her departure from the villa.

It may be asked, how could Wallis communicate so easily with Ribbentrop at the time? The fact is that it didn't require more than the slightest of efforts. The German Foreign Minister was still in France, moving to and from the Ritz and the Château d'Ardenne near Dinant, which could both be reached either by telegram or by telephone; when communications became difficult, a messenger could at once be sent by car or motorcycle. Ribbentrop was present for the signing of the French armistice at Compiègne on 22 June and of course was in touch with all foreign ambassadors, including Bullitt, who had moved into Charles Bedaux's Château de Candé, a buzzing vespiary of Nazi spies and collaborators.

The Tamm report went on to state that in view of the leakage of information to Ribbentrop, the Windsors were told by the SIS to leave for Spain at once. Even at this early stage it was decided they must go to the Bahamas; an appointment in South Africa or New Zealand would have been more appropriate but there was a clear-cut reason, stated directly in the Tamm report: as the most prominent figure of the Bahamian island colony, Jane Williams-Taylor would once again be able to spy on them.

Back at La Croë, the Windsors left the incriminating documents from Fort Belvedere with Herman and Katherine Rogers for safe keeping; still acting for the Secret Intelligence Service, the couple locked them in a safe instead of handing them to the Italian or German authorities as the Windsors would have wished; along with the records of collusion went the contents of the official red dispatch boxes sent to Windsor when king, an act of theft for which he cannot be excused. The abdication documents went to Switzerland.

The duke cabled Sir Samuel Hoare in Madrid for a ship, but Hoare could do nothing without authorization from the Foreign Office. Finally, according to Winston Churchill's secretary, the late Sir John Colville, the Windsors persuaded Hugh Dodds, consul general at Nice, to leave his post and take them across the border. When Churchill found out that a number of wounded war veterans who needed assistance in Nice had been denied it, he went, Colville says, 'through the roof'. Colville mentioned that Dodds was his uncle by marriage. 'I couldn't care less!' Churchill exploded. But, while Churchill was furious at the duke and duchess's behaviour, it was clearly essential that they should leave Europe as soon as possible.[3]

NOTES

1 £25,000 less the pensions for the disabled staff.
2 Though officially kicked upstairs, Vansittart was permitted to continue operating, largely behind the cover of London Films, his own special spy system.
3 Hardinge wanted the duke posted to Egypt; the Archbishop of Canterbury to the one place where he might be rendered safe: the Falkland Islands.

14

A DARK PLOT

The duke and duchess, driven by the chauffeur Ladbroke, began the long and difficult journey to Spain. Accompanying them in a fleet of cars were the equerry Captain George Wood and his wife, Gray Phillips, Major Hugh Dodds and Martin Dean, vice-consul at Menton. They had an uncomfortable night in Arles, and were not pleased to be removed from the hotel in Perpignan by the sudden arrival of the chief of French intelligence, who had no time for them, probably because of their Nazi connections, and unceremoniously commandeered their suite.[1]

Unable to find any other accommodation, they proceeded irritably through the night and were twice almost stopped. The British embassy in Paris had failed to obtain authorization from London or Madrid to secure the necessary safe-conduct passes, and the party was barely allowed to scrape through. At midnight on the 20th the group arrived at Barcelona.

Sir Stewart Menzies was concerned about the arrival of the Duke of Kent on an official visit to Lisbon. It was feared that he would contact the Windsors for purposes that would be inimical to British interests in the region. Such concern was conveyed through William Strang, a special agent of the Foreign Office in London reporting to Sir Alexander Cadogan of the FO; Strang made it clear, through Arjando Monteiro, Portuguese ambassador to the Court of St James, to President Salazar of Portugal in a letter dated 21 June, that Kent's exact whereabouts must be kept secret during his visit.

There was a double reason for this; Prince Philipp of Hesse was in Lisbon to see Kent. It is clear from a letter sent by Kent to Prince Paul of Yugoslavia shortly after his return to London on 17 July that he wouldn't have wanted to meet the Windsors; that he considered his brother's behaviour disgraceful – a classic case of the royal pot calling the kettle black – and that he was greatly relieved he and the duchess (whom he, like Churchill, called, 'the Bitch') hadn't come back to England. With false naivety he wrote to Paul that he was surprised that his brother would accept so lowly a position as governor of the Bahamas. 'W[inston] C[hurchill] doesn't want him back,' he wrote.

And he added that he had fought against his brother's possible return.

On 16 May, Bullitt wrote to Cordell Hull, US secretary of state, in Washington, that as the British ambassador was leaving Paris, and burning all his papers, he would take over the operation of British message systems in the city; at the same time he would transmit everything of a political nature through the German embassy and thus through the Berlin Foreign Ministry of Ribbentrop – Wallis's continuing associate, who was now at the Ritz in Paris. Thus, all British–American secret affairs would be known in Berlin before they were sent to Washington.

On the 22nd, Churchill cabled the duke, care of Sir Samuel Hoare: 'We should like Your Royal Highness to come home as soon as possible. Arrangements will be made through His Majesty's Ambassador at Madrid with whom you should communicate.' On the same day Eberhard von Stohrer, German ambassador to Spain, cabled Ribbentrop in Berlin seeking advice on how the Windsors were to be treated. The question arose whether 'we might perhaps be interested in detaining the Duke . . . here, and eventually in establishing contact with him'. The next day Ribbentrop replied, 'Is it possible . . . to detain the Duke and Duchess of Windsor before they are granted an exit visa? It would be necessary at all events to be sure that it did not appear in any way that the suggestion came from Germany.'

On 24 June, Sir Alexander Hardinge wrote from Buckingham Palace to W. I. Mallet of the Foreign Office that it had been observed by the king that in certain correspondences the duke and duchess were referred to as 'Their Royal Highnesses'. Hardinge added: 'For obvious reasons it is very undesirable that this incorrect description of the Duke and Duchess should be included in any official communication, and the King trusts that steps will be taken to prevent this mistake being repeated.' It was not repeated.

In the meantime the Windsors arrived on the 23rd in an impoverished, beggar-haunted, shabby Madrid. Sir Samuel Hoare had arranged accommodation for them at the Ritz. The slippery British ambassador conveniently suspended all activities of the Secret Intelligence Service in the Spanish capital for the duration of the Windsors' visit. They were thus free of surveillance, which must have greatly aggravated the authorities in London.

Pieter G. Hansen, of the Abwehr, German military intelligence, in 1940, writes from Germany, basing his information on a clear memory of the subject under discussion in his office at the time:

> Dansey had been handling private jobs for Churchill and [the British secret agent Claude] Churchill's henchman Professor Frederick W. Lindemann; he had been caught misappropriating government funds for his personal advantage and charging expenses to the government. He would have been fired if he hadn't continued to do jobs for Churchill.

According to Hansen, the ferocious Claude Dansey, acting on orders that were emphatically not from Churchill but from Sir Stewart Menzies of the Secret Intelligence Service, made a terrifying threat at a meeting with the duke and Wallis. He told them they would be murdered in cold blood if they did not leave Europe for the Bahamas as soon as it could be arranged.

Hansen goes on to state that it was known in the Abwehr that the duke and duchess were making financial and other demands of Ribbentrop towards their assuming the English throne which had to be approved by Hitler himself. Hitler was hesitant to pay them, as he 'wanted a German in charge (in London) and not some figurehead'. This caused the Windsors considerable concern; if they weren't going to be paid to resume the throne in the event of a negotiated peace, they certainly weren't going to cooperate. Soon Hitler changed his mind.

The Windsors' old friend Don Javier Bermejillo had escorted

them into Madrid and was proving to be a good samaritan. The Spanish fascist government under Franco was prepared to offer its hospitality for an indefinite period. Characteristically, the duke arranged with Bermejillo to deal directly with the enemy. Bermejillo went to the German and Italian embassies and asked them to be sure that the Windsors' properties in the south of France and Paris were protected and carefully maintained. Actually, neither house was in danger; La Croë was in unoccupied France and Boulevard Suchet was of course being maintained by Bullitt, who had just moved into Charles Bedaux's Château de Candé, which he used as the embassy. Even after Pearl Harbor and after the German occupation of France and Italian guardianship of La Croë, the Windsors' requirements were still met. This breach of the Trading with the Enemy Act was described by Michael Bloch in his book *Operation Willi* as 'indiscreet'. The Windsors' account at the Banque de France was never confiscated by the German alien property custodian, Carl Schaefer.

The duke was determined that he would not go to England unless the duchess was accorded her proper rank. In what looks very much like a device to avoid going to London, he insisted upon her being given full status with other members of the family. He knew by now that any such request must meet with a direct refusal. Churchill was furious at the Windsors' intransigence, and he cabled the duke on 28 June: 'Your Royal Highness has taken active military rank, and refusal to obey direct orders of competent military authority will create a serious situation. I hope it will not be necessary for such orders to be sent.' Sentimentally, Churchill struck out the following suggestive sentence: 'Already there is a great deal of doubt as to the circumstances in which Your Royal Highness left Paris. I most strongly urge immediate compliance with wishes of the government.' The duke now shifted his ground to ask only that he and the duchess should be received for a short meeting by the king and queen. Again, he knew that such a request was totally out of order, and it was of course rejected outright. Also on 28 June the Italian chargé d'affaires in Spain, Count Zoppi, cabled Wallis's former lover Count Ciano with the request that La Croë should be committed to the protection of the Italian government in the event of Italy invading France. The request was promptly granted. On the 30th, Ribbentrop instructed Otto Abetz 'unofficially and confidentially' to provide 'an unobtrusive observation of the [Paris] residence of the Duke'. The ambassador to Spain was instructed to inform the duke that Ribbentrop was taking care of the house's protection.

Late that week, the US ambassador to Spain, A. W. Weddall, sent a secret memorandum to the State Department. It read:

> In conversation last night, the Duke of Windsor declared that the most important thing now was to end the war before thousands more were killed or maimed to save the faces of a few politicians.
>
> With regard to the defeat of France . . . the Duke stated that stories that the French troops would not fight were not true. They had fought magnificently, but the organization behind them was totally inadequate. In the past ten years Germany has totally reorganized the order of its society in preparation for this war. Countries which were unwilling to accept such a reorganization of society and concomitant sacrifices should direct their policies accordingly and thereby avoid dangerous adventures. He stated this applied not merely to Europe, but to the United States also.
>
> The Duchess put the same thing more directly by declaring that France had lost because it was internally diseased and that a country which was not in a condition to fight a war should never have declared war.
>
> These observations have their value, if any, as doubtless reflecting the views of an element in England, possibly a growing one, who [sic] would find in Windsor and his circle of friends a group who are realists in world politics and who hope to come into their own in the event of world peace.

Sumner Welles, undersecretary of state, forwarded this document to Whitehall, with the inevitable result of increasing the disfavour in which the Windsors were held.

Hoare was anxious for the Windsors to leave Madrid. They were an embarrassment and a burden to the embassy, particularly since there were widespread and probably well-founded comments in the European press that he and the Windsors were having meetings with Germans to arrange a negotiated peace. Nevertheless, Hoare did his best to make them comfortable. He arranged introductions for them to such figures as a member of the royal family, who had flown in the Franco air force, bombing villages, and seemed not to object to their association with the fascistic Don Miguel Primo de Rivera, civil governor of Madrid.

As the Windsors began the next stage of their journey of exile, the German ambassador to Spain cabled Ribbentrop to tell him that the duke was about to leave. The duke planned eventually to return to Spain, where he had been offered as a residence the Palace of the Caliph at Ronda. The Windsors arrived in a still glittering and raffish, refugee-filled Lisbon on 3 July.

In his book *Total Espionage*, the political journalist Curt Riess gave a vivid picture of that city, and the fashionable district of Estoril, at the time. No less than 200 German agents were housed at the Nazi legation; the Link, the dangerous pro-Nazi organization in London that had supported the duke and duchess for years, was active in the area, particularly its leader, Sir Ivone Kirkpatrick, who flooded his contacts at the Park and Palace Hotels with appeasement literature.

Others present included Camille Chautemps, whose craven abandonment of his premiership of France had occurred in the week of blackmail and intrigue involving the Windsors in March 1938, and who had now betrayed his country's cause; the Windsors' close friend and fellow intriguer, the French airplane tycoon Paul-Louis Weiller; Prince Philipp of Hesse; Friedrich Sieberg, right-hand man of Otto Abetz, Hitler's ambassador to Paris . . . and soon to arrive, William Bullitt himself, up to no good as usual.

Meanwhile, Sir Stewart Menzies in London, clearly without the newly appointed Winston Churchill's knowledge, had by now discovered from a source that is believed to be secret agent and member of the Windsor entourage, George Wood, that Wallis continued to be in touch with Ribbentrop from Madrid, as Edward Tamm wrote, 'without difficulty because of the pronounced Nazi sympathies in Spain'.

On 29 June, Bullitt, still using Berlin Foreign Ministry facilities, left Paris and travelled to unoccupied France, where he set up the collaborationist government at Vichy, conferred with Marshal

Pétain and Pierre Laval, the betrayers of France, and assured them of Washington's cooperation. Staying at the home of the American millionaire Frank Jay Gould in Vichy, he advised Washington by radio via Berlin that all the necessary arrangements for full-scale collusion were in place. Ribbentrop could not have asked for more.

The situation in Portugal was explosive. Members of the Himmler-trained secret police were on guard everywhere. There was a German plan afoot to bring about a coup d'état which would overthrow the ineffectual neutralist Salazar. The British ambassador, Sir Walford Selby, the Windsors' old friend from Vienna, was bombarding the Foreign Office with anxious cables on the matter. The Portuguese government, fearful that any close association with Britain might result in such a coup, was refusing to allow the Secret Intelligence Service to have access to encoded telegrams; by June, Selby had been trying to organize a British landing force to forestall German plans. The Germans were contemplating an attack on Portuguese East Africa; the Japanese, already contemplating war, were pushing for oil concessions in Portuguese Timor.

A villa had been arranged for the Windsors at the appropriately named Boca di Inferno (Mouth of Hell) at Cascais. The couple's host was Ricardo Espírito Santo e Silva, owner of a private bank and a friend of the Rothschilds; he was also of Jewish origin. The Duke of Kent had stayed with him until his departure a few days earlier. Silva was under constant watch by the Secret Intelligence Service and it turned out that he had considerable Nazi connections. It seems incredible in the circumstances that such a residence had been authorized by Selby. Asked to explain his father's curious action at that time, Ralph Selby replied:

> The Windsors were originally booked in Lisbon's main hotel, the Aviz. As the flood of refugees from occupied Europe grew larger, the hotel manager contacted my father and told him he would find it difficult to provide the Duke and Duchess with adequate accommodation and he wondered whether it would not be preferable to house him in a suitable villa. He thought he would be able to find him one. My father agreed, and the house at Cascais was found. As my father drove to the airport with his air attaché to greet the Duke, the air attaché said that

he had heard that the villa's owner had the reputation of being a Nazi sympathizer. My father said that he had heard the same thing but did not see what they could do about it now.

It was thought at the time that the Duke would only be in Lisbon for 48 hours or so, and that he would be taking one of the York aircraft sent out to bring him back to England. Little harm could be done in so short a time. My father's papers reveal how surprised and pained he was to see the owner of the villa on its doorstep to greet the Duke on his arrival there. Neither before nor afterwards did my father have any reason to suppose that the manager of the hotel who had made the arrangement was in any way a Nazi sympathizer.

On 4 July, the duke telegraphed Churchill, 'I will accept appointment as Governor of Bahamas, as I am sure you have done your best for me in a difficult situation. I am sending Major Phillips to England tomorrow, and will appreciate your receiving him personally to explain some details.' Churchill replied, 'I am very glad Your Royal Highness has accepted the appointment, for I am sure useful service can be rendered to the Empire at the present time. I will arrange all details with Major Phillips if you will send him home. Sincere good wishes.' The appointment was published in London on the 10th. However, Sir Alexander Hardinge was worried about the duchess's activities in Lisbon. He sent a memorandum on 9 July to Eric Seal of the prime minister's staff at 10 Downing Street: 'As I told you once before, this is not the first time that this lady has come under suspicion for her anti-British activities, and as long as we never forget the power she has exerted over [the duke] in her efforts to avenge herself on this country, we shall be all right.'

It is clear from this extraordinary message that Hardinge remained unshakable in his conviction that the duchess was a Nazi collaborator or agent. Evidently the Secret Intelligence Service in Lisbon had reported unfavourably on her activities. These cannot have been merely associating with Nazis, who certainly would be welcome in the house in which the Windsors were staying. The activities would have to have been more serious than that.

Among the numerous acquaintances of the Windsors at the time was the German ambassador, Oswald Baron von Hoyningen-Huene, a career diplomat of the old school. Polished and ingenious, he was anxious to promote cultural exchanges between Portugal and Germany. An OSS Intelligence report on him dated 11 October 1945 reads, 'His self-appointed task of cultivating the Portuguese [for political objectives] was facilitated by the lax British practice of regarding Portugal as traditionally within the British orbit.' He found that Portuguese distrust of Germany sprang largely from a fear that Germany might wish to compensate itself for the loss of its colonies at Portugal's expense. It was his main objective to allay this distress.

Huene was, the OSS reports confirm, an instrument of the Nazis. He reported to Berlin on 10 July that the duke was convinced that 'had he remained on the throne, war could have been avoided and [he] describes himself as a firm supporter of a compromise peace with Germany. The Duke believes with certainty that continued heavy bombing will make England ready for peace.' Was this possible? The duke certainly loved the English people. But perhaps his bitterness and hatred of the war, his conviction that an alliance with Germany was the only way to avoid a total conquest of his nation, had driven him to make such a rash and brutally thoughtless statement. Hoyningen-Huene was certainly not the type of diplomat who was prone to irrational and unsubstantiated reports. And it is worth noting that not too long after the cable was received in Germany, the heaviest bombing of England began.

On 7 July, a secret Foreign Office report signed L. (Reginald Leeper) to Sir Alexander Cadogan at the Foreign Office read:

> Germans expect assistance from Duke and Duchess, latter desiring at any price to become Queen. Germans have been negotiating with her since June 27th. Status quo in England to expect undertaking to form anti-Russian alliance. Germans propose to form opposition government under Duke of Windsor having first changed public opinion by propaganda. Germans think King George will abdicate during attack on London.

Ribbentrop decided that it was important to make the duke and Wallis return to Spain on some pretext, no matter what money they demanded from Hitler. At that stage Germany would put pressure on Windsor to collaborate, resulting in 'the assumption of the English throne by the Duke and Duchess'. The message added, 'Should the Duke have other plans, but still be prepared to cooperate in the restoration of good relations between England and Germany, we would likewise be prepared to assure him and his wife an existence which would enable him, either as a private citizen or in some other position, to lead a life suitable for a King.'

Ribbentrop added that he had received information from a London source that the duke would be killed on official instructions as soon as he reached the Bahamas. Ribbentrop sent for Walter Schellenberg, head of the SD, German secret intelligence, and instructed him to make an offer to the duke based on the Windsors' proposals. Schellenberg was to deposit 50 million Swiss francs in an account in the duke's name. The Windsors were to be invited across the Spanish border, from where they would be conducted to an appropriate location at which the necessary arrangements with Germany could be made. Ribbentrop said that if the British Secret Intelligence Service gave any trouble, it should be dealt with by force, but that the duke should be treated similarly only if he were seized by 'a fear psychosis'. If 50 million francs wasn't enough, the figure could be increased. At that moment in the conversation the telephone rang. Hitler was on the line. Schellenberg was given the extension so that he could listen in. He heard Hitler say, 'Schellenberg should particularly bear in mind the importance of the Duchess's attitude and try as hard as possible to get her support. She has great influence over the Duke.'

There was concern in London that the Windsors might wish to go to the United States on their way to the Bahamas. Such a visit would be highly undesirable. With their immense following in America, they might easily influence public feeling towards the isolationists who wished to keep the United States out of the world conflict. It was Winston Churchill's unequivocal policy to involve America in the war. The 1940 elections were looming, and even within the Democratic party such extreme right-wing figures as Senator Burton K. Wheeler of Montana were determined that Roosevelt's policy of collaboration with Britain should see no chance of fruition. The Windsors had a double reason for wanting to go to the United States. Not only did they wish to make contact with isolationists and appeasers, but the duchess had the mundane motive of wanting some surgery done on her nose. By now, Major Gray Phillips was in London at the Bath Club, and the duke was cabling him via Sir Walford Selby that it was essential that the duchess see the 'specialist' in New York.

At the same time, the Windsors were worried about getting their property out of Paris and Antibes. Joseph Kennedy, the US ambassador in London, cabled Cordell Hull in Washington about the matter on 10 July, stating that the Foreign Office was requesting the US consul at Nice to make arrangements for the shipping of many of the personal effects, clothing and linen from La Croë. This would be taken care of, on Kennedy's authorization. However, Paris presented slightly more of a problem since it was in the occupied zone. The duchess, seemingly confident of her reception from Otto Abetz and the other Nazi figures there, actually planned to go back to the Boulevard Suchet and supervise the packing of her belongings. Fortunately this plan was prevented by Selby, who clearly saw the outrageous nature of the request.

Wallis contacted one of her former chefs in Vichy and asked him to pick up the rest of their effects from La Croë; at the same time she asked the Germans to allow her maid, Jeanne-Marguerite Moulichon, to proceed to Paris to collect silver, china and linen for shipment to the Bahamas. This, of course, was in breach of the British Trading with the Enemy Act and, under the provisions of the recently amended British Defence Regulations, would normally result in imprisonment without trial. Don Javier Bermejillo undertook to act as a go-between in this peculiar act of outright treason. In Madrid he spoke to the German ambassador, Eberhard von Stohrer, who in turn contacted Ribbentrop. He sent Ribbentrop two telegrams, the first of which dealt with the duke's appointment to Nassau, the capital of the Bahamas, and revealed that Churchill had threatened the duke with court-martial if he did not obey orders. The second (11 July) read as follows:

The Duke of Windsor, through the confidential emissary of the Foreign Minister, has again expressed thanks for cooperation in the matter of his house in Paris, and has requested that a maid of the Duchess be allowed to travel to Paris in order to pick up various objects there and transport them by van to Lisbon, as they are required by him and the Duchess for the Bahamas.

The German ambassador continued by stating that these wishes should be acceded to because the maid could always be held as a hostage against the Windsors' decision to cooperate with the German government in the event that they hesitated.

At the same time, the duke met an emissary of Ribbentrop's in Lisbon and told him that Churchill had threatened a court-martial by telephone if the duke did not proceed to the Bahamas.

On the 15th, William Bullitt met the Windsors and, in a conversation which President Roosevelt repeated to the writer Fulton Oursler, referred to their imminent departure. 'We sail for our St Helena,' Wallis said. St Helena was, of course, the island location of Napoleon Bonaparte's final exile and death.

On 17 July, Wallis planned Madame Moulichon's trip to Paris with the expertise of a general. Armed with a German passport and clearance documents stamped by the Gestapo, the adventurous maid flew to Madrid to obtain further documents from the German consulate. She was held up by red tape; the authorities in Vichy Paris and Berlin were questioning this matter of collaborating with their own enemy. In the meantime, Wallis was worried about acquiring a new secretary. She cabled Johnny McMullen at the St Regis Hotel in New York, asking him whether the girl he had recommended knew shorthand, typing and accountancy. 'Would she be free to meet us in New York on 7 August?' the duchess wanted to know. She also asked McMullen to find her a butler 'as London impossible'. Apparently even Wallis quailed at the thought of having to take on a butler in London when Great Britain was fighting for its life.

Meanwhile, at 10 Downing Street, Sir John Colville recalled that Churchill was furious at being bothered by such trivial matters as the Windsors' requests at this time of crisis. The duke was bombarding Churchill with requests for the proper transportation, complaining that the neutrality laws made it difficult for him to find passage on an American ship. There was always the danger of attack or boarding parties when British subjects were aboard American vessels. The duke advised Major Phillips that he should send all

British luggage to New York direct and that he wanted a member of the Scots Guards as a soldier servant. He ruled out a recommended maid, and asked Phillips to continue the search. He wanted a second cook hired in Nassau. He was sending his other equerry, the probable SIS agent George Wood, to London with further instructions that his cigarettes and tobacco were to be sent to Lisbon on the next flying boat.

It is possible that at this stage the Windsors may have had a narrow escape from death. Squadron Leader Frederick W. Winterbotham, head of air intelligence of the Secret Intelligence Service, co-creator of the famous 'Ultra' system that broke the German Enigma code, specialized in sabotaging airplanes by the simple device of dropping sulphuric acid through a drip bottle onto the insulation wires, a device he would, by his own assertion (to the late author Peter Allen), apply in disposing of the Duke of Kent and of General Wladyslav Sikorski, exiled premier of Poland and his Nazi associate Victor Cazalet.

On the advice of David Eccles, who worked with Winterbotham and with Sir Stewart Menzies in the Secret Intelligence Service, the Windsors were, the SIS decided, to return from Lisbon to London by Sunderland flying boat, the same make of plane in which Kent was to die in 1942 and which could easily be tampered with. Churchill may have got wind of this and cancelled the trip. On no account must the Windsors return to England; they must not carry out their plan to stay there with the Duke of Westminster, the most powerful property owner in London, setting up his country estate Eaton Hall as a second Buckingham Palace.

By 17 July, when Wallis's maid was waiting in Madrid for clearance, it was settled in London that the Windsors would sail to Bermuda and be conveyed from there by warship to Nassau. Lord Lothian, the British ambassador to the United States, would be taking care of the necessary arrangements. However, there must be no question of the ship's touching American ports or even entering US territorial waters. Cordell Hull was adamant about this. Reservations were made on the Export Lines' vessel *Excalibur*, sailing from Lisbon on 1 August. This meant that passengers who had already booked for that day would have to be rebooked for a later sailing. At the same time, with considerable difficulty, Wallis arranged for furniture and paintings to be moved from La Croë to storage in Italy, yet another breach of the Trading with the Enemy Act.

On 18 July, Gray Phillips sent a telegram from London saying that the duke could not be granted the services of various non-commissioned officers whom he wanted to accompany him, because they were required for immediate wartime service, and under no circumstances would he be permitted to go to the United States. Lord Lloyd cabled the duke, 'War Office represent that to take fit and efficient soldiers out of Army at this junction would set an unfortunate precedent.' The Foreign Office cabled Lord Lothian that it would be necessary for the *Excalibur* to make a 350-mile diversion from its normal route to Bermuda. The British government would, of course, be ready to meet any extra expense involved.

That same day, the duke, impatient with a number of frustrations vis-à-vis his voyage, sent an irritable telegram to Churchill which included the words, 'Have been messed about quite long enough and detect in Colonial Office attitude very same hands at work as in my last job. Strongly urge you to support arrangements I have made, as otherwise will have to reconsider my position.'

On 20 July, Herbert Claiborne Pell, US minister to Portugal, had dinner with the Windsors at the house of Espírito Santo e Silva at Cascais. Another of the guests was David Eccles. After dinner the duke and duchess said several extremely unwise things. Pell sent a top-secret telegram to Cordell Hull that night. It read:

> Duke and Duchess of Windsor are indiscreet and outspoken against British government. Consider their presence in United States might be disturbing and confusing. They say that they intend remaining in the United States whether Churchill likes it or not and desire apparently to make propaganda for peace. If Department cancels their visas, they can take clipper to Bermuda, thence to Bahamas. Visas were given by Consulate General.

This devastating telegram made its way through the normal channels to London. Written by an impeccable personage, it set the seal of doom on the Windsors forever. The fact that they would be prepared to press for peace with Hitler in the United States, against the expressed policy of Churchill and Roosevelt, made both of them about as welcome in the US and British corridors of power as a resurrected Bonnie and Clyde.

On the 22nd, there was a secret communication to Ribbentrop from his agents in London stating that the duke had addressed a memorandum to King George VI urging upon him the appointment of a new pro-Hitler appeasement cabinet which would replace the existing coalition cabinet headed by Churchill. The report said that a new cabinet was also being pressed upon the king by Lloyd George. The German ambassador to Ireland cabled Ribbentrop the same day, saying that such a revised cabinet would be prepared to make immediate peace with Germany. Among those who would be willing to make such a peace were Lord Halifax, Sir John Simon and Sir Samuel Hoare ('whose delegation [as ambassador] to Spain was viewed in the appropriate perspective').

Also the same day, neutral Italy's newspapers headlined the story. The *Gazetta del Popolo* of Turin provided a detailed account in which it was stated, rightly or wrongly, that the duke wanted Lloyd George as prime minister of a fascist England. The actual telegram remains classified to this day.

On 23 July, it was determined in London that the cost of the diversion of the *Excalibur* would be £1,500, plus £10,000 in insurance premiums, when Britain needed every penny. By now, the telegrams to and from Major Phillips were assuming a fantastic absurdity in time of war. That day he cabled the duchess: 'Have choice of two maids, one hundred pounds. One nine years Lady Duncan, seven Countess Vitetti. Recommendations excellent. Other five years Clare Beck. Since then dressmaking four years, appearance distinctly plain. Either could leave Sunday with me.'

The same day, Ambassador Stohrer reported to Ribbentrop that his emissary had learned the following from the Windsors:

In Portugal [the duke] felt almost like a prisoner. He was surrounded by agents, etc. Politically he was more and more distant from the King and the present English government. The Duke and Duchess have less fear of the King, who was quite foolish, than of the shrewd Queen, who was intriguing skilfully against the Duke, and particularly against the Duchess. The Duke was considering making a public statement and thereby disavowing present English policy and breaking with his brother.

It was also reported to Ribbentrop that the duke and duchess would be willing to go to Spain instead of to the United States, but it is probable that the Windsors were only talking about this possibility and had no intention of actually returning.

On the 24th, arrangements were made for another vessel, the Canadian *Lady Somers,* to meet the Windsors in Bermuda and take them to Nassau. They would have to be accommodated for several days in Hamilton, the Bermudan capital. In the meantime, after several postponements due to the pressure of other work, Walter Schellenberg at last made preparations to depart for Lisbon. On 26 July, apparently still uncertain of what he would do, the duke began playing desperately for time. He stated that the American Export Lines agent wanted him to sail with Wallis on the 8th instead of the 1st, because they would 'create bad feeling' by displacing other passengers. This was a blatant lie, easily exposed. But a later departure would provide the chance of perhaps getting some possessions from La Croë. He urged Phillips to obtain an 8 August sailing for them. He remained very cross at the refusal to let him disembark in New York. That day he cabled Churchill:

> Regarding not landing in the United States at this juncture, I take it to mean that this only applies until after the events of November [the presidential election]. May I, therefore, have confirmation that it is not to be the policy of His Majesty's government that I should not set foot on American soil during my term of office in the Bahamas? Otherwise I could not feel justified in representing the King in a British colony so geographically close to the United States if I was to be prevented from ever going to that country. I appreciate your successful efforts regarding my soldier servant.

In other words, he would not take up his position if he were to be forbidden visits to America indefinitely.

Walter Schellenberg arrived in Lisbon on the 26th, carrying with him Hitler's authority to do everything in his power to discourage the Windsors from leaving Lisbon for the Bahamas and to persuade them to return to Spain and thence to Germany prior to the duke's reassuming the English throne following a negotiated peace. Schellenberg had some reason to be optimistic. The following telegram was sent from Ambassador Stohrer to Ribbentrop that day:

> Strictly secret. A wire message from the Spanish Embassy in Lisbon is now in the Spanish Ministry of Foreign Affairs. According to it, the Duke and Duchess of Windsor have had their visas [for Spain] organized for them after considerable pressure on the British Embassy in Lisbon. Confirming messages to be awaited ... The plan, as developed in previous telegram, will under all circumstances be followed through, since even after issue of visas, counteraction Intelligence service is possible.

In a separate telegram of the same date Stohrer made it clear that, if the British Secret Intelligence Service intervened, the Windsors could be taken by plane to Spain. Schellenberg's intermediaries pointed out to the Windsors the danger that when they went to the Bahamas they would be killed by British intelligence agents.

It now became imperative in London that the Windsors leave at once. Churchill cabled the duke on the 27th:

> I have seen your telegram to Major Phillips suggesting postponement for one week. I believe Lord Lloyd is telegraphing to you in reply suggesting that you should sail on August 1 as arranged, and I do very much hope that you will be able to fall in with this proposal. As regards to your visiting the United States, we should naturally wish to fall in with Your Royal Highness's wishes. It is difficult to see far ahead these days, but in accordance with the standing royal instructions to colonial governors which you already have, you would no doubt consult the Secretary of State of the colonies before leaving the colony, and we should naturally do our best to suit Your Royal Highness's convenience.

At the same time, the Windsors talked of moving to the Hotel Aviz in Lisbon, probably under pressure from Sir Walford Selby, who must have learnt through the Secret Intelligence Service of Schellenberg's arrival. The SIS had complete control of the Aviz. Needless to say, the house at Cascais with its pro-Nazi owner was a more convenient location from the German point of view. An associate of Schellenberg's warned the Windsors that the Aviz was dangerous and that they might be murdered there on British orders. The duchess was particularly frightened by this suggestion. That same day a Spanish agent delivered to the Windsors a letter signed by Miguel Primo de Rivera, civil governor of Madrid, directly proposing the Schellenberg plan for them to go in the guise of a hunting expedition to Spain, where they would be met by the appropriate contacts. The duke read this document in a state of bemusement; it would of course be impossible for him to take such a risk since, were he to do so, he could easily be arrested by the British authorities in Lisbon and shipped to London for court-martial. That same night Gray Phillips and the duke's newly appointed valet, Piper Alistair Fletcher, were flown into Lisbon by Edward Fielden. Sir Walter Monckton had accompanied them, on Churchill's instructions, to make sure that the Windsors left on the scheduled sailing.[2] Monckton was greeted warmly by the Windsors; they had never forgotten his help to them during the abdication crisis. They were also pleased by his moderating influence in London. What they did not know was that he was under orders to deactivate and remove them.

Monckton carried with him to the house at Cascais several documents, including a letter from the king stating that he was pleased the duke had agreed to accept the post in the Bahamas, and one from Churchill, dated the 27th, warning the duke in the friendliest spirit to be extremely careful: 'Many sharp and unfriendly ears will be pricked up to catch any suggestion that Your Royal Highness takes a view about the war, or about the Germans, or about Hitlerism, which is different from that adopted by the British nation and Parliament.' He went on to refer to various reports that might have been used to the duke's disadvantage. Churchill's cleverness in the matter is undeniable. He had followed his original threats of possible action with an indirect command that the duke should not make his Nazi sympathies public. At the same time, he had expressed respect along with his concern, which was sure to appeal to the duke's inflated ego. The duke told Monckton that he was pleased with the communications but was still concerned that certain figures in the British government might wish to remove him. In this he was entirely accurate. Monckton warned the Windsors that Churchill had discovered a plot to put them on the throne in the event of an invasion of England and a negotiated peace. Monckton felt Churchill was right.

Monckton also felt it desirable for a CID detective from Scotland Yard to accompany the Windsors on the *Excalibur*, both to keep them under surveillance and to protect them in case there was an attempt to abduct the duke and duchess at sea. Meanwhile, the duke was determined to go to America despite instructions to the contrary; as early as 29 July, he booked a whole floor of New York's Wickersham Hospital and the services of Dr Daniel Shorell to give the duchess her nose job. Apparently the Secret Intelligence Service got wind of this, because further communications between London and Lisbon indicated that there was no relinquishing of fears that the Windsors would make a trip to New York.

Amazingly, Sir Walter Monckton, true-blue British to the core, actually stayed in the Nazi household at Cascais, where he and the Windsors were watched day and night by an odd variety of amateur and professional secret agents. Presumably unknown to Monckton, the duchess's maid, Jeanne-Marguerite Moulichon, had obtained the necessary documentation in Madrid from the German embassy and was on her way to Paris. When she arrived at the house in Boulevard Suchet she and the butler and his wife carefully packed the silver, china and linen in numerous cabin trunks and boxes. Nobody knew the combination to the safe, so it remained closed for the duration of the war. The German High Command in Paris and the German embassy were, of course, privy to Jeanne-Marguerite's arrival, turning a blind eye to this breach of the Trading with the Enemy regulations.

Meanwhile, in Lisbon, Schellenberg was growing desperate. He was even thinking of kidnapping the Windsors, but this of course was absurd. His next idea was to advise the Windsors that a line of communication would be opened up to the German government. But the warnings from Churchill via Monckton again rendered any such action impossible. Schellenberg cabled Berlin for instructions. He later claimed that Ribbentrop had ordered a kidnapping after all, but this was almost certainly sheer invention on Schellenberg's part. However, it was leaked by someone that a similar idea was being discussed. The Americans shared the alarm. A week later, on 6 August, a confidential report to Ribbentrop by a member of his staff stated, 'The American fears are at present along the following lines: That [there could be] intermediate negotiations with Germany through the Duke of Windsor, and thus via Spain, with the goal of removing the Churchill government and achieving a cease fire pact with strong colonial concessions.'

On 30 July, from his special train at Füschl in Germany, Ribbentrop fired off a long telegram to Schellenberg that amounted to a last-ditch effort. The duke's pro-Nazi host was to talk to him in an effort to persuade him that Germany would now, following the British rejection of the Führer's last peace speech, force Britain to a position of surrender. Germany would be willing to cooperate with the Windsors in any future alliance between Germany and Britain, and in response Hitler would ensure their future. They should be warned that Churchill would keep the Windsors permanently in the Bahamas in order to be in complete control of them.

The duke's response to this message was that, though he was in favour of the Führer's policy, the present moment was 'inopportune ... to manifest [myself] on the political scene'. On the other hand, his departure for the Bahamas need not imply a rupture, since he could easily return to Europe in twenty-four hours via Florida. The next day, the 31st, Detective Sergeant Harold Holder of Scotland Yard and a maid named Evelyn Fyrth arrived in Lisbon by flying boat. According to a German report of that date, Miss Fyrth was a British Secret Intelligence Service agent; if this is true she almost certainly did not make it known to the duchess, but was used to carry out a surveillance on the couple during their voyage.

At the eleventh hour, the duke sent a letter to Churchill, sourly stating that he didn't consider his appointment first class, but since it was clear that his brother the king and Queen Elizabeth would not bring the family feud to an end, he would agree that the Bahamas post was 'a temporary solution'. Shortly after sending this letter he went to the Spanish embassy to discuss the entire matter with the ambassador, Nicolás Franco Y Bahamonde. The ambassador urged him to stay, to assist those Britons in favour of a negotiated peace to find a new leader. The Duke listened carefully, but realized he could still do nothing.

That night, Selby gave a farewell party for the Windsors at the Hotel Aviz. The next day Primo de Rivera warned the Windsors that if they left they would be risking their lives. Other warnings were delivered. The duke told Santo e Silva that he was impressed by the Führer's desire for peace, which was in complete agreement with his own point of view; he was convinced that if he had been king it would never have come to war; it was too early for him to come forward with such a plan at the present time; and he would make himself available to Germany immediately once he received a particular code word. He concluded with an expression of admiration and sympathy for the Führer.

Meanwhile, Schellenberg acted with incredible stupidity. Highly strung, overwrought and afraid of repercussions in Berlin over his abject failure, he arranged for Gray Phillips to receive a passenger list of the *Excalibur* on which the names of the Jews aboard were marked, suggesting that danger might come from them. The wife of a Portuguese official called on the duchess and told her that, if the Windsors sailed, her husband would lose his job. A bouquet of flowers arrived at the Cascais house with a warning on the enclosed card. An anonymous letter advised the duchess she was in grave danger. An English driver told the Windsors he was afraid to go to the Bahamas because of a murder plot. A scene was staged on board the *Excalibur* in which there was a fake arrest of a German agent disguised as an ordinary passenger, who informed the Portuguese police that a bomb intended for the Windsors had been hidden on board. A plan to fire shots in the night, breaking the Windsors' bedroom window, was abandoned.

Dr Salazar, the prime minister of Portugal, who had been advised to neither encourage nor discourage the duke's travel plans, received the duke on the day of the sailing while the duchess completed the packing. The Spanish Ambassador had warned Salazar that the duke was a probable peace mediator 'in spite of his temper' and that he could have an important role to play: 'As peace mediators are not many, the ones that are left should not be disregarded nor should we allow them to be destroyed.' At the meeting, which quite improperly was not reported to Sir Walford Selby, it appears that such proposals were put forward by the duke and that Salazar most skilfully avoided any kind of commitment. Up to the very last minute, the Windsors were still trying to play for more time, and even requested the *Excalibur* to be held for a week for their convenience. This, of course, was impossible. All ideas of going to Spain at last abandoned, the duke and duchess finally made their way on board on 1 August as scheduled.

The British authorities had imposed rigid censorship on the Windsors' every movement. Sir Samuel Hoare turned up at the last minute to see them off; recently declassified US State Department documents suggest that he too was still discussing with them the potential of peace arrangements between Britain and Germany. There was some talk of a convoy being supplied for the *Excalibur*. But the American undersecretary of state, Sumner Welles, absolutely rejected any such idea as a breach of neutrality arrangements. The Windsors, who had made a thorough inspection of their ten cabins and veranda suite the previous week, were driven to the ship in the early afternoon. The vessel was crowded with British and American citizens making their way out of Lisbon to safety in the United States. Among the passengers were Anthony J. Drexel Biddle, US ambassador to Poland and a friend of the Windsors, George Gordon, US minister at The Hague, and William Phillips, US ambassador to Italy. The Windsors' party included Major Gray Phillips, the mysterious Evelyn Fyrth, Captain and Mrs George Wood and Harold Holder. All were accommodated in the veranda suite of cabins.

The *Excalibur* sailed slowly in a north-westerly direction. The Windsors were advised by telegram that their baggage had arrived in New York from Liverpool aboard the Cunard White Star liner *Britannic*. They had an early night, followed by a leisurely day on the 2nd. In the afternoon, they strolled on the deck, chatting informally with their fellow passengers. They visited the bridge to see the captain and looked out at a flat, brilliantly blue sea.

The next day, the Windsors were on the bridge when the Pan American Yankee Clipper, en route with wealthy refugees to New York, flew overhead at a low altitude. Baron Eugene de Rothschild and Kitty were on board the flying boat. Captain Sullivan of the

Clipper descended to within 200 feet of the *Excalibur* and greeted the Windsors by wireless. They waved and sent a message back: 'Thank you . . . We reciprocate and bon voyage.'

The Windsors entertained the Drexel Biddles and William Phillips and his daughter at dinner that evening; the next day, they answered their correspondence, the duchess by hand and the duke on a portable typewriter. The sea remained calm. The duke and duchess sunbathed and watched films in the ship's cinema. They might have been on holiday; there was no suggestion that they were going to an awkward and disagreeable exile.

NOTES

1 In order not to reveal his presence, the intelligence chief told the Mayor of Perpignan to tell the Windsors that 'the entire French government' was arriving.
2 Monckton was a member of the appeals committee in the matter of the fascists aiming for a negotiated peace in Britain.

15

ELBA

The *Excalibur* steamed into pale green Bermudan waters on 7 August, as Sir Charles Dundas, retiring governor of the Bahamas, and Lady Dundas left Nassau for Rio de Janeiro, from where they would fly to a new appointment in Uganda. Sir Charles had not wanted to leave. His wife was ill, and the journey would be exceedingly uncomfortable for her. But Churchill had given him no alternative.[1]

The Windsors came ashore by tender to the Royal Bermuda Yacht Club at 2.45 p.m.; hundreds of spectators burst into applause as the duke stood to attention on a small palm tree-flanked grass oval while the national anthem was played. Wallis remained at the dockside, talking to Mrs Francis Hastings-Brooke, sister of the governor, Lieutenant-General Sir Denis Bernard. Among the welcoming party was Frank Giles, aide-de-camp to the governor. Detective Inspector Holder, the royal bodyguard, advised Giles that the Windsors were in danger every moment of the day and night and should never be allowed out of sight.

The duke carried out an inspection of the guard of honour, pausing briefly to talk to a youth in the Bermuda Volunteer Rifle Corps. He then departed for Government House in a state carriage with Sir Denis and the ADC, while Wallis and Mrs Hastings-Brooke followed with the rest of the entourage in another carriage. Although the duke seemed to be cheerful, composed and in the best of tempers, in fact he was not. The reason was that Mrs Hastings-Brooke and the ladies accompanying her had so far failed to curtsey to Wallis and that nobody had addressed her as 'Your Royal Highness'. At dinner that night they again failed to do what he wanted. Instructions had come from London that on no account was Wallis to be treated as royalty and that, in extremis, the most that could be accorded to the duke would be a half-curtsey. The duchess was to be addressed as 'Your Grace'.

Red-faced and flustered at the lack of respect for his wife, the duke sulked all through the banquet. After dinner, when the ladies repaired to the drawing room and the gentlemen made their way to the library for brandy and cigars, the duke burst out with, 'If I had been King, there would have been no war.' This characteristic statement at a time when Britain had her back against the wall so infuriated Sir Denis Bernard that he almost lost his temper. The duke's former equerry, Charles Lambe, who was now commander of a British cruiser, stepped in and changed the subject, but the governor remained furious.

The pleasant and relaxed Frank Giles accompanied the Windsors day and night during the following days. In his memoirs, *Sundry Times*, he wrote: 'I had ample opportunity for observing them and every night made some copious notes about my impressions. They included the curious fact, imparted by seeing the Duke take a shower after a game of golf, that he had absolutely no hair on his body, even in the places where one would most expect it to be.' Giles further observed:

> It was fascinating to watch this famous couple together and assess the impact of each personality upon the other. He [was] more in love with her than she with him, I noted, though her feelings assumed a watchful, almost maternal devotion. Each night, before the Government House party went to bed, she would ask me about arrangements for the next day, in particular the time of the Duke's first engagement – for I am the alarm clock in this family. As well as timekeeper, she was also watch dog.

Giles recalled that a game of bridge was in progress one evening. The duke was supposed to be preparing a speech that he would make upon assuming his new position at Government House in Nassau, but instead he was chatting away while the duchess played cards. She left the table and walked into the drawing room, saying, 'Now, David, what about that work?' He replied sheepishly, 'All right, darling, I'm going up now.' As it turned out, he didn't go up to his bedroom to work until close on midnight. When he told Wallis that he was at last going to attend to his work, she looked at him like a nanny 'whose charge had forgotten the precepts she had taught him, thereby grieving more than annoying her'.

Although day after day the duke insisted that Wallis should be curtseyed to and addressed as 'Your Royal Highness', his wishes went unsatisfied. The governor did his best to suppress his finer feelings and made the couple as welcome as possible in the circumstances. After a lengthy press conference on the night of 9 August, Mrs Hastings-Brooke gave a dinner party for the famous guests; it was attended by Admiral and Lady Kennedy Purvis, Colonial Secretary Eric Button and Mrs Button, Charles Lambe and the George Woods.

The next day, while the duke reviewed the Canadian troops stationed on the island, and then played a game of golf, Wallis visited the local aquarium. At a cocktail party that night an American woman, Mrs Beck, caused considerable adverse comment when, followed by three other Americans, she curtseyed to the duchess. The Englishwomen present glared at them. A notable absentee from the cocktail party was the Bishop of Bermuda, the Right Reverend Arthur H. Browne, who had personally ripped the couple's photographs from a shop window in Hamilton, Bermuda, at the time of the abdication. However, the Windsors boldly attended the service at the cathedral on Sunday the 11th.

During the sermon, the bishop made a very curious reference. At some stage during the previous two days, the duke had sent a treasonous telegram to Lisbon indicating to his Nazi contacts that he would be willing to return as agreed to discuss the negotiated peace arrangements. Censorship was very strict in Bermuda; even if the duke had sent a message via a neutral consulate or in a diplomatic bag for transmission from a neutral island, it is doubtful whether he could have evaded interception. Looking directly at the Windsors the bishop said, as he analysed St Paul's Epistle to Philemon, 'St Paul's letters reveal much. As censors these days come to know, correspondences can afford the most intimate revelation of the writer's personality.'

On the night of the 11th, the duke visited St George's Island and spoke with the officers and crew of an interned French vessel; next day he inspected many troops on the island. He also planted a poinciana tree next to the mango that his father had planted in 1880. In the meantime Wallis took several cruises around the bays and inlets, and had tea with Aunt Bessie's good friend Jeffrey Dodge, of the Dodge car family.

On 15 August, the couple sailed for the Bahamas. Nassau had been scrubbed, repainted and extensively brushed up for the royal arrival. The Windsors were taken aboard the Canadian vessel *Lady Somers*, in normal circumstances a risky procedure for royalty in time of war. However, a British destroyer did keep the *Lady Somers* in sight the whole way. Among the other passengers was, by chance, Eugene Rothschild's cousin the Baron Maurice, who proved to be a genial companion on the voyage.

Thousands were lined up behind the police cordons along the wharf at Nassau as the official welcoming party, led by the Colonial Secretary and John W. Dye, the American consul, all dressed in white suits, stood along the pier with their wives beside them. American and British flags flapped feebly in the slight breeze. The heat was enveloping and stifling.

The duke was in general's uniform; Wallis wore a navy blue silk coat, a simple print dress and a white cap stitched with mother of pearl. The Windsors gave no inkling of the discomfort they were feeling in the humidity as they shook hands with the officials. Without further ado the duke and duchess made their way directly to the council chamber, where, watched by 150 fascinated citizens, they sat under a red canopy bearing the insignia of the crown in gold. Wallis sat one step below the duke, but one above the place normally reserved for the wife of a governor. It was a discreet touch that the local authorities had taken hours to work out.

The duke removed his army cap and wiped his perspiring brow with a large white linen handkerchief withdrawn from his left sleeve, while Lieutenant Colonel R. A. Erskine-Lindop, commissioner of police of the Bahamas, read the commission of office.

Then Chief Justice Sir Oscar Daly stepped forward to administer the sacred oath. Reflected in a huge mirror that filled much of the wall opposite him, the duke swore his allegiance to his brother the king and with a tortoiseshell pen signed a written form of the same declaration. Wallis stood to watch him, thereby breaking protocol. As he completed his second signature, he looked directly at her. Neither smiled.

The duke delivered the official speech he had worked on in Bermuda, which contained an extremely veiled reference to his desire for peace: a remark about 'the changed conditions which hostilities have imposed'. The couple then shook hands with 285 people, all of whom were visibly wilting in the airless, suffocating chamber. The couple proceeded to the balcony as the band played the national anthem and the crowd cheered.

At the official reception, Lady Jane Williams-Taylor's husband, Sir Frederick, gave a stiff and awkward welcome speech. Apparently the shock and distress Sir Frederick felt over Wallis's treasonable activities conveyed through his wife were such that he forgot the importance of pretending to be favourable to her in order to assist his wife in milking her of secret information; he even, to the duke's fury, could not bring himself to mention Wallis.

He would continue to snub Wallis for weeks until Jane convinced him that his attitude was unhelpful if secret information was to be obtained; she would begin to be friendly with Wallis and even, to make her feel better, invited her to her magnificent estate of Star Acres, reminding her of other times together in Paris. Later, she would show her in her drawing room, as a false picture of her true sympathies, the oil painting of Hitler that the Führer, whom she had pretended to admire, had given her on her visit to Munich in 1934. That even outdid Wallis's photograph of Ribbentrop on her own bedroom dressing table, the first thing the duke and she saw when they got up in the morning.

The Windsors arrived with their hosts at Government House. Wallis was appalled by its condition. Unlike the Nassau building, which was spruce, well constructed and attractively furnished, their new residence was crumbling into decay. The swimming pool was disused and filled with brown palm leaves blown there during a recent storm. The Windsors could barely make out the 'HM King

Edward VIII' accompanied by the royal seal that a previous governor had painted on the bottom.

By 19 August, the Windsors had already given three press conferences. The duke made it clear that his official activities for the rest of the war would be confined to these islands, and it was only with the greatest effort that he was able to keep the bitterness out of his voice. The couple at least had some good news in their state of depression: the Bahamian assembly had voted a sum of $8,000 to restore Government House. Wallis immediately began removing the hideous wicker furniture and the ugly portraits of Queen Mary and Queen Victoria that dominated the drawing room. The Windsors employed painters to redo the pale pink stucco front. They started repairs on the ceiling and took on specialists to deal with the damp patches and flaking plaster. But there was not much they could do for the time being about their bedroom, with its stolid cabinets, monstrous brass bed and an imposing desk. They began talking with the American consul general about wanting to go to Canada to visit the Alberta ranch, and an anxious John W. Dye cabled Washington to give warning of this possibility. There were great fears that the Windsors might move from Alberta to Washington, and the State Department advised Whitehall that any such idea must not be entertained. When the duke cabled the Colonial Office asking to be allowed to go to Canada, Lord Lloyd got in touch with Ambassador Lothian, who instantly stated that there must be no question of the Windsors making the journey. Lothian's telegram to the Colonial Office, dated 24 August, read in part:

If the Duke and Duchess visit the United States en route to Canada, they will certainly attract a great deal of publicity and much commercial interest of a rather undesirable character. But reaction of the press might be even more unfortunate if it were thought the Duke was being prevented from visiting this country . . . In view of great pressure on the President and for other reasons, it is obviously undesirable that any such visit should be made until after the elections, and I think, therefore, that the idea of His Royal Highness coming to this country should be postponed until after that date. In any case, public opinion here might well be surprised if His Royal Highness were to leave his post now, so soon after his arrival there. It is most desirable that the general public here should not get an impression that he is not taking his public duties seriously.

On the 25th, the Windsors attended a reception at which three-quarters of the Bahamas' twenty thousand citizens turned up. Unable to endure Government House a moment longer, the couple moved to the temporarily vacant home of Frederick Sigrist, aircraft-designing genius and creator of the Hurricane, one of the most famous fighters used by the RAF against Hitler. It was a pleasant house on Prospect Ridge, its large, high-ceilinged rooms cooled at night by the intermittent trade winds. The heat still left the couple totally exhausted. Even at Prospect Ridge, the lack of air conditioning was painful. The Windsors hated the petty colonial atmosphere and inbred gossip. Nassau was extraordinarily cramped, claustrophobic and provincial. Its faded colonial charm and pleasant quasi-American shops, its palm trees and coral beaches, scarcely compensated for the sense of remoteness and futility it engendered. Moreover, Secret Intelligence Service agents were watching them, and they knew it. They were somewhat cheered by the arrival from New York of a newly appointed equerry, Captain Vyvyan Drury, and his wife, Nina. The Drurys proved to be congenial companions as well as loyal servants.

Wallis began to look round the island, trying to make the best of a bad job. The duke and duchess grew even closer now to Lady Jane Williams-Taylor, who was still spying on them. Sir Harry Oakes, the wealthy uncrowned king of the Bahamas, offered them the use of his house, Westbourne; they stayed there for weeks, and Wallis gratefully gave him her favourite Chinese screen she had brought from Peking. He had been a penniless gold prospector in Canada when, after years of futile searching, he had at last discovered the world's second-largest goldmine. His coarse, loud-mouthed, vulgar personality had not changed from the days when he had explored the wilderness armed with a pick and shovel. A big man, with massive shoulders and a once-powerful physique that had run to fat, he had a harsh, grating voice and a strident, challenging manner that were excused only because of his money. His Australian wife, Eunice, was by contrast a gentle charmer, and he had a pretty daughter, Nancy, who would soon marry the playboy and

Bahamian businessman Alfred de Marigny. Oakes also had two handsome sons.

Oakes's partner in Nassau and in the Nazi Banco Continental in Mexico was a very sinister character. Swarthy, green-eyed, muscular Harold Christie was a former rum-runner who had bootlegged alcohol during Prohibition. He had become the leading real estate dealer in the islands. Christie lived extravagantly, running an expensive household and travelling to and from the United States, ceaselessly trying to rustle up interest in his properties. But it was wartime, and in spite of the allure of living in a tax-free zone many potential investors were concerned that, because the Bahamas were British colonial property, they might be seized in a German attempt to obtain airfields from which the American mainland could be attacked. Thus Christie was running into considerable financial difficulties at the time. He tried to take up the slack by wheeling and dealing in large numbers of low-priced properties, making loans to blacks. He was a prominent and aggressive figure in the Bahamian Assembly, using his considerable influence in Bay Street, the business and shopping district, to push through his various shady or legitimate projects.

Axel Wenner-Gren, the notorious multi-millionaire Swede, was a very powerful figure of the Bahamas; at the time he was sailing around the United States after the US authorities had denied him permission to land in Alaska. He was Christie and Oakes's partner in the Bank of the Bahamas and the Banco Continental. A tall, fleshy, pink-faced man with white hair, Wenner-Gren had made his vast fortune through inventing the vacuum cleaner and the refrigerator, which he had patented early in the century. His Electrolux industries had spread all over the world. An internationalist with a foot in every camp, Wenner-Gren dealt openly with Nazi Germany, Britain and the United States, preaching a convenient doctrine of peace, and manoeuvring behind the scenes to preserve his massive interests. On 25 May 1939, he had had a meeting with Goering in Berlin. He had listened sagely as Goering called for a permanent peace with England that would entail the restoration of German colonies in Africa, confiscated after the First World War, and no interference in the Polish Corridor, the strip of territory granted to Poland in 1919 which gave the Poles access to the Baltic but divided Germany; the

Germans had reoccupied it in 1939. Wenner-Gren had carried Goering's message directly to Neville Chamberlain, to secure a negotiated armistice; but, as Chamberlain remarked in an undated memorandum, all the Swede's ideas favoured Germany and offered only futile promises in return. Wenner-Gren was also in ceaseless conference with Krupp, whose interests he protected in Sweden. He manufactured munitions for the Germans through his Swedish company, Bofors, which was protected by Sweden's neutrality. He also had a share in SKF ball bearings, the company which supplied commodities to the belligerents on both sides of the war.

Wenner-Gren owned the *Southern Cross*, which he had bought from Howard Hughes for $2 million. The largest yacht afloat, the vessel was magnificently furnished and had a private radio station on board. He had settled in Nassau at the end of 1939 and had founded the Bank of the Bahamas; he also bought Hog Island, renaming it Paradise Island and creating a luxury resort there. Wenner-Gren was constantly changing the registry of the *Southern Cross* to avoid seizure on the high seas, and from aboard the vessel he tried to sell arms to the Latin American republics at a time when the Panama Canal was under threat of seizure by Nazi-controlled elements in the Panamanian republic.

Wenner-Gren's agents in Nassau advised him of the Windsors' arrival and he left messages for them to be welcomed, albeit belatedly, on his behalf. He had in fact been in touch with them before, corresponding via Charles Bedaux in the matter of a negotiated peace. Soon he would return and form a close friendship with them.

In mid-September, Wallis was fretting over the whereabouts of her maid, Jeanne-Marguerite Moulichon. The State Department's division of European affairs cabled the American embassy at Vichy to approach Maynard Barnes of the American embassy in Paris on the matter. Madame Moulichon had had a dramatic series of experiences. In August, a German official had met her in Paris and helped her carry the precious trunks containing linen, silver and china to the Spanish frontier. Although he left her before the frontier was actually reached, she succeeded in getting a removal company to complete the rest of the journey to Spain; then she was held up for a month by the British consul in San Sebastian. Meanwhile Gray Phillips in Lisbon, working with Bermejillo and the US consulate in Madrid, had organized the shipment of the trunks from La Croë to the Bahamas. After further vicissitudes, Jeanne-Marguerite at last managed to make her way to Nassau in November with the aid of Gray Phillips. Simultaneously, the duchess, who was determined to find some way of getting into the United States, had succeeded in securing an American passport via the head of the visa division of the State Department, Breckinridge Long.[2]

On 19 September, an urgent message was sent by Lord Lothian to the Foreign and Colonial Office in London. Headed '*Possible visit of the Duke of Windsor to USA*' it read: 'President Roosevelt's opinion [is] that in no circumstances should HRH come to America *before* the election. He himself hopes soon to visit Eleuthera Island and meet him there. Possibility of the Windsors visiting Washington later.' The reference in this secret message was to the fact that Roosevelt was interested in establishing a base at Eleuthera where American warships could be berthed in expectation of US involvement in the war. In a written memorandum, John Balfour of the Foreign Office provided a footnote to this cable, saying:

> It seems to me that the President is going ahead rather fast. In the first place, we have not yet agreed that the Americans shall have a base on Eleuthera Island, though we know that they have cast tentative eyes on it. Secondly, the President can surely not visit a British dependency without finding out first from us whether such a visit is agreeable. Nothing is said as to the date of the visit.

Copies of Balfour's memo and the telegram were sent to, among others, Sir Alexander Hardinge at Buckingham Palace. Later that month, the duke had somehow influenced Lord Lothian to the point that Lothian himself was pressing the Colonial Office to allow the duke to visit America. On 28 September, Lord Lloyd sent a memorandum to the Foreign Secretary, Lord Halifax, which read: 'I think Lothian is being a nuisance in sounding the President about a possible visit of the Duke of Windsor to the USA. I have just got the Duke, as I thought, clamped down securely in the Bahamas for a while, and now Lord Lothian is stirring up the waters again.'

An appropriate memorandum was sent to Lothian, suggesting

that it would be advisable to discourage any further ideas along these lines. On 8 October, a German newscast in English, relayed to England, stated that the duke might play a part in possible peace negotiations in Europe by President Roosevelt. The report added: 'The government sent him to the Bahamas to get him out of the way, but he accepted the appointment so that he could be within easy access of the USA. He will shortly leave the Bahamas for the US in order to talk with the President.' John De La Vautry of the censorship division of the intelligence unit of the ministry of information wrote in a memorandum of the same date, forwarded to Sir Walter Monckton, 'The Germans have . . . started a peace rumour campaign. Now they are again linking it up with the Duke of Windsor, and bringing in his announced trip to USA – which, for that if no other reason, might usefully be put off.'

On 9 October, Monckton sent Sir Alexander Cadogan a secret memorandum which read:

I have seen the telegrams passing between the office and Lothian about the suggestion that the Duke and the President might meet in the apparently not too distant future. The . . . German broadcast in English . . . sent to me by the Censorship Intelligence Unit, may suggest some confirmation of the Office view that even discussion of such a meeting is not without risk. You may have heard from the Secretary of State of the efforts made by some circles in Spain to prevent the Duke from leaving Lisbon. I had and have no doubt this was because the Germans could make use of his presence, particularly after an expressed intention to go away – in much the same way as they are now using the possibility of his meeting with the President.

Cadogan added a handwritten footnote: 'We might perhaps inform Lord Lothian of the broadcast to illustrate the danger of this.' Lothian sent a telegram to London on the 10th, saying that he had no intention of implying that he wished to encourage an early visit of the duke to America; he reassured the Colonial Office that the president's visit to the Bahamas would be of a purely private character and would not take place until after the election. Winston Churchill personally confirmed the necessity for caution in the matter, and in a secret memorandum dated 15 October he approved the Colonial Office's and Monckton's attitudes. Four days later, the duchess sent two shipments of personal effects to Miami, including clothing for cleaning and repairing. The following memorandum was sent on the 19th by an FBI staff operative to Clyde Tolson, second-in-command to the head of the organization, J. Edgar Hoover:

> In the course of my duties as classifier, I noticed that the Duchess of Windsor was reported as being violently pro-German; on subsequent date I noticed that her clothes were sent to New York City for dry-cleaning. The possibility arises that the transferring of messages through the clothes may be taking place.

Improbable though this was, she was prevented from sending any more.

In October, an incident occurred at the Château de Candé, still being used as the American embassy, with supposedly secret current files and archives still available to the German government as Bullitt had wished. On the 23rd of that month, Hitler met with General Franco of Spain at Hendaye on the French border for a meeting intended to involve Franco in the war; the meeting failed.

Next day, he met Marshal Pétain at Montoire, with the result that Pétain offered him full support in the war against England in return for the promise of certain British dependencies in Africa. From there, Hitler, accompanied by Goering and Ribbentrop, made a pilgrimage to the Château de Candé, where, seeing the duke and duchess's portraits in oils hanging in the library, they stood solemnly side by side and gave those loyal supporters in exile the Nazi salute.

The matter was reported by Whitney Shepherdson, American agent in France, to William Donovan, the OSS leader in Washington, on the 25th.

On 29 October, the duke opened the parliament in Nassau. He delivered a carefully worded speech calling for certain reforms in legislation and discussing electricity and communications, the sponge fisheries and unemployment problems. It was all conventional material, of little or no significance.

On 11 November, after several postponements because of bad weather, the Windsors sailed on a six-day visit to the Out Islands of the Bahamian group to make property deals with Harold Christie. In the meantime, Whitehall remained concerned about the Windsors having any contact with Roosevelt, who was still determined that they should not come to Washington. Secret message after secret message crossed the Atlantic, all inevitably forwarded to Alexander Hardinge at the palace. Lothian even went to see the president's secretary, General 'Pa' Watson, to confirm that no immediate meeting would take place.

In November, Jeanne-Marguerite Moulichon arrived, and on the 15th, John W. Dye sent a message to C. W. Gray, assistant to Cordell Hull in Washington:

> The maid arrived in Nassau some days ago and according to her, the British authorities were not very helpful. In fact she declares that she was unnecessarily delayed nearly a month in Spain because of their inaction, and during this time no effort was made to recover her lost luggage. The Duke expressed his sincere thanks for the real help rendered by all the American officials concerned.

That same week, Axel Wenner-Gren arrived in Nassau aboard the *Southern Cross*. He was accompanied by his wife, the American singer Marguerite Liggett. A Department of State official, G. A. Gordon, wrote on 20 November to Fletcher Warren of the same department: 'Axel Wenner-Gren has since November 1, 1939 been constantly steaming in and out of Nassau Harbor on his yacht, equipped with high-powered radio antennae. This yacht is manned by ex-Swedish Navy officers, all of whom, according to my informant, are definitely and professedly pro-Nazi.'

In meetings with Wenner-Gren, the Windsors agreed with him on his policy of supporting a separate peace with Nazi Germany. They also arranged for him to meet the pro-Nazi General Maximino Camacho, brother of the Mexican president, an improper act since Anglo-Mexican diplomatic relations had been broken off. The purpose was to transfer money to Mexico.

Early in December, Wallis suffered from a severe dental problem which needed to be treated immediately. She would, she said, have to be operated on by a periodontist, Dr Horace Cartee, in Miami. The Windsors were stubbornly bent upon going to the mainland.

Of course, Cartee could have been flown to Nassau. In the mean-time President Roosevelt had been triumphantly re-elected, and it was now agreed in Washington that he should go to the Bahamas for the long-deferred meeting to forestall the duke's coming to see him. The Colonial Office was still opposed. Lord Lloyd pressed the couple to avoid the encounter, and also skilfully engineered the duke's requested leave dates to coincide with the very period in which the president was due. Then, by a quirk of fate, the *Munargo*, the passenger ferry to Miami, had to be dry-docked because of engine trouble. Ironically, in order to get rid of the Windsors during the week of 9 December, the Colonial Office had to authorize them to sail on Axel Wenner-Gren's *Southern Cross*. They were thus pitched directly into a situation that under normal conditions would be considered highly inadvisable.

The party sailed on schedule. It included Harold Holder, who was under investigation for anti-British sentiments, Piper Alistair Fletcher and Evelyn Fyrth. The *Southern Cross* docked in Miami, causing a great deal of critical comment in the left-wing press. Twelve thousand people were gathered at the docks to greet the couple, and eight thousand more were lined up along the eight-mile route to the St Francis Hospital. Wallis was in great pain, but showed no sign of it; when she arrived in the outpatients' room, Dr Cartee told her it would be a difficult operation as her jawbone was in a serious condition. She was operated on immediately, and her lower right molar was extracted. There was considerable infection, and her post-operative recovery was miserably slow. That same week Lord Lothian died unexpectedly; a Christian Scientist, he was suddenly taken ill and refused treatment that might have saved him. Stubbornly seizing the advantage of his death, the duke flew in a US naval patrol bomber to the Bahamas. He met Roosevelt after all, in a three-hour visit on board the presidential cruiser *Tuscaloosa* which was anchored off Eleuthera. The duke, with characteristic determination and along with many defeatist state-ments, asked the president on the spot whether he could visit the camps set up for young people during the Depression. This was a way of ensuring that he and Wallis would at last make their way farther on to the American mainland. The question of base sites for the US Navy was discussed, but the results were inconclusive.

The duke flew back to Miami to join Wallis for the return voyage on the *Southern Cross,* and they sailed on 17 December. The duke announced to reporters that he would be happy to accept the post of British ambassador to the United States if he was appointed, a remark that caused disapproval in Whitehall. After a brief cruise of the western Bahamas, Wenner-Gren took the couple back to Nassau.

The trip to Florida had been undertaken in defiance of Churchill's orders and as an act of defiance also against Jane Williams-Taylor's efforts to stop it, seconded by her husband, Sir Frederick, and by her friends Marjorie Merriweather Post, and the Maryland Senator Millard E. Tydings. Soon, the British Secret Intelligence Service would engage the unlikely agents Greta Garbo and her friend, the diet authority Gayelord Houser, to keep an eye on Wenner-Gren and his royal associates.

When the Windsors returned to Nassau, they were told that Fulton Oursler, the prominent American isolationist editor and author whose magazine *Liberty* was owned by that other leading diet guru, Bernarr McFadden, was waiting to see the duke for an interview.

Oursler was unaware of the Windsors' Nazi associations – or at least so it seems. In turn, the Windsors admired *Liberty*, which had engaged Errol Flynn in 1937 as a cover for his Nazi adventures in the Spanish Civil War. What the duke overlooked was that, isolationist or not, Oursler was a loyal, anti-Nazi American.

Oursler had been seeking the interview for weeks. The White House had discouraged it, probably because Roosevelt didn't want Windsor to spout his defeatist views in print at a time of Lend Lease to Great Britain. The British government had similarly vetoed the idea. But Oursler was determined to press ahead. He obtained the support of one of the Windsor's social acquaintances, the wealthy Thomson Rich, who promised to do what he could.

On the plane to Nassau, Oursler had as travelling companion Charles A. Taussig, head of Roosevelt's presidential mission to investigate labour conditions in the Caribbean. Taussig snubbed him and did everything possible to stop the Windsor interview from taking place.

But then, Thomson Rich turned up suddenly and showed

Oursler a letter which Captain Vyvyan Drury, the duke's aide-de-camp, had written to Roosevelt saying that the duke would be pleased to receive Oursler at any time. Just how Rich had obtained the letter he chose not to explain.

Oursler secured a meeting with Drury on the 18th; he was astonished to see the ballroom walls at Government House lined with much of the Windsors' luggage – still unpacked after more than four months. Drury was cordial and said that the duke would be pleased to receive him at six o'clock that night.

The duke strolled into the drawing room at the appointed hour, shook Oursler's hand and offered him a seat. Oursler plunged right in. He asked Windsor what he thought of the collaborationist Marshal Pétain's act of removing his second-in-command Pierre Laval; in fact, Laval had been reinstated in a matter of days, but the question brought a hoped-for expression of approval of Pétain that proved Windsor's support of Vichy. Oursler also spoke of Italy's 'defeat' – actually, a minor frontier setback – and put forth the deliberately absurd statement, designed to provoke his interviewee, that Italy's collapse before the Allies would cause an anti-war revolution in Germany that would result in Hitler's removal by the masses. The Duke fell into the trap. He said, irritably:

> That is wishful thinking, Mr Oursler. There will be no revolution in Germany and it would be a tragic thing for the world if Hitler were to be overthrown. Hitler is the right and logical leader of the German people. It is a pity you never met Hitler just as it is a pity I never met Mussolini. Hitler is a very great man.

He added:

> Do you suppose your president would consider acting as a mediator when and if the proper time should arrive?

Oursler replied that the president would do so if he thought it in humanity's best interests. But he hadn't seen him in three months and that was only a guess.

Windsor plunged in deeper:

> Few people are aware what a serious situation Britain is in. England is blockading Germany but Germany is blockading

England. The submarine losses are enormous and getting worse, and creating havoc. The time is coming when something has to be done. Someone will have to make a move.

His pulses racing, Oursler flew to Washington where the president granted him an audience at the White House. He repeated every-thing Windsor had said and Roosevelt shook in anger, mentioning the high-level appeasement group in England that Windsor repre-sented. The president was appalled by the duke's expression of Hitler's greatness and the certainty of a revolution in England; he knew that such a revolution would ensure Windsor's placement on the English throne.

It was then that he delivered the bombshell about the nine short-wave Paris radio broadcasts to Berlin that relayed information supplied by Windsor to the German government. The president discreetly made no mention of Bullitt, whom he despised and had now dismissed. He said:

After [the broadcasts] it was suggested to the duke he go to Cannes with his wife and stay there.

Oursler never published the whole story. His son, Fulton Junior, says he feared for his life if he did so. Instead, he published a much milder version, which in itself annoyed Churchill and King George VI; had the full account appeared it would, in Oursler Senior's words in his diary, have 'blown the lid off the English throne'.

It is clear today, from recently declassified documents of the British Foreign Office, that Roosevelt deceived Oursler in the matter. So far from being appalled by appeasement policies of Hitler, he had been involved up until May, when the new prime minister Winston Churchill swayed him, in continuing attempts to appease Nazi Germany and bring the war to an end. The only difference was that, instead of initiating such a plan, as Windsor suggested, he would support Britain under the table, and once Whitehall had put out the feelers to Berlin, he would bring the matter to Hitler.

The inspiration for this ignoble idea came from Sumner Welles of the State Department, an old friend of Roosevelt's who had been at school with him at Groton. Welles, as special emissary to

Italy, had been unduly impressed by Mussolini, King Victor Emmanuel and Count Ciano, and believed that they might act as intermediaries with Hitler, as (he said) none wanted war, despite the fact that Italy had entered it that summer – the Führer's incompetent ally.

Lord Lothian had met Roosevelt secretly on 5 April to discuss the president's plan for a negotiated peace. Roosevelt ironically matched and echoed the Duke of Windsor's fundamental hope that in any peace arrangement, Germany would retain its 'living space' and would never be cut up into sections then or in the future. All that Roosevelt would require was that Hitler would agree to a European peace force arranged jointly with the United States; the president even went to the unique and improper length of drafting a memorandum for Chamberlain to convey to Hitler on the matter.

The Foreign Office in London was appalled. On 8 April 1940, Sir Robert Vansittart wrote in disgust to Chamberlain, 'We should on no account go into this. It would be a real trap.' He added, 'Let us go on fighting the war. Let us not be drawn into this embarrassing rigmarole by these distant and inexperienced amateurs [Welles and Roosevelt].' He went on:

> These loose ideas [in Washington] are very dangerous. No sane man will consider disarmament unless (a) Prussia is broken up and (b) the German military caste is destroyed. Both these conditions are absolutely indispensable to anything resembling peace and Roosevelt and Welles never mention them. On no account must His Majesty's government be influenced by tyros.

That winter, Frazier Jelke, a well-known New York stockbroker, paid several visits to the Windsors. He was astonished to hear them stating quite categorically to their guests that they were totally opposed to America entering the war. On one occasion, the duke said to Jelke, 'It is too late for America to save democracy in Europe. She had better save it in America for herself.' In view of the expression of such sentiments, which were conveyed by Jelke to Churchill, it is hardly surprising that Churchill felt very strongly, along with the king and Roosevelt, that in no circumstances was the duke to go to the United States, where he might give strength to the isolationists. It is worth noting that at the time many of those isolationists were not merely well-meaning but misguided pacifists, bent upon protecting the lives of young Americans, but were in the direct pay of the Nazi government, a fact that was generally known in Whitehall and to the intelligence services in Washington.

Christmas of 1940 was spent informally, with parties at Government House for the poor children of the islands. The winter season began; now that the weather was more comfortable society flocked as usual from the mainland to Nassau for a series of major events. Axel Wenner-Gren entertained aboard the *Southern Cross*, anchored off Paradise Island; among the guests with whom the Windsors became very close was the extrovert James D. Mooney, European chief of General Motors.[3] After failing to obtain a visa for London because of the intercession of Sir Robert Vansittart, Mooney was travelling in the Americas with a charter from Goering to negotiate peace on Hitler's behalf. Now he was visiting Cat Cay, an island to the north of Nassau, along with another Nazi sympathizer, Alfred P. Sloan, the chairman of General Motors, aboard Sloan's yacht the *René*. According to American intelligence reports, the duke had several meetings with Mooney to discuss plans for a separate peace with Hitler. To protect himself Mooney, according to several sources, had been a double agent for Vansittart for several years; he may possibly have reported on the Windsor–Nazi connections in the Bahamas.

An actual eyewitness of the Windsors' malfeasances in the matter of evading currency restrictions was the British secret agent H. Montgomery Hyde, then on the staff of Sir William Stephenson of British Security Coordination. Montgomery Hyde visited Nassau at the time, observing much to his annoyance that Harold Christie and Maximino Camacho were blatantly having meetings with the duke to discuss arrangements with the Banco Continental that would illegally benefit the Windsors in time of war. Montgomery Hyde declines to state whether he reported this matter to the British and US Treasuries; however, it was already known both in Washington and Whitehall, as numerous documents of the time reveal.

On 25 January 1941, Sumner Welles sent a confidential memorandum to Fletcher Warren of the State Department:

The most recent information I have regarding Mr Wenner-Gren indicates that he is in constant and close touch with the Duke of Windsor and that both of them are seeing a great deal of prominent and influential businessmen, particularly from the Middle Western states, where a strictly commercial point of view would appear to prevail in business circles with regard to relations between the United States and Germany.

There would appear to be certain indications that Mr Wenner-Gren, as well as the Duke of Windsor, is stressing the need for a negotiated peace at this time on account of the advantages which this would present to American business interests. This angle, I think, should be closely observed.

The other information I have is that the brother of the new President of Mexico, General Maximino Avila Camacho, is due to arrive in Nassau early in February, apparently to confer with Mr Wenner-Gren. Reports have reached me that Mr Wenner-Gren is anxious to participate in an American consortium planning the investment of a considerable amount of new capital in Mexico. For all of these reasons I think it is highly important that we have more than the customary routine reports of Mr Wenner-Gren's activities.

Camacho would in fact soon be back in the Bahamas as the Windsors' guest for discussions about setting up a complex of German, American and British interests in Mexico in which the Windsors would be involved.

On 5 February, James B. Stewart, American consul general in Zurich, sent a strictly confidential memorandum to Fletcher Warren. The document, headed 'Alleged Nazi Subversive Activities in the US of James D. Mooney', read in part as follows:

Mr Eduard Winter, formerly General Motors distributor in Berlin, and at present this company's representative in Paris, acts as courier in delivering communications from Mr James D. Mooney, president of the General Motors Overseas Corporation, to high German officials in Paris. Mr Winter has a special passport which enables him to travel freely between occupied and unoccupied France. Mr Mooney is known to be in sympathy with the German government, and the persons who supplied this information believe that the General Motors official is transmitting information of a confidential nature through Mr Winter.

In other words, Mooney was involved in espionage on behalf of Germany. Messersmith, who was now US minister in Cuba, wrote a long report, dated 4 March 1941 which contained this passage:

Something has fundamentally gone wrong with Mooney's [brain], and I consider him a dangerous individual. He is one of those Irishmen who is so against England that he would be prepared to see the whole world go down in order to satisfy his feelings with respect to England. In my opinion, he is as mad as any Nazi and is one of those who nourishes the hope that when the United States may turn fascist he will be our Quisling or our Laval.

Messersmith, unbriefed on Mooney's role as a double agent, also added that the General Motors executive had recently had an affair with the daughter of a well-known German official, 'the girl being somewhat unbalanced in character and a pronounced Nazi'. Mooney was an 'even more dangerous person than Wenner-Gren for the Duke and Duchess of Windsor to be associated with'. The American government intensified its watch on the Windsors. The FBI was not empowered to operate in the Bahama Islands and the OSS was newly formed and somewhat restricted from operating in British territories. Nevertheless, various US secret agents flew to and from Cuba, Florida, Bermuda and Haiti in an effort to try to unravel the truth of what was going on. Meanwhile, German propaganda never ceased to emphasize the Windsors. It was asserted on the radio that in the new order of things the duke would be Viceroy of America and (again) that the British royal family would be banished to the Bahamas in his place. Yet another visitor to Cat Cay at this time was Errol Flynn, ostensibly for deep-sea fishing but in fact to be the guest of Alfred P. Sloan and James Mooney. That egregious film star, with his extensive Nazi connections, had reason to support the discussions of future negotiated peace.

Harold Christie deepened his associations with the Windsors. On 6 February, he gave them the first big party of the season and the first ever by a Bahamian for a governor and his wife. Among the guests were Aunt Bessie, Sir Harry and Lady Oakes, Captain and Mrs Vyvyan Drury, and the Wenner-Grens.

On 4 March, US consul John Dye sent a memorandum marked 'Confidential' to the State Department, indicating that the duchess had been making secret visits to San Juan in Puerto Rico; the source of the information was Mrs William Leahy, wife of the former Puerto Rican governor Admiral Leahy, who was currently US ambassador to Vichy France. Oddly, it was Aunt Bessie who conveyed this information to the authorities. Dye dismissed the report as baseless, but was it? The Foreign Office had grave suspicions in the matter, and it was anxious to prevent either the duke or the duchess from visiting Santo Domingo, where other undesirable contacts might be made; President Trujillo was particularly anxious to have them there; he had important Nazi connections. The British embassy in Washington expressly forbade the Windsors to travel to the island.

With the aid of an extra increment of some £5,000 and an interior decorator from New York, Wallis gradually converted Government House into a comfortable residence. The atmosphere was American rather than British, undistinguished, but at least adequate. But her modest pleasure in improving her living conditions, and her typically energetic work in the Red Cross and in the hospitals and orphanages of the islands were at all times undermined by her deep bitterness and misery in exile. She and the duke never ceased to rail against everyone who had put them into their present predicament, although the duke, to his credit, would not tolerate direct criticism of his brother, sister-in-law or mother, even from Wallis. Wallis had no such sense of restraint. She breathed fire at the merest mention of the British royal family in her presence. Many of her insults made their way back to the palace, with the inevitable results.

On 4 March, the duchess wrote to a friend, P. G. ('Nick') Sedley of the Carter Carburettor Corporation in St Louis, Missouri. Sedley had been assisting her in communicating with Sir Pomeroy and Lady Burton, owners of La Croë, who were living under house arrest in France; in the letter she revealed that she had been paying the rent for La Croë to the Burtons' account at Coutts Bank in

London. She also revealed that she had been sending money to Herman Rogers to pay the wages of Antoine and Anna, her staff at the villa. She was concerned about rumours that the house had been sold. She was determined, she said, to keep La Croë going, no matter what happened in the future. Sedley was acting as a go-between in the matter. He was married to Lady Burton's sister, and his mother, Mrs Sedley, was living at her house at Dinard in northern France. In a letter dated 5 March to a contact of his, Hugh R. Wilson of the State Department, Sedley wrote the following message, which made its way to the Special Intelligence Service:

> I know nothing of these things, but conceivably there might be some German in authority at Berlin who would permit this copy [of the duchess's letter] to be *delivered as a courtesy to you or to the Duke of Windsor, or to both* [author's italics]. It is said that an occasional 25-word message may be sent through and I am trying that, asking whether my people need ready money, but obviously the Duchess of Windsor's message could not be compressed to 25 words, because if I tried to do that, with mention of names and places, the German censor would no doubt hold it up because of lack of understanding, whereas the complete message, as written by the Duchess, is quite clear and harmless from any point of view.

US assistant secretary of state Breckinridge Long, in a note dated 4 April to Mr Sedley, stated that he would be glad to transmit the text of the letter to France, but only with the authority of the British. He would have to get in touch with the British embassy in Washington before he could proceed, since clearly this was on the edge of breaching the security regulations and could be interpreted as going beyond the limitations of the Trading with the Enemy Act. The duchess's letter was forwarded to the Foreign Office in London, where it proved to be of particular interest to Wallis's old enemy Sir Robert Vansittart. As far as it can be determined, the letter was stopped. The fact that Wallis would countenance obtaining the support of the Berlin authorities in order to get a letter through concerning her house was naturally frowned upon in Whitehall.

On 18 March, Churchill sent a cable to the duke saying that the proposed visit to the United States was neither in the public interest nor in the duke's own. Churchill did not object to his cruising the West Indian islands, as long as it was not done in Wenner-Gren's yacht. He continued:

> This gentleman is, according to reports I have received, regarded as a pro-German international financier, with strong leanings towards appeasement, and suspected of being in communication with the enemy. Your Royal Highness may not perhaps realize the tensity of feeling in the United States about people of this kind and the offence which is given the administration when any countenance is given to them.

Referring to the watered-down article in *Liberty*, he added:

> The language, whatever was meant, will certainly be interpreted as defeatist and pro-Nazi, and by implication approving of the isolationist aim to keep America out of the war . . . I could wish, indeed, that your Royal Highness would seek advice before making public statements of this kind.

Churchill had not forgotten his investiture as the Prince of Wales at Caernarvon Castle, and he was still a sentimental godfather and guardian in the last sentence: 'I should always be ready to help as I used to be in the past.'

There could be no relinquishing of the secret watch on the duchess as long as such activities continued. It was not until July that H. Freeman Matthews, first secretary at the US embassy in Vichy, informed the State Department that the telltale letter had actually slipped through the mesh despite the stoppage in London. Breckinridge Long, who had frequently breached the Trading with the Enemy regulations himself (while precluding foreign payments for Jewish refugees because, he said, such payments would be in breach of the act), had passed Wallis's letter under the table via the diplomatic pouch. Ironically, however, as Matthews reported on 16 March:

> Due to the interruption of the pouch and ordinary postal services by the German authorities between the Embassy at Vichy and the American Consular offices in occupied France, the

Embassy has unfortunately been unable to communicate copies of the letter from the Duchess of Windsor to our Consular offices in the occupied zone for transmission to the persons concerned.

On 17 March, Winston Churchill sent a secret message to the duke urging him not to continue his association with the 'pro-Nazi' Wenner-Gren. At the same time as Churchill was issuing his warnings and admonitions to the duke – and, by extension, to Wallis – he was also taking care of the duke's property in France. The following memorandum (X2153/188/503) in breach of wartime regulations was sent by the Foreign Office on 7 April 1941 to the American embassy in Paris:

> Mr Winston Churchill presents his compliments to the United States Ambassador, and has the honour to request that His Excellency may be so good as to ask the United States Consul at Cannes, to pay, from British funds at his disposal, the sum of 44,156.25 Francs (being the equivalent of 250 pounds at 176.625 Francs to the pound) to Mr Herman Rogers, Villa Lou Viei, Cannes, against his receipt for the upkeep of the property of His Royal Highness the Duke of Windsor, for whom Mr Herman Rogers is acting as agent.

Following the watered-down Fulton Oursler interview publication in *Liberty* magazine, on 27 March the duke had dashed off an angry note to Churchill, care of Lord Moyne at the Colonial Office. He began, 'Any repudiation of Oursler article in American press would only serve to attract attention and publicity. Besides, were I to hold views at complete variance with your policies, I would use more direct means of expressing them.' (Of course, he had.) He went on:

> I wonder if [ambassador] Lord Halifax has been long enough in America to be able to predict that a visit of ours would become a show ... In Miami last December ... our visit was most dignified and no harm was done to British interest that I am aware ... The importance you attach to American magazine articles prompts me to tell you that I strongly resent and take great exception to the article in the magazine *Life* of the 17th

The Duke and Duchess of Windsor
in Paris, 1937.

Above: During the controversial trip to Germany in 1937.

Left: The famous meeting with Hitler on 22 October 1937.

Opposite top: Sir Harry Oakes and his wife, Lady Eunice. Sir Harry was murdered in bizarre circumstances on 7 July 1943.

Opposite right: Harold Christie, who many think was behind the murder. He was never charged.

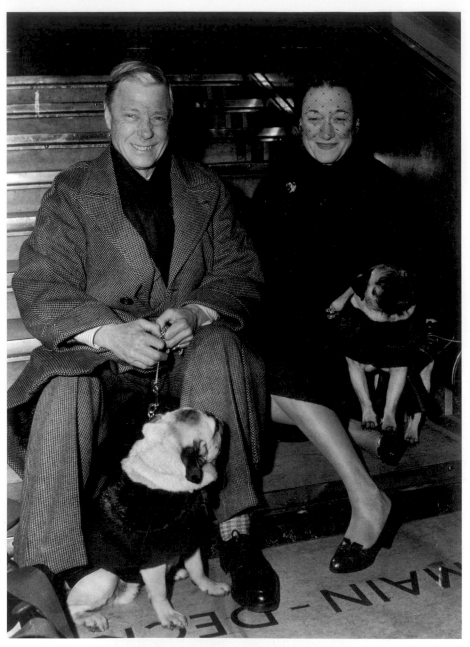

Above: The Windsors arrive in New York in January 1955
on the *Queen Mary*, with two of their pugs.

Opposite top: William Bullitt, US Ambassador to France.
Opposite right: With President Nixon in April 1970,
as guests of honour at a party in the White House.

Above: Receiving Emperor Hirohito of Japan at their
Bois de Boulogne house in October 1971.

Opposite top: The Duchess peers through a window of
Buckingham Palace, five days after her husband's death.

Opposite right: The funeral service for the Duke of Windsor
was held on 5 June 1972 at St George's Chapel.
This photograph shows HM the Queen, the Duchess of Windsor
and the Duke of Edinburgh, followed by the Queen Mother
and King Olav of Norway.

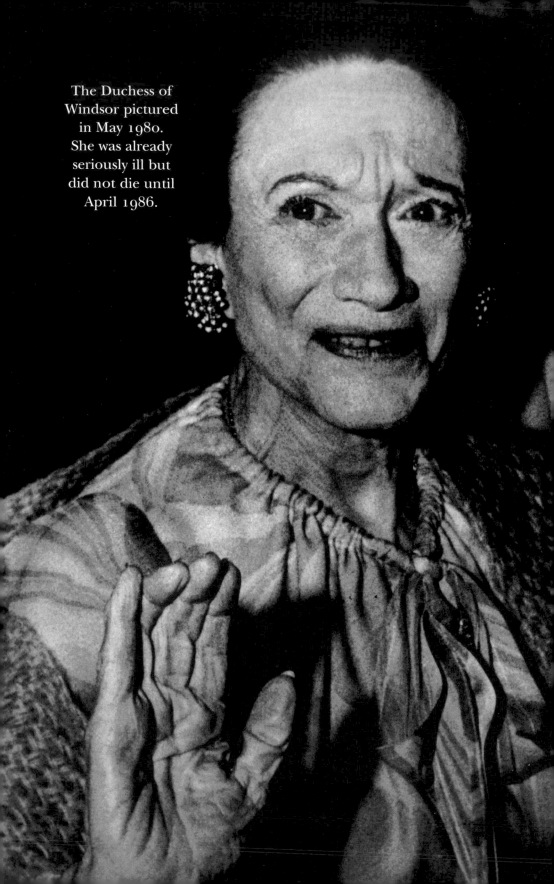

The Duchess of Windsor pictured in May 1980. She was already seriously ill but did not die until April 1986.

March entitled 'The Queen' in which the latter is quoted as referring to the Duchess as 'that woman'. I understand that articles about the Royal Family are censored in Britain before release, and this remark is a direct insult to my wife and is, I can assure you, no encouragement in our efforts to uphold the monarchical system in a British Colony. Added to this is the chronic anomaly of my wife not having the same official status as myself, which is not without its unpleasant and undignified [aspects]. It is not necessary for you to remind me of the sacrifices and sufferings that are being endured by Great Britain ... Had my simple request conveyed to you by [ambassador to Spain] Sam Hoare been granted by my brother, I would have been proud to share these sad and critical times with my countrymen. I have both valued and enjoyed your friendship in the past, but after your telegram FO No. 458 of the 1st July and the tone of your recent messages to me here, I find it difficult to believe that you are still the friend you used to be.

Sir John Colville told the present author of Churchill's fury at this missive; no reply was sent.

On 23 June, a meeting took place in Washington between Hoyer Millar, first secretary at the British embassy, and J. W. Hickerson of the US State Department on an extremely urgent matter. With the collusion of the Windsors and Harold Christie, Wenner-Gren was planning to buy large tracts of land in the Bahamas. Word of this had been transmitted by Hickerson to the war and navy departments. Both departments had informed Hickerson of their hope that the British government would not allow Wenner-Gren to gain control of land in the vicinity of proposed American naval and military bases. Millar was pleased to hear of these responses, and he gave the concurrence of the British government that Wenner-Gren must not be permitted to continue with his plans. The duke rashly interceded on behalf of Wenner-Gren, thus giving his whole game away. He actually wrote to Lord Halifax, British ambassador in Washington, asking him to find out what it might be that the United States government had against Wenner-Gren. The duke claimed that Wenner-Gren was disposed to make large investments in the Bahamas which would be very helpful to the native population, and said that as governor of the islands he, the duke, desired to know officially what reason there might be for 'not approving and encouraging such activities on the part of Wenner-Gren'.

Halifax took this note to Sumner Welles, and they had a discussion in the State Department the same day. Welles explained to Halifax that Wenner-Gren's associations with high-ranking members of the German government were intimate, and he made it clear to Halifax that the Swede's activities could only be regarded as suspicious in view of the world situation. As a result of this meeting Halifax replied to the duke on the 23rd, 'I will look into the matter, but since it is a delicate subject I doubt if I can obtain any information.' The duke's furious reaction can easily be imagined. At the same time Wenner-Gren had joined, along with Sir Harry Oakes, Harold Christie, former senator John D. Hastings, Wall Street speculator Ben Smith, and Ed Flynn, Democratic boss of the Bronx, the Banco Continental in Mexico City. According to US Treasury reports, in the spring of 1941, Camacho yet again had a meeting with the duke and duchess to discuss ways and means of evading British currency regulations at a time when diplomatic and political relations between Great Britain and Mexico had been discontinued following a dispute over oil concessions in 1938. For the Windsors even to confer with such a person on banking matters was entirely in breach of British regulations. It was widely believed that the Windsors had succeeded in siphoning over a million pounds of illegal currency to the Banco Continental through the medium of its various shareholders.

At a Bundles-for-Britain party in Nassau on 21 April 1941, the socialite William Rhinelander Stewart reported to Percy Foxworth of the FBI that the duke had been vigorously singing the words, 'There'll always be an England,' when he suddenly stopped and said, freezing the room, 'There'll always be a Scotland Yard,' almost as if he knew that his hostess, Lady Williams-Taylor, was a British spy. At another dinner party, at Government House, a bagpipe player working for the Secret Intelligence Service accompanied the guests' arrivals. Making an inflammatory anti-British remark to someone at the table, the duke turned to the bagpipe player and said, sharply, 'You can report what I've said to 10 Downing Street.'

Prime Minister Winston Churchill, in a second breach of the

Trading with the Enemy Act, made arrangements of so disturbing a character that only a complete quotation of the appropriate document can fully illustrate it. Restricted by the Foreign Office, the document, dated 7 April 1941, made its way into the State Department and was declassified, for the present author, for the first time on 28 October 1986, under the enumeration NND 70032L. (Biographers since then have ignored it.)

No. X1937/188/503

Mr Winston Churchill presents his compliments to His Excellency the United States Ambassador and, with reference to Mr Achille's letter of 1st March to Sir George Warner of the Foreign Office concerning the property in Paris of His Royal Highness the Duke of Windsor, has the honour to request that the United States Embassy in Paris may be asked to be so good as to make the following payments on behalf of the Duke of Windsor, from British funds at their disposal, the payments to be shown as separate items in their account with the Foreign Office:

1. Rent of 55,000 Francs for the current year, but not to continue the purchase option.

   Renew the insurance, costing 10,000 Francs.

   Pay back wages to Fernand Lelorrain at the rate of 2,000 Francs monthly to 31st December, 1940 and at the rate of 1,000 Francs monthly for January, February and March, 1941, plus 30 Francs daily for food for the whole period. It should be explained to Lelorrain that this latter rate is the rate paid to the servants at La Croë, His Royal Highness's house at Antibes.

   Continue to pay Lelorrain monthly, upon presenting himself, his 1,000 Francs, plus 30 Francs a day for food.

2. The Duke of Windsor would also be grateful if the United States Embassy could enquire the situation regarding his possessions in the Banque de France and pay 15,000 Francs for the current year's rent of his strong room there, which expired last November.

3. Mr Churchill would be obliged if an expression of His Royal Highness's appreciation could be conveyed to the United States Embassy in Paris for the able assistance they are giving to his affairs.

Paris was fully occupied by the Nazis, of course; the Banque de France was totally under Nazi control.

On 11 April 1941, at dinner at Government House, Windsor told his guests that it would be very unwise for America to enter the war against Germany as Europe was finished anyway, and what little help she could give would be too late. Several nights later at another party, the duchess said that if the United States did come into the war it would go down to history as 'the greatest sucker of all time'. And they both spoke of their admiration of Hitler.

The Windsors succeeded in obtaining permission to land once more on United States soil. On 18 April, they sailed to Miami aboard the SS *Berkshire*; they were met by a welcoming crowd estimated at two thousand. The purpose of the trip was to have a meeting with Sir Edward Peacock, head of the British Purchasing Commission and a director of the Bank of England, to discuss financial matters. The British Purchasing Commission was under surveillance by both British and American intelligence. The prominent financiers Montagu Norman, Sir Otto Niemeyer and F. W. Tiarks[4] of the Bank of England were all partners in the Bank for International Settlements in Basle; also on the Swiss bank's board of directors was Dr Walther Funk, president of the Hitler-controlled Reichsbank. The Bank of England had also played a crucial role in stealing the Czechoslovakian gold reserve, sent from Prague in 1938 for safe keeping in London. Montagu Norman had sent the gold of that defeated country directly to Berlin.

The meeting with Peacock was thus scarcely encouraging to Vansittart and the Windsors' other enemies. Not surprisingly, the duke issued a press announcement through Gray Phillips on 19 April, saying, 'The talk [with Sir Edward Peacock] will be private, and no announcement of its contents will be made.' In Palm Beach the Windsors had a meeting with the mysterious Walter Foskett, lawyer to Sir Harry Oakes and Harold Christie, and a partner with both men in a consortium called the Tesden Corporation that was suspected of shady dealings in both the United States and the Caribbean. Foskett also had another connection with the Windsors. He was a member of the board of directors of Alleghany, the massive railway empire of which the presiding genius was the

Windsors' great friend the multi-millionaire Robert R. Young. Young warmly welcomed the couple.

While the Windsors were in Palm Beach in May, they saw a good deal of the handsome socialite Captain Alastair ('Ali') MacKintosh, one of Wallis's first friends of London days; he was a self-appointed informant for the FBI and was about to enlist in the British army. On 2 May, he issued a secret report to J. Edgar Hoover. As a result, Hoover wrote next day to Roosevelt via the presidential secretary, Major General 'Pa' Watson:

> Information has been received at this Bureau from a source that is socially prominent and known to be in touch with some of the people involved, but for whom we cannot vouch, to the effect that Joseph P. Kennedy, the former Ambassador to England, and Ben Smith, the Wall Street operator, had a meeting with Goering in Vichy, France, and that thereafter Kennedy and Smith had donated a considerable amount of money to the German cause. They are both described as being very anti-British and pro-German.
>
> This same source of information advised that it was reported that the Duke of Windsor entered into an agreement which in substance was to the effect that if Germany was victorious in the war, Herman Goering through his control of the Army would overthrow Hitler and would thereafter install the Duke of Windsor as the King of England.

After that memorandum, the Windsors were, in the words of a presidential aide of the time, 'about as welcome at the White House as two pickpockets'. Yet they were allowed to tour the nearby army air base at Morrison Field, which was nearing completion. It was during that visit that the duchess made her first-ever flight, aboard Harold S. Vanderbilt's air transport piloted by Benjamin Thaw's brother Russell. She seemed to enjoy the tour of naval and military installations.

Another event that May was the flight of Rudolf Hess to England. The Windsors' old friend Ernst Wilhelm Bohle was partly responsible for this, though it was generally believed that Hess made the decision on his own. The flight had originally been planned for Spain, where Hess would undoubtedly have conferred with Sir Samuel Hoare.

The Windsors celebrated their birthdays in very severe heat. The day before the duke's birthday Hitler invaded Russia. On 30 June, the duke sent an immensely long letter to Winston Churchill pouring out his feelings. While admitting that 'banishment to these islands was as good a war-time expedient for a hopeless and insoluble situation as could be found', he complained that his services were not rated 'very high by any [*sic*] British government' and that 'I have the same old court clique to thank for keeping me out of my country. I hope the latter is the correct conclusion, but whatever the true facts of the case, I have learned a very good lesson, and that is never to become involved with official England again, from which I intend to extricate myself the day the "cease fire" is sounded.'

He promised to continue in the Bahamas, 'so long as I can conscientiously feel that I am pulling as much of my weight as this restricted appointment allows'. He mentioned the duchess's work for the Red Cross and other local charities, and he complained because Churchill had not advised the king to grant the duchess royal rank. He said his demand was not based upon snobbery, since he would readily drop his own title if the occasion arose, 'but it is to protect her from the world being able to say, and indeed they do, that she has not really got my name. Some newspapers have even gone so far as to infer that ours is a morganatic marriage.' The letter continued to press for the American trip, urging the establishment of a steamship line to the islands and saying that it was important for him to visit the president. He assured Churchill he would not speak against British policy, and he said, 'I have no desire whatsoever to make any speeches outside the Bahamas or to discuss politics, for in these days it is far too dangerous a topic with people's emotions keyed to such a high pitch.' He asked, 'I only wish you would do something to dispel this atmosphere of suspicion that has been created around me, for actually there is a good deal more I could do to help on this side of the Atlantic.'

The Windsors bought a cabin cruiser, the *Gemini*, and toured around in her against orders, meeting their various questionable friends. Wenner-Gren departed for Peru, using the excuse of an archaeological expedition to the Inca ruins, to help set up (or so the FBI believed) a network of pro-Nazi connections in that region. Vincent Astor turned up, on his yacht the *Nourmahal*, on an unofficial investigative mission for Roosevelt; Astor was an unpaid special agent for the president, and the reports that the millionaire sent back to the White House were of great assistance in determining the Windsors' activities.

Meantime, the Windsors stubbornly began planning yet a third trip to America, this time an extended tour that would take them all the way to Canada and the ranch in Alberta. It was virtually a reworking of the cancelled trip of 1937, with a few cities left out. The Foreign Office was understandably alarmed by such a proposal, and in fact Vansittart once again influenced policy against the Windsors. At Buckingham Palace Sir Alexander Hardinge felt equally disturbed by the idea. The anxiety in London was exacerbated by the fact that the Duke of Kent was due to make an official visit to America in August, and on no account must the two brothers be present on the American mainland at the same time. There was still fear of a double kidnapping. It was felt once again that, given their great popularity among an unsuspecting public, the two dukes might easily try to swing their weight behind the various senators and congressmen who wanted to keep America out of the war. But it was virtually impossible to refuse the Windsors' request for the appropriate visas and travel documents. All that could be done was to deny them, once more, full-scale diplomatic assistance or the hospitality of the embassy and the various consulates. They must on no account be given the impression that their visit had even the most tacit approval in Whitehall.

Lunch at the White House was inevitable, since to decline the Windsors' suggestion that they should be entertained there would create unfavourable publicity against the president at a time when it was necessary for him to have complete public support. He was already fighting an undeclared war with Hitler in the Atlantic and was under a storm of criticism in Congress over it. He had begun Lend-Lease, which enabled Britain to be supplied with much-needed war material, and in everything except name was Britain's ally against the Nazis.

At the last minute, Churchill sent the duke a long and deeply felt memorandum, urging him to do everything in his power to influence the Roosevelts – not that they needed influencing – in Britain's cause.

> [Remind the president that] the whole British Empire is one in its inflexible, unwearying resolve to fight against Hitlerism until the Nazi tyranny has been forever destroyed ... This time of struggle and of sorrow might be long, but it cannot last forever. It will only last until victory of the righteous cause has been won.

There was, of course, no chance that sentiments of this noble sort would be conveyed, and in any event the meeting with the president was called off because of a bereavement of Mrs Roosevelt's that week.

By an odd and rather disagreeable coincidence, the week the couple arrived in the United States so did Wallis's Paris lawyer, the Nazi agent Armand Grégoirc. A huge FBI file, accompanied by State Department documents and OSS records, appeared on the desk of Adolf A. Berle, assistant secretary of state, an able and patriotic man who reported directly to the president on secret intelligence matters at regular weekly meetings. Often bypassing the FBI, Berle used his own information, gleaned from a network of cypher-trained vice-consuls acting as spies in neutral countries overseas. He was in many ways the equivalent of Sir Robert Vansittart, who had now retired. Berle shared Vansittart's unfavourable view of the Windsors; he was certain they were Nazi collaborators. He found an ally in George Messersmith, now minister to Mexico, who no longer adhered to his moderate view of the duke and duchess. Their connections with Wenner-Gren, whose Nazi links were known to Messersmith in Berlin and Vienna, had been sufficient to make that accomplished diplomat their enemy.

The Grégoire file proved to be of interest to Berle. It spelled out the French lawyer's representation of the duchess in 1937, and it revealed his handling of Ribbentrop and Sir Oswald Mosley as well as Ernest Simpson's French and German shipping contacts. Berle kept a watch on Grégoire for the next twelve months, tracing him to Berkeley, California; he authorized Grégoire's seizure and imprisonment by the department of justice in March. In jail for the rest of the war, defined as a Nazi agent, Grégoire was tried and found guilty of collaboration with Germany by the French government in 1946 and sentenced to hard labour for life.

The Windsors' position was not aided by the fact that they were taken from Miami to Washington on a special train supplied by the millionaire president of Alleghany, their old friend Robert R. Young. John Balfour, basing his statement upon evidence,[5] wrote in his memoirs that Young was a Nazi sympathizer. Young was yet another in the long line of wealthy people who wished to create a negotiated peace with Hitler. He had been introduced to the Windsors by a member of the Alleghany board of directors, Walter Foskett, the prominent and questionable Palm Beach lawyer who was both partner and friend of Harold Christie and Sir Harry Oakes in the much-investigated, allegedly shady Tesden Corporation.

In view of the nature of the Windsors' host, whose bulging file was already on Berle's desk, it is not surprising that the couple received a chilly welcome when their train chugged into Union Station, Washington, on 25 September. The chargé d'affaires was notable by his absence, the other British and American officials cold and unwelcoming. The unsuspecting public, always the last to know about anything, cheered the duke and duchess as they made their way to the embassy. On this occasion, the ambassador, Sir Ronald Campbell, proved to be at least polite. In the wake of President Roosevelt's re-election the previous year the Foreign Office, presumably under Churchill's guidance, this time did not refuse to allow the ambassador to give at least the appearance of hospitality to his erring visitors. Despite the cancelled lunch at the White House the Windsors actually made their way there; the president, unaccompanied by his disapproving wife and no doubt apprised of their activities to the full, gave them a token welcome. His motive was still the securing of those troubled bases in the Bahamas.

At the National Press Club the duke, with the duchess looking smilingly on, delivered a much watered-down version of Churchill's suggested patriotic address; unwisely but predictably, he removed the more aggressive elements and replaced them with an outrageous call for peace, in direct contradiction of Churchill's insistence on unconditional surrender and the total destruction of Germany. That evening, a number of high-ranking officials of Roosevelt's cabinet came to a party for the duke and duchess at the British embassy. Among the guests were Berle, seeing first-hand what he was up against, and the strongly anti-Nazi secretary of the Treasury, Henry Morgenthau, who also had highly damaging files on the Windsors on his desk and feigned friendliness in order to lay the ground for obtaining more information in the future.

The duke and duchess gave a party for old friends and relatives, including Lelia Barnett and several Warfields. Then they left for Canada to see the royal ranch in Alberta. They were rapturously received, the duchess noted excitedly, as they travelled through the Midwest, the centre of isolationism. The crowds were filled with large numbers of German-Americans who had elected pro-Nazi politicians as senators and congressmen, including the dangerous Montana senator, Burton K. Wheeler, the best friend of Robert Young. The isolationist *Chicago Tribune* announced the Windsors' arrival in huge headlines, embarrassingly endorsing their appease-ment stance. They crossed into Canada whose prime minister, Churchill's friend Mackenzie King, was in an embarrassing position, since he had not wanted the Windsors to come; he knew their record too well. The Royal Canadian Mounted Police not only guarded the Windsors but kept an eye on them throughout their visit. Finally they arrived at the ranch, handsomely situated in magnificent countryside, and Wallis much enjoyed the rest of the trip. The duke dreamed of striking oil on the ranch; there was much discussion with the duchess of selling the property in return for his retaining fifty per cent of the petroleum rights. He was to call this off at a later stage, on her advice, and start to drill for himself.

In the couple's absence the Bahamas were swept by a disastrous hurricane. It would have been advisable for the Windsors to have returned to take care of the situation, but they did not, causing much criticism among the blacks whose properties had been wiped out.

The Windsors went on to Baltimore, where they visited Lelia Barnett. Wallis was delighted to see her uncle, General Henry M. Warfield, at Salona Farms in the Harford hunting country. Uncle Henry was waiting for the couple at the station, along with a large crowd of cheering people. The duke and duchess very much enjoyed their stay at the farm, which was only a few miles away from Oldfields School and Solomon Warfield's house, Manor Glen. Wallis was delighted to show the duke paintings of the clan. She did not go to Oldfields; the reason may have been that Mary Kirk Raffray had recently died. The Windsors returned to Baltimore for a full-scale motorcade attended by two hundred thousand cheering people. During the procession, Wallis caught a glimpse of 212 Biddle Street, in which she had spent so much of her youth. She was delighted at a country club reception when an elderly lady came up to her and announced that she was Ada O'Donnell, her kindergarten mistress.

While the Windsors were enjoying the delights of Baltimore, a naval intelligence report on them, dated 14 October, appeared on the desks of Adolf Berle and J. Edgar Hoover. Supplied by Major Hayne G. Boyden, naval and air attache of the US Marine Corps, it read:

> During conference in German Legation [in Washington D.C.] Duke of Windsor was labeled as no enemy of Germany. [He was] considered to be the only Englishman with whom Hitler would negotiate any peace terms, the logical director of England's destiny after the war.
>
> Hitler well knows that Edward at present cannot work in a matter that would appear to be against his country and he does not urge it (a reliable informant on close terms with a Nazi agent reported). But when the proper moment arrives he will be the only one person capable of directing the destiny of England.

That weekend, the couple stayed with Wallis's old friend, Mrs Sterling Larrabee, at Oakwood, Warrenton, Wallis's home during the first weeks of sitting out her divorce from Winfield Spencer. The Windsors continued to New York City for a five-day visit that at first turned out to be something of a disappointment. Fewer than twenty people, all of them reporters or railway workers, were on the platform when the duke and duchess stepped off the train. They made their journey through almost deserted streets to the Waldorf Towers in a custom-built limousine supplied to them by GM's Alfred P. Sloan. Vyvyan Drury met them at the hotel; they were delighted with their twenty-eighth-floor suite, a magnificently preserved art-deco masterpiece overlooking the sweep of Park Avenue. The duchess was suffering from recurrent stomach ulcer pains and she saw three specialists during the stay. Either separately or together, the duke and duchess visited various housing developments, baby crèches and clubs. When they went to City Hall, they received a welcome from a much larger crowd as they were greeted by the mayor, the ever-popular Fiorello LaGuardia, whom Wallis loved.

She was delighted that the Herman Rogerses were in town. Rogers had finally left France after initiating the Voice of America broadcasts that were proving to be of great value in stimulating anti-Nazi feeling in the Americas.

By now, thousands of people had poured in from out of town in response to widespread publicity of the royal visit, and they swept down on the Windsors en masse everywhere they went. The duke and duchess continued to Detroit. There, they happily joined Guy Trundle's employer Henry Ford for tea; they had much in common with Ford, who had been a favourite of Hitler's and had published in his *Dearborn Independent* a reprint of the notorious forgery 'The Protocols of the Elders of Zion', an outrageous anti-Semitic tract. Hitler had Ford's photograph on display in his Brown House in Munich. At the time of the duke's visit, and even after the United States entered the war a few weeks later, Ford was building trucks and armoured cars for the Nazis in occupied France, a procedure he would follow until the end of the conflict.

The duke also visited General Motors, which likewise retained German connections even after Pearl Harbor; James D. Mooney received them.

On 18 November 1941, Sir Ronald Campbell, now the ambassador in Washington, sent a personal and secret memorandum to Anthony Eden in London, saying that Henry Morgenthau, Jr, Secretary of the Treasury, was inquiring about the dollars which the Windsors used during their visit to the United States. The memorandum stated: 'The Secretary of the Treasury made it plain that he was not asking the question for frivolous reasons but because there were stories going about in connection with which information was required ... The United States Treasury are checking on any dollar accounts which the Duchess may have in the United States.' Campbell continued, 'If you wish to avoid supplying any information, can you give me a formula for reply?' The surrounding documents are missing from Lord Avon's files at the Public Record Office in London, but it is clear from this memorandum that the gravest suspicions had yet again been aroused of the Windsors' improper use of currency against all the restrictions in force at the time. Documents located in the National Archive in Washington, DC, indicate that the couple had obtained even more black market currency through Wenner-Gren.

Eventually, the Windsors returned to Miami. For the second time in her life the duchess got into a plane, for the return to Nassau.

On 7 December, the Japanese attacked Pearl Harbor. Immediately, President Roosevelt declared that a state of war existed with Japan. However, despite the fact that Japan was part of the Axis, the United States did not declare war on Germany. Hitler consulted Ribbentrop, asking him whether it would now be necessary for Germany to declare war on America. Ribbentrop advised the Führer that the terms of the present Tripartite Pact between Germany, Italy and Japan called for aggressive action by each partner if another partner was subjected to attack or invasion. Since Japan was the aggressor in this instance, the terms of the pact did not apply. However, Hitler decided to declare war because of information that the *Chicago Tribune* had published on its front page. Based on a leak from the US War Department, the article stated that Roosevelt planned, in an operation entitled Rainbow Five, to invade Europe and defeat Germany in 1943. The leak was made by Robert R. Young's close friend Senator Wheeler.

After Pearl Harbor, Charles Lindbergh held a meeting of the pro-Nazi America Firsters, at which he stated that, although he had no quarrel with Germany, he was disgusted by the yellow hordes of Japan threatening the United States; the duke expressed an equal horror of the 'Nipponese hordes'. While he was appalled by news of the attack, because clearly it would end forever the chance of a negotiated peace with Germany, he would, like Lindbergh, fight Japan. The duchess was, according to her biographer Michael

Bloch, 'thrilled by the news' of Pearl Harbor. What does this mean? Was she delighted that America was entering the war, thus ensuring a swift end to the conflict, or was she pleased it had been attacked?

Seven days after Pearl Harbor, under the most severe pressure from Whitehall and Washington, Axel Wenner-Gren was blacklisted for the duration of the war. In view of the fact that the Swede was a resident of the Bahamas, the duke was placed in the awkward position of having to sign the blacklisting document himself. Among the companies included in the document was the Bank of the Bahamas, in which the duke and duchess had a substantial interest. Other companies were listed, all quite clearly having German connections. Wenner-Gren was on his way to Mexico at the time, aboard the *Southern Cross*, and he was compelled to stay at his house in Cuernavaca until the end of the war. All his operations in the Bahamas were closed down. President Roosevelt, under-secretary of state Sumner Welles and Adolf Berle were jointly responsible for the action that was taken. As stated by Berle in a memorandum to the president, dated 9 February 1942, the purpose was 'to put Wenner-Gren out of the general promoting business to make it perfectly plain that he was politically unacceptable in the United States. I should not think it necessary to go further at this time.'

There were other reasons. A British intelligence report dated 29 January 1941 stated, 'Wenner-Gren is ... attempting to form in America a cartel to control the wood trade, and this has been discussed with various persons who have got the impression that his real object is to cut off Britain's supply of wood.' Most seriously, Wenner-Gren was a partner in the H. A. Brassert Company, which had multi-national connections and had offices in both New York and Berlin; it was handling Goering's affairs in the steel industry. The Treasury was interested in the possibility that, through Brassert and the Bank of the Bahamas, Wenner-Gren had assisted the Windsors with investments and had transferred laundered money owned by them through the Banco Continental.

There was much discussion in 1942 of U-boat sightings in the Out Islands of the Bahamas. The duke said he was still fearful that he and the duchess would be kidnapped and exchanged for Rudolf Hess. As a result the guard, both British and American, was greatly increased in the islands. The duke bombarded London with tele-grams expressing the gravest concern over the situation.

Wallis was afraid to go out of doors; there was considerable labour unrest in Nassau and throughout the rest of New Providence island. Conditions, already very bad, were not helped by the depar-ture of Wenner-Gren, whose tenants in many cases were left home-less. The Windsors once again ran into trouble with the British Secret Intelligence Service and the FBI. William Stephenson, head of British security coordination in New York, found out through his censorship office in Bermuda that a letter addressed to Prince Rudolfo del Drago in Rome from Wallis's close friend Mrs Harrison (Mona) Williams, later the Countess von Bismarck, contained a card from Government House used only by the Windsors. On the card was a message, the contents of which are still classified in 2004, from Major Gray Phillips, who used the code name Grigio. For Phillips to communicate with a resident of an enemy country was in breach of the Trading with the Enemy Act. By now, British and American authorities on both sides of the Atlantic, all the way up to the White House and Buckingham Palace, were finding their worst suspicions of Wallis and her contacts confirmed. However, the matter was allowed to drop. In a memorandum to the Nazi agent Charles Howard Ellis, planted on Stephenson's staff and occupying the role of British consul general in New York, the duke wrote, with unconscious humour:

> I am entirely satisfied with [Major Phillips's] explanation of this incident, and that his endeavour to communicate with an Italian was in no way prompted by any sinister motive . . . I can vouch for his integrity. I hope, therefore, that under the circumstances British Security Coordination will overlook the serious breach of security regulations which he has unfortunately committed.

In April 1942, Harold Christie was negotiating with Sir Harry Oakes to sell him a substantial stretch of land, which in turn would be sold to the British government for use as an RAF base. The land adjoined the existing Oakes Field, which was used as a civil airport. Oakes was quibbling over the price and Christie went behind his back, making arrangements to sell the property at a high price to a questionable American syndicate. The syndicate, in turn, would make a substantial profit by reselling land that in the first place should have been given to Britain in support of the war effort. It was not until several months later that Oakes realized he had been double-crossed.

In May 1942, the Windsors were thinking of visiting South America, but Anthony Eden sent Churchill a memorandum dated the 14th strongly discouraging such a move. Latin America was torn apart by Nazi influences and, Eden added, '[such a visit] would certainly arouse suspicions in Washington'.

On 28 May, the Windsors returned to Miami aboard the *Gemini*; they went on to Washington and joined the Rogerses at a small luncheon at the White House. In their absence the long-smouldering fires of anti-white hatred and resentment burst into flames in Nassau.

On 1 June, there was a full-scale riot. Wallis was appalled when the duke told her that black workers had looted and pillaged Bay Street. The US Marines arrived, in the guise of military policemen, on direct instructions from the president; all businesses closed down and there was a general strike. Soon the rioters had swelled to two thousand in number, demanding that the government act immediately to improve their conditions. Finding no response, they used anything they could carry, from broken bottles to antique swords snatched from the local museum, to smash the shop windows, hurl the contents into the street and invade the bars where they consumed large quantities of liquor. When British troops, led by the Cameron Highlanders, confronted them, they beat up one of the Scots soldiers violently. The Highlanders shot at random into the crowd, killing seven and injuring forty others. In a lull in the fighting there was a hysterical meeting of leading businessmen, who demanded that the acting governor, Colonial Secretary Leslie Heape, act immediately. Lieutenant Colonel R. A. Erskine-Lindop, commissioner of police, was under particular fire from Christie, Oakes and the other business leaders for not having acted promptly. A curfew was instituted in Nassau. That night, two blacks were shot and killed. Reports reached Government House that the mob had set fire to the local Grant's Town public buildings, including the police and fire stations.

Leaving the duchess behind in Washington to shop and visit

friends with Aunt Bessie, the duke returned to Nassau immediately. Despite the fact that he was opposed to blacks joining local clubs or having any place in government, his personal charisma in a British colony, his charm and presence, ensured a sudden cessation of the local insurgence. To give him credit, the duke did his best to achieve a semblance of order. He no doubt enjoyed his first serious challenge as governor, and it must not be forgotten that the blood of Empire ran in his veins. Although he would undoubtedly rather have been Viceroy of India, he still took pleasure in making high decisions even in this unlikely place. He calmed down the jangled nerves of the ruling clique, the Bay Street boys, and, on advice well taken from Eric Hallinan, Attorney General of the Bahamas, set up a commission of inquiry. On 8 June he broadcast to the people of the islands in a tone of imperial authority and not a little condescension, urging general cooperation and somehow contriving to give his listeners the impression that, while he was intensely pro-black, he would not tolerate any further displays of rebellious lack of discipline.

The duke telephoned Winston Churchill in London and told him of these events. Churchill's response, on 10 June, was to offer him slyly the governorship of Bermuda, describing it, in a letter of that date, with a certain amount of tongue in cheek, as 'a key point in the relationship between Great Britain and the United States with a better climate than Nassau'. Since this was an even more meaningless post than his present one – Bermuda was not more than a flat and featureless holiday resort with a naval base – he rejected the idea on the 10th. As it happened, President Roosevelt had a motive the duke no doubt saw through: Bermuda was the headquarters of the British censorship and espionage operation in the North Atlantic and whereas Lady Williams-Taylor had failed in her authorized mission to keep Windsor away from Wenner-Gren, Sir William Stephenson, head of the Secret Intelligence Service in North America, with frequent stays in the Bermudan capital of Hamilton, perhaps would not.

Windsor seized the opportunity to return to the United States on 12 June to obtain advice from Roosevelt. As in all their previous encounters, the president gave the impression of sympathy and interest, acting with his customary skill a role meticulously rehearsed and typical in its fully realized falsity. In fact he said nothing of interest; with great geniality he left the duke to fend for himself in the situation.

Meanwhile, Nassau looked as though it had been struck by another hurricane, with storm shutters hastily nailed to the great gashes and holes in the public buildings. The duke joined Wallis in New York on the 17th, celebrating her birthday there two days later, followed by his own on the 23rd. On 27 June, they joined Herman and Katherine Rogers aboard the *Gemini*, sailing through a storm.

No sooner had they returned to Nassau than a new and dramatic incident occurred. The duke and duchess were sitting with Mr and Mrs Rogers, celebrating Katherine's birthday on the 28th, when they were astonished to see fire bursting out of Bay Street and flaring against the sky. Accompanied by Sergeant Harold Holder and a butler from Government House, the duke, as excited as a schoolboy, ran along the street and began helping the volunteer groups and the fire brigade. In a fit of heroics, he began running in and out of buildings to see if anyone was trapped. He and the duchess formed chains with numerous citizens to try to salvage furniture and equipment. The culprit turned out to be a local businessman seeking to collect on his fire insurance.

The Bay Street boys were furious with the duke for failing to take extreme measures against the looters and arsonists in the riots. His own policy – to avoid a full-scale revolution which would place himself and the duchess in mortal danger – was sensible enough: pragmatic rather than liberal, as some people considered it. While he faced many angry complaints, the summer heat once more intensified unbearably. Then came shattering news.

At 1.15 p.m. on 25 August, the Duke of Kent had taken off with eleven other people in a Sunderland flying boat from Invergordon, Scotland, en route for Iceland.

Shortly afterwards, the plane crashed, killing all except one man aboard, Rudolf Likus, Ribbentrop's chief of intelligence in the German Foreign Ministry, made a statement, issued widely through the various media, that:

> The so-called accident has been engineered by the nefarious
> British Secret Intelligence Service to get [Kent] out of the way

before he would embarrass the royal family any further with his outspoken sympathies for the German cause.

Ladislas Farago, formerly of the US Office of Naval Intelligence, recorded this fact in his book *The Game of the Foxes.*

The biographer Martin Allen wrote to the present author on 4 July 2003:

> The Duke had descended into the murky world inhabited by British Intelligence, and so it is not impossible that he was becoming a problem, had outlived his usefulness. My father knew Freddy Winterbotham [of the SIS], and in a discussion they had in the late 1970s, asked him about the matter. My father said that all Winterbotham would say was that 'We got rid of Kent as we got rid of the Sikorski problem.'

The reference was to an almost identical air crash of July 1943 involving Wladyslav Sikorski, premier of Poland in exile. According to Winterbotham, the method used was sulphuric acid on the insulation wires.

How was this supposedly done? With no knowledge of the actual murder, Georg von Zirk, a former Luftwaffe pilot, explains:

> If you wanted to destroy a flying boat in those days, a member of the ground crew would be engaged to carry out the job. He would fit a bottle, rather like those used in hospitals for intra-venous feeding, to a section of the internal insulation wiring, and, using a timer, allow it to drip, drop by drop, until the connections were burned through. Then, when the plane took off, it would only be a matter of minutes before it lost altitude; the pilot would try to make a forced landing but it would already be too late.

What reason can there have been for Sir Stewart Menzies of the SIS to take so desperate a step as eliminating the king's brother, a possible heir to the throne?

According to Martin Allen, there was a primary reason in Kent's increasing drunkenness and outspokenness on his missions. Bitter and disappointed in tasks in navy and air force, and jealous of his royal cousin Lord Louis Mountbatten, he was unhappy in his life.

The war he had so desperately wanted to avoid, hence his many missions to Germany, filled him with horror; his numerous letters to Prince Paul of Yugoslavia, exiled under arrest to Kenya by Winston Churchill, show hatred of Germany for betraying his trust, but at the same time no love of his own country either. Instead of the burning patriotism expressed by his brother King George and sister-in-law Queen Elizabeth, his letters are full of misery. And misery and drunkenness can cause so egregious a personage to be a dangerous potential security leak, especially since he was privy to both British and American air-force activities and German spies were active in his frequent destinations of Canada and Iceland.

Kent had an intriguing connection to William Bullitt, over-looked by historians. In a dissertation for a master's degree in economics at Cornell University in the United States, the scholar Jonathan Victor Marshall showed the two men involved in a highly questionable matter concerning the purchase of bomber planes in Canada, which led to personal profit and to security leaks to Germany that caused considerable concern in Whitehall. By their working with French contacts, over a million dollars was extracted from the Banque de France in one swooping measure; in view of Kent's comparative lack of grasp of money matters, Bullit must bear the brunt of the blame for this. But Kent's close contact with General Spaatz of the US Army air force in terms of securing vital information as liaison was thought to be highly dangerous by the British Secret Intelligence Service, especially in view of his drinking and looseness of mouth.

Another motive for murder (if murder it was) can be found. Allen says that Kent had been involved in a complex scheme to lure to England the same British-born Nazi agent Ernst Wilhelm Bohle who had met with the Windsors in Germany; the purpose was to pretend to set up a negotiated peace, while capturing Bohle on a flight to Scotland. Bohle could be a fount of information on Hitler's high-level tactics. Kent had been chosen for the task because of his links to Nazis in the 1930s, particularly in Munich; he was allowed to work with the Duke of Buccleuch, recently dismissed from the royal household for his Nazi sympathies, because Buccleuch also had made connections in Germany.

As it turned out, Rudolf Hess flew famously to Scotland in

Bohle's place; his flight and landing were put down, by both German and British government sources, as the random trip of a madman. Martin Allen states that the truth of his coming as a result of an invitation by Kent towards peace discussions had at all costs to be hidden from the world – and the Germans also wanted it hidden. Thus, if Kent was getting drunk and talking loosely, was it not possible that, particularly in Iceland, where the American press had representatives, and in Newfoundland, his next port of call, the biggest secret of the Second World War might leak and bring disgrace on the English government? Nigel West (Rupert Allason), the authority on the Secret Intelligence Service, believes the crash was caused by the fact that the duke and the captain and some crew members were drunk on takeoff. Yet the reliable Winterbotham's account, in the absence of any other explanation, has the ring of authenticity. The final truth may never be known. As for Kent's role in the Hess mission, West and other historians have dismissed it out of hand. Until further documentation emerges, that matter too must remain a case in which the jury is still out.

Once Kent was dead, his chief German contact towards negotiated peace in Hitler's favour was no longer of value to the Führer. Prince Philipp of Hesse, his brother Wolfgang, his cousin Princess Viktoria Luise, her daughter, now Princess Friederike of Greece, and all other royals who had been involved with Hitler were summarily dropped and in some cases punished. Behind Hitler's dissatisfaction with his former favourites which rapidly turned to hatred was the implacably anti-royal and petit bourgeois propaganda minister Dr Joseph Goebbels, whose diaries of the time show the relentless process whereby he destroyed Philipp of Hesse and Hesse's wife, Princess Malfalda.

Philipp was certain, and not without reason, after the German defeat by the Russians at Stalingrad, that Hitler was a definite liability towards a knitting together of the royal families in the interest of anti-communism and the destruction of Russia. Only by a hasty replacement of Hitler by Himmler and Goering could Germany ally with England and create a new state, in which the German royals could flourish and Russia be defeated. With Kent dead, he was finished, as no doubt Sir Stewart Menzies and Winterbotham knew when they killed Kent; Hitler sent both Philipp and

Malfalda (whom Goebbels accused of poisoning to death the collaborationist Tsar Boris of Bulgaria) to concentration camps.

Ironically, Malfalda died in an Allied bombing raid; Philipp's imprisonment was coincidental with that of the double agent and intelligence chief Admiral Canaris, who was hanged in the same camp and for years had been Menzies's and Winterbotham's contact in Berlin.

The news of his brother's death was a devastating shock to Windsor. Scarcely able to believe his ears, he sobbed like a child when he heard it on the radio. He was in tears again at the memorial service on the 28th. He was so distraught that he forgot to send a letter of sympathy to the Duchess of Kent, an oversight for which he was unfairly criticized. Wallis also failed to write.

Meanwhile, an extraordinary report had been made, now in the Axel Wenner-Gren file of the State Department (RG 59/Box 2682/ K/1940–1944). The following statement is dated 21 July 1942:

> Axel Wenner-Gren is supposed to have according to my information the following sums of money on deposit and now all frozen:
>
> | *London* | $50 millions. |
> |-----------------|------------------|
> | *Bahamas* | $2,500,000. |
> | *United States* | $32 millions. |
> | *Mexico* | Two millions. |
> | *Norway* | $32 millions. |
>
> It is understood that the deposits of $2,500,000 in the Bahamas were made at the express request and *in part for the benefit of* the Duke of Windsor . . . he is a very close friend of the Duke.

Subpoenaed accounts later confirmed the statement, proving the duke's previously mentioned evasion of currency restrictions and his partnership in questionable business organizations.

In the meantime, Churchill continued through the Foreign Office to be concerned with the upkeep of La Croë, the Windsors' property in France. On 11 August, a memorandum was sent from the American consulate in Nice to John G. Winant, American ambassador in London. Marked confidential, it reads in part:

It will be recalled that the Foreign Office authorized payments sufficient for the upkeep of the property up to June 30, 1942. I am now informed by Mr Antoine Carletti, the personal servant of the Duke, that the funds deposited to Mr Herman Rogers' account with the Société Générale at Antibes for the upkeep of the Duke's property are now exhausted. He states that he will be able to manage until about September 15, and accordingly hopes that the money will arrive by that time.

Sometime back, Antoine called to report that he was becoming anxious to know what to do to protect the movable property belonging to His Royal Highness. He referred to eight cases of silver which he had packed up and hidden in his own villa situated nearby, which he recently rented. He has also packed up the china and glassware and is attempting to find a suitable place for the storage of the twenty cases involved. I informed Antoine that there was little this office could do to assist him. However, I expressed approval of the precautions he had taken, to allay his fears. Nevertheless, as he is very conscientious, he is very much concerned at the possible seizure of the silver in the event of occupation by enemy forces.

Antoine asked that His Royal Highness be informed that everything is in good order and that there have been no changes in the personnel.

In the midst of all this high-level improper finagling the duchess was running the local Red Cross in temporary quarters, making charity arrangements for orphans.

The duke opened the Bahamian Legislature on 1 September. At a stormy meeting, members of the House demanded that Colonial Secretary Leslie Heape, Sir Eric Hallinan, senior commissioner for the Out Islands, John Hughes, and Lieutenant Colonel Erskine-Lindop be summoned for immediate action for their disgraceful role in failing to quell the June riots. It was at this moment that, as so often before, the Windsors' guardian angel Sir Walter Monckton turned up from England. He stayed for several days, advising the Windsors to refuse to allow the House to gobble up these officials in any form of kangaroo court. Instead, he said he had made arrangements for a British judge to appear to conduct the authorized commission of inquiry. Sir Alison Russell, retired

Tanganyika chief justice, turned up on 1 October, and the commission convened on the 5th. The report was completed by the end of the month. Erskine-Lindop stood condemned by the evidence for inadequate treatment of the rioters. However, Mr Justice Russell also condemned the wholesale corruption of Bay Street for having brought about the riots in the first place. This pitched the Bay Street figures still further against the duke; in order to avoid a direct confrontation, he sent the report to London with very little comment.

On 8 May 1943, the Windsors undertook their third tour of the United States. The day they arrived at Robert R. Young's Palm Beach house, word reached them that the US government was deporting the Reverend Jardine, who had conducted their religious marriage ceremony in France, and his wife for outstaying their visas. Since there was some suspicion attached to them, the duke said he could do nothing; he let them be sent home. The Windsors travelled again to New York and saw the Ringling Brothers Circus.

They continued to Washington, where the duke took a drastic and revealing step. On the morning of 18 May, he visited the secretary of state, Cordell Hull, not the most sympathetic person in the circumstances, and asked him if he would be good enough to discontinue censorship of Wallis's letters. The request was made under great pressure from Wallis. The duke's own letters were uncensored because he had royal and diplomatic status. Unfortunately for him, the matter wound up on Adolf A. Berle's desk. In a memorandum dated 18 June, addressed to all appropriate government departments, Berle wrote:

> I believe that the Duchess of Windsor should emphatically be denied exemption from censorship. Quite aside from the shadowy reports about the activities of this family, it is to be recalled that both the Duke and Duchess of Windsor were in contact with Mr James Mooney of General Motors, who attempted to act as mediator of a negotiated peace in the early winter of 1940; that they have maintained correspondence with [Charles] Bedaux, now in prison under charges of trading with the enemy, and possibly of treasonous correspondence with the enemy; that they have been in constant contact with Axel Wenner-Gren, presently on our blacklist for suspicious activity, etc. The Duke

of Windsor has been finding many excuses to attend to private business in the United States, which he is doing at present.

Permission for exemption from censorship was denied.

Bedaux, whose desire to maintain his international businesses despite the interruption of war had put him in a position where he was charged with treason, was in prison in north Africa; he would be brought to Miami in 1944. His son, Charles Eugene Bedaux, insists to this day that his father was innocent, saying he was deliberately fooling the Germans about supplying them with plans of pipelines in Africa in order to protect his Jewish friends in France. In support of his case, Bedaux Jr states that his father was, along with his companies, posthumously awarded the Légion d'Honneur and had a street named after him. Berle, J. Edgar Hoover and General Sherman Miles of US military intelligence took a less favourable view. And it is worth noting, too, that after the first wave of condemnation and revenge, the postwar De Gaulle government began reinstating certain figures of Vichy; De Gaulle attended the funeral of Marshal Pétain; and the Académie Française did not eject those of its members who had been of fascist sympathy. By the 1960s, more had been forgiven, and former supporters of the Vichy regime were given certain awards and raised to high office after convenient periods of exile.

Winston Churchill was visiting Washington at this time, and, on 19 May, he delivered a characteristically resounding address to Congress. The duke had two meetings with Churchill, who had never relinquished his belief in his beloved prince. The duke begged Churchill for a new appointment. The prime minister contacted the Foreign Office, the Colonial Office and the Palace, and the result had more than a little black humour.

At that time, Sir Stewart Menzies, tirelessly vigilant in his efforts to obtain still more damaging evidence on Wallis Windsor, sent Eddie Chapman, one of his most peripatetic agents, on a special mission from his native Channel Islands to Germany to retrieve the duchess's files from the Abwehr, showing her continuing contacts with Ribbentrop until at least August 1940. Operating out of Jersey, which was under German occupation, Chapman, posing as a Nazi spy, had undertaken several similar missions for Menzies during the war; he succeeded in bringing not only the duchess's but the duke's Abwehr files back to London, along with Errol Flynn's – no doubt because of the Windsor–Hess–Flynn meeting at the Hôtel Meurice in Paris in March 1938.

On 12 June 1943, the duke cabled Anthony Eden:

> Mr [George] Allen has informed me that my fourteen boxes of documents have been removed from South of France to Switzerland. Will you please convey to the Swiss Government my gratitude and sincere appreciation of their actions in removing my documents to their archives, and their continued interest in the security of my belongings at Cap d'Antibes.

On 4 July, in an echo of the death of the Duke of Kent, the exiled and deposed premier of Poland Wladyslav Sikorski took off from Gibraltar on a secret mission in a Liberator flying boat with the Windsors' and the Duke of Kent's close friend and Pro-Nazi associate, Victor Cazalet of the Anglo–German Fellowship and The Link; Frederick Winterbotham claimed all aboard were killed in a crash arranged by him through the use of sulphuric acid on the insulation lines.

Cazalet, who had acted as Churchill's special emissary in visits to the United States, and Sikorski himself had become security problems because they were playing a dangerous game against the Allies' Russian partners. As in the case of Kent, within an hour the German radio stations accurately announced that Sikorski had been killed by the British Secret Intelligence Service; it is clear that someone at very high level in the SIS was a German/British/Soviet triple agent. Denials were issued very swiftly from Whitehall.

Shortly after the Windsors returned to Nassau, the newspapers announced that Win Spencer had been found bleeding on the porch of his house in San Diego, a knife protruding from his chest. He announced feebly that he had been 'peeling fruit'. Nobody believed him; it was probably a clumsy attempt at suicide. He survived.

NOTES

1 Dundas was known to be anti-American, another reason for Churchill's desire for change.

2 The same day that he authorized the passport, 9 September 1940, Long refused permission for a Jewish refugee ship to land her passengers at Norfolk, Virginia, with the result that many who would have left Germany died in the concentration camps.

3 Protective of his company's substantial holdings in Nazi Germany, Mooney was directly in charge of Hitler's enormous Adam-Opel factories, manufacturing armoured cars and tanks of the type which had led the invasions of Czechoslovakia and France. On 22 December 1936, in Vienna, Mooney had told the Windsors' acquaintance George Messersmith, 'We ought to make some arrangements with Germany for the future. There is no reason why we should let our moral indignation over what happens in that country stand in the way.' In an interview with the *New York Times* on 8 October 1937, the US ambassador to Germany, William E. Dodd, reported that Mooney was part of a 'clique of US industrialists hell-bent to bring a fascist state to supplant our democratic government'. In 1938, Mooney received the Order of the Golden Eagle from Hitler. In April 1939, he conferred with US Ambassador Joseph Kennedy in London, arranging for a visit to that city by Emil Puhl, of the Hitler-controlled Reichsbank, and Helmuth Wohlthat, Goering's American-educated economic adviser. In a series of conferences these men organized a plan: Germany would be given a secret loan of £100–200 million in British gold, and in a future reorganization of Europe Germany would control all currencies through a restoration of the gold standard. Mooney proposed a scheme whereby, in a negotiated peace with Hitler, Germany would receive back her lost African colonies.

4 Friend and adviser of Prince Otto von Bismarck.

5 Balfour was privy to the Windsors' secret file in London, and the whole mass of telegraphic correspondence between the Windsors in Nassau and the Foreign and Colonial Offices in London was automatically sent to him.

16

MURDER IN NASSAU

Despite the many conflicts arising with Bay Street, the Windsors remained friendly throughout the spring and summer of 1943 with Sir Harry Oakes and his partners, Harold Christie, Walter Foskett and (in Mexico) Axel Wenner-Gren. They were also fond of Eunice Oakes and gave a small farewell party for her when she left in June with her sons and daughter for Bar Harbor, Maine, to escape the Nassau summer heat.

However, the duke emphatically did not like Nancy Oakes's husband, Alfred de Marigny, though the duchess had a soft spot for him. He was a prosperous, up-and-coming young businessman in the Nassau community. The brisk and fun-loving de Marigny, facing much criticism in a then racist and anti-Semitic community, was involved in building apartments to which he admitted Jews. He even managed to persuade restricted local clubs to accept Jews as members, and, with a determination that many people found maddening, he pushed for an improvement of water supplies to the impoverished blacks during the many months of drought outside the hurricane season.

Born in Mauritius, de Marigny was a tall, lanky, attractive man with a wide mouth that often curled into a mischievous, challenging and crinkly smile. A charming but opinionated gadfly, possessed of immense vitality, he made the mistake in a tiny, tight community of talking far too loudly and far too often against the people he disliked. Most notably, the objects of his detestation were Oakes and Christie; but above all he hated the Duke of Windsor.

That summer of 1943, de Marigny had become infuriated because water rights had been granted to the well-known travel writer Rosita Forbes, who had bought a large property on New Providence island. As a result of this diversion of the supply, many poor blacks were threatened with thirst and perhaps disease from polluted springs. De Marigny stormed into Government House and demanded to speak to the duke, who listened with barely concealed impatience as he puffed away at a briar pipe. Vyvyan Drury stepped in and said coldly, 'The audience is at an end.' De Marigny shouted, 'You may be impressed by His Royal Highness! He doesn't impress me! Here he is ruling this pimple on the ass of the British Empire! If he amounted to anything, he would be in high office in England or the United States!' From that moment de Marigny was a marked man.

At the same time, Sir Harry Oakes had found out that Christie had sold the land for a new RAF base behind his back to an American syndicate, thus cutting him out of the deal. In revenge, Oakes began to make preparations to call in Christie's IOU notes and repossess Christie's only fully owned asset, his beloved island of Lyford Cay. Christie realized that his whole world was falling apart. With the blacklisting of Wenner-Gren, Christie's partnership in the Banco Continental, the Tesden Corporation and Bahamas General Trust was useless. Oakes was talking about going to the mainland to join his family, planning not to return until the autumn, by which time Christie would be ruined.

What follows is based upon a minute re-examination of the evidence of what would turn out to be one of the most famous unsolved murder cases of the century. Dr Joseph Choi, chief of forensic medicine of the Los Angeles County Coroner's Office; the late John Ball, well-known writer and special adviser to the Los Angeles Police Department homicide division; and Sergeant Louis Danoff of the LAPD all assisted the author in reaching the conclusions presented here. This analysis of the case is based on an inspection of the original autopsy reports obtained from the Bahamas, the evidence given under oath by the Nassau forensic specialists, the recently declassified FBI files, the photographs hitherto unavailable and the judge's notes in the subsequent murder trial transcript. No detail offered here departs from the fully documented (and only now available) facts; the late Alfred de Marigny has also contributed much valuable information and has confirmed the guilt of the murderer, of which he knew from the beginning, but his opinion differed from the present author's in the matter of the murder weapon.

On the evening of 7 July, Sir Harry Oakes entertained a small party of visitors at Westbourne, including Harold Christie, a friend of Christie's Mrs Dulcibel 'Babs' Heneage and Charles Hubbard, a retired Woolworth's executive. Dinner was prepared by the cook, Mrs Fernandez, and served by the maid, Mabel Ellis, at 8.45 p.m. The guests finished eating shortly before ten. They played Chinese checkers until 11 p.m. Christie announced unexpectedly that he had decided to stay the night; a tropical storm was blowing up, and he did not feel like driving home. He had also stayed at Westbourne the previous night. At about 11.15, Hubbard drove Mrs Heneage to her house, which was close by on Eastern Road; Hubbard then drove back to his own house, just a few doors away from West-bourne.

Meanwhile, Christie had dismissed the two night watchmen, one of whom doubled at the Country Club next door, saying that he would take care of the house and grounds. The only people within both view and earshot of the house now were Mrs Newell Kelly, wife of the property's manager who was on a fishing trip to a remote Out Island of the Bahamian group, and her mother, an elderly lady. They were housed in a small guest cottage in the grounds.

It was Oakes's custom to have no doors or windows fastened, bolted or locked at any time, despite the fact that he was so nervous of possible intruders that he constantly changed his bedroom and at all times kept a gun in the drawer of the bedside table, with his pound notes fixed in a Canadian gold money clip underneath the weapon. Like many of pioneer stock, Oakes seemed to invite the prospect of confronting a potential burglar or would-be murderer with a firearm; a very light sleeper, he would often rise several times in the night to prowl around, keeping his weapon ready. He liked having Christie for company, despite the fact that Christie was already plotting against him and that he had never forgiven Christie for going behind his back in the airfield deal. Lady Oakes and their children were still in the United States.

After Mabel Ellis had left at 11.30 p.m., having washed up the dishes and laid the table for breakfast, the wind increased from the sea, sending black waves pounding against the beach below the house. Lightning began to flash in a murky sky. Thunder burst in enormous peals. Rain beat down with the intensity typical of the region. As the storm broke, Christie went up to see Oakes in the master bedroom where the Windsors had slept almost three years before. They talked for a while; at some stage during the conversation Christie laced Oakes's nightcap with a drug that would be sufficiently powerful to give Oakes – a very light, nervous sleeper – a deep, not easily disturbed sleep. Christie watched. After a while Oakes began to show signs of drowsiness. Satisfied, Christie left the room. Sir Harry fell into a profound slumber with a feather pillow pressed for comfort against his body, an oddly childlike habit for a man of sixty-nine. Another pillow was tucked at an angle under his head, with a third tossed aside on the floor. The doomed millionaire tucked the *Miami Herald* for 7 July, which he had been reading, under his right thigh as he turned over on his right side, his face buried in the pillow.

Christie had no time to waste. Leaving all the lights on to give Mrs Kelly and her mother the impression, if they should wake up and look out of the guest-house windows (they did), that he was still inside Westbourne, he went out through a back door and along a newly constructed connecting passage that led to the country club. He walked to the front of the club, looking to right and left to make sure he was not observed. His car was parked there, allegedly to save petrol because of wartime rationing, but actually to enable him to drive off without the sound of his engine alerting Mrs Kelly and her mother. He made his way through the storm into Nassau.

It is not certain where he contacted the hit man whom he had engaged to dispose of Oakes. However it is most likely, in view of his subsequent movements, that he met him at his own Bay Street offices, where any such encounter would be safe from detection. It is possible to reconstruct the nature of the hired killer from accumulated indirect evidence. He was a very short but powerfully built spear fisherman, expert – as Christie was – in the art. He was a member of the Brujeria sect of south Florida, which figured prominently in the Bahamas and emanated from the Congo region of Africa. Its members practised the diabolical cult of Palo Mayombe. An initiate who wished to be involved in murder was required to wear the dead man's clothes. Christie was wearing Sir Harry's pyjamas before, during and after the murder. In Palo Mayombe murder, the head must never be injured except for the precise purposes of the killing itself. It must not be burned, decapitated or in any other way molested. Feathers, spears and gunpowder were invariably used; the gunpowder was placed traditionally in small piles on the floor near the victim and set on fire, causing tiny explosions that would make burns in the carpet and smoke smudges on the walls. Stab wounds to the head were intensely characteristic, because the figure of the diabolical Palo Mayombe god, Eleggua, was portrayed in drawings and paintings with swords or arrows embedded in its cranium. The use of a fishing spear in such killings was common; it was a symbol of the interwoven Abaqua cult, also of south Florida and the islands, a symbol of that particular sub-sect which was committed to ritual assassination and which denied membership to homosexuals.

Palo Mayombe murderers were available for hire in the region. Christie, who was probably, if only for convenience, an adherent of the cult (few who did not belong could obtain hit men for any price), must have imported the nameless killer from south Florida. It would have been too risky to engage the services of a local resident. In so crammed and closeted a society as Nassau, and with so much drinking common in the bars and shanties of Grant's Town, the native district, word of such a person being in the neighbourhood would have spread very quickly.

In a station wagon borrowed for the purpose, the hit man, or an accomplice with the hit man as a passenger, drove Christie through the driving rain and wind along Bay Street, preparing to head towards the beach. As the station wagon swung out round a corner, it was stopped by a traffic light. At that exact instant, Edward Sears, chief of police of Nassau, passed it going in the opposite direction at a distance of six to eight feet and at fifteen miles per hour. He saw Christie clearly through the side window of the passenger seat, but the visibility was not good enough to enable him to make out the driver's face or colour.

The driver took Christie to a girlfriend's house, where he stayed for several hours. His overnight stays at Oakes's two or three nights a week were mere disguises, in a community noted for gossip, for his nocturnal sojourns at that house. His girlfriend was married to a man in the forces.

In the meantime, the station wagon was driven round the back of Westbourne, near the country club, in order not to disturb Mrs Kelly and her mother in the guest house. The hit man climbed the long wooden staircase that led up from the beach to the three levels of the house, his footsteps on the creaky wooden slats muffled by the sounds of the storm. He was carrying with him a fishing spear, gunpowder, matches and an insecticide spray can.

Sir Harry had not moved; overcome by the drug, he still had his face in the pillow with his body pressed against the second pillow. The hit man walked soundlessly across the thick brown carpet towards the bed. He now stood almost exactly level with Oakes's head in its prone position. At extremely close range he hauled back and struck with the fishing spear exactly four times, with ritualistic precision; each time the apex of the triangular spearhead faced in the same direction towards the nose, and the wounds formed were almost exactly equidistant from one another. They made, according to Palo Mayombe tradition, a sort of crescent pattern around and above the ear.

The cuts were at different depths, none deeper than an inch, and were insufficient to kill. The arteries and veins spurted in fountains, drenching the killer in blood. The murderer tried to wipe away the blood from his eyes. He took out his insecticide can and aimed the nozzle at Oakes's chest. Oakes stirred a fraction; at that moment the killer flung a match so that the petroleum-based inflammable liquid caught fire. Then the hit man stabbed the second pillow against the body with his spear. He pulled handfuls of feathers from it and scattered them over the burning body in the time-worn practice of the exponents of the Palo Mayombe black arts.

According to the autopsy report, Oakes died of shock combined with a fractured skull and the fierce heat of the flames. He probably never knew what had happened. At the moment of death, he evacuated so completely that the mattress was soaked through. The burning flesh and the heat made the feathers adhere to him, as the killer had wished. But the effort of committing the murder, and perhaps the effect of drink or drugs, temporarily affected the assailant. He staggered to the opposite wall of the room, leaving his bloody, smoky finger marks at his full height of just over four feet. He tried to wipe the blood from his face and body, using a towel that Sir Harry had left on the second of the two twin beds. Then he flung the towel impatiently on to Sir Harry's bed and began looking for the bathroom, groping through the smoke and still unsteady on his legs.

In doing so, he took a wrong turn and left more bloody marks on the walls of the corridor – even, ironically, on the glass handle of the door to Christie's room and on a panel of the door itself. He turned back, realizing he had made a mistake; at last he found a bathroom and began washing off the blood, leaving some specks on the basin. Meanwhile, Sir Harry's bed had burnt only in small patches; though his body had collapsed under the blazing feathers and the force of the flames, the window had burst open in the storm and the mattress was merely smouldering in its rain-dampened state. In a reflex action the dying man had swallowed some smoke, which, mixed with mucus, had formed a viscous black substance in the digestive tract that (they alleged) puzzled investigating medical personnel and police later on. He hadn't breathed the smoke in; his lungs were unblackened. His nose was too buried in the pillow to allow him to inhale.

The killer had more work to do. Remembering his ritualistic task, he began dropping small mounds of gunpowder on the floor of Oakes's bedroom and the corridor outside, igniting them with his store of matches so that they burned and exploded but did not spread fire through the house. Had arson been his purpose, or an attempt to conceal the crime rather than give it an unmistakable signature, the killer would have brought a blowtorch and used it on curtains, draperies, inflammable chairs, woodwork, paintings and tapestries; none of these was touched. Sometimes he sprayed small amounts of insecticide on the walls or floors, lighting them one by one; again, the fire did not spread. In one place he tried to set a small gunpowder charge on an inside windowsill and, significantly, another giveaway of his height, had to climb up on a chair to do so.

He left at last, again using the back door to escape any possible sighting by Mrs Kelly or her mother. He drove the station wagon to pick up Christie and take him back into Nassau to collect Christie's car. Before dawn he was on his way back to the mainland; the storm had blown out and the sea was navigable by motor launch.

Christie returned to Westbourne. As he walked through the hall, he found numerous small burnt patches where the powder or inflammable liquid had made holes in the carpet or smoke smudges on the walls. He went upstairs. Oakes was still in the position in which the murderer had left him; theoretically, all Christie now had to do was call the police. But he couldn't reveal that he had been absent from the house. He had planted the idea that he would be staying there when he spoke to the other guests at the party the night before; moreover, he had to protect his girlfriend, who could be ruined by gossip and might turn against him. He must turn the body over and go through a pretence of trying to revive Sir Harry, deliberately leaving his fingerprints on the thermos flask and the glass by the bed. He would say that he had tried to make Sir Harry drink the water and that in order to do so he had raised his head. He overlooked the fact that rigor mortis had long since set in, given Oakes's weight and the temperature of just over seventy-five degrees Fahrenheit, and that in order to raise the head he would have had to break the neck. The jaws would have been clenched, even without the teeth, which still lay in a second glass on the bedside table. No one on earth could have managed to force a glass of water between the dead man's lips.

Christie dared not wait until the maid, Mrs Ellis, appeared at her usual time of between 7.00 and 7.30 a.m. He shouted from the veranda to waken Mrs Kelly and her mother; sleeping, they did not respond, so he called them on the telephone in Sir Harry's room. Mrs Kelly came to Westbourne immediately. Next, Christie telephoned Government House; he reached Gray Phillips, who awoke the Windsors with the news. The duke cannot have doubted for a moment that, given Christie's description, this was a black crime with sinister overtones. The riots were fresh in his memory, and the fire, the feathers, the wound or wounds to the head clearly spelt ritual murder. If this indeed were the case, then any arrest or punishment would lead to further bloodshed and great danger for him, Wallis and every other white person in the Bahamas. It cannot be doubted that the duke was in an agony of indecision. Unquestionably, Wallis shared that agony. In desperation, to give himself time to think, the duke told Gray Phillips to put a total censorship on all news of the case. Phillips was to call Sir Etienne Dupuch, publisher of the *Nassau Tribune*, at home to tell him to suppress the story; he was to contact the local radio station and say that on no account was it to beam the news out on the morning broadcast.

But Phillips was too late. Christie, playing to the full his role of frantic and bereaved friend, had already called Dupuch who, scenting the story of the century, rushed an immediate announcement on to the wire services. Dupuch also advised the local radio station. In the meantime, Christie called Erskine-Lindop, who arrived twenty minutes later, summoned by his wife from the police headquarters where he had gone on an early morning call. At 7.30, Mrs Kelly telephoned Dr H. A. Quackenbush, a rather curious choice since Quackenbush was a post-mortem surgeon normally called in only by the police. Oakes's own local doctor was never summoned, nor was his mainland doctor flown in. Two minutes after 7.30, Christie called Charles Hubbard, who in turn called Mrs Heneage. Christie dared not risk a direct call to her because the wires at Westbourne were tapped by the US State Department. At 7.40, Erskine-Lindop, now at Westbourne, summoned his colleague Charles Pemberton. Five minutes after that, Mrs Ellis reported for work an unusual thirty minutes late. Meanwhile, urgent messages were sent to the Out Islands to find Mrs Kelly's husband on his fishing trip.

By 8 a.m., the murder room was filled with people milling about the body and discussing the mysterious crime. This was totally against all possible regulations. Erskine-Lindop and Pemberton should immediately have sealed the room and ordered everyone out. By having all and sundry move around the room touching everything, there would be so complete a puzzle of fingerprints that nobody would ever be able to make out the nature of the intruder. Dr Quackenbush did not examine the head fully. He announced to all concerned, including Sir Eric Hallinan, the Attorney General, who arrived at 10 a.m., that there was only one wound, and he put his finger into it. He concluded that the death must be 'suicide disguised as murder'. The other three wounds were obscured by blood. It was not until his abler colleague Dr FitzMaurice arrived at Hallinan's behest at 11.30 that it was determined through swabbing that there were in fact four wounds.

Neither Quackenbush nor FitzMaurice was able, it seemed, to determine that the wounds were caused by a sharp, triangular instrument, either an arrow or a fishing spear. Yet both talked from that moment on about 'blunt instruments' and bludgeons. No blunt instrument or bludgeon existed with that shape of head. Christie, then and later, repeated his story that he had tried to waken Sir Harry, had lifted his head and forced water between his lips. Nobody questioned his statement, despite the accepted effects of rigor mortis.

At 10.30 a.m., after much tortuous indecision and many conferences with Wallis, Erskine-Lindop, Pemberton, Christie and everybody else available, the duke called the Miami Police Department. It is clear that he dared not call Scotland Yard or the FBI because too much would have been disclosed by the expert investigative methods of either one. Neither would have hesitated to reveal that this was a black crime, a disaster for island unity. The duke had already established an association with Captain Edward W. Melchen, chief of the Miami homicide department, who had accompanied him on some of his more questionable journeys in Florida, in particular to meet Walter Foskett at Palm Beach. He could trust Melchen; moreover, Melchen had a long record of criminal associations, and for that reason J. Edgar Hoover had had him on his suspect list for years. The duke's telephone call was intercepted by the Foreign Activities Correlation branch of the State Department under Adolf A. Berle; the intercept file, declassified for the first time for the present author in 1986, still exists. The duke did not, as every historian has said he did, speak to Melchen of 'suicide disguised as murder'; rather, he spoke of a crime of 'a most extraordinary character', without specifying either victim or method of murder. Melchen must come at once, he said, and he was 'not in any circumstances to obtain a passport'. The Pan American Airways noon flight from Miami would be held for Melchen and one or two of his men; the duke would arrange it – he knew Juan Trippe, chairman of PanAm. Melchen applied to the State Department for immediate passport-free clearance despite the duke's instruction; he was aware that not to do so could cost him his badge. He brought with him Captain James O. Barker, supervisor of the Miami police laboratory and his number-one fingerprint expert. According to the recently declassified FBI file on the Oakes case, J. Edgar Hoover was convinced that Barker also had strong contacts with criminals and confidence men in south Florida.

The two detectives clearly knew that a cover-up would be involved, since they deliberately left behind the fingerprint identification camera that was mandatory in every examination of the circumstances of a violent crime. They later used the lying excuse that the duke had told them on the telephone that this was a suicide case. Even when they arrived, met at the airport by Erskine-Lindop and Pemberton, they failed to pick up the perfectly usable fingerprint camera maintained by the Nassau police, and apparently neither Erskine-Lindop nor Pemberton offered it to them, nor did they fly in their own camera from Miami on the next plane. The danger of using such a camera was that, by mandate, they would have to photograph every object in the murder room; therefore, it would be impossible for them to plant any fingerprints there once the photographic coverage was completed.

Contrary to every published report, Erskine-Lindop and Pemberton were not instructed by the duke or anyone else to place Melchen and Barker in exclusive charge of the case. First, in a British colony such a situation would be out of the question. Second, it was necessary for everyone concerned to hold together in this difficult predicament. However, there is no evidence that either Erskine-Lindop or Pemberton were privy to the conspiracy that followed.

It was decided by all concerned that the killer, whoever he was, must have signs of singes or burns. This was an entirely arbitrary decision since the killer could easily have used a fire helmet, a mask and asbestos-lined gloves. Indeed, anyone not committing a ritual murder would have obtained such protection. Naturally, Christie came through the examination of his body hair with his reputation unscathed. None of the rest of the staff, including the black groom at the stables, was asked to submit to such examination. By now everyone had decided on the identity of the person who would be declared a suspect. Inevitably, it was Alfred de Marigny. He was the perfect fall guy. he had annoyed almost every major figure of Bay Street; he was known to have had violent quarrels with Oakes; he hated Oakes as much as Oakes hated him; and he had an irritating gadfly presence that most people would be happy to see removed. Most important, he would take the heat off the black issue that was threatening to plunge Nassau into bloody violence. A white man as the accused would be perfect in every way.

Yet there wasn't a shred of evidence on which to arrest him. He stood to inherit nothing if Oakes died; Nancy, his wife, had herself been cut out of the will. He had no record of crime; he wasn't the type to stab and burn an old man in his bed, no matter what people thought of him; and he had a perfect alibi. He himself had given a party on the night of the murder. And his closest friend, Georges de Visdelou, had been with him at the time the murder was committed.

Yet de Marigny was arrested, on the pretext that some hairs on his forearms were lightly singed; he had been putting a match to a hurricane lamp at the house during the party, and the lamp had flared up. He was charged and placed in Nassau prison. Bail was not granted. In the meantime, the duke visited the murder room. Barker announced that he had found a fingerprint of de Marigny's on the Chinese screen that Wallis had left at Westbourne. He had chosen to overlook the fact that the screen had been removed from the room when de Marigny was brought to it and encouraged to pick up a glass, leaving the print that was later and most improperly transferred.

At the preliminary magistrate's hearing in the first week of August, the ritual of folly was repeated: Christie's lying statements, Quackenbush's inadequate summation of the forensic evidence, and the ineptitude of the successive police reports. Not a soul tried to look through hardware or sporting goods stores to match the size and shape of the weapon head; nobody came forward to contradict the blunt-instrument story; there wasn't an inkling in the press either in Nassau or overseas (the story made headline news even in the middle of the war) to draw attention to the sinister, black magic elements of the murder. At the preliminary hearing, Melchen, rapidly embroidering his fake story, insisted without producing a shred of evidence that Oakes, after being struck the first blows, had staggered into the hall (*sic*), his clothes on fire, before being dragged back to his bed and finished off. No one exposed this lie for what it was; even the most amateurish student of medicine would have seen that Oakes had died without moving.

The Windsors took off to the mainland for a tour that included a visit to Aunt Bessie, who had broken her hip and was lying in a hospital in Boston. They left de Marigny to his fate; Erskine-Lindop, who was clearly disturbed by the nature of what he was involved in, was transferred to Trinidad as he had wanted to be since the riots. The fingerprints were taken to New York for analysis in a laboratory; by a curious irony, just as the trial began, on 17 October 1943, the Windsors turned up at FBI headquarters in Washington and were given a conducted tour by a grimly humorous J. Edgar Hoover of the very fingerprint laboratories whose expertise they had so skilfully avoided using. The duchess was feeling ill, perhaps because of strain over the case, and the duke proceeded alone to the Quantico base where marines were being trained. While de Marigny fought for his life, the duke inspected the honour guard, the shower facilities, the dormitories, the gun vaults and the rifle ranges.

The trial, which the Windsors followed closely, was a sinister farce from beginning to end. De Marigny's able counsel, Godfrey Higgs, KC, exposed Christie as an outright liar in the witness box. Again and again Higgs pressed him on the matter of his pretending that he thought Sir Harry was alive; thrusting a picture of the dead man in front of Christie, the figure burned away and covered in feathers, the face streaked with blood. Higgs asked him if anyone could think that such a burnt and devastated corpse could possibly have any life in it. He attacked Christie on the issue of his sleeping through fire, blood and storm; Christie screamed at him in anger, yet never cracked, holding firmly to the exact letter of his evidence at the preliminary hearing. Disgracefully, Christie's girlfriend was never called to give evidence on the matter of his whereabouts. Higgs made one major mistake: he did not summon to the witness box an independent doctor to testify to the effects of rigor mortis, evidence which would have shattered Christie's credibility at a blow. Higgs did effectively destroy Barker; he showed him up to be a liar and revealed to everyone in court that Barker had planted de Marigny's fingerprint. He as good as stated that the duke was an accessory to the planting. The following exchange took place:

HIGGS   Did not His Royal Highness visit you at Westbourne and come to Sir Harry's room at the time you were processing for fingerprints?

BARKER   Yes, he came up to see the crime scene.

HIGGS   I do not think it would be proper for me to inquire as to why he came or to what was said.

De Marigny was saved by the fingerprint evidence. However, three jurymen held out against nine. In Great Britain the result would have been a hung jury; in the United States, a mistrial. But in the Bahamas a nine-to-three verdict was sufficient. De Marigny was acquitted. In the tremendous hubbub that filled the courtroom, few people heard the jury foreman's addendum: the absence of Erskine-Lindop from the trial was deplored, and it was recommended that de Marigny and his friend Georges de Visdelou Guimbeau should be deported at once. Such a recommendation was unprecedented in law and was totally unsupported by any existing statute. However, the duke acted upon it immediately. Having returned to Nassau, he besieged the Colonial Office in London and the authorities in Washington to make sure that the deportation suggestion was implemented. Meanwhile, Harold Christie returned to his normal role on the executive council.

After several attempts to find de Marigny a new domicile, the duke packed him off to Cuba. The duke's extreme impatience is conveyed in a telegram dated 25 November 1943, addressed to the secretary of state for the colonies:

Immediate confidential.
De Marigny and Guimbeau. I will telegraph the Governor of Mauritius ... De Marigny has made inquiries as to the chances

of his getting [to Haiti], but must point out that, unless the government has the means to transport him compulsorily, de Marigny may remain in this Colony, as the only inducement for him to leave of his own volition is the threat that he may be sent to Mauritius. I, therefore, very greatly regret your decision that transport by Royal Air Force cannot be justified, and I very strongly urge that Air Marshal Bowhill be given an opportunity to consider my request, and that copies of all telegrams which have passed between us be sent to him for consideration. I am sure that you will meet me thus far. Although I would be loath to worry the Prime Minister at this time, I feel so strongly on this question that I would not hesitate, as a last resort, to approach him direct, because I am convinced that unless the Bahamas Government is armed with the power to move both deportees, the British Colonial Administration will be subject to derision in the United States, and the relations of the Government with the local people strained to a breaking point.

De Marigny recalled to me in 1986 that within a few weeks more than one attempt was made on his life; on one occasion a series of shots was fired into his bed. He charges that the duke was accessory to this attempted murder. De Visdelou Guimbeau went to Haiti, securing a permit to enter Great Britain. De Marigny led a vagabond life for years, threatened, pursued, repeatedly refused documents because of ducal influence, repeatedly denied the right to emigrate anywhere. He is convinced the duke was responsible for his appalling plight. He went to Canada, and thence to South America, on a seemingly endless journey until, at last, with the duke's death, he seemed to find relief in exile. He and Nancy divorced; subsequently he married the daughter of one of Roosevelt's trusted aides and found much happiness with her and in raising a family; at last he found safe haven in the luxurious suburb of River Oaks in Houston, Texas.

Over the years, Christie was repeatedly asked why he was absent from Westbourne on the night of the crime; nobody believed he could have slept there and not heard the murder. He always held to the story that he was trying to protect his girlfriend's reputation, an odd way of protecting her since, as a result of his false alibi, she spent the rest of her life under a cloud of gossip.

There was a theory, propounded in three books on the case, that Oakes had been killed by the Mafia, and that the Florida godfather Meyer Lansky had ordered the crime from his head-quarters in Key West. The motive was supposed to have been that Oakes was refusing to allow the mob to run a gambling concession in Nassau. But in fact Oakes had no power to make that decision, and no Mafia crime has ever been committed in the manner in which Oakes was disposed of. The same authors suggested that Oakes was killed somewhere else, probably with a winch lever on his boat or at the dock, and carried back to the house, placed on the bed and then set on fire. Yet these theorists overlook some important details. No man leaves home without his false teeth; Oakes's never left the glass by his bed. Moreover, if he had been struck with a winch lever the nails would all have gone in to the same depth; additionally, the nails of a winch lever do not match either the size or shape of the implement used on Oakes. Further-more, if he had been hit while standing or sitting, as was suggested, the blood would have flowed vertically down his cheeks, instead of horizontally from left to right as in fact was the case.

The great unsolved murder case refused to die. On 26 June 1944, Raymond Schindler, a famous private eye of the era whom Nancy Oakes had brought in on the case, asked the duke to reopen it. The request was refused. Schindler responded by exposing some new evidence unearthed in Nassau establishing certain elements in the case.'[1] His reputable colleague Leonard Keeler, inventor of the lie detector, and Homer S. Cummings, a distinguished former US Attorney General, also appealed to the duke, but both were refused. They were told in a memorandum that 'the matter is closed'.

On 18 April 1946, de Marigny called for a new investigation, claiming that Oakes died from a bullet wound. By then the duke had left the Bahamas; there was no response to de Marigny's request. Then something startling happened. On 16 September 1950, Edward Majava, a New York docker on holiday in California, got drunk in a bar in Berkeley and said that he knew the killer's name. It had been given to him by Mrs Hildegarde Hamilton, a society portrait painter of Fort Lauderdale, who had heard the story on the local grapevine and perhaps had been told it by friends of Walter Foskett.

It seemed a highly dubious lead, but the Berkeley police decided to take action. They contacted Augustus Robinson, the Nassau police chief, who was rushed to Berkeley to interrogate Majava. Majava told him (recently declassified FBI files reveal for the first time) that the killer was Harold Christie. Robinson confirmed that Majava was correct. However, Robinson did not explain how he had obtained this information, or why he had failed to act on it by charging Christie with murder. The press never printed Christie's name; it revealed only that Robinson had confirmed the guilt of the person whom Majava had named. According to FBI rules, if the bureau had not been involved in a case in the first place it would not deal with it in the future, so the FBI chose to do nothing. Scotland Yard remained silent; royalty was involved.

Five days later, a young woman in Toronto reported to the FBI (which has not declassified her name) that Christie had hired a killer; that Christie was a secret mulatto, son of a white father and a black mother; and that he had acted in concert with a still more powerful figure. In a recently declassified FBI report that figure was named as Walter Foskett.

In the late 1950s, Cyril St John Stevenson, a prominent figure in the Bahamian government, directly charged Harold Christie with the murder in the assembly. Christie did not reply. The press still refused to name Christie; Stevenson applied to Scotland Yard to begin a full-scale inquiry, for which the upper and lower houses of the Bahamian assembly uniformly voted. Christie himself, to avoid risk of exposure, had to vote along with the rest. Scotland Yard refused to act, and the file was closed. Christie became immensely rich after the war, and he was knighted by Queen Elizabeth II for his services to the islands. He died peacefully of a heart attack in 1973, in bed in Munich.

The Oakes case remains closed.

At a party in a house in the south of France in the 1960s, the newspaper magnate Lord Beaverbrook asked Christie, 'Harold, now that you're free and clear, why not tell us all how you did it?' Christie only smiled. He spent the rest of his life seeking to convince anyone who would listen that the crime had been committed by a voodoo priest out of jealousy – the opinion that Schindler had expressed. Many still believe him.

A final question remains. Were the duke and duchess accessories after the fact? There is no proof that they were. But there is circumstantial evidence that the duke knew this was a black crime and that therefore his treatment of de Marigny remains a mark against him forever. And it is impossible to believe that he did not share this guilt with Wallis.

NOTE

1 Though he strongly believed a voodoo priest killed Oakes because Oakes was having an affair with the priest's wife.

17

RETURN TO EUROPE

In the wake of this horrific event came Christmas; while de Marigny, his marriage shattered, languished in Cuba, Wallis worked very hard to cast off the shadow of the murder and supervise special dinners for a thousand enlisted men. Despite the fact that she was unregenerately convinced that there should never have been a war, Wallis tried to make the best of a bad job and flung herself with all her customary energy into the Red Cross work, the infant welfare clinics and the Nassau canteen. From Pearl Harbor onwards she had been tireless in her efforts to improve conditions in the islands, and so had the duke, except for his mysterious blind spot over the water supply issue. It was one of the many paradoxes of their personalities that the Windsors still retained the fascination with the question of social reform that had helped propel them so disastrously into Hitler's camp.

However, in one of his local concerns the duke was not entirely liberal and altruistic. He still had a consuming interest in developing the Out Islands, and in this he was more than ever secretly hand-in-glove with his friend's murderer Harold Christie. Because of the war scare, and now the lack of money available to him to make something of the distant Cays, Christie feared his land would have no future. By pressing constantly in the Upper and Lower Houses in Nassau for the Out Islands development scheme, the duke clearly hoped to profit from rake-offs from Christie. In consistently blocking the duke in the matter, at least until the middle of 1943, the assembly was bearing in mind the nefarious involvement of its own member, Christie, in get-rich-quick property schemes. To the duke, stubborn as ever, the colonial government was being stupid, obstructive and pig-headed.

There were symbolic changes in the administration at the outset of 1944. Sir Eric Hallinan, worn out by the stress of the riot and the murder trial, followed Erskine-Lindop to Trinidad, where no doubt those embattled gentlemen had a great deal to discuss. Colonial Secretary Leslie Heape applied for a transfer and was granted the depressing post of acting governor of British Guiana. He accepted it immediately.

In the early months of the new year, Wallis received a series of shocks. At Verona, on 11 January, Count Galeazzo Ciano, her long-lost lover of China days, went to the firing squad on the instructions of his father-in-law, Mussolini, who accused him of treason. Ciano died bravely, refusing a blindfold, and made a request to look directly at his executioners as they fired. The first round of shots failed to kill him. The chair in which he was bound toppled over and he lay on the floor, groaning. Even when the commander of the firing squad shot him in the temple with a revolver, the stubborn young man did not die. It was only with a second shot that his life was terminated. How Wallis responded to the news is unknown. It takes no great feat of the imagination to envisage the torment she must have felt and the flood of memories that must have poured into her mind. Soon, the Windsors' dear friend Pierre Laval would be dragged, half-fainting with terror after an abject attempt at suicide, before another firing squad for betraying France. There was another echo of the past when the newspapers anounced that Alberto da Zara, Wallis's other old flame from China, who was now admiral of the Italian fleet, had handed his ships over to the Allies at Malta and that her Nazi former lawyer Armand Grégoire had been tried and imprisoned for treason.

Charles Bedaux, who had been arrested and imprisoned in north Africa on suspicion of treason against the United States, and had then been brought to Miami for incarceration, died by his own hand. He had managed to hoard a supply of sleeping pills, probably in his rectum, a practice later adopted by Field Marshal Goering. On 10 February, he retired to bed and swallowed the lot. Max Lerner and I. F. Stone disclosed in the newspaper *PM* and in the

Nation that they were convinced Bedaux had been encouraged to take the easy way out. Had he stood trial, he might have exposed a whole network of internationalist American businessmen (and a royal duke) who traded on both sides of the war.[1] Again, no record exists of Wallis's reaction to this second and shattering piece of news. She could not communicate with Madame Laval, the Lavals' daughter Renée, Edda Mussolini-Ciano or with Fern Bedaux, her beloved hostess of the days at the Château de Candé, because all her mail was still censored and even the telephone was monitored by the State Department Foreign Activities Correlation staff.

On 10 March, a flash fire mysteriously swept through the top floor of a luxury hotel in Richmond, Virginia; among those who were burned to death was Wallis's friend and lawyer from Warrenton days, Aubrey 'Kingfish' Weaver. This news must have been a terrible shock to Wallis; she always felt that Weaver had waved a magic wand over the judge who had granted her divorce from Spencer.

She was driven almost beyond endurance by stress during the spring of 1944. In her exasperation, her increasing irritation with everyone and everything in Nassau, she even let her racism slip into a letter to Aunt Bessie ('Government House with only a coloured staff would put me in my grave!'). She increased the white staff. Later she wrote, not for the first time, that she and the duke had been 'dumped here solely by family jealousy!' – a refrain to which Aunt Bessie was scarcely unaccustomed. In another missive Wallis wailed about 'being a prisoner of war or worse' – and there she was closer to the mark. She told Rosita Forbes, 'They [*sic*] only murdered Sir Harry Oakes once. They will *never* stop murdering the Duke of Windsor.'

The duke tried one last desperate ploy to improve his embarrassingly pathetic position. He urged Whitehall to approve his becoming viceroy of a new Caribbean federation over which he would preside. The Germans had been announcing in their propaganda broadcasts that he was to be viceroy of an America that lay conquered by Germany and Japan. He applied for this position through friends in London. His lawyer, George Allen, and his long-term economic adviser, Professor Henry Richardson, ran into a brick wall. Even the reliable Sir Walter Monckton proved unhelpful.

The duke had the nerve to take the matter to Buckingham Palace. Sir Alexander Hardinge had resigned his post the previous year because of ill health, and perhaps Windsor hoped that Hardinge's successor, Alan (by now Sir Alan) Lascelles, would take a more favourable view of him. This seems incredible. Hardinge had thoroughly briefed Sir Alan in the matter of the Secret Intelligence Service files on the Windsors. Like Hardinge, Lascelles had been trained in cyphers and had been privy, like Sir John Balfour, to all the intricate manoeuvrings of the Windsors on the international Fascist scene. Moreover, Lascelles had never liked the duke from the time he had known him in the First World War, and surely the duke, self-centred though he was, must have known this. Sir Alan was also devoted to King George VI and Queen Elizabeth and shared their horror of Wallis. Nothing came of the application, and the federation concept was never acted upon.

That summer, the Allied forces reoccupied Paris. There was word of both Windsor properties in France: the Foreign Office files were a-brim with intercepted telegrams and secret reports. Although all of these have conveniently disappeared, due to an oversight the Foreign Office printed a synopsis of what was going on in its published indexes that were unwisely issued in 1972. The furniture still remained stored at Maple's in Paris. More was at Antibes and Grenoble; still more remained at the Hôtel Majestic and the Maison Camerlo at Cannes. Other effects were hidden in the fastnesses of the Alpes Maritimes. Some objects were stored at the town of Tarn, others – with audacious disregard for the rules of war – in Italy. The strong room at the Banque de France was still being paid for on Churchill's orders, at this time through Switzerland. The Germans had of course hardly touched the Boulevard Suchet. Otto Abetz had planted soldiers at the gate to make sure nothing was disturbed. Even if the Windsors had not been on Hitler's special list of favourites, the house would have been preserved – at least until Italy made a negotiated peace with Britain and the United States in 1943 – because it had an Italian owner, the Countess Sabini.

As for La Croë, it too was scarcely disturbed. Even when the Germans occupied all of France, the chateau remained carefully kept up, its lawns leading to the sea laced with landmines to protect it still further. According to Foreign Office indexes, the Germans had paid rent on the property throughout the latter part of the war, when it was no longer possible for America to filter through funds to Sir Pomeroy Burton. The Swiss had paid the rent for the Boulevard Suchet house out of British funds.

Sailings to Europe were prohibited at the time, so the Windsors had to remain in a state of frustration, unable even to take a holiday to inspect their property. And perhaps it was just as well that they couldn't go, because two of Wallis's intimate friends and sometime designers, Coco Chanel and Elsa Schiaparelli, came under suspicion of espionage. Schiaparelli was able to scrape through because her many powerful friends in high places used their influence on her behalf. But Chanel had actually worked for the enemy, and Walter Schellenberg had been her employer. In a British intelligence secret report, declassified in 1985, she stands revealed as a participant in a negotiated peace plan in April 1944. The report reads, in part:

> [I was] told of the existence of a certain Frau Chanel, a French subject and proprietress of the noted perfumery factory. This woman was referred to me as a person who knew Churchill sufficiently to undertake political negotiations with him as an enemy of Russia and as desirous of helping France and Germany, whose destinies she believed to be closely linked together.

The report continues in the following vein: Chanel had been brought to Berlin, where Schellenberg briefed her as a direct agent of foreign intelligence, the SD; a friend of hers, a Signora Lombardi, was released from internment in Italy to go to Madrid to lay the groundwork for Chanel with Sir Samuel Hoare. She would bring with her a letter from Chanel urging Hoare to contact Churchill. But no sooner was Signora Lombardi in Madrid than she reported that Chanel was a Nazi agent. Chanel was charged with treason against the French state and arrested as soon as she arrived in Paris. She was held by the American authorities for twenty-four hours. Then, with amazing swiftness, she was released. It seems that she had several aces up her sleeve. Had she been forced to stand trial with threat of execution as an employee of an enemy government, she could easily have exposed as Nazi collaborators the Windsors and dozens of others highly placed in society. Despite the hatred of the Windsors at Buckingham Palace, the royal family would not willingly tolerate an exposé of a member of the family.

In August 1944, Wallis and the duke stayed once more with their great friend Robert Young, both at Palm Beach and at Newport, Rhode Island. Wallis was stricken with stomach pains; on this occasion they were symptoms not of perforated ulcers but of cancer. She moved into a ten-room suite with six full-time nurses at the Roosevelt Hospital in New York, where she was attended by Dr Henry W. Cave and by Dr Lay Martin of Baltimore.

She went through a successful operation with her usual resolution and strength and left the hospital on 11 September: as she walked shakily down the steps to her car, she was met by a carefully organized group of cheering children from a nearby high school. The Windsors stayed at their favourite Waldorf Towers for several weeks. The duke was still bombarding London with requests for a different job. Finally, and with negligible chance of success, he asked to be engaged in intelligence work, presumably against the Russians: the application only suggested to his enemies at court that he couldn't have applied for such work unless he knew something about it.

The duke and duchess returned to the Bahamas in a depressed mood that autumn. They were disappointed when after many attempts at drilling it was proved that there was no oil at the ranch in Alberta. There was a small consolation prize in January 1945 when, at long last, the Bahamian government approved the sum of £77,000 for developing the Out Islands, an investment which finally paid off and incidentally paved the way for Harold Christie's financial future and his ultimate knighthood. After many threats the duke finally resigned his post on 15 March 1945, and handed over his seals of office to the mild-mannered William L. Murphy, Colonial Secretary and frequent acting governor of Bermuda. The duke's brother, King George, personally signed the papers authorizing the resignation some months before the actual appointment term would normally expire. The duke stayed on for a few weeks to tie up any loose ends. On 5 April, he held meetings in both houses of the legislature to sign bills passed during the previous session.

President Roosevelt died that month. The Windsors sent conventional condolences, but in letters given to this author by Kenneth de Courcy the duke deplored Roosevelt and blamed him for what the duke called his intervention in the Second World War. He spoke with contempt of the great man whose statue would later stand in Grosvenor Square. As Frank Giles, his former aide in 1940, reported in his memoirs, the duke complained that the war could have been avoided had it not been for 'Roosevelt and the Jews'.

On 4 August 1945, John Balfour, who was now chargé d'affaires in Washington, made arrangements for the duke (Wallis was ailing) to meet President Truman at the White House. Balfour, like Sir Alan Lascelles, was still in the anti-Windsor camp in London and had been privy to all the many encoded documents relating to the couple. He liaised with Adolf A. Berle (before the latter's resignation that year) in keeping a constant watch on the couple.

It was a dramatic moment for the duke's encounter with the president. Truman had issued an ultimatum to the Japanese calling for unconditional surrender. That morning, the Japanese government replied through Switzerland that it would not accede to the request. When the duke and Balfour walked into the Oval Office, Truman told them the news. He said, in a voice dark with foreboding, 'I now have no alternative but to drop the atomic bomb on Japan.'

In the next few days, at the Balfours' house, the news came through that Hiroshima and Nagasaki had been destroyed and that Japan had given in. The duke tried to call Wallis at the Waldorf Towers in New York, but the lines were engaged and he could not get through. He took a hot bath, trying to relax and gather his thoughts together. As he lay in the water, the Balfours' Irish maid burst into the bathroom and, without turning a hair, shouted at the top of her voice, 'Get out of the water at once! Yer wife wants to speak to yer on the telephone!'

Two nights later, Robert and Anita Young came to dinner with Wallis and the duke. Balfour's purpose in having the duke stay with him was to keep an eye on him. The Youngs showed their true colours that evening. Balfour wrote in his memoirs, 'They all seem to be oblivious of Nazi misdeeds and seem to feel that if Hitler had been differently handled war might have been avoided.'

It was in that period that Young, always weaving in and out of the Windsors' lives, assumed a temporary predominance. From 1937, he had been in virtual control of Alleghany. This had been Wallis's favourite investment; her Warfield uncles had managed to secure her some of the preferred stock issued in a storm of controversy by the banker J. P. Morgan, who had earlier been a principal investor for King George VI and Queen Elizabeth at the time when they were Duke and Duchess of York. Alleghany stock was among the few to survive the Wall Street crash. Young had risen higher and higher, keeping Wall Street in a constant state of turmoil as he fought the investment banks and Capitol Hill to plunge forward with his wild and reckless schemes for a multi-billion-dollar railway empire that would link the nation coast to coast without the necessity to change trains. His particular obsession was Chicago, where travellers had to stop, often for a whole night, before proceeding to the west or east coast. But despite every effort he was unable to cut through red tape and vigorous opposition by rival railway tycoons; the need to change trains continues to this day.

The Windsors were intoxicated by Young. In particular, the duke, who clung to the past of his youth, longed to see the railways combat what would undoubtedly be the postwar rise of commercial domestic airlines; because of her only partly conquered fear of flying, as well as her love of trains, Wallis also found Young a crusader and a hero. The Windsors decided to invest substantial sums in him.

In August 1945, the embattled couple ran into further trouble. At his trial for treason in France, Pierre Laval testified of his dangerous political association with the duke. He mentioned their secret meeting in Paris to discuss the handing over of Abyssinia to Mussolini and to secure the permanence of fascist alliances. The duke responded to this sworn statement with fury. When an alert *New York Times* called him for comment, he lied, saying that, although he had met Laval at 'a social function at the British Embassy in Paris in 1935', it was 'untrue that any conversation on political matters took place between us'. Quite apart from the fact that British government documents, published after the war, contained an apparently doctored but revealing paragraph disclosing the very text of the political conversation at that luncheon presided over by Ambassador Sir George Clerk, Laval's son-in-law, the indispensable Comte René de Chambrun, emphatically states that the Mussolini plan was laid down at the subsequent secret meeting.

That month, a very curious and since much discussed mission was instigated at Buckingham Palace. Owen Morshead, archivist of Windsor Castle, that formidable catch-all for every document likely to be even marginally threatening to the British royal family, was dispatched to Friedrichshof, the traditional home of the Hesse family in Germany. His seemingly innocuous purpose was to retrieve letters by Queen Victoria to her eldest daughter, Princess Victoria, wife of Emperor Frederick I of Prussia, and grandmother of Prince Philipp and his twin brother Wolfgang of Hesse, as well as their Nazi brothers. The ostensible purpose was to extract the letters from the American army, which might misuse or destroy them.

No indication of such vandalism had reached Buckingham Palace, and if the letters were required, Margarethe, mother of Philipp and Wolfgang, could have supplied them. They were of no great value, nor was King George VI a student of his ancestor Victoria's progeny. Therefore, why was Morshead sent on so expensive and difficult a mission?

Further questions could be – and have been – asked as to why Anthony Blunt, of the British Secret Intelligence Service, was also sent.

At the time, Philipp was a prisoner of the Allies. The existing interrogatory reports, most of which concern Hitler's imprisonment of him on suspicion of treason and his wife's similar imprisonment, naturally and completely avoid, no doubt on high-level orders, any discussion of his prewar (and during the war) role in appeasement arrangements with the Duke of Kent and Prince Paul of Yugoslavia – the royal mafia.

No mention was made then or later of the blackmail plot in Paris in March 1938, or who was behind it, namely the supposed Madame Maroni, or the role in it of her architect uncle, Gian Carlo Maroni, and his cousin Fernand, the editor of the *Journal des Débats*. Certainly, records of the matter, the documents and photographs for sale, would have been known to the Secret Intelligence Service, which also failed to act upon the denazification interrogatories in which Philipp disclosed his meeting with a Hitler-pacifying Duke of Kent in July 1940, with the war having been on for over ten months.

Only royal orders could have so completely squelched any proper talks with Philipp, and it was not until 25 November 1979, more than fifteen years later, that his twin, Prince Wolfgang, revealed to the London *Sunday Times* Insight team that Blunt and Morshead were looking for the Philipp–Windsor–Hesse documents that showed collusion among all three.

The likelihood is that the documents, thought by the royal family to have been returned to the Hesses by the Germans when they seized the files of the Paris Sûreté at the Quai d'Orsay in June 1940, and shipped by them to Berlin, were, in fact, not at Castle Friedrichshof at all. The evidence suggests that, busy fighting a war, the Germans didn't have time to sift through the vast mass of materials of the Paris police, and simply stored them away for the duration.

In 1945, the Russians seized them and took them to Moscow; some records have been returned to Paris over the years, but these have yet to be fully sorted and filed. If the records of Inspector Gilbert Rochès's investigation into the Maroni affair survive, they are undoubtedly still in the French capital, either at the archives of the Sûreté at Fontainebleau, or in the Deuxième Bureau files at Versailles. It will be many years before they are catalogued and released for public inspection, but it is doubtful if more details than are available from the indispensable Coolidge diaries will surface, even then.

This still doesn't answer the question of what became of the records of the Windsor–Kent–Philipp connections *after* April 1938. The answer very probably is that the Duke of Windsor, in collusion with the Duke of Kent, made sure that no records of meetings were preserved, and most certainly no photographs. And there the matter rests.

October offered more embarrassments. British and American forces seized the archives of the German Foreign Office, including a high proportion of the documents relating to the Portuguese episode. The telegrams, now decoded and clearly readable, lay on the desk of every appropriate official in London and Washington.

Also disclosed was the more serious matter of the duke's leaking the contents of the War Cabinet meeting of January 1940, at which the defence plan for Belgium and France was discussed. John Balfour was put in charge of the matter in Washington. Dean Acheson, in the wake of Adolf A. Berle (who was thereby cheated of his prey), was in constant touch with Balfour in the matter. Top-secret memoranda flew to and fro. London requested that all documents be forwarded to the appropriate authorities. The documents were considered highly embarrassing to the royal family, and Winston Churchill stepped in, making every effort to suppress them entirely. He did not want the public to get wind of what had been going on. However, the Windsors' enemies in Whitehall were moving rapidly, and the advent of a Labour government under Clement Attlee ensured that the documents would see the light. It was to be emphasized that the disclosures were totally without the approval of King George VI or Queen Elizabeth. Once again, much as they disliked Wallis and were uneasy about the duke, they did not want to have the royal family's dirty linen washed before the world.

*

During this curious series of events, with incriminating documents either about to be published or buried in royal archives, the Windsors, with impeccable timing, sailed to France for the first time in nearly six years. They travelled aboard the troopship *Argentina,* one of the first vessels permitted to make the journey at the end of the war. The ship anchored in the Channel outside Plymouth, where she was boarded by thirty British and American reporters who came by launch to interview the duke. They noted that by now he had a pronounced American accent. The duchess was not with him in the purser's cabin, where the press conference took place.

Asked if he planned to visit England, the duke said, 'I'm certainly not going to hide, and people will have a chance to see me.' After the press conference Wallis joined the duke on deck and smilingly posed for photographers and newsreel cameramen. 'It will be lovely to be back in England,' the duchess said.

The ship docked at Le Havre at 5 p.m. on the 22nd. The

Windsors were met by a British embassy chauffeur, who drove them to the Boulevard Suchet. They discovered that the Countess Sabini was going to sell the house, but they were allowed to stay on to organize their furniture and bring it out of storage. They were given at least six months' grace, a remarkable consideration in the circumstances.

As it turned out, Wallis did not accompany the duke to Britain. She was, it would be reasonable to suppose, uncertain of how she would be received, and of course it would be embarrassing to receive a direct snub from the Palace. Certainly, the Attlee government would not make her feel welcome or comfortable.

The duke arrived at Hendon airfield in a Royal Air Force Transport Command Dakota, and was driven to Marlborough House to see his mother. A crowd was waiting for him; as the car approached the royal residence, hundreds burst through the police cordon and shouted at him joyously, 'Good old Edward!' and 'You must come back, Teddy, we want you back!' So violent was the crush that a number of very young children were almost trampled underfoot. At last, the car entered the courtyard of Marlborough House.

That evening, there was a partial family reunion. The Duke of Gloucester was in Australia and was unable to attend. However, King George did appear, unaccompanied by his wife. The Duchess of Kent was also notable by her absence. It has been claimed that she had never forgiven the Windsors, who had disliked her from the 1930s, for not writing a letter of condolence to her and her children upon her husband's untimely death. The Princess Royal, who still adored the duke, had been in residence at Marlborough House for several days.

It was on the whole a pleasant evening. Old enmities and strains were temporarily forgotten, and the conversation was brisk. On 7 October, the duke and his mother went to the East End, exploring the bombed areas. They visited the home of James Kirby, a forty-seven-year-old gas company clerk, to see a new prefab – a special venture of the Labour government. On the 11th, the duke flew back to Paris, announcing ominously, 'I shall certainly be back, and next time the duchess will be coming with me.'

Both in London and in Paris the duke saw a good deal of

Winston Churchill, who showed little or no interest in meeting the duchess. The Windsors stayed on in Paris through the winter. They began house-hunting, aware of the fact that they had long outstayed their welcome at Boulevard Suchet, and they also discovered, on a visit to La Croë, that although they would spend a good deal of time there it was unlikely to be their permanent home. The costs of upkeep in more expensive times would be crippling.

In January 1946, Wallis, to her delight, topped the New York Dress Institute's list of the ten best-dressed women in the world. She had been on the list for years, tying on one occasion with Courtney Espil, who had replaced her in the affections of the Argentinian diplomat she had once loved. On 7 January, the duke was again unaccompanied as he revisited London to see his mother. Once more, he was greeted by excited crowds; on the 8th he went to visit his brother at Buckingham Palace. He had what must have been very uncomfortable meetings with his enemies Attlee, Ernest Bevin and other Labour government figures, regarding his desire to be made ambassador at large in the United States, or perhaps Viceroy of India. But he was offered nothing; eventually, Governor General of Australia was suggested. He unwisely refused the post.

Unfortunately, while the duke was in London another disagreeable echo of his past was heard. The *New York Times* reporter Tania Long, stationed in Nuremberg to cover the International Military Tribunal's trial of the major Nazi war criminals, got hold of a secret document from the files of Alfred Rosenberg. The document referred to Sir Samuel Hoare's interest in Nazism, to Rosenberg's 1931 visit to London, in which he found many pro-Nazi figures on the general staff, and to the visit of the special agent de Ropp to London in January 1935 to discuss National Socialist philosophy with the Duke of Kent, who had conveyed the details directly to his brother. This was most embarrassing, and the article appeared in the *New York Times* on 10 January, while the duke was still at Marlborough House. On this occasion he declined to make any comment.

The Windsors spent the next few months in Paris and at La Croë. The arrangement that enabled them to stay on at Boulevard Suchet was in fact extended until 1948. The duke was ceaseless in his requests to return to Great Britain in some official capacity. He was keenly supported in this by Wallis and by public feeling; his popularity still worried Buckingham Palace greatly.

The Windsors' chief concern during 1946 was as always the Russian threat. At the outbreak of the Second World War, when he heard the news at La Croë, the duke had told Wallis that it would mean the influx of Bolshevism and the destruction of Europe as he knew it. He was not entirely mistaken, of course, no matter how misguided the political principles which had provoked the remark. The notorious decision at the Yalta Conference to give almost all of eastern Europe to Stalin was of course of the gravest concern to every thinking person not of the far left. The hysterical fear that the Russians would move rapidly westwards and absorb all of European civilization did not have an equal foundation in logic, but the duke cannot be blamed for his fears at the time, nor for his continuing belief that the only possibility now was to launch an immediate attack upon the Soviet Union. The fact that such an attack would be totally illegal, unprovoked and unsupported by international regulations and restrictions, did not have the slightest interest for him; he believed to the end of his life (and many agree) that the Russian people would have been freed by the defeat of Stalin. Soon the world would be plunged into a cold war, and that year Churchill's famous 'Iron Curtain' speech on Russia at Fulton, Missouri, found the Windsors in total concurrence.

Finally resigned to the fact that the duchess would never be accepted at the palace, the Windsors arrived in London for a private visit on 1 October 1946. It was the duchess's first appearance on British soil for more than eight years. The Earl and Countess of Dudley, whom the Windsors had entertained at La Croë on the eve of the war, had offered them Ednam Lodge, their country house at Sunningdale, Berkshire, only a stone's throw from Fort Belvedere. The Dudleys were staying at Claridges in London.

Gray Phillips and the reliable Thomas Carter, who continued to represent the Windsors' interests vis-à-vis the royal allowance in London, met the duke and duchess at Dover and drove them to Ednam Lodge, where they were very comfortable. They made a brief and nostalgic drive to Fort Belvedere, which they found in a sad state of disrepair; later, it would be restored and occupied by Mr and Mrs Gerald Lascelles. Lascelles was the duke's nephew, the son of his sister, the Princess Royal. The duke had been quietly disposing of the furniture at the Fort piece by piece through private channels, anxious that no word of the matter would leak out. George Allen arrived from London to pay his respects and reassure the duke on that score. On 16 October the Windsors made a visit to London and stayed, like the Dudleys, at Claridges.

The duchess kept a large number of her jewels in a box, almost the size of an overnight suitcase, which was normally placed under her maid's bed. The night before she and the duke left for London she moved the box, placing it in front of the fireplace in her bedroom, where it could not have been more conspicuous. The excuse she later gave was that her maid was going on holiday to Scotland and that the following day the box would be placed under the bed of Lady Dudley's maid. She had completely ignored Lord Dudley's urgent request to put the jewels in the well-protected and burglar-alarmed strong room where the family silver was stored. Burglaries concerning celebrities were in the headlines every week that season.

At 6 p.m. on the night of the 16th, the detective on watch outside Wallis's bedroom apparently joined the rest of the staff for an early dinner in the kitchen. It was still twilight when thieves climbed up a white rope attached to a window in the room of Lady Dudley's daughter. Ignoring all other rooms and the strong room, they walked down a corridor directly to the duchess's bedroom. Without touching any of the items on the dressing table or in the drawers, searching through cupboards or even taking Lady Dudley's gems, which were on her dressing table in the neighbouring room for all to see, they picked up the jewel box and carried it back down the same corridor. Despite the fact that the Windsors' cairn and pug dogs were upstairs, neither barked. Is it possible that they recognized the thieves?

The duchess's maid went to her mistress's room to fetch something and noted the absence of the box. She immediately called the police. Soon the house was in uproar. It seemed incredible that burglars could have made their way into the house in daylight, walked across an entire floor, picked up a heavy box and made their way down the rope without disturbing anyone. The maid advised the Windsors, who instantly drove down to Ednam Lodge, where the police were already interrogating everybody. The Dudleys followed immediately. Assistant commissioner R. M. Howe and Chief Inspector Capstick from Scotland Yard were in charge of the investigation.

A golf caddie reported that he had found a number of earrings, none of them matching, scattered among the bunkers. Members of staff reported finding expensive Fabergé boxes lying about on and near a windowsill. There was no trace of the jewel box itself. There was talk of people seeing a large Canadian armoured car parked in the vicinity, and it was mentioned that a somewhat demented individual seen prowling around the local golf club might have been responsible. The duke reacted very much as he had done in the Oakes case. He decided on the spot that the madman was responsible and had him arrested on the flimsiest evidence and held in prison; after a brief arrest the unfortunate man was released, on the grounds that it was clear that the crime had been carried out by highly skilled professionals.

Lady Laura Dudley, later Duchess of Marlborough, recalled that the duchess behaved with artificial fury. Much to the Dudleys' annoyance, she insisted that all their valued retainers and maids, as well as their cook, be thoroughly searched and subjected to a police grilling. Only one scullery maid was new to the household. The police questioned her mercilessly, but they could prove nothing against her.

One of the duchess's brooches, supposedly not in the box, proved to be missing that night. The duchess compelled the duke to search high and low for it, turning over cushions, getting on all fours to peer under chairs, ransacking cupboards and generally turning a beautifully ordered and elegantly maintained house upside down. This inelegant and humiliating performance ended with the duke at last recalling that he had hidden the brooch, for some inexplicable reason, under a vase on a mantelpiece. He produced it, pale, exhausted and on the verge of tears, to Wallis's cold, shrugging approval.

The Duchess of Marlborough remembered how extremely annoyed she was by Wallis's misbehaviour in the matter. A few days after the theft, she had been walking in Mayfair when, to her astonishment, she was stopped by a plain-clothes policeman who asked to inspect her diamond clip. It was in the form of the Prince of Wales's feathers and was a family heirloom. He had evidently mistaken it for the sapphire and diamond 1936 Cartier clip which the duchess had worn at her wedding.

Summers, Henderson, the insurance assessors, issued under pressure a list of the items in the jewel box. It was extremely brief and was followed by the tantalizing word, 'etcetera'. In view of the fact that the Duchess of Marlborough had already examined the contents of the box and seen a vast number of items in it that were not included on the assessor's list, it is possible that Summers, Henderson chose not to reveal the vast majority of the items. The reason for this is mysterious. Among the very significant pieces that went unlisted, but which the duchess mentioned to reporters, was the magnificent diamond tiara that the duke had given her as a wedding gift; made by Cartier in 1936, it included four large centre diamonds and three curved upright fingers of smaller diamonds mounted on platinum. The tiara had been intended for wear at the wedding, but this idea was decided against at the last moment because of the implied insult to Buckingham Palace. It was worn only for photographs.

Later in 1946, Frances Goldwyn, wife of the famous movie tycoon Samuel Goldwyn, was in a jeweller's in Bond Street, asking to see a book of samples of important items that were offered for sale. She was astonished to see in the book certain gems that were supposed to have been stolen. The book was hurriedly removed with the words, 'We regret, madam, this sample was offered to you in error.' For years, people claimed they saw the duchess wearing gems, now in different settings, which were supposed to have been in the stolen box.

A rumour flew around London, not discouraged by the Windsors, that Buckingham Palace was responsible for the robbery. The reason put forward was that the mysterious and fictional Alexandra emeralds were in the box and that the Palace wanted them back at all costs. This absurdity has persisted to the present day.

A number of theories have been suggested. Among them is that of the official historian of the queen's jewels, Leslie Field, who says:

I believe the Duchess of Windsor defrauded the insurers by overstating the numbers and identifications of the jewels which had been disposed of. At least thirty items she named as being stolen turned up in the Sotheby's catalogue at Geneva in April 1987 and were sold for high prices. She clearly could never wear those jewels again after she and her husband had collected the insurance. They had from the beginning been in a strong-box in Paris and remained there.

According to Suzy Menkes, author of a major book on the duchess's jewels, a thief confessed to the crime in 1960. However, he appears not to have revealed to which fence he disposed of the gems.

With the theft officially unsolved and Scotland Yard in a great state of embarrassment, the Windsors wisely sailed for the United States on the *Queen Elizabeth* on 6 November. The sailing was rendered uncomfortable by the presence on board of Sir Alexander Korda, the close friend and colleague of Sir Robert Vansittart. Sir Alexander had been in the Secret Intelligence Service throughout the war, and he was well aware of Vansittart's investigations of the Windsors. Korda was coolly polite, but the Windsors generally gave him a wide berth.

When the ship docked, the Windsors were met by Robert and Anita Young. Young was still locked in his continuing battle to obtain ultimate control of the New York Central Railroad; questioned by reporters, both Young and the duke denied that royal money was invested in the struggle. It was a futile denial.

On 21 November, the Windsors attended with the Youngs the world premiere of William Wyler's classic movie *The Best Years of Our Lives.*

They spent Christmas happily at the Waldorf Towers. In January 1947, a new and remarkable personality entered their lives. Tiny, sharp-eyed, twinkling, Guido Orlando was one of the ace publicists of his era. Among his clients had been Mussolini, Greta Garbo and Aimée Semple MacPherson. Dapper and fast-talking, he could buy or sell any gimmick.

The duchess met Orlando at the Waldorf Towers and told him that the duke was worried because the German diplomatic records relating to their pro-Hitler activities might see publication despite Winston Churchill's determined efforts to suppress them. Orlando recalls that, without thinking twice, he immediately cooked up an

enterprising 'patriotic' scheme. He would arrange a party at Del-
monico's Hotel which would be attended by a hundred wounded
Purple Heart veterans and the duke and duchess. Photographs
would be taken and distributed to the foreign press; the domestic
press would be there in full force. At the end of the party, the
veterans would send bouquets to Wallis with notes of thanks; she
would, of course, pay for these.[2]

The party went off according to plan. The official hostess was
the wealthy Mrs Sailing Baruch, sister-in-law of the important
political figure Bernard Baruch. At a certain stage during the
evening, the New York playboy Jimmy Donahue turned up and said
to Mrs Baruch, 'I understand the Duke likes you very much. He
always did have a weakness for sailors!'

The Windsors had not met Donahue before. Orlando introduced them. Slim, oval-faced, with slicked-down hair, Donahue was
a remarkable personality. His mother, Jessie, with whom he lived at
834 Fifth Avenue, was the daughter of the billionaire Frank Woolworth; Barbara Hutton was her cousin. His father had committed
suicide in April 1931, taking an overdose of mercury tablets. The
elder James Donahue had been noted for his homosexual activities,
and he had allegedly taken his own life because he had been jilted
by a young serviceman. His oldest son, Woolworth Donahue, had
seen the suicide.

By 1947, when he met the Windsors, Donahue was as notorious
in society as his father had been. Despite the fact that press agents
organized numerous women for him as well-publicized dates, he
remained exclusively interested in men. With unlimited cash, he
could afford the most expensive call-boys; he staged elaborate
orgies during his mother's absences in Palm Beach. A close friend
was Cardinal Spellman, the leading Catholic dignitary in the United
States, whose indulgences with male prostitutes and handsome
young priests were an open scandal in Manhattan. On one memorable occasion Donahue gave a dinner party for the cardinal and
appeared at the table in a ball gown. The stories about him were
legion. An informant who wishes to be anonymous says that Donahue and a friend had cornered a waiter at the Waldorf Towers and
tried to rape him; when the man resisted their advances, they
allegedly castrated him.

An extraordinary incident took place on 18 March 1946. Donahue walked into the elegant Cerutti's, a gay bar on Madison
Avenue. It was full of men in uniform. Accompanied by the
jewellery designer Fulco di Verdura, Donahue took a number of
sailors, soldiers and marines to a party at Mrs Donahue's Fifth
Avenue apartment. They stripped a GI and began shaving off his
body hair. They were using an old-fashioned cut-throat razor. Then
Jimmy castrated the soldier. Everyone became hysterical; the man
was thrown into Jimmy's car, driven to the 59th Street Bridge and
tossed on to the pavement. Donahue was arrested but released
when Mrs Donahue paid the unhappy victim close to a quarter of
a million dollars to drop charges. Donahue fled for two years to
Mexico.

According to the author Stephen Birmingham, when a male
prostitute failed to satisfy Donahue's requirements, he forced him
to eat an excrement sandwich. Guido Orlando claimed that, after
he introduced Donahue to the Windsors, the duke fell in love with
Donahue and that within a year they were involved in an affair.
Certainly, the three were notoriously inseparable for the next
several years. Orlando says that he encouraged Donahue to flirt
continuously with the duchess in public places in order to give the
impression that it was they, not Donahue and the duke, who were
interested in each other. At the same time, Orlando claims, he
urged the duke to put on a full-scale display of detesting all homosexuals; he was to throw up his eyes in despair in restaurants when
Jimmy flirted with the waiters.

The Windsors' surviving friends deny Orlando's story. Certainly,
gossips suggested that Wallis was seeking to convert Donahue to
heterosexuality by having a surreptitious affair with him. There is
no proof whatsoever of either occurrence. But there is no question
that their association with Donahue was the most sordid of the
Windsors' lives, more sordid even than the episode involving Sir
Harry Oakes, and, if Orlando is correct, Wallis must have hated the
situation. Not even Orlando's most determined efforts could make
the Windsors acceptable at the highest levels of society; true, they
never ceased to go to parties, but many people would not receive
them if Donahue were with them. As for England, it would clearly
be insupportable for Donahue to accompany the duke and duchess

to the homes of those few members of the aristocracy who would be generous enough to receive them.

By 1947, the duke, perhaps because of stress over his relationships with Wallis and Jimmy, was drinking heavily for the first time since the mid-1930s. In February 1947, the Windsors found a temporary escape from this ghastly liaison and travelled to Florida. Here the Youngs joined them at the Horse Shoe Plantation, Tallahassee, owned by the millionaire banking heir George Baker and his mother, Edith, to shoot turkey, quail and pigeons. Surprisingly, they returned to the hated Bahamas to stay with friends of the Baker family, the explorer Arthur Vernay and his wife, at Los Cayos. They returned to attend the Hialeah Park Handicap race meeting at Miami, and throughout March they were at the Youngs'. Back in New York, they were reunited with Donahue and, at Orlando's behest, formally opened the New York Book Week, designed to refurbish the Merchant Marine Coast Guard Station libraries. They visited the east side settlement and toured the New York police headquarters, where unflattering files on the Oakes case were inconveniently maintained.

On 15 April, an episode not organized by Guido Orlando put the duke in a heroic light. A fire broke out in one of the suites of the Waldorf Towers at 11.55 p.m. and the hotel alarm went off. The duke, always attracted by fires, made his way, followed by the duchess, from the twenty-ninth to the thirty-fifth floor, where flames were emerging from the apartments of the Baron and Baroness Egmont van Zuylen of Holland. The duke helped an emergency crew of hotel employees break open a firebox and carry the long hose down the corridor, aiming the water into the suite. By the time firemen arrived, the worst of the problem had been solved.

Six days later, Mr and Mrs Harry Truman arrived at the hotel, and the Windsors saw a good deal of them. On 26 April, they watched the Maryland Hunt Cup at Glyndon, the first time Wallis had seen the race since childhood. On 10 May, Aunt Bessie saw the Windsors off for England on the *Queen Elizabeth*, this time with only eighty-five pieces of luggage, a secretary, a valet and a maid. They renewed their happy relationship with Commander Grattidge. In England the duke again made efforts to secure some form of employment but without success. He was greatly hurt by the fact that he was forbidden to attend his mother's birthday celebrations on 27 May; he was allowed only to go to Marlborough House alone to present his greetings. That same week the engagement of Princess Elizabeth to Lieutenant Philip Mountbatten was being widely discussed. It was made clear that there would be no question of the Windsors being asked to the wedding. Asked for his comments, the duke said only that he wished the couple the very best. The duchess found herself unable to make any comment.

That autumn, London was *en fête* for the royal wedding. Through the pages of his own *Evening Standard*, Lord Beaverbrook urged Britain to demand that Buckingham Palace invite the Windsors. 'What has the Duchess done that she should be held up to ridicule in this way?' the *Standard*'s Londoner's Diary columnist asked. 'As the wife of the bride's uncle, if for no other reason, the Duchess should be accorded the dignity of an invitation to her niece's marriage.' There was no response to the plea.

NOTES

1 According to Charles Bedaux, Jr, his father committed suicide to protect his wife and family in France; if he made an admission that he had aided Jews in his companies, his family would have been punished.
2 In the end, she did not.

18

WANDERING YEARS

By the late 1940s, the Windsors were adrift. Their lives had begun to assume a circular monotony as they moved between Paris, the south of France, London and New York. Their list of true friends remained limited: the Youngs, George and Edith Baker and, in Paris, the Mendls and the Rochefoucaulds. The duke tried to alleviate Wallis's frequent periods of depression by bestowing on her a whole new series of gifts of jewellery. In 1947, he presented her with a magnificent gold, turquoise, amethyst and diamond bib necklace, set in a lattice design on a chain of Prince of Wales linking, signed by Cartier. In 1948, he presented her with the first of a series of panther clips, which were to become legendary. That first piece was made of gold, enamel and emeralds; the whole was crouched upon a single cabochon emerald of 90 carats. It was Cartier's first use of the motif. In 1949, it was followed by a sapphire and diamond panther clip, the cabochon sapphire of 152.35 carats, the whole including 106 sapphires. For many years after that the Duchess would accumulate a marvellous menagerie of similar gems.

In 1948, a new presence entered the restricted inner circle of the Windsors. By a curious coincidence, the arrival of this new personage on the scene coincided with the punishment of her predecessor. On 8 October 1947, Armand Grégoire was found guilty in absentia, in a judgment of the Court of Justice, First Subsection, Department of the Seine, of the crime of intelligence with the enemy in 1940 and 1941. He was sentenced to hard labour for life, and his property was confiscated; the court declared that he was in a state of national indignity, of which the penalty was national degradation.

The Windsors' new lawyer was the remarkable Maître Suzanne Blum. Then Madame Paul Weill, she was the sister of André Blumel, a lifelong friend, law partner and associate of France's former premier, Léon Blum. Blumel had been administrative assistant or chef de cabinet in the socialist and Russian-allied Blum administration during Edward VIII's reign. A convinced left-winger, he was, like Blum, Jewish. During the Second World War, when Léon Blum was imprisoned following the preposterous Riom trial in which the Vichy government sought hypocritically to blacken his name as an aide in the downfall of the Third Republic, Suzanne Weill and her husband managed to reach New York, where she altered her name to Blum. During her exile she tirelessly sought to obtain public support to alleviate ex-Premier Blum's conditions of imprisonment. Before America had entered the war, on 9 April 1941, she had secured over a hundred signatures, among them that of Eleanor Roosevelt, to a telegram of goodwill that was forwarded to the distinguished prisoner in his cell. The following year she organized another telegram to celebrate his seventieth birthday. Maître Blum, as she became known, never ceased to give what support she could to the Resistance movement from her distant position in Manhattan.

It seems peculiarly ironic that Blum, as a socialist, a relation of Blumel whom the Windsors politely deplored, and an apparent disliker of all Nazis, could attach herself to them, or that they would want her to handle their affairs. How did she manage, in short, to obtain an influence over the Duchess of Windsor that she never relinquished until the duchess's death?

The answer can be given in two words: William Bullitt. As his intimate friend, from the first day she and her late husband met him in Paris, perhaps misunderstanding his political role which on the face of it seemed publicly opposed to Hitler, a driven, self-deceiving woman who believed only what she wanted to believe, she worshipped Bullitt. He had the cunning, since he was being connected dangerously to Armand Grégoire, Laval and other traitors, to take her up in wartime America and to co-edit, write the introduction to and help her publish a book of Léon Blum's writings in French in Montreal in 1943.

Thus she was privy to Wallis's greatest secret, the secret her besotted Duke of Windsor would (and must) never find out: the Bullitt affair, which, according to Eleanor Davies Tydings Ditzen, even went on in Washington during the Bahamian exile period and later. Had the truth come out, the greatest love story of the century would have seemed a brutal sham – the story of a ruthless woman who manipulated a hapless cuckold as her slave.

When I wrote the original edition of this book in 1987, I stated that Maître Blum was clearly oblivious of the duke's and duchess's politics. I no longer hold this view; Maître Blum wanted these rich and famous clients and cared nothing about their political associations, whatever those may have been.

During 1946 and 1947, though still hovering around the fifty mark, the duke felt that impulse which usually seizes upon older men: the desire to write his official memoirs. He engaged for the purpose an accomplished journalist, Charles J. V. Murphy, a frequent contributor to *Life* magazine. Despite the fact that Clare Boothe Luce, wife of Henry Luce, chairman of TimeLife Incorporated, remained convinced that the Windsors were Nazi collaborators, Henry was less fussy and encouraged Murphy to go ahead with the assignment. It proved, like many arrangements of the sort, to be somewhat of an ordeal for both partners. The duke proved to be maddeningly skittish and unreliable in terms of schedules; he would say a great deal that appeared to be revealing and would then withdraw it. He fussed over every detail. Sometimes he would appear to be involved in the work, but at other times he would be totally abstracted and indifferent. Murphy pressed on doggedly, clearly realizing that the book could be a bestseller. In the midst of the writing Robert Young, George Baker and Kenneth de Courcy all indicated to the Windsors that war with Russia might break out at any minute. They began to make arrangements to sell La Croë and shifted a lot of their personal belongings to the United States. All of this absorbed a great deal of their time, and the matter of the memoirs kept being delayed.

Moreover, according to Murphy the duchess proved to be infuriatingly interruptive, constantly irritable and resentful of the irregular absorption of her husband in the task in hand. She would burst into the study in the various homes they occupied, dragging the duke off to this or that luncheon; she would scream out, 'Stop talking about the past!' and she would insist that the duke go, with or without Jimmy Donahue, to nightclubs and restaurants very late, so that he would be too exhausted to tackle the business of writing in the morning.

It was only by sheer main force that the determined Murphy squeezed a series of articles out of the duke; they appeared in *Life* magazine beginning on 8 December 1947. It gives some indication of the laboriousness of the task in hand that it was 1950 before the second part of the series appeared.

In April 1948, following a winter with the Youngs at Palm Beach, the Windsors took a lease on Severn, the elaborate estate of Mrs Brooks Howe at Cedar Creek, Locust Valley, Long Island.

In June, with 120 pieces of luggage, they sailed for England aboard the *Queen Mary*; among the other passengers was Lord Beaverbrook, who no doubt had much to discuss with them at the captain's table about the abdication years.

They made a second visit later in the year, and on each occasion the duke paid a loving visit to his mother, to whom he had grown closer and closer over the years. Whenever Wallis made a sharp remark about his family he would gently but firmly reprove her, and it is clear that despite all the differences between the members of his family they began to draw closer together in the late 1940s. Only Queen Elizabeth stood firm in her resolution never to forgive the duchess for her activities on behalf of the enemy or for provoking the abdication.

Much of Queen Elizabeth's concern and sense of unforgiving-ness still centred upon her husband's health. Although still not far advanced into middle age, by the late 1940s King George VI was suffering from declining strength. Always lacking his older brother's athleticism, energy, drive and sheer charm, he had, with courage, decency and resolution, sustained his royal duties without flinching, and his role in the Second World War had been nothing short of heroic. But the stress of working against his shy nature as the most conspicuously exposed of public figures had at last worn down his health.

By November 1948, he was suffering from a failure of arterial circulation in his legs, which had become a mass of swollen varicose veins. A lifelong smoker, like the Duke of Windsor, he was also showing symptoms which Lord Horder, the royal physician, would two years later indicate to his family might suggest a possible carcinoma. Further bronchoscopic examinations in 1950 suggested that this supposition was not without basis. The king was not informed of this discovery.

The Duke of Windsor was disturbed and moved by the news of his brother's ill health. The duchess's indifference made him fretful, even though there were perfectly understandable grounds for it. While in England he stayed either with his mother at Marlborough House or, when Wallis accompanied him that year, again with the long-suffering Earl and Countess of Dudley at Ednam Lodge.

He showed no forgiveness of his enemies. He wrote to Kenneth de Courcy on 28 August 1948, referring to the Franklin D. Roosevelt stone figure in Mayfair, London:

> I would not be surprised if you by-passed Grosvenor Square nowadays to spare yourself the disgust of having to look at the statue of the man most responsible for the jam in which the Western Powers now find themselves.

In the rest of the letter he said characteristically that 'if we had given a free hand to Hitler, we would have destroyed the Soviet Union, instead of America forming a wartime alliance with the Soviets'.

At the end of 1949, the Windsors stayed with Margaret, Mrs Anthony Drexel Biddle, their old friend from Paris days, at her Mayfair home.

They had by now given up their Paris residence and had moved to a rather unsatisfactory house at 85 Rue de la Faisanderie, near the Bois de Boulogne, which by mid-1949 was ready for occupancy. It was in essence the gift of an old friend, Paul-Louis Weiller, a French millionaire and controller of the airline that was later nationalized and became Air France. This leader of French commerce had continued to be the mentor and patron of Sir Charles and Lady Mendl, and he made it possible for this perennially charming pair to sustain their exquisite house, the Villa Trianon, near Paris.

These friendships and associations with people of very different political backgrounds proved to be highly supportive at the time. Yet it cannot be said that the Windsors were ever entirely comfortable during those years. The Palace's continuing refusal to accept the duchess still nagged and irritated. There were people who avoided them at parties or aboard the Cunard ships they favoured. The Donahue situation continued to be maddening to everyone. The gossip column items on the trio were increasingly unflattering; the ferocious Walter Winchell in particular rejoiced in exposing the ghastliness of the ménage à trois while discreetly failing to reveal its true nature.

Laura, Duchess of Marlborough told me that she found Donahue's very presence insupportable, and recalled a dreadful episode at the popular Paris nightclub Scheherazade some time in 1950. There was a Windsor party of twelve, all of them watched most closely by the other diners, who barely attended to their food. Jimmy and the duke had drunk far too much wine. Donahue had placed large numbers of red roses in front of all the plates, including his own. Suddenly, in an extravagant gesture, Wallis flung her Prince of Wales feather fan into Jimmy's roses. The duke turned to Lady Dudley in horror, his eyes full of tears. Lady Dudley naturally assumed that his jealousy was provoked by the alleged affair between Jimmy and the duchess, and did not understand the true reason for his discomfiture.

Charles Murphy recalled that one evening:

> at the [restaurant] Monseigneur ... the Duke left early, after buying the Duchess a gardenia from the flower girl's tray. Jimmy had bought her one, too. As soon as the Duke had gone, the Duchess snatched his flower from her corsage, flung it into the champagne bucket, and tamped it down in the ice with a bottle. Jimmy's flower she then tucked into its place ... [Jimmy] took her hand and they wept.

According to Murphy, Donahue was determined to have Wallis become a Roman Catholic. He enlisted the aid of the popular Monseigneur Fulton J. Sheen, who had already won Clare Boothe

Luce, the journalist Heywood Broun and the communist Louis Bedunz to the faith. Wallis somewhat frivolously discussed the matter, but of course to have entered into any such arrangement would have caused extreme offence to her husband; it was clear at all events that she was by now entirely agnostic. She also carried with her some odd echoes of the past. Nancy Mitford, gifted author and sister of Lady Mosley, wrote to Evelyn Waugh on 11 January 1950, saying that during a dinner party at the Windsors' she had gone into the bedroom and had seen there an erotic painting by Boucher of two lesbians making love. Surprised, she had asked Wallis what the painting signified. Wallis replied, 'Well it seems there was some god called Neptune, who could change himself into anything he liked – once he was a swan, you know – and this woman liked other women so he turned himself into one.'

The seemingly endless work on the duke's memoirs was finally completed, and the rights were sold to G. P. Putnam's Sons in December 1949. Kennett L. Rawson, vice president and editor in chief at Putnam's, made the necessary arrangements. He flew to Paris to obtain the duke's signature on 21 January 1950. Later that month the Windsors took off on an elaborate trip to New York, Florida, Louisiana, Texas and Mexico. As usual, they used the private railway coach of Robert Young. En route they stayed with the Bakers at their Tallahassee Horse Shoe Plantation. In Mexico City they were the guests of President Miguel Aleman, who discreetly made no reference to their association with his rebellious and pro-Nazi former associate, General Maximino Camacho. In association with Axel Wenner-Gren, who had survived blacklisting to continue acting as a cloak for Krupp in Europe, Aleman and his close friend Bruno Pagliai had acquired many of Wenner-Gren's interests; the Windsors thus moved back rapidly into the orbit of the very group they had allegedly broken with nine years earlier. After spending three days in Mexico City they proceeded via Texas and other points (many of which Wallis described in letters to her old friend Corinne Murray) to Alberta, to the ranch they had not seen for nine years. All efforts to strike oil there had of course long since failed. They returned to Europe on 24 May, the duke still labouring at the third draft of the autobiography. News of King George VI's health was very bad.

In July 1950, Herman Rogers wrote to Wallis to invite her to his wedding. Katherine had died in May 1949, and he was marrying Lucy Wann, widow of a retired RAF officer. The date was set for 6 August, but Wallis was unable to attend that day and asked Herman to put back the date by several days. According to friends of Wallis's, she was not at all happy about this new union. In various telephone conversations she criticized Herman for becoming involved with another woman so soon after Katherine had died. When Wallis did arrive at the Villa Lou Viei to attend the wedding, she presented the couple with a sterling silver salver, having deliberately omitted any mention of Lucy in the inscription. The Windsors turned up late for the wedding breakfast at a restaurant near Antibes, and during lunch Wallis ignored Lucy and talked across her to Herman. As the Rogerses set off on their honeymoon, a yacht cruise on which the Windsors accompanied them, Wallis pulled at Lucy's dress, twisting the cloth until the whole collar was totally ruined.

Wallis became a little more polite during the voyage, and at last began talking to Lucy. After dinner at the Hôtel de Paris in Monte Carlo, the two women found themselves in the powder room together. Wallis stared at a ring of gold and diamonds on Lucy's finger. Lucy said she felt she had enough jewellery and was going to insist that Herman return it for a refund. Wallis revealed herself all too clearly when she exclaimed, 'Don't send it back! Don't be a fool! It's money!'

At the beginning of 1951, Wallis, without knowing it, faced a new threat: the emergence from the secret files of the 1935 China dossier. The Hon. John Coke, son of the Earl of Leicester, who had originally taken the dossier to Queen Mary, and had himself examined its contents and kept a copy, felt that sufficient time had passed (and the old queen had little time left to live), to discuss it with Winston Churchill. Churchill was painting and writing in Marrakesh, Morocco, on a month-long stay throughout January of that year.

Churchill made no comment; he told Coke he had had heard about the dossier in 1936, when it was much discussed in the circles that wanted to see the removal of Edward VIII from the English throne; he certainly knew that Prime Minister Stanley Baldwin on instruction from George V had obtained it; and that when Queen

Mary saw it, in shock and outrage she decided Wallis would never be queen. It will be recalled that it was she, with the Duchesses of Gloucester and Kent, who resolved after the abdication that Wallis would never receive the title of Her Royal Highness.

From Marrakesh, Coke came to stay with the Windsors' old friend and confidant, Kenneth de Courcy, Duc de Grantmesnil, who was renting the Windsors' old home, the Villa La Croë, in the south of France. The Duke and Duchess of Westminster joined Coke as de Courcy's guests for lunch on 9 March and Coke described the contents of the dossier to the group. He added that Queen Mary, whom he still served as attendant gentleman-in-waiting, had never forgotten the dossier and thus would not even now relent in the matter of agreeing to Wallis having the title of HRH. He added that there was no question at any time of the queen receiving in her home a former prostitute who indulged in 'perverse sexual practices'. Coke asked de Courcy whether, after hearing such facts, he could expect Queen Mary to relent? De Courcy replied that in the circumstances he could not.

Later, after forming a friendship with the Windsors' lawyer Maître Suzanne Blum, de Courcy wrote to her frequently, attempting to appease her by saying that the dossier did exist but was 'a forgery'. But it was conceivable, indeed it fitted with his investigation into Guy Trundle via Scotland Yard, that King George had the dossier obtained; what is inconceivable is that he and the Secret Intelligence Service would have provided false witnesses and faked Hong Kong, Shanghai and Peking police reports in Chinese – a criminal act indeed. When the National Archives of Great Britain (then the Public Record Office) opened the Scotland Yard files on Trundle in 2003, it issued an official statement that the China dossier never existed. No further comment seems necessary.

The house at the Rue de la Faisanderie was proving less and less satisfactory. Wallis was not at all happy with it. Although its salon was large and its bedrooms spacious, the house suffered from a smallish dining room, a particular drawback in view of her desire to give large dinner parties. It was a somewhat cold, unwelcoming residence, and she decided they must move. They finally left the house in 1953. They had already given up their residence on Long Island.

It was unfortunate that the publication of the excellent royal autobiography *A King's Story* in the spring of 1951 coincided with King George VI's total collapse and disintegration. The book, however, was very successful, earning the duke a much needed $1 million. He apparently invested part of this in Robert Young's continuing venture in railway acquisition.

In September, King George was found to have a malignant growth in his throat. His left lung was removed on the 23rd. The Windsors were in London that October, staying with Margaret Biddle. Perhaps unfortunately, the duke chose the occasion to press Winston Churchill once more for a position in government. When the stricken monarch sharply refused any such suggestion, the duke was obliged to inform the duchess. She stood at the window of the house gazing out into the foggy day and said, with intense bitterness, 'I hate this country. I shall hate it to my grave.' Soon after that, when the Windsors' nemesis John Balfour happened to visit them at Biarritz and the duchess dropped something on the floor, Balfour, unfailingly British and polite, got on his knees to pick it up. 'I always did like to see the British grovel,' the duchess said.

On 12 November, C. L. Sulzberger of the *New York Times* attended a dinner party at the Windsors' house in Paris. Among the guests were French prime minister René Pleven and Senator Warren Austin of the UN delegation. According to Sulzberger, the other guests consisted of 'a weird collection of social derelicts'. The dinner comprised ten courses and was 'heavily spiced with sherry, white wine, red wine, pink champagne, and huge slugs of brandy'. At the seventh course, a string orchestra appeared and played nostalgically in the mode of the bands the Windsors had admired in 1930s Vienna. The guests all sang a birthday song to Senator Austin. After dinner everyone disappeared except the Sulzbergers. The Windsors insisted on buttonholing them and launching into a diatribe against the British royal family, the duchess saying she would never return to England because of the shabby treatment of her husband. The duke complained that when he had recorded a speech for a publisher's dinner announcing his book of memoirs, he was told to cancel it because of the king's illness. Yet on the same afternoon that the speech was to be delivered, Princesses Elizabeth and Margaret had gone to the races. Both the Windsors repeatedly said it was disgraceful that the princesses had gone to see the horses despite their father's condition while the duke was forbidden to promote his book.

The Sulzbergers were now invited to listen to the forbidden recording. At the end of it, the duchess exclaimed, 'What hypocrisy! What jealousy!' And she repeated her critique of the princesses going to the racecourse. The Sulzbergers left in a state of numb boredom.

In December 1951, the king gallantly made a Christmas broadcast. He rallied a little in January, but on 6 February 1952 his valet found him dead. The Windsors received the news in New York. The duke sailed at once aboard the *Queen Mary* for England. At the press conference which he held in the Veranda Grill on the sun deck of the ship, before sailing on 7 February, he said:

> This voyage, upon which I am embarking on the *Queen Mary* tonight, is indeed sad – and is indeed all the sadder for me because I am undertaking it alone. The Duchess is remaining here to await my return. I am sailing for Great Britain, for the funeral of a dear brother, and to comfort Her Majesty, my mother, in the overwhelming sorrow which has overtaken my family and the commonwealth of British nations.

Referring to the fact that he had participated in the funerals of three previous British monarchs – his great-grandmother, his grandfather and his father – the duke added hypocritically and falsely:

> The late King and I were very close, and the outstanding qualities of kingship he possessed made easier for me the passing on of the interrupted succession to the throne of the United Kingdom. That was over fifteen years ago – a turbulent decade and a half during which my brother's reign ran its noble course. Harassed by the dangers and tribulations of a second world war, and beset by more than his share of political strife, King George VI steadily maintained the highest standards of constitutional monarchy...
>
> But Queen Elizabeth is only twenty-five – how young to assume the responsibilities of a great throne in these precarious times? But she has the good wishes and support of us all.

Throughout the voyage, Commander Grattidge reported, the duke's misery was enhanced by Wallis's absence, and he paced the decks day and night like a lost soul, yearning for her. Others reported that he tied up the radio telephone and cable rooms of the liner talking with Wallis through the crackling interference or besieging her with messages of affection. He was still as much in love with her as ever.

As the *Queen Mary* sailed past the Isle of Wight, the duke stood on the bridge, pointing to the outlines of Osborne House where Queen Victoria had died. He spoke to Grattidge with tear-filled eyes about his many bereavements. Then he went down to the Veranda Grill to meet the press representatives, who had come out by launch and climbed a Jacob's ladder to talk to him. 'God save the Queen,' he said to the reporters, who spontaneously applauded.

He drove straight from Southampton docks to Marlborough House, where he found Queen Mary in mourning, stricken with grief. He gave her what comfort he could. She was too infirm, too advanced in years at eighty-four, to go to the funeral. Instead, she accompanied the duke to Westminster Hall, where, with the Princess Royal, they stood and looked at the royal catafalque, covered in a purple and gold pall, while the crowd of visitors was held back. It was the same dais upon which King George V's remains had lain in 1936. Later in the day, after leaving his mother and sister at Marlborough House, the duke went to Buckingham Palace for his first meeting in many years with the young queen. They were joined for tea by the Queen Mother and the Duke of Edinburgh. As at the time of King George V's state funeral, London was filled with royalty: Prince Paul of Yugoslavia, King Paul of Greece, the Spanish pretender Don Juan, King Gustav and Queen Louise of Sweden and many others poured into London to pay their last respects. Queen Juliana of the Netherlands flew in by plane, piloted by her husband Prince Bernhard. The King and Queen of Denmark arrived by ship. Prince Albert of the Belgians represented his brother King Baudouin, who for controversial reasons had refused to attend. The King of Norway and the Crown Prince of Ethiopia were also in attendance.

The duke arrived at 10 Downing Street on the night of 14 February for a private conference with Winston Churchill. At the funeral procession, the duke was accompanied in the long walk behind the royal coffin by the Duke of Edinburgh, his brother the Duke of Gloucester and his young nephew the Duke of Kent. Thousands of people dressed in black lined the streets, and many were weeping. The Duke of Windsor caused unfavourable comment by walking out of step, pushing forward, possibly in an attempt to draw attention to himself.

Wallis remained at the Waldorf Towers, listening to the broadcast of the funeral and perhaps remembering with sadness that other occasion long ago at which she had urged the then king to wear his father's greatcoat to block out the intense and bitter winter cold.

In the wake of this tragic hour, a controversy blew up. The duke was back in New York with Wallis in May; they returned to Paris later that month. It was then that Lord Beaverbrook rashly embarked upon a BBC broadcast on the subject of the abdication. He charged the late Geoffrey Dawson, former editor of *The Times*, with having terrified King Edward VIII and swayed public opinion against him. He accused him of having used methods 'which many would condemn', and said that Dawson 'pursued his quest with a vigour that seemed more like venom'. The broadcast immediately provoked an outburst of fury from every direction. Wickham Steed, who had been a colleague of Mr Dawson's, denounced the broadcast in the pages of *The Times* itself. He claimed that the charges were 'wholly fantastic'. The *Daily Telegraph* and almost every other paper rallied to the support of the deceased editor. The truth was, of course, that Dawson had played a role in the abdication, but in the long run he most certainly could not be blamed for it.

Following what turned out to be something of a storm in a teacup, the Windsors took off on their first yacht cruise of the Mediterranean in many years. They chartered the *Amazon* and sailed to Genoa, Portofino and other Italian coastal towns, proceeding to Rome, where they were received in audience by a person of like political views, Pope Pius XII. They were accompanied by Sir Walter Roberts, British minister to the Vatican. They avoided, for obvious reasons, Clare Boothe Luce and Edda Mussolini-Ciano. On the next leg of the cruise the duke went down with a severe case of gastro-enteritis and had to be taken by train from Montecatini to

Paris for immediate treatment. Still feeling ill, he was stricken with a severe attack of lumbago, and even a trip to Biarritz did not prove to be particularly reviving. At close to sixty, he was feeling the first symptoms of approaching old age. His temper cannot have been helped by the publication that year of a book entitled *Lese Majesty: The Private Lives of the Duke and Duchess of Windsor,* by Norman Lockridge. Chapter 1 was entitled 'The Worst of the Charges: Homosexualism'. The book, with a degree of readable scurrilousness, contained alleged interviews by the author with Sir Edmund Gosse (whom the author claimed knew the Windsors) and with a psychiatrist; the former denied the charge that the duke was homosexual, while the latter confirmed it. There was no suit for libel.

In late 1952, the Windsors finally wearied of the Rue de la Faisanderie. They began house-hunting, deciding that at last they must obtain a residence which would satisfy their every requirement and from which they would never have to move. They settled at first upon 29 Rue Barbey-de-Jouet, but discovered that this was French government property and was not available. There was some discussion of their obtaining the historic home that had once belonged to Madame du Barry, the famous mistress of Louis XV, but the notoriety of its previous occupant finally made them decide against it. They had continued their friendship with Paul-Louis Weiller, and it was this benign personage who recommended to the Paris municipal authorities that they should be allowed to live, at a peppercorn rent, in a magnificent house, 4 Route du Champ d'Entramement. The rent was only £10 a year; a magnificent establishment, the house stood in a two-acre park on the edge of the leafy Bois de Boulogne. The metal gate was flanked by two stone posts and gave on to a small gravel driveway. A spiked fence completely surrounded the property, which was planted with old oak trees. The structure was of characteristic French grey stone. The overall effect was at once grand and sombre, without the gloom of the Rue de la Faisanderie house.

It was in these years that the duchess again set the tone of the style of life that defied postwar austerity and would forever be associated with her name. She embarked upon close to thirty years of a fine degree of extravagance in households in which she saw herself as surrogate queen. Sydney Johnson, a black man who had been with the couple since the Bahamas, would greet arrivals with great circumstance, dressed attractively in scarlet and gold. He was accompanied by a French butler, Georges Sanègre, who customarily wore white tie and tails. As always, Wallis ran the household with fanatical expertise. As a hostess, she was more dazzling than ever. She supervised every detail of her perfect dinner parties, even making sure that the lettuce leaves were trimmed to a standard size and shape. At the cocktail hour, the staff, in livery, carried fine silver trays with such Legros delicacies from prewar years as grapes individually hollowed out and filled with tiny dollops of cream cheese, bacon bits fried in brown sugar, cabbage leaf pieces with shrimps or prawns attached to them by toothpicks, fried mussels and chipolata sausages. Dinner was customarily served in the blue chinoiserie dining room at two round tables set for eight. Wallis did not copy her prewar habit of having flowers on the tables. She always made sure that, following a tradition she had learned in Britain, there would be delicate savouries for the guests following the dessert. There were, of course, silver and gold monogrammed cigarette boxes and exquisite cut-glass fingerbowls; the dinner service and silver were souvenirs of York House and Fort Belvedere. According to Suzy Menkes, Wallis especially favoured as main courses roast partridge, chicken Maryland – a nostalgic touch – grouse and faux filets and then, for dessert, the luscious dark chocolate cake known to the world as Sachertorte.

The Windsors decided that they also needed a country home, a gentle and subdued place of escape; despite the fact that the Paris house had its tiny park and its greenhouses, the duke yearned for a garden. From the beginning, one of his greatest pleasures in life had been pottering about among flowers, cross-breeding, vigorously applying a watering can and dibbling the soil for new plantings. Under his green fingers even the most reluctant earth would let plants flourish and multiply. Give him a packet of seeds and a set of instructions and he was in seventh heaven.

With great good fortune, the duke and duchess managed to locate the house which, of all the houses in their lives, they were to love the most. It was known familiarly as the Mill. Only the Fort approached it in terms of the magic it held for the duke. Its real name was the Moulin de la Tuilerie, and it was just fifteen miles south-west of the fashionable Paris suburb of Neuilly, outside the charming but rather gloomy village of Gif-sur-Yvette. It was a seventeenth-century structure, brown with white shutters, redolent of a more comfortable era when kings were kings and a leisurely aristocracy ruled France. It was owned by the distinguished designer and creator of theatrical spectacles Etienne Drian; it was rented initially, and then bought, for no more than £16,000.

Fastidious visitors like Cecil Beaton and Kitty Bache (Mrs Gilbert) Miller made some criticisms of the house to Charles Murphy as they walked through it. Beaton thought the whole thing excessive, and he disapproved of the use of war medallions, bamboo chairs and gimmicky pouffes. Kitty Miller hated the clutter; like many Americans she objected to the British habit, now mimicked by Wallis, of wanting to fill every bit of space in the Victorian tradition. There was one fantastic import from York House: the immense illuminated war map that had embellished the duke's rooms there, representing the world from sea to sea, from pole to pole, and marked with all the journeys he had undertaken in his lifetime. From as early as 1933 such visitors as Gloria Vanderbilt and her mother had been captivated by the map, and now another generation of friends and acquaintances would stand transfixed before it. Two Grenadier bass drums formed the coffee table in the living room. The stables and cowsheds became a guest wing. There the atmosphere was exceptionally military and nautical, with Highland banners and tartars, trophies, Great War buttons and other souvenirs everywhere. The abdication table formed part of this private museum. It was said that years later, when the duchess died, the table was offered to the British royal family. 'The queen needs the abdication table like a hole in the head,' a Palace representative is, with unaccustomed informality, supposed to have said.

Much of 1952 and 1953 was absorbed in work on the two houses. During this period the duke resumed and the duchess acquired a warm friendship. They became very close to Sir Oswald and Lady Mosley, who lived at the Temple de la Gloire, only a few miles from the Mill. Since the duke had first known them in the 1930s, they had had a checkered career. It will be recalled that in

May 1940 Winston Churchill, acting on the recommendation of Sir Robert Vansittart and Clement Attlee, had imprisoned them in London for activities that were considered inimical to the public safety under the provisions of the specially introduced Regulation 18B. They had suffered considerable privations in jail. For a long time Lady Mosley did not see her children, because she was anxious that they should be kept away from the scandal. The effects of an icy winter of 1940, the bad food and the insanitary conditions seriously affected Sir Oswald's normally robust health; by 1943, he was a victim of phlebitis, and it was felt that he might not survive another year.

A much embattled home secretary, Herbert Morrison, and Winston Churchill apparently decided that Mosley must not be a martyr, and they arranged for both his and Lady Mosley's release. At the end of the war it was the Mosleys' misfortune that Attlee was elected prime minister as head of the Labour government; he made sure that life continued to be uncomfortable for the pair. According to Lady Mosley, she and her husband were forbidden the use of passports and had to flee the country aboard a chartered yacht for Ireland. They later went to France, where they at last settled in the Temple. It had once been the property of General Moreau, chief of the armies of the Rhine, who was considered to have been a rival of Napoleon's until his death in 1810. For years the building had belonged to the family of the Comtes de Noailles. When the Mosleys purchased it in 1951, it was in a state of extreme disrepair, a dank and pathetic structure that had lost most of its character. They proceeded to remodel it with great taste and style, and the Windsors very much enjoyed going there.

It was unwise for the Windsors to associate with the Mosleys at this particular juncture. The Mosleys not only were persona non grata in London but were not to be received by British diplomatic representatives in Europe. One would have thought that, in the wake of all they had been through, the Windsors would have wished to associate only with those who were apolitical, or who by no stretch of the imagination could recall the disastrous commitment to a now vanquished and deceased Adolf Hitler and Mussolini. Instead, they chose to enjoy a public friendship with the man most clearly associated with Nazism in the minds of thinking Britons. In fact, Lady Mosley's sister Unity Mitford had been notorious among the more celebrated British supporters of Hitler, had flung herself at the Führer himself and had attempted suicide following public condemnation.

Still resident at the Temple de la Gloire, retaining the delicate beauty of a moonbeam in her old age, the late Lady Mosley recalled to me in December 1986 her friendship with the Windsors. She made it clear that, starting in the 1930s and right up until their deaths, the Windsors shared her views on politics. They felt, as she and her husband did, that if a separate peace had been made with the Führer in 1939 and Hitler had been given a free hand against the Soviet Union, the world would have been saved from communism and the British Empire would never have fallen into decay. She said:

> The Windsors agreed with me, and the Duchess was certainly politically sophisticated and knew exactly what she was doing and saying, that World War I had been a total failure, that it was a disaster the Austro-Hungarian Empire had been broken up, that the Versailles Treaty was grossly unfair, and that Germany should never have been encircled in the 1930s. If Hitler had been given a free hand to destroy Communism, and if he had been allowed to deport the Jews, if Britain and America had accepted them, there would have been no need for a holocaust. There was of course no room in Palestine for them. Hitler felt the Jews behaved abominably in Germany after World War I, and all he wanted to do was be rid of them. And one mustn't forget that anti-Semitism was endemic everywhere in Central Europe: the Poles hated them, the Czechs hated them, everyone did. Of course, my husband and the Windsors and I felt that we could not exonerate Hitler for being impatient and provoking World War II. With two egos like Churchill and Hitler, there was little chance for peace in the world. But still, if the right people had been in power in England, particularly Lloyd George, there could have been a negotiated peace.

The Mosleys dined at the Mill twice a week, and the Windsors almost that frequently at the Temple de la Gloire. One of their perennial topics of conversation was the idea that after the Second

World War ended the Allied forces should have occupied what were now the satellite countries of the Soviets before the Russians got to them, and should have proceeded to conquer the Soviet Union itself. In none of these retrospective views were the Windsors in any way exceptional in aristocratic or royal society. Such opinions were bruited about clubland and right-wing dinner tables from shore to shining shore, and still are in 2004.

In April 1950, Wallis learned of the death of Win Spencer at sixty-two. During the early 1950s, she continued to suffer from poor health. In February 1951, she was at the Harkness Pavilion at the Columbia Presbyterian Medical Center in New York for tests, followed by surgery to remove her apparently cancerous ovaries. Dr Benjamin P. Watson, Fellow of the Scottish Royal College of Surgeons and an eminent gynaecologist, assisted the American doctor, Henry Wisdom Cave. Wallis was depressed and miserable. After she had gained sufficient strength, she began desultory work on her own memoirs, using a variety of collaborators, including Cleveland Amory, who later became the author of the witty and perceptive *Who Killed Society?*, and the hard-working Charles Murphy. Like so many authors of memoirs, she naturally selected from the past those facts which would flatter her, omitting those which would not. She was particularly evasive in the matter of China. That entire chapter of the book was so completely fabricated that she even altered the name of the hotel at which she stayed in Shanghai from the Astor House to the Palace; she scarcely mentioned the Chinese civil war, and, apart from her arrivals on the *Chaumont* and the *Empress of Canada*, she scrambled her dates completely. One might legitimately conclude that, concerned over her oath of secrecy, she was anxious to disguise the fact that she had been working for US naval intelligence, and of course she would also have been concerned about hiding her affair with Count Ciano.

Throughout the book, however, facts were remorselessly rearranged in what amounted to a self-performed face-lift. The Oakes case was dismissed in brief paragraphs; only in the passages dealing with her childhood and her flight to France at the time of the abdication did she rise to the drama of the occasion. Yet in spite of everything the book, finally published in 1956 under the excellent title *The Heart Has Its Reasons*, had enormous charm, reflecting in abundance its author's politically misguided but winning and desirable personality. Though it did not equal the critical success of the duke's own volume, the book sold well and attracted a new generation of readers to this charismatic, electric and compulsively ambitious personality.

Old friends turned up in the 1950s, and new friendships were formed. One of the most embattled of these was with the dumpy, smart, sophisticated hostess and society mascot Elsa Maxwell. She had, of course, encountered the Windsors before, most notably when they arrived in Vienna on one of their visits in 1935, when she was riveted by the duchess's strong, forceful stride across the lobby of the Hotel Bristol on her way to the lift. Miss Maxwell had known the duke when he was Prince of Wales, and like everyone else was captivated by him. By the late 1930s Miss Maxwell was the party organizer par excellence of her era. Despite her phenomenal lack of personal attractiveness and a figure that resembled a doughnut, she was called upon by everyone who mattered to organize spectacular occasions that people talked about for decades.

Miss Maxwell had a knack for engaging the most skilled caterers, the finest decorators, the very best chefs, waiters and attendants, the most glittering dance bands, and the most exotic and beautiful young men and women. She created, for the bored and exhausted members of high society, a range of stimuli in the form of soirees attended by a mixture of movie stars, playwrights, authors, politicians, composers and artists. She brought them all together and moved among her guests with a somewhat toadlike but persistent waddle, fixing everyone in sight with her charming, always fascinated, stare, snapping out deliciously squalid gossip, and making sure that all the guests were happy with their company and that their champagne or cocktail glasses were never empty.

Elsa Maxwell was infuriated by the Windsors' interest in Hitler and strongly felt that the duke should never have abdicated, but should have retained Wallis as his mistress. She would even confront them at parties and tell them point-blank what she thought of them, her effrontery causing them only to smile. She ran into them in both New York and Europe during this period – they enjoyed a mutual friendship with Mrs George Baker. In December 1952 Mrs Lytle Hull, sister-in-law of the former secretary of state,

Cordell Hull, gave a tremendous benefit party in New York and invited the Windsors. Wallis asked that her name should not be mentioned as a sponsor; she was always crying poor and trying to find ways out of paying income tax. Elsa, who was making all the arrangements, was annoyed about this, as she had expected to display the duchess as her trump card, showing not only the end of a long hostility but also her capacity to attract the very greatest to her occasions. She was even more annoyed the following year when Mrs Hull queened it over a similar Maxwell-organized benefit. On this occasion Miss Maxwell chose the beautiful Duchess of Argyll, the Duchesse de Brissac, the Duchess of Alba and the Duchess Disera as her sponsors. Cholly Knickerbocker, the popular society gossip columnist, asked Wallis her opinion of the choices. Wallis snapped back, 'It would take four ordinary duchesses to make one Duchess of Windsor.' Elsa was phenomenally upset about that. And she was also annoyed because, despite many pleadings, she could never get the Windsors to speak publicly in her favour. However, she was mollified when the duchess hired her to present the Windsor Ball at the Waldorf Astoria in 1953, with decor by Cecil Beaton. It was a tremendous occasion: the duchess caused a flurry when she entered the ball, not on the arm of the duke but on that of the socialite Prince Serge Obolensky.

The Windsors and Elsa quarrelled again soon afterwards, chiefly over the omnipresent Jimmy Donahue, whom Elsa could not abide and whose behaviour, particularly in front of his adored mother Jessie, the somewhat prim and proper Miss Maxwell found insupportably offensive, despite the fact that she herself was a lesbian. She begged the duchess not to drag Jimmy along on a Mediterranean cruise in 1954, and she was continually worried that his ménage of male prostitutes and other low-life might threaten the Windsors' safety or make off with their possessions. As it turned out, these fears were groundless, but that did not prevent Miss Maxwell from retaining them.

By the mid-1950s, the Windsors were growing tired of Donahue. He was losing his looks all too rapidly under the onslaughts of drinking, smoking and endless late nights. A ghastly incident to which Charles Murphy was privy brought the whole miserable matter to an end. The embattled trio were at Baden Baden in

Germany, staying at a hotel and apparently taking the waters. During a quarrel in the hotel restaurant one evening, Jimmy kicked the duchess so hard that she bled. She screamed in combined shock and fury, and the duke, scowling and red-faced, assisted the duchess to a sofa. He screamed at Jimmy to get out. Soon after Jimmy left the dining room, the unembarrassable playboy telephoned the duke and said, 'I can't find my valet to pack. He's off with yours.' The duke slammed down the receiver: the most atrocious relationship of the Windsors' lives was almost at an end. According to the author Hugo Vickers, basing his findings upon the diaries of Cecil Beaton, the final rift was caused by a petty detail: Donahue was eating too much garlic, and his breath offended the duke and duchess.

19

LATE AFTERNOON

In the early months of 1953, Queen Mary, then in her mid-eighties, began to fail. On 6 March the duke, accompanied by the Princess Royal, who had been visiting New York, sailed aboard the *Queen Elizabeth* for England to see his stricken mother. The duchess again stayed behind at the Waldorf Towers.

No sooner had he arrived than the old queen passed away. The duchess heard the news on the radio at the hotel; her secretary, Anne Seagrin, recalled later that, to her surprise, the duchess wept when she heard the news. It was a remarkable feature of the duchess's character that, despite all the calumny heaped upon her from the Palace, and her own hatred of England, knowing how much Queen Mary meant to her husband she shared his grief almost as though she had known the queen herself. For years afterwards she kept a picture of the deceased queen on a table in her bedroom in Paris.

The coronation of Queen Elizabeth II was to take place on 2 June. This presented a unique problem because the normal period of court mourning was six months of full mourning followed by six more of half mourning. The Duke of Windsor as monarch had set a precedent by shortening the entire mourning period to six months. Elizabeth had reduced the period to four months for her father. In order not to upset the arrangements for the coronation, the new mourning period was reduced to one month. Queen Mary had left explicit instructions that in the event of her death nothing must affect the coronation; this was typical of her.

For the second time in a little over two years, London was draped with black mourning banners. Flags flew at half-mast again. A long stream of visitors appeared at Marlborough House to leave notes of condolence along with visiting cards. Members of both houses of parliament convened in black suits. The prime minister, Churchill, again moved the duke to tears as he delivered a BBC broadcast, stating incorrectly that Queen Mary was the last living link with Queen Victoria. It was yet another excruciating reminder to the duke of the world of his childhood, a world now irrevocably lost in an increasingly pragmatic and democratic age, with the Soviets looming and dangerous. He can only have realized the poignant irony contained within Churchill's statement:

> She [Queen Mary] died in the knowledge that the crown of these realms, worn so gloriously by her husband and by her son, and soon to be set with all solemnity on the head of her granddaughter, is far more broadly and securely based on the people's love and the nation's will than in the sedate days of her youth, when rank and privilege ruled society.

The duke can scarcely have failed to note that only one son of his late father was mentioned by the prime minister.

Lord Beaverbrook seized the occasion to express through his newspapers an urgent request to the world at large that the long exile of the Duke and Duchess of Windsor should be terminated. The *Daily Express* stated in an editorial, 'It is the deep and earnest desire of the nation that [the former king] should make his home in this, the land that gave him birth.' Other newspapers pointed out that, while Queen Mary was alive, the duke had announced repeatedly to her that he would take up residence in Great Britain only if the duchess were to be received by his family. Queen Mary, the newspapers stated had remained unalterably opposed to the duchess's reception. These were painful things for the duchess to read.

Once again, thousands of saddened Londoners filed past the royal coffin lying in state in Westminster Hall. The drums sounded; the salute of guns rang through the air; the gun carriage, drawn by six black horses, lumbered through the streets. Behind the carriage the Duke of Windsor walked in company with the Duke of Edinburgh, the Duke of Gloucester and the Duke of Kent. At West-minster Hall the new Queen, Princess Margaret, the Princess Royal, the Queen Mother and the Duchesses of Kent and Gloucester were waiting. The burial at St George's Chapel, Windsor, was a further ordeal for the duke. As at the time of his brother's interment, he could not hold back the tears. At the end he stood quietly beside the tomb and then made a deep bow towards it, whispering words of farewell to the mother he loved. He sailed on the *Queen Elizabeth* the following day for the United States, and for most of the voyage remained confined to his cabin. He would not attend his niece's coronation since, despite all his pleas, it was decided not to invite the duchess. According to some sources, the duke himself was not invited. The Windsors remained in New York during the June celebrations, listening with mixed feelings to the skilful running commentaries by Richard Dimbleby and others in the broadcasts from London.

Soon afterwards, the couple faced the unpleasant ordeal of the publication of the German Foreign Office documents which dis-closed the duke's leakage of the discussion that had taken place at the War Cabinet meeting of February 1940 on the matter of the Belgian invasion plan. Confronted with the matter by reporters during a visit to London on 9 November, the duke denied the entire affair and said that he was not responsible and that the documents were false. No one had the temerity to cross-question him or to seek further investigation, and his denial was allowed to stand. Churchill, as always, defended him. When a question was asked in parliament, Churchill stated that the charges against the duke were, 'of course, quite untrue'. He added: 'I naturally thought it proper to show [the documents] to the Duke of Windsor and, on May 25, told him they were to be published in the United States and in this country later in the year. His Royal Highness did not raise any objection. He thought, and I agree with him, that they can be treated with contempt.'

In January 1955, the Windsors visited President Eisenhower at the White House. They had first encountered him as a colonel on their first wartime visit to Washington in 1941. In March they were present at White Plains, New York, where they exhibited their favourite three-year-old pug, Goldengleam Trooper, in the fifteenth championship of the Saw Mill River Kennel Club. The dog won against 950 competitors. However, it lost the gold rosette to Mr and Mrs Arnold J. Canton's Golden Note.

In October 1955, Mrs George Baker gave a party for the Windsors at her elaborate home at Locust Valley, Long Island. Fifty-eight guests attended for a banquet and dancing. Among the guests were two recent acquaintances of the duchess, the wealthy and handsome thirty-five-year-old sportsman and racehorse owner William Woodward, Jr, and his wife, Ann. Wallis very much liked Woodward's mother, the still glamorous and fascinating former Elsie Ogden Cryder. The Woodwards left the party at 1 a.m., returning to their house at Oyster Bay. Mrs Woodward was nervous that night because there had been talk of prowlers in the neighbourhood.

At 2.08 a.m., the operator answered an emergency call from the Woodward house. Ann was shrieking hysterically. Lieutenant Haff arrived at the house and found Mrs Woodward in a state of desperation; Woodward was lying naked on his face on his bedroom floor, shot through the right temple.

It was discovered that Ann Woodward had taken a duck-hunting rifle and loaded it with shells, placing it next to her bed. She said through floods of tears that she had heard her watchdog barking and was convinced there was an intruder. She turned on the lamp next to her bed, picked up the rifle and made her way to the door. Seeing a man standing there, she fired twice, right into his face.

The Windsors, who were staying with Mrs Baker, were advised of the shooting that night. The news was of course a considerable shock to them. Wallis had even danced with Bill Woodward at the party. The duke shared Woodward's interest in horses, and they had enjoyed their meetings socially over the previous months. The Windsors followed the subsequent events with deep interest; Wallis was questioned twice by the police. Mrs Woodward was held for questioning while society flew into an uproar. The Windsors were asked about the killing wherever they went. They wisely decided not to get involved, and made no attempt to contact Ann during her long ordeal, though they did remain in close touch with Mrs Baker and Elsie Woodward.

On 25 November, a Nassau County grand jury heard Mrs Woodward tell her story. On the advice of her lawyers, she appeared voluntarily and signed a waiver of immunity against the possible consequences of what she might say. In a state of great distress, sobbing helplessly, she told her version of the facts simply, poignantly and with apparent honesty, her face devoid of make-up, her cheeks drained of colour. The jury accepted her account and reached the conclusion that she was not guilty of a crime. However, many refused to believe her. The most persistent sceptic was Truman Capote, who in the late 1960s and 1970s would pursue the matter. He made clear that his book then in preparation, *Answered Prayers*, would disclose the fact that Ann Woodward was guilty of murder.

Capote's destructive campaign achieved results. Ann Woodward, met by suspicious glances from those who believed Capote's story, and still haunted by the horror of what she had done, committed suicide. As a result, Capote himself was adversely affected. His whole life hinged upon society; and many members of society closed their doors to him. The Windsors were as angry with Capote as everyone else.

The late 1950s brought two further bereavements. Herman Rogers, whose first wife Katherine had passed away in 1948, died of cancer in the south of France. He left a son from his second marriage. Ernest Simpson died, also of cancer, in 1958. Wallis did not visit him in hospital in London when he lay dying. She sent a large bouquet of his favourite chrysanthemums, a reminiscence of their early times together, with a note that said, 'From the Duchess of Windsor'.

In April 1956, the Windsors embarked on the first of a series of charitable projects that did much to restore their tarnished image in the eyes of thinking people. They set up a clinic for the rehabilitation of handicapped people in New York. In this they were assisted by Dr Howard A. Rusk, director of the Institute of Physical Medicine and Rehabilitation at the New York University Bellevue Medical Center. They also set up a similar clinic in Paris with the aid of Dr Jacques Hindermayer, director of the rehabilitation programme at the Paris Children's Hospital.

But while their public relations image was being burnished by these adventures in charity, the Windsors, with apparent perversity, seemed to encourage relationships which could only reconfirm the more unfair suspicions of those who wished to cast aspersions on them. They resumed their prewar friendship with Prince Otto and Princess Ann-Mari von Bismarck. The Princess von Bismarck recalls today that she lent the Windsors her home in Marbella and stayed with them at their house in Paris. Her husband had been cleared of Nazi associations at the end of the Second World War, but nevertheless the fact that the prince had been a representative of Germany in London as chargé d'affaires at the embassy throughout much of 1936, the year of Edward VIII's reign, emphasized the duke's persistent political interests, memories and concerns.

In 1960, the duchess made another of her rather serious mistakes. She decided to embark upon a critique of the British royal family and government for its 'twenty-four years of persecution' against the duke. In an article in *McCall's* magazine, published in January 1961, she wrote, 'My husband has been punished like a small boy who gets a spanking every day of his life for a single transgression.' She continued, 'I think the monarchy's lack of dignity toward him [at the time of the abdication crisis] and occasionally now, has been resented.' She also wrote,

> It suddenly occurred to me how ridiculous it is to go on behind a family-designed, government-manufactured curtain of asbestos that protects the British Commonwealth from dangerous us . . . This man, with his unparalleled knowledge, trained in the affairs of State . . . was first given an insignificant military post. Eventually, he was 'put out of harm's way' with an appointment of little consequence – the Governorship of the Bahamas.

This outburst was singularly ill-advised and, had it not been for the consideration of the queen, might have closed the door to the Windsors at Buckingham Palace forever. It seemed almost deliberately designed to infuriate the Queen Mother, who continued to tell people that it was the influence of Wallis that had forced her husband to assume the throne, thereby destroying his health. For the duchess to portray the royal family as mean, vindictive and destructive on some absurdly hypocritical moral basis was a falsification of the truth.

In Paris in the 1960s, the Windsors surpassed even their own previous record as party givers. Sir John Colville recalled that everything at the Bois de Boulogne house was 'perfection itself'. The food, the service, the exquisite elegance of the hostess, the collection of French aristocracy and representatives of the diplomatic corps, all in a setting of matchless elegance created by Boudin, made an unforgettable impression. Lady Mosley in her turn will not forget those evenings, the candlelight shining on polished mahogany, the period mirrors glowing from the walls, the paintings and tapestries and fine silver.

The guests were served by footmen dressed in royal scarlet livery. The table was decorated with six immense Venetian sterling silver candelabra. Each guest had beside his or her plate a small, perfectly fashioned snuffbox, containing either cigarettes or small gifts. If there were Spanish or German guests present, the duke would talk to them expertly in their own language. Oddly, in view of their place of residence, neither of the Windsors could manage more than fourth-form French.

The duke remained more outspoken than the duchess on political themes. He continued to say, at these dinner parties preaching in some cases to the converted, that a negotiated peace should have been made with Hitler in 1940 and that England should have retained a neutral position, as Sweden did, while the Germans and Italians were free to destroy communism. He would point out that all his predictions had come true and that now, because there had been no Third World War in 1945 and Russia had not been crushed, one had to face the menace of communism. If the Rothschilds or other figures of the Jewish community were not present, he would drag out his old theme of blaming Roosevelt and the Jews for the confrontation and total surrender policy of the Second World War.

As the 1960s wore on, the duke acted with an increasing eccentricity, watched with disapproving frowns by his more composed and restrained wife. Charles Murphy has recorded that the duke would rather awkwardly attempt to conduct the dance band hired for the evening or would suddenly stand up and perform as though on an invisible cello or violin. He would join the band, clumsily tapping away at the drums. He would even sing, most raucously, in reprises of the hit numbers of *Annie Get Your Gun* or

South Pacific. At times he would break out in Spanish or German. During one party he danced a clumsy charleston with Noël Coward.

While Wallis shopped or went to fashion salons, was massaged or spent hours at the hairdresser's, the duke continued to display his passion for golf. He remained rather a poor hand at the sport. He had been through the hands of numerous golfing pros but still, according to Murphy, could only manage to score in the nineties. He was as stingy as ever, failing to tip even the caddies, who in France depended upon largesse to exist. At the same time he never ceased going over his accounts books, watching everything meticulously, jiggling his knee in a state of nervous tension. Chainsmoking, he would scatter ash over the ledger pages, brushing it irritably aside as he found some real or imaginary mistake in his accountant's work. He remained shrewd in his investments, taking the money he had pulled out of the Central Railroad and investing it in reliable blue-chip stocks. The money from his memoirs was expertly placed in a varied portfolio. His lawyers and London advisers on his royal interests were on their toes day and night to satisfy him. But, above all, the garden of the Mill absorbed him and satisfied him. He still loved working there, pottering about in old shoes and a large, floppy hat, blissfully cross-pollinating.

Much of the mid-1960s was taken up with elaborate social events: parties at the New York World's Fair of 1964; major functions in honour of President Lyndon B. Johnson; benefits at the Waldorf, including the big Heart of America Ball, held in the Sert Room, where a columned gazebo, covered with elder vines, was ablaze with multicoloured lights. In June 1964, the duke and duchess celebrated their birthdays. The magnificent party in Paris is still talked about by everyone who attended it.

But at the same time, life was not without its many problems and moments of anguish. The duchess had two face-lifts but she did not respond well to surgery, and the post-operative recovery period caused her considerable distress. The duke was suffering from severe eye problems; ever since he had read the difficult and complex official documents during his reign in 1936 he had had almost consistent strain in his eyes, and now the ravages of advancing age had drastically affected his vision. The retina of his left eye had become detached in late 1964, and an operation was recommended in London. It was feared that he might go blind in that eye and that the other eye might be affected in what was known as sympathetic blindness.

In August 1964, Aunt Bessie turned a hundred, and Wallis's cousin Lelia Noyes gave a big party for her at Wakefield Manor. The house was as beautifully preserved as it had been during Wallis's childhood. Twenty-five relatives and friends attended the dinner, at which Mrs Noyes proposed the toast, saying, 'This is for Aunt Bessie to all the world, a great lady, once called by the King of England a "wise and gentle woman".' The Windsors' health problems prevented them from attending the dinner. According to Wallis's cousin, Mrs Dale St Dennis, Aunt Bessie was very disappointed. The family was upset when Wallis failed to attend Aunt Bessie's funeral; she died on 29 November. But at the time Wallis, recovering from surgery on her right foot, was in hospital in New York. She was bitterly disappointed that the doctors would not let her go. However, the duke did put in an appearance.

To Wallis's distress, he was ailing seriously by this stage, suffering from an aneurism in the aorta – the abdominal artery – below the branches that led to the kidneys. The decision was made to have an immediate operation, because the weakening of the artery wall through which blood was circulated from the heart could present serious danger; it could rupture suddenly, with at least a seven per cent chance of immediate death. Only in recent years has the corrective surgery become available, in which a synthetic fibre graft or section could be used. The pre-eminent expert in the field was Dr Michael de Bakey, professor of surgery at Baylor University College of Medicine in Houston. On 11 December, the Windsors arrived by train in that city and were met by the British consul general, Peter Hope. They decided to take up residence in the Methodist Hospital together, arriving with a police motorcycle escort in a $35,000 Rolls-Royce grey Phantom limousine. Despite their personal distress the Windsors gave a buoyant interview to reporters, carrying off the situation with their customary style and grace. They were touched and surprised when, on entering the suite of rooms, they found bouquets of flowers from the queen and the Princess Royal. This was yet another subtle and welcome indication of the present queen's moderate attitude towards the Windsors, or at least towards the duke.

The operation took place on 16 December; it began at 7.35 a.m. and lasted exactly sixty-seven minutes. Though the duke was thin and generally devoid of body fat, the operation was still strenuous and delicate for a man of his age. Had he been over-weight, it would have been much more problematical. De Bakey found that the aneurism was the size of a large grapefruit, and there was severe erosion of the aorta wall. In fact, the duke had been in more danger than had been expected. The duchess was not present during the operation itself – she was stoical and calm as she waited – but she was with the duke every other minute. As he came round from the anaesthetic he was remarkably perky, and talked to the duchess and de Bakey with an eager smile. Letters and telegrams poured in from all over the world. Two days after-wards, the duke managed to struggle to his feet and take a few steps, feeling chipper but undeniably and understandably weak. He sat down hard on the bed, breaking into a charming laugh at his own expense.

Everyone in the hospital adored him. He was the best possible patient, considerate of the nurses and always ready with a joke. He never complained about the liquid diet or the subsequent soft foods. His eye was still giving him much trouble, and when he waved to the cameras during this first Christmas photo session, his left eye, sadly, was closed. He pulled himself together for the traditional turkey dinner on Christmas Day.

On New Year's Day, the Windsors left the Methodist Hospital and moved into a ninth-floor suite at the Warwick Hotel. Six days later they flew to New York, accompanied by the duke's personal physician, Dr Arthur Antenucci. This was the first time the duchess had set foot on a jet plane: it was a Delta Airlines Convaire 880. The couple sailed for Europe on 29 January aboard the *United States*. They were greatly saddened by the death of Winston Churchill; because of the medical problems of the moment, they were unable to attend the funeral, and the duke was represented by Sir John Aird. The persistent eye trouble would be taken care of at the London Clinic under the supervision of the distinguished Sir Stewart Duke-Elder, surgeon oculist to the queen herself. Again, the queen sent a magnificent bouquet to the clinic. The operation, which took place on the night of 26 February, was successful. Sir Stewart Duke-Elder used recently improved high-intensity laser beams, now a standard in eye surgery, to weld the troublesome retina to the back of the eyeball. A second operation was involved, treating the membrane that delivered the images to the eye's optic nerve. On 15 March, after the duke had had a third session of corrective treatment, the queen arrived at the London Clinic with her principal private secretary, Sir Michael Adeane, and her body-guard, Detective Inspector Albert Perkins. Sir Stewart Duke-Elder and two of his colleagues greeted her as she arrived at the suite. It was made clear that she would accept the duchess's presence, and in a historic act she greeted Wallis, who curtseyed deeply. They had not seen each other since that awkward moment when Wallis appeared at the Royal Lodge in 1936 and suggested that the garden be rearranged according to her specifications.

The duke presented a smiling but sad figure as he sat in an armchair, wearing a robe over his pyjamas, his left eye concealed behind bandages. The meeting was somewhat strained, but both the queen and the duke behaved with appropriate royal composure and refused to allow past differences to affect them. The duke seized the occasion to ask the queen if she would permit him to be buried, when death came, in the private burial ground of the royal family at Frogmore. And he had a further request – a request of the highest moment that would call upon the monarch's consideration. The duke understandably wanted Wallis buried next to him, and he wanted both of them to be accorded the privilege of funeral services at St George's Chapel.

The queen promised to attend to the matter. She felt favourably disposed to the thought of the duke's being buried at Frogmore, but she was said to have been opposed to the idea of the duchess's being buried there. The Queen Mother is said to have felt even more strongly on the matter. Of course, in the eyes of the queen and her mother Wallis still was not 'Her Royal Highness', nor by any stretch of the imagination could she be called a royal person, nor was she acknowledged even at that late hour as a member of the family. But the queen, who was fond of her uncle, could not bear to hurt him. She was faced with a considerable quandary, which she did not immediately resolve.

The Duchess of Kent turned up, quite disguising her ill feelings about the failure of the Windsors to send her a note of condolence following the death of her husband. The Duke and Duchess of Gloucester were in Australia; the Queen Mother, who did send flowers, was not present at the hospital. Nor, so far as is known, did she speak to the duke on the telephone.

On 19 March, the Windsors left the London Clinic; caught by a cruel camera, the duke was wearing dark glasses and looked pathetically frail. The queen visited the duke and duchess at Claridges, and she brought with her pleasing news. She would grant the duke permission to be buried at Frogmore, and the Duchess would be accorded an identical privilege. Moreover, both would be given the special funeral service requested at St George's Chapel. This indication of understanding from the Palace was of the utmost importance to the Windsors.

But in the wake of this display of forgiveness came bad news. On 28 March the Princess Royal died of a coronary thrombosis during a walk through the grounds of her home in Yorkshire. Doctors advised the Windsors not to attempt the journey to Leeds to attend the funeral. The couple sent a white carnation wreath; the duke was deeply distressed by his beloved sister's death. However, they did attend the memorial service at Westminster Abbey, their first 'royal' outing in Britain. The stricken Lady Churchill, still overcome by her husband's death, was also present. These were grievous, stressful times. Death and the prospect of death seemed to haunt the Windsors every hour: the inevitable burden of growing old.

The Queen Mother remained adamant in her attitude towards the duchess. Wallis's disdain for the Queen Mother was equally intense. The duchess did nothing to overcome the problem when, following the Queen Mother's stomach operation in 1966, she said, 'It must be all those chocolates she's eating.'

Like Errol Flynn before her – forgiven his wartime treason, he had been used as a CIA agent against Castro in Cuba – Wallis joined the same agency in the winter of 1966. She used her position as a famous hostess to determine whether certain of her regular dinner guests was acting as a mole in the Paris headquarters of NATO, leaking secrets of American conventional and atomic weapons to Moscow.

Her control was John Derby, code name Jupiter, head of the CIA operation in France; she was to report to her friend Aline, Countess of Romanones, who had been an American secret agent since the war years. Ironically, Wallis was accorded the code name Willy, almost exactly the German code name for the Duke of Windsor in 1940. Smartly, she she did not mention this to the countess.

Wallis settled on the American NATO officer Paul Ferguson as the possible mole, but efforts to have him make a slip in conversation at her dinner parties failed. His wife, Maureen, proved to be a mistress of the legpull: realizing Wallis was investigating her husband, she talked of mysterious visits out of town, attendance at classical concerts – thought at the time to be used for conveying information through music scores – and claimed that he was actually his twin brother Peter, exchanged for him in her marital bed without a demur.

Following this, Wallis targeted a certain spy in NATO; according to the Countess of Romanones, as soon as she did so a CIA agent was found murdered, his death staged as a suicide by gas oven. A letter from him arrived at John Derby's office the next day saying that 'Willy' should find out if the man would be in Paris on 1 February, and for her to 'beware'. Unafraid, Wallis invited him and his wife to dinner on the 2nd; they didn't turn up, and after that, according to Romanones, they fled – to Austria, Hungary and then Russia, without the secrets Romanones alleges they had promised the Soviet KGB. At lunch at Maxim's soon after, 'Gilbert' congratulated Wallis on her feat.

In the summer of 1967, the Windsors were invited to attend the unveiling of a plaque in honour of Queen Mary's memory. When they announced that they could not get to England from New York in time for the originally scheduled date of 26 May, the centenary of Queen Mary's birth, the monarch postponed the unveiling until 5 June. Lord Mountbatten, who had apparently softened in his attitude towards the Windsors, greeted them at Southampton as they disembarked from the United States. He invited them to stay with him at his house, Broadlands, at Romsey. The next day, the Windsors appeared at York House for the first time in thirty years, where they lunched with the Duke and Duchess of Gloucester. The Duke of Gloucester, too, was suffering from the ravages of time: he was partially deaf, his circulation was sluggish and his memory poor. It was a tormenting meeting for all concerned.

The following day, the streets were crowded with well-wishers as the Windsors drove from Claridges to St James's Palace for the unveiling. There was a tremendous cheer from the hundreds of people thronging the street as the duchess, in an exquisite Givenchy costume, blue coat and pillbox hat, and the duke, haggard, with an expression of deep sadness, left the royal limousine and made their way to the wall where the plaque had been inserted. The Queen Mother was present; the duchess stared at her intently, no doubt to the recipient's annoyance. According to the Countess of Romanones, the duchess appeared to be counting the berries in the Queen Mother's hat. The countess described the scene as told to her by Wallis. The Queen Mother graciously, if coolly, extended her hand to Wallis, who with great audacity and singular lack of taste failed to drop a curtsey. When asked about this later, the duchess snapped, 'She stopped people from curtseying to me. Why should I curtsey to her?'

With great composure the elder Queen Elizabeth gave no inkling of the displeasure she must have felt at this outrageous breach of etiquette. She talked to her old bête noire with all the seeming warmth and dignity which she, above all others save the queen herself, could summon up when necessary. Her private thoughts, it goes without saying, must have been another matter. It is most unfortunate that the duchess, when curtseying to the queen, could not resist a direct glance at the queen's already offended parent.

After the service of dedication, the Queen Mother said a temporary farewell to the Windsors. Once again, Wallis failed to curtsey. 'I do hope we meet again,' the Queen Mother said, probably not meaning it. Wallis rudely replied, 'Oh? When?'

The Windsors attended a small luncheon given at Kensington Palace by Princess Marina (as the former Duchess of Kent called herself now that her son, the present duke, was married). Then they returned on a plane of the Queen's Flight to Paris. Prince Michael of Kent, followed by Prince William of Gloucester, came to see the Windsors; they now addressed the duchess as 'Aunt Wallis'. Her apparent rehabilitation continued. *Burke's Peerage* urged that she be granted the title of 'Royal Highness', as the previous refusal to accord her this title was 'the most flagrant act of discrimination in the whole history of our dynasty'. But flagrant or not, the act of discrimination was not revoked. The duchess was never accorded the title of HRH.

20

EVENING AND NIGHT

In a determined effort to stave off the advance of old age, the duke yielded to suggestions from several of his friends and, emulating Somerset Maugham, travelled to Switzerland on more than one occasion in the late 1960s to attend the Paul Niehans Clinic at Vevey, near Lausanne. The duchess apparently did not undertake Niehans's rejuvenating treatment until later.

He and the duchess indulged themselves with an extraordinary degree of extravagance. By the late 1960s, they had a staff of thirty servants; they had separate chauffeurs to drive them on shopping trips, and the kitchen staff alone was seven-strong, including the chef, assistant chef, washers-up and scullery maids. When guests arrived, they were greeted by seven liveried footmen. Needless to say, when they addressed the duchess her household members invariably used the title 'Your Royal Highness'.

By 1969, the Windsors were forced to put their beloved Mill up for sale. The reason was not only that they needed to obtain some extra capital; the journey from Paris to the country was proving excessively tiring for the now shockingly fragile Windsor.

He was improved in spirits by the investiture of Prince Charles as Prince of Wales on 1 July 1969. He and the duchess watched the ceremony on television in Paris. It must have brought back vivid memories of his own investiture at the same Caernarvon Castle, at which Winston Churchill had presided.

In October 1971, the Windsors received Emperor Hirohito of Japan with the empress at the Bois de Boulogne house. The duke had not seen the emperor since 1922, when he had gone on a tour of Japan. He showed the emperor the screen that Hirohito had given him. The emperor recalled that on the previous occasion he had been too young and too shy to utter a single word to the Prince of Wales. Albin Krebs of the *New York Times* affectionately recorded this pleasant and relaxing reunion.

But by now the duke was in a more grievous state of health. Even when the emperor and empress visited him he was suffering from almost complete loss of his voice. His French doctors performed a biopsy and found that he had a cancerous tumour in his larynx. A further biopsy on 17 November confirmed that the cancer was deep-seated and beyond direct surgery. He was to be given a series of cobalt treatments which would last a total of forty-one days. Despite this horrifying news, which left him and the duchess in a severe state of shock, the duke was as stubborn and childish as ever, insisting upon smoking an expensive cigar after dinner every night. His doctors were in despair.

Lord Mountbatten came to visit the duke in February 1972 when the duchess had gone to Switzerland for what was described as an operation but may well have been a Niehans treatment. (Some sources place the meeting four years earlier, in 1968.) According to Charles Murphy, the duke complained about the fact that Mountbatten had not attended his wedding. Mountbatten replied that he had not been invited. The truth was, of course, that he had been invited but that the royal family was adamant that he must not go. Murphy says that at midnight the duke croaked to Mountbatten, 'There's something I bet you don't realize. If I hadn't abdicated, I'd have completed thirty-six years of my reign by now – longer than either my father or my grandfather.' Mountbatten left with the conviction that the duke had finally buried the last traces of bitterness towards him and the rest of the family in London.

In March, the duke was operated on for a double hernia at the American Hospital in Neuilly. He had lost a good deal of weight and now weighed a mere 100 pounds. Wallis, in anguish, hardly left his side. Her constant concern for him was touching to everyone who observed it. Word was conveyed to the queen in London that she should visit her uncle while there was still time. Lady

Monckton (Sir Walter had died) visited the Windsors; she urged Her Majesty's principal private secretary, Sir Martin Charteris, to advise the queen of the urgency of the situation. Elizabeth was due to visit Paris anyway for a state visit in connection with Britain's joining the Common Market.

At first, the queen was adamant she would not revise her schedule to see her uncle. One of Wallis's doctors, Jean Thin, called Buckingham Palace to report that the duke might not live more than a few days. He received a telephone message from Christopher Soames, Churchill's son-in-law and ambassador to France; Soames told Dr Thin that the duke must die 'before or after the royal visit – but not during'. It was another indication that royalty would even seek to influence the Grim Reaper – just as King George V, the queen's grandfather, had been disposed of before his death overtook him in order to make the morning edition of the London *Times*. When Thin became irritable, the Palace issued a statement to him saying that, '*You* know he's dying. *We* know he's dying. But WE [meaning the queen] don't know he's dying.' Then the queen did the unthinkable and changed her schedule to see him.

By now, the duke was being fed glucose intravenously. He hated the idea that Lilibet, her childhood name by which he affectionately called the queen, would see him in this condition, with tubes descending from his nose and a bristle of radium needles. He demanded that Dr Jean Thin have the nurses remove the 'damn rigging'. Thin agreed.

According to Murphy, it took close to four hours for Thin and Wallis to prepare the duke for the royal visit. She was impressed by his marvellous control, and he gave the performance of his lifetime. Wallis, curtseying as the queen entered the room, took her to the chair where the duke sat. He had carefully dressed in his favourite navy blue, brass-buttoned blazer, and he struggled to make a small, wan smile. The queen was determined to show no inkling of her shock at his appearance. She too played out her part with expertise. She spoke warmly and consolingly, while the duchess sat nearby. Then the duchess withdrew to join Prince Philip and Prince Charles for tea, while the queen and her uncle remained *à deux*. The visit gave the duke great pleasure and eased his suffering somewhat.

On 27 May, according to Murphy, the duke asked his nurse, 'Am I dying?' She replied, with alarming briskness, 'You're quite intelligent enough to decide that for yourself.'

Dr Arthur Antenucci, the duke's favourite doctor, from Roosevelt Hospital in New York, flew to Paris. The duke was able to take feeble hold of his hands. On Saturday, 28 May, Sydney Johnson told the British writer Ingrid Seward that the Duke had asked Johnson to take him to his desk so he could write some letters. Johnson added:

> I got him up and sat him at his desk, but he couldn't hold his pen as he was shaking too much. I suggested that he have something to eat – perhaps his favourite finnan haddock and scrambled eggs, but he insisted that it wasn't food he needed. [He said] 'They're feeding me through my veins, Sydney. All that is behind me now, and I don't want anything. I don't feel like anything . . . except maybe some peaches and cream.'
>
> I ran downstairs to the kitchen and got some fresh peaches and cream and put [them] in front of him. He started putting the spoon to his mouth, but he was trembling so much he couldn't eat. So I fed him and he drank all the cream. Then he felt tired and wanted to go back to bed, so I sponged him down as I always did and put him to bed with the curtains drawn. It was the last time I ever saw him alive.
>
> At two or three in the afternoon, the Duke was still sleeping. I went to see Her Royal Highness and told her it was getting late and he was still sleeping. 'Don't worry, Sydney,' she said. 'Let him sleep.' But I knew she was worried as I heard her mumbling, 'This is a bad sign.'

That evening, the duke woke and again feebly requested stewed peaches, a favourite of nursery days. Then he began to sink into his final coma. The duchess was determined to remain in control of her emotions, refusing to break into tears in front of the staff.

There is more than one version of the duke's death. The late John Utter told his friend Hugo Vickers that Wallis was asleep in the early morning hours of 29 May when the duke quietly passed away. It fell upon Utter to waken her with the sad news. She took it with stoical resignation.

According to the Countess of Romanones, soon after 2 a.m. on the 28th, the doctors called the duchess from her rooms to the bedside. As life drained away from the man with whom she had shared most of her days, the duchess took him tenderly in her arms. He let out a deep breath; his blue eyes gazed tenderly into hers; he uttered the one word 'Darling', and then he was gone. According to Sydney Johnson, the duke also said, 'Mama, Mama, Mama, Mama.' Johnson apparently felt that he was referring to Wallis, but of course he could also have been addressing his long-lost parent, Queen Mary. The duchess was frozen, paralysed, speechless. She was gently taken to her room, where she sat silent, staring into space. She still refused to display hysterics. And from then on, she never for an instant lost her dignity.

The news was relayed on the late-night radio and television services. Millions of people, remembering the golden image of the Prince of Wales, the man who gave up his throne for the woman he loved, felt a wave of grief. Young people, who were scarcely aware of the abdication crisis and all that followed, had not forgotten their history. The queen ordered a period of mourning.

According to Sydney Johnson, when the embalmers arrived from London the duchess was crying and told him to take care of everything. Johnson advised the embalmers that he proposed dressing the duke in nightshirt and robe. The embalmers said this was impossible because of rigor mortis and he would be covered, naked, with a satin sheet. The clothes should be given away to the needy. The appalled Johnson asked the duchess about this. She allegedly said, 'Don't interfere. Just brush his hair the way he does it and leave him. They know what they're doing.'

Through the media, the public was requested by the grief-stricken but outwardly composed Wallis not to besiege the house; people answered that request with appropriate consideration. Those who wished to express their sympathies were asked to come to the British embassy in Paris, where they would be able to sign a book bound in black leather. On 29 May, hundreds turned up close to an hour before the embassy opened to make their tender and deeply felt endorsements. Not a few of the signatures were accompanied by special notes of remembrance. A flock of private visitors did turn up at the house, led by the duchess's favourite hairdresser, Alexandre, King Umberto of Italy, and Maurice Schumann, French Foreign Minister and former journalist, who had been present at the wedding at the Château de Candé in 1937. Hubert de Givenchy arrived to fit her mourning dress and coat. The next day the body was taken by motorcycle escort to Le Bourget airport, where it was accompanied by a special French guard of honour before being taken to England on a plane of the Queen's Flight to RAF Benson in Oxfordshire. The duchess was not in a condition to accompany the coffin.

At Benson, the Duke and Duchess of Kent led the party that greeted the dead former monarch. The national anthem was played. The next morning the body was carried in a sombre procession to Windsor Castle, for the special lying in state at St George's Chapel. Some indication of the affection in which the duke was held by the people of England can be given by the fact that a crowd of mourners stood for many hours outside the chapel to pay their last respects. The catafalque, draped in royal blue, stood at the centre of the sixteenth-century nave. Wallis had sent a cross formed of Easter lilies picked from the gardens of the Mill; the coffin was flanked by tall black candles. Thousands of people an hour filed past the catafalque. Alvin Shuster of the *New York Times* reported that many in the long line, which stretched from the Henry VIII gate down Castle Hill past the railway station and beyond, remembered the abdication speech as though it were yesterday. Joan Hutchison, who had stood for twelve hours in line, told Shuster that she was fifteen years old and working in a knitwear factory when she heard the speech. 'I cried and cried,' she said. 'He should have stayed on. The wife he wanted would have just slipped into the background. We wouldn't have cared at all. She's a lovely woman.'

With great determination, the stoical and courageous but miserable duchess managed to summon up the strength to go to London. The Queen's Flight pilot took her to Heathrow; with her were her friend Grace, Countess of Dudley; Winston Churchill's daughter Mary, wife of British ambassador Sir Christopher Soames; Dr Antenucci; and John Utter, her secretary. Upright, her face a mask, the duchess stepped down the ramp to be greeted by Lord Mountbatten. She was reported to have asked Utter, 'Why couldn't

Prince Charles have been here?' She said querulously to Mountbatten, 'I am afraid of the Queen Mother. She never approved of me.' Mountbatten did his best to reassure her.

Even in her extremity the duchess was appalled (as she had been in 1936) by what she felt to be the lifeless and gloomy interior of Buckingham Palace. She was accommodated in the State Suite at the front of the palace. The royal family did everything possible to make her comfortable, making sure that the bathroom was very well equipped; the suite itself was exceptionally comfortable and her later complaints about it quite unjustified. Princess Anne was reintroduced to her, and she was very touched and happy to see her. A revealing newspaper photograph showed the duchess at a window of the palace, her face stamped with grief. But in her Givenchy mourning dress, exquisitely fashioned in black silk, she succeeded in being among the most elegant and fashionable members of the royal family – even though that membership was still denied to her.

The queen had an unfortunate and difficult decision to make. For many years, 3 June had been her official birthday. This was always a major public event, at which she went on horseback to take the salute at the Trooping of the Colour. She had thought of cancelling the event this year, but was prevailed upon not to do so. Instead, she introduced the touch of having the pipe bands play a dirge, an appropriate reminiscence in view of the duke's love of the bagpipes. It didn't work; the duchess still hated them.

Still barely able to move or talk, the duchess watched the ceremony on television in the State Suite. It was her wedding anniversary. She was under sedation, but even so the playing of the bagpipes provoked uncontrollable tears. She was so badly shaken that she could hardly remember what was said to her from one moment to the next. Finally, pressed hard by Lady Monckton, she agreed to go with Lady Dudley to the official lying in state after the public had gone. At 8.52 p.m. on 3 June, the duchess left Buckingham Palace in a royal car to go to St George's Chapel at Windsor. Accompanied by the Prince of Wales and Lord Mountbatten, she walked slowly around the catafalque on which her husband's coffin lay in the centre of the nave. She stood staring at the flower-heaped coffin before moving on to examine the many wreaths in the cloisters. She said, over and over again, to Mountbatten and Prince Charles, 'Thirty-five years! Thirty-five years!' and added, 'He was my entire life. I can't begin to think what I will do without him, he gave up so much for me, and now he has gone. I always hoped I would die before him.' Before her, 57,903 people had by now stood in line to pay their last respects. The queen, Prince Philip and Princess Anne had also paid visits to the chapel earlier that day.

The service, on 5 June, lasted half an hour. It began at 11.15 a.m. and the public was not admitted. The duchess sat next to the queen, with the Duke of Edinburgh to her right. The Queen Mother did appear. The prime minister, Edward Heath, was there. So was the Earl of Avon, Anthony Eden, who had so radically disagreed with the duke during the time he was king. Lord Mountbatten, Prince Charles, the Duke of Kent, Princes William and Richard of Gloucester and King Olav of Norway were also present. The Duke of Gloucester was too ill to be there.

The Dean of Windsor, the Very Reverend Launcelot Fleming, presided. The blessing was given by Dr Michael Ramsey, Archbishop of Canterbury. The coffin stayed in the chapel while the royal family accompanied the duchess to luncheon, after which the Queen Mother made a sudden decision to attend the interment at Frogmore. The mourners continued to the place of burial. The duke was lowered gently into the rich English earth, alongside his beloved George, Duke of Kent, Princess Marina, his adored great-uncle, the Duke of Connaught, and his father's favourite sister, Princess Victoria. The duchess was reassured that when the time came she would be laid beside her husband, but she did note, with an old, characteristic touch of cynicism, that the space available to her was exceptionally tiny and cramped. She told the Archbishop of Canterbury, 'I realize that I'm a very thin, small woman, but I do not think that even I could fit into that miserable little narrow piece of ground.' The duchess told her friend the Countess of Romanones (who is the source of this story) that the archbishop then replied, 'I don't see that there's much that can be done about it. You'll fit, all right.' To which the duchess responded that she didn't think she would. She wanted the hedge removed to give her more room. 'After all, I am not a hedgehog, you know.' This Alice-in-Wonderland conversation concluded with the archbishop's promise to move the hedge. He did; there was, at last, more than ample space for both graves.

There followed an unfortunate lapse. The Lord Chamberlain, who was in charge of the arrangements, did not arrange for any member of the royal family to go to Heathrow Airport to see the duchess off on her flight to France. Instead, and touchingly, all the members of the family who were present bade her farewell at Windsor Castle. Fighting back tears, Wallis was accompanied by the Hon. Mary Morrison, lady-in-waiting to Her Majesty, and by the Lord Chamberlain. The third member of the party was Lieutenant Colonel John Johnston, who happened to be Sir Alexander Hardinge's son-in-law. The Hon. Mary Morrison was not permitted to curtsey to the duchess even at this stage. Summoning a remarkable amount of energy, the duchess walked unaided up the ramp to the plane, filmed as she did so by the television crews. She then proceeded, with her beloved Lady Dudley doing her best to console her, on the Queen's Flight to Paris. In the House of Commons Edward Heath spoke movingly of the death of the former monarch, concluding with words of praise for the duchess, 'who has repaid his devotion with an equal loyalty, companionship and love. His death is, above all, her loss, and to her the House will wish to extend its profound sympathy.' Harold Wilson, leader of the opposition, added words of admiration, saying, 'We hope that she will feel free at any time to come among and freely communicate with the people whom her husband, Prince of Wales, King, and Duke, lived to serve.' The ill-fated Liberal leader Jeremy Thorpe confirmed these sentiments. However, despite the feelings of the entire House, and the considerable softening towards the duchess of several important members of the royal family, she was emphatically not permitted the title of 'Her Royal Highness' even now. She would still be addressed as 'Her Grace, the Duchess of Windsor'.

Exhausted, the duchess returned to her house in Paris. Disturbingly, she dismissed Sydney Johnson, allegedly because he had asked to go home early one evening to be with his family. These sudden twists of behaviour were uncharacteristic and suggested the adverse effects of certain medical preparations, the imminent onset of senility, or both.

The duke left her his entire fortune of £3 million, and of course there was her brilliant collection of jewellery. She was informed by Maurice Schumann, representing the French government, that she would not be charged death duties and that she would continue to live free of income tax for the rest of her life. Moreover, the house would be hers in perpetuity. The Mill was still for sale, but in June 1973 a buyer was finally found: Edmond Antar, a Swiss business-man, paid close to $1 million for it. Yet burdened by the duchess's expenses, Maître Blum deemed it necessary to sell many Windsor possessions during the next decade.

For some weeks, the duchess remained in almost complete seclusion, tended to by a dedicated small staff led by her elegant French butler Georges Sanègre and his wife Ofélia. John Utter, a former American diplomat who had once, ironically, been emissary to the Emperor of Ethiopia, Haile Selassie,[1] continued his duties as secretary. Johanna Schutz assisted him. Maître Blum was constantly at the house attending to all the complex details of the estate. She also assumed a protective role, discouraging members of the press from prying into the duchess's solitude, seeking to prevent them from invading the duchess's territory and taking shots of her through the windows. She gradually became the guardian that the late Walter Monckton had once been.

The duchess had hoped to go to a wedding in Salzburg, but her old problem of ulcers flared up again and prevented the trip. Instead, she invited the newly-weds, the son and daughter-in-law of the Countess of Romanones, to stay with her when they concluded their honeymoon. In one of her rare public appearances, she took them to Maxim's for dinner. They were astonished when she ordered a hamburger. Now that her life seemed to all intents and purposes to have come to an end, she saw no reason to put on any pretence and her old, intense American feelings and appetites were resurfacing.

She continued to fret about the size of her grave at Frogmore. At last she was reassured by a letter from her solicitors in London, stating, somewhat bizarrely, 'There is plenty of room between the Duke's grave and the border, approximately nine yards.' The letter added that there were six yards on the other side to the base of the plane tree which overshadowed that part of the garden. A sketch was enclosed showing the exact position. The duchess sent a note to the Countess of Romanones asking her to be sure 'when my rock-a-bye time comes' that the tree would not fall on the two adjoining graves.

Wallis's attorney, Maître Suzanne Blum, still had the supreme advantage of knowing of Wallis's affairs with Guy Trundle and William Bullitt from 1937 to 1940; of her use of Armand Grégoire as Nazi lawyer; of her true connection to Ribbentrop; of all of her espionage activities, and surely of the China dossier. The duchess would never dare let her go, and the lawyer's overwhelming influence increased by the day, the week, the month. The dominatrix ruled her willing victim from a grim and gloomy nineteenth-century apartment on the Rue de Varenne. The few visitors intrepid enough to visit her and risk her flaring wrath had to make their way up to her quarters in an arthritic, creaky elevator that seemed in imminent danger of crashing to the basement. When visitors arrived, a maid, hobbling and bent with age, opened the door to a dusty chamber with six imposing doors, furnished in the familiar browns and dull ochres of the 1930s.

Despite the smudges of age, the liver spots and wrinkled hands, the tiny monster had benefited from facial surgery and looked younger than her eighty-four years. She hated meeting journalists or would-be biographers; she would hiss at them threateningly, like a cobra. She dismissed every book or article written about the duchess as 'ordure' or stew made out of discards from a second-rate kitchen. She insisted absurdly that the duke had never had sex with the duchess; that the duchess was a virgin the day she died and even that she was actually a man – despite the operation on her ovaries, which Blum chose to forget. When the late Irish novelist Caroline Blackwood had the temerity to mention the fact that the duke, after a team of porters carried as many as eighty-six pieces of luggage to various suites, had tipped none of them, she snapped, 'Tip! Him tip! Tipping would have been demeaning!' She went on to call Miss Blackwood a 'jackal'. Then she suddenly weakened and trembled, looking old and shaken when the question of the duchess's medical bills came up. 'They are fearful,' she groaned.

Slowly but surely, the duchess began to experience a minimal social life once again. Patrick O'Higgins, close friend and biographer of the perfume tycoon Helena Rubinstein, took her out to small dinner parties in Paris. She occasionally saw Sir Oswald and Lady Mosley and the Rochefoucaulds. She gave very intimate, limited soirees, with never more than eight guests. When she went out to dinner, she always made sure that there was a guard on duty outside the restaurant. She was terrified of murder or kidnap; there was no doubt that she remained extremely unpopular in communist circles, although it is doubtful whether at this stage she would have been considered seriously as a target. She talked about having a Duchess of Windsor museum set up at Oldfields School, where she had spent so much of her childhood. But the scheme lay fallow, and finally disintegrated. Sometimes her memory would fail, and she would forget names or even faces. Obsessed with a fear of burglars, she had a toy revolver placed next to her bed (she thought it was real) and increased the complexity of her electronic warning system, threaded through every inch of the doors and windows. She would sometimes rise in the night and peer out of the window with her increasingly myopic eyes, trying to see whether the former French soldier she had hired was standing on duty. She stumbled and broke her hip. Admitted to the American Hospital in Neuilly, she was petulant, muddled and difficult, searching in vain for her light switch, besieging the staff with questions over and over again and ignoring the answers. Sometimes her old, flashing humour would re-emerge in an eccentric form. An old friend came to see her. He was limping heavily on a stick and told her that he too had broken his hip. She hooted, gleefully, 'Hip, hip, hooray!'

The duchess kept everything in the house exactly the way it was when her husband died. She even retained the cigarettes she hated; the pipes were still in their racks, and the cigars lay neatly in their expensive boxes. The desk was exactly preserved, even down to the full inkwells. The duke's room remained crowded with pictures of Wallis from one end to the other. Visitors noted that almost all the pictures were of her alone; only a few showed the duke with her. Even the wardrobe was unchanged. In the cupboards hung all the duke's suits, immaculately preserved in mothballs.

The duchess worried constantly about her pug dogs, adoring them as passionately as ever and drastically concerned that they were not getting the right food. She began cutting down her staff, applying the same principles of somewhat ruthless economy that she had applied to the staffs at Fort Belvedere and York House in London. While visiting Biarritz, still one of her favourite resorts, she fell once more, breaking some ribs. It proved to be difficult to place an anaesthetic tube down her throat because of the extensive plastic surgery that had been done on her neck.

Even in hospital, she still had considerable style. She rejected the hospital food outright, introducing her own three-star menu supplied by her personal chef. Appalled by the inexpensive linen used on the bed, she brought in her own pillows and sheets. She freshened up her rooms with magnificent displays of flowers and, at one stage, her favourite motto cushion which carried the legend, 'You can't be too thin or too rich.'

The absurd story appeared in the French newspaper *France-Dimanche* that she was going to marry John Utter in 1972. This gave her a much needed laugh. Utter, a warm and lovable man, could always be relied upon, despite some misgivings about the duchess, to cheer her up and give her satisfactory company. He did not live at the house, but had his own home in the country at Osmoi, where he had established a foundation for up-and-coming musicians who could not afford to pay the high rents of Paris. Utter was not impressed with Lord Mountbatten, who had a tendency to turn up at the duchess's house and, acting as though he owned the place and was Utter's employer, would say to him, 'Get your notebook out, John,' and then proceed to dictate letters to him. This infuriated the retired diplomat.

Mountbatten annoyed John Utter in those years by walking around the rooms of the house in Paris, pointing out this or that expensive objet d'art, particularly the Fabergé gold boxes that had been left behind by the burglars at Ednam Lodge, saying that the duke had intended those for him and that he proposed removing them. Utter and Johanna Schutz advised Maître Blum of this, and she accordingly made sure she was present during Mountbatten's visits to preclude any possible theft. Another who was asked to be present was Aline, Countess of Romanones. The duchess told Aline, '[Mountbatten's] always asking for things. And after my kind husband bestowed all those honours on him! Even Georges [Sanègre]

I suspect dreads his visits . . . But what can one expect from a man who threw his wife into the sea?' This was a reference to the fact that Lady Mountbatten, after dying in Borneo, had been committed to the waves.

According to the duchess, Mountbatten insisted upon her making out a will during one of his visits, in 1973, leaving everything to the royal family. Naturally, she alleged, Mountbatten wanted to be included in the legacy. He had even drawn up a working version of the document himself, stating where everything should go. The duchess apparently intended that certain legacies would be left, in particular to Prince Charles, but, she told the Countess of Romanones, 'They [all] did David out of properties which were his own.' This, of course, was a false charge. In fact, as the duchess well knew, she had enjoyed the benefits of a life income from the act of blackmail her husband had performed against the members of the royal family in forcing them to pay him an income as a reward for ceding his life interest in Sandringham and Balmoral.

According to Maître Blum, Mountbatten now tried to make the duchess sign a document in which she placed all her property in a foundation which Mountbatten would administer, with the Prince of Wales as its chairman. He urged her to reinstate her dismissed English firm of solicitors, Allen and Overy. The duchess authorized certain innocuous papers and military and other insignia of her husband to be taken back to London for the benefit of the queen; these were housed, as far as can be determined, at Windsor Castle. But later, Maître Blum made extremely serious charges in a series of letters dated 24 March, 5 April and 7 April 1979, to the Windsors' old friend Kenneth de Courcy, Duc de Grantmesnil. She stated that whereas the duchess was perfectly willing to have letters from King George VI and Queen Elizabeth to the duke, historical souvenirs, and other documents given to the Palace, that was the limit of the duchess's agreement.

Maître Blum stated to Grantmesnil that two individuals, authorized either by Lord Mountbatten or 'some other person', acting upon what she alleged to be royal authority, had somehow obtained the keys to the duke's boxes and confidential filing cabinets and burgled the contents, placing everything in packing cases which had been carried under secret conditions to the concierge's lodge, where a van appeared to remove them as night fell. The contents included the duke's private correspondence, the documents of divorce from Win Spencer and Ernest Simpson, bills from trades-men and department stores, and a certain amount of the duchess's personal correspondence. Maître Blum confirmed her charges with supporting statements in writing from John Utter, Sydney Johnson and Johanna Schutz. Each supported Maître Blum's claim that when the duchess requested her filing cabinets and boxes to be opened, she was appalled to find them empty.

Grantmesnil decided to take up the matter of the alleged royal burglary with Sir Robin Mackworth-Young, the librarian at Windsor Castle. On 11 April, Sir Robin replied, stating that the allegations were without foundation. He said that the first consignment of documents had been given to him by Utter on 15 June 1972, in the presence of Maître Blum. The duchess had received Sir Robin personally. She herself had given permission for the transfer of the papers. The second consignment had been delivered, again in person and again by Utter, on 13 December that year. The third had been handed over on 22 July 1977. On this occasion the duchess had not been present and John Utter had left her employ. In 1987, in response to a question a similar letter was sent to the present author by the Windsor Castle librarian who had succeeded Mackworth-Young. The late Maître Blum did not act further on the charges of theft and the matter remains open.

On 30 March 1973, Wallis made a gift to the French state of her collection of Louis XVI furniture, with some paintings and pieces of porcelain. Some of the items were put on display at Versailles, some at the National Ceramic Museum at Sévres, and some at the Louvre.

In 1974, she was able to muster the strength to take a ship to New York. Accompanied by Johanna Schutz and two of her pugs, she sailed aboard the Italian liner *Rafaello*, arriving on 9 April. A *New York Times* reporter managed to obtain a brief quote from her. She said, 'I don't go out as much and I'm much lonelier. [The royal family] made a fuss at the time of the abdication, but I don't think they would make a fuss now. I get on well with the royal family.' Her old wit flashed again. The reporter ignorantly asked her, quite forgetting the publication of *The Heart Has Its Reasons*, whether she would one day write an autobiography. 'That would be the most dreadful thing to do!' she snapped back, and the reporter still didn't understand. She was fascinated, while at the Waldorf Towers (in Suite 40F, twelve floors above her old beloved 28A, a suite which belonged to the millionaire art collector and food tycoon Nathan 'Nate' Cummings) to learn that Prince Charles had recently been in San Diego, scene of that memorable night when she had glimpsed the Prince of Wales across the room.

She rallied a little under the vibrant stimulations of Manhattan. Princess Margaret and Lord Snowdon called upon her and were photographed with her. Nate Cummings freshened up the Waldorf suite with a Sisley painting and a Renoir. The duchess bought a few decorative pieces to improve the rather sombre furnishings, and she again filled the rooms from end to end with her favourite flowers. Walking on a cane, ravishingly dressed by Givenchy, she always caused a flurry in the lift and the lobby during her arrivals and departures. Stooped, visibly frail, staring straight ahead, her voice somewhat tremulous, she carried with her an atmosphere of extraordinary dignity, resolution and intrinsic power. Even in her precipitate decline, she was undoubtedly *someone*.

The duchess made a private visit to her husband's grave at Frogmore. She sent a simply but beautifully worded letter of thanks to the queen for her consideration, and she was touched to receive a thoughtful and sensitive telegram from Prince Charles. She adored Charles and again talked of leaving him some small but significant legacies, but on 9 December 1974 she wrote to Mountbatten stating categorically that the efforts to retrieve objets d'art of the duke were permanently rejected. John Utter was helpful to the duchess when she fell seriously ill on 13 November 1975 and went back into the American Hospital. She almost died from her old problem of bleeding ulcers. In May 1976, she wanted to take some sunshine, and her two nurses carried her out on to the terrace of her house. Two cameramen took cruel and devastating photographs of her, looking thin, weak and sunken-checked. The photographs were published in *France-Soir*. Maître Blum sued the paper for invasion of privacy and was awarded 80,000 francs.

That summer Wallis began to suffer from the characteristic hallucinations of senility. She cried out, 'I'm frightened! They've been here again! They've moved my things! This is the second time they've hijacked me!' This did not seem to be a reference to the missing documents; the duchess appeared to be convinced that certain of her decorative objects had been stolen by Mountbatten.

There was again talk that June, when she had her birthday, that a left-wing political group was planning to kidnap her, and she increased the guard on the house. When John Utter retired, disturbed and uncomfortable with the duchess's sudden alarming shifts of mood, he continued to see her from time to time, taking her to dinner about once every eight weeks and calling her every day to see how she was. Then, quite suddenly, and without the slightest explanation, the duchess brought the curtain down on him. When he telephoned from his country house, the receptionist informed him that Johanna Schutz had given out instructions that his call must not be put through. It was the same fate that had befallen Freda Dudley Ward when she had tried to reach the Prince of Wales at York House some forty years earlier.

The duchess grew weaker and weaker. The American Hospital doctors succeeded in having her cut down her consumption of alcohol to a minimum; she had been drinking more and more heavily during the previous years. She ate scarcely anything and lost so much weight that by 1976 she was positively emaciated. Her mind continued to wander. Unable to reach the telephone, she would pick up an imaginary instrument and ask quietly, 'Miss Schutz, please come up here immediately!' Everyone in her circle felt that it would be very important to her if the Queen Mother would finally relent and pay her a personal visit. It says much for the Queen Mother's character that, despite all that had taken place in the 1930s, she was prepared to oblige.

The Queen Mother was due to come to Paris in October 1976, and it was decided that she would undertake her mission of compassion at that time. On the 25th, she was at the British embassy for an official luncheon in her honour. The next day, she opened the British Cultural Centre in Paris. It was agreed that at 4 p.m. she would drive to the duchess's house in the embassy car. But at the last minute the duchess was too ill to receive her. Johanna Schutz called the embassy and stated that the duchess would not, as a result of her poor state of health, be able to receive Her Majesty. It was later explained to the Queen Mother that the duchess was suffering from severe hallucinations and that Dr Jean Thin and Maître Blum both felt that the moment was not opportune for the meeting. The Queen Mother then displayed the splendour of her character in full force. She sent the duchess a bouquet of two dozen roses, red and white, with a note that read, 'In friendship, Elizabeth'.

Late in 1976, on behalf of the duchess, Miss Schutz agreed to lend a number of the duke's personal possessions for a special exhibition at Windsor to commemorate the fiftieth birthday of the queen. Hugo Vickers, the well-known biographer, flew to Paris on 14 September to pick up the twelve items on loan. According to Vickers, 'The Queen Mother examined the abdication items with interest, while she expressed disapproval at seeing Mussolini and Hitler on display.'

In May 1978, Verity Lambert, director of drama at Thames Television, went to see Maître Blum to inform her that Simon Raven would be writing the script for the seven-part series *Edward and Mrs Simpson*, based on the biography of Edward VIII by Lady Frances Donaldson. Maître Blum was not at all happy with Lady Donaldson's book, but apparently under the existing laws was unable to intervene. She certainly would like to have done so. She demanded to see the scripts, but was told that this was out of the question. The duchess too hated the idea of being portrayed on the screen, and perhaps it was fortunate that her mental and physical condition precluded her from knowing about the series.

She was now very seriously ill. Maître Blum took over everything. The house was like a morgue. There remained only the butler, Georges Sanègre, and his wife; a maid, Germaine, the receptionist, and the day and night nurses. The duchess had lost the use of her hands and feet and had to be carried from her bed to a clinical couch. Visitors were for a time forbidden, because when they arrived she seemed to become excited and her blood pressure reached a dangerous height. She had to be spoon-fed. John Utter told a friend, 'For everyone's sake, the sooner she dies the better.' She was for periods in a world of her own. Eventually, she had to be fed intravenously because in her semi-paralysed condition she was unable to swallow. Tragically, she was not in a coma, which at least would have rendered her oblivious to her fate. She had moments of vivid awareness, which to anyone of her essential vitality and love of life must have been very nearly unendurable.

According to the Countess of Romanones, the duchess called her, saying, 'Aline, you must come to see me right away. I need you desperately.' The countess was up to her eyes organizing the first free elections in Spain since General Franco had taken over the government. He had died; King Juan Carlos had assumed the throne. The countess asked Wallis if she could possibly come the following week. The duchess said that was fine. The next day, the countess called to give the exact hour of her arrival so that the chauffeur could pick her up at the airport. Johanna Schutz answered the phone. The countess asked to be put through to Wallis. Ms Schutz replied that it was out of the question; if there were any messages for the duchess, she would be glad to convey them. The countess was shocked and upset. She said she intended to come anyway. Any further effort to contact the duchess proved fruitless. The Countess of Romanones wrote several times and telephoned, but there was no response.

The duchess was not even able to read; she was almost completely blind. Sometimes she would ask feebly to be taken to the window, where she could hear the birds singing. Hugo Vickers, observing the house from the road, wrote in his diary:

> Over the wall through the grey, misty atmosphere one could see a kind of living tomb. All the windows on the ground floor were shuttered from the outside world, but I thought the drawing room window was open. Upstairs where what remains of the Duchess [sat] surrounded by nurses, there were two lights – one on the side, which is her bedroom, and one in the far window of what I think is the upstairs sitting room.

The duchess was unaware of her birthday in June 1980. A new person entered the scene: Michael Bloch, the scion of a well-to-do family resident in Ireland. Born in 1953, he was a graduate of St John's College, Cambridge. He had written to Maître Blum for assistance on a book he was writing on the historian and biographer Philip Guedalla, an old friend of the Duke of Windsor's. He wanted to interview Maître Blum and obtain access to certain papers. The Paris lawyer became very fond of him and appointed him her assistant; he had been admitted to the English Bar. Bloch took over as official custodian of the Windsor papers and also as authorized biographer. He was appointed editor and annotator of the duchess's letters, most of which had escaped the alleged removal of the papers to Windsor Castle by unauthorized persons.

By the time he assumed his position, the duchess was quite unable to talk to him or assist him in his researches. However, she signed full power of attorney to Maître Blum, allowing the lawyer to publish whatever she chose. In answer to certain queries Maître Blum has stated that the duchess wanted her correspondence to be made public. Many of the letters which appeared after the duchess's death (with great success, particularly in England) were of a painfully personal character. But they are of indispensable value to the biographer.

After two years of trying to see the duchess, the Countess of Romanones at last succeeded in obtaining permission from Maître Blum to pay a visit. This was an extremely rare privilege. The duchess had had several haemorrhages. When the countess arrived at the house, she noted an eerie, disturbing silence. She knew at once what was missing: the loud, excited barking of the pug dogs. Sadly, the duchess had no longer been able to tolerate the sound that she had once adored, and the pugs had been given away. When the countess entered the boudoir, the exquisitely furnished room that stood between the two main bedrooms, she found the duchess, seated with immense and majestic poise in her wheeled chair, wearing a handsome brocade dressing gown the colour of her blue eyes. Her hair was elegantly drawn back behind her ears, showing the still impressive cheekbones and the firm line of the jaw. She was wearing her favourite sapphires. Surprisingly and for the first time in weeks she was coherent, and when the countess said she looked like a Chinese empress, Wallis sparked up with an old, significant memory. 'People told me that when I was living in Peking in 1924,' she said.

Even when the countess returned several months later, the duchess was still able to talk to her. Her hearing was so amazingly sharp that she even caught the countess's footfall as her visitor entered the room. The countess was saddened to see that Wallis had not been manicured or made up and that her hair was white and lifeless now. But she still had an appreciation of beauty. Staring out of the window, she said, 'Look at the way the sun is lighting the trees. You can see so many different colours.' But then she uttered a sentence that for the countess was like a knife to the heart. She said, 'Tell David to come in. He wouldn't want to miss this!' On her third and fourth visits, the countess heard not a single word from the duchess's lips.

Wallis did not leave her house after 1981. Dr Thomas Hewes, senior physician at the American Hospital in Neuilly, answered a question about her condition with the following words: 'The duchess is a vegetable. She is in a pitiable state. I don't believe she suffers anything at all any more.' A pianist was engaged to play, hour after hour, a medley of popular songs once beloved of the duke, including 'Bye Bye Birdie' and 'I Get a Kick out of You', in an effort to stir her moribund mind. The effort was useless. Interested people would walk past the house and stare across the wall at the bedroom window beyond which her silent figure lay immobile. Occasionally, they would see nurses in white moving to and fro, but otherwise there was no sign of life. Bizarre rumours began to circulate, that she was already dead and had been refrigerated, or that she was on a sophisticated computer that could tell Maître Blum what sustenance she needed and whether the nurses had fulfilled their duties.

At last all the unwelcome publicity surrounding her illness ceased. For months nothing appeared in the press. Then, on 24 April 1986, her heart finally and mercifully gave out. She was ninety years old.

The Lord Chamberlain flew to Paris to escort the body home in its plain oak coffin. The Duke of Gloucester, her nephew by marriage, whose father had died some years before, greeted the remains at RAF Benson and accompanied them to Windsor Castle. The castle was closed and a guard of honour was waiting to salute the duchess on her last journey.

There was a twenty-eight-minute private service in St George's Chapel, attended by 175 people. Queen Elizabeth II entered the chapel with Prince Philip and the Queen Mother. The American ambassador, Charles Price, was among those present. Sixteen members of the royal family sat in the choir, directly opposite the coffin, which was flanked by the Military Knights of Windsor in red uniforms with gold braid. The duchess was accorded the honour of lying in the same position and place as King George V, King George VI, Queen Mary and the Duke of Windsor had done. The queen's wreath of yellow and white lilies lay at the centre of the coffin. The words 'Her Royal Highness' did not appear upon the plaque; the duchess's name was absurdly omitted from the service. The St George's Chapel choir sang the anthem 'Thy will keep him in perfect peace'. Among those who mourned that day were Lady Mosley, whose husband had died in 1980; the Countess of Romanones; the Princess Ann-Mari von Bismarck; Grace, Lady Dudley; Lady Alexandra Metcalfe; the Duke and Duchess of Marlborough; and Laura, Duchess of Marlborough. Very few others of the duchess's friends were still alive.

At the end of the service, the coffin was taken in procession from the choir, led by the constable of Windsor Castle, Marshal of the RAF Sir John Grandy, and the Military Knights of Windsor, and preceded by the dean of the American Pro-Cathedral in Paris, the Archbishop of Canterbury, the dean and canons of Windsor, and the Lord Chamberlain. The queen, the Queen Mother, Prince Philip, Princess Anne and the Prince and Princess of Wales followed the coffin through the nave and down the Great West Steps. And then the duchess was at last lowered into the grave next to that of the duke.

The obituaries for the duchess in both Great Britain and the United States were on the whole respectful. Indeed, more than one newspaper incorrectly stated that any suggestion that she had Nazi connections was without foundation. The Countess of Romanones published an article in the June 1986 issue of *Vanity Fair* in which, amidst a great deal of colourful – and contested – reminiscence, she included some shockingly unflattering remarks that the duchess had allegedly made about the Queen Mother. The duchess had apparently mocked the Queen Mother in conversations with the countess, calling her 'Cookie' and saying that she resembled 'a pudding'. With considerable ingratitude in view of the Queen Mother's consideration towards her at the time of the duke's death, she insultingly described that great lady's black hat as having a 'white plastic arrow sticking up through it'. She said that she almost laughed in the Queen Mother's face even though she was stricken with grief. Elsewhere in the piece the countess, who as a former OSS agent in Spain should have been better informed, said that the duchess had been falsely charged with Nazi associations. Although seeming to be in the duchess's favour, the article turned out in the end to be somewhat unflattering.

The love letters were serialized in newspapers during the very week of the duchess's death, which some have regarded as an error of taste. Soon they were published in book form. An important letter by Alistair Cooke appeared in the *New York Times* of 9 May. Mr Cooke pointed out that the real reason for the abdication was that, according to the terms of the Statute of Westminster passed in 1931, any alteration in the law touching the succession of the throne required the assent of the parliaments of the dominions as well as of the parliament of the United Kingdom. Thus the secretary of state for the dominions was required to put the matter before the Commonwealth parliaments. Whereas New Zealand was prepared to follow the majority decision of the British parliament, and India was divided between Hindus and Moslems, Canada, Australia and South Africa were adamant that they would neither sanction Wallis as queen nor permit her to enter into a morganatic marriage. The Labour party in London was, of course, equally opposed.

Although it is questionable, to say the least, whether the duke and duchess would have wished their romantic correspondence to have been examined by a large and interested public, it is probable that the duchess (though not the duke) would have been happy to have had her magnificent jewellery displayed to the world. The decision was made by Maître Blum to auction the entire collection at Sotheby's; at least twelve major items had been sold before the duchess's death, along with the duke's royal silver, the china pug dogs and the wines. The sale of the jewellery took place in Geneva on 2 and 3 April 1987.

The spectacular and dazzling array consisted of 230 lots valued at more than $7 million and including eighty-seven Cartier pieces and twenty-three emanating from Van Cleef and Arpels. According to Nicholas Rayner of Sotheby's, the duchess's favourite piece was a Burmese ruby and diamond necklace given to her by King Edward VIII on the occasion of her forty-first birthday on 19 June 1936, and inscribed, 'My Wallis from her David'. The Mogul emerald engagement ring given by the king to Wallis on the evening after her decree nisi was granted at Ipswich was another major item.

From the 1930s came a platinum and diamond necklace, a diamond dress suite of great beauty; a pearl, emerald and diamond bracelet; the diamond and sapphire Prince of Wales feathers clips; and the diamond bracelet which included the many Latin crosses inscribed with mementoes of various occasions, including a visit to St Wolfgang in 1935 and Wallis's appendectomy in 1944. An 18-carat gold and gem-set cigarette case by Cartier had a map of the couple's travels from London via Calais, Paris, Biarritz, Spain and Cannes to Italy, Germany, Austria, Yugoslavia, Turkey, Bulgaria and Hungary and then back to London, a grand prize for whoever acquired it. An exquisite gold and gem-set powder compact was studded with sapphires, rubies, emeralds, citrines and amethysts; on the back was another map, identical to the one on the cigarette case.

From the 1940s came a sapphire bracelet; a gold, sapphire, ruby and diamond hinged bangle; golden ruby ear clips; sapphire and diamond ear clips; a sapphire, emerald, citrine and diamond clip in the form of a flamingo; and the gorgeous panther clips designed by Jeanne Toussaint, the beloved friend of Jacques Cartier, who had nicknamed Mademoiselle Toussaint his 'Panther'.

From the 1950s there were an onyx and diamond panther bracelet, an onyx and diamond tiger clip, and pearl and diamond ear clips; from the 1960s, a superb gold, cultured pearl and diamond choker necklace, an emerald and diamond pendant designed by Harry Winston, a Cartier emerald and diamond necklace, and ruby and diamond ear clips.

Included in the auction were many historic items of the Duke of Windsor's, including legacies of extreme value. There were gold snuffboxes, silver cigarette cases, an 1820 silver-gilt seal box, a 1910 silver-gilt inkstand, an 1823 desk seal and a motley collection of clocks, watches and even gold replica train tickets supplied by the Canadian Pacific Railway Company in 1919 and 1927. One of the most splendid items was a cigar box presented to the Prince of Wales in 1915 by the members of the king and queen's households while the prince was on active service in the First Battalion Grenadier Guards in northern France.

The Mogul emerald went for $2.1 million, and the 1936 birthday present, the ruby and diamond necklace, for $2.6 million. A tiny cigar piercer raised a staggering $3,700. Mohamed al-Fayed, the Egyptian owner of Harrods who had just been granted by the French government a continuing lease on the Windsors' house in Paris, obtained the memento charm bracelet. The Los Angeles divorce lawyer Marvin Mitchelson paid over half a million dollars for the amethyst necklace. He bought sapphires for $300,000 apiece. Elizabeth Taylor snapped up the Prince of Wales feather brooch for $575,000. According to some sources she also obtained the panther brooches, outbidding Prince Charles, who was determined to obtain them for the Princess of Wales, who had set her heart on them.

At the end of the second day, the total realized by the sale was $50,281,887. This was seven times what Sotheby's had estimated. The highest price of all was paid by an anonymous buyer: it was $1,466,653 for a Royal Navy sword presented by King George V to the Prince of Wales, and it was, of course, vastly beyond its true value. All the money from the auction went to the Louis Pasteur Institute in Paris, where it would be applied to research into AIDS. In view of the fact that two of Wallis's her husbands were bisexual and that many of her friends and admirers were gay, this seemed appropriate.

Thus, in death, the duchess was more famous than ever, and the jewels that were her main love in life became her monument.

Unhappily, Mr al-Fayed did not keep the Windsor house's contents for long. He decided to close the residence after its brief spell as a museum and to sell the furniture, paintings and china to support his son Dodi's charities. After announcing an auction at Sotheby's in New York City, in 1997, he had to postpone it because of the death of Dodi and Diana, Princess of Wales, his son's lover. When the auction did finally take place, in 1998, it fetched considerably more than anticipated; but it entirely lacked the glamour and excitement of the jewellery auction and, attended by almost no celebrities, came as a sad anticlimax to the duchess's life.

On 6 June 1995, Prince Edward, the nephew of the Duke of

Windsor, who had been working for Andrew Lloyd Webber's Really Useful theatre company, embarked on a documentary on his uncle for ITV. Housed in Mohamed al-Fayed's Ritz Hotel in Paris, appropriately in the Duke of Windsor Suite (at $5,120 a night), Edward, on the first day of shooting, found himself, perhaps for the first time in his life, compelled to make himself a sandwich.

Although the documentary, as shallow and misguided as its royal subject, was a typical example of Buckingham Palace spin-doctoring, it gave rise to at least one entertaining story, told by Wendy Leigh, author of *Edward Windsor: Royal Enigma*. According to Leigh, the prince told Desmond Wilcox, his producer, that contrary to the 'facts' presented in the finished work, his great-uncle was a thief, and took into exile oil paintings and furniture that belonged to the royal family. In this, the duke had inherited his great-grandmother Queen Mary's tendencies: the rooms of her various residences were notoriously magpies' nests of stolen items and 'lock up the silver' was the watchword when she came to visit.

A series of protective books appeared in the 1990s. Philip Ziegler's *King Edward VIII* was a result of the authorization of the queen, who allowed him access to the collection of papers at Windsor Castle. Careful and cautious, with notable omissions, the biography failed to deal satisfactorily with any of the controversial aspects of the Windsors' life, using the time-worn device of other somewhat dim authorized chroniclers in replacing any suggestion of treasonable activities with the lesser charges of foolishness and naivety (the duke) and greed and selfishness (the duchess). This had the effect of diminishing the couple; at least their espionage and treason had shown a degree of intelligent enterprise, if entirely in the wrong direction.

The most ill-advised biography to date was Michael Bloch's hagiography *The Duchess of Windsor* (1996) which suggested, like Maître Blum, his mentor, that Wallis was a man, despite her cancer of the ovaries. *Hidden Agenda* by Martin Allen (2000), though much contested, is interesting; but only one book, *Hostage to Fortune, The Letters of Joseph P. Kennedy*, edited by his granddaughter Amanda Smith (2001), can be said to provide astonishments for the seasoned Windsor biographer, revealing as it does at first hand the true nature of the figures of the abdication crisis.

The last words must go to an anonymous poet. Among the items found in the inventory of the duchess's house in Paris, and not included in the Sotheby's auction, was a small gold-framed illuminated manuscript; the verse text was surmounted by a coronet. The words were:

> My friend to live with thee alone
> I think t'were better than to own
> A crown, a sceptre or a throne.

NOTE

1 A victim of the king's (Edward's) finagling with Mussolini; the king refused to receive the Abyssinian monarch at Buckingham Palace.

Notes on Sources

1. A Baltimore Childhood

The details of Bessie Wallis Warfield's childhood are based upon research conducted by the genealogist Robert Barnes of Perry Hall, Maryland. Mr Barnes has obtained census reports for Baltimore for 1900 and 1910 listing both the Warfield and the Montague families; an autobiographical document by Solomon Davies Warfield incorporated into his last will and testament dated 22 August 1927; an administration account book of Anna E. Warfield, giving details of house and land transactions, deeds and certifications; the will of Anna Emory Warfield incorporated into a document dated 26 March 1929, and found in the papers of Solomon Davies Warfield; and birth, marriage and death certificates for the principal figures, along with Baltimore *Sun* newspaper reports of these events. At the time of the Orphans' Court hearing in which Josephine Metcalf Warfield filed against the estate of Solomon Warfield on 9 August 1929, numerous other documents were subpoenaed and have been examined, giving a clear picture of the family history. Dr Beale Thomas, with the assistance of numerous officials of the Episcopalian church of Baltimore, searched all church records and conclusively determined that Bessie Wallis Warfield had not been baptized. This was subsequently confirmed by the local archdiocese; Dr Winthrop Brainerd, Mrs Jewel Vroonland, John Zeren and Dr Beale Thomas supplied more information. Dr Thomas also obtained the confirmation record and was able to establish that, in entering it, the Warfield family falsified the truth concerning the lack of a baptism. Todd Dorsett did research at Blue Ridge Summit, Pennsylvania, searching valuable records. *The American Dictionary of Biography* contained exhaustive biographies of the principal figures of the Warfield clan. City directories disclosed addresses. Baltimore guidebooks gave particulars of the schools that Bessie Wallis attended. The Baltimore fire was extensively covered by the Baltimore *Sun* and by the *New York Times*.

The Baltimore Historical Society supplied documents of Oldfields School published at the time of the fiftieth anniversary in 1917. These included memorabilia of members of Bessie Wallis's class. A Warfield genealogy in handwriting, accompanied by a Montague genealogy, was also obtained from the Baltimore Historical Society. Society visiting lists for the period proved to be of use. *The Heart Has Its Reasons* provided much valuable detail. Articles in *Harper*'s magazine, *World's Work, Good Housekeeping*, the *Delineator*, and *The North American* were illuminating. Cleveland Amory's book *Who Killed Society?*, F. F. Beirne's *Baltimore: A Picture History* and his indispensable *The Amiable Baltimorians*, and S. E. Greene's *Baltimore, An Illustrated History* were all good sources. Mrs Edward D. Whitman gave a vivid interview. Charles F. Bove's fine book *A Paris Surgeon's Story* was consulted. Archdeacon Moseley of the Los Angeles Episcopalian archdiocese provided me with details of the religious issues involved in the failure to baptize Wallis and confirmed that according to the orthodoxy of the 1890s, condemnation to hell was the consequence of not being baptized.

2. A Stubborn Young Lady

The substantial number of letters written by Mary Kirk to her mother, at a rate of three or four a week, describing her school days with Bessie Wallis proved to be a treasure trove. The correspondence has been preserved at Radcliffe. Records of the du Pont family maintained at the Eleutherian Mills library in Delaware have been drawn from. Cholly Knickerbocker ran a series of articles at the time of the abdication crisis in which he interviewed many of the then-living contemporaries of Bessie Wallis, including Lloyd Tabb, Tom Shyrock and the principals of Wallis's schools. Robert Barnes obtained records on John Freeman Rasin. Mrs (Douglas) Dale St Dennis, granddaughter of Corinne De Forest Montague Mustin Murray, was very kind in handing me the substantial and extraordinary correspondence between her grandmother and Bessie Wallis. *The Amiable Baltimorians* is the best source on the Bachelors' Cotillon.

3. RUNNING UP THE LADDER

Here again *The Heart Has Its Reasons* was very helpful and the Anna Warfield and Solomon Warfield accounts and probate records proved to be of value. In the matter of Pensacola, I had the invaluable help of a navy wife, Anna Irwin, who spent weeks checking up on descriptive details of the naval base in the second decade of the century, talking with various survivors of that era and searching the microfilms of the Pensacola *Journal,* which supplied many of the particulars. Professor George F. Pearce was most helpful. The US Navy Air Force records in Washington were obtained, along with the correspondence files, kept in boxes at the Library of Congress, of Henry Mustin and Mark L. Bristol, among others. Annual reports of the US Navy were searched, along with the files of the naval academy at Annapolis. Several railway historians were contacted for descriptions of the journey to that region in 1916, and an examination of maps and street directories showed the journey that a visitor would take to reach specific destinations at that time. Brochures of the San Carlos Hotel came to light in the Pensacola public library. The history of Earl Winfield Spencer's father was found in Chicago records searched by Eleanor Campbell, a qualified genealogist in that city; she also visited Highland Park, Illinois, to obtain more information on the spot. Obituaries of the members of the family revealed much; these appeared in the *Chicago Tribune.* Annapolis supplied the class, demerit and graduation records of Spencer. The case of reckless driving and manslaughter in which he was involved with Ensign Chevalier was obtained from the Maryland Hall of Records on an application for the criminal docket. I was assisted in this by Rick Swanson and Rita Molter, in charge of the records. An account of the hurricane of 1916 appeared in the Pensacola *Journal.* Once again, Professor Pearce was most helpful; his excellent book *The US Navy in Pensacola* was consulted and all footnoted sources obtained and read.

4. A STYLISH MARRIAGE

The best description of the wedding appeared in the Baltimore Sun and was supplemented by the wedding certificate obtained by Robert Barnes. The resident historian of the Greenbriar Hotel at White Sulphur Springs, West Virginia, Dr Robert Conte, was kind enough to send me prospectuses of that period, the room number, location and view of the Spencers' honeymoon room, and other particulars. Rear Admiral George Van Deurs, US Navy (retired), supplied more information in his little-known book *Wings for the Fleet*. Mrs Fidelia Rainey and Mrs Lottie Gonzalez reminisced. Records of the US Navy aeronautic station at Pensacola were searched. Paolo E. Coletta, working on the editing of the unpublished manuscript *The Goonie Bird*, sent me notes. Katherine Carlin King, daughter of Gustav and Katherine Eitzen, left memorabilia, now to be discovered in San Diego. The Boston Historical Society was helpful. Again, railway historians were consulted for an account of the train journey to California at the time.

The San Diego *Tribune, Union* and *Transcript* files were searched for details of that city in the second decade of the century. I had a very pleasant visit in San Diego, assisted in both driving and research by John Baron of the University of California. I enjoyed visiting the houses rented by the Spencers at the time. Eileen Jackson, veteran journalist of the San Diego *Union*, supplied me with the addresses. I then contacted the owners of the houses, T. Hyrum Callister of 1143 Alameda Street, Mr and Mrs Leo Hansen of Pinewood Cottage, and Mr and Mrs Jennings Brown of 1023 Encino Row, and they were good enough to allow me to visit them. I stayed at the Hotel del Coronado, where the publicity staff generously supplied me with period information. The manager of the Palomar apartment building was equally helpful. Members of the Fullam and Spreckels families cooperated with me, as did Neil Morgan, editor of the *Tribune*, and the aforementioned Mrs (Douglas) Dale St Dennis, who was most hospitable. Captain Arthur Sinclair Hill showed me a moving photographic gallery of his tragically star-crossed Montague family, with bereavement after bereavement in every generation and so many magnificent-looking young people struck down. Mary Carlin King and her family were extraordinarily hospitable. Vastly changed though it is, San Diego still has the sense of warmth and welcome it had when the young Mrs Spencer lived there. The San Diego newspapers all described the Armistice Day celebrations of 11 November 1918 and the Prince of Wales's visit on 7 April 1920. I obtained the complete guest list of the party at which he was received by the local citizens, thus determining that Wallis was not on the special shortlist. Joan Alban of the Coronado Chamber of Commerce and the staffs of the San Diego and Coronado Historical Societies provided much material.

Back in the east, the Chevy Chase Country Club was cooperative; so was the Army and Navy Club. The divorce files of Spencer v. Spencer, unsealed for me at Warrenton, Virginia, contain the important depositions of Wallis and her mother which provide transcripts and conversations between them and Earl Spencer. The best source on the *Pampanga* was Commander Bernard D. Cole's *Gunboats and Marines*. I interviewed Commander Cole several times by telephone to his home in Honolulu, Hawaii. Mrs Milton E. Miles, widow of Rear Admiral Miles, gave me her recollections as a young navy wife. I interviewed Professor Immanuel C. Y. Hsue, author of the excellent *The Rise of Modern China*, at his home in Santa Barbara, California, on the general background. Navy annual reports were drawn from. Record Groups 24 and 38, containing general correspondence of the Navy Department and records of the chief of naval operations, were searched. So were files of Record Group 45, the naval records collection of the Office of Naval Records and Library. The government of Argentina supplied background information on Don Felipe Espil; the best sources on his relationship with Wallis are her own *The Heart Has Its Reasons* and Ralph G. Martin's *The Woman He Loved.*

5. CHINA

The Operational Archives Branch of the Naval Historical Center of the Washington Navy Yard supplied declassified data. So did Evelyn M. Cherpak, head of the Naval Historical Collection, Department of the Navy, Naval War College, Newport, Rhode Island. Oral histories of wives of that time in China were used. An obituary of Mrs F. H. Sadler in the *New York Times*, 20 June 1951, and OAB materials on Rear Admiral Sadler were used. The Biographies Branch of the US Department of the Navy supplied details of Admiral Luke McNamee. US Navy intelligence files and the US State Department passport files on Mrs Earl Winfield Spencer were declassified under the Freedom of Information Act and were available on production of her death certificate. These established circumstantial evidence that she was on government business. Record Group 59 of the State Department, records relating to internal affairs in China, MF 329 rolls 38, 39, 40, 43, 103, 128 and 163, were consulted. So were boxes 6432, 6254 and 930. More specific frame references can be obtained in the author's collection of documents at the University of Southern California. The complete log of the USS *Chaumont* was obtained. The author drew from his experience as press liaison officer on British merchant passenger ships to analyse these complex pages. It was possible to determine the description of Hong Kong at the time from numerous travel books. The *Pampanga* log was examined for coincidental dates. Professor Hsue was again helpful on the political background. Files of the *Hong Kong Telegraph, North China Herald, China Press, Celestial Empire* and

North China Daily News were read on microfilm. Details of the China dossier were determined through interviews and correspondence with the Duc de Grantmesnil and Mrs Leslie Field. Fortunately the passenger lists of the *Empress of Russia*, the *Empress of Canada*, the *President Garfield* and the *Shuntien* were published in the local newspapers. US military intelligence reports at the University of Southern California were examined. The guest lists of the Astor House Hotel in Shanghai and the Grand Hôtel de Pékin were also published, a curious lapse of security for US citizens in time of civil war that was amended by 1925. US State Department consular records were searched to obtain details of Mrs Spencer's movements. Several members of Herman Rogers's family, most notably his nephew, Richard D. Schley, and his niece, the former Mrs Edmund Pendleton Rogers (Mrs Beatrice Tremain), were interviewed at length on Rogers's background in intelligence work. The US State Department maintained quarterly lists of US citizens resident in Peking, which enabled the author to discover the address at which Herman Rogers was resident. This was quite at variance with that given in *The Heart Has Its Reasons*. FBI files were examined, along with published railway timetables preserved at the Library of Congress. Naval and Marine files were looked at on the matter of Commander Little. The Ciano relationship was confirmed by Mrs Miles; an oblique reference to it, with Wallis's name omitted, is in Giordano Bruno Guerri's *Galeazzo Ciano, A Life 1903/1944*. The most difficult task was determining the date of Wallis's return to the United States, which she described quite incorrectly in her memoirs. James P. Maloney spent a week searching US Department of Justice immigration and naturalization records for vessels arriving in Seattle before, late one night, he at last lit upon her name as a passenger aboard the *President McKinley*.

Logbooks of the USS *Wright* were examined. US Navy records of Spencer (RG 1959: 1930–1939, box 79) established his Mussolini connections. The public library of Warrenton, Virginia, and the local genealogical society unearthed brochures of the Warren Green Hotel, today a government office building. They also obtained for me the number of the room in which Wallis lived, while files from the local newspapers disclosed her movements, including her visit with Mrs Larrabee. Mrs Edward Russell and Mrs Henry Poole left reminiscences. Ralph G. Martin in *The Woman He Loved* interviewed Hugh Spilman.

6. ERNEST

The New York Genealogical Society has confirmed Ernest Simpson's Jewish origins. Barbara Goldsmith, in *Little Gloria, Happy At Last,* disclosed details of the Vanderbilt and Morgan families. The Pittsburgh Historical Society and Pennsylvania Historical Society supplied information about Mary Thaw. The divorce records of Spencer v. Spencer, preserved at Warrenton, Virginia, were unsealed for the author on request. *The Times* and *New York Times* helped me to clarify the social background in London in 1927. Luc Nemeth in Paris, a specialist in Italian political history, and John Hope in London unravelled the pro-Italian background. Kenneth Rose and Lady Donaldson in interviews in London helped illuminate the character of the Prince of Wales. The *New York Times* files revealed the engagement to Lady Elizabeth Bowes-Lyon and the Max Beerbohm caricature which created such a fuss. Samuel Marx revealed the prince's affair with Marguerite Laurent in his entertaining book *Queen of the Ritz.* The author visited the various addresses in London where Wallis and her husband lived; they are scarcely changed today. Barbara Goldsmith was the best source on the relationship of the prince with Thelma Furness. Contemporary photographs in the *Tatler,* the *Sketch* and the *Bystander* revealed the contents of 5 Bryanston Court. The dual memoir of Gloria Vanderbilt and Thelma Furness entitled *Double Exposure* was an excellent source. *The Heart Has Its Reasons* was also drawn from here.

7. THE PRINCE

Barbara Goldsmith was excellent on Thelma Furness and the prince. Mary Kirk, later Mary Kirk Raffray, wrote vivid letters home on her visit to London. Again, these were obtained from Radcliffe. The account of the trip to the south of France was obtained from Goldsmith. The Windsor letters edited by Michael Bloch supplied more information. The *New York Times,* a great source neglected by all Windsor biographers, gave particulars of the prince's movements in those years. *The Times* gave a more censored calendar of events, notably avoiding the Italian connections. The *New York Times* had no such compunctions. Henry Flood Robert of San Diego supplied the anecdote about the ill-fated afternoon party. Sir Robert Bruce Lockhart revealed in his diaries the particulars of Prince Louis Ferdinand's visit to London. Kenneth Rose kindly supplied me with diary excerpts of Graf Albert Mensdorff, former Austrian ambassador to the Court of St James. The Duke of Windsor's *New York Daily News* article was indispensable. The biography of Aly Khan by Leonard Slater was a witty source on the Furness–Khan affair. Stanley Jackson's *The Sassoons* filled me in on the background of that remarkable family. *The Long Party* by Stella Margetson was vivid. John Costello supplied me with details of Admiral Wolkoff and his daughter Anna, supplemented by information obtained from transcripts of the trial of Tyler Kent, available at Yale University. Donatella Ortona interviewed her father, who in turn interviewed his close friend and colleague Count Dino Grandi at the count's home in Bologna for an irreplaceable first-hand account of the Italian connection in London. I spoke with the Princess Ann-Mari von Bismarck at her home in Marbella, Spain, on the matter of the German connection, and she followed up our conversation with a letter, of great historical value, which has been somewhat adapted in the actual wording to conform with current English usage. Paul Schwarz's excellent book *This Man Ribbentrop* supplied much information. The *Tatler* had a memorable full-page photograph of the guests at the 27 May January Club dinner (only William Joyce was without a black tie). The biography of Elsie de Wolfe by Jane S. Smith was a good source on her and was supplemented in my research by Tony Duquette, her protégé and today a leading California decorator and artist, and his associate Hutton Wilkinson. Frederick Corbitt, in charge of catering for the royal household, left an entertaining memoir entitled *Fit for a King*. This book has been much neglected by historians. *The Times* and *New York Times* followed the prince's movements throughout Europe. Several members of Lord Moyne's family, including his son and the Duchess of Normandy, have filled me in on matters relating to the *Rosaura*.

8. MOVING TOWARDS THE THRONE

Laura, Duchess of Marlborough, was the authority on the matter of the illegitimate child of Prince George. She married Michael Canfield, who died tragically young. The affair with Noël Coward was discussed in Michael Thornton's *Royal Feud*. The memoirs of Prince Christopher of Greece have been consulted. Thornton is the best source on Wallis's burlesque imitation of Princess Elizabeth. Frederick Winterbotham, through correspondence and telephone calls, and the late Ladislas Farago, both on the telephone with me and in his *The Day of the Foxes*, discussed the de Ropp episode.

The account of the journey to Europe is drawn in part from the *New*

York Times; the collection of George Messersmith, American minister to Austria, housed at the University of Delaware, contains more useful information. The British journalist G. E. R. Gedye's book *Betrayal in Central Europe* gives a vivid picture of the Prince of Wales in Vienna. Austrian newspapers of the period, including the *Arbeiter Zeitung* and the *Neue Freie Presse,* supply further details. Prince Otto von Hapsburg has confirmed the Prince of Wales's interest in him. Research in the Budapest newspapers *Kis Ujsag, Neps Java* and *Budap* has brought to light useful information. The diaries of Henry Channon have been consulted. A most helpful article by Francis Watson in *History Today* (December 1986) has supplied excerpts from the Wigram diaries, which are not at present open to public inspection. *Loyal to Three Kings* by Lady Hardinge is the source of the anecdote about Wallis at St James's Palace. The diaries and letters of Mrs Belloc Lowndes have also been used here. The *New York Times* expertly covered the Silver Jubilee and pointed to the involvement of Princess Cecilie in the prince's German connections. Further information on the matter of the British Legion was drawn from the Legion's official history by Graham Wooten. Hansard was referred to for the questions asked by Aneurin Bevan. The Londonderry connection is dealt with in many sources, including *England's Money Lords* by Simon Haxey, a most useful work. The Windsor letters have again been consulted.

Once again, the *New York Times* exhaustively covered the royal tour. George Messersmith was on the case as always. The matter of Armand Grégoire is dealt with in the FBI and army intelligence files on Grégoire and in the Sûreté files in Paris, now lodged at the Diplomatic Archives along with numerous other reports on him drawn from a variety of intelligence sources. The magazine *La Franciste* has been read, and so has the book *Bucard et le Francisme* by Alain Deneiel. *Deadline* by Pierre Lazareff, former editor of *Paris-Soir,* and *Campaign of Treachery* by the distinguished Paris lawyer Henry Torres confirm FBI and State Department reports that Wallis engaged Grégoire as her lawyer. The Laval connection was established by the evidence given by Laval at his trial for treason in France after the Second World War, and both transcripts and *New York Times* accounts have been drawn from. Comte René de Chambrun has confirmed the relationship, which he has discussed in his book *Pierre Laval: Traitor or Patriot?* British Foreign Office documents have been looked at. *Current Biography* for 1942 gives particulars of Mainbocher. Again, Kenneth Rose supplied the Mensdorff diaries.

Kenneth de Courcy (Duc de Grantmesnil) and Mrs Leslie Field were, of course, the main sources on the China dossier. George Seldes discussed in *In Fact* the matter of Dr Frank Buchman and his Nazi connections. The biography of Sir Oswald Mosley by Robert Skidelsky supplies much information, supplemented by additional details in Colin Cross's book *The Fascists in Britain* and in the memoirs of Nicholas Mosley, Lord Ravensdale. The matter of Simpson's cotton concessions, referred to in the indexes to the documents of the Foreign Office published in 1972, is recorded in the existing Foreign Office files at the Public Record Office at Kew. Frederick Corbitt's aforementioned memoirs supplied the avocado story. Kenneth Rose's *King George V* is excellent on the old King's decline. The *History Today* article was most valuable here; it confirmed from both Lord Dawson's and Lord Wigram's documents the fact of the euthanasia matter. *Business Week*, 21 March 1936, supplied the details of the royal income based on careful research in British archives. Helen Lombard's *Washington Waltz*, a most reliable work, gives details of the royal investments in Lyons. Henry Grattidge's book *Captain of the Queens* includes the story of the disturbing event that took place during the funeral procession. Paul Schwarz's *This Man Ribbentrop* contains the account of the secret films taken of the king and Wallis and sent to Hitler. Schwarz was among the few people in a position to know about this.

The German Foreign Ministry documents contain descriptions of the meetings between the king and his German visitors at the time. *Loyal to Three Kings* was consulted. Hitler's memorial service for King George V was recorded in the *New York Times*. So was the party at Buckingham Palace, notably played down in the British press. The idea of Lady Mendl's redecorating the palace came from a *New York Times* article. So did the interview with my father, Sir Charles Higham. The love letters were once more a good source. *Time* magazine expertly covered these events. The papers of J. C. C. Davidson, former chairman of the Conservative party and later Chancellor of the Duchy of Lancaster, were consulted on the Masonic issue.

9. Almost Glory

The intelligence files on Mrs Cartwright are in the diplomatic records branch of the National Archives in Washington. Mary Kirk Raffray's letters were again a good source. Paul Schwarz dealt with the matter of the seventeen red roses, and Channon gave a detailed account of Ribbentrop in England. Harold Nicolson's diaries have been consulted. Again, Sir Robert Bruce Lockhart's diaries provide much colourful information. Keith Middlemas and John Barnes's *Stanley Baldwin* is a most reliable basis. The FBI files have been looked at in connection with the documentary leakage. Schwarz confirms it. John Connell gave the best account of Vansittart in his book *The Office*. John Costello has provided more information from intelligence sources in Britain. Nigel West has filled me in on zu Putlitz. The Phipps leak is confirmed in British Foreign Office document indexes. The Baldwin papers have been consulted. Marion Crawford's controversial book *The Little Princesses* supplied the anecdote about Wallis's visit to the little princesses. The matter of the secret submarine war between Italy and Russia has been confirmed by Donatella Ortona in discussions with her father, and by Henry Gris, journalist, who interviewed Count Ciano at the time. The attempted assassination was well covered by *The Times* and the *New York Times* and by *Time* magazine. Yet again, the *New York Times* was the best source on the royal tour. J. Charlet in *The Living Age* described the political significance of the trip, basing his information on interviews on the spot. The *New York Times*'s George Weller, its indispensable correspondent in Athens, dealt with the political purposes of the journey in the issue of 20 September 1936, and so, once again, did the invaluable George Messersmith. The British press and subsequent historians have swept aside much of this information, dealt with further in the Windsor State Department files. John Balfour's memoirs *Not Too Correct an Aureole* are of great value to the historian in this connection. The biography of Sir Percy Loraine by Gordon Waterfield has been consulted. Lady Hardinge continued to be a good source on the couple's activities. The *New York Times* kept a constant watch on Wallis at Cumberland Terrace, and at Felixstowe and Ipswich. *Time* magazine also expertly covered the divorce matter. Mrs Belloc Lowndes revealed the provenance of the Mogul emerald.

10. ABDICATION

Here, the *New York Times* was especially indispensable. Copies of the *Daily Mail* for the period have been read. Rudolph Stoiber, the leading authority on Princess Stephanie Hohenlohe, has supplied background on the Rothermere family. Lord Birkenhead provided judicious comments and much information in his excellent life of Walter Monckton. Birkenhead was the source of the anecdote about Monckton's 'secret' visits to Buckingham Palace. The Duc de Grantmesnil is the source on the attempted assassination of Wallis. He has also described meetings of the Imperial Policy Group. The diaries of Blanche Dugdale were drawn from. The account of Wallis's flight from England was obtained from a great variety of sources, including her own memoirs, the *New York Times*, *The Times*, the memoirs of Diana Vreeland, a close friend of Lord Brownlow, Lady Donaldson's *Edward VIII*, etc. Martin Gilbert's monumental biography of Winston Churchill has been a great source. Copies of all London newspapers for the period have been examined. So have the Scotland Yard reports. (The cabinet minutes on the abdication crisis will remain classified for many years.) The journey to the south of France was exhaustively discussed by the *New York Times. The Times* was notably inadequate on the subject. Birkenhead was again an excellent source. French newspapers, especially *Paris-Soir, Le Figaro, Le Matin* and *Le Temps* were indispensable. Michael Bloch's annotations on the love letters filled in many useful details. Kenneth Rose is the chief source on the matter of Sandringham and Balmoral, as well as on the Civil List issue concerning the royal income. Charles Bedaux, Jr, Betty Hanley and the former Mrs Edmund Livingston Rogers have been marvellously helpful in the matter of Wallis's stay in France.

11. EXILE

Donatella Ferrario Ortona, in consultation with her father, obtained the quote from Count Grandi. Birkenhead on Monckton was the best source on the king's journey to Europe. *Orient Express* by E. H. Cookridge gave a good account of the duke's travels aboard that legendary train. The former Mrs Edmund Livingston Rogers gave me an exhaustive description of Lou Viei at the time. Douglas Reed in his memorable book *Insanity Fair* covered the duke's activities in Vienna. Frederick Morton's book on the Rothschilds was a useful source. The *Sunday Referee* contained the article by Ellen Wilkinson. Newbold Noyes's pieces in the *Washington Star* and *Paris-Soir* were read. The *New York Times* covered every inch of both the duke's and Wallis's movements at the time. So did *Time* magazine. Aunt Bessie's letters included in the Windsor love-letters book were valuable; Corinne Murray's granddaughter Mrs (Douglas) Dale St Dennis supplied me with several of her notes from the south of France. Lady Donaldson obtained exclusive access to the Metcalfe letters and quoted them in her *Edward VIII*. The *New York Times* covered the concert in Vienna and the visit of the Princess Royal and the Earl of Harewood. Mrs Leslie Field has effectively disposed of the Alexandra emeralds theory. For her book on the royal jewels Mrs Field spent years of research at Buckingham Palace. Betty Hanley has been indispensable on life at the Château de Candé. She is one of the very few surviving eyewitnesses, and Charles Bedaux, Jr, read these passages and confirmed their authenticity. *The Times* and the *New*

York Times covered the hearing on the divorce. Reporters from the *New York Times* were present every day at Enzesfeld. The State Department file 033.4111 on the Duke of Windsor contains information on his relationship with Bedaux and on the problems that relationship provoked.

12. WEDDING OF THE DECADE

A good source on the wedding was the hitherto neglected memoir *At Long Last* by the Reverend Jardine. Constance Coolidge's account is to be found in her correspondence at the Maryland Historical Society. The London *Gazette* was consulted. So were Aunt Bessie's letters to Corinne, supplied by Mrs (Douglas) Dale St Dennis. As always, the *New York Times* was in the forefront in covering the wedding. Betty Hanley obtained many details from her Aunt Fern, even though she herself was not present. The *New York Times* covered the visit to Italy, largely ignored by *The Times*. The stay at Wasserleonburg was drawn from aforementioned Austrian papers as well as British and American newspapers. The *Daily Express* was an especially good source. Messersmith's report on the duke's leakage of information regarding the armaments shipment was to be found in his collection at the University of Delaware. The further travels were covered by the *New York Times* as usual. The Duke of Windsor State Department files exhaustively document in letters and telegrams the preparations for the American tour. None of these files had been consulted by historians in 1986–1988. The Earl of Crawford's diaries are an excellent source for the grave concern of the king and queen in the matter of the Windsors' Nazi connections. The *New York Times* and Austrian and Italian newspapers covered the German tour in detail. The Duchess of Windsor's account in her memoirs was grossly distorted and self-serving. Nerin E. Gun in his entertaining biography of Eva Braun was a good descriptive source; William Bullitt's *Personal and Secret*, his correspondence with President Roosevelt, was also a much ignored source of information. So was J. Paul Getty's *As I See It*. The late Adrian Liddell Hart interviewed Frau Hess, who told him of her meeting with the duchess. Army intelligence, OSS and State Department files were consulted on the matter of Bohle. Martin Gilbert is the source of the Churchill letter on Germany; it is reproduced in the accompanying volume of Gilbert's biography that includes correspondence. Files of the Protocol Division of the State Department were drawn from. So were the documents of Sir Eric Phipps; the Hardinge–Vansittart correspondence cited is from the Lord Avon files at the Public Records Office at Kew.

13. Outer Darkness

The loyalist newspaper *Voz* was examined. Vincent Sheean's admirable book *Between the Thunder and the Sun* provided the best account of the events at Maxine Elliott's house in the south of France. The *New York Times* continued to follow the Windsors' every move. The late Tony Duquette supplied much information, as well as telegrams and correspondence relating to Lady Mendl and the Windsors. George Seldes has exposed William Bullitt definitively in *In Fact*. The *New York Times* dealt with the Louis Rothschild matter in some detail; the duke's involvement in the ransom arrangements has been supplied by a confidential source. The Ribbentrop document on the Duke of Windsor's involvement with the Sports and Shooting Club at Schloss Mittersill is included in the German Foreign Ministry Dienststelle Ribbentrop documents entitled 'Personliche Inlander File', volume II, period: 17 December 1936–31 August 1940, serial number 3 i 4, negative frame numbers 190707–190708 T120/roll 250. The document may be found in the Charles Higham collection at the University of Southern California or at the National Archives in Washington. The *Sunday Dispatch* report has been examined. Nigel West was most helpful on the matter of the Duke of Kent. The attempted murder of the King and Queen of England by Sean Russell can be traced through the Russell documents in the author's collection at USC or in the files of the FBI, Diplomatic Records Branch of the National Archive, and State Department files. Mrs Smith's life of Lady Mendl and the French newspapers were combined for my account of the party which signalled the end of an era in Europe. The death of Bedrich Benes was described by the *New York Times*. John Hope in England pulled together details of the many fascist-oriented groups functioning at the time. Donald McCormick in his biography of Lloyd George described the dangers that existed in Wales and at Hindhead. The Earl of Crawford's diaries were again consulted. The French Military Archives at Vincennes, the State Department files, *The Gravediggers of France* by Pertinax, Lady Donaldson's *Edward VIII*, Major General Pownall's diaries, my interviews with Lord Ironside in London, the memoirs of Hore-Belisha, the German Foreign Office documents, War Cabinet meeting transcriptions, and massive numbers of documents from the Public Record Office were consulted vis-à-vis the duke's service in France. Boelcke's book on war propaganda was read. The Red Cross security problems are exhaustively dealt with in files in the Diplomatic Branch record room at the National Archives in Washington.

14. A Dark Plot

Michael Bloch's *Operation Willi* contains much original research in this controversial area. The former Public Record Office's files were consulted, including the all-important Portuguese file, to which Mr Bloch first drew attention. State Department files on the Windsors proved to be another source. The Portuguese government archives supplied material relating to the Duke of Kent's visit. Martin Gilbert, completing in many volumes Randolph Churchill's unfinished biography of his late father Winston Churchill, has given the historian a fine record to draw from. The memoirs of David Eccles were useful. OSS reports on Serrano Suñer and Baron von Hoyningen-Huene were declassified for the author. John Taylor of the National Archives in Washington was helpful. German Foreign Ministry documents were re-examined. I also drew from previously unavailable and specially declassified reports on and by Walter Schellenberg, obtained under the Freedom of Information Act from US intelligence sources. The late Sir John Colville granted me an all-important interview. Hutton Wilkinson, on behalf of the late Tony Duquette, gave me the duchess's cables to Johnny McMullen. The Herbert Claiborne Pell telegram is in the Windsors' US State Department documents. These apparently were not consulted by Michael Bloch. The Schellenberg memoirs were used. Birkenhead's biography of Monckton was again a good source. Portuguese files of Dr Salazar had not hitherto been available. The *New York Times* had a reporter on board the *Excalibur* and on the *Yankee Clipper*. Thus it was possible to reconstruct the events of the voyage and the air-sea encounter with the Rothschilds.

15. Elba

The Windsors' declassified State Department files indicate that on a day-to-day basis the local authorities were keeping constant surveillance on the couple. Frank Giles wrote amusingly about the duke and duchess in his memoir *Sundry Times*. The Nassau *Tribune* covered the duke and duchess's activities, and so, from a defending counsel's point of view, did Michael Bloch in his *The Duke of Windsor's War*. The Public Record Office had substantial files on the Windsors in the Bahamas. Not all of these were consulted by Bloch. The FBI files on Sir Harry Oakes, Harold Christie, Walter Foskett, Axel Wenner-Gren, Mrs Wenner-Gren and the Bahamas as a whole were declassified after many years. J. Edgar Hoover,

frustrated by the restrictions of his activities in the Caribbean, characteristically embarked upon a full-scale separate investigation to the details of
which other historians have not obtained access. The Wenner-Gren FBI
files alone amount to almost three thousand pages. Bloch's account of
the journeys of the duchess's maid have been supplemented by reference
to the State Department files. The Windsors' FBI file contains the report
on the duchess's alleged shipping of messages to New York City. John W.
Dye reported on them somewhat unfavourably. The *New York Times* filled
in details of their travels to the mainland, supplemented by the Miami
Herald files. The James D. Mooney documents were drawn from his
collection at Georgetown University. The State Department and FBI files
on Mooney were also of value. Previously undiscovered letters written by
the Duchess of Windsor to Churchill were located by Daniel Re'em in the
file of the late Earl of Avon at the Public Record Office in Kew. Messersmith's documents at the University of Delaware were again used. Errol
Flynn's movements were determined from the Warner Bros files at the
University of Southern California Doheny Library, Department of Special
Collections. The duchess's letters to P. G. Sedley are in her State Department files. The *Liberty* magazine article has been read and annotated.
Churchill's telegram concerning it is in both the State Department files
and Martin Gilbert's. The material concerning the Banco Continental is
to be found in the Diplomatic Records Branch of the National Archives
in Washington. The substantial Mexico files in that same record room
were drawn from. Churchill's memorandum concerning the Windsors'
property in France is in the Windsors' State Department files. FBI files on
the British Purchasing Commission are included with the massive documentation on Princess Stephanie Hohenlohe, declassified on appeal.
Details of the Tesden Corporation were also obtained from the FBI. The
MacKintosh report is to be found in the Franklin D. Roosevelt Memorial
Library at Hyde Park, New York, in the J. Edgar Hoover collection. Hoover
reported each Wednesday afternoon to the president. The Hess documents were been obtained from Madeleine Sorel, who in turn obtained
them from Hess's jailer at Nuremberg. Adrian Liddell Hart has supplied
more information. The Windsor letters have been used. Vincent Astor's
investigative mission is recorded in files in the Diplomatic Records
Branch. The *Washington Post* and *New York Times* have been consulted.
Once again, the Armand Grégoire FBI files and his OSS file have been
useful. The Adolf Berle documents are at the Diplomatic Records Branch.
John Balfour's *Not Too Correct an Aureole* has been a source. The Chicago
Tribune, Toronto *Star,* and Montreal and Ottawa papers have been consulted. For a more detailed account of the Windsors' tours, read Bloch;

but he has missed some details supplied by the *New York Times* and incorporated here. The Ribbentrop–declaration of war matter was found only in the Ribbentrop documents declassified by the Department of Army Security and Intelligence Command at Fort Meade, Maryland. The British intelligence report on Wenner-Gren is quoted in US intelligence reports; the British report is still unavailable in England. The Brassert Company files are with the US Treasury. The information on the Williams–del Drago correspondence comes from Bloch. It is supplemented by material in the Windsors' State Department files. The information about Christie's conflicts with Oakes came from interviews with the only surviving eyewitness, the late Alfred de Marigny. The account of the riot is drawn from the Nassau *Tribune*; so is the account of the subsequent fire. The description of the death of the Duke of Kent comes from a declassified report recently available from the Public Record Office. The Axel Wenner-Gren State Department files yielded particulars of the Windsors' improper investments. The Berle memorandum re censorship is available from the Diplomatic Records Branch. The FBI and army intelligence files on Charles Bedaux were examined, and his son has in fairness been allowed his say in the matter. The judicious historian will examine the intelligence records before reaching a conclusion. The account of Spencer's near death came from the San Diego *Union* and *Tribune*.

16. MURDER IN NASSAU

In 1986, Alfred de Marigny gave excellent interviews discussing the entire scene in Nassau in 1943 and his collisions with the Duke of Windsor. He also explained in full Christie's motive for murder. As stated in the text, it was necessary to re-present all the forensic and circumstantial evidence, along with details of the judge's previously unavailable handwritten trial transcript, to those best able to analyse them. In Los Angeles these were Dr Joseph Choi, former assistant to the famous Dr Thomas Noguchi, and John Ball, an expert on murder and author of that admirable *roman policier In the Heat of the Night*. The moment I mentioned the size and shape of the wounds to Mr Ball he identified them as being caused by a fishing spear, and he also knew from other cases with which he had dealt that this method of killing was exclusive to the Santeria-Palo Mayombe cult. On approaching Dr Choi, I had exactly the same response. In Los Angeles in recent years there have been a number of murders that can be described in precisely identical terms. I also showed both gentlemen the photographs of the deceased, and they confirmed instantly that nobody seeing that body could have believed the victim was alive. Thus, Harold Christie was proved to have committed perjury. Alfred de Marigny, as indicated in the text, believed Oakes was killed by a bullet. He avers that the two pathologists lied in court about it. But there is nothing to indicate that they did, and in fact the wiser policy would have been to lie, saying that the crime was committed by gunshot, so as to remove any suggestion of a black ritual murder, which could only cause another riot in the islands. Dr FitzMaurice's testimony was especially valuable since he precisely stated the details of the wounds and declined to give an opinion on the cause of them. The author visited many ship's chandlers in Los Angeles and Newport Beach, examining winch levers and other possible instruments of murder, ruling them all out and returning confidently to the conclusion of Choi and Ball. The precise details of everyone's movements on the night of the crime were obtained both from the judge's notes and from the Nassau *Tribune*'s files. None of the participants appears to have survived. Sergeant Louis Danoff of the LAPD Homicide Division kindly sent me detailed printed brochures, normally for use only by the police force itself, with diagrams and descriptions of Palo Mayombe killings. I consulted experts on arson in the matter of the gunpowder, an inevitable feature of Palo Mayombe. The matter of rigor mortis was explained to me by Dr Choi. The Foreign Activities Correlation Department of the State Department kept records of the duke's conversations, carefully monitored through RCA and Western Union sources in Miami. The Windsors' mainland visit was extremely well covered by the FBI and is contained in the FBI files. The visit to the FBI headquarters in Washington was discreetly ignored by all newspapers. Alfred de Marigny directly charged the Duke of Windsor with being an accessory after the fact of the crime and claimed that the duke pursued him through intermediaries who made attempts on his life, and also that the duke prevented him from emigrating. *Inside Detective*, November 1944 has been read. That fine detective Raymond Schindler got part of the story right. The Majava report is in the J. Edgar Hoover special file on the case. Whereas the newspapers neglected to mention whom Robinson identified as the killer, the FBI files specifically name him. Surprisingly, the FBI declassified this information for this author in 1981 without requesting Christie's death certificate, an indication to the historian that they had conclusive proof of his guilt. The Toronto report is in the Windsor FBI files. Stevenson's charges were recorded by *Time* magazine and the *Saturday Evening Post*.

17. RETURN TO EUROPE

Ciano's death was recorded in newspapers all over the world. The demise of Charles Bedaux was also extensively reported. The Richmond newspapers gave an account of Aubrey Weaver's death in a fire. *The Duke of Windsor's War* by Michael Bloch shows Wallis's increasing distress in Nassau and the duke's efforts to reinstate himself in Britain. (As usual, Bloch blames the British royal family for their pettifogging attitude, an incorrect approach in my opinion.) The Foreign Office Indexes published in 1970 list the whereabouts of the Windsors' properties. The Chanel file comes from the Schellenberg report. Balfour's memoirs again are excellent on the Young matter. Joseph R. Borkin's biography *Robert R. Young: The Populist of Wall Street* is a carefully documented source. The State Department Windsor files give uncomfortably revealing details of the attempts to suppress the German Foreign Office files. The trip to England was covered by the *New York Times* and most other newspapers. Tania Long covered the Nuremberg–Rosenberg matter thoroughly. The Duc de Grantmesnil supplied me with all correspondence of the period housed at the Hoover Institution at Stanford University, California. The Duchess of Marlborough was a main source on the jewel robbery; her account is supplemented by *The Times*, *New York Times*, *Daily Mail*, *Daily Express*, Scotland Yard reports and an interview with Mrs Leslie Field. Captain Harry Grattidge's *Captain of the Queens* supplies much little-known information. An interview with Guido Orlando has proved invaluable. Stephen Birmingham in his *Duchess* gave an amusing picture of Jimmy Donahue. The New York newspapers covered the Windsors' movements thoroughly in the late 1940s, including the fire episode at the Waldorf Towers. Mrs Eleanor Miles's letter about the Windsors in the south of France is to be found at the Maryland Historical Society. The Henry M. Warfield will is obtainable from the Maryland archives.

18. WANDERING YEARS

Sotheby's catalogue of the famous jewellery auction at Geneva in April 1987 has been examined. The details of the history of Suzanne Blum are contained in several existing biographies of Léon Blum. *The Windsor Story* by Charles J. V. Murphy and Birmingham's book reveal Murphy's problems with the duke and duchess in the matter of working on the memoirs. The late Laura, Duchess of Marlborough and the late Margaret,

Duchess of Argyll have supplied much new information. Details of the tour of the southern states and Mexico are to be found in the Corinne Murray correspondence; it has only been possible to include some highlights in this account. Balfour provided the Biarritz anecdote. C. L. Sulzberger in his memoir *A Long Row of Candles* gave the strong description of the Windsors incorporated here. Most newspapers recorded the duke's speech about Queen Elizabeth's accession, as well as the subsequent controversy. Hugo Vickers admirably described the Windsors' successive homes in Paris. Cecil Beaton wrote characteristically of the couple in his diaries, drawn from by Vickers in his definitive biography of Beaton. Lady Mosley granted the author one of the most memorable interviews of his life at her home near Paris. I drew from this rather than from her biography of the duchess, which was based almost entirely on published sources. Elsa Maxwell wrote with a surprising sharpness and intelligence about the Windsors in her neglected memoir *RSVP*, one of the best books of its kind and an indispensable guide to the social life of an era. Cholly Knickerbocker's syndicated columns were read. The story of the collapse of the Donahue relationship is drawn from Birmingham and Murphy, and supplemented with an interview conducted in 1980 with Jerome Zerbe.

19. Late Afternoon

The *New York Times* dealt expertly with the matter of Queen Mary's death. Biographies by Anne Edwards and James Pope-Hennessy were consulted. The *Daily Express* was read. The *New York Times* was the most reliable source on the Woodward killing, the Capote account the least reliable. *McCall's* magazine, January 1961, was read. The late Sir John Colville and Lady Mosley were the best sources on the Windsors' social life and brilliant capacity to entertain in those years. Murphy's accounts were also valuable. Members of the Murray and Mustin families described Aunt Bessie's hundredth birthday party and her funeral. The New York and Texas newspapers covered the duke's surgery at Houston. Michael Thornton's *Royal Feud* brought together most reliable sources on the visit to the London Clinic and on the events that immediately followed. Hugo Vickers has filled in more information.

20. EVENING AND NIGHT

The Niehans Clinic information was researched in Switzerland. Charlene Bry gave her account in *People* magazine in 1987. The *New York Times* covered the visit to Portugal. Hugo Vickers kindly showed me the Kenneth Harris interview. The Nixon banquet was recorded in detail in the Washington *Post*. Murphy was the best source on the Mountbatten matter. Thornton supplied more details. Hugo Vickers and the late Ginette Spanier confirmed or corrected published information. The best account of the death of the duke and the subsequent service is to be found in the *Times*, with additional details supplied by Thornhill. Vickers has given me long and invaluable interviews on the final years. The Countess of Romanones, in an article in *Vanity Fair*, June 1986, gave an intimate if controversial memoir of that difficult time. Most importantly, the Duke de Grantmesnil Collection at the Hoover Institution at Stanford, contains the extraordinary correspondence between himself and Maître Blum on the matter of the removed documents. The late Laura, Duchess of Marlborough, Princess von Bismarck and Hugo Vickers discussed the duchess's funeral with me. Alistair Cooke in the *New York Times* provided the last word on the reasons for Wallis's being denied the throne. Once again, the Sotheby's jewel catalogue was used as a source on the auction, and various newspaper and television reports were drawn from.

A final note: US Department of Justice criminal files on the Duchess of Windsor were destroyed, allegedly for space reasons, in the 1960s.

Notes on the New Material

The late Sir Dudley Forwood was the source on Edward 'Fruity' Metcalfe, in an interview at his house in the New Forest at Ringwood, Hampshire, on 9 October 1987, which was to be kept confidential until his death. *The Kaiser's Daughter*, the memoirs of Princess Viktoria Luise, Duchess of Brunswick provided the details of the proposed marriage of Princess Friederike of Prussia and the Prince of Wales. The matter of Prince Philipp of Hesse was drawn from the denazification files on the prince (1945–6) supplied by Professor Jonathan Petropoulos of Claremont College, California, the world authority on the subject; from the *New York Times* from 1924–45; from seized German records on microfilm at the National Archive and Records Service in Washington, DC, Modern Military Branch; from the Foreign Office files at the National Archive of Great Britain; and from State Department files, obtained by Jill Cairns-Gallimore, courtesy John Taylor. The Sandra Rambeau matter comes from the State Department official files on her and on Frederick G. McEvoy and Errol Leslie Flynn; from the files of the Los Angeles *Herald-Examiner* at the University of California; and from her master FBI file. Jane Singer supplied her birth and death (1987) records.

The connections of the Duke of Kent, Prince Paul of Yugoslavia, Prince Philipp of Hesse, Goering and Hitler are clearly stated in the State Department files on each and in Philipp's denazification files as well as from private information. Records of the affair with Guy Trundle, in the Albert Canning reports at Scotland Yard to Lord Trenchard and then to Sir Philip Game, were originally classified until 2037 but were released in January 2003. The matter of the China dossier can be found discussed in the correspondence and diaries of Kenneth de Courcy, Duc de Grantmesnil, housed at the Hoover Institution of Peace and War at

Stanford University, California. The actual dossier may or may not exist in the closed (until 2017) de Courcy files or in the archives of Windsor Castle, where its presence even at the time of the abdication has been consistently denied by Buckingham Palace sources and all official biographers. Sir John Coke can be regarded as reliable and the record stands. The conversations of Sir Edward (Robert) Peacock and Joseph P. Kennedy are contained in the aforementioned *Hostages to Fortune: The Letters of Joseph P. Kennedy*, edited by his granddaughter Amanda Smith. They represent the only leak to date of the most careful cover-up in the royal chronicle – the matter of the Windsors' finances and of the queen's (later the Queen Mother's) attitude to the Windsors, which has also been carefully hidden to date, with one entire box of files removed from the Bodleian Library at Oxford – it is alleged on royal orders. Happily, her letter on the matter to Prince Paul of Yugoslavia (2 October 1940) survives at Columbia University, along with her acid comments recorded in the Kennedy diaries. The involvement of Prince Paul with the Nazis, hidden by generations of busy whitewashers, is exhaustively dealt with in his former minister Ilija Jukie's *The Fall of Yugoslavia*, the only insider's account available to date. The Prince of Wales's behaviour at the time of his father's death is described in the Kennedy diaries. His egalitarian actions when he became king – hailing taxis and so forth – are to be found in an anonymous but reliable report at Churchill College, Cambridge, and confirmed as authentic by the son and grandson of Sir Louis Greig.

The Maundy Thursday occasion was mentioned in the *New York Times*. The 4 May 1936 letter of complaint from Wallis to her aunt Bessie Merryman is at the Baltimore Historical Society. The report on communist activity regarding the king is in the Scotland Yard reports by Albert Canning. The minutes from the Privy Council meeting regarding Ethiopia are in the Royal Archives at Windsor Castle. The Blenheim Palace divorce conspiracy is discussed in the anonymous report at Cambridge. The Bulgarian visit was published in the *Bulgarian Monthly Review* as cited in the narrative, and in *Crown of Thorns, the Reign of King Boris III of Bulgaria* by Stéphane Grovet. Wallis's continuing affair with Trundle when her future husband was king is recorded in the Kennedy diaries; the source, as given, was Sir Edward Peacock; the visit to Wales is in the Anne Fremantle book cited in the narrative. The account of the Duke of York's horror at being king is shown in a long and anguished confession preserved in the Royal Archives at Windsor Castle. The desire to reverse the abdication is in the Peacock–Kennedy discussions. The Cockburn matter is to be found without a solution in his memoirs *A Discord of*

Trumpets; the account of the king's blackouts at dinner and the meeting with Peacock comes from the Churchill papers at Cambridge.

Sir Horace Wilson's sixty-four-page report on the abdication in the British National Archives is indispensable, and damning in its conclusions. Dismissed as 'inaccurate and ill-advised' by the royal spin doctors when declassified in 2003, it is based upon exhaustive research by a devoted and reliable royalist civil servant. The report also contains documentation on cabinet discussions as to whether Wallis should be bribed, confirming my findings on the matter in the 1987 edition of this book. The visits to Count Toerring by the Duke of Kent are recorded in the Foreign Office files of the British National Archives. The exhibition on Wallis in the Baltimore museum was recorded in that city's newspapers.

Sir Dudley Forwood supplied me with details of the duke's grief on the HRH issue at his home at Ringwood, Hants, England, on 9 October 1987. The Helga Stultz matter is in the FBI files on the Windsors in Washington, DC. The meeting with Errol Flynn, Hesse and Bormann at the Hôtel Meurice is in the Flynn SIS files described in detail to the writer Gerald Brown at the Ministry of Defence in February 1980. The entire Flynn file has conveniently disappeared since. The historians Martin and Peter Allen have since enlarged the picture from reliable eyewitness sources in the intelligence services. The Horchers banquet and the visit to Goebbels were recorded in the van Owen work cited in the narrative. The Peacock–Windsor discussion over money by telephone from London to Paris is in the Peacock–Kennedy conversations in the Kennedy diaries.

Wallis's love affair with William Bullitt was described to the author in telephone interviews with Eleanor Davies Tydings Ditzen, a close friend of Lady Jane Williams-Taylor, at her home in Washington, DC, on 4, 8, 12, and 19 March 2003, and referred to in her memoirs, *My Golden Spoon*. Bullitt's background can be found discussed in various issues of George Seldes's weekly *In Fact* (1940–45) and is closely documented in the Bullitt State Department files at the National Archives in Washington, including the illicit use of the German Foreign Office for transmitting top-secret messages to Washington. The details of Bullitt's sexual life are to be found in *Friend and Lover, a Life of Louise Bryant*, by Virginia Gardner, the Freud connection is documented in Peter Gay's biography of the doctor. The Bullitt–Offie affair comes from Rosemary Murphy, actor daughter of Bullitt's close friend and diplomatic associate Robert Murphy, who was in Paris at the time. The secret rendezvous at Schiaparelli's is from Mrs Ditzen; details of Lady Williams-Taylor come from Gioia Diliberto's *Debutante, the Life of Brenda Frazier* and from the records of the Bank of Montreal and the Montreal Historical Society. The Maroni blackmail story, as stated in the narrative, is given in the Constance Coolidge diaries, courtesy Andrea Lynn of the University of Illinois; it is supplemented by Coolidge's letters to her father at the time, maintained at the Massachusetts Historical Society in Boston; and from research in the social registers *Bottin Mondain* and *Tout Paris*, sundry books in French, and Pierre Lazareff's *Deadline*, as well as the files of *Le Matin* in Paris, records of the Sûrêté at Fontainebleau, and interviews in Paris, plus an exploration of that city in October 2003 for all the appropriate addresses. The meeting at the funeral of Queen Marie of Romania is in the Romanian newspapers and in the *New York Times*; the letter from King George V to Baldwin regarding the Windsors is in the Royal Archives at Windsor Castle; the insult following Rose's refusal of the dinner invitation is in the Kennedy diaries. The resuming of the Kent–Rambeau relationship is in the files of the Los Angeles *Herald-Examiner* for 1939; the meeting of Prince Philipp of Hesse and the Duke of Kent in July of that year is in the files on Philipp maintained by Professor Jonathan Petropoulos; the letters of the Duke of Kent to Prince Paul on the subject of Prince Friedrich of Prussia are at Columbia University. The conversation between the queen and Kennedy on the American tour is in the Kennedy diaries. The letter dated 2 October 1939 from the Queen of England is the only record of her contempt of Wallis to have been rescued from generations of royal weeders and is as stated at Columbia University in the Prince Paul papers. A unique and invaluable picture of her personality, it also displays a surprising homophobia in its mocking picture of the society photographer and designer Cecil Beaton. The fake broadcast on 11 October 1939 is recorded in the Goebbels diaries housed at the National Archives, Washington, and in the book by Christabel Bielenberg, *The Past Is Myself.* The treasonable note sent to Hitler by the Duke of Windsor via Bedaux is in the possession of Martin Allen. It was given to his father Peter Allen by Albert Speer, who said he obtained it from Hitler in the last days of the Führer's life in the Berlin bunker. The Bullitt–Assergio–Mussolini connection is in the US State Department file of Bullitt's letters. The report of Fulton Oursler's conversations with Roosevelt is recorded in his diaries and private papers at Georgetown University, Washington, supplied courtesy Fulton Oursler, Jr. The Bullitt mention of British assets in Paris is in the State Department files. The Edward A. Tamm report on the Windsors, classified when I wrote the original book, was declassified by the FBI in March 2003. However, the name British Secret Intelligence Service was blacked out. My assistant Jill Cairns Gallimore found the same document with the SIS name not excised as the source in a long-lost file on Axel Wenner-Gren at the Washington, DC, National Archives, thus supplying the indispensable fact that the report came from Sir Stuart Menzies and not from some unreliable and superficial society source.

The information on Claude Dansey and the Windsors came by letter from the former Abwehr agent Pieter Hansen, who is at work on a memoir, courtesy of Harry Cooper of the Sharkhunters Society of Submarine U-boat. The Bullitt–Vichy story is in the Bullitt files at the State Department. The Strang report is in the files of the British National Archive (formerly the Public Record Office). The July memorandum is also at the National Archive Frederick W. Winterbotham spoke of his killing of the Duke of Kent on SIS orders to historian Peter Allen – courtesy of Martin Allen, in a letter dated 4 July 2003. German comments on the crash are in the *New York Times*.

The Williams-Taylor matter is from Eleanor Davis Tydings Ditzen. The William Rhinelander Stewart story is in the Windsor FBI files first declassified in March 2003. The Bullitt–Welles matter is in the files of secretary of the interior Harold L. Ickes at the Franklin D. Roosevelt Memorial Library at Hyde Park, NY. The Eddie Chapman mission is from Chapman himself, in an interview with Gerald Brown of the Murdoch newspapers at an Arab health farm near London on 3 February 1980. The Sikorski death was recorded in the *New York Times* on 5 July 1943; the cause was given by Frederick W. Winterbotham to Peter Allen. Windsor's comment on Roosevelt is from the de Courcy papers at Stanford. So, too, is the revival of the China dossier issue in Marrakesh and in the south of France in 1951.

The Susan Mary Alsop story is from her *To Marietta from Paris*. The story of Wallis as a CIA agent comes from Aline, Countess of Romanones's *The Spy Went Dancing*. The matter of the duke being required to die on schedule is from my interview with Dr Jean Thin in Paris in December 1987. The matter of the auction of furniture and effects by Mohamed al-Fayed is supplied courtesy of Sotheby's, New York.

Bibliography

Abend, Hallett, *My Life in China*. New York, Harcourt, Brace, 1943.

Acland, Eric, *Long Live the King*. Chicago, Winston, 1936.

Alsop, Susan Mary, *To Marietta from Paris*. New York, Doubleday, 1975.

Amory, Cleveland, *Who Killed Society?* New York, Harper, 1960.

Balfour, John, *Not Too Correct an Aureole*. Wilton, Salisbury, M. Russell, 1983.

Beaverbrook, William Maxwell Aitken, Baron (ed. A. J. P. Taylor), *The Abdication of King Edward VIII*. New York, Atheneum, 1966.

Beirne, F. F., *The Amiable Baltimoreans*. New York, Dutton, 1951.

Beirne, F. F., *Baltimore, A Picture History*. Baltimore, Beaudine, 1968.

Bielenberg, Christabel, *The Past Is Myself*. London, Corgi, 1968.

Birkenhead, F. W. F. S., Second Earl of, *Walter Monckton: The Life of Viscount Monckton of Brenchley*. London, Weidenfeld and Nicolson, 1969.

Bloch, Michael, *The Duke of Windsor's War: From Europe to the Bahamas, 1939–1945*. London, Weidenfeld and Nicolson, 1982. New York, Howard McCann, 1983.

Bloch, Michael, *Operation Willi: The Plot to Kidnap the Duke of Windsor*. London, Weidenfeld and Nicolson, 1984. New York, Weidenfeld and Nicolson, 1985.

Bloch, Michael, *Wallis and Edward: Letters 1931–1937: The Intimate Correspondence of the Duke and Duchess of Windsor*. New York, Summit Books, 1986.

Bolitho, Hector, *King Edward VIII: An Intimate Biography*. New York, Literary Guild of America, 1937.

Borkin, Joseph R., *Robert R. Young: The Populist of Wall Street*. New York, Harper and Row, 1969.

Bove, Charles F., *A Paris Surgeon's Story*. Boston, Little Brown, 1956.

Brody, Iles, *Gone with the Windsors*. Philadelphia, Winston, 1953.

Brookman, Laura L., *Her Name Was Wallis Warfield*. New York, Dutton, 1936.

Brunswick, Princess Viktoria Luise, Duchess of, *The Kaiser's Daugher*. New Jersey, Prentice Hall, 1977.

Bryan, J. and Charles J. V. Murphy, *The Windsor Story*. New York, Morrow, 1979.

Bullitt, William, *Personal and Secret: Correspondence Between Franklin D. Roosevelt and W. C. Bullitt*. Boston, Houghton Mifflin, 1972.

Chambrun, Comte René de, *Le Procès Laval*. Paris, Editions France-Empire, 1984.

Channon, Sir Henry 'Chips', *The Diaries of Sir Henry Channon*. London, Weidenfeld and Nicolson, 1967.

Christy, Jim, *The Price of Power: A Biography of Charles Eugene Bedaux*. New York and Garden City, Doubleday, 1984.

Cockburn, Claude, *A Discord of Trumpets*. New York, Simon and Schuster, 1956.

Cole, Bernard D., *Gunboats and Marines*. Delaware, University of Delaware Press, 1983.

Colville, Sir John, *The Fringes of Power: Downing Street Diaries*. New York, Norton, 1985.

Connell, John, *The Office*. London, Wingate, 1958.

Cookridge, E. H., *Orient Express*. New York, Random House, 1978. London, Allen Lane, 1979.

Corbitt, Frederick, *Fit For a King*. New York, Harcourt, Brace, 1950.

Crawford, David, Earl of Lindsay (ed. John Vincent), *The Crawford Papers: The Journals of David Lindsay, 27th Earl of Crawford and 10th Earl of Balcarres*. Dover, New Hampshire, Manchester University Press, 1984.

Crawford, Marion, *The Little Princesses*. New York, Harcourt, Brace, 1951.

Cross, Colin, *The Fascists in Britain*. London, Barrie and Rockliff, 1961.

De Leeuw, Hendrik, *Cities of Sin*. London, Noel Douglas, 1934.

Deniel, Alain, *Bucard et le Francisme*. Paris, J. Picollec, 1979.

Dennis, Geoffrey, *Coronation Commentary*. London, Heinemann, 1937.

Diliberto, Gioia, Debutante: *The Life of Brenda Frazier*. New York, Simon and Schuster, 1987.

Ditzen, Eleanor Davies Tydings, *My Golden Spoon*. New York, Lanham Books, 1997.

Donaldson, Frances, *Edward VIII*. New York, Ballantine Books, 1976. London, Omega Books, 1976.

Eccles, Sybil, *By Safe Hand: Letters of Sybil and David Eccles*. London, Bodley
 Head, 1983.

Edwards, Anne, *Matriarch: Queen Mary and the House of Windsor*. New York,
 Morrow, 1984. London, Hodder, 1984.

Farago, Ladislas, *The Game of the Foxes*. New York, McKay, 1972.

Forbes-Robertson, Diana, *My Aunt Maxine: The Story of Maxine Elliott*. New
 York, Viking Press, 1964.

Gardner, Virginia, *Friend and Lover: A Life of Louise Bryant*. New York,
 Horizon Press, 1982.

Garrett, Richard, *Mrs Simpson*. London, Arthur Barker, 1979.

Gay, Peter, *Freud: A Life For Our Time*. New York, W. W. Norton, 1988.

Gedye, G. E. R., *Betrayal in Central Europe*. New York, Harper, 1939.

Getty, Jean Paul, *As I See It: My Autobiography*. Englewood Cliffs, New
 Jersey, Prentice Hall, 1970.

Gilbert, Martin, *Churchill* (many volumes). London, Heinemann,
 1967–87. Boston, Houghton Mifflin, 1967–87.

Giles, Frank, *Sundry Times*. London, John Murray, 1986.

Goldsmith, Barbara, *Little Gloria, Happy at Last*. New York, Alfred Knopf,
 1980. London, Pan, 1981.

Grattidge, Captain Harry and Richard Collier, *Captain of The Queens*.
 London, Oldbourne Press, 1956.

Greene, Suzanne E., *Baltimore: An Illustrated History*. Woodland Hills,
 California, Windsor, 1980.

Grovet, Stéphane, *Crown of Thorns: The Reign of King Boris III of Bulgaria*.
 New York, Madison Books, 1987.

Guerri, Giordano Bruno, *Galeazzo Ciano: A Life 1903–1944*. Milan,
 Bompiani, 1979.

Gun, Nerin E., *Eva Braun: Hitler's Mistress*. New York, Meredith Press, 1968.

Hardinge, Helen, *Loyal to Three Kings*. London, William Kimber, 1967.

Hibbert, Christopher, *Edward: The Uncrowned King*. London, Macdonald,
 1972.

Hore-Belisha, Leslie, *Private Papers*. London, Collins, 1960.

Hsue, Immanuel C. Y., *The Rise of Modern China*. New York, Oxford
 University Press, 1983.

Jardine, The Reverend H. A., *At Long Last*. New York, Murray and Dore/
 Ambassador Books, 1943.

Jukie, Ilija, *The Fall of Yugoslavia*. New York, Harcourt Brace Jovanovich,
 1971.

Lazareff, Pierre, *Deadline*. New York, Random House, 1942.

Lockhart, Sir Robert Hamilton Bruce, *Diaries*. London, Macmillan, vol. 1,
 1973, vol. 2, 1981.

Lombard, Helen, *Washington Waltz*. New York, Knopf, 1942.

McCormick, Donald, *The Mask of Merlin: A Critical Study of David Lloyd George*. London, Macdonald, 1963.

Mackenzie, Compton, *The Windsor Tapestry*. New York, Stokes, 1938.

Maine, Basil, *Our Ambassador King*. London, Hutchinson, 1936.

Martin, Ralph G., *The Woman He Loved*. New York, Simon and Schuster, 1974.

Marx, Samuel, *Queen of the Ritz*. Indianapolis, Bobbs Merrill, 1978.

Maxwell, Elsa, *RSVP*. Boston, Little, Brown, 1974.

Middlemas, Keith and John Barnes, *Baldwin: A Biography*. London, Weidenfeld and Nicolson, 1969.

Mortimer, Penelope, *Queen Elizabeth: A Portrait of the Queen Mother*. New York, St Martin's Press, 1986.

Morton, Frederic, *The Rothschilds*. New York, Atheneum, 1962.

Mosley, Diana, *The Duchess of Windsor*. London, Sidgwick and Jackson, 1980.

Mosley, Sir Oswald, *My Life*. London, Nelson, 1968.

Muggeridge, Malcolm, *Chronicles of Wasted Time*. New York, Morrow, 1973.

Pearce, George F., *The US Navy in Pensacola*. Pensacola, University Presses of Florida, 1980.

Pertinax (André Géraud), *The Gravediggers of France*. New York, Doubleday, 1944.

Pool, James and Suzanne, *Who Financed Hitler?* New York, Dial Press, 1978.

Pye, Michael, *The King Over the Water*. New York, Holt, Reinhart and Winston, 1981.

Recd, Douglas, *Insanity Fair*. New York, Random House, 1938.

Romanones, Aline, Countess of, *The Spy Went Dancing*. New York, G. P. Putnam's Sons, 1990.

Rose, Kenneth, *George V*. London, Weidenfeld and Nicolson, 1983. New York, Knopf, 1984.

Rose, Norman, *Vansittart: Study of a Diplomat*. London, Heinemann, 1978.

Schumann, Frederick L., *Europe on the Eve*. New York, Knopf, 1939.

Schwarz, Paul, *This Man Ribbentrop: His Life and Times*. New York, Messner, 1943.

Sheean, Vincent, *Between the Thunder and the Sun*. New York, Random House, 1943.

Skidelsky, Robert, *Oswald Mosley*. New York, Macmillan, 1975.

Slater, Leonard, *Aly, A Biography*. New York, Random House, 1965.

Smith, Amanda (ed.), *Hostages to Fortune: The Letters of Joseph P. Kennedy*. New York and London, Viking, 2001.

Smith, Jane S., *Elsie de Wolfe*. New York, Atheneum, 1982.

Sulzberger, C. L., *A Long Row of Candles: Memoirs and Diaries 1934–1954*. New York, Macmillan, 1969.

Thornton, Michael, *Royal Feud: The Dark Side of the Love Story of the Century*. New York, Simon and Schuster, 1985.

Torres, Henry, *Campaign of Treachery*. New York, Dodd-Mead, 1942.

Trevor-Roper, H. R., *Hitler's Table Talk 1941–1944*. London, Weidenfeld and Nicolson, 1953.

US Military Intelligence Reports, *China, 1924–1925*. Frederick, Maryland, University Publications of America, 1975.

Vickers, Hugo, *Cecil Beaton: A Biography*. Boston, Little, Brown, 1986.

Vreeland, Diana, George Plimpton and Christopher Hemphill, *D. V.*, New York, Knopf, 1984. London, Weidenfeld and Nicolson, 1984.

Warwick, Christopher, *Abdication*. London, Sidgwick and Jackson, 1986.

Waterfield, Gordon, *Professional Diplomat: Sir Percy Loraine of Kirkharle*. London, Murray, 1973.

West, Nigel, *The Circus: MI5 Operations 1945–1972*. New York, Stein and Day, 1983.

West, Nigel, *MI6: British Secret Service Operations 1909–1945*. London, Weidenfeld and Nicolson, 1983. New York, Random House, 1986.

White, J. L., *The Abdication of Edward VIII*. London, Routledge, 1937.

Windsor, Duchess of, *The Heart Has Its Reasons*. New York, McKay, 1956. London, Chivers Press, 1983.

Windsor, Duke of, *A King's Story: The Memoirs of the Duke of Windsor*. New York, Putnam, 1951.

Winterbotham, Frederick, *Secret and Personal*. London, William Kimber, 1969.

Wooton, Graham, *The Official History of the British Legion*. London, Macdonald and Evans, 1956.

Index